"Should you get hooked on Tuscan villas, half-timbered taverns, Swiss chalets, and Scottish country houses, you will want to buy a copy of EUROPE'S WONDERFUL LITTLE HOTELS AND INNS."

—STEPHEN BIRNBAUM, *Europe 1983*

"Appeals to those who prefer to stay in small, comfortable places, surrounded by antiques, fragrant gardens, and a friendly staff." —*Washington Post*

"Delightful...A useful guide that's fun to read."

—*Library Journal*

"The range is exciting...An excellent idea."

—*Publishers Weekly*

"Agreeably quirky...Will well serve adventuresome Americans." —*The Kirkus Reviews*

"I wage an eternal search for the small, personal, idiosyncratic hotel, the establishment with charm and character, and this book has suggested a number of them which I would like to try."

—CASKIE STINNETT, Travel Editor, *Signature*

"On quaint lodging places, [one of] the best." —*Harper's*

"An indispensable travelling companion."

—*The Times* of London

EUROPE'S WONDERFUL LITTLE HOTELS AND INNS
1983

Edited by
Hilary Rubinstein

Fifth Edition

CONGDON & WEED, INC.
New York

Fifth Edition, copyright © 1983 by Hilary Rubinstein Books Ltd.
Illustrations copyright © 1983 by Ray Evans
Maps copyright © 1983 by Consumers' Association

Library of Congress Cataloging in Publication Data

Main entry under title:

Europe's wonderful little hotels and inns.

   Includes index.
   1. Hotels, taverns, etc.–Europe–Directories.
I. Rubinstein, Hilary.
TX910.A1E95   1983   647'.9401   82-19864
ISBN 0-86553-071-8
ISBN 0-312-92193-4 (St. Martin's Press)

Originally published in England as *The Good Hotel Guide 1983* by
Consumers' Association and Hodder & Stoughton

Published by Congdon & Weed, Inc.
Distributed by St. Martin's Press
Published simultaneously in Canada by Thomas Nelson & Sons Limited

All Rights Reserved

Printed in the United States of America

First Printing

Contents

A note for new readers

This is an annual guide to hotels in Britain and the continent of Western Europe that are of unusual character and quality. The entries are based on reports from readers who write to us when they come across a hotel which has given them out-of-the-ordinary satisfaction, and who also send us their comments, critical or appreciative, when they visit places already included in the Guide. Our task is to collate these reports, check and verify them, making inspections where necessary, and select those which we consider make the grade. No cash changes hands at any point: contributors are not rewarded for writing to us; hotels do not pay for their entries; the editor and his staff accept no free hospitality.

The Guide operates on the same principle as *The Good Food Guide*, but is independently owned and edited. We have no say in the hotels and restaurants chosen by our sibling publication, nor are they involved in our choices. But we are keen to share our correspondence where appropriate, and, unless asked not to, we will pass on to *The Good Food Guide* reports on any British hotel where the restaurant is an important feature. Hotels which are included in the 1983 *Good Food Guide* have [GFG] after the hotel's name.

The hotels in the book cover a wide range. People want different things from a hotel according to whether they are making a single night stop or spending a whole holiday in one place, whether they have young children with them, whether they are visiting a city or staying in the remote countryside, and according to their age and means. We make no claims of universal compatibility or comprehensiveness, but we hope that our descriptions will help you to find good hotels that suit your tastes, needs and purse. If an entry has misled you, we hope you will use one of the report forms at the back of the book, and tell us in order that we can do better next time; and we hope equally that, if you have found the Guide useful and a hotel has fulfilled your expectations, you will also write to us: endorsements and criticisms are both essential if the Guide is to achieve its purpose. A hotel is dropped unless we get positive feedback.

Introduction

This Guide is committed to finding out and reporting on hotels of individual excellence. We cherish places that are dedicated to giving their guests value for money, and a personal touch. It is often thought that these special cossetting hotels must cost the earth. But expensive hotels are not necessarily special, and special hotels need not be expensive. Whatever price you are prepared to pay, you can have an enhancing experience or leave feeling robbed. Why pay more when you can have an even better time *and* pay less?

This is the Guide's fifth annual edition, and our largest yet. We would also claim that it is our strongest. The total number of entries has gone up by just over 100 to almost exactly 800, of which nearly one-third, 250 in all, are hotels new to the Guide this year. But 1982 has also seen a very big jump in the number of reports we have received. This has not only enabled us to extend our coverage, but has helped us to achieve much finer tuning in our descriptions. We have also extended the range of our inspections, which this past year covered hotels of every class in 11 different countries.

England and Scotland have both increased their entries by 10%, but the really significant growth area, this year as last, has been in the French section, which has grown by no less than 30%. From the start, the Guide has tended to reflect holiday trends, and the expansion of the French section is a natural consequence of the growing popularity of France for holiday-takers of many different tastes and dispositions – skiers, sun-lovers, gourmets and culture-seekers – a process hastened by the relative cheapness of a holiday in France, especially since the devaluation of the franc. Moreover, France has a long tradition of good hotel-keeping, so it is natural that Guide correspondents, as they travel in ever greater numbers through the French countryside, should be constantly telling us of some delectable new 'discovery'.

The other major change in the 1983 edition also relates to the French section, which has been edited this year by the well-known writer and broadcaster on French affairs, John Ardagh. He has brought to the formidable task of collating and assessing all our French reports his profound knowledge of every region of France.

A remarkable feature of the British section this past year has been the sighting of a number of potential new super-stars in the country hotel galaxy: notable among these are *Cromlix House*, Dunblane and *Arisaig House*, Arisaig in Scotland, *Bodysgallen Hall*, Llandudno (a particularly welcome addition since good country house hotels are thin on the ground in Wales), *Thornbury Castle*, Thornbury (already a famous restaurant, now a hyper-elegant restaurant with rooms), *Ston Easton Park*, at Ston Easton near Bath (can Bath support yet another luxury hotel, one asks: there are already five of the best and dearest in that area), and *Lainston House* at Sparsholt near Winchester (a fine city that has patently been lacking a fine hotel). All these new enterprises, most in substantial parklands, represent huge investments on the part of their owners. Unless they are all tax-loss operations (which some of them may be), these openings reflect a remarkable confidence in the economy. But whether they can survive in the immediate future, charging London prices, remains to be seen. Of less concern to Guide readers perhaps is the announcement that Holiday Inns, the world's largest hotel chain, is intending to open five new hotels in the UK at a cost of up to £90 million, and that another American chain, Sheraton, has plans for a further eight hotels in Britain and Ireland.

To set against this eloquent display of entrepreneurial optimism, there is evidence from our files that many of the hotels in which the Guide is particularly interested – not just in Britain but throughout Western Europe – are having a very tough time indeed. Among warmly-appreciated Guide hotels which have had to close or sell out this past year have been *Beaconside House* at Monkleigh (the subject of last year's Appendix, *Mrs Brand's Dream Hotel*), *Nichols Nymet House* at North Tawton, *Milton Ernest Hall*, Milton Ernest and *Dunmor House*, Seil, Argyll. The special places in this book, just because they tend to be off the beaten track and out of the ordinary, with just a few rooms, are often worryingly dependent on a listing in the Guide. Readers who hesitate to endorse an existing entry or to recommend similar places they have come across for fear of their becoming spoiled, are doing the hotels as well as fellow-travellers a disservice. These hotels need all the support and help we can give them.

When is a hotel not a hotel?
We have always taken a relaxed view as to what constitutes a hotel, and from the start have included many establishments – guest-houses, *pensions* and *pensiones*, restaurants with rooms, farmhouses – which are outside official hotel classifications. We are strongly influenced in what we put in by what our readers say they like and are looking for in the Guide.

This year in particular we have included a number of places which are far removed from traditional notions of a hotel, and where the visitor is essentially a paying guest rather than a customer. It is hard to know where to draw the line with this relatively new hybrid. There are places in the Guide this year, such as *Chilvester Lodge* at Calne, where you will find yourself sitting down to dinner with your host and hostess. Does that rule them out of court? Certainly the rooms at *Chilvester Lodge* are as elegant as those of any country house hotel. Places that call themselves 'Bed and Breakfast' or *Chambres* or *Zimmer* cover a wide spectrum of standards of accommodation, including rooms that are clearly used by members of the resident family when there is no guest around and bathrooms that are shared with the owner-occupiers.

We are reluctant to draw any hard-and-fast rules. We welcome houses, whether they have a hotel sign outside or not, which offer discriminating travellers an unusually agreeable experience and good value for money.

9

This last phrase is a key one at a time when so many people, who would like to take a break, can no longer afford conventional hotel prices. We shall continue to select the unhotel-like places, alongside the regular ones. And we shall continue to welcome news of new enterprises, however small and however way out.

Drop-outs

Hotels are dropped from the Guide when they change hands as well as when they go out of business. A significant departure this year because of change of ownership has been *The Elms* at Abberley, which had been our opening entry since our first edition. Hotels are also left out when there is evidence that their standards have been slipping. But there are many hotels, especially in the more remote areas of the Continent, which are omitted simply because we lack adequate feedback. We often discover subsequently that our entry in a previous edition has attracted many Guide readers who have told the hotel-keeper how much they have enjoyed their stay but have not bothered to write us an endorsing note. We cannot emphasize often enough how vital it is for our Guide to be kept up to the mark by readers' reports. We also urge readers to tell us of their 'finds'. In the case of hotels on the Continent, we should be very grateful if such reports could be accompanied by brochures. These are invaluable in preparing entries for those foreign hotels which fail to return our questionnaire. The deadline for new nominations is 1 June, and for comments on existing entries 31 July. This is earlier than in previous years because the next British edition of the Guide will be published in the autumn of 1983.

Complaints, complaints

We naturally appreciate it if correspondents write to us when they feel they have been fleeced or poorly treated. We don't necessarily agree, however, with all the snorts or grumbles that reach us. It is pleasant for a hotel to supply morning papers free, but not a black mark in our book if they choose to make a charge even if their tariff is a high one. It is the same with breakfasts: many of us are not used to coping with a full English breakfast and are perfectly content with the continental variety. Writers who complain about having to pay extra for their bacon and eggs are in effect asking the rest of us to subsidize their larger breakfast appetites. It is surely the hotel-keeper's prerogative to decide what to make inclusive and what to treat as an optional extra.

It is equally the hotel's business whether it imposes a small or a large mark-up on its wine list. But we would like to see more well-chosen cheaper wines available generally, also more half-bottles and more wines by the glass (with some indication in the latter case of what quantity of wine is being offered).

We take a dimmer view of hotels that pride themselves on their restaurants but take little or no trouble with their breakfasts – offering canned or cartonned rather than fresh fruit juice, inferior bread or rolls, wrapped pats of butter and commercial rather than home-made preserves, often in awkward little plastic containers. Guests who care about what they eat and are prepared to pay for it should be regarded as equally discriminating at the breakfast table as they have been the previous evening at dinner.

A shamefully common cause of complaint is poor heating. Sometimes hotels, especially those which close in the winter, are simply not equipped to cope with sudden spells of cold weather. But often hotels are too slow (or too mean) to heat rooms adequately in time before a guest arrives. We regard proper heating and ventilation as *sine qua nons* of a good hotel, irrespective of its price bracket, and would be glad if readers would make a point of letting us know wherever they have found rooms uncomfortably cold or stuffy.

In 1982, the papers alerted the public to the fact that many hotels were making extortionate charges for phone calls. One West End London hotel was reported to have charged £15 for an inland trunk call which British Telecom had subsequently confirmed should have cost no more than £1. This insidious practice is hard to nail down unless you carry a stop-watch. But it underlines again the need to scrutinize your bill at the end of a visit and to query any item that seems unreasonable. We should always be glad to hear from readers about any allegedly unfair charges levied by a hotel in the Guide.

Guidelines for gourmets

We get more complaints about food than about any other single item. We are of course a Guide to good hotels not to good restaurants, but for many of us the quality of a hotel's kitchen is crucial to the pleasures of a visit. Unfortunately, sensitivity to ingredients, like a feeling for words, is not an innate human characteristic: some people never take an interest in what is put before them; for many others a capacity to distinguish between outstanding and mediocre cooking comes only after much grazing in rich pastures. When a new correspondent tells us that 'the cuisine at the *Grand Hotel* was of cordon bleu standard', we have no way of knowing whether that reader knows his or her onions. We are not, however, dependent on our reports. We invariably ask hotels to send us sample menus, and these are often informative of an establishment's gastronomic literacy – and we don't just mean whether they can spell *Boeuf Bourguignon* or *Schwarzwälder Kirschtorte*.

In deciding what we print about the quality of a hotel's meals, we also study how its restaurant is rated in other Guides, we have access to many of the Good Food Guide's reports, and when we are in doubt, we make our own inspection. Nevertheless there is a limit to how much we can say about food when there are so many other features to be described. British hotels which have an entry in the Good Food Guide have [GFG] after their name – a shorthand way of indicating that you can expect above-average standards of cooking. On the Continent we have usually mentioned if a hotel has one or more Michelin rosettes – and, in the case of France, we have also in many cases shown its rating in that invaluable guide to good eating, Gault-Millau.*

---

*Gault-Millau awards *toques* (chef's hats) which roughly correspond to Michelin rosettes and likewise range from one to three. They are rather more liberal with their 3-toques than Michelin: in 1982, they awarded 3-toques to sixty-six establishments compared to Michelin's twenty. Toques are either red or black. Red indicates what they call 'inventive cuisine' (they avoid the increasingly outmoded expression 'nouvelle cuisine') and black, 'classic cuisine'. They have a clear penchant for the former: all but six of their 3-toque establishments are red.

Next year
We are keen, with readers' help, to have many more budget-priced hotels next year – in all areas, but especially in cities where hotels are so frequently business-oriented and priced accordingly.

Among the other innovations we have in mind to introduce in our 1984 edition is a Consumer's Guide to Hotel Law (bookings, deposits, cancellations, suits of negligence and suchlike). We hope to announce the winner of the first Report of the Year competition (see page 558). We should also like to start a regular feature called *These Hotels*, reprinting such revelations as:

Peter Milner likes to describe his wines rather than just leave the diner with a list of names and vintages. The Chateau Latour 1967 (£28.80), for example, he confidently calls 'a wonderful wine'. (From *Caterer and Hotelkeeper*, 30 July, 1981)

All such contributions gratefully received.

If there are other features which readers would like to see in the Guide would they please let us know?

America's Wonderful Little Hotels and Inns
The Guide is published in the United States and Canada under the title *Europe's Wonderful Little Hotels and Inns*. Its success in North America has led to a sister publication on American and Canadian hotels based on the same principles. As with this Guide, the text is revised regularly. Readers with first-hand recent experience of good hotels in North America are urged to write to the American publisher, Congdon & Weed, 298 Fifth Avenue, New York, NY 10001, USA. Report forms at the end of the book may be used, but regrettably Freepost is not available for transatlantic use.

HILARY RUBINSTEIN
London, October 1982

How to read the entries

As in previous editions, entries are in two parts – a citation, usually endorsed by one or several names, followed by relevant information about accommodation, amenities, location and tariffs.

We must emphasize once again that the length or brevity of an entry is not a reflection on the quality of a hotel. The size of an entry is determined in part by what we feel needs to be said to convey a hotel's special flavour and in part by the character and interest of the commendation. In general, country hotels get more space than city hotels because the atmosphere of the hotel matters more with the former and also because it is often helpful, when a hotel is in a relatively remote or little-known area, if the entry says something about the location.

The names at the end of a citation are of those who have nominated that hotel or endorsed the entry that appeared in a previous edition. Some entries are entirely or largely quoted from one report; if several names follow such an entry, we have distinguished writers of quoted material by putting their names first. We do not give the names of those who have sent us adverse reports – though their contributions are every bit as important as the laudatory ones.

The factual material also varies in length. Some hotels provide a wide variety of facilities, others very little. But the paucity of information provided in some cases may derive from the fact that the hotel has failed to return our detailed questionnaire or send us a brochure. All hotels in the British Isles have completed our form, but the same is not true for continental hotels, despite the fact that we send out our questionnaire in five languages, and repeat the operation for the recalcitrant a month later. Perhaps a quarter of the hotels in the second half ignore our form or return it months later when the Guide has gone to press. In these instances, we have to rely on the information available from national tourist offices. The fact that no lounge or bar is mentioned in an entry is not evidence that a hotel lacks public rooms or a licence – only that we can't be sure. The same applies to availability of parking, which we aim to mention in the case of town and city hotels. As to tariffs, in those cases where we have had no communication with a hotel, we have added a percentage increase on present tariffs according to informed views about the present and likely future trend of inflation in each country.

There is a limit to the amount of 'nuts and bolts' that can be given in any guide book, and we are against providing, as some other guide books do, a lot of potted information in complicated hard-to-decipher hieroglyphic form. [GFG] after the hotel's name indicates that the hotel has an entry in the 1983 *Good Food Guide*. The only other shorthand we use is 'B & B' for bed and breakfast and '*alc*' for *à la carte*; the 'full *alc*' price is the hotel's estimate per person for a 3-course meal and a half bottle of modest wine, including service and taxes. This year, as last, we have employed the convention of a symbol (&) for the disabled. We hope next year, however, to persuade hotels to be more explicit about the particular facilities available – the number of ground-floor rooms available and so forth.

There is one crucial point that must be emphasized with regard to the tariffs: their relative unreliability. We ask hotels, when they complete our questionnaire in the summer of one year, to make an informed guess as to their tariffs the following year. For the last few years, however, because of fluctuating inflation and changes in taxation, the task has become much harder. We must warn readers not to attach too much credence to the figures printed. In many cases prices may be steeper than those shown, though there may well be some hotels whose rates we have overestimated. *In all cases, we would urge readers to check at the time of booking and not to blame the hotel*, or the Guide, *if our prices are wrong*.

Terms are difficult enough to cope with at the best of times. A few hotels have a standard rate for all rooms regardless of season and length of stay, but most operate a highly complicated system which varies from low season to high (and some have a medium-high season as well), according to length of stay, whether there is a bathroom *en suite* and, in the case of most British hotels, whether a room is in single or double occupancy. And on top of all that, most British hotels operate breaks of one kind or another, but rarely of the same kind. We try to give the essential information: what you may expect to pay for bed and breakfast either in a single room on your own or sharing a double room. When two figures are given, they indicate, unless otherwise stated, the range of prices per person for B & B, full board and so on. When a hotel has low and high season rates, the range shows the lowest price in the low season and the highest price in the high season. In the case of many hotels on the Continent, particularly in France, we have given a rate for rooms, indicating the range between a single room (preferably with bath or shower) and the equivalent for a double room; but the B & B, pension and meals prices are still per person. But we do beg you to check your tariff with the hotel when you book, more especially in the case of hotels on the Continent. If you are going for two days or more to a hotel in the British Isles, it will pay you to find out the exact terms of any special offers available. Sometimes these bargain terms are amazing value, and can apply throughout the year, not just in the winter, but they may call for some adjustment in your holiday plans in order to qualify.

We must end with our customary exhortation; we implore readers to tell us of any errors of omission or commission in both the descriptive and the information parts of the entries. We make constant efforts to improve our information under 'Location', especially with the more out-of-the-way places, but would be very grateful if readers would let us know of any cases where they have found our directions inadequate. We recognize what an imposition it is to be asking readers to write us letters or fill in report forms, but it is essential that people do let us know their views if the Guide is to meet consumer needs as well as it can.

14

Part One

ENGLAND
WALES
SCOTLAND
CHANNEL ISLANDS
NORTHERN IRELAND
REPUBLIC OF IRELAND

Plumber Manor, Sturminster Newton

England

ALFRISTON, Polegate, Sussex   **Map 2**

Deans Place Hotel   *Telephone:* Alfriston (0323) 870248

The Brewsters, who had owned and run this easy-going, fairly shabby,
clearly much-loved family hotel for many years, sold out at the end of
1981. Michael and Janet Pritchard have now taken it over. The house
dates back to Tudor times, but is essentially 18th-century. It stands in
seven acres of grounds by the river Cuckmere in the heart of the South
Downs, and, as the details under 'Facilities' below indicate, it has a lot to
offer on the spot as well as being only three miles from the coast. The news
about the Pritchard regime seems, from early reports, encouraging. They
have cut down the creeper, presumably for structural reasons, and have
also taken out the indoor bowling green, which had been a unique claim to
distinction on the part of the previous owners. We understand that a big
room for functions is intended to take its place. Otherwise, they have
been busy redecorating and cleaning the place up. The staff look smarter
in a brown uniform. The food has improved. Prices have gone up, but are
felt still to be reasonable. It is probably a bit less idiosyncratic than it was,
though still sometimes disorganized. One reader remarked on the provision of paper bath-mats; apparently a small pile of the things, coyly
labelled 'Your own personal bathmat' was delivered outside her door
every morning alongside the morning papers. Another wrote: 'Happily,
children, including the owners' daughter and two sons, still reign,
together with the elderly, and long may that continue. One old lady was

17

obviously delighted at being dragged into a game of snooker by a ten-year-old-boy!' 'It *is* still a children's paradise – our 14-year-olds loved it,' was the comment from a third correspondent. *(Heather Sharland, AJV Baker, Deirdre Tilley)*

Open: All year, except January.
Rooms: 35 double, 11 single – all with bath, tea-making facilities and baby-listening.
Facilities: 2 lounges, dining room, games room, TV room; snooker, table tennis. 7 acres grounds with tennis court, outdoor swimming pool (heated in summer), croquet, putting. 3 miles from beach; golf, riding nearby. Glyndebourne 5 miles. &.
Location: Heading for Eastbourne on the A22, take the right-hand turning for Seaford.
Restriction: 'Well-behaved' dogs allowed, but not in dining room.
Terms (no service charge): B & B £14–16; dinner, B & B £17–19 (3 days), £16–18 (7 days). Set meals: lunch £4.50, dinner £7. Special winter and Christmas breaks. Reduced rates for children.

AMBLESIDE, Cumbria   Map 4

Rothay Manor Hotel [GFG]   *Telephone:* Ambleside (096 63) 3605
Rothay Bridge   *Telex:* 65294 Telecom G

As in previous years, there has been no shortage of commendations and re-commendations for the efficiency and friendliness of this handsome Regency hotel which lies in a secluded position at the head of Windermere, a few minutes' walk from the centre of Ambleside. This is a traditional establishment in more ways than one; waitresses are mob-capped and pinafored when waiting at meals, and Bronwen Nixon, assisted by her two sons, keeps a vigilant eye on the flowers, silver, napkins, table settings and the like, as well as maintaining a high standard of ambitious cooking. But it is also a go-ahead set-up: throughout the winter months, when other hotels are half-empty or close down, *Rothay Manor* provides a full programme of 'events' – wine tastings and the like, as well as weekend breaks. The only negative note in this year's crop of reports referred to the breakfasts – tepid porridge, only warm coffee and poor croissants. Another reader took a different line: 'Breakfast was a real feast, and the Cumberland platter – bacon, kidney, fried bread, tomato, mushroom, black pudding – just couldn't be beaten!' Finally, an extract from a reader who sums up the general view: '*Superb*. It is totally comfortable and we could not fault the food. £73 for dinner, bed and breakfast for two for one night [1982] sounds expensive, but at that level of food, accommodation and caring attention we considered it good value for money.' *(Jean and Malcolm Seymour, John Taylor; also R A Riley, Alfred Knopf Jr, Dr J Biggs, Kevin Myers)*

Open: 4 February 1983–8 January 1984.
Rooms: 10 double, 2 single – all with bath, telephone and colour TV, 4 with radio.
Facilities: 2 lounges, 1 with bar, dining room. 1 acre gardens with croquet. Near the river Rothay. Steamer services, sailing and water-skiing nearby; also riding and golf.
Location: Lake Windermere ¼ mile; on the Langdale outskirts of Ambleside.
Restriction: No dogs in public rooms.
Credit cards: American Express, Diners.
Terms (service at guests' discretion): B & B £26–36; dinner, B & B £39–50. Set

meals: lunch from £3.50 (Sunday lunch £7); dinner £14. Reduced rates for children sharing parents' room; special meals provided. Winter events such as wine tastings, 'Humour of Dickens', fashion shows, etc. Victorian Christmas dinner and party.

AMBLESIDE, Cumbria   Map 4

Wateredge Hotel   *Telephone:* Ambleside (096 63) 2332
Borrans Road

The address is Ambleside, but the *Wateredge* is a mile from that bustling busy village. As its name suggests, it is right on the water at the northern tip of Windermere, and most of its bedrooms look over the lakeside garden and down the length of the lake – a very pleasing prospect indeed. Don't confuse this hotel with its larger neighbour, the *Waterhead*, which is on the main Windermere–Keswick road, whereas one of the pleasing aspects of *Wateredge* is that it is on a quiet byroad. It has been skilfully converted from two 17th-century fishermen's cottages, well grafted on to some modern extensions. There are several public rooms of differing sizes – enough to accommodate all the guests in comfort when the hotel is full. There is nothing flash about the *Wateredge*, and no special 'treats' in the bedrooms. But the cooking is ambitious without being pretentious or particularly pricey, and the helpings are generous alike for the full English breakfasts and the 5-course evening meal. There is a popular buffet lunch. Staff are friendly and efficient. *(HR; also Shirley Williams and others)*

Open: Early March–early November.
Rooms: 15 double, 3 single – 8 with bath, 2 with shower, all with baby-listening.
Facilities: Lounge, TV room, dining room. 1½ acres grounds with 200 ft lake frontage, private jetty, free sailing in Flying Fifteen and 2 dinghies, rowing boat, fishing and safe bathing. Good centre for walkers and climbers.
Location: ½ mile from town; just off the A591 at Waterhead on Kendal–Keswick road.
Credit cards: Access/Euro/Mastercard.
Terms (no fixed service charge):   B & B £14.50–22; dinner, B & B £24.50–32. Set meals: lunch £4.80, dinner £10.90. Reduced rates and special meals for children.

ASHFORD, Kent   Map 2

Eastwell Manor   [GFG]   *Telephone:* Ashford (0233) 35751
Eastwell Park   *Telex:* 966281 EMANOR

Eastwell Manor opened its doors in 1980 with a *sforzando* trumpet blast. It could have fallen flat on its face, but has triumphed. Though the house has a history that goes back to Domesday and beyond, it is, for practical purposes, a 1920s reconstruction of an old manor house, with no expense spared – either in the Twenties or in the late Seventies when it was converted to its present incarnation as a luxurious country hotel. Matthew Bates, the young owner, has also spent a fortune on the garden, taming at least 14 acres of a 3,000-acre estate in the North Downs of Kent to form a suitably grand outdoor decor for the Manor itself. The restaurant, under Ian McAndrew, formerly sous-chef at the *Carlton Tower*, is of a piece with everything else. Of course, with a place like this, questions are raised about value for money, and not everyone would subscribe to an encomium as unreserved as the one we print below – in particular, there have

19

been mutterings about slow service at dinner – but in general we feel that those who don't have to count the cost and who like to live in the grand style from time to time, will find that *Eastwell Manor* delivers the goods.

'The hotel cannot be faulted. My wife and I have stayed on three occasions and we feel we are guests in a country manor rather than in a commercial hotel. The food is superb, the service friendly and the bedrooms comfortable and modern. The wine list is extensive. Everything in the hotel is in the very best of taste and the young owner and staff are unobtrusive and efficient. I have stayed at several five-star hotels in London and elsewhere and have found nothing remotely to compare with the comfort and general atmosphere of *Eastwell Manor*. My wife does not like hotels in general, but loves this place, and so do I. For what you get, it is not, in my opinion, expensive. In a word, *Eastwell Manor* is *unique*. On our last visit, the welcome note, with the basket of fruit in the bedroom, simply stated "Welcome Home" – and that's how we felt, exactly.' *(P J Gordon; also Alfred Knopf Jr)*

Open: All year.
Rooms: 20 double – all with bath, direct-dial telephone, radio and colour TV.
Facilities: Lift, 2 halls, lounge, lounge bar, restaurant, snooker room; conference facilities. 14 acres garden in 3,000 acres estate; tennis, croquet. &.
Location: Off the A251, 3 miles from Ashford.
Restrictions: No children under 7. Dogs allowed only in kennels and grounds.
Credit cards: Access/Euro, American Express, Barclay/Visa, Diners.
Terms: B & B £27.50–59.50. Set meal: lunch from £9; full *alc* £15–20. Special bargain rates for 2-night stays; special winter rates; 4-day Christmas programme.

ASTON CLINTON, Buckinghamshire　　　　　　　　　　　　　　　**Map 2**

The Bell Inn　[GFG]　　　　　　　　　　*Telephone:* Aylesbury (0296) 630252
　　　　　　　　　　　　　　　　　　　　　　　　　　　　　Telex: 82617

A famous old coaching inn on the A41, four miles from Aylesbury on the London side (London 41 miles), now a thoroughly sophisticated restaurant with rooms. Its restaurant does a roaring trade locally. Prices are high, but the panache of the service, the agreeable ambience, the quality of the cooking and a remarkably good wine list, keep the restaurant thriving; it can serve 140 people at a sitting and at weekends is often booked out. Across a minor road from the restaurant is a converted stable block with rooms that are as elegant (also as pricey) as the restaurant.

The Bell doesn't suit everyone. One reader this year, while recognizing many special qualities about the place, complained that she felt on a production line because of the number of covers. Some people, we imagine, enjoy eating in a large flourishing company and others prefer a quieter, perhaps also less touristy, hotel. But *The Bell* scored full marks with another reader, an elderly lady travelling on her own and a vegetarian to boot: 'A really good hotel. Reception pleasant and efficient. Luggage carried and car parked. Extremely well-appointed bedroom with everything one could wish for. The same applied to the bathroom. The *maître d'hôtel* ordered a well-thought-out vegetarian dinner for me. I was put at a nice corner table in the dining room, not pushed into "widows' corner" and made to feel like one. The chamber-maid service was the best I have ever had. Even my untidy clothes were all folded for me while I was at dinner. In the morning the maid didn't keep on coming to do the room either. First class all round.' *(Mrs M D Prodgers)*

Open: All year.
Rooms: 21 double, 4 suites – all with bath, telephone, radio and colour TV. (7 rooms on ground floor.)
Facilities: Drawing room, bar, restaurant; conference facilities. 3 acres grounds at the foot of the Chiltern Hills.
Location: On the A41, 4 miles on the London side of Aylesbury.
Restriction: Dogs not allowed in public rooms.
Credit cards: Access/Euro, Barclay/Visa.
Terms (excluding VAT):   B & B £23–38. Full *alc* £18.

BARNSTAPLE, Devon   **Map 1**

Downrew House Hotel   *Telephone:* Barnstaple (0271) 2497
Bishops Tawton

'The aim at *Downrew*', say Desmond and Aleta Ainsworth in their mouth-watering brochure, 'has always been that of perfection, whether for a family holiday in the summer months or for guests who require a quiet break out of season.' When we first read those words, we thought that the Ainsworths were sticking their necks out, but now, three years on, reading our file of gratified reports, we recognise that the aim is realistic. *Downrew House* is chiefly Queen Anne (some parts older), with a lodge and a west wing. It's a few miles inland and 500 feet above Barnstaple, on the southern slopes of Codden Hill. The Ainsworths have been running the hotel for the past 18 years; they say that it is unashamedly orientated to the comfort and well-being of their adult guests, though children of all ages are welcomed and all sorts of special amenities provided for them, including their own tea at 5.30. The nearest beaches are eight to ten miles away. Hotels that provide successfully for the welfare of children and their parents are not all that common, but, as the report below indicates, *Downrew* appears to achieve this aim, too – as well, of course, as its target of perfection:

'Totally delightful. Having one child, five years old, it was lovely to have so many facilities for her, and yet to be able to enjoy the food, drink and peaceful surroundings in a holiday location tailored for adults. Even when the hotel was almost full, it still felt like a private house with ourselves as the principal guests.' *(James Dubois)*

Open: Mid March–end October.
Rooms: 14 double, 4 suites – all with bath, radio and colour TV. 5 rooms in West Wing, 2 in Lodge. (2 rooms on ground floor.)
Facilities: Drawing room, 2 lounges, 1 with colour TV, bar, dining room, library, games room, solarium. 14 acres grounds with golf, croquet, tennis court, heated swimming pool. Free fishing within 1½ miles; beaches within 8–10 miles. ᕷ.
Location: Travelling to Barnstaple on the A361, turn left on to the A377 to Exeter. After Bishops Tawton take the left fork off the A377 on to the Chittlehampton road. Then 1¼ miles to *Downrew* on right.
Restriction: No dogs except in Lodge.
Terms (excluding VAT; no service charge):   Dinner, B & B £23.50–34. Reductions for stays of 3 days or more. Special autumn and spring breaks. Reduced rates and special meals for children.

Don't rely on our printed tariffs! Check before booking.

Cavendish Hotel   *Telephone:* Baslow (024 688) 2311

There is no other hotel in the Guide whose entry gives us as much trouble. We left it out last year because, though the hotel had delighted some of its guests, the number of detailed criticisms made it impossible for us to write a recommendable entry. This year, the plusses have outweighed the minusses, but we should be glad of further reports. First on the plus side is the hotel's enviable location. Although on the A619, in the centre of Baslow village, all the rooms overlook Chatsworth Park – a noble vista. And these rooms, though they vary in size, are without exception elegantly furnished, warm and comfortable. The public rooms all have beautiful flower arrangements. Also on the plus side is the eagerness of Eric Marsh, who runs the Cavendish, to please. The Paxton Room Restaurant is another matter. The brochure speaks of 'its perfect view and its controversial menu of individually prepared dishes featuring home-made and local produce eaten from Wedgwood china and Sheffield plate'. We wouldn't quarrel with any of that, not least the word 'controversial': our readers have indeed differed about the quality and pretensions of the food – also about the prices which are 15% higher than they look because, as with the room tariff, they are quoted exclusive of VAT.

So ran, in an expanded form, the 1982 entry for the *Cavendish*. It would be pleasant to record a significant improvement in this year's crop of reports. Changes there have indeed been: the designer Nina Campbell, who made such a success of *Hambleton Hall* (q.v.), has been brought in to give a facelift to the Paxton Restaurant; and, sadly, Eric Marsh's genial brother Peter, who was formerly the barman, has left with Eric's mother to start their own hotel in Glossop. But our readers continue to feel ambivalent about the place – about the quality of the cooking, and also about uneven service. We are aware of the striking lack of entries in Nottinghamshire and Derbyshire. The *Cavendish* is an oasis in an otherwise barren land; we mind having to give it once again no more than a qualified entry.

Open: All year.
Rooms: 12 double, 1 suite – all with bath, direct-dial telephone, radio, colour TV, tea-making facilities, refrigerated bar and baby-listening. (2 rooms on ground floor.)
Facilities: Lounge, bar, restaurant. 1 acre grounds, with golf practice (putting green and driving net); fishing in rivers Derwent and Wye. ⛄.
Location: On the A619 Chesterfield–Bakewell road.
Restriction: No dogs.
Credit cards: American Express, Barclay/Visa.
Terms (excluding VAT; no fixed service charge): Rooms about £38. Set meal: breakfast from £3; full *alc* from about £12. Winter breaks. Cots/extra beds available for children; special meals provided on request.

B & B prices, unless otherwise specified, are per person. Where two figures are given, they indicate the range of prices. The lower figure is for one person sharing a double room in the low season, the higher figure is for one person occupying a room alone in the high season. We have also given full- and half-board prices when available.

BASSENTHWAITE LAKE, Cockermouth, Cumbria   Map 4

The Pheasant Inn   *Telephone:* Bassenthwaite Lake (059 681) 234

The Pheasant Inn is an old-fashioned country inn, of a kind not so easily found these days. It is 16th-century, with lots of genuine inn trimmings. The bar is thoroughly atmospheric, with oak panelling and honest pub furniture, real ale and good bar snacks, though it does have a carpet instead of spit and sawdust. It stands at the head of Bassenthwaite Lake, below Thornthwaite Forest. Our first entry for *The Pheasant* was last year, from a correspondent who found every prospect pleasing except that the manager never once showed himself during a three-day visit and she wished the heating, during a miserably cold April spell, could have come on earlier in the morning. The manager, Mr Barrington Wilson, in returning our questionnaire, included two completed report forms from his guests, testifying to *their* complete satisfaction with the visibility of his management and the adequacy of the heating. 'It is for you to assess the amount of duress needed to extract these,' he added disarmingly. We do discount testimonials which we suspect are solicited – and it usually shows, even if the solicitor doesn't declare his hand. Here, however, is a genuine, if qualified, tribute to the pleasures of *The Pheasant*: 'The Inn is very comfortable in traditional style, with pleasant rooms and excellent service. It is conveniently situated in a quiet location but near to the main Keswick–Cockermouth road. There is a choice of three lounges for residents, all with real fires, and the bar is very popular with the locals. My main criticism was with the dinners, for although the menu showed some imagination and care, the food was rather variable. For example one of the desserts was excellent, fresh strawberries Romanoff, but there were failures elsewhere, and rather mean portions. It seems that they try to produce something above average, but do not often succeed. Still, breakfast was better, with a choice of trout, Arbroath smokie, kippers, Cumberland sausage, etc. Overall, excellent value. No problem with the coldness of the rooms, as mentioned in your report. Provided with constant central heating *and* electric blankets. You can't please all the people: my mother was too hot!' *(Pippa Norris)*
    Another reader praises heating of a different kind: '*Wonderful*. Full of natural warmth and atmosphere. Food excellent. I couldn't help but relax.' *(J B Aultermann; also Kevin Myers)*

Open: All year except Christmas Day.
Rooms: 13 double, 4 single – 11 with bath, 1 with shower. (3 rooms in annexe on ground floor.)
Facilities: 3 lounges, bar, dining room: facilities for private parties and small conferences, 15 acres grounds with 2 acres garden. Sailing, fishing, pony trekking nearby. &.
Location: 7 miles NW of Keswick just off the A66 (on the W side of Bassenthwaite Lake); parking for 80 cars.
Restriction: No dogs in bedrooms.
Terms: B & B £18–20. Set meals: lunch £5.50, dinner £8.50. Reduced rates and half portions for children.

If you consider any entry incorrect, inadequate or misleading, you would be doing us and your fellow travellers a service by letting us know as soon as possible.

The Hole in the Wall   [GFG]   *Telephone:* Bath (0225) 25242/3
16 George Street

What Michelin calls 'a converted Georgian kitchen and coal hole' has recently undergone a further act of conversion and become an elegant restaurant with rooms. It is in the best part of the city, equally convenient to the Pump Room and Abbey below and the Crescent and Assembly Rooms above. The restaurant has been famous for decades past – originally under George Perry-Smith, who has since moved to the *Riverside*, Helford (q.v.). Sue and Tim Cumming trained under George Perry-Smith, then moved to their own restaurant in Salisbury, returned to the *Hole* in 1980 and have now restored the upper floors of their fine Georgian house to make eight double bedrooms, all with bathrooms adjoining. Here is a first report: 'I had what must have been one of the nicest rooms, on the front corner of the third floor, with views over rooftops to the hills beyond. Not a huge room, but comfortably furnished. Biggest white bath sheets I've ever seen, lots of other towels too and face flannels. Bed made down and shutter and curtains closed while you're at dinner. Dinner quite splendid. A fixed menu which is in reality utterly flexible, hardly even decided till they start to cook. Good wines properly served. Service throughout coolly efficient, but reserved rather than unfriendly. One admired the professionalism and integrity. Breakfast very pleasant in a sunny room, tables far apart and large padded chairs, so that one could have a leisurely wallow with the papers (delivered) and the excellent croissants and coffee. Home-made marmalade and jam looked odd but tasted good.' *(BI)*

Open: All year, but B & B only during Christmas and New Year (residents' meals by arrangement). Restaurant closed Sunday to non-residents, and 2 weeks after Christmas.
Rooms: 8 double – all with bath, telephone, colour TV, tea-making facilities and baby-listening. (Warning: light sleepers may find one or two of the rooms rather noisy.)
Facilities: Reception, 2 lounges, 2 bars, 2 dining rooms; function/banqueting facilities.
Location: Central; no private parking.
Restriction: No dogs.
Credit cards: All major credit cards accepted.
Terms: B & B (continental) £19–33; dinner, B & B £31–46. Set meals: English breakfast from £2, lunch £5–14, dinner £14; full *alc* £18. Reduced rates and special meals for children. Special weekend, midweek breaks.

The Priory Hotel   [GFG]   *Telephone:* Bath (0225) 331922
Weston Road   *Telex:* 44612

The Priory has long been a favourite of discriminating hotel-users in Bath. It is not as central, or as spectacularly sited, as the *Royal Crescent* (see below), but some would regard its position – a mile out of the town centre – as a positive advantage; you could hardly expect to find a well-tended 2-acre garden (tea on lawn served under gigantic cedar tree) and a heated swimming pool closer in. The interior of the 1835 Gothic house has also much to recommend it: large comfortable public rooms, individually decorated bedrooms, dependably courteous service and a first-rate restaurant. John Collom, who arrived as the *Priory*'s chef in early 1981, seems to be giving general satisfaction – 'outstanding' and 'superb' were among this year's crop of appreciative adjectives.

But, as with the *Royal Crescent*, there has been more than one reader who has raised eyebrows at the prices charged – more particularly for the rooms. The bedrooms vary in size and quality, but the prices vary relatively little. Adequate hot water for pre-prandial baths has been a problem; breakfasts have disappointed; bedside lighting (at least in some rooms) has been found wanting; and one reader, who had read in a previous edition about 'fresh flowers everywhere', commented that the nondescript little plant in his room was clearly in transit to its maker. Sadly, this entry has to be a 'Recommended – but with reservations'.

Open: All year, except 1–10 January (approx).
Rooms: 12 double, 3 single – 14 with bath, 1 with shower, all with telephone, radio and colour TV.
Facilities: Sitting room, lounge opening on to the garden, bar, restaurant, 2 acres garden with heated outdoor swimming pool.
Location: ¾ mile from town centre; ample parking.
Restrictions: No children under 10. No dogs.
Terms: B & B £34.70–37.50. Full/half board terms on request. Set meal: lunch £8.50; full *alc* £18. Special winter rates November–April. 3-day Christmas programme.

BATH, Avon　　　　　　　　　　　　　　　　　　　　　**Map 2**

The Royal Crescent Hotel [GFG]　　　　*Telephone:* Bath (0225) 319090
Royal Crescent　　　　　　　　　　　　　　　　　*Telex:* 444251

The incomparable position of this hotel – at the exact centre of the peerless Royal Crescent, with views across the city from the front and the Avon hills from the back – together with its impeccably restored and beautifully decorated 18th-century interior, make this one of the most exquisite of English city hotels. Add to this a large and well-kept garden, in which you can recover from the city's crowds with afternoon tea or pre-dinner drinks, a friendly and entirely unstuffy staff, and a skilful if not faultless chef, and there is no doubt that the *Royal Crescent* earns its entry.

But there are some flaws in the crystal. While the suites are stunningly beautiful, pearls beyond price, the smaller rooms, though skilfully converted and generously appointed, and especially the tiny ones under the eaves, seem over-priced and under-insulated. A reader tells us that she heard every word spoken by her neighbours, including a spirited discussion at 6 a.m. as to whether the price of the dinner had been inclusive of VAT. The same reader reported inadequate hot water on the top floor for her pre-prandial bath at 7.30 p.m.

The restaurant, too, has been a partial let-down for several readers. Some dishes have given total satisfaction, but there have been frequent grumbles about this and that: burnt croutons in an uninteresting fish soup; a charred croissant and unfresh orange juice at breakfast; mean helpings of vegetables which were undercooked even by the most 'nouvelle' of standards; an unexciting sweet trolley. At the prices charged, defects are

25

less easy to forgive. And perhaps, too, the disappointments are felt keenly because the hotel has so much going for it. It could be a supreme hotel experience in a supremely beautiful city. At the moment, it falls some way short of that summit.

Open: All year.
Rooms: 19 double, 4 single, 5 suites – all with telephone, radio and colour TV; baby-sitting by arrangement. (3 rooms on ground floor.)
Facilities: Lift, drawing room, cocktail lounge, restaurant. ½ acre grounds. &.
Location: 5 minutes' walk from town centre; parking for 7 cars.
Restriction: No dogs.
Credit cards: All major credit cards accepted.
Terms: B & B £29.75–59.75. Set meals: lunch and dinner £16; full *alc* £19.50. Sundays November–March: dinner, B & B £50. Reduced rates for children sharing parents' rooms, special meals provided.

BATH, Avon   Map 2

Somerset House   *Telephone:* Bath (0225) 66451
10 Dunsford Place, Bathwick Hill

A small reasonably-priced guest house in a listed Georgian terrace, ¾ mile from the Abbey and the Pump Room in a quiet residential area. Jean and Malcolm Seymour are the hosts, and they serve simple well-regarded three-course dinners, specializing in English traditional dishes, with everything home-made and most of the produce (including Mendip snails) home-grown. One couple, while enjoying their visit and feeling it very good value for money, had been mildly put out at the set mealtimes, 8.30 breakfast and dinner at 7 p.m. prompt, and taken aback further when the Seymours said they were going to the theatre, would the couple like to join them and did they mind eating at 6. 'We did, but didn't dare to voice our objection. In fact we decided to make the best of it and go to the theatre too.' His conclusion was that it was an excellent place, but that he had gone expecting a bit too much. Another reader had no qualification: 'Having expected much, anticipation was more than fulfilled.' *(Derrick C Turner)*

Open: All year, except Christmas, New Year and annual holiday (usually October).
Rooms: 3 double (2 can be used as singles).
Facilities: Lounge with TV, dining room. Small garden. 2 minutes from Kennet & Avon Canal – angling for temporary members of Bathampton Angling Club. 12 minutes from Abbey, Roman Baths, shops, etc.
Location: Bathwick Hill runs SE from A36 up to Claverton, University and American Museum; plenty of kerbside parking.
Restrictions: Normally no children under 5. Small dogs allowed in bedrooms only. No smoking in this hotel.
Credit card: Barclay/Visa.
Terms (hotel is not VAT rated): B & B £9.50–9.75; dinner, B & B £15–16. Table d'hôte menu (residents only). Special-interest weekends: Somerset Heritage, Georgian Bath, etc. Reduced rates for children sharing parents' room; special meals available.

Procrastination is the thief of the next edition.

BATTLE, East Sussex   Map 2

Netherfield Place   [GFG]   *Telephone:* Battle (042 46) 4455/7

Several warm reports of this new hotel reached us by almost the same post earlier this year. Since these correspondents had never written to the Guide before and used almost identical words to advocate the attractions of *Netherfield Place*, it was not hard to discern a collusive hand at work. No matter. From reports since, and from a test inspection, we are confident that this handsome 1924 Queen Anne-style mansion set in 30 acres of strikingly beautiful grounds merits inclusion – the more welcome because of the relative paucity of good hotels in this luscious county. (Battle Abbey, the site of the Battle of Hastings, is well worth a visit.)

The hotel is owned and run by the Katnic family – Rajko, Megan and June: new names in the hotel business, but familiar to London gourmets from their years at the *Oslo Court Restaurant*. All our reports speak eloquently of the quality of meals here: the breakfasts, with home-made croissants and rolls and excellent coffee, as well as the three-course dinners. But other things seem to be right too: 'The warmth of the welcome, pretty universally bestowed on all so far as I could see, was altogether unusual. The atmosphere of the place was set by the beaming pleasantness of father, mother and daughter: Saturday dinner felt as if you were at a private even if rather large (70 covers, I think) occasion, where, though the surroundings were distinctly elegant and spacious, a good time really was being had by all.' *(DL; also Eric McKenzie, Dr Douglas Woolf, I S E Wood, R West)*

Open: All year.
Rooms: 7 double, 4 single – 11 with bath, all with telephone, radio and colour TV.
Facilities: Lounge, bar, restaurant, sun-loggia; musical evening and dinner dance once a month. Indoor swimming pool planned for 1983. 30-acre grounds. 15 minutes' drive from the sea, fishing nearby.
Location: 1½ miles from town centre; parking, including 3 lock-up spaces.
Restriction: No dogs.
Credit cards: All major credit cards accepted.
Terms: B & B £24–30; full board £44–50. Set meals: lunch/dinner £11.50; full *alc* £15.50. Reduced rates for children sharing parents' room. Special Christmas break.

BEANACRE, Melksham, Wiltshire   Map 2

Beechfield House Hotel   [GFG]   *Telephone:* Melksham (0225) 703700

The area around Bath is exceptionally well-provided-for with rewarding hotels. *Beechfield* is not as grand as some of its neighbouring rivals – *Hunstrete*, say, or *Homewood Park* at Hinton Charterhouse (q.v.) – but not as expensive either. Architecturally, the house is a gem, provided you have a taste for the ornate Victorian. And Peter Crawford-Rolt has given the same loving attention to the decor as he does to the preparation of his meals. The following report conveys the flavour as well as uttering a warning:

'If Beechfield House had been planned for the pleasure of Guide readers it would be no surprise. It's the archetypal Guide "find". To begin with, it's a rarity . . . a Victorian house which is charming and yet has all the modern comforts. Pretty papers set off the most elegant Victoriana, from brass bedsteads to wine-glasses, and there seems to be an extended family of pretty girls who tend and serve. If you like seafood especially the food is wonderful – and even if you don't, the noisette of lamb I had was worth the whole journey. Well done *Beechfield* for having a proper radio in each room. Only one quibble: it's the only place I've ever been to where the lighting is so absurdly subdued that I had to crouch on the floor under a bedside lamp to do my make-up. It was as bad in the bar area, where elderly guests had to lean over the log fire to peer at the menu. Still, I would advise anyone to go there . . . just take a torch.' *(Di Latham; also C R A Jackson)*

Open: All year except Christmas. Restaurant closed for lunch on bank holidays.
Rooms: 16 double – all with bath, telephone, radio, colour TV, baby-listening. (8 rooms in annexe on ground floor.)
Facilities: Resident's lounge, bar, restaurant, 8 acres grounds with outdoor heated swimming pool, tennis, croquet, all-weather riding ring, stabling, paddock and riding lessons available. Coarse fishing on River Avon 300 yards away. &
Location: On the A350 Melksham–Chippenham road, 2 miles N of Melksham.
Restriction: No dogs in public rooms.
Credit cards: All major credit cards accepted.
Terms (excluding 10% service charge): B & B £20–40. Set meal: lunch £6.50; full *alc* dinner £15. Special meals for children. Special winter breaks.

BIBURY, Nr Cirencester, Gloucestershire   **Map 2**

Bibury Court   *Telephone:* Bibury (028 574) 337

A fine example of a Cotswold manor, dating from Tudor times, but with its main part Jacobean, built in 1633, set in six acres of parkland, with the river Coln (trout fishing rights available) running through the southern boundary of the grounds. 'Our hotel,' writes the owner Mr Collier, 'is run on country house lines, but in order to keep the rates as low as possible, we do not have an excessive staff, so we do not appeal to the "money-can-buy-anything type" or the people who regard staff as inferior people.' Nicely said, but in fact one of the compliments paid to *Bibury Court* this year was from a correspondent who said that he had only to ask to receive anything he wished for and that, as he liked to stay in bed late in the morning when away, *Bibury* got a big plus for schooling the chambermaids not to try to get people to leave their rooms at an early hour. This same writer also reported his amazed surprise, having rung up in March to ask about a winter-break weekend, and, being told that the break bargains had ended in February, had then booked at regular prices, only to be rung back an hour later by the owner to say that he had decided to extend the break prices in his case – at a not inconsiderable saving. He tells us that the food was extremely good, better than on a previous visit and he had much appreciated being given the run of the *à la carte* menu at set rates: a change from treating break visitors as second-class citizens.

Here is another view of *Bibury* which catches the unusual flavour of the place: 'It's a beautiful Jacobean house standing in its own grounds next to a river (stocked with trout) and inside it's comfortable with the air of a not-too-rich friend's country house. There are flagged floors, log fires and a panelled lounge, but absolutely no "hotel touches" in the bedrooms – none. But there are some surprises. My bath was quite the biggest I have ever seen and my bedroom, some 20 feet square, was marvellously furnished in original 1920s down to its joyful grey and blue fruit-design carpet. Dinner was a treat and very cleverly cooked. I didn't manage to see the wine list; it was hogged by a greedy friend who announced it 'stunningly good value' and certainly both the wines we drank were delicious and bought very reasonably. One caveat: I suspect *Bibury Court* may be erratic in its standard of rooms (I notice that previous Guide correspondents have sometimes been dissatisfied). I can certainly vouch for the comfort of rooms 9 and 10, but since the house is a series of nooks and crannies it may be worth asking about your room when you book. Otherwise it's a peaceful and friendly place to stay with lovely surrounding countryside.' *(Gillian Vincent; also John Bennett)*

Open: All year, except Christmas.
Rooms: 13 double, 2 single, 1 suite – 14 with bath, 5 with telephone, 1 with TV; intercom available to residents for baby-listening.
Facilities: TV lounge, residents' lounge, cocktail bar, dining room. 6½-acre grounds with dry fly trout fishing. Golf courses nearby.
Location: On the outskirts of the village; parking.
Restriction: No dogs in dining room.
Credit cards: All major credit cards accepted.
Terms: B & B (continental) £15–18. Set meal: English breakfast £2.50; full *alc* £11.50. Reduced rates and special meals for children. Special winter breaks November–February.

BIDEFORD, North Devon   **Map 1**

Yeoldon House   *Telephone:* Bideford (023 72) 4400/6618
Durrant Lane, Northam

The prospect is invigorating: a great sweep of lawn overlooking the river Torridge, a short distance from where the estuary opens out into the Atlantic at Bideford Bay. The pleasant old market town of Bideford is some two miles downstream; about the same distance in the opposite direction and you will come to the hard golden sands of Westward Ho! beach, with safe bathing as well as Malibu surfing and fishing facilities. (The famous Westward Ho! championship golf course is 1½ miles away.) The hotel is run by the owner-managers, Chris and Judi Fulford – Judi being a Cordon Bleu-trained cook. They celebrate their tenth birthday at *Yeoldon* this year. It's an enterprising place, with all kinds of special activities at various times of the year: guided coastal walks, moorland rambles, birdwatching weeks (with instruction), gourmet weekends in the winter, and so forth. The hotel has consistently enjoyed good reports from our readers. Here is a recent example:

'The baby-listening service offered in the *Guide* was much improved by the installation of our wireless baby alarm, which intrigued other guests and impressed the ubiquitous and jolly owner of the hotel, Chris Fulford, while his wife and co-owner, Judi, paused from her Cordon Bleu creations to provide for our baby son. Nothing was too much trouble for them, and if cauliflower cheese for the baby's lunch meant cauliflower was on the dinner menu later that day, there was every reason for the other guests to praise our son's discerning tastes (it was cooked perfectly). The hotel caters for the fads of young and old alike (though one couple were bemused to find their regular sleep-inducing glasses of warm milk cold in parts until they discovered they were warmed up in a microwave oven to save washing the saucepan). Everything was provided to ensure a restful and peaceful holiday, with our hosts and their capable staff on hand to meet our every need. Apart from fine weather, what more can one ask?' *(Joshua Rozenberg)*

Open: All year, except 4 days over Christmas and 20 January–14 February.
Rooms: 9 double, 1 single – all with bath or shower and WC, radio and colour TV; 1 four-poster bed; baby-listening if required.
Facilities: Sitting room, bar, restaurant, 2 acres grounds surrounded by fields and river. At nearby Westward Ho! there are 2 miles of sandy beach with safe bathing and Malibu surfing; golf at the championship Westward Ho! course, and at Saunton; sailing on the estuary, sea and river; fishing, riding and pony-trekking; birdwatching.
Location: 2 miles downstream from Bideford.
Restriction: No dogs.
Credit cards: Access/Euro, American Express, Barclay/Visa, Diners.
Terms: B & B £19.50–26; dinner, B & B £19.75–34.50. Full board (for 1 week) £132–205. Set meal: dinner £8.50; full *alc* £11. Bargain breaks and special gourmet weekends in winter. Special honeymoon rates and golf holidays. Reduced rates and special meals for children; babies and small children free.

BISHOPS TACHBROOK, Leamington Spa, Warwickshire   Map 2

Mallory Court   [GFG]   *Telephone:* Leamington Spa (0926) 30214
Harbury Lane

We said last year that this luxurious Twenties mansion (with spacious richly-furnished rooms to match), set in ten acres of beautifully land-scaped gardens, was by far the most attractive place to stay within a 25-mile radius of the National Exhibition Centre outside Birmingham. We would say the same again. As one reader puts it: 'It is a superb civilized oasis in this area. Very expensive but very comfortable. Immacu-lately maintained and with magnificent food.' One reader protested, when paying £45 for single occupancy of a double room, at having to pay extra for morning tea and a further 20p for a morning paper. The question of what a hotel should 'throw in' with the basic charge is always tricky. In general, we don't think the prices, though high, are excessive for what is offered, though we would like to see the hotel offer more wines at the lower end of the scale: there is little to be had for less than £10, and £14.50 for a 1978 Chablis seems pretty steep. But the only serious drawback about *Mallory Court*, for the non-business user, is that its location and the absence of competition, does give the place at many times of the year, an over-businesslike air. *(Pat and Jeremy Temple; also Bernard Theobald, Julia de Waal)*

Open: All year, except 25–30 December, 1 January, 2 weeks in January.
Rooms: 6 double, 1 single – 6 with bath, all with telephone, radio on request and colour TV.
Facilities: Lounge, drawing room, oak-panelled dining room, sun lounge. 10 acres grounds and landscaped gardens, water garden, rose garden, terraces; outdoor swimming pool, squash courts, croquet; golf 2 miles.
Location: 2 miles S of Leamington Spa off the A452.
Restrictions: No children under 14. No dogs.
Credit cards: All major credit cards accepted.
Terms: B & B (continental) £25.50–39.50. Set meals: English breakfast £5.50; lunch £10; dinner £18.50.

BLAKENEY, Nr Holt, Norfolk

Map 2

The Blakeney Hotel
Telephone: Cley (0263) 740797
Telex: 975465

Built by the formidable Sir Henry Deterding of Shell fame in 1920, *The Blakeney* has a particularly agreeable site: it is a low rambling building right on one of the more picturesque of Norfolk harbours, looking out over flotillas of small craft to Blakeney Point and the sea. A lot of people are attracted to Blakeney as a centre for sailing and fishing, but it is also a mecca for ornithologists, with three bird sanctuaries close by. The hotel is large by the standard of the Guide, but has a reputation for being well-run and friendly, and sympathetic to families with children. There is a heated indoor pool and a large garden behind the hotel. No special claims to culinary distinction. *(David R W Jervois, Ann Carr)*

Open: All year.
Rooms: 37 double, 17 single, 2 suites – 36 with bath and TV, all with telephone, radio, tea-making facilities and baby-listening. 13 rooms in annexe. (Some rooms on ground floor.)
Facilities: 2 lounges, 4 bars, TV room, games room; heated indoor swimming pool, sauna, 6 acres garden with outdoor children's play area; safe bathing, fishing. &.
Location: On the quay.
Restriction: No dogs in public rooms.
Credit cards: All major credit cards accepted.
Terms (no fixed service charge): B & B £16–24. Set meals: lunch £6, dinner £8: full *alc* £9.50. Free accommodation for children under 12 sharing parents' room. Special bargain breaks all year. Christmas house party.

BLANCHLAND, Nr Consett, Co Durham

Map 4

The Lord Crewe Arms Hotel
Telephone: Blanchland (043 475) 251
Telex: 53168

Blanchland is on the river Derwent, about 30 miles north-west of Newcastle-upon-Tyne, and six miles west of Consett – though, with a hill providentially in between, Consett's dark satanic mills might not exist. It is surrounded by moors, fields, forests and a lake – some of the loneliest scenery in Britain. The name of the village comes from the white robes of the monks who inhabited Blanchland Abbey from its founding in the 12th century until its dissolution in the 16th. And *The Lord Crewe Arms* was once the Abbot's lodgings, guest house and kitchen, before becoming a manor house and now, its latest transformation, a small country hotel. There is a Priest's Hole lounge, a Crypt Bar, and, reputedly, a 250-year-old ghost.

The place is run by Ermes Oretti and his English wife. In a long report on the charms of the hotel, we particularly liked this account of Signor Oretti in his role as maître d': 'The Manager, Ermes Oretti, presides – reigns, rather – in the dining room like the monarch of the place that he is, in pullover and trousers at breakfast time and neatly suited in the evening. He is the doyen of all Italian head waiters. He must have ten pairs of eyes arranged all round, and he encompasses his dining room in a series of graceful noiseless swoops (one cannot help but be reminded of the hawks

31

one sees on the moors). He meets you at the door, escorts you to the table, draws back the chairs, sweeps the napkins off the table and places them on your lap as you hit the chair, the table is shifted into position and the menu appears like a rabbit out of a hat – and all with an affability, style and economy of motion that is a joy to behold and must have taken years to perfect. All this with a full house too! Breakfast starts at 8 a.m. and they were still rolling in to dinner up to 9 o'clock at night but that unforced courtesy and critical omnipresence never varied by a shadow's breadth all day. The food is sound rather than inspired cooking, very enjoyable and better than one would expect, the north-east being something of a gastronomic wasteland. *The Lord Crewe* is not the *Ritz*. It is not in the Grand Hotel bracket, and is certainly not in the modern, plastic and glass class either. Among its other roles, it is the only village pub, but it has much character and charm, and is run by people who know their job and put their backs into doing it. My wife and I have been there three times in the past year. It suits us and we think it will suit a lot of other people too.' *(Jeff Driver)*

Open: All year.
Rooms: 15 double, 2 single – 9 with bath, 11 with shower, all with telephone, tea-making facilities and baby-listening. 12 rooms in annexe.
Facilities: Lounge, TV room, bar, restaurant; 1-acre garden. Near Derwent reservoir. Sailing, trout fishing available nearby; golf, horse racing 10 miles.
Location: On the B6306 S of Hexham. From the E you can turn off the A68 – there is a hotel warning sign on the main road.
Restriction: No dogs in restaurant.
Credit cards: All major credit cards accepted.
Terms: B & B £13–20; dinner, B & B £18–22 (minimum 2 days). Set meals: lunch £5, dinner £7.80. Special winter and summer bargain breaks. Reduced rates and special meals for children (they are charged only for food if they share their parents' room).

BLOCKLEY, Moreton-in-Marsh, Gloucestershire   **Map 2**

Lower Brook House   *Telephone:* Blockley (0386) 700286

If you want a good central base from which to tour the Cotswolds, you could fare worse than spending a few days at Lower Brook House. *Blockley, once famous for its silk trade, is full of handsome Cotswold houses and cottages; it has little or no tourist passing trade itself, but is within a few miles of such resonant names as Chipping Campden, Broadway, Moreton-in-Marsh, Hidcote with its famous gardens – not to mention Stratford-upon-Avon.* Lower Brook House *is a delightful cottagey hotel, with pretty cosy rooms, and a small terraced garden leading down to the brook which gives the place its name. For several years past, it has been in the caring and capable hands of John and Mavis Price. As we go to press, we learn that the hotel has been sold. The new owner is Ewan Wright, who has been in the hotel business most of his life, but has come to Blockley by way of Achaba, where he has been in charge of the Royal Summer Palace of the Royal Jordanian Household. He tells us that he has no plans for structural changes, but will be introducing a more 'English cuisine' than the Prices. Reports welcome.*

If you have difficulty in finding hotels because directions given in the Guide are inadequate, please help us to improve them.

Open: All year except approx. end December–end January.
Rooms: 7 double, 1 single – 6 with bath, all with tea-making facilities; colour TV on request.
Facilities: Lounge, bar, restaurant. ½ acre garden.
Location: On edge of village; turn off the A44 2 miles N of Moreton-in-Marsh.
Restriction: No dogs.
Credit card: Access.
Terms (service at guests' discretion): Dinner, B & B £31; full *alc* £15. Winter breaks: November–mid March. Special meals for children.

BOLTON-BY-BOWLAND, Clitheroe, Lancashire   **Map 2**

Harrop Fold Farm Guest House   *Telephone:* Bolton-by-Bowland
Harrop Fold   (020 07) 600

A thoroughly enterprising set-up, even if not quite a hotel. As the name implies, Harrop Fold is a working farm in a secluded and remote hamlet in the heart of the Pennines, run by various members of the Wood family, who also look after the guest side of things. They organize several special occasions, such as an Old English Game weekend, and Lancashire and Scandinavian evenings. Their menus are ambitious and exotic, including a dish called Surf and Turf which revives an old-fashioned idea of combining seafood and red meat. They are keen to encourage their guests to enjoy their countryside, and even offer in their brochure to pick up walkers at the end of the day if they find the return journey too much. One guest, arriving at 9.45 in the evening, was immediately asked if he would like a meal; he ended his report: 'We have never found a more friendly hotel or one offering better value for money.' A second report is given below:

'Calls itself a guest house, but with chef ex-*Miller Howe* it is definitely a cut above the others in the area. Rooms have rather twee names (I was in Meadow Suite) but are more than adequate with nice bathrooms and all sorts of extras. It is a working farm and Mr Wood Senior is not much in evidence, but Mrs Wood and her son make the guests very comfortable. It is hell to find (I resorted to asking a policeman) but once there it was lovely. The public rooms are tiny but beautifully restored and there are only five bedrooms (one of them is suitable for the disabled as it is on the ground floor and has a shower and handrails instead of a bath, and twin beds instead of a double). Dinner was very good with nicely cooked duckling and profiteroles that a puff of wind would blow away. Breakfast was enormous, and to sit gazing out of a window on to rolling hills whilst enjoying homebaked bread, fresh honey and home-made marmalade and jam was bliss.' *(Mrs S Chait; also Ian Whitney)*

Open: All year.
Rooms: 5 double – 4 with bath, 1 with shower, all with colour TV and tea-making facilities. 2 rooms in annexe. (1 room on ground floor with extra wide doors, and weight bars.) &

Facilities: Large loft lounge, bar/lounge, dining room. Small conference facilities. 280 acres grounds.
Location: 6 miles from Clitheroe. Harrop Fold Hamlet is located on the Grindleton-Slaidburn road (Ordnance Survey Map No. 103 *75 × 49*).
Restrictions: No children. Small dogs at management's discretion.
Terms: B & B £11.60–15. Packed lunches/bar snacks available. Full *alc* £10.50. Game weekends November–Easter (excluding Christmas); Lancashire/Scandinavian/Game Buffet evenings; 4-day Christmas house party.

Peacock Vane [GFG]   *Telephone:* Ventnor (0983) 852019

'Those who cherish *Peacock Vane* will argue over its chief attraction: whether it is the elegant Regency house nestling on the Bonchurch rock face; the finely simple English cooking and classic, inexpensive wines; or the ability of John and Rosalind Wolfenden to make one feel like a guest in a private house, though with no obligation save to rest, eat and listen to the twin songs of wood pigeons and the sea. The atmosphere is less that of hotel than old-fashioned manor house, growing its own vegetables, baking its own bread, bottling its own preserves – a fortress, protecting its inhabitants against all the usual hotel's homogenized impersonality. The charge of about £20 per head for bed, breakfast and four-course dinner seems almost worryingly moderate, and the house rule against hidden extras makes one frequently scan one's final (hand-written) bill in anxiety that the Wolfendens may have charged too little. The few bedrooms, booked solid during summer weekends, are offered at even more moderate terms early in the week. To sit in the beautiful upper drawing room, sipping drinks served from a grand piano-top, before the traditionally lavish Sunday night cold table, is the quintessential *Peacock Vane* experience – taste combining with unpretentiousness, comfort with excellence, happy anticipation with absolute tranquillity of mind.' *(Philip Norman)*

Open: Easter–November and 2 weeks at Christmas. Restaurant closed midday Monday/Tuesday.
Rooms: 8 double – all with bath, mono TV and tea-making facilities; baby-listening by arrangement. (4 rooms in 3 annexes.)
Facilities: Large drawing room, dining room. 3 acres grounds with heated swimming pool. Sea at Bonchurch Shore, ¼ mile away.
Location: 1st drive on left after pond, coming from Ventnor (1 mile away); parking.
Restrictions: Children over 7 preferred. No dogs in public rooms.
Credit cards: All major credit cards accepted.
Terms: Dinner, B & B £20. Set meals (no fixed service charge): lunch £7.50, dinner £12. Negotiable rates for children.

Winterbourne Hotel   *Telephone:* Ventnor (0983) 852535

'The location is quite delightful. It is situated next to the tiny old church in a quiet cul-de-sac and, behind the buildings, enchanting gardens slope down the hillside in interlocking terraces of beautiful lawns, gravel paths, herbaceous and rose borders. Hidden away are sheltered areas to sunbathe and a completely secluded modern 40-ft heated swimming pool. A

We should be glad to hear of good hotels in Olympia.

stream and waterfall gurgle away downhill, and one can go down to the beach through a gate at the bottom of the garden opening on to a footpath which meanders down to the shore. The decor of the house is Regency. There are everywhere, even in the ladies' loo, profuse and magnificent flower arrangements. The reception rooms are light and airy, and the furniture comfortable.'

So runs part of an inspector's long report on the *Winterbourne*. It sounds like a corner of paradise, and in fact Charles Dickens, who leased the house in 1849, while writing *David Copperfield*, called it, 'The prettiest place I've seen at home or abroad.' There is no doubt that it could be one of the most idyllic country-house hotels in the book. We don't think it is that at present. Service seems to be very variable, with staff that lack experience or a firm co-ordinating hand. One visitor commented on customers being kept waiting at dinner on a busy Saturday night while the owners were being attended to at another table. The food, though not expensive, also lacks distinction. We suspect that many of the guests have the kind of English good manners which make them shy about complaining. All that having been said, we believe many readers would enjoy a visit, even if the hotel doesn't quite live up to its pretensions. But we should welcome more reports.

Open: 22 January–5 November.
Rooms: 16 double, 3 single – 17 with bath, all with colour TV. 6 rooms in annexe.
Facilities: 2 lounges, cocktail bar, restaurant, terrace. 4 acres terraced gardens overlooking sea with pools, stream and heated swimming pool. Paths to coves, safe bathing, sand/shingle beach; riding, fishing, tennis, bowls, golf, etc, available nearby.
Location: 1 mile from town centre; from Yarmouth, Fishbourne, East Cowes, follow signs to Ventnor, then Bonchurch. Parking.
Restrictions: No children under 7. No dogs in dining room or annexe; allowed in garden and other public rooms if on lead.
Credit cards: All major credit cards accepted.
Terms: B & B £12–24.20; dinner, B & B £20.50–34.50. Set meals (excluding 10% service charge): lunch £5.75, dinner £9.50. Children sharing parents' room: ⅔ adult rate. Bargain rates October–end March (2 nights minimum).

BORROWDALE, Keswick, Cumbria   **Map 4**

Seatoller House   *Telephone:* Borrowdale (059 684) 218

As we went to press last year, we learnt that Geoffrey and Gillian Trevelyan were giving up the active running of this well-known much-loved guest house at the foot of Honister Pass, and that David and Ann Pepper would now be in charge, even though the house continues to be owned by a Trevelyan family trust. Reports on the Pepper regime, we are glad to say, are all as enthusiastic as one could wish. 'Be not afraid,' writes one old Seatollerian: 'The Pepper regime *is* maintaining the house's traditional style of hospitality. Need I say more? We have been addicts for the last four years and remain addicted.' Another Old Boy goes further: 'My fears were groundless: Mr and Mrs Pepper are if anything friendlier than the previous incumbents, making the atmosphere more relaxed, the

---

Are there no good hotels in Bristol? Write *now* if you have suggestions.

---

standard of food has been maintained and the general cleanliness improved.' Warning (for some): *Seatoller* is a simple house. Bathrooms and lavatories are shared. The evening meal is at 7, breakfast is at 8.45, and at these times you must stand by. Everyone sits together. For some, staying here is like being at some small house party, but it won't be to everyone's taste. *(Dr David Ball, J M Leigh; also Heather and Roy Sharland, John Hills, Dr and Mrs N J Hodgson)*

Open: Approx. mid March–mid November. No dinner Tuesday evening.
Rooms: 8 double (2 rooms on ground floor).
Facilities: 2 lounges, tea bar, picnic shop. Small conference facilities. 2 acres grounds.
Location: 8 miles from Keswick on the B5289. Regular bus service from Keswick.
Restriction: No children under 5.
Terms (service at guests' discretion): Dinner, B & B £15.50–£16.50; weekly board £94–101. Dinner £5. Reduced rates for children of 12 and under sharing parents' room (⅔ adult price).

BOSHAM, Nr Chichester, Sussex   **Map 2**

The Millstream Hotel   *Telephone:* Bosham (0243) 573234
Bosham Lane

An attractive red-brick and flint building, mostly modern, with a major overhaul ten years ago, that fits happily into the landscape of this popular picturesque sailing village. There is a stream with ducks that runs by the hotel's well-kept front lawn, where you can sit with drinks or bar snacks. Rooms are full of little extras, including bubble baths and a trouser-press. 'I enjoyed a delightful stay. The staff are pleasant and helpful; they don't advertise room service but were happy to bring some sandwiches to our room on a Saturday afternoon. The food at breakfast and dinner was first-class and beautifully presented, though the toast might have been crisper and a greater selection of breakfast jams would have been appreciated; also the dining room could do with a facelift. But the attention and care of the Italian waiters overcame the surroundings. It really was a pleasure to stay here. Most of the guests seem to have been before.' *(Susi Coben)*

Open: All year.
Rooms: 19 double, 3 single – 19 with bath, 20 with colour TV, all with telephone, radio and tea-making facilities. (3 rooms on ground floor.)
Facilities: Lounge with TV, bar, restaurant. Conference facilities. ½-acre garden. Sailing, fishing, riding, golf nearby. ♿.
Location: 4 miles W of Chichester off the A27. Follow signs to Bosham Quay. Car park.
Restrictions: No children under 7. No dogs in public rooms.
Credit cards: All major credit cards accepted.
Terms: B & B £18–23. Full *alc* £13. Special winter/spring weekend breaks, 4–7 day Christmas programme, theatre packages, sailing weekends.

If you have had recent experience of a good hotel that ought to be in the Guide, please write to us at once. Report forms (Freepost in the UK) are at the end of the book.

BRAMPTON, Cumbria   Map 4

Farlam Hall   [GFG]   *Telephone:* Hallbankgate (069 76) 234

Once again nothing but praise for the welcome, comfort and outstanding board provided by Mr and Mrs Quinion in their part 17th-century Border manor house four miles from Hadrian's Wall. The building itself, once a farmhouse, has historical interest: Wesley is thought to have preached there, and George ('Rocket') Stephenson was a visitor. The country around – despite its castles and abbeys as well as its great scenic beauty – continues to be wonderfully unspoilt by tourist invasion even in the height of summer. 'Tremendous place to stay – extremely comfortable room with luxurious private bathroom. No possible complaints about dinner – everything was fresh and carefully cooked, and it had the best cheese board we have encountered. The dining-room service was excellent. Again, we were delighted with our breakfast, especially the mushroom omelette. The whole Quinion family combined to make our stay an exceedingly pleasant one: we cannot praise them too highly.' *(Harry and May McIver; also Roy and Norah Hill)*

Open: All year, except first two weeks November, Christmas, and February; also closed Monday–Tuesday in November, December and January.
Rooms: 9 double, 2 single – 4 with bath, 2 with shower.
Facilities: 3 lounges, 1 with TV, bar, dining room seating about 50. 2 golf courses nearby.
Location: On the A689 2½ miles SE of Brampton; Carlisle 9 miles W; Hadrian's Wall 4 miles. The hotel is on the A689, *not* in Farlam village.
Credit cards: Access/Euro, American Express.
Terms (service at guests' discretion): B & B £17.50–20.50. Set meals: lunch £8, dinner £10.50. Reduced rates mid November–mid April.

BRIXHAM, South Devon   Map 1

The Quayside Hotel   *Telephone:* Brixham (080 45) 55751/2/3/4
King Street   *Telex:* 42962

In our entry last year, we described this conversion of five 17th- and 18th-century cottages as 'overlooking the inner harbour of this small fishing village on the southern headland of Torbay' and we went on to recommend the front rooms 'even if you are woken at dawn by a cacophony of seagulls meeting the incoming fishing boats.' One reader felt our entry had misled him: the hotel does overlook the harbour, but it also overlooks a busy noisy road. He minded, too, that the car park available to *Quayside* guests should be some 300 yards away. And he did not much care for the food either, which he dubbed 'bland', while the surcharge for local fish on the menu seemed to him excessive. We should be glad of further reports, but in the meantime note that another *Quayside* guest felt very differently. He would have agreed with the first correspondent about the food, which was nothing out of the ordinary but warmed to the character and feel of the hotel, which he felt was much above the norm for the locality. *(Alan Ross)*

Please don't just leave the feedback to others.

Open: All year.

Rooms: 28 double, 4 single – 26 with bath, all with telephone, radio, colour TV, tea-making facilities and baby-listening. 2 rooms in annexe.

Facilities: Lounge, 2 bars, restaurant; live entertainment several times a week. Shingle beach and seawater swimming pool nearby; deep sea and mackerel fishing trips during season.

Location: 200 yards from town centre; ample parking (300 yards away).

Credit cards: All major credit cards accepted.

Terms: B & B £16.68–25.88; dinner B & B (min. 3 days) £21.74–32.20. Set meals: lunch £4.85, dinner £8; full *alc* £12. 2-day bargain breaks; Christmas programme. Reduced rates for children sharing parents' room; special meals provided.

BROAD CAMPDEN, Chipping Campden, Gloucestershire   Map 2

The Malt House   *Telephone:* Evesham (0386) 840295

Many owners of small country hotels would like their guests to feel that they were staying in a private country house even though paying for the privilege. Mrs Pat Robinson, whose *Malt House* is a conversion of three mellow Cotswold 17th-century cottages in an unspoilt hamlet a mile from Chipping Campden, is particularly keen to foster this atmosphere: her guests – the house can accommodate no more than six – will often sit together round a large single table for the evening meal, though they can opt for separate tables if they wish. 'Mrs Robinson gave us a marvellous welcome, beaming and helpful like a sensible favourite aunt. Throughout our visit she was attentive, ever-present but never obtrusive. We found the food to be excellent. We arrived having forgotten to ask for a special meal as I am vegetarian (husband not), and it was simply an exciting challenge for cheerful Mrs Robinson; we were served soufflés, one haddock, one mushroom, followed by masses of superbly cooked fresh vegetables, and an imaginative watercress salad; my husband had pheasant and after the sweet (nothing to rave about) there was the best Stilton we'd ever eaten. Generous, wonderful food. The garden with ha-ha, stream and sheep-filled orchard are a delight. The atmosphere was very relaxed and easy; we felt at home. Though not highly sociable people, we really enjoyed sharing the long farmhouse table near the vast open fire for breakfast and dinner. Although the GHG had the stipulation "Children over 10 preferred", Mrs Robinson has no strong objection to younger children – as long as they are well-behaved and don't jump on the furniture! As our baby was ten months at the time, she was very welcome!' *(Joanna C Melzack; also Jill Bickerton, HR)*

Open: All year, except 24, 25, 26 December.

Rooms: 3 double – all with private bath, 1 single, only let *en suite* with double.

Facilities: Drawing room, restaurant. 4 acres grounds with large gazebo and small brook. Spinning workshops held occasionally.

Location: Leave Chipping Campden by Sheep street, turn first left after garage on left into Broad Campden; *Malt House* second on left after the *Baker's Arms* pub; parking.

Restrictions: Children over 10 preferred. No dogs.

Terms (no fixed service charge): B & B £13–17; dinner, B & B £23. Set meal: dinner from £8.

> Hotels are dropped if we lack positive feedback.

BROADWAY, Worcestershire   Map 2

Lygon Arms   [GFG]   *Telephone:* Broadway (0386) 852255
                                           Telex: 338260

Ever since we started work on the Guide, we have been inundated with conflicting reports on this famous and sophisticated hostelry. Many visitors have felt that it had become too successful, that it was resting on its laurels. Often, we suspect, the complaints came from English people who were reacting against a hotel so blatantly popular with overseas visitors. When a hotel is constantly being recommended to tourists, as the Lygon Arms is, as the hotel to stop off at in the Cotswolds, it is bound to alter its native colouring. Nevertheless, this is how the hotel strikes one English visitor:
'Broadway has become almost too famous for its own good – the Cotswold village par excellence with razor-trimmed grass verges and mellow stone buildings of picture postcard perfection lining its broad curve of street. The Lygon Arms is one of these buildings and something of a showpiece in its own right. Starting life as a modest inn in the 16th century, it has developed into a distinguished and fairly luxurious hotel without losing its venerable charm. The older parts of the building are furnished with fine antiques with everything from log-fired inglenooks to a great hall with minstrel's gallery to delight the romantic eye. Unobtrusive wings of modern bedrooms, in garden settings, provide sleek contemporary comfort. Douglas Barrington runs the hotel with ceaseless devotion and a sharp eye for detail. He inspires his staff with a capacity for friendly and personal service rare enough in this age of diminishing standards. (Roger Smithells)

We have printed the above in italics because it is taken from the 1979 Guide. *The Lygon Arms* then disappeared from these pages, the opposition having become more vociferous. We are delighted to welcome it back. The fabric and character of the place have changed little, though perhaps the word 'luxurious' above no longer needs to be qualified by 'fairly'. But there has been a radical improvement in the restaurant since Shaun Hill, formerly head chef at the *Capital*, joined *Lygon* in 1980. There is a distinguished wine list. And the charge of snootiness, which used to be heard, happily no longer seems to apply. But we should be glad of further reports.

Open: All year.
Rooms: 62 double, 5 single, 4 suites – all with bath, telephone, radio, colour TV and baby-sitting by arrangement. (9 rooms on ground floor.) (1 four-poster bed.)
Facilities: Numerous lounges including Gin Lounge and residents' drawing room with TV, bar, restaurant. Conference/function facilities for 100 people. 2-acre garden with tennis court.
Location: In Broadway High Street; especially quiet rooms available on request; parking for 200 cars and 2 garages.
Restriction: No dogs in restaurant or in other public rooms without manager's permission.
Credit cards: All major credit cards accepted.
Terms (service at guests' discretion):   B & B (continental) £33–39. Set meals: breakfast £3.30, lunch £8.25 (buffet £3.30), dinner £14; full *alc* £20. Children: extra bed in parents' room, £5.50; special children's menu. Reduced rates November–end April (min. 2 nights), May–end October (min. 3 nights).

Don't keep your favourite hotel to yourself. Hotels are *glad* to be in the Guide. Good hotels need all the support they can get.

Hell Bay Hotel   *Telephone:* Scillonia (0720) 22947

Bryher is somewhat overshadowed by its larger and more sophisticated neighbour, Tresco. It shares with all the other islands in the group a warm climate and ruggedly beautiful scenery, but will appeal specially to some just because it is less well-known and therefore emptier. *Hell Bay* is so far the only hotel on the island – a conversion by its engineer owner, Mr Philpot, of an old farmhouse. The somewhat functional bedrooms, which are round a courtyard, are designed also to be let as self-catering units if required: ideal for families.

'Excellent position with three beautiful beaches within five minutes' walk; view of freshwater lake (nature reserve) from hotel, but no view of the sea. Beaches this year almost always empty – island quite unspoilt – birds, butterflies, wild flowers, and no traffic. Staff at hotel extremely friendly and helpful, service at meals good and quick, but it is a new hotel and so far not many guests, so it is difficult to tell what it would be like if full. Food plentiful though not exciting; a well-supplied bar. Our two-room apartment had full equipment for self-catering – stove, sink, refrigerator, pans, china, etc. – all details carefully thought out. We particularly noted the good quality of all fittings. There was a toilet and shower, and two armchairs in the sitting room converted easily into extra beds. Duvets on beds, but sheets were provided on request. Bryher has no facilities for entertainment in bad weather, nor are there any in the hotel. In good weather (which we had) there are interesting daily trips by launch to lighthouse, outer islands, etc., and to St Mary's where there are shops; one very good shop on Bryher itself.' *(Lady Sinker; also Mrs A Pirie)*

Open: 1 March–30 October.
Rooms: 2 double, 10 suites with shower, all with tea-making facilities. (All rooms on ground floor.)
Facilities: TV room, reception-lounge, bar, dining room. 3½ acres garden. Sandy and rocky beaches, good sea fishing.
Location: Access by air or sea from Penzance to St Mary's; launch service to Bryher. Parking facilities at Penzance.
Restriction: No dogs.
Terms: Dinner, B & B £18.50–21.50. Suites (with self-catering) from £78 per week. Set meals (excluding service): lunch £3, dinner £7. Reduced rates for children sharing parents' suite. (Convertible chair/bed in sitting room.)

Budock Vean Hotel   *Telephone:* Mawnan Smith (0326) 250288

Budock Vean is best described as a resort hotel. Converted from an 18th-century manor, but with modern extensions, it has 53 bedrooms, 65 acres leading down to the Helford river, a golf course, and plenty of other facilities listed below. By the standard of this Guide, if not by the standard of many resort hotels in the States, it is a substantial establishment. At one stage, we thought that it had no place in the book, but a campaign of 'Put *Budock Vean* back!' convinced us otherwise. The description below admirably characterizes its appeal: 'My wife and I have spent many happy holidays at this delightful hotel, where service and courtesy predominate.

Mr and Mrs Whiteside, assisted by other members of the family, set out to provide an atmosphere of a country house filled with invited guests. Each year we leave after a satisfying holiday, believing it can never be as good next year, but it is always better. The chefs may change, but the cuisine always improves, and you would have to be very fastidious not to find something to your taste at every meal. I believe there is an *à la carte* menu, but I have never needed to ask for it. For the connoisseur there are plenty of wines from which to choose, but the house wines, at very reasonable prices, underline the quality and acceptable costing of the whole enterprise. The bedrooms are tastefully decorated, and have both splendid views and every modern convenience. The recently decorated lounges are graceful and comfortable, and provide a separate room for non-smokers. Being golfers we enjoy the splendid 9-hole course with cunningly devised 18 tees which produce a challenge to the tyro and weekend golfer alike. If your pleasures are sailing, fishing, walking, country interests, folklore, photography or gardening, all are within easy reach. If this is insufficient to entertain you, there is a Golfers' Bar, with a gaming machine, snooker table, and all the atmosphere of your favourite inn, including snacks. Nearby there is the best indoor pool I have ever seen, and if still anxious for exercise a games room for the pleasure of young and old. We have visited many hotels in Europe and the States, and will return to *Budock Vean*, as we still think it best in location, value for money and friendliness.' *(A Furber Murphy; also F W Grant, V Thynne, B W Croft, Rev. M Osborne, D J Bratt)*

Open: All year.
Rooms: 42 double, 10 single, 1 suite – all with bath and telephone; TV on request.
Facilities: Lift, 4 lounges (2 with TV), restaurant, games room, sun lounge; heated indoor pool. Weekly dance in restaurant and weekly disco in bar August/September. 65 acres grounds with gardens leading down to Helford River; golf course, private sandy tidal foreshore with sailing, windsurfing and fishing; horse riding and fly fishing nearby. &.
Location: 7 miles from Falmouth; take the A39 from Truro to Penryn Cross, then proceed to Mabe Bunrthouse, then to Mawnan Smith, and from Mawnan Smith to the hotel.
Restrictions: No children under 5. No dogs.
Credit cards: All major credit cards accepted.
Terms (service at guests' discretion): B & B £17–27; dinner, B & B £22–37. Set meals: lunch £3.50, dinner £12; full *alc* £18. Off-season weekend rates and half-term breaks. Reduced rates and special meals for children.

BURFORD, Oxfordshire   **Map 2**

The Bay Tree   *Telephone:* Burford (099 382) 3137
Sheep Street

The Bay Tree, a noble Elizabethan house (it was once the home of Elizabeth I's unpopular Lord Chief Baron of the Exchequer) in a small street off Burford's magnificent High Street, looks in every way a fitting place to stay in what has been called the most beautiful village in England. Inside, too, there is no shortage of atmospheric detail: oak panelling, huge stone fireplaces, galleried stairs, sloping floors and some fine antique furniture. The hotel has been owned and run for many years by Sylvia Raven, and has, over the years, had many enthusiastic supporters as well as some passionate detractors. This year has been no exception. As

41

before, there have been complaints about stuffy staff, shabby poky rooms, and some poor cooking. Clearly, the hotel lacks a dependable standard of service, accommodation and meals, but that it can provide satisfaction is evidenced by the following report, among others:

'I cannot fault this hotel on any score but if one wants to be super-niggly then: bath towels too small; no tumblers, or possibly just one, in bedroom and Sunday paper not brought with breakfast but left on dining room table! Very warm and courteous welcome by efficient receptionist, apologizing for inability to accommodate us in main hotel. Room in annexe next door very pleasant if small, good genuine antique furniture, comfortable bed, sufficient hanging and drawer space, good bathroom, well heated, boiling hot water. No keys to rooms which seems to be a feature of the establishment and as far as I'm concerned this touch of old-world trust is very welcome as is the absence of radios, televisions and telephones. The set dinner, by candlelight, at £5.75 per person [1982] for three courses each with a choice of four different dishes is very good value indeed; food was well prepared, completely unpretentious, with stress on good ingredients and high quality rather than indigestible disguising sauces smothering inferior products. The service was quick and friendly, executed by young Englishwomen who replace professionalism by charm and helpfulness – a pleasant change from pompous overbearing frequently foreign waiters! Same applies to bar service where drinks were not over-priced. Various comfortable lounges with roaring wood fires which were burning even in the morning.' *(Uli Lloyd Pack)*

Open: All year, except 4 days in January.
Rooms: 15 double, 9 single – 17 with bath. 10 rooms in annexe.
Facilities: 4 lounges (3 with log fires), restaurant. 2–3 acres garden.
Location: In town centre; parking.
Restriction: No dogs in public rooms or garden.
Terms: B & B £15–21.50; full board (weekly) £130–160. Set meals (excluding service): lunch £3.50 (Sunday £6), dinner £6. 3-day budget breaks available. Reduced rates for children, depending on age. Special meals provided. Bargain breaks November–end March.

BURY ST EDMUNDS, Suffolk   **Map 2**

The Angel   [GFG]   *Telephone:* Bury St Edmunds (0284) 3926
Angel Hill   *Telex:* 81630 (Angel G)

The chief hotel in this handsome market town, rich in historical associations. *The Angel* is an old coaching inn dating back to the 15th century. It's a fine creepered house, four-square with what used to be the market place and opposite the great abbey gate, one of the architectural glories of the town. (Note: rooms in the front tend to be a bit noisy.) Its most famous visitor was Charles Dickens. You can sleep in his very room (No. 15), complete with four-poster. There are four other rooms with similar beds if No. 15 is occupied and four-posters are your thing. One restaurant, Regency in style, overlooks the abbey gate, and there is another in a

Are there no good hotels in Cambridge? Write *now* if you have suggestions.

cellar-like basement, with tables set under arches, now called the Angel Grillroom. It's a thoroughly well-run market town hotel – would that all attractive historical towns had inns as hospitable as *The Angel* – and, as usual, has not lacked enthusiastic endorsers for our entry. *(D A Tibbenham, Miss M Cox, Iain McKinlay)*

Open: All year.
Rooms: 32 double, 11 single – 32 with bath, 1 with shower, all with telephone, radio, colour TV and baby-listening. (5 four-poster beds.)
Facilities: 2 lounges, 2 restaurants (one conventional, one in arched basement), 2 ballrooms, private dining room, Pickwick Bar, Main Bar.
Location: In town centre, facing Abbey Gardens; parking for 20 cars.
Restriction: No dogs in public rooms.
Credit cards: All major credit cards accepted.
Terms (no fixed service charge): B & B £23–40. Full *alc* £15. Reduced rates and special meals for children. Special weekend breaks; Antiques weekends, Christmas/Easter house parties.

CALNE, Wiltshire **Map 2**

Chilvester Lodge *Telephone:* Calne (0249) 812950

Another example – one of several among this year's new entries – of owners of country houses opening their doors to paying guests. Neither 'hotel' nor 'guest house' effectively describes the character of *Chilvester Lodge*, a small elegant Georgian building in an attractive garden with lily pond just off the A4 west of Calne. It is the home of Francis Reiss and his wife, and their house is agreeably furnished with antiques, paintings, a Tang horse in the dining room and original Hiroshige prints in the bedrooms. The owners dine with their guests at one long table. There is no choice on the menu, but a list of possible main dishes (including Greek, Indian, Japanese and vegetarian dishes) which are available on 24 hours' notice. Breakfast, including optional waffles with maple syrup, is taken in the Reiss's kitchen. Prices for four-course dinner and coffee, bed and full English breakfast are reasonable. The success of these ventures depends on the mutual congeniality of hosts and guests. Our nominators enjoyed their stay and were impressed by the standards of food and comfort. More reports welcome. *(G G and E M Coleman)*

Open: 1 February–31 December.
Rooms: 3 double, 1 single – 2 with bath, 1 with shower, all with radio, colour TV and tea-making facilities.
Facilities: Study/library with bar, drawing room, dining room. 1-acre garden and paddock. Indoor swimming pool, badminton and squash available at Calne Sports Centre; golf club 2 miles.
Location: On N side of A4 1 mile from town centre in direction of Chippenham; *Chilvester Lodge* is on the right-hand side shortly after the de-restriction sign and opposite the sign for Bremhill; if coming on the A4 from the W, watch out for the second Bremhill turn off after Chippenham, at the top of the hill before coming down into Calne, and *Chilvester Lodge* is the 2nd entrance on the left on the A4 after the Bremhill turn-off. Parking.
Restrictions: No children under 12. No dogs in public rooms.
Credit cards: American Express, Diners.
Terms: B & B £15–22; dinner, B & B £23.50–31. Set meal: dinner £9.50. Special *Let's Go* rates October–end December, 4 February–26 May.

Bly House Hotel   *Telephone:* Chagford (064 73) 2404

'This small country hotel, although not highly sophisticated, is lovingly cared for and professionally run, and for my money represents one of the best in terms of value in England today. Mr and Mrs Thompson, hoteliers of many years' experience, have recently bought and refurbished this Victorian rectory standing in several acres of well-tended gardens at the edge of Chagford. For more than 40 years Mrs Thompson has collected antiques and the house is full of her treasures – furniture, mirrors, paintings, china, bric-à-brac – all arranged in a manner which pleases but does not overpower. Bedrooms are large and airy, most with four-poster beds, private baths and delightful views. The charmingly-furnished drawing room has french doors opening onto a spacious terrace, and there is a separate television lounge. Mrs Thompson does all the cooking and the food is simple, unpretentious English fare at its best. Service by Mr Thompson is pleasant and efficient. The hotel is unlicensed but guests are welcome to bring their own wine.' *(Lynn Hay)*

Open: January–end October.
Rooms: 7 double, 1 single – 5 with bath, all with tea-making facilities. (4 four-poster beds.)
Facilities: Lounge, TV room, dining room, terrace. 5 acres grounds with tennis court. Fishing, riding, bowls, swimming (outdoor pool in Chagford) available nearby.
Location: ¼ mile from town centre. Turn left in Chagford Square, passing the *Three Crowns* on your right. Turn left at the *Globe Hotel*, and *Bly House* is the second house on the right past the public car park. Private parking.
Restrictions: No children under 12. No dogs in public rooms.
Terms: B & B £8.25–10.50; dinner, B & B £13.50–15.75. No lunches served or meals to non-residents. Weekly rates available.

Gidleigh Park Hotel   [GFG]   *Telephone:* Chagford (064 73) 2367 or 2225

Gidleigh Park is a phenomenon. Now in its sixth year, it is constantly adding fresh laurels. One star already in Michelin, and one suspects that Paul Henderson, the American owner and creator of the *Gidleigh* experience, won't rest till he has won a second. The food, prepared by John Webber, who learnt his skills at *The Dorchester* under Anton Mosimann, is, to quote from one of this year's letters, 'faultless', from another '*better* than – (damn it, even if comparisons are unfair, I'll still make the comparison!) – *Miller Howe, Sharrow Bay, Thornbury Castle*, etc., etc.' A third writes: 'We could praise the restaurant to the hilt. We have rarely dined so well.' We must also mention the remarkable wide-ranging wine list – 367 wines at the last count – with an exceptionally modest mark-up. (Warning: contrary to what we had been told last year, there is no *à la carte* menu as yet. In other words, whatever the size of your appetite you must be prepared to take the four-course set menu (three or four choices per course) for dinner or at least pay the 1983-estimated price of £19 per head, exclusive of VAT. *Caveat emptor!*)

What makes *Gidleigh* phenomenal is the visible sense of the owner's dedication to the pursuit of excellence, and a willingness to raise the tariff to achieve that aim. The hotel is one of the most expensive country-house hotels in the Guide, but no one who has written to us has felt outraged at the prices charged. Of course there have been things that could have been better. The 30 acres of park and woodland that surround the house have had their scruffy side, and we are glad to know that garden renovation is planned. Bedroom refurbishment, badly overdue in some cases, is also in hand. One guest gave as his only real criticism that the Marks and Spencer bath towels were not big enough: 'M & S do sell larger ones than those provided.' But the important elements of an outstandingly good hotel, including 'capably casual service', are all palpably present. *(Kenneth Dowden, Sue and Geoff Page, S M Gillotti, Alfred Knopf Jr)*

Open: All year.
Rooms: 12 double – all with bath, telephone and colour TV.
Facilities: Front hall, large lounge, bar loggia, 2 dining rooms. 30 acres grounds and gardens with croquet lawn. North Teign river 50 yards in front of the house; 14 miles of trout, sea trout and salmon fishing. Golf, riding and walking nearby.
Location: Approach from Chagford, *not* Gidleigh. Take the M4 or M5, then the A30 to Whiddon Down. Then go to Chagford. From Chagford Square facing Webbers with Lloyds Bank on right, turn right into Mill Street. After 200 yards fork right and go downhill to Factory Crossroad. Go straight across into Holy Street and follow lane 1½ miles to end.
Restrictions: No children under 10. Dogs sometimes allowed.
Credit cards: No credit cards accepted.
Terms (excluding VAT): B & B (continental) £25–65. Set meal: dinner £19. 25% reduction on stays of 3 days or more November–March. 4-day cooking courses, and wine-tasting weekends November–March.

CHAGFORD, Devon   **Map 1**

Thornworthy House   *Telephone:* Chagford (064 73) 3297

One of those hostelries that is hard to classify: certainly not a hotel, but too sophisticated for a guest house. Despite the address, it is three miles out of Chagford, down many a twisting lane to the very edge of Dartmoor – a place of exceptional tranquillity. There are only four rooms, three double and a single of the kind about which it could be said: 'Would suit a tiny French maid.' It is a thoroughly personal house, the success of which greatly depends on the rapport which Peter and Daphne Jackson establish with their guests. We reported last year on a thoroughly dissatisfied customer, and on reflection think that this unhappy experience may have been because the Jacksons were away from the shop at the time. No such complaints have reached us this year. Instead, compliments like: 'In our recent holidays, the Jacksons were the most amenable and friendly of the proprietors we had the pleasure of meeting, and *Thornworthy* was the only hotel of five prepared to offer us an early breakfast on the day we departed.' 'The quietness of the surroundings and the comfort of the house combined to give us the most restful and relaxing holiday we have had for years.' 'The whole place – house and garden – has a splendid relaxing atmosphere. The Jacksons' hospitality is first-class . . . they were always available but never hovering over us. Food . . . excellent. With such cooking, no choice of main course is necessary. Breakfasts are marvellous and set you up until dinner – with only a liquid lunch necessary in between. Unbelievable value compared to prices at other hotels.' *(Dr and Mrs M J Denton, John and Marion Hamlin, Michael and Julia Potter)*

Open: March–end October.

Rooms: 3 double, 1 single – 2 with bath; additional 3 double bedrooms in barn cottage, mainly used for self-catering.

Facilities: 2 sitting rooms (1 with colour TV), dining room. 2 acres grounds with hard tennis court. Excellent walking, hill climbing and trout fishing, swimming in open-air pool at Chagford or, for the hardy, in moorland pools. No disturbing noises.

Location: 3 miles from Chagford. From Chagford Square turn right into Mill Street. After 150 yards fork left at sign to Kestor Rock. At top of Waye Hill road curves to left. Immediately after, take right turn signposted to Thornworthy. From there on, follow signposts to Thornworthy, via Thorn and Yeo.

Restriction: No dogs.

Terms: B & B £13–13.75; dinner, B & B £19.25–20. Set meal: dinner £7.75. 10% reduction for children under 10; special meals provided.

CHEDINGTON, Beaminster, Dorset   Map 1

Chedington Court   [GFG]   *Telephone:* Corscombe (093 589) 265

When a well-respected restaurateur decides to branch out into hotel-keeping, he is sure to attract to his door loyal supporters from his former vocation. As will be seen from the number of names below, the Chapmans have made many devoted friends from their six years in South Petherton, Somerset. The report below is typical. Sometimes when we get a batch of letters supporting a new enterprise, we suspect that the unfortunate signatories have been held at gun-point and press-ganged into writing to us. The endorsements for *Chedington Court* are not of this kind, but clearly written *con amore*.

'The Chapmans moved here from *Oaklands*, South Petherton, where their delicious food and considerable service established them in the Good Food Guide over many years. The standard of service and food are just as high, but now their home is *Chedington Court*. Set in about ten acres of gardens containing a variety of mature trees and shrubs on the edge of the peaceful village of Chedington, the house, built in the Jacobean style in 1840, stands 700 feet above sea level and commands magnificent views of the surrounding countryside. A stone's throw away from the A356 at Winyard's Gap (National Trust). A perfect place to relax in with the elegant comfort of well-appointed spacious bedrooms (all with bath, etc.), log fire in lounge, books and magazines, excellent food and wine and unobtrusive service. Mr and Mrs Chapman deserve every success with their move into the hotel business which is why I send this report; otherwise I'd like to keep the knowledge of this haven to myself and the few friends to whom I have so warmly recommended it.' *(Dilys Pinion; also Roy and Norah Hill, Dinah Morrison, Peter S Davis, Mrs D J Ferrett, Dr and Mrs Brian Webb, A J F Andrews)*

Open: All year. Restaurant sometimes closed to non-residents for dinner Sunday/Monday. Light lunches available to residents only.

Rooms: 8 double – all with bath, telephone, radio, colour TV and tea-making facilities; baby-listening on request. Large lounge and library; billiards/snooker. 10 acres garden with croquet, clock-golf and putting; golf, birdwatching, fishing nearby; coast 10 miles.

Location: ¼ mile off A356 at Winyards Gap, 4½ miles SE of Crewkerne.

Restriction: No dogs (except perhaps at Christmas).

Credit card: American Express, except for Special Break terms.

Terms (excluding 10% service charge): B & B £20–27.50; dinner, B & B £32–39.50 (2 nights or more: £24–35.50). Set meal: dinner £12. Reduced rates for children at management's discretion; special meals provided. Special Bargain Breaks 2 or more nights October–June, 3 or more nights July–September.

CHESTER, Cheshire   **Map 2**

The Grosvenor Hotel   *Telephone:* Chester (0244) 24024
Eastgate Street   *Telex:* 61240

The biggest and best hotel (the two are not often synonymous) in Chester. It is a dignified mock-Tudor Victorian building in the centre, close to the Rows, and has all that you would expect from a thoroughly well-run four-star establishment (except perhaps a few pictures or embellishments to humanize the otherwise well-equipped rooms), a recommended restaurant with an exceptional wine list (they catered admirably for a vegetarian guest), elegant and immaculate public rooms, and – one of the points that recur in our reports – a dependably high standard of courteous service. Only (mild) snag: if you want to avoid paying a parking charge you have to arrive after 6 p.m. and leave before 9 in the morning. *(Mrs M D Prodgers and others)*

Open: All year, except Christmas and Boxing Day.
Rooms: 60 double, 40 single, 6 suites – all with bath, direct-dial telephone, radio, colour TV, mini-bar and baby-listening; 1 four-poster bed.
Facilities: Lifts, lounge, 2 bars, restaurant, ballroom, conference and banqueting facilities; in-house video films. &.
Location: Central; large NCP car park adjoins the hotel.
Restriction: No dogs.
Credit cards: All major credit cards accepted.
Terms (service optional): Rooms from £35 (single), from £49.50 (double); B & B from £29.50. Set meal: lunch (buffet) approx. £6.50; full *alc* £13.50. Special mini-weekend tariff 1 October–2 May. Reduced rates and special meals for children.

CHICHESTER, West Sussex   **Map 2**

Clinchs' Hotel   *Telephone:* Chichester (0243) 789915
Guildhall Street

Patrons of theatre festivals often look for a civilized bed-and-breakfast in preference to a long drive home or a flash motel. *Clinchs'* – so called because Daphne and Tom Clinch are the resident owners – is an elegant town house in a small quiet street adjoining Priory Park and no more than 300 yards from the Festival Theatre. You can park just behind the hotel. 'A delightful small hotel, serving the best English breakfast I have enjoyed in 60 years. The atmosphere is more that of a private home than a hotel, with a higher level of comfort than many private homes.'

> The length of an entry does not necessarily reflect the merit of a hotel. The more interesting the report or the more unusual or controversial the hotel, the longer the entry.

Since last year, *Clinchs'* have opened a restaurant for lunch and dinner. Reports would be welcome. *(Christopher Calthrop)*

Open: All year. Restaurant closed Sunday.
Rooms: 5 double, 2 single – 5 with bath, 2 with shower, all with telephone, radio, colour TV and tea-making facilities.
Facilities: Lounge, restaurant.
Location: In town centre adjoining Priory Park; 300 yards from Festival Theatre; parking.
Restrictions: Not suited to children. No dogs.
Credit cards: Access/Euro/Mastercard, American Express, Barclay/Visa.
Terms (excluding service): Single room with breakfast £27.50–30.50; double room with breakfast £35–40. Full *alc* £11.

CHIPPING CAMPDEN, Gloucestershire   Map 2

Kings Arms Hotel   [GFG]   *Telephone:* Evesham (0386) 840256

Even by Cotswold standards, Chipping Campden is exceptional – and a lot less touristy than Broadway and Burford. Its main street is a parade of spectacularly beautiful houses, all in delectable honey-coloured Cotswold stone. *The King's Arms* is in the centre of things, beside the old Market Square. It is made up of two adjoining buildings – one Georgian, the other 17th-century, both stone-built, with a pleasant garden. It went through a bad patch, and was left out of the Guide one year, but for the last two or three years past it has been in the capable and sympathetic hands of Vincent and Rosemary Willmott who have been busy with refurbishments of the rooms. It is now, in our view, as good as it had ever been – if not better. It isn't one of those well-heeled Cotswold hotels, with TV, radio clocks and tea-making facilities in the bedrooms; only two of the bedrooms have their own bathrooms, and bedroom lighting could be improved. But in other important respects, the *Kings Arms* scores heavily: it has a first-rate restaurant, also serves outstandingly good bar lunches (in the garden when the weather is suitable) and generally exudes a sense of cheerful welcome. 'A winner in every respect: charming reception, friendly rooms (nice flower pots) and excellent meals. . . . We know few country places in France which could exceed this standard.' *(Dr Wilfrid G Harding)*

Open: All year.
Rooms: 9 double, 5 single – 2 with bath.
Facilities: Sitting room, bar, dining room. ½-acre garden. Golf courses nearby; horse racing locally during spring.
Location: In town centre, facing Market Square; parking for 30 cars.
Restriction: No dogs in public rooms.
Credit cards: All major credit cards accepted.
Terms: B & B £13.75–16.50. Bar/picnic lunches available. Set meal (excluding 10% service charge): dinner £8.95–9.95. Reduced rates for children on camp bed in parents' room; special meals by arrangement. Winter weekend breaks November–March, spring midweek breaks March–May.

'Full *alc*', unless otherwise stated, means the hotel's own estimate of the price per person for a three-course dinner with half a bottle of house wine, service and taxes included.

CLEEVE HILL, Cheltenham, Gloucestershire   Map 2

Malvern View Hotel   *Telephone:* Bishops Cleeve (024 267) 2017

Very devoted readers of this Guide, if they exist, may have noticed a
boring year-in year-out similarity of entry for certain hotels. *Malvern
View*, a restaurant with just seven rooms, 750 feet up on the edge of
Cleeve Common, is one such. 'With no serious dissent, once again a
chorus of praise for the special quality of Paul and Mary Sparks' hospitality,' we wrote last year. 'Compliment after compliment for the special
hospitality offered' appeared the year before. And once again we are
faced with the same problem. Well, one flaw has been recorded this year:
the floorboards of Room 7 are 'appallingly creaky' and the occupant
believes that another room suffers from the same problem. Another
reader remonstrates against the 'grotesque' portions of the main helpings,
but goes on to admit that they seemed to be thoroughly acceptable to the
other diners. Otherwise – once again – it is roses roses all the way.
'Excellent in all respects.' 'Excellent – all you say it is.' 'Completely to our
liking – not a single complaint.' 'Our beds were so comfortable, it was like
sleeping on a cloud. The meal was like eating ambrosia – the best food that
I have ever had in a restaurant.' *(G C Brown, May Clarke, T Halsall, Jean
E Bricksel, Ivor Hall, Ivor C Storey)*

Open: All year, except 3 weeks at Christmas. Restaurant open to residents only
for dinner on Sunday.
Rooms: 7 double – all with bath or shower and colour TV.
Facilities: Lounge, bar, restaurant. 1 acre garden leading on to Cleeve Common;
excellent walks; golf nearby.
Location: On the A46 to Broadway, 4½ miles NE of Cheltenham.
Restrictions: No children under 6. No dogs.
Terms: B & B £16.50–22.50. Set meal: dinner £11.50. Special meals for children.
Winter breaks November–March.

CLIMPING, Nr Littlehampton, West Sussex   Map 2

Bailiffscourt Hotel   *Telephone:* Littlehampton (090 64) 23511

We continue to receive good reports on the new management of this
celebrated medieval manor, in an impressive 20-acre estate close by the
sea, a mile from Littlehampton on the Bognor road. A million pounds, we
are told, was spent by Lord Moyne in the late Twenties on reconstructing
the Norman ruins and producing the present highly plausible result. We
believe the report below does the place justice; the minor reservations
about the food are echoed by other readers.
'We took a two-day "Bargain Break" at *Bailiffscourt* (March 1982) –
£45 for BB and evening meal for two days and including early morning tea
(we had delicious fresh orange juice instead) and daily paper – good
value. It's a lovely building – elegant and ancient without being imposing.
The low ceilings and panelled walls give it a friendly intimate feel. Very
tastefully furnished – every detail in keeping with the period – attractive
fabrics, etc. Comfortable bedrooms combining atmosphere with practi-
cality – good lighting – comfortable beds and thoughtful details like a
hairdryer, Badedas, etc., supplied. The service is efficient and friendly.
The owner, whom some of the guests knew, was away when we were there

but everything ran smoothly under the very helpful, friendly manageress's eye. Grounds are beautiful – primroses and wild daffodils and a newly born foal. For summer, a lovely swimming pool and plenty of chairs and tables to sit outside even in seclusion. A short attractive walk through the grounds to the sea – glimpses of which are available from some upstairs windows. Excellent breakfasts, good starters and sweets at dinner but rather disappointing main courses – rather tough meat somewhat under-cooked, but a peaceful, restoring place to stay. We would go again.' *(SR; also Barbara Bennett; Mr & Mrs K W Mills)*

Open: All year except 3 January–13 February.
Rooms: 16 double, 3 single – all with bath, telephone and colour TV.
Facilities: 3 sitting rooms/lounges, TV room, restaurant; function/meeting rooms; table tennis and pool table. 20 acres grounds with tennis, heated swimming pool and riding stables; own path to beach.
Location: Near Arundel; turning to beach off the A259, 1 mile from Littlehampton on the Bognor Regis road.
Restrictions: No children under 10. Dogs by arrangement.
Credit cards: All major credit cards accepted.
Terms: B & B £24–33. Set meals: lunch £10.25; dinner £12.75.

COATHAM MUNDEVILLE, Darlington, Co Durham   Map 4

Hall Garth Country House Hotel   [GFG] *Telephone:* Aycliffe (0325) 313333

We had a qualified entry for *Hall Garth* in our 1981 edition, but left it out last year because, on balance, critical comments outweighed the positive ones. As has happened in other cases, supporters of the hotel have risen staunchly to its defence. The hotel is 3½ miles north of Darlington and no more than a ½ mile from the A1(M). It's in a part of England sadly lacking in recommendable hotels. But we are satisfied that this rambling old house, dating from 1540, with Georgian and Victorian extensions – not to mention a very recent conversion of a stable block to provide a further 8 rooms – earns its place in the Guide on its own account and not because of the paucity of competition in the neighbourhood. What guests at *Hall Garth* can count on is a warm friendly informal welcome from the proprietors, Ernest Williamson and Janice Crocker, and a standard of cooking above the regional average. The reservations we expressed in 1981 referred largely to the shabbiness of the rooms and the fabrics. These reservations continue to be expressed in some of our reports, though we took note of the correspondent who assured us that 'comfortably faded' would be a much kinder and more accurate description. The same correspondent also wrote to tell us of generosity, beyond the call of duty, that had been shown him when he had fallen ill during a visit. Finally, we quote from one reader who, as a result of a first visit after our last entry had appeared, rose to the defence: 'I entirely disagree about the impression of neglect. While, thank goodness, the place has none of the slick and brittle repro-antiquity of a south coast tourist trap, it is totally unshabby and obviously a good deal of money has been spent on it. Your reader is perhaps unfamiliar with French hotels where food and unobtrusive service are properly considered, as I believe at *Hall Garth*, to be of much

---

Please write and confirm an entry when it is deserved. If you think that a hotel is not as good as we say, please write and tell us.

---

more importance than glittering new upholstery and hangings.' *(Derek Priestley; also C J B Walls, Teresa Biggs, Joan and Gordon Feetenby, Mr and Mrs R Langford)*

Open: 3 January–23 December. (Restaurant closed Sunday but bar food available.)
Rooms: 15 double, 3 single, 1 suite – 11 with bath, 8 with shower, all with telephone, radio, and colour TV. 8 rooms in annexe with tea-making facilities. (4 four-poster beds.)
Facilities: 3 lounges, dining room in main building, public bar (with TV), lounges in annexe. 10.5 acres gardens with putting green, croquet and children's play area; swimming pool under construction.
Location: ½ mile from the A1, 3½ miles N of Darlington. Leave the A1 at the A167 junction, go towards Darlington, take first left at brow of hill signposted Brafferton; *Hall Garth* is 200 yds down the road. Parking.
Restrictions: No dogs in public rooms.
Terms (no fixed service charge): B & B (continental) £22–26. Set meals: English breakfast £2.50, lunch £7.50, dinner £10.50; full *alc* £9. Reduced rates for children sharing parents' room; special meals provided. Weekend rates: 25% reduction for nights or more.

CONSTANTINE BAY, Padstow, Cornwall   **Map 1**

Treglos Hotel   *Telephone:* Padstow (0841) 520727

A traditional seaside hotel – but a superior example of its kind – blessed with a choice position overlooking Constantine Bay. Golfers will be glad to know that it is very close to Trevose Golf Club. It is about ¼ mile from the sea, and there is of course superb walking along the Cornish Coastal Path. The furnishing is chintzy rather than trendy, and the menus, though they carry French names, are English in conception and execution. It's one of those hotels that get a high return rate – an addictive sort of place. The quality of service is superior: shoes are cleaned, luggage is carried, breakfast, and indeed all meals can be served in your room if desired. *(Peter Wade)*

Open: 20 March–2 November.
Rooms: 33 double, 6 single, 3 suites – with bath, all with telephone, radio and colour TV (1 suite on ground floor).
Facilities: Lift, 4 lounges, bar lounge, restaurant, 2 acres garden with croquet and heated swimming pool; sandy beach 300 yards.
Location: Follow signs to St Merryn, then to Constantine Bay. The hotel advises you to avoid Bodmin and Wadebridge and will send directions.
Restrictions: No children under 3 in restaurant. Dogs at proprietors' discretion.
Terms (no fixed service charge): B & B £18–26; dinner, B & B £20.50–28.50; full board £23–31. Set meals: lunch £6.50, dinner £8.50; full *alc* £14. Reduced rates for children sharing parents' room; special meals provided.

The terms indicate the range of prices in each hotel. Some have a low and high season, some do not. The lower price is likely to be for someone sharing a double room, and the higher price the maximum for a single occupant.

Crantock Bay Hotel   *Telephone:* Crantock (0637) 830 229

A jolly family hotel, owned by Mr and Mrs David Eyles, a mile outside the village of Crantock, in a beautiful and absolutely quiet position on the West Pentire headland, facing four-square on to the Atlantic: sandy and rocky beaches, caves and pools, easily accessible on both sides. Good surfing. Nothing fancy in the decor, and the food is traditional English fare. But it's the kind of hotel that tends to be habit-forming: lots of regulars. From one correspondent this past year, we learn that the Eyles tradition of hospitality goes back over two generations: 'My grandmother used to take me there as a teenager, and our last visit there was when she was 86 and I was a young mum with small babies and a husband away at sea. Since then, my husband and I have been there with under-tens. The bliss of coming out of breakfast to find our day's picnic ready, and at the end of the day returning to find tray suppers for tired children, time for a bath after they had crashed out, a quiet dinner together, a walk round the headland at sunset, then a nightcap at the bar. The Eyles are exceptional hoteliers, and if you ever receive any complaints, one suspects they would be from the sort of people whom the fellow-guests end up feeling sorry for because they are unable to appreciate anything.' *(Diana Taylor)*

Open: Easter–end October.
Rooms: 19 double, 12 single – 22 with bath, most with sea views, all with radio, tea-making facilities and baby-listening. (1 room with bath on ground floor.)
Facilities: Lounge, TV room, games room, bar; dancing, slide shows, children's parties 2–3 nights a week. 4½ acres grounds with putting green, croquet, children's play area. Sea with sandy beach and safe bathing (lifeguard service) 200 yards from the hotel, reached through the grounds; tennis, riding, golf nearby.
Location: 1 mile from Crantock, 5 miles from Newquay.
Credit cards: Barclay/Visa.
Terms (excluding VAT; no charge for service): B & B £7.50–12.50; dinner, B & B £11.25–19.50. Set meals: lunch £2.50, dinner £6.75. Bargain spring and autumn breaks. Children under 1, no charge; 1–5, 33% of adult charge; 6–12, 66% of adult charge; special meals provided.

DEDDINGTON, Oxfordshire   **Map 2**

The Holcombe Hotel   *Telephone:* Deddington (0869) 38274
High Street

Deddington is one of the charming little-known villages of the East Cotswolds on the A423 between Oxford and Banbury. 'A good country hotel hugs you when you go in, and that's precisely how you feel when you walk into the *Holcombe*,' wrote a correspondent last year. Since then, the hotel has undergone major improvements – almost all rooms now have baths *en suite* and front rooms have triple glazing. A recent visitor warmly endorses the entry: 'This small, well-situated, well-appointed spotlessly clean and endearingly unpretentious village inn deserves its place in the Guide. The service is quick and friendly, the rooms very comfortable and prettily decorated, the food adequate for a traveller though no magnet for a gourmet. Something is being done to reduce traffic noise in front rooms; something ought to be done to produce more air in back ones. But further improving their desirable domain is unlikely to faze the highly professional Osborns.' *(Di Latham, PG)*

Open: All year.
Rooms: 11 double, 1 single – 8 with bath, 2 with shower, all with baby-listening.
Facilities: TV lounge, bar, restaurant; facilities for meetings and seminars of up to 30 people.
Location: In village centre, front rooms triple glazed and sound-proofed; parking.
Restriction: No dogs in public rooms.
Credit cards: All major credit cards accepted.
Terms (no fixed service charge): B & B £15–25. Set meals: lunch £5.50, dinner £9.50; full *alc* £13. Special weekend breaks and activity weekends; Christmas package. Reduced rates and special meals for children.

DEDHAM, Colchester, Essex   **Map 2**

Dedham Vale Hotel   [GFG]   *Telephone:* Colchester (0206) 322 273
Stratford Road

A new (opened April 1982) extension of the mini-empire of Gerald Milsom, proprietor of the *Maison Talbooth* and *Le Talbooth* restaurant (see below) and a smart, well-reputed fish restaurant in Harwich, *The Pier.* Like *Maison Talbooth*, *Dedham Vale* is a much-modernized Victorian country house; it is set in three acres of landscaped garden just out of earshot of the A12. Rooms tend to be smaller and slightly less opulent than those in its older sibling up the road; the prices are rather less, too. But, when it comes to pampering, there is not much to choose. Residents at *Dedham Vale* are all provided with a similar profusion of extras – bowls of fresh fruit and vases of fresh flowers in the bedroom, not to mention remote-control colour TV; thick towels, face flannels, carafes of bubble bath, etc., are standard items in the adjoining bathrooms. The restaurant, called *The Terrace*, much bedecked with hanging plants, is a light and airy room, roofed high like an elegant greenhouse or small-scale Crystal Palace, to give the illusion of alfresco eating without taking any chances with the British weather. There is a splendid wall-grill where all kinds of spit-roasting and barbecuing goes on. The wine-list, as at *Le Talbooth*, is also impressive. As one might expect with a hotelier as experienced as Gerald Milson, everything appears to have been working smoothly from the start, with a minimum of teething-troubles. The cooking has earned high praise in the first few reports to reach us. The only complaint from one otherwise rapturous correspondent: that the portions were grossly excessive in quantity – 'fit for ravenous trencher-persons!' *(MBR, Cynthia Oakes and Ben Rauch, Elisabeth Lambert Ortiz)*

Open: All year. Restaurant closed for lunch, except Sunday.
Rooms: 6 double – all with bath, telephone, radio, colour TV and private bar.
Facilities: Lounge, bar, restaurant; function facilities. 3 acres grounds.
Location: Off the A12 Ipswich–Colchester road, 8 miles from Dedham; parking for 50 cars.
Restriction: No dogs.
Credit cards: All major credit cards accepted.
Terms (excluding 10% service charge): Single room with breakfast £30–35, double £40–45. Full *alc* £13–14. Reduced rates for children sharing parents' room; special meals by arrangement.

Maison Talbooth   [GFG]   *Telephone:* Colchester (0206) 322367
Stratford Road

The Vale of Dedham is in the heart of Constable country, and Constable
himself painted *Le Talbooth*, the fine old building rich in gables and
exposed beams on the banks of the Stour – though you will have to go to
the National Gallery of Scotland to see it. *Le Talbooth* was the hotel *and*
the restaurant when Gerald Milsom bought it in 1952, but for many years
now the two have been separated. The original building is now pure
restaurant, one of the best in this part of the country and attracting plenty
of outside custom. The residents stay half a mile away in a luxuriously
modernized Victorian house, *Maison Talbooth*, on the other side of the
A12, close to Dedham. *Maison Talbooth* has ten opulent bedrooms or
suites, furnished with accessories such as fresh fruit and flowers and
remote-control colour TV which maximize the cossetting experience.
Breakfast only is served in this latter establishment; other meals being
taken at *Le Talbooth* – and, if you haven't a car, the hotel itself provides
suitably grand transport. It's not an ideal arrangement, one would have
thought, but it seems to work and the hotel has always received high marks
from our readers. 'Elegant perfection,' as one guest puts it. One correspondent this year, however, wanting to put his feet up in *Maison
Talbooth*'s sybaritic lounge, found that a small conference was in residence and the lounge door locked. Perhaps the hotel reckoned that, with
such luxurious bedrooms, the lounge would not be missed. But, like
Queen Victoria, the visitor was not amused. *(Elisabeth Lambert Ortiz and
others)*

Open: All year.
Rooms: 8 double, 1 single, 1 suite – 9 with bath, 1 with shower, all with telephone,
radio, colour TV and baby-listening. (5 rooms on ground floor.)
Facilities: Large hall with french windows on to the garden, drawing room with
open fire. The hotel stands in 2 acres of grounds, the restaurant in 3 acres on the
banks of the river Stour; boating; seaside within half an hour by car.
Location: Off the A12, 7 miles NE of Colchester at Stratford St Mary.
Restriction: No dogs.
Credit cards: All major credit cards accepted.
Terms (excluding 10% service charge):   B & B (continental) £27.50–47.50. Set
meals: lunch £11; full *alc* £22. Special meals provided for children.

DOVEDALE, Ashbourne, Derbyshire   **Map 2**

The Izaak Walton Hotel   *Telephone:* Thorpe Cloud (033 529) 261

'The hotel is in a stunning position at the entrance of Dovedale, with
beautiful views all around. There are walks for the faint-hearted as well as
the hardy (Ilam Country Park nearby is exceptionally lovely), excellent
climbing, and fishing as you might guess from the hotel's name (the *Izaak
Walton* has fishing rights on about 3 miles of the river Dove). On the
peaceful residents' lawn we had a snack lunch in the sunshine without
noticing the Sunday trippers and campers in the valley below. The hotel
was originally a farmhouse, built in the 17th century. It has been extended
and modernized but retains the sturdy character of the original building.

It is not beautiful, and looks its best at night floodlit against the darkening sky. This is a straightforward place; no Roger et Gallet soap in the bathroom or his-and-hers bathrobes, but a good-sized bath and plenty of very hot water; no trouser-presses or sewing kits in the not very large bedroom, but plenty of storage space, good reading lights and comfortable bed (not very comfortable chairs though). We had a view of hills and cattle; it would be wise to specify on booking that you don't want to overlook the car park. We had a peaceful night; not a sound to be heard from inside or outside the hotel. Dinner (£7.50 each for the *table d'hôte*) was good. We chose avocado julienne and onion soup, spring chicken and delicious pink-fleshed local trout *au bleu*, cauliflower nicely *al dente*, apple mousse with thick cream, and fruit salad. Our Piesporter was not properly chilled but they brought a bucket of ice. Good service in a well-staffed dining room. Not a beautiful room, but with big windows looking out at the lovely view. And you could eat at any time between 7.30 and 9.30 – a welcome change from those authoritarian establishments which tell you when to dine and give you no choice of menu while charging considerably more. At breakfast there were some problems: no-one took our order for some time and the tea and toast arrived long after the rest had been eaten; we don't know what went wrong there. It was quite adequate, though butter was wrapped, jams in plastic containers, and bread pre-sliced. But the atmosphere was so friendly and the service so unassuming and kind we forgave them.' *(Adam and Caroline Raphael)*

Open: All year.
Rooms: 23 double, 4 single – all with bath, telephone, radio, and colour TV; baby-listening by arrangement. (2 rooms on ground floor.)
Facilities: 3 lounges, bar, restaurant, conference room. Saturday night dinner dance. Spacious grounds; fishing rights on River Dove. &.
Location: 5 miles from Ashbourne, off the main Ashbourne–Buxton road; car park.
Restriction: No dogs in restaurant.
Credit cards: All major credit cards accepted.
Terms: B & B £20–30. Set meals: lunch £6, dinner £8; full *alc* £12. Special rate 30 October–2 April: dinner, B & B £20; special summer breaks (4 days minimum); 3-day Christmas package. Children sharing parents' room, £5 extra, irrespective of number of nights; high teas available.

EAST GRINSTEAD, Sussex   **Map 2**

Gravetye Manor   [GFG]   *Telephone:* Sharpthorne (0342) 810567
                                                Telex: 957239

Until this year if we had to elect one hotel in the Guide to represent the platonic idea of a country-house hotel, we should probably have chosen *Gravetye*. This Elizabethan manor house, built in 1598, has been lovingly preserved over the centuries, and especially since it has been in the care of its present owner, Peter Herbert, who recently celebrated his silver jubilee here. The gardens and 30-acre grounds are in their way as historical as the house. William Robertson, the man who created the English natural garden, lived here from 1884 to 1935, and the Robertson heritage outside has been as faithfully maintained as the Elizabethan interior.

For many years *Gravetye* has enjoyed a reputation for its restaurant as well as for the other features which go to make a hotel of true excellence.

With Michael Quinn as the chef, it won a Michelin star. In late 1981 however, Michael Quinn moved to London's *Ritz*, and his place as *chef de cuisine* was taken by Quinn's *sous-chef* for the previous eight years, Allan Garth. First impressions of the new regime are encouraging, though the question of value for money, always a tricky area, has been raised. We should be glad of further reports.

There has been another feature of this year's reports which has to be recorded: a falling-off in the previous high standards of reception and service. One reader commented on the impersonality of the place: there had been no sense of cordiality on the part of any of the staff during his stay. Another told us of the snootiness she had repeatedly encountered at reception. A third reported deplorable delays, when arrangements for a special occasion had all been confirmed a week earlier. Not all our reports have been negative. Some have found the place all that it has ever been, and singled out for special praise the quality of service under pressure. But top prices provide an expectation of perfection. Some hotels can be depended on to provide the elysian experience. In view of these adverse opinions, however, the entry for *Gravetye* must necessarily be a qualified one.

Open: All year. Restaurant closed to non-residents on Christmas evening.
Rooms: 12 double, 2 single – 12 with bath, 2 with shower, all with telephone and colour TV.
Facilities: 2 sitting rooms, club members' bar, 2 restaurants (public and private dining room separate). 30 acres grounds and superbly planned and maintained pleasure gardens with croquet, clock golf; private trout fishing in nearby lake.
Location: 5 miles SW of Grinstead off the B2110 at West Hoathly sign. Glyndebourne opera 40 minutes' drive, Gatwick Airport 9 miles.
Restrictions: No children under 7. No dogs.
Terms (excluding VAT): B & B £27.75–47.75. Full *alc* about £27.

EAST PORTLEMOUTH, Nr Salcombe, South Devon   **Map 1**

Gara Rock Hotel   *Telephone:* Salcombe (054 884) 2342

A converted coastguard station in a stunning situation in National Trust land on cliffs overlooking the sea near Salcombe. Everything is structured to make life pleasant for both parents and children and many families make regular return visits. In recent years the addition of 13 self-catering units has meant that the swimming pool gets rather crowded in the high season, and we get the impression that the food is better at the less crowded times of year. Here is a report from a first-time Easter visitor:

'A tolerant family hotel on the south coast of Devon. It overlooks, and a winding path leads down to, a sheltered sandy beach at the bottom of the cliff. The meals are large enough to satisfy a teenage boy and tasty enough to please all but the most jaded palates. Afternoon Devon teas and picnic lunches can and should be taken. The cliffside walk to the ferry that goes to Salcombe is about three miles long and the short-cut to the ferry across fields with cows and through dappled woods about half that distance. It is the sort of hotel that grows on you and to which after one visit you are almost sure to return.' *(Tony Thomas and others)*

> Report forms (Freepost in the UK) will be found at the end of the Guide.

Open: April–October.
Rooms: 53 double, 9 single – 41 with bath or shower, some with TV; baby-listening service; 13 self-catering flats.
Facilities: 3 lounges (separate TV room), weekly dances and regular entertainment in summer; laundry for use of guests. 5 acres grounds with heated swimming pool, tennis court, adventure playground and garden games; 2 acres vegetable gardens. Large beach with safe bathing; boating and fishing immediately below the hotel and 5 minutes away. 10-metre motor cruiser for charter; trips round Salcombe estuary organized in hotel boats.
Location: Take A38, then B3196 to Kingsbridge, then the road to Frogmore, East Portlemouth and Gara Rock, off the A379 between Kingsbridge and Dartmouth.
Credit cards: Access/Euro, Barclay/Visa.
Terms (excluding VAT): B & B £12–22.50; dinner, B & B £19.50–26.50. Set meals: lunch £2.75; dinner £9.50; full *alc* £8.75. Special 3-day breaks out of season. Reduced rates for children.

EVERSHOT, Dorset   **Map 1**

Summer Lodge   *Telephone:* Evershot (093 583) 424

When we publish a specially mouth-watering entry, we sit back and wait for brickbats. *Summer Lodge* appeared for the first time in our 1981 Guide, soon after it had been taken over by Nigel and Margaret Corbett, and we were well aware that our description would attract a lot of new customers. Our entry last year was much the same. 'What a task you set us!' writes Mr Corbett. 'We wondered if we could ever live up to it, every day throughout the year!' From the evidence in our files, he is making a very good job of living up to it. Rarely have we come across so many unreserved endorsements: clearly the Corbetts, in the Earl of Ilchester's former dower house, understand what people want when they spend a weekend or a week in a country-house hotel. And of course the glorious unspoiled Dorset countryside is a natural setting for this sort of recuperative break.

A few characteristic compliments: 'Must surely be among the best small country hotels in Britain. Certainly it is the very best that I have encountered.' 'Splendid and imaginative cooking of a standard seldom now met with. . . . Extraordinary attention to detail in the luxurious and pretty bedrooms. . . . Kindness and enthusiasm of the young owners.' 'The atmosphere of a country house matched with the professionalism of a first-class hotel.' And, finally, one that pulls out all the stops: 'This just has to be the loveliest, friendliest and most English hotel in this part of the country. The food, on the other hand, has to rate with the best anywhere.' (Warning: the tributes to the cooking might suggest an elaborate menu; in fact, *Summer Lodge* serves a no-choice menu, though the owners are always willing to substitute another dish if asked.) *(Terence Lancaster, Pamela Holmes, Douglas Gluckstein, Jennifer Clarke; also Professor C H Vereker, Keith Symons, D E Padfield, Di Latham, R L Mobbs)*

Open: 1 February–30 November.
Rooms: 8 double, 1 single – 9 with bath, all with tea-making facilities.
Facilities: Large lounge, TV room, bar, dining room. 4 acres grounds with ping pong, grass tennis court, croquet, badminton, heated outdoor swimming pool, stables. Golf, fishing; 15 miles from the sea and pebble beach; sandy beach at Weymouth and Lyme Regis, 20 miles.
Location: 10 miles S of Yeovil. (Note: the entrance on the village street is for

pedestrians only; cars must turn left on reaching the village and then right into the drive to the house.)
Restrictions: No children under 8. Dogs by arrangement.
Credit cards: All major credit cards accepted.
Terms (service at guests' discretion): B & B £17.50–24; dinner, B & B £23.50–32.50. Set meal: dinner £10. Bargain 2-day breaks February–end May, October–end November. Reduced rates for children sharing parents' room.

EVESHAM, Hereford and Worcester   **Map 2**

Evesham Hotel   [GFG]   *Telephone:* Evesham (0386) 49111
Coopers Lane, off Waterside   *Telex:* 339342

What looks like a Georgian manor house, about five minutes' walk from the centre of Evesham, is in fact one of the oldest buildings in this historical and pleasant town: it was built as a Tudor Manor in 1540 and has undergone various transformations since. More are expected in early 1983 with an extension which will add a further 16 bedrooms. One of the attractions of the hotel is its 2½-acre garden, with six venerable mulberry trees and a magnificent Cedar of Lebanon, and plenty of comfortable deck chairs. (The hotel tells us that the original 1540 purchase price of the house and its then 100 acres is roughly the same as a winter break for two in the 1980s.) For the past seven years the hotel has been owned and managed by the Jenkinson family. They have made a feature of their restaurant and an exceptional wine list, with special attention to less familiar wines from California, South Africa and Australia.
'The owners could not be more friendly, welcoming and generally helpful. The Jenkinsons, *père et fils*, carry in luggage. Bedrooms are large enough to afford the space carved out between two rooms to provide a well-equipped bathroom each. Colour TV, tea- and coffee-making equipment are provided but without making one feel as though at a motel or Post House. The bedrooms also contain the dinner menu, a selected take-away wine list, hotel tariffs and booklets about the Shakespeare country and the Cotswolds. Lots of books downstairs to help the sightseer. Excellent dinner. The wine list introduced in the bar consists of two mighty leatherbound tomes, one consisting of wines from the Old World and the other the New with photographs of the bottle and comments on each item. Breakfasts are exceptional. The menu allows any combination of the items listed, and includes just about everything one might want. My husband was able to have the cold ham with scrambled eggs he used to have at his late-lamented London club and I had excellent grilled kidneys, bacon and mushrooms. Very tempting winter terms on offer.' *(M M G Jennings; also A J Benbow)*

Open: All year.
Rooms: 28 double, 5 single, 1 family suite – 28 with bath, 5 with shower, all with telephone, radio, colour TV, tea-making facilities and baby-listening.
Facilities: 2 lounges, bar, restaurant. 2½-acre garden with putting green.
Location: 5 minutes' walk from town centre. Large car park. Just off the A44 Oxford–Worcester road. Ask for easy directions when booking.
Restriction: No dogs in public rooms.
Credit cards: All major credit cards accepted.
Terms: B & B £21.50–29. Set meal: lunch £7.60 (buffet £4.60); full *alc* £12.15. Reduced rates and special meals for children. Special bargain breaks (minimum 2 nights) £18.75–33. 4-day Christmas holiday.

FOWEY, Cornwall   Map 1

The Fowey Hotel   *Telephone:* Fowey (072 683) 2551

When a well-known seasoned traveller recommends a hotel, we take note. *The Fowey Hotel* is one of those solidly virtuous Victorian seaside hotels about which one often has to say that it has seen better days. We are glad to know that the *Fowey* is an exception. It has a superb ring-side view over the estuary of this famous yachting town. Readers should note that Jonathan Raban did not sample the hotel's restaurant. We should be glad to hear from readers who have dined here. The hotel itself claims to provide good English cooking, with local trout, salmon and crab. (We hope the chef's cooking is rather better than his spelling. . . .)

'It's a long time since I've stayed at a hotel that I haven't wanted to complain about. Last week, though, I had to stop in Fowey without a reservation and landed up at 9 p.m. at the *Fowey Hotel*. An immaculately furnished room, with a splendid view out over the estuary. Although the dining room was closed, I was told that they'd be happy to bring supper to my room. Room service was excellent: I had a full cooked breakfast, with freshly squeezed orange juice, a copy of *The Times*, two local telephone calls. Total bill at the end was £18.50 [1981] – which I count as the best hotel value that I've had for ages. The building itself is a handsome piece of Victorian seaside gothic, *c* 1880, built into the cliff. There's still a faint air of old-fashioned plush about it. The bar has gone rather too plastic; but the dining room, staircase, lift and rooms are all good Victorian. My £18.50 was on the hotel's "summer tariff": out of season, it's even cheaper. I very rarely want to revisit hotels, and I have a generalized loathing of the seaside-holiday sort; but I mean to go back to the *Fowey Hotel*, and I really think it's worth a reference in your book, just for its good value, good service and comfortable furnishing.' *(Jonathan Raban)*

Open: All year.
Rooms: 29 double, 5 single, 1 suite – 13 with bath, 9 with shower, all with telephone, radio, tea-making facilities, baby-listening and colour TV on request. (5 rooms in annexe.)
Facilities: Lift, TV room, sitting room, 2 bars, dining room; small conference/ function facilities. Large garden. Safe bathing, sand/rock beach, fishing, golf 5 and 8 miles. &.
Location: Directional sign board near Esso garage on road into Fowey. In centre of town; parking.
Restriction: Dogs on lead only and not in dining room.
Credit cards: All major credit cards accepted.
Terms (no fixed service charge): B & B £20–22. Set meals: lunch £6, dinner £8. Reduced rates for children, depending on age, sharing parents' room; special meals on request. Bargain breaks (2 nights or more) October–April.

FRENCHBEER, Nr Chagford, Devon   Map 1

Teignworthy   [GFG]   *Telephone:* Chagford (064 73) 3355/6/7/8/9

The address is Frenchbeer, a minuscule hamlet three miles from Chagford via a characteristic maze of narrow Devon lanes. The house is Lutyens style, built as a gentleman's residence by the same craftsmen that built Castle Drogo nearby, in a sheltered south-facing position. Six of the rooms are in the main house, three more in a converted stable: all enjoy glorious moorland views. The Newalls took over *Teignworthy* as a hotel five years ago, at about the same time as the Hendersons moved into Chagford's *Gidleigh Park* (q.v.). Both couples have made an outstanding success of their very different operations. *Teignworthy* doesn't have the panache of *Gidleigh Park*, nor the latter's outstanding restaurant. The rooms tend to be smaller, and less sophisticated in their decor. The prices are a lot less steep too. As Jeeves would say, the Newalls endeavour to give satisfaction – and succeed. 'Outstanding – lived up to every (and more) word in the Guide, the Newalls have achieved a rare combination of professional hotelkeeping and personal ease. The furnishing and fittings are of the highest quality – and there is no atmosphere (or smell!) of public or commercial premises. . . . All in all, totally indulgent.' *(Anne Morris; also Diana Blake, H C Hunter, J M Chandler, W A Collins)*

Open: All year except January.
Rooms: 9 double – all with bath, telephone, radio and TV.
Facilities: Drawing room with large log fire, small bar, dining room; some conference facilities; sauna and sunbed. 14 acres grounds, which include woodland, heathland and lawned garden; ¼ mile of the river Teign; fishing in the river at the bottom of the garden or in the Fernworthy reservoir; golf at Moretonhampstead; riding available. Dartmoor on the doorstep.
Location: 3½ miles SW of Chagford. Follow signs to Kestor Rock and Thornworthy.
Restrictions: No children under 14. No dogs.
Terms (no service charge, gratuities not expected): B & B £18.50–27; dinner, B & B £29.50–38. Set meals: Sunday buffet lunch £11; dinner £13; full *alc* £13. Reductions for winter stays, 2 nights minimum. Christmas and New Year house party at normal rates.

GITTISHAM, Nr Honiton, Devon **Map 1**

Combe House Hotel *Telephone:* Honiton (0404) 2756
Telex: 42563 (Ticlav G) Attn Combe

Some country house hotels are homely and some are stately. *Combe House* belongs emphatically in the latter category. It is a grand and beautiful Elizabethan mansion standing in its own grounds at the head of a steep and typical Devonshire combe (marvellous walking country) with lovely views to the west, and beautiful gardens with some exceptional trees, especially cedars. Gittisham village now belongs in its entirety to the National Trust and is full of historical associations.

Combe House has its own associations, but they are Scottish. The hotel is owned and run by a direct descendant of James Boswell, John, who has restored *Combe House* with great fidelity to its present elegant incarnation, and has filled it with furniture, books and pictures from the ancestral home of the Boswells, Auchinleck House in Ayrshire. His wife Thérèse runs the kitchen – and the restaurant draws plenty of visitors from the surrounding neighbourhood.

Last year, we heard mostly from satisfied customers, though there was one severe minority report, and it has been the same this year too. The couple who hadn't enjoyed their visit had had to ask for the music in the staff room above them to be turned down so that they could get some rest, and had been equally unhappy in the restaurant: 'We sent back almost everything virtually untouched and no-one asked why.' In contrast, another reader reported: 'Excellent accommodation, delicious food, dining room service perhaps a little unnecessarily pompous, but the vista from the bedroom sheer paradise. One would pay particular respect to John, whose other name was never made known to us, but who plays the multiple role of hall porter, head waiter, accountant and receptionist with an undisturbed, charming aplomb.' *(Dr R Million; also J M French, Mrs P Baldwin-Thrower, Ivor Hall, Robert Robinson)*

Open: All year.
Rooms: 13 double – 8 with bath, 3 with shower, all with colour TV.
Facilities: Large reception room, panelled log-fired drawing room, cocktail bar. 8 acres gardens in the 3,000-acre estate, with croquet. Trout fishing on the river Otter. Nearest beach Sidmouth 11 miles; sandy beach at Exmouth 16 miles; golf and riding nearby.
Location: 3 miles SW of Honiton.
Restrictions: No children under 10 in the dining room at night. No dogs in public rooms.
Credit cards: All major credit cards accepted.
Terms: B & B £20–27.50. Set meal: Sunday lunch £8. Full *alc* £15. Reduced rates for children sharing parents' room; special meals provided.

GRASMERE, Ambleside, Cumbria   Map 4

Michael's Nook   [GFG]   *Telephone:* Grasmere (096 65) 496

Just outside Grasmere, in a beautiful garden, with view of hills and valley, *Michael's Nook* looks like a quintessential Guide hotel: it has a strong Victorian character, its public rooms are elegant and filled with antiques, *objets* and rewarding paintings, its bedrooms tend to be extra-spacious and well-equipped, and its restaurant has long enjoyed a reputation both among residents and locals who care about good food. But this year, as before, there have been murmurs of complaint. Mr Reg Gifford, the owner, is an idiosyncratic character – and some take to him more than others (and no doubt vice versa). There have been complaints about unprofessional service in the dining room and, as last year, about uncomfortable over-crowding when the restaurant is stretched to capacity. Like many other hotels, we suspect that *Michael's Nook* is a better bet away from the high season. More reports welcome.

Open: All year.
Rooms: 10 double – 9 with bath, 1 with shower, all with telephone, radio and colour TV. (1 room on ground floor.)
Facilities: Spacious hall with seating, drawing room, residents' and diners' bar, dining room. 3 acres grounds. Indoor heated swimming pool, sauna, solarium and games-room facilities available at the *Wordsworth Hotel*, 1 mile away, which is under the same ownership. &.
Location: On outskirts of Grasmere; turn away from Grasmere village off the A591 Windermere–Keswick road up a narrow road by the side of the *Swan Hotel*.
Restrictions: No children under 12. No dogs in public rooms.
Terms (service at guests' discretion): Dinner, B & B £34–48. Full board on application. Set meals: lunch £11.95, dinner from £14.95. 10% discount for stay of 6 nights or more, except Bank Holiday periods. Winter off-peak and mid-week terms. 4-day Christmas house-party.

Please don't just leave the feedback to others.

White Moss House [GFG]   *Telephone:* Grasmere (096 65) 295
Rydal Water

White Moss has been in the Guide since our first edition, and has on the
whole been well liked by our readers though this past year has brought
more criticism than previously. It is a conversion of three stone cottages
overlooking Rydal Water – five rooms in the main house and a separate
cottage called *Brockstone*, five minutes' drive or an energetic walk up the
fells, which can accommodate two to four people and is only let on a single
booking. There are no radios, TV sets or telephones in the rooms – indeed
no TV at all except for one set in *Brockstone*. But the rooms, though
mostly small, lack little else in the way of sophisticated home comforts –
sewing kits, hair-dryers and trouser-presses as well as books, magazines
and guides. Bathrooms may be tiny, but all have splendid large towels and
bath oil as well as dependable hot water. The whole house is immaculately
maintained – 'gleaming' is a word that occurs frequently in descriptions –
and is also full of personal touches and agreeable furnishings. A drawback
for some will be the house's proximity to the A591, though there are few
cars at night and heavy traffic uses the A66; double-glazing provides
sound as well as heat insulation, even if it can make rooms a bit stuffy at
night.

The house has long been owned and run by the Butterworths, Jean in
charge of the restaurant and Arthur front of house. In the past two years,
the Butterworths' daughter, Susan, and her husband, Peter Dixon, have
joined them in the enterprise. The Butterworths are no longer in residence, though they are still active, but Peter Dixon is playing an increasingly important role in the kitchens. Dinners are five-course no-
choice occasions, served punctually at 8 p.m., with very soft background
music to ease the constraint of conversation in the small, sometimes
cramped, dining room. Up till a year or two ago, readers were unanimous
in praise of their meals, both dinner and the full English breakfast. For
many, *White Moss* has been a kind of model of really good English
cooking, but critical notes have been sounded in some recent reports –
about the balance of the menus (cream with everything), the size of
helpings ('they don't cater for hearty appetites') and the actual quality of
individual dishes. Not all reports are negative – many readers are still
warm in their enthusiasm for *White Moss*'s special brand of hospitality and
the many things the owners do to provide for their guests' comfort. We
regret that these other notes have been sounded, and would be glad of
more reports.

Open: Mid March–early November.
Rooms: 7 double – all with bath and radio. 2 rooms in cottage which also has TV.
Facilities: Lounge/hall, lounge, dining room. Garden.
Location: On the A591 just outside Grasmere in the direction of Ambleside.
Restrictions: No children under 15. No dogs.
Terms (service at guests' discretion): Dinner, B & B £36–43. Set meal: dinner
£13.

Unless otherwise stated, prices are per person and indicate the
range offered by a hotel.

GULVAL, Penzance, Cornwall   Map 1

Trevaylor   *Telephone:* (0736) 2882

A dignified somewhat staid 18th-century granite manor a mile above Penzance and well away from the tourist hurly-burly and traffic jams. *Trevaylor* has had an entry in the Guide since our first edition, and it continues to get appreciative reports from readers, many of whom are helplessly addicted to the charms of the house, its ten-acre informal gardens and its stunning views. The cooking is unashamedly English.

'All that has been said about this lovely establishment can be thoroughly substantiated. The charming private country-house ambience, and its eminently civilized owner, Mrs Ellen Fleming, make you unaware of 'hotel living', without, however, foregoing any of the comforts. Rooms are large, individually elegantly and adequately furnished; and if you feel sociable, you are sure to find like-minded sociable guests.' *(Uli Lloyd Pack)*

Open: Easter–October.
Rooms: 5 double, 2 single – 4 with bath, 1 with shower.
Facilities: 2 lounges (1 with TV), large hall, small bar, dining room. 10 acres grounds and gardens with pretty woodland walks; vegetable garden and fruit trees. 1½ miles from sandy beach with safe bathing; fishing, riding, golf nearby.
Location: To reach Trevaylor from the A30, just before entering Penzance and after the speed-limit sign, turn right at the horse trough on to the B3311, signposted Nancledra, Zennor, St Ives. In just under half a mile, and before Gulval, turn left and after a few hundred yards turn right following signs for New Mill and Zennor. *Trevaylor* is on the left in just over half a mile.
Terms (no service charge): B & B £10–14. Set meals: Sunday lunch £4.50, dinner £6.50. Reduced rates for children sharing parents' room; special meals provided.

HAMBLETON, Oakham, Rutland, Leicestershire   Map 2

Hambleton Hall   [GFG]   *Telephone:* Oakham (0572) 56991
                                            Telex: 341995 Ref 207

This substantial mansion opened its doors as a hotel in the summer of 1980, and almost immediately began to command what theatre managers call rave notices. It's close to the centre of England in an untouristy area, though near a number of famous open-to-the-public houses, such as Burghley House, Rockingham Castle and Belvoir Castle. It stands on a tongue of land that leads out from Oakham into the centre of Rutland Water and there are fine views from the main windows of the lake scene. From our large and, without exception, enthusiastic file on *Hambleton*, we select three extracts which reflect contrasting facets of Tim and Stefa Hart's outstanding success in the art of hotelmanship: 'Wonderful! Our room was a gentle buttercup and coral pink with pretty pieces of Chinoiserie furniture and a stained-glass bathroom door; one of the many original touches found throughout the hotel which is beautifully decorated to high, Nina Campbell, standard.' 'Dinner was an enjoyable experience of the type only rarely met. Raw materials, preparation, inventiveness of dishes, all scored 100%. But it was in the preparation that the chef rose most above his peers – 150% for preparation.' 'A genuine and efficient welcome. Delicious food, and I even had a specially cooked

63

vegetarian dish. Never was I made to feel "A woman alone; put her in the widow corner". I felt really welcome. There were never any chi-chi affected mannerisms hiding incompetence!' *(Gillian Vincent, JET, Mrs M D Prodgers; also Charles Osborne, Lady Martin, Miranda Barlow and others)*

Open: All year.
Rooms: 15 double – all with bath and shower, telephone, radio and colour TV.
Facilities: Lift, drawing room/bar, dining room; small conference facilities; private dining room. 20 acres grounds with tennis court; overlooking lake with trout fishing and sailing.
Restrictions: No children under 8. Dogs by arrangement.
Location: Off the A606 1 mile SE of Oakham.
Credit cards: All major credit cards accepted.
Terms: B & B (continental) £25–40. Set meals: lunch (Sunday) £14 (weekday) £12.50, dinner £18. Reduced rates for children; special meals on request.

HARROGATE, North Yorkshire

Map 4

Russell Hotel [GFG] *Telephone:* Harrogate (0423) 509 866
Valley Drive

A small-to-medium-sized hotel owned and managed by various members of the Hodgson family. Richard Hodgson is in charge of the admirable *Hodgsons* restaurant, adjoining the hotel. The building is a row of converted terrace houses overlooking Valley Gardens: corridors run at all sorts of angles, so you may need some navigational aid first time around. Not everyone appreciates the colourful decor of the public rooms, but much else gives satisfaction. The service seems to be consistently efficient and amiable, even when the hotel is full of conferees, but the restaurant is what tends to get singled out for special commendation, e.g. 'Fantastic value, excellent service, comparable in quality to *Sharrow Bay* on Ullswater (q.v.) or even better from our point of view because helpings not so *vast!' (M G and B A Furse)*

Open: All year, except 28–30 December.
Rooms: 26 double, 14 single – 8 with bath, 12 with shower, all with telephone, radio, colour TV and baby-listening.
Facilities: Lift, lounge, bar/lounge, bar, restaurant. Conference/banqueting facilities. Small garden. Golf, swimming, squash, tennis, cricket, fishing, riding, racing nearby.
Location: ½ mile from town centre, by Valley Gardens; no special parking facilities.
Restriction: No dogs in public rooms.
Credit cards: Access/Euro/Mastercard, American Express, Barclay/Visa.
Terms (no fixed service charge): B & B £13.25–18.95; dinner, B & B £21.20–27.45. Set meal: dinner (3-course) £8.50, (4-course, inc. ½ bottle wine) about £15. Reduced rates and special meals for children. Special weekend breaks (2 days minimum) 14 October–31 March. Special 3-day Christmas programme.

> Most hotels have reduced rates out of season and for children, and some British hotels offer 'mini-break' rates throughout the year. For details you should write direct to the hotel.

HELFORD, Helston, Cornwall   Map 1

Riverside   [GFG]   *Telephone:* Manaccan (032 623) 443

'It is said to be difficult to convey saintliness in words; it is certainly difficult to convey perfection in a hotel. But we could not wish for a more comfortable place to stay, or better food, or more civilized and agreeable managers or more pleasant service.' *(T M Wilson)*

One of those places which inspire superlatives, *Riverside* is an enchanting conversion of two white-washed cottages bordering a small creek winding into the Helford River. George Perry-Smith and his partner Heather Crosbie made their names in the Fifties and Sixties running Bath's famous restaurant *The Hole in the Wall*, and have made a fresh reputation with this tiny restaurant with rooms in deepest Cornwall. Here is another typical salute:

'If the definition of a good hotel is one that makes you feel at home, then *Riverside* is surely an excellent hotel for offering all those small luxuries you normally manage without. I accept that it is false to assess *Riverside* as a hotel, especially as it does not claim to be one, but this little restaurant with rooms put our more expensive accommodation of the night before well and truly to shame. The room was spotless, the bathroom seductive with not one but two varieties of foam bath available and the coffee and tea-making facilities included Nescafe Gold Blend, Lapsang Souchong tea, Rich Tea biscuits and fresh milk. I will not describe our dinner in detail – suffice it to say that I rate it the best meal I have ever had. Please tell your readers not to be put off by the fact that *Riverside* only serves continental breakfast. Ours consisted of half a fresh grapefruit, fresh fruit salad, a bowl of the biggest juiciest prunes I have ever seen, croissants that melted in the mouth, freshly cooked wholemeal rolls, home-made jam and marmalade, a whole pot of coffee for Shelagh and a whole pot of tea for me. I swear I ate more than many hotels provide for what they call a full breakfast!' *(Roger and Shelagh Utley)*

Open: Mid March–end October.
Rooms: 6 double – all with bath. 2 rooms in annexe.
Facilities: Residents' lounge, restaurant. 1 acre grounds on Helford creek off the Helford river and Falmouth bay, with beaches, sailing, and fishing.
Location: 12 miles from Helston off the B3293.
Restriction: No dogs.
Terms: B & B from £22. Set meal: dinner £17.50. Full *alc* £20. Reduced rates and special meals for children.

HINTON CHARTERHOUSE, Bath, Avon   Map 2

Homewood Park   [GFG]   *Telephone:* Limpley Stoke (022 122) 2643

If we were in the business of awarding accolades, then *Homewood Park* would certainly be a candidate for the most attractive new country-house hotel to have opened in Britain so far this decade. Stephen and Penny Ross launched themselves as hoteliers in December 1980, but they had already made their mark as restaurateurs with *Popjoys* in Bath. *Homewood Park* is by no means as expensive as other hotels offering similar facilities, and all our reports display the same enthusiasm. Here is a typical view: 'This exquisite hotel and restaurant is set in ten acres of beautiful grounds. It provides the most friendly personal service afforded to me in 16 years of high-quality hotel travelling throughout Europe. Every member of the staff addresses you by name and makes you feel as one of the family. There are only eight rooms, but they are all beautifully appointed. The food is wonderful, and there is a superb yet realistically priced wine list. I shall stay here whenever I can.' *(Peter Cook; also Pat and Jeremy Temple, JET, HR, Lottie Freedman)*

Open: All year except 25 December–14 January.
Rooms: 8 double, all with bath, colour TV and telephone.
Facilities: 2 lounges, TV room, dining room. 2 acres grounds with tennis court; riding can be arranged with stables next door. Near wooded hills and Norman border castle of Hopton.
Location: 12 miles NW of Ludlow, 6 miles SW of Craven Arms via the B4368 and B4385 (sign to Hopton Castle just after Twitchen).
Restriction: No dogs.
Terms: B & B (continental) £18.75–35 (cooked breakfast £3 extra). Set lunch: £8 Monday–Friday (£5.50 on Sunday); fish dinner Thursday £10; full *alc* £17. Reduced rates and special meals for children by arrangement. *Let's Go* breaks November–March, 2 nights between Monday and Thursday £62, dinner B & B.

HOVINGHAM, York   Map 4

Worsley Arms Hotel   *Telephone:* Hovingham (065 382) 234

'The valuable Medical Properties of the Spring, manifested in numerous well authenticated cases, the convenient locality of the Town of Hovingham, the healthiness of the situation (being on a fine gravelly soil), the beauty of the Scenery, its vicinity to the unrivalled ruins of Rievaulx Abbey, and other celebrated remains of Gothic Architecture, and to the splendid Mansions of Castle Howard, Duncombe Park, &c, must, it is presumed, render a visit to this Spa as agreeable as it will be found salubrious, in many prevalent Complaints – Sores, Lameness, Gravel, Loss of Appetite, &c.'

So runs an early 19th-century advertisement for the *Worsley Arms* when Hovingham enjoyed fame as a popular spa. No one these days comes to Hovingham to take the waters, but the *Worsley Arms* continues to flourish, and perhaps specially since *Brideshead* put Castle Howard on the international tourist map. But this old coaching inn in a pleasant unspoilt village has never needed adventitious fame to prosper: it has enjoyed a consistently good press since the first edition of the Guide because it practises so dependably the arts and skills of good hotelmanship, not least in its restaurant. *(John M Mitchell, Dr John Lunn, RCS)*

Open: All year, except Christmas.
Rooms: 11 doubles, 3 single – all with bath.
Facilities: 3 lounges (1 with TV), cocktail bar, public bar, restaurant. Facilities for small meetings, conferences, etc. ½ acre garden with croquet lawn.
Location: In Hovingham village, 18 miles NW of Malton and Castle Howard; Scarborough 26 miles E.
Credit cards: Access/Euro, Barclay/Visa.
Terms: B & B £18–20; dinner, B & B £26.50–28.50. Set meals: lunch £5.50, dinner £10. Special meals for children on request.

HUNSTRETE, Chelwood, Nr Bristol, Avon   Map 2

Hunstrete House   [GFG]   *Telephone:* Compton Dando (076 18) 578
                                                       Telex: 449540

The 1983 examiner's report on this outstandingly beautiful 18th-century manor house in its 90 acres of parkland has to be almost exactly a repetition of last year's: First Class Honours, *summa cum laude*, for the Lodging, and – sadly! – a Second Class Degree only for the Board. Here is a citation for the former:

'It was pelting down when we arrived, the worst gales to date. This did not interfere in any way with the comforts of the hotel. I fell in love with the huge room, with its large double bed, simply but attractively decorated with beautiful paintings and attractive pieces of old china. In fact the whole place has been done up with the unerring hand of a true artist – which indeed Mrs Dupays is since she gives lecture weeks in painting, and her works, displayed all over the hotel, are beautiful and highly original. Every care was given to one's comfort – bubble bath, hot towels, hair dryer, etc. – and we also appreciated the separate dressing room. The service was impeccable. *Hunstrete* is a joy to stay at if only for aesthetic reasons.' *(Francine and Ian Walsh)*

In our report last year, we had said that the only significant reservation among our correspondents referred to the food, which 'many find does not really match the perfection of the decor'. One couple rose gallantly to the defence. They felt we had been too sweeping and should have said that the food does not *quite* match the decor – and that it would have been hard to meet that standard. But even they conceded that the chef often 'failed to enhance the flavour of meat or fish, and was too fond of sweet sauces'. Other correspondents spoke about poor coffee, undistinguished veal chops, overcooked vegetables. All these criticisms were made more in sorrow than in anger. *Hunstrete* continues to inspire superlatives: if only the restaurant could live up to the excellence of other features.

Open: All year, except 4–21 January.
Rooms: 15 double, 3 single, 2 suites – all with bath, telephone and colour TV. 6 rooms in annexe. (4 rooms on ground floor.)
Facilities: Drawing room, bar, dining room. 90 acres grounds and walled garden; outdoor heated swimming pool, hard tennis court, croquet lawn. &.
Location: On the A368 8 miles SW of Bath.
Restriction: No children under 9.
Credit cards: American Express, Barclay/Visa.
Terms: B & B (continental) £29–50.40. English breakfast £2.60. Set meal: buffet lunch £9.20; full *alc* £20. Special winter rates November–31 March (min. 3 days). Winter courses on antiques and oil painting. Christmas programme.

HUNTINGDON, Cambridgeshire   Map 2

The Old Bridge Hotel   [GFG]   *Telephone:* Huntingdon (0480) 52681
High Street   *Telex:* 32706

The main snag about *The Old Bridge*, we have said in previous issues, is that its front rooms are close to the road, and suffer from the noise of passing traffic. It has a lot going for it otherwise. It is a fine ivy-creepered Georgian building, with a garden running down to the river Ouse, is admirably run by the same outfit, Poste Hotels, that also owns *The George* at Stamford and *Bailiffscourt* at Climping (both q.v.) and it has a distinguished restaurant as well. Our latest correspondent, however, has one caveat – the vegetables let the place down badly. 'I have stayed half a dozen times in the past few months. The idea and philosophy of the place is good. Pleasant humans run it. Early-morning tea and newspaper are *delivered*. Good breakfasts – have you seen so many varieties of marmalade? Very good food – apart from those vegetables. I hope this report is not neurotic or paranoid. I just want the vegetables to be better!' *(Brian Chapman)*

Open: All year.
Rooms: 15 double, 8 single – 17 with bath, all with telephone and colour TV.
Facilities: Main lounge, bar, restaurant; conference/banqueting facilities. 1 acre garden leading down to the river Ouse; private jetty.
Location: Near town centre; parking for 100 cars.
Restriction: No dogs in public rooms.
Credit cards: All major credit cards accepted.
Terms: B & B £21.50–29.50. Full *alc* £17.50. Special weekend rates out of season from £7.50 per person per day. Christmas programme.

HUNTSHAM, Nr Tiverton, Devon   **Map 1**

Huntsham Court   *Telephone:* Clayhanger (039 86) 210

A thoroughly intriguing, unconventional establishment, the creation of a Danish former travel agent, Mogens Bolwig, and his Greek wife, Andrea. It is in a secluded setting in rural Devon, between Exmoor and Dartmoor; by car, it is five slow meandering miles from the M5 at the Tiverton exit, roughly halfway between Taunton and Exeter. It is a choice example of High Victorian architecture, built in 1869 by Benjamin Ferry, with awe-inspiring room dimensions.

Huntsham is an unashamedly amateur enterprise, dedicated to making its guests forget that they are in a hotel at all. It eschews such mod cons as colour TV and direct-dial telephones or locks on bedroom doors. There is a TV room, but no-one uses it. The Bolwigs opened *Huntsham* in early 1981, after what must have been a Herculean task of renovating and furnishing these potentially spooky rooms. The furniture is eclectic: much of it comes from local antique shops and auction rooms – Victorian sideboards and outsize armchairs of the Twenties and Thirties which are out of favour these days. Our first reaction was 'Ghastly!', but we came to realize that these fruity period-pieces somehow worked in this setting. The bedrooms are all named after composers. Most have bathrooms *en suite*, not the skilfully accommodated modern baths you find in other hotels, but free-standing old tubs with silver claws, and the bathrooms tend to be as big as other people's drawing rooms. Beethoven has two such baths side by side in the middle of the room and a log fire. All the rooms are provided with pre-war radio sets resurrected by some local enthusiast who learned his craft running a radio station in the jungle of Nicaragua. We were sweetly lullabyed in Brahms. Dinner is a five-course affair eaten communally round one huge table in the oak-panelled Hall: it's enthusiastic and generous cooking, if not gastronomically distinguished. *Huntsham* has a modest wine list, but a huge musical repertoire. There are over 2,500 records and cassettes, mostly classical with a leaning towards the operatic, which are free for guests to play on a high hi-fi. There's also a sauna, a mini-gym and lots of bicycles; a Jacuzzi is coming shortly. Tea and coffee are free for guests to help themselves to night and day in the butler's pantry. And if you are thirsty for something stronger, and there's no-one around at the Bar, you help yourself and enter details in a book. Booze is really the only extra there is at *Huntsham*. The price for a double room varies from Beethoven down to Chopin, but that price includes the five-course dinner, a whopping full English breakfast – the complete works, but two of everything – served in bed if you wish and as late as you wish, morning papers and everything else. The minimizing of extras is one of the pleasant things about the place; the absence of hotel notices of any kind inside or out is another. If *Huntsham* is nothing like a normal hotel, it is also, with its many unconventional features, a far remove from domestic life. A conventional hotel in this Gothic setting could only too easily be a morgue. But as soon as you enter the place, you feel its verve: it hums with life. The Bolwigs may appear laid-back; but they are also relaxedly attentive to their guests' needs and moods. *(HR; also Alex Macovich)*

Open: All year.
Rooms: 15 double, 2 suites – 10 with bath, all with pre-war radios, tea-making facilities and babysitting.
Facilities: Hall, TV room, drawing room, library, music room, billiard room, bar, dining room; occasional music and dancing; sauna, gym. 3 acres garden with croquet; bicycles. Trout fishing in private lake; riding, golf nearby.
Location: M5 Motorway to Taunton, then the A361 towards Rampton until Huntsham is signposted; alternatively, leave the M5 at Junction 27 towards Tiverton and turn off to Huntsham when signposted; parking. Collection from Taunton station or Exeter airport.
Restriction: No dogs in public rooms.
Credit cards: All major credit cards accepted.
Terms: Dinner, B & B £22–52 (1st night), £20–38 (extra nights). Set meal: lunch from £5 (no fixed service charge). Packed lunches £2. Reduced rates for children, depending on number and whether sharing parents' room. Special Christmas programme; February–April prices include extras, e.g. ½ day trout fishing.

ILFRACOMBE, North Devon   **Map 1**

Langleigh Country Hotel   *Telephone:* Ilfracombe (0271) 62629
Langleigh Road

Langleigh became a hotel in 1980, started by David Darlow, a Granada producer, and his wife Tessa. It is, we are told, the oldest inhabited house in the town, built in 1570, but it had an extensive facelift in the early 19th century and is now effectively Regency. It has an attractive setting at the foot of a wooded valley, but it is only a few minutes' walk from the town centre and Ilfracombe's sandy and rocky coves.

We had our first entry last year, enthusiastic about every aspect of the place and especially about Tessa Darlow's cooking. Most reports this year have been enthusiastic too, *viz:* 'Extremely comfortable – food excellent – staff attentive but not pushy. Exclusive but not pretentious. Thoroughly re-recommendable.' Another writer mentioned how ideal the hotel was for couples with babies or young children. A third liked the furnishings: 'Jane Austen would have been at home in the quiet, elegant drawing room.' Another singled out for special commendation Tessa's brother

Charles, 'a genial barman'. As pleasant a bunch of reports as one could wish for. The only detracting factor – and this may be grossly unfair to the parties concerned – several of them were written on consecutive pages of the Report Forms. This always makes the Editor suspicious about the spontaneity of the feedback, though in the present instance, the reports do have a genuinely gratified air. *(Mavis Macdougall, J Silverman, Brenda Finn, Diana Morgan, R J and S A Nickolls, G M Pooley)*

Open: All year, except Christmas week.
Rooms: 5 double, 1 single – 8 with bath, 2 with shower, all with intercom, radio, colour TV, tea-making facilities and baby-listening. Also 2 family cottages each with 2 bedrooms, living room and bathroom.
Facilities: Lounge, bar, dining room, 2 games rooms. 3 acres grounds. Badminton, solarium. Within walking distance of sandy and rocky coves in Ilfracombe. &.
Location: Off the A361 from Barnstaple, on the corner of Broad Park Avenue and Langleigh Road.
Restriction: No dogs in public rooms.
Terms (no service charge): B & B £11–16; dinner, B & B £16–21. Family cottage £17–19. Children half-price if sharing parents' room; special meals provided.

IPSWICH, Suffolk **Map 2**

The Marlborough [GFG] *Telephone:* Ipswich (0473) 57677
73 Henley Road *Telex:* c/o Bury St Edmunds, Angel Hotel 81630

An admirably enterprising hotel, with a well-reputed restaurant, housed in a red-brick Victorian residence a few minutes' walk from the town centre, opposite Christchurch Park. It has many business users during the week, but offers 'Old English Weekends' and various other inducements and attractions for the non-business visitor, including – for those with a taste for it – a Champagne Breakfast in Bed from 8 a.m. onwards at £3.50 per person. 'I have visited on average two nights per week at this hotel for the last eight months. In 30 years of business travel, I have never encountered such a consistently high standard of cuisine, room facilities and cheerful efficient service from all the staff. This reflects the utmost credit on the managerial skills and personality of the manager, David Brooks. 101%!' *(J A Paget-Brown)*

Open: All year. (Restaurant closed Christmas evening.)
Rooms: 17 double, 4 single, 1 suite – 21 with bath, all with telephone, radio, colour TV and baby-listening.
Facilities: Lounge, bar, restaurant; function room. Small garden. 20 minutes by car from the sea at Felixstowe; convenient for exploring Constable country.
Location: 10 minutes' walk from town centre; 200 yards to the right from the A12 and Henley Road crossroads.
Restriction: No dogs in public rooms.
Credit cards: All major credit cards accepted.
Terms (no service charge): B & B £22–34. Set meal: dinner £8.25; full *alc* £20. Old English Weekends and 5-night breaks available at reduced rates. Reduced rates for children over 5 sharing parents' room. No charge for children under 5. Special meals by arrangement.

> Please write and confirm an entry when it is deserved. If you think that a hotel is not as good as we say, please write and tell us.

JERVAULX, Masham, Ripon, North Yorkshire — Map 4

Jervaulx Hall *Telephone:* Bedale (0677) 60235

Our index cards for some hotels tell a chequered story; not so *Jervaulx Hall* which, consistently since its first entry in 1981, has attracted warmly appreciative responses. The number of such reports this past year has been particularly pleasing because Shirley Sharp had a major operation a year ago, and an exceptional load fell on her husband John. Terrible hiccups can occur in these circumstances, but if they did, we never heard of them.

Jervaulx Hall is in Wensleydale, between Masham and Middleham, and within easy driving of the Dales National Park. The hotel is on the site of one of the famous Cistercian abbeys, and adjoins the ruins, with only a ha-ha between; guests enjoy the run of the substantial Abbey Park. The Hall itself is early Victorian, and maintained in style – with all that that implies in terms of spaciousness and solid comfort. When the hotel opened there were only three rooms with baths *en suite*, but two more have been converted this year, and possibly more by next season.

'The Guide brings us a steady number of customers,' writes Mr Sharp, 'and I must say that, almost without exception, they are the type of person for whom we are looking.' His guests, through their correspondence with us, have clearly returned the compliment: almost without exception – there were slight niggles about weak coffee and poor lighting in the bedrooms – the under-mentioned have shown that *Jervaulx Hall* is the type of hotel for which they are looking. *(Hugh and Anne Pitt, Kenneth and Mary Habershon, Edward Hibbert, Peter R Copp, J G Fenwick, Frances Perry, H F King, C J Bosanquet)*

Open: 1 March–22 December.
Rooms: 8 double – 5 with bath, all with tea-making facilities and baby-listening. (1 room with bath on ground floor.)
Facilities: Residents' lounge, TV room, dining room. 8 acres garden with Abbey ruins; trout and grayling fishing available in nearby river Ure. &.
Location: 12 miles N of Ripon on the A6108, between Masham and Middleham.
Credit cards: Access, Barclay.
Terms (no fixed service charge): Dinner, B & B £26.75–29. Set meal: dinner £8.50–9. Reduced rates and special meals for children.

KESWICK, Cumbria — Map 4

Lodore Swiss Hotel *Telephone:* Borrowdale (059 684) 285
Telex: 64305

The Lodore Swiss, with its 72 bedrooms and its huge range of facilities (see below) is one of the larger and grander hotels in the Guide. It has an exceptional position, standing in 40 acres of ground, including the famous Lodore Falls, on Derwentwater. It has been run for more than 30 years by a Swiss family named England, and its attention to the small details of customer-cossetting represent Swiss traditions of hotelmanship at their best. Last year, in a generally favourable entry, we quoted one critic of the hotel who had described it as possessing 'the intimate charm of London Airport'. A correspondent this year springs to the defence: 'I had a good laugh at the reference to London Airport, but frankly the *Lodore* is too good to be guyed in this way. The atmosphere is perfect. Our room was not very big, but was very cleverly arranged with good lighting and a first-rate bed. The evening meal, in the dining-room window, was an unforgettable experience. Between the table and Derwentwater were the water meadows with sheep, lambs, cows. It sounds banal, but it was great. The impeccable friendly service from the time we arrived until we left, was faultless.' Another correspondent pulled out a similar stop: 'They don't miss a trick. . . . Quite the best hotel I've stayed in for years.' *(John Hills; also Peter J Williams and Conrad Dehn)*

Open: Mid March–November.
Rooms: 60 double, 11 single, 1 suite – all with bath or shower, telephone, colour TV and baby-listening.
Facilities: Lift, lounge, writing room, bar, dining room, ballroom; health and beauty suite, sauna, exercise rooms, hairdressing salon, shop, indoor swimming pool, children's nursery with resident nanny. Dancing every Saturday; disco twice-weekly during July and August. 40 acres grounds going down to Derwentwater and the river Derwent; outdoor swimming pool, tennis court, children's playground.
Location: 3½ miles S of Keswick.
Restrictions: Children under 6 not allowed in dining room; special meals provided in nursery. No dogs.
Terms (excluding service): B & B £25; full board (minimum 3 days) £36. Set meals: lunch £6.50; dinner £8.50; full *alc* £13.50. Reduced rates and special meals for children.

KILDWICK, Nr Keighley, West Yorkshire   **Map 4**

Kildwick Hall   *Telephone:* Cross Hills (0535) 32244

We had our first entry last year for this imposing Jacobean manor house which comes complete with atmospheric creepers, mullioned windows, embossed lead pipes, ornate plasterwork, oak panelling, huge fireplaces and the like, and are glad to say that reports since have all confirmed the original verdict that there is the stamp of quality and caring about the place. It is high above the main road from Keighley to Skipton, overlooking Airedale, and makes a thoroughly civilized centre for touring the Yorkshire Dales. 'Very comfortable, attentive and friendly service and charming bedrooms. The dining-room is very beautiful as are the gardens and surroundings – and the food is imaginative and first class.' *(James Hill; also G J Warburton, John Hills, Angela and David Stewart, Mrs Robert Hanna)*

Open: All year.
Rooms: 9 double, 3 single – 10 with bath, 2 with shower, all with telephone and colour TV; 2 four-poster beds.
Facilities: Main hall, lounge (including bar), dining room. 3 acres garden in own surrounding woodland. Ideal centre for the Yorkshire Moors and Dales.
Location: In Kildwick village. Take road between *The White Lion* and church, cross canal and turn left at top of hill.
Credit cards: All major credit cards accepted.
Terms: B & B £24–45; dinner, B & B £180–270 per week. Set meals: lunch £6.95; dinner £9.95; full *alc* £14. Special diets catered for by arrangement. Special weekly and off-peak rates available; special Christmas break. Reduced rates for children sharing parents' room; special meals provided.

KINGHAM, Oxon
Map 2

The Mill *Telephone:* Kingham (060 871) 255

Once again, it has been a good year for John and Val Burnett's guests at this simple but thoroughly well-maintained country inn just outside Kingham village. It's not in a much-travelled area, but Burford, Stow-on-the-Wold, Chipping Norton and Moreton-in-the-Marsh are all within a ten-mile radius. A typical report: 'Extremely hospitable and exceptionally friendly service. Tasty food, generous portions, somewhat limited menu for stay of more than two days, but freshly and individually cooked. Very pleasant decor, from king-size log fires in the bar to immaculate and very pretty table settings in the dining-room. The charming hosts were much in evidence.' In our entry last year, we mentioned that opinions had varied as to the quality of the food. Another correspondent rises staunchly to the defence: 'The comment about unimaginative meals could not be sustained at the time of our visit without the adoption of quite excessive standards of gastronomic fantasy!' *(Dr and Mrs C G H Newman, Dr C P Spencer; also A M Street, Mr and Mrs J Kavanagh, E Brazier, Peter Cornall)*

Open: All year.
Rooms: 9 double, 1 single, 2 family – 7 with bath, 3 with shower, all with tea-making facilities. 3 rooms in annexe. (1 room on ground floor.)
Facilities: Residents' lounge, TV lounge, dining room. 10 acres grounds with golf practice range and trout stream – fishing available. Horse-riding nearby. &.
Location: Between Stow-on-the-Wold and Chipping Norton on the B4450.
Restrictions: No children under 3. Dogs by prior arrangement only.
Credit cards: American Express, Barclay/Visa, Diners.
Terms (excluding 10% service charge): B & B £14–19; dinner, B & B £23–28; full board £28–33. Set meals: lunch £5.95, dinner £9.95; full *alc* £13. Two-day winter breaks October–May. 3-day Christmas programme.

KINTBURY, Nr Newbury, Berkshire
Map 2

Dundas Arms [GFG] *Telephone:* Kintbury (0488) 58263

We are constantly being asked to recommend small quiet recuperative hotels, within an hour or so's drive from London. We wish we knew of more, but the *Dundas Arms* fits the bill, even though Kintbury is 73 miles from the capital, so you will have to belt along the M4 slightly above the speed limit to get there within an hour. The qualities that recommend it to our readers are twofold: it is in a quiet backwater between the river Kennet and the Kennet and Avon canal; the rooms are in a converted stable-block, each with its own private patio. And the restaurant, which is out of earshot of the bedrooms, has a deservedly high reputation (though we had one report of slow off-hand service) and is, for what you get, reasonably priced. 'A short fishing holiday on the Kennet was made doubly enjoyable: we had a memorable dinner, imaginatively planned and superbly cooked, and a refreshingly different bedroom, with ducks for company on the patio in the morning!' *(Anne Voss-Bark)*

Open: All year, except Christmas and New Year. (Restaurant closed Sunday and Monday.)

Rooms: 6 double – all with bath, 5 with telephone and colour TV. 1 room in annexe. (All rooms on ground floor.)
Facilities: Bar, restaurant. Kennet and Avon canal alongside. &.
Location: In the Kennet Valley, S of the A4 and M4, 5½ miles W of Newbury.
Restrictions: No children under 18 months. No dogs.
Credit cards: All major credit cards accepted.
Terms (no fixed service charge): B & B £15–25. Set meal (dinner) from £13.50. Special meals for children.

KIRKOSWALD, Eden Valley, Cumbria   Map 4

Prospect Hill Hotel   *Telephone:* Lazonby (076 883) 500

This small hotel was converted a few years ago by Isa and John Henderson from a complex of old farmhouses. It is in the unspoilt Eden valley, ¾ mile north of the pretty village of Kirkoswald and 20 minutes' drive from the M6 at Penrith. We were glad to get the report below, but would like to hear from other visitors to *Prospect Hill*, especially from those who have dined as well as stayed the night.

'Very tranquil, with not even farm noises. Good old furniture and interesting "junk" abound. One room had enormous brass bedstead and stained glass in adjoining bathroom door. Our room was smaller, equally comfortable, but slightly marred by ugly shower cabinet; however, water good and hot. The night was cold, but central heating more than adequate. Superb views towards Pennines. We only had breakfast, but it was best English in local china – honey particularly good. The hotel bar was furnished with chapel furniture – well done, and local clergy asked about it beforehand. Staff helpful, everything spotless and clean. Good information on walks, etc., in each bedroom. Owners are to be congratulated. Prices most reasonable. We could easily return.' *(S D Carpenter)*

Open: All year except February. Restaurant closed to non-residents on Tuesday.
Rooms: 9 double, 3 single – 4 with shower, all with tea-making facilities; TV available at nominal charge. (3 rooms in annexe.)
Facilities: Porch, TV lounge, reading room, lounge bar, restaurant; occasional dinner dances; indoor games; 1-acre garden with 3 ornamental pools; summer house planned for 1983. Bicycles for hire; trout and salmon fishing nearby; golf 9 miles. Good walking country: maps, wellingtons and waterproofs supplied.
Location: ½ mile N of Kirkoswald on the Armathwaite road; Kirkoswald usually approached on the B6413. Parking.
Restriction: No dogs.
Credit cards: American Express, Barclay/Visa, Diners.
Terms (no service charge): B & B £11–16.50; dinner, B & B £18.10–24.10. Set meals: lunch from £3.30, dinner from £7.10; full *alc* £9.50–12.50. Reduced rates for children. 2-day honeymoon breaks; discounts for 3, 7 days; Christmas and New Year packages.

LAMORNA COVE, Nr Penzance, Cornwall   Map 1

Lamorna Cove Hotel   *Telephone:* Mousehole (073 673) 411/564

Lamorna Cove is very near the end of England: Penzance is six miles away to the north-west and Land's End not much farther to the north-east. Land's End is a shambles, but this part of the coast has been vigilantly protected against development and is rich in spectacular scenery. Not far away to the north are ancient boulders and the gaunt silhouettes of ruined tin mines. Lamorna itself is wonderfully peaceful, a small fishing cove at the end of a wooded valley – designated, as the jargon puts it, an area of natural beauty. Don't expect much in the way of sandy beaches, though there's a bit at low tide. But the hotel has its own heated outdoor pool, and a splendid beach is close at hand at Sennen Cove. And of course the toe of Cornwall is a paradise for walkers and birdwatchers. The hotel, part an old chapel and part a former quarryman's home, with a modern extension, stands at one side of the cove in five acres of grounds, with glorious seaward views in the direction of the Lizard. It changes little from year to year, one reason no doubt why it attracts a lot of loyal regulars, who appreciate its welcome to children and its dependable friendliness and comfort, and who don't mind the fact that some of the rooms are on the small side and not very well insulated. One reader this year wrote: 'If they must play muzak in the dining room, could they please buy a second tape?' But the only regular grumble, this year as before, is from those who care about the quality of meals on holiday and have found Lamorna Cove's cooking no more than average. *(Julian M Roberts, Rob and Lisa Thirlby, Mrs Sheila Williams, David R W Jervois)*

Open: February–31 November.
Rooms: 19 double, 2 single, 2 suites – 19 with bath, 4 with shower, 6 with telephone, all with radio, colour TV and baby-listening. 4 rooms in annexe.
Facilities: Lift, 4 lounges, bar, restaurant. Cottages for 4 and 5 in hotel grounds. 5½ acres garden in a wooded cleft leading down to the sea, 300 yards away; heated outdoor swimming pool.
Location: 6 miles S of Penzance.
Restriction: Dogs by special arrangement.
Credit cards: All major credit cards accepted.
Terms: B & B £12.50–£21.95; dinner, B & B £17.50–26.95. Set meals: lunch £5.25, dinner £8, full *alc* lunch £7.95. Winter breaks. Reduced rates for children sharing parents' room; special meals provided.

LASTINGHAM, North Yorkshire   Map 4

Lastingham Grange   *Telephone:* Lastingham (075 15) 345

'A peaceful backwater' is how Major and Mrs Wood describe their consistently popular small country house, stone-walled and creeper-covered, which lies in ten acres of garden at the end of a road which leads straight out on to the Moors and becomes a bridle path stretching to Rosedale. There is nothing flash about the quality of hospitality offered here, no gimmicky cooking: just two people who understand how to run *their* kind of hotel and succeed in attracting and retaining the affection of their visitors. Some 90% of their guests, they tell us, have stayed with them before – an exceptional figure by any reckoning. *(Piers and Rosemary Raymond)*

Open: All year, but weekends only mid November–March.
Rooms: 11 double, 1 single – 9 with bath, all with radio and baby-listening.
Facilities: Large entrance hall-cum-reception, spacious lounge with log fire; sheltered terrace. 10 acres grounds with croquet, swings and slides. In the heart of the National Park, near moors and dales, 20 miles from the coast, riding, golf and swimming nearby.

Location: Off the A170 N of Kirkbymoorside. Turn N towards Appleton-le-Moors, between Pickering and Kirkbymoorside.
Restriction: No dogs.
Terms (no fixed service charge): B & B £18.50–20.50; dinner, B & B £24.75–27.75; full board £28.50–32.50. Set meals: lunch £6 (picnic lunches available), dinner £9.75. Reduced rates for long stays. Children under 6 free; special meals provided.

LEDBURY, Hereford and Worcester   Map 2

Hope End Country House Hotel   [GFG]   *Telephone:* Ledbury (0531) 3613
Hope End

'This charming place is all that it sets out to be – a *quiet haven* for *adults* with *good food*,' writes one thoroughly satisfied guest at John and Patricia Hegarty's remote small hotel set in 40 acres of parkland in the Malvern Hills. Elizabeth Barrett Browning lived here for 23 years, and makes many references to the house in her poetry. There is not much that remains of the original building, except for a room, specially recommended for honeymoon couples, in the courtyard at the foot of a minaret reminiscent of Brighton Pavilion. A tribute from a honeymooner appears below. We have kept in the reference to John Hegarty because a similar reservation appears in other reports. It is also clear from our extensive postbag on the house that *Hope End* doesn't suit everyone. Some guests are put off by the owners' enthusiasm for organic foods, and mind being offered a no-choice menu, however carefully prepared each course may be. More than one guest has felt the portions were on the mean side. But those who like the special quality of hospitality offered here, often tend to be fervent in their enthusiasm.

'We went for a long weekend after our wedding in April and asked for the minaret room which was beautiful with lovely wood-panelled bathroom and modern prints. The modern decor in elegant surroundings was beautifully done. The food was entirely excellent, and all cooked freshly for each person. This delayed dinner somewhat, but the sitting room is so comfortable it doesn't matter. Breakfast choice off a table of muesli, yogurt, fruit juice, etc., before delicious cooked mushrooms and scrambled eggs, exceedingly yellow and fresh. Fresh croissants on Sundays and home-made bread, all delicious. Vegetables cooked to perfection and steak in wine, and lettuce, almond and grapefruit salad a revelation. Only one small criticism. Mr Hegarty's general fussing around and waiting at table fairly irritating to begin with, but after a day we even forgave them that. All-inclusive price with no extras – very good value for perfection.' *(Mrs S J Bailey; also Sean and Eithne Scallan, Z N Powell, Angela and David Stewart, Ivor Hall, Roger Smithells, Robin Morton-Smith)*

Open: March–November.
Rooms: 7 double – all with bath. 1 double with bath in annexe.
Facilities: 2 sitting rooms, dining room. 40 acres wooded parkland and nature reserve; 1 acre walled garden.
Location: 2 miles N of Ledbury, ¼ mile W of Wellington Heath.
Restrictions: No children under 14. No dogs.
Credit cards: Access/Euro, American Express, Barclay/Visa, Diners.
Terms: B & B £18–25; dinner, B & B £32–37. Set meal: dinner £12. Full *alc* (5-courses) £28. Reduction of £3 per person for dinner, B & B for 5 nights or more.

LIFTON, Devon   **Map 1**

The Arundell Arms   *Telephone:* Lifton (056 684) 244

The Arundell Arms celebrates a double birthday this year: 50 years as a leading fishing hotel and 21 years since Anne Voss-Bark became its proprietor. It's a much-creepered early 19th-century stone building, once a coaching inn, on the A30 (the five rooms in the front have double-grazing). It has 20 miles of its own water on the Tamar and four of its tributaries, a special beginner's course in fly-fishing, trout fishing week-ends in the spring, a hire shop for equipment, and much else besides. There are indeed other activities available, such as golf, riding, shooting – not to mention walking on Dartmoor. But most of the *Arundell* regulars come with a rod in hand. The hotel has consistently enjoyed a good press from our readers, with one reservation – the food was a let-down. We are delighted to learn from Anne Voss-Bark that the hotel recently brought in as chef a young French-trained Devonian, Philip Burgess, who was previously *sous-chef* at the *L'Ecu de France* in London. We look forward to hearing how the guests are biting.

Open: All year, except 3 or 4 days at Christmas.
Rooms: 20 double, 7 single – 16 with bath, 5 with shower, all with radio, tea-making facilities and baby-listening. 4 rooms in annexe.
Facilities: Sitting room, TV room, 2 bars, restaurant; games room, skittle alley. Small terraced garden. Lake and river with salmon, trout and sea-trout fishing.
Restriction: No dogs in dining room.
Location: 3 miles E of Launceston on the A30.
Credit cards: Access/Euro/Mastercard, American Express, Barclay/Visa.
Terms: B & B £16.50–23; dinner, B & B £20–32 (minimum 2 nights). Set meal: dinner £9–9.50; full *alc* £13. Bargain breaks; sporting courses. Reduced rates and special meals for children.

LINCOLN, Lincolnshire   **Map 2**

D'Isney Place Hotel   *Telephone:* Lincoln (0522) 38881
Eastgate

'*A* must *for the Guide! A family-run establishment, 100 yards from the Cathedral, opened by Judy and David Payne two years ago; it was formerly a run-down Georgian building, but the hotel has lovely elegant rooms and beautiful furniture, fabrics, bedcovers, curtains, etc. No meals served except cooked or continental breakfast – brought to your bedside on Minton bone china – and no bar. But there's a good bar next door and Harvey's Restaurant close by. The friendliest and most satisfying place I've stayed in for a long time.*' (Christopher Portway)*
So ran last year's hyperbolic commendation. A recent visitor endorses the entry, though with two minor reservations: his room had been very pleasant, but he would have preferred eating in a breakfast-room if there had been one available; also, a common complaint, he had found the walls thin and the party next door noisy. We don't know whether the Paynes

---

Procrastination is the thief of the next edition.

---

have plans for a breakfast room, but what is promised for 1983 is a half-size snooker table and a four-poster bed for honeymooners.

Open: All year.
Rooms: 11 double, 1 single, 1 suite – 11 with bath, 1 with shower, all with telephone, radio, colour TV, tea-making facilities and baby-listening. (6 rooms on ground floor.)
Facilities: Lounge. 1 acre garden with children's slide and swing. &.
Location: 100 yards from Lincoln Cathedral; parking.
Credit cards: Access/Euro/Mastercard.
Terms (no service charge): B & B (single) £22, (double) £32. Reduced rates and special meals for children. Weekend breaks November–April.

LITTLE LANGDALE, Nr Ambleside, Cumbria   Map 3

Three Shires Inn   [GFG]   *Telephone:* Langdale (096 67) 215

A small friendly inn in an unspoilt Lakeland valley halfway between Ambleside and Coniston – roughly five miles in each direction – and at the foot of Wrynose Pass. The *Three Shires* has had a tradition, through several successive ownerships, of simple hospitality with a quality of cooking that simple inns rarely attain. Readers have found that the present owners, John and Joan Smith, have well maintained these traditions. 'It is, if anything, cleaner, more comfortable, more welcoming and fires are lit even more readily at the slightest suggestion of a chill,' writes one old-timer, who added that her son, daughter-in-law and eight-year-old granddaughter had all enjoyed their stay. Only snag, reported by one correspondent: Rooms 6 and 7 (and possibly 5 and some others) are disturbed by a high whining of what could possibly be beer pumps. *(Professor P J Scheuer and others)*

Open: 1 March–1 November, weekends only in winter.
Rooms: 7 double, 1 single – 1 with bath.
Facilities: TV lounge, reading lounge, bar lounge, restaurant. Hunting, climbing.
Location: 4 miles west of Ambleside on the Coniston road, turn left and follow signs for Wrynose Pass.
Restriction: No dogs.
Terms (no fixed service charge): B & B £12; dinner, B & B £21.50. Set meal: dinner £10. Children sharing parents' room £8 B & B; special meals provided. Special 2–4 day spring breaks, winter weekend breaks.

LITTLE SINGLETON, Nr Poulton-Le-Fylde, Blackpool, Lancashire   Map 2

Mains Hall   *Telephone:* Poulton-Le-Fylde (0253) 885130
Mains Lane

A small hotel in a pastoral setting five miles east of Blackpool off the A585, run by Bob and Beryl Owen in a friendly unassuming non-hotellish way. The house itself has character and history: the Heskeths lived here in Elizabethan times, and George IV, when Prince of Wales, courted Maria Fitzherbert, a virtuous widow, here. One couple, while appreciating the welcome and helpfulness of the Owens, had felt that the dinner had lacked distinction. We don't think this is a place for highly discriminating eaters, but most readers have found *Mains Hall* a pleasure, especially after 'the neon glories of Blackpool, the chip buttys and mushy peas' to quote a previous visitor. *(HR, Anthony Benger, Gordon Cole, Elizabeth William Logan)*

Open: All year. (Restaurant closed for dinner during owners' holiday.)
Rooms: 5 double, 1 single – all with bath or shower and tea-making facilities.
Facilities: Hall with log fire, lounge bar, dining room; dogs allowed 'if well-behaved'. 4 acres grounds with croquet. Access to tidal river with birdwatching and fishing.
Location: 1½ miles from village, just off the A585. Leave the M55 at Junction 3. Take the A585 and follow signs for Fleetwood. *Mains Hall* is ½ mile past the 2nd set of traffic lights.
Terms (no fixed service charge): B & B £11–16; dinner, B & B £16.50–21.50. Set meal: dinner from £5.50. Reduced rates for children sharing parents' room; special meals provided. Special weekend breaks.

LONDON

Athenaeum Hotel
116 Piccadilly, W1

Telephone: (01) 499 3464
Telex: 261589 ATHOME

The Athenaeum, overlooking Green Park, has all the trimmings that one expects of an expensive and de-luxe West End hotel – 24-hour service, excellent restaurant, hyper-elegant decor – but also consistently pleases our readers for less tangible virtues. 'We stayed here regularly before moving to London in 1980, and now recommend it to friends. We often visit the bar for its handsome club-like ambience and wide selection of hard-to-find whiskies. The staff are unfailingly courteous and the service outstanding.' *(S M Gillotti; also Jane Isay)*

Open: All year.
Rooms: 81 double, 9 single, 22 suites – all with bath, shower, telephone, radio, colour TV, baby-listening and double-glazing.
Facilities: Lifts, lounge, cocktail bar, restaurant; conference facilities, facilities for private parties. &.
Location: Central; parking.
Restriction: Dogs only by arrangement.
Credit cards: All major credit cards accepted.
Terms: Rooms £49.50–81 per person. Set meals: breakfast £5.60, lunch £10, dinner £14; full *alc* £22.

LONDON

Basil Street Hotel
8 Basil Street, Knightsbridge, SW3

Telephone: (01) 581 3311
Telex: 28379

The Basil Street Hotel entered our pages for the first time last year, though we had known and appreciated its quality for many years past. It is in a quiet central location just off Sloane Street and within a few minutes' walk from Hyde Park and Harrods. It caters with dependable friendliness and efficiency both for what used to be called folk up from the shires and visitors from overseas. It is a hotel with old-fashioned virtues, and its prices are reasonable by contemporary London standards.

As will be seen from the names below, we have been collecting an uncommon number of reports on the *Basil Street* in recent months – all unfailingly complimentary. Since some of the reports were written on photostats of our original forms, we are sure that the hotel's enterprising manager, Stephen Korany, has been press-ganging his guests into writing to us. No matter: we would not consider an entry if we were not convinced that the hotel merited a mention in our pages. *(C H Lawson, Geoffrey Toney, Bette Dunmore, Lester M Shulman, Mr and Mrs Thomas Roberts, G D Paris)*

Open: All year.
Rooms: 39 double, 62 single, 2 suites – 66 with bath, all with telephone and radio, some with TV.
Facilities: 2 lounges/writing rooms, TV room, coffee shop, wine bar, 3 restaurants; facilities for conferences and functions.
Location: Central; public car park nearby.
Restriction: No dogs in public rooms.
Credit cards: All major credit cards accepted.
Terms: Rooms £23–58. Set meals: breakfast (continental) £2.50, lunch £8; full *alc* £13. Special weekend rates. No charge for children under 16 sharing parents' room; special meals provided.

LONDON

The Connaught [GFG]
16 Carlos Place, W1

Telephone: (01) 499 7070

The incomparable *Connaught* continues to be a paradigm for all city hotels – in London or anywhere else. It has natural advantages – like being in the heart of Mayfair and a strolling distance from Piccadilly and Oxford Street, but in a relatively unbusy street. It has advantages of another kind in its altogether admirable restaurant, even if Michelin has now reduced it to single-star status. But what makes it a great hotel is something else as well: 'fantastic service, stunningly professional *and* friendly, quiet perfection.' *(Barbara Bennett)*

Open: All year.
Rooms: 105, including suites – all with bath, direct-dial telephone, and colour TV; 24-hour room service.
Facilities: Lounges, cocktail bar, grill/restaurant.
Location: Central; no private parking.
Restriction: No dogs.
Terms (excluding 15% service charge): Rooms £51–66 single, £82–104 double, £154–198 suite. Set meal (no fixed service charge): breakfast (continental) £3.75; full *alc* about £28.

> B & B prices, unless otherwise specified, are per person. Where two figures are given, they indicate the range of prices. The lower figure is for one person sharing a double room in the low season, the higher figure is for one person occupying a room alone in the high season. We have also given full- and half-board prices when available.

LONDON

Duke's Hotel *Telephone:* (01) 491 4840/3090
35 St James's Place, SW1 *Telex:* 28283

A sophisticated elusive small hotel with the special attraction of being right in the centre but also very quiet, in a cul-de-sac off a cul-de-sac off St James's Street. One visitor this year, who found Duke's in other respects excellent, complained of a very poor bed which she felt should have been retired years ago. Another wrote: 'Since two years I have been staying with the lovely *Duke's Hotel* for reason of complete satisfaction and greatest pleasure I feel happy about. As I worked in the hotel business a long time, I faced details most critically. I must admit that the staff is very well-trained and their efforts offering the guests the most attentive services are highly recommended. And one gets the opportunity to enjoy a real good meal in the St James's Room.' *(Shirley B L Müseler)*

Open: All year.
Rooms: 26 double, 15 single, 14 suites – all with bath, shower, telephone, radio and colour TV; tea-making facilities in suites; babysitting service; 24-hour room service.
Facilities: Lifts, lounge, bar, restaurant; banqueting and conference facilities. Courtyard.
Location: Central; off St James's Street, between Piccadilly and Pall Mall; 4 minutes' walk from Green Park station; parking facilities nearby.
Restriction: Dogs at manager's discretion.
Credit cards: All major credit cards accepted.
Terms: Rooms £70 single, £81–90 double; suites from about £165, depending on number of people. Set meals: breakfast (continental) £4, (English) £6.50; full *alc* £16–19. Children using cot in parents' room additional £7; special meals on request.

LONDON

Durrants Hotel *Telephone:* (01) 935 8131
George Street, W1 *Telex:* 894919 DURHOTG

Durrants continues to be a dependably recommendable hotel for anyone wanting to stay in a hotel of genuine character in the centre of London (it's three blocks north of Oxford Street, and 100 yards from the entrance to the Wallace Collection in Manchester Square) without paying top London prices. Last year, we reported some murmurs of discontent about the full English breakfast, and there have been further complaints this year from a minority of correspondents – about the breakfasts and about dinners too. Most readers have been content to express their satisfaction with the hotel itself, the pleasant rooms, and the reliably agreeable service. *(Sydney Downs, Mary Lawrence and others)*

Open: All year, but restaurant closed for lunch and dinner Christmas Day/ Boxing Day.
Rooms: 78 double, 26 single – 88 with bath or shower, all with telephone, radio and colour TV. (4 rooms on ground floor.)
Facilities: Lift, 2 lounges, breakfast room, dining room, conference and banqueting room.

Location: Central; no private parking.
Restriction: No dogs.
Credit cards: Access/Euro/Mastercard, American Express, Diners.
Terms: B & B £25–44. Set meals (excluding 10% service charge): lunch £11, dinner £16; full *alc* (excluding 10% service charge) £16.

LONDON

Ebury Court   *Telephone:* (01) 730 8147
26 Ebury Street, SW1

Among the dozens of small hotels within a radius of half a mile of Victoria Station, *Ebury Court* is one of the only two that have been recommended to the Guide. It's been run for nearly half a century in a thoroughly personal way by Diana and Romer Topham. One reader wrote angrily this year to complain of discourtesy because (she believed) she was wearing jeans and a sweater, but this was an isolated grievance. Most readers have written gratefully about their friendly reception. Over the years, Mr and Mrs Topham have slowly expanded their operation into neighbouring houses. There is a maze of narrow corridors, and though the rooms are individually furnished with good pieces, they vary in size – some might be called very cosy indeed – and, for one reader, a little too pink. But the place is full of character, there is a more than decent restaurant, the hotel is dependably helpful with messages and the prices for such a pleasant central London hotel are decidedly reasonable. *(Elisabeth Sifton and others)*

Open: All year.
Rooms: 16 double, 23 single – 11 with bath, 2 with shower, all with telephone, radio and colour TV to hire.
Facilities: Lift, front hall, writing room with TV, club bar (visitors may become temporary members), restaurant; theatre suppers served.
Location: 3 minutes from Victoria Station; parking difficult.
Restriction: Dogs allowed, if small and well-behaved.
Terms (no fixed service charge): B & B £17.25–24.70. Full *alc* £12.

LONDON

Elizabeth Hotel   *Telephone:* (01) 828 6812/3
37 Eccleston Square, SW1

A modest (for London), centrally-placed hotel in a quiet position overlooking the square's well-maintained garden. Only one of the rooms has its own bath and another six have showers – so the hotel won't satisfy all-comers. Another snag: the *Elizabeth* is a five-storey Belgravian terrace house, with no lift or porter, so you must be prepared to carry your bags up steep stairs. 'I have sampled both their cheapest (£15 a night in 1982) and most expensive rooms. In neither was I disappointed. For this friendly family hotel must represent the best value for money available in Central London. Rooms are comfortable and clean. A substantial English

We should like to be able to recommend more budget-priced hotels in London.

breakfast is included in the cost. Warmly recommended.' *(W Lloyd-George; also J Gilbert)*

Open: All year.
Rooms: 14 double, 10 single – 1 with bath, 6 with shower, all with internal telephone, some with colour TV.
Facilities: Lounge with colour TV, breakfast room. ½ acre garden with tennis court.
Location: Central; National Car Park for 400 cars nearby.
Restriction: No dogs.
Terms (no service charge): B & B £15–19. Weekly terms off-season by arrangement. Reduced rates for children sharing parents' room.

LONDON

Number Sixteen   *Telephone:* (01) 589 5232
16 Sumner Place, SW7   *Telex:* 266638

Called *Number Sixteen*, this small exclusive hotel in fact now comprises three contiguous early Victorian terrace houses in Sumner Place, which runs between the Old Brompton Road and Fulham Road, close to South Kensington Underground. The hotel – bed and breakfast only – is intended for people spending more than a day or two in town. The rooms are stylishly maintained, the house is full of paintings and antiques, there are lounges and a help-yourself bar as well as a garden. Prices are substantially below the norm for more conventional establishments in central London.

Open: All year.
Rooms: 20 double, 4 single – 11 with bath, 13 with shower, all with direct-dial telephone and colour TV on request.
Facilities: Reception, bar/lounge. Garden.
Location: Central; no private parking.
Restriction: Children over 12 preferred.
Credit cards: Access/Euro/Mastercard, American Express, Diners.
Terms (excluding service): B & B (continental) £17.50–29.

LONDON

The Portobello Hotel   *Telephone:* (01) 727 2777
22 Stanley Gardens, W11   *Telex:* 21789/25247 Attn: Portobello Hotel

The Portobello is certainly not as raffish and bohemian as the *Chelsea* in New York, but it has long enjoyed a reputation as a hotel of singular character in one of the most colourful and enjoyable parts of the city – a stone's throw, as its name implies, from the Portobello Road, with its famous flea-market, and within ten minutes' strolling distance of Kensington Gardens. For those without their own transport, there are plenty of buses and tubes close by to take you to any part of the town quickly. There is a comfortable ground-floor lounge looking out over private gardens, though without access. The decor is distinctive: lots of flowers, large mirrors and plants, some antique furniture, and cane, wicker and satin furnishings in the bar and the 24-hour restaurant. Service in the restaurant – indeed throughout the whole establishment – is admirable: chatty without being intrusive. The food is ambitious – there is a menu which changes daily – but a bit erratic in its execution, and pricey for what is offered. The bedrooms vary a lot in size; they are all well-equipped with drawer and hanging-space, mini-fridge and everything you need for a d-i-y continental breakfast, including freshly wrapped croissants, but some are decidedly cramped. To sum up, it is a relaxing and unusual base for a city visit, though it would be worth asking for one of the larger rooms and trying out some of the many excellent restaurants of every possible ethnic variety in the Portobello area.

Open: All year, except 24–30 December.
Rooms: 8 double, 8 single, 9 suites – 4 with bath, 21 with shower, all with telephone, radio, colour TV and drink-stocked fridge. (2 rooms on ground floor.)
Facilities: Lift, lounge, bar/restaurant (open 24 hours a day to residents).
Location: Central; meter parking only.
Restriction: Dogs allowed at the proprietor's discretion.
Credit cards: Access/Euro, American Express.
Terms (no fixed service charge): B & B (continental) £20–40. Full *alc* £15. Special meals for children.

LONDON

The Sandringham Hotel   *Telephone:* (01) 435 1569
3 Holford Road, Hampstead, NW3

Maria and Bertie Dreyer, with their son Anthony, run this five-storey Victorian family house in a quiet street on the edge of Hampstead Heath as a small highly personal B & B hotel – the most modest in price, by quite a margin, of our London entries. Guests are given the front-door key as well as a bedroom key. There are several 'house rules': e.g. turn off TV lounge lights but not stair-landing lights, no baths after 11 p.m., no breakfast after 9 a.m., etc. Lots of helpful advice given to young travellers. No frills, but rooms are kept spotlessly clean and are adequately furnished. Abundant large towels. Generous breakfasts in garden-floor dining room. Prices are exceptionally reasonable. 'The Dreyers obviously run this hotel with pride and care, and it shows.' *(DG)*

Open: All year.
Rooms: 10 double, 4 single – 2 with bath.
Facilities: Lounge with TV, breakfast room. Small garden.
Location: 15 minutes by underground from centre; parking on forecourt of hotel.
Restriction: No dogs.
Terms (excluding VAT and service charge): B & B £9–10. Reduced weekly rate during off-season.

If you have difficulty in finding hotels because directions given in the Guide are inadequate, please help us to improve them.

Important reminder: terms printed must be regarded as a rough guide only to the size of the bill to be expected at the end of your stay. For latest tariffs, check when booking.

LOOE, Cornwall   **Map 1**

Klymiarven Hotel   *Telephone:* Looe (050 36) 2333
Barbican Hill, East Looe

Daphne Henderson has been running this seaside hotel for many years, and with conspicuous success. For those who don't know Looe, it is an idyllically picturesque resort, though crowded in the high season. Happily, *Klymiarven* is away from the throng, a handsome old house, *circa* 1800, five minutes' walk from the centre up a steep hill (no place for the elderly or disabled). One of the attractions of the hotel is its heated swimming pool in three acres of grounds. In a letter accompanying the completed questionnaire, Daphne Henderson writes: 'Perhaps you would be kind enough to mention our glorious views across the harbour upon which almost every guest comments.' We are delighted to comply, and indeed, from the evidence of a new brochure, the view is unquestionably a fine one. Our postbag has never lacked compliments, and they come from all over: the USA, Canada and Austria, as well as tributes from the home side. Since we get so few letters from abroad, we suspect that these testimonials are hardly unsolicited, and the suspicion of some gentle arm-twisting grows a little stronger when we receive this letter: 'Daphne Henderson works hard and it shows. Please put our names in the book or she won't believe we write to you after each visit.' *(Alan and Maggie Telford; also Katharine and Luis Molina, Dr and Mrs Charles Carter, Mrs A Entwistle, Pixie and Al Underwood, Josephine Wrigley, Josephine Burr)*

Open: All year except 29 December–mid February.
Rooms: 12 double, 1 single, 2 suites – 6 with bath, 2 with shower, all with radio, colour TV and baby-listening.
Facilities: Lounge, cocktail bar, terrace bar, cellar bar with pool table, darts and table tennis; pool tournaments and disco as required by visitors (but no disturbing noise); recreation room. 3 acres grounds with heated swimming pool. 5 minutes from sandy beaches with safe bathing. Tennis, riding, para-kiting and fishing nearby.
Location: 5 minutes' walk from centre of East Looe; parking for 15–30 cars. Approach via Barbican Road.
Terms (excluding 10% service charge):   B & B £9.50–18.50; dinner, B & B £15.50–24.50. Set meal: dinner £6.50. No fixed *alc* but special meals can be cooked by arrangement. Hot and cold bar lunches available. Bargain breaks October and March–April. Special Christmas programme; art and micro-computer courses. Reduced rates and special meals for children.

LOWESWATER, Nr Cockermouth, Cumbria   **Map 4**

Scale Hill Hotel   *Telephone:* Lorton (090 085) 232

A former coaching inn in one of the less populous parts of the Lake District – in the Loweswater–Buttermere valley, near the National Trust land at Crummock Water. Don't expect anything fancy in the cooking, and only some of the rooms have central heating. But the report below makes the case for inclusion.

'A good honest little lakeland hotel in a supremely beautiful spot. Mr

and Mrs Thompson provide a warm and friendly atmosphere with all the necessary comforts, without sacrificing the homely feel. The food is plain, plentiful and beautifully cooked. The garden is lovely, and the guests all seemed to be there for return visits. Unless one absolutely requires a lake on the doorstep or a daffodil in the soup, I can't imagine anything nicer.'
(Mrs F Newall; also Chris and Dorothy Brining, C J Bosanquet)

Open: 26 March–4 November.
Rooms: 9 double, 3 single – 9 with bath, 1 with shower. (2 double rooms on ground floor.) 2 double, 1 single in annexe.
Facilities: 4 lounges, entrance hall, dining room. ½ acre grounds. Fine walking and climbing; fishing, swimming, golf, pony-trekking nearby. &.
Location: 30 miles from the M6 at Penrith; 12 miles W of Keswick. Just off Lorton–Rosthwaite road.
Terms: B & B £14–20; dinner, B & B £23.50–29.50. Set meals: Sunday lunch £6, dinner £9.50. Reduced prices for long stays and for children.

LUDLOW, Shropshire   Map 2

The Feathers   *Telephone:* Ludlow (0584) 2919/2718
                                                     Telex: 28905 Ref 685

One of the showplace inns of Britain, with an eye-stopping half-timbered front elevation and plenty to catch the eye inside as well – carved mantelpieces, elaborately ornamented plaster ceilings, fine panelling, oak beams and the like. The Edwards family who have owned the place since the war have been mindful of their civic trust obligations and have kept the place in spick-and-span condition, while contriving to give all the bedrooms their own bathrooms, as well as the gamut of radio, TV, hair-dryers and tea-making facilities. It's a busy bustling town hotel, catering for plenty of tourists by car and coachload, but the message, this year as before, is that *The Feathers* succeeds in welcoming all-comers with equal brio. There's a new head chef, we are told, who was formerly a pastry cook member of the Buckingham Palace kitchens – a recommendation, we hope, to those who are used to taking tea with the Queen. *(S M Gillotti and others)*

Open: All year.
Rooms: 29 double, 1 single, 1 suite – all with bath, radio, colour TV and tea-making facilities.
Facilities: 2 lounges, 2 bars, TV and writing room, stone and timbered restaurant with inglenook fireplace. Dances, private parties, wedding receptions catered for; conference facilities.
Location: In town centre; parking for 40 cars.
Restriction: No dogs.
Terms: B & B £23–33; dinner, B & B £32–42; full board £37–47. Set meals: lunch £5.50, dinner £9; full *alc* £12. Special Bargain breaks. Reduced rates and special meals for children.

We ask hotels to estimate their 1983 tariffs some time before publication so the rates given here are not necessarily completely accurate. Please *always* check terms with hotels when making bookings.

LUNDY ISLAND, Bristol Channel, via Ilfracombe, North Devon   Map 1

Millcombe House   *Telephone:* Woolacombe (0271) 870870

Our practice is to drop hotels from the Guide if we lack feedback. We have had no reports on *Millcombe House* since our first entry appeared in the 1981 edition. We recognize that, with limited accommodation as well as restricted accessibility, not many of our readers may have had a chance to visit the island. If any have, could they please let us know? Otherwise, sadly, this will be *Millcombe's* last appearance. Meanwhile, we reproduce a slightly revised version of last year's entry.

'For those who have never heard of Lundy Island, it rises 400 feet out of the sea in the Bristol Channel, with tremendous views of England, Wales and the Atlantic. It is just over three miles long by about half a mile wide, and the nearest practicable harbours are at Ilfracombe and Bideford, each about 24 miles away – further than England is from France. Sailings on the island supply ship are normally on Tuesdays, Thursdays and Saturdays. There is also a Saturday only helicopter service from Hartland Point.

You will need to be fairly fit to stay at *Millcombe House*, the only hotel (or guest house) on the island, since it is set on a hill and there are no made-up roads or paths. Other creature comforts, basic for some, are also missing here: the hotel provides no TV or radio. "We aim," writes the hotel, "to provide an atmosphere more of a house party than an ordinary hotel." Guests sit at one table, and talk is mainly about the island, its history and wildlife (over 425 different birds have been recorded here, as well as Grey Seals, Sika deer, Soay sheep and Lundy ponies). To stay at *Millcombe House* is a mixture of mild adventure – it is certainly unique in the hotel world – and being thoroughly spoiled. Our full board rate – there isn't any other – includes such things as early morning tea, afternoon tea and coffee after dinner, so once you have paid, you have no need to put your hands in your pockets again except for wines and spirits.' *(Ray and Beverley Williams)*

Open: Easter–mid October.
Rooms: 5 double, 2 single.
Facilities: 1,100 acres grounds. Sea ¼ mile with rock beach and safe bathing.
Location: In the Bristol Channel, 24 miles by ferry from Ilfracombe or Bideford.
Restriction: Dogs not allowed to land on Lundy.
Terms (no service charge): Full board £19–27. Set meals: lunch £5, dinner £7.50. Reduced rates and special meals for children.

LYME REGIS, Dorset   Map 1

The Mariners Hotel   [GFG]   *Telephone:* Lyme Regis (029 74) 2753
Silver Street   *Telex:* 46491. I.C.C.G.

Connoisseurs of watering places have long appreciated the special charm of Lyme Regis. It also has literary connections. Jane Austen partly wrote and set *Persuasion* in the town and John Fowles wrote and partly set *The French Lieutenant's Woman* here. A more recondite literary fact: Beatrix Potter used *The Mariners Hotel* as the background in her illustration of *Stumpy the Dog and Susan the Cat* in the *Tales of Little Pig Robinson*. *The Mariners Hotel*, formerly a 17th-century coaching inn, is on the Axminster Road at the end of the town, with fine views from its garden, its lounge and many of the bedrooms of the sweeping Dorset coastline. (Warning: front rooms, though double-glazed, can be a bit noisy and steep stairs won't suit the elderly or infirm.) It's an unassumingly pleasant hotel, but is run with personal enthusiasm by Leo Featherstone, who is also the chef patron and takes his cooking seriously. 'We have stayed several times. The accommodation and service are very good, the menus imaginative and varied and the cooking absolutely first class. . . . In every way a well-run and charming hotel.' *(Miss D Powell and L Satchwell; also K C Turpin, M J Corner, Claire Rayner)*

Open: All year except December/January; weekends only November to February.
Rooms: 14 double, 2 single – 8 with bath, 4 with shower, all with radio and baby-listening. (2 rooms on ground floor.)
Facilities: 2 lounges, bar, restaurant. Small garden overlooking sea. &.
Location: Coming from London on A35 through Lyme Regis take right fork at top of main street (Broad Street); hotel on right; large car park.
Restriction: No dogs in public rooms or garden; allowed in bedrooms at management's discretion.
Credit cards: All major credit cards accepted.
Terms (excluding service): B & B £15.50–19.50; dinner, B & B £21.50–26. Set meal: dinner £9.75. Bar lunches only. Reduced rates for children sharing parents' room: under 6 years with supper tray at 5.45, 40%; 6–12 years, ⅔ adult rate; 12 years up, ¾ adult rate. Bargain breaks (min. 2 days) in winter, spring and autumn.

LYMINGTON, Hampshire   Map 2

Passford House Hotel   *Telephone:* Lymington (0590) 682398
Mount Pleasant

A part 17th-century white-fronted country house, once a hunting lodge, in eight acres of grounds, with a hard tennis court, croquet, putting, child's play area – and the New Forest on or near its doorstep. It's hard to find: see directions below. By the standards of the Guide, it is on the large side, and there are no pretensions in its cooking. We include it because of the evidence from our files of a thoroughly well-run establishment, catering equally for the needs of adults and children – and, one reader adds, 'Dogs are really made to feel welcome too.'

'Three comfortably furnished lounges to choose from, immaculate bedrooms elegantly equipped, and a restaurant which supplies straightforward English food, well cooked and well served, at a pretty reasonable price – the lunchtime *table d'hote* has four or five very acceptable choices for each of the three courses for an all-in price of £5 [1982] including service and VAT. What impressed me even more was that the same high standard was maintained at the dinner for 100 guests at which I was speaking in the evening. Mr Hermitage, the owner, is very much in evidence, but it seemed to me his staff needed no prompting. And when they learned I had to leave at 6 a.m. as part of my eccentric working hours, in the absence of any night porter they supplied a breakfast tray and a kettle (normally the tea would have been delivered to the door). All this seems to add up to the sort of service and facilities you ought to find in any decent hotel – but how often do you?' *(John Timpson; also Veronique Twine)*

Hotels are dropped if we lack positive feedback.

Open: All year.
Rooms: 46 double, 5 single, 1 suite – all with bath, shower, telephone, radio, colour TV and baby-listening; tea-making facilities in de-luxe rooms. (Some rooms on ground floor.)
Facilities: 3 lounges, lounge bar, restaurant, banqueting and conference facilities, games room; 8 acres grounds, sunken garden, with heated swimming pool, hard tennis court, children's games area, croquet and 9-hole putting green. Beach 4 miles, river 2 miles; sailing, golf, riding available nearby. &.
Location: 2½ miles from town centre; parking including 3 lock-up garages. Take A337 from Brockenhurst. Nearing Lymington after 3½ miles, take first turning right after railway bridge, signpost to New Milton (short of the Monkey House pub) along Sway Road for ½ miles, take first turning to the right, Mount Pleasant Lane; the hotel is approx. 1 mile up the lane on the right-hand side.
Restriction: No dogs in de-luxe rooms.
Credit card: American Express.
Terms (no fixed service charge): B & B £21–27. Set meals: lunch £5.50, dinner £8.50. Mini-breaks from November–end May; 4-night Christmas programme. Special meals for children; no accommodation charge if sharing parents' room.

LYNDHURST, Hampshire   **Map 2**

Parkhill Hotel   *Telephone:* Lyndhurst (042 128) 2944
Beaulieu Road

The Guide has been poorly represented in the New Forest. There's *Chewton Glen* at New Milton (q.v.), but that is on the fringes rather than in the forest centre. *The Parkhill*, half a mile from the nearest road, has the advantage of greater rurality.

'An elegant Georgian mansion, surrounded by beautifully kept lawns, in the heart of the New Forest, presents a welcome refuge for a quiet weekend or holiday. It is within easy walking distance of the tourist-crowded Lyndhurst, 'capital' of the New Forest, yet deserves the symbol of the birdie on a rocking-chair (or is it a fat little man on a deck chair?) which Michelin bestows on a hotel that is *très tranquille ou isolé*, or both. The bedrooms are well furnished and equipped (the rooms in the main building are preferable to those in the outbuildings) and the public rooms are comfortably furnished in traditional English chintzy country house style. The food is well presented and nicely served, and particularly the *à la carte* presents some ambitious specialities. The greatest attraction is taking tea or a drink on the terrace facing the tranquillity of the lawn and considering the competitive temptations of the well-kept swimming pool, a walk in the forest, or the relaxing deck chairs on the lawn.' *(Arnold Horwell)*

Open: All year, except 1 week in January.
Rooms: 15 double, 1 single, 2 suites – 16 with bath, 2 with shower, all with telephone, colour TV and tea-making facilities.
Facilities: Writing room and library, residents' lounge, bar lounge, dining room; private function room. 9 acres grounds with heated swimming pool; golf, tennis, riding, yachting nearby.
Location: On the A337 S of Cadnam.
Restriction: No dogs in public rooms. (3 rooms allocated to dog-owners, 2 with access to gardens.)
Credit cards: All major credit cards accepted.
Terms (no fixed service charge): B & B £18–35; dinner, B & B £25–40. Set meals:

lunch £5.50, dinner £9.25; full *alc* £15. Reduced rates and special meals for children. Spring/winter breaks April–June, 15 October–March (excluding bank holidays); reduced rates for stays of 2 days or more.

MERSHAM, Nr Ashford, Kent   **Map 2**

Stone Green Hall   *Telephone:* Aldington (023 372) 418

'An exquisite Georgian house set in about five acres of garden and fields. It was privately owned until about two years ago, when it was bought by Mr and Mrs James Kempson, who opened it as a small restaurant and hotel. There are only three bedrooms, each individually furnished and large. One has a four-poster *bath* set in the middle of the room. The Kempsons have kept the country house atmosphere. The cooking is original, individual and nearly always delicious. The service is friendly and professional. James Kempson does the cooking – a dedicated amateur turned successfully professional. The house itself, which is so beautiful, has retained its personal feeling – flowers are fresh, linen crisp, every comfort – even delightful china displayed in the huge downstairs wooden loo. There is an Edwardian conservatory, full of gardenia and camellia, extending right across the back of the house – wonderful for summer drinks. A ha-ha, a gazebo, yew hedges, grass tennis court and croquet lawn. Nothing to touch it for a romantic weekend.' *(Ian and Joan Curteis)*

Open: All year.
Rooms: 3 double – 2 with bath, 1 with shower, all with TV.
Facilities: Writing room, drawing room, conservatory, private dining room, restaurant; Saturday dinner dance approx. every 2 months. 5½ acres garden with croquet and tennis. Sissinghurst, Great Dixter and Leeds Castle nearby.
Location: Turn W off the A20 S of Ashford at Mersham signpost. Hotel is 1¼ miles on the left, just past cricket pitch.
Restrictions: No children under 12 in hotel, under 6 in restaurant. No dogs.
Credit cards: Access/Euro/Mastercard, American Express, Barclay/Visa.
Terms (no fixed service charge): B & B £15–25; dinner, B & B £24.50–34.50. Set meals: lunch £8.50, dinner £9.50 (cover charge £1); full *alc* £16. Reduced rates for children, according to age; special meals provided. Winter weekend breaks 1 October–1 May.

MIDDLEHAM, North Yorkshire   **Map 4**

Millers House   *Telephone:* Wensleydale (0969) 22630
Market Place

A handsome greystone Georgian house, once a finishing school for young ladies, just off the market square of this friendly Dales village, famous for its racing stables. 'Wake to the sounds of horses clip-clopping through the village on their way to the high moor training grounds,' writes one cheerful light sleeper. The hotel changed hands two years ago, and the enthusiastic new owners, Richard and Jean Nicholson, have on the whole made good impressions on our readers. One old-timer, it is true, considered things didn't compare with the former regime, but another felt the change had not at all affected previous high standards. Tributes have been paid in particular to breakfasts ('definitely for serious walkers – portions more than ample') and dinners ('unexpectedly high standard'), also to the general comfort and upkeep of the house. Warning: bookings necessary at weekends. *(Joan and Gordon Feetenby, C Weinstock)*

Open: All year.
Rooms: 5 double, 1 single – 5 with bath, 1 with shower, all with mono TV.
Facilities: Lounge, lounge bar, dining room. Small secluded garden for summer meals. Golf, fishing.
Location: Middleham is on the A6108 NW of Ripon between Leyburn and Masham; the hotel is central; car park.
Restriction: No dogs.
Terms (no fixed service charge): B & B £14.50. Set meal: Sunday lunch £7; full *alc* £9; bar snacks available. Special Christmas break.

MIDDLE WALLOP, Stockbridge, Hampshire   Map 2

Fifehead Manor   *Telephone:* Wallop (026 478) 565/566

'My husband was recuperating from an operation, and we needed somewhere quiet. We thought the food was both excellent and unusual. The owner, Mrs Leigh Taylor, was very concerned that we should enjoy ourselves. The bedrooms with bathrooms *en suite* were simply furnished, but comfortable – and everything worked. And the countryside was really beautiful.'

A characteristic tribute from this year's mail. Another reader was impressed when the staff stayed up almost till midnight to serve his dinner as a result of a delayed arrival.

Fifehead Manor is a handsome but not overbearing manor house, in part dating from the 11th century. It's conveniently close to Winchester and Salisbury, and its proximity to the M3 makes it not much more than 1½ hours' drive from London. There are some rooms in the main house, mostly spacious, light and comfortably furnished, and others, more functional and smaller, in a converted stable block. The beamed and (in the evening) candle-lit dining room is particularly attractive. There has been extensive redecorating and refurbishing of the public rooms this past year, but the things that have appealed to our readers about *Fifehead* have always been more the welcome and caring of the owner and her staff, the atmosphere of the place and the imaginative and rewarding meals rather than the standard of the decor. A final plus: they are not planning to put prices up in 1983. *(Diana Weir; also H C Hunter, Arthur Hoare, L Fletcher-Trebas)*

Open: All year, except 23 December–5 January. (Restaurant closed Sunday evening to non-residents.)
Rooms: 6 double, 6 single – 7 with bath, 5 with shower, all with telephone, mono TV and tea-making facilities; baby-listening can be arranged. 5 rooms in annexe.
Facilities: Lounge, bar/reception, conference room for up to 25 persons. 3 acres grounds with croquet and bowls. Fishing in the river Test 1 mile, riding 4 miles.
Location: On the A343 between Andover and Salisbury.
Credit cards: All major credit cards accepted.

Deadlines: nominations for the 1984 edition should reach us not later than 1 June 1983. Latest date for comments on existing entries: 31 July 1983.

Terms: Rooms with breakfast, single £25, double £38. Set meal: lunch (Sunday only) £7.80; full *alc* £10.50–13.50. Reduced rates and special meals for children. Cheap weekend/weekday breaks: £50 for 2 nights, dinner B & B.

MINCHINHAMPTON, Stroud, Gloucestershire   Map 2

Burleigh Court Hotel   *Telephone:* Brimscombe (0453) 883804

Mr and Mrs Benson took over this decidedly pedigree (listed in Pevsner) Georgian country-house hotel a few years ago, when it was badly run down. They have evidently made a success of their new-broom work, not only internally but also in the 5-acre garden which has been restored with the help of old photographs and is now featured in the National Gardens Guide. The house is spectacularly sited on a hillside between the Stroud valley and Minchinhampton Common, with a dramatic view across the valley from the terrace. 'The staff were there when you wanted them and not there when you didn't' was a compliment paid by one correspondent. 'It's not a place that would appeal to those who like a highly organized grand-hotel style,' writes another, 'but we appreciated the informal, friendly family-run atmosphere, which manages to combine an absence of pretentiousness with gracious surroundings. And we also liked the owner's enthusiasm and enterprise in renovation and restoration.' *(L Fletcher-Trebas, J & J W; also John Simpson)*

Open: All year, except Christmas.
Rooms: 10 double, 1 single – 5 with bath, 5 with shower, all with radio; TV, tea-making facilities and baby-listening available on request.
Facilities: TV room, reception/lounge, lounge/bar, dining room; conference/function facilities. 5 acres landscaped garden with heated swimming pool and putting green. Riding, tennis, golf available nearby.
Location: ½ mile S of A419 at Brimscombe, follow signs for Minchinhampton and Burleigh Court.
Restriction: Dogs by arrangement only.
Credit cards: Access/Euro/Mastercard, Barclay/Visa.
Terms (no fixed service charge): B & B £15–23; dinner, B & B £23–32; full board £26–37. Set meals: lunch from £2, dinner £8.95. Reduced rates for children sharing parents' room; special meals provided. Bargain breaks at most times of the year (min. 3 days).

NEWLYN, Penzance, Cornwall   Map 1

Smuggler's Hotel   *Telephone:* Penzance (0736) 4207

Don't be misled by the word 'hotel': this is a true old-fashioned inn, with rope-railed ship's stairs, uneven floors, exposed beams and lots of nautical paraphernalia to add to the local colour. It borders Newlyn's busy fishing harbour, with picturesque views looking out to St Michael's Mount in the distance. 'Public rooms are small, but comfortable and intimate. Bar in the basement with a lot of character. Dining room, half-timbered, a bit cramped, but atmosphere cheerful and cosy. Service particularly friendly. Bedrooms are simple, but pretty – and some have good views. Hotel parking a bit awkward. Otherwise a very enjoyable place to stay – comfort, character and charm.' *(PM)*

Open: All year.
Rooms: 16 double – 2 with bath, 4 with shower, all with radio and baby-listening. TV and tea-making facilities on request.
Facilities: TV lounge, cocktail bar, restaurant. Deep sea and harbour fishing.
Location: 1½ miles from town centre, on the front; parking.
Restriction: Dogs in bar only.
Credit card: American Express.
Terms (excluding service): B & B £11–13. Full *alc* £7. 50% reduction for children sharing parents' room; special meals provided. Special Christmas programme.

NEW MILTON, Hampshire   Map 2

Chewton Glen Hotel   *Telephone:* Highcliffe (042 52) 5341
                                    Telex: 41456

We had an ambivalent entry last year for this most luxurious of English country-house hotels not far from the New Forest. Every one agreed about the quality of the restaurant under the young chef Christian Delteil, but – partly no doubt because prices were so high – eyebrows were raised at charges for small items which correspondents felt should have been included in the room price, about the upkeep of the gardens, and also about the cordiality of the welcome – a special problem, we suspect, with very smart hotels when some of the customers may prefer formal even starchy service. We also queried whether the active marketing of the hotel in the States might have had deleterious consequences.

For many months after the 1982 Guide appeared, we had – unusually – no reports at all on Chewton Glen. Then, shortly before the book had to go to press, we received two very different letters. The first, while praising the excellent food and the delightful pre- and post-prandial piano music in the comfortable lounge, complained strongly of poor service and of 'a staff more concerned with their own status and staff politics than the guests'. The writer may have hit an unfortunate week: certainly its tone could not have been in greater contrast to the second letter, reproduced below. We were particularly glad to read it, because women travelling on their own so often get shoddy treatment. Note: Christian Delteil left Chewton Glen in May 1982, and his place as *chef de cuisine* has been taken by Pierre Chevillard, who had been *sous-chef* at the hotel for the previous three years. We should be glad to hear readers' views about the restaurant under the new regime (Mrs Arnold's visit had taken place under the old), and of course about the hotel in general.

'I am not used to staying alone in large hotels, I am usually on a business trip with my husband who copes with everything. I cannot praise the hotel too highly for the charm and sheer friendliness of their welcome which made me feel like somebody arriving to stay in a very grand country house where they had stayed since a child. The receptionist takes one up to the room, to be sure it is OK. It is super, comfortable, *clean*; small good details like a rack to hang out undies over the bath which is such a help when one is travelling about. A friendly lady in a flowery overall turns down the bed, and kindly pressed my rather tired tweed suit. I somewhat nervously tried the bar, was talked to in a friendly and companionable but not familiar way by the French barman who made my American cocktail perfectly, and served it with a hot delicious dainty. Dinner was superb, service exactly right, swift but not hurried. I was very impressed by the fact that the manager had a "bleeper" so that he could always be found. I am very sad about the tone of your comments about *Chewton*

Glen. Is it not good that there should be hotels where visitors who have money to spend in England will find the standards they can expect abroad *plus* a certain English charm? We have Italian friends who write for an Italian Food Guide who stayed here and have not stopped raving about it. I should be enchanted to take any friends of any nationality there, knowing that the bill would be no larger, maybe even smaller than elsewhere, but that I would be certain that the standard would be superb.' *(Mrs A M Arnold)*

Open: All year.
Rooms: 39 double, 2 single, 7 suites – all with bath, telephone, radio and colour TV. 6 suites in annexe. (7 rooms on ground floor.)
Facilities: 1 large lounge, 2 small lounges, bar, dining room, shop, terrace. 30 acres grounds with croquet lawn, putting, swimming pool and tennis court. The sea is ½ mile away, with safe bathing from shingle beach; the New Forest spreads to the north. Fishing, riding, sailing close by; 12 golf courses within a radius of 20 miles.
Location: Do not follow New Milton signs. Take turning to Walkford and Highcliffe off the A35; go through Walkford to fork junction. Take left fork (A337 to Lymington). *Chewton Glen* is ¼ mile round corner to the left.
Restrictions: No children under 7. No dogs.
Credit cards: All major credit cards accepted.
Terms: B & B (continental) £31–75; dinner, B & B £52–85 (high season, 7 nights minimum; off-season terms on application). Set meals: English breakfast £3, lunch £9, dinner £17.50; full *alc* £26. Special 3- and 5-day stays offered at reduced rates from 13 April to 31 October.

NORTHIAM, Rye, East Sussex   **Map 2**

The Hayes Arms Hotel   [GFG]   *Telephone:* Northiam (079 74) 3142
Village Green

It sounds like the village pub, but the *Hayes Arms* is a hotel of verve and style, as well as a restaurant. Architecturally, it is a hybrid: a mixture of a 15th-century farmhouse, with inglenook fireplaces, leaded windows and ancient low beams, a Georgian wing which houses the dining room, as well as two of the seven bedrooms. The house is well set back from the road, surrounded by magnificent trees, and facing Northiam's 12th-century church. It is about eight miles north of the coast at Rye and five miles from Bodiam Castle.

We first heard of the *Hayes Arms* from the following report: 'Hadn't booked, but liked the look of the outside and the setting and called on chance about mid-morning. Given an enormous front room in the Georgian bit; armchair, sofa to seat four, writing bureau, twin beds, large private bathroom. We installed ourselves and disappeared until tea-time, when we returned to find complimentary sherries waiting for us in the room. The place is run by a Canadian couple, Douglas Butt and Carol Jackson, and their enormous shaggy dog Siegfried. The dog is quite a character, but after more than two days his buffoonery might get a bit trying; he has learnt to unlatch the front door from the outside, but not to close it again after himself.' The report continues with a long detailed and appreciative resumé of the five-course set dinners eaten during a two-day

Are there no good hotels in Oxford? Write *now* if you have suggestions.

94

stay, and concludes, 'We would most certainly come back here and recommend it to our friends. The dining-room standards and cooking are well up to an entry in the Good Food Guide and certainly qualify for an entry in your Guide too.' *(David and Patricia Martin; warmly endorsed by Maureen Foster)*

Open: All year except December–January. (Restaurant closed Sunday/Monday evenings to non-residents.)
Rooms: 7 double – all with bath and telephone; radio and colour TV available on request. (1 four-poster bed.)
Facilities: Tudor bar and lounge, Georgian restaurant; indoor games. 1½ acres grounds. Many historic towns and houses in the vicinity.
Location: Behind village green; parking. Rye 8 miles.
Restrictions: No children under 12. Dogs in bar only.
Credit cards: All major credit cards accepted.
Terms (excluding 10% service charge): Dinner, B & B £32–48. Set meals: lunch (Sunday only) £7, dinner £11. Reductions for stays of more than one night, particularly in off-season.

PENZANCE, Cornwall **Map 1**

The Abbey Hotel *Telephone:* Penzance (0736) 66906
Abbey Street

We have always resisted suggestions that we should grade or categorize hotels symbolically as is the fashion in most other guides. Run-of-the-mill establishments can easily be put into one slot or another, but there are other hotels – and *The Abbey* is a good example – which defy routine classification. It is a very unpretentious small private hotel, essentially a family house with hotel facilities, close to Penzance's town centre in one of the old streets running down to the harbour. It is in fact one of the oldest buildings in the town, being mainly 17th-century. Large gothic windows have magnificent views across the harbour and Penzance Bay to the front, and there is a lovely walled garden at the back. There are no more than six bedrooms, and only one has a bath *en suite*. Michael and Jean Cox, whose house it is, have filled the place, the bathrooms as well as the bedrooms and the public rooms, with antiques and interesting objects collected from all over the world. There is a small dining room, which is only for residents if they are in. Menus normally consist of a soup, followed by a choice of two entrees and a couple of sweets. There is a short wine list, keenly priced. Cooking, Michael Cox's province, is basically English but excellent of its kind. Breakfast is virtually whatever you like. *The Abbey* is decidedly informal, and for that reason alone will attract some visitors and emphatically not appeal to others. There is no real 'service'; if you need anything you must find someone to ask (but they could be out!). On arrival, you are given a front-door key as the door is often locked during the day as well as at night. One other detail needs to be mentioned: Jean Cox was formerly the model Jean Shrimpton. Perhaps not surprisingly, her new incarnation as a hotelkeeper has attracted the attention of the glossies, both here and in the States. Don't be surprised if the house is full of Americans. *(Pat and Jeremy Temple)*

Open: 1 March–31 October.
Rooms: 5 double, 1 single – 1 with bath, TV and tea-making facilities on request.
Facilities: Large drawing room with TV, panelled dining room, both with open fires. Small walled garden.

Location: 200 yards from town centre. Courtyard parking.
Restrictions: The hotel is not really suitable for children. Dogs discouraged.
Terms (excluding service):   B & B £12.50–20. Set meal: dinner £7.50 (lunch not served). 10% reduction for stay of 7 nights or more.

PEVENSEY, Eastbourne, Sussex   Map 2

Priory Court Hotel   *Telephone:* Eastbourne (0323) 763150/761494

A part 16th-century timbered house looking out on the Roman walls of Pevensey Castle. It also overlooks the A27; double-glazing mitigates the rumbles, but the better rooms are at the back. There has been a change of ownership since the 1982 edition. New owners, the Robinsons, took over the hotel early in 1982. They have kept on many of the previous staff, though there is a new chef who was formerly (for 25 years) on the *Queen Mary*. A correspondent who knew the hotel in its previous incarnation reports: 'The general high standard is *at least* being maintained – and may even be going up a little. The food seemed better – and I think this is the only hotel in which I have stayed where the bacon and egg at breakfast was hot enough to make one jump. Bargain breaks are astonishing value. Service is attentive and most cordial. Tiny grumble: canned music at breakfast is a bit much – particularly *Zorba's Dance* at 8.30 a.m.! Slightly chilly evening produced a real fire in the bar – and the fearsome Victorian portraits which observe one's every move up and down the stairs give the place a period charm of its own.' *(G H Booth)*

Open: All year.
Rooms: 9 double – 4 with bath, all with colour TV. (1 room on ground floor.)
Facilities: Residents' lounge with colour TV, public lounges, dining room, William Room for private parties or meetings. 2 acres grounds. Safe sea bathing 1 mile; golf, riding, sailing, fishing nearby; walks across the Pevensey Marshes, noted for wide variety of birds.
Location: In village; parking for 38 cars.
Restrictions: No children under 12. No dogs.
Credit cards: Access/Euro, Barclay/Visa.
Terms (excluding 10% service charge):   B & B £11–13.50. *Alc* lunch £4, dinner £10 (excluding wine). Bargain breaks, special weekend rates (excluding bank holidays); reduced rates and special meals for children.

PILTON, Shepton Mallet, Somerset   Map 1

The Long House   *Telephone:* Pilton (074 989) 283
Pylle Road

One of those unassuming small hotels, offering a warm welcome and good simple food (though on a no-choice menu), which are a lot rarer than they should be. The Long House, a 17th-century building of character, is in a quiet and beautiful village halfway between Glastonbury and Shepton Mallet, and not on any well-trodden tourist path. It is owned and run by Paul Foss and Eric Swainsbury. Some of the rooms are on the modest side – and don't expect anything new-fangled like TV or a sauna.

The descriptive part of last year's entry, reproduced above, can bear repetition: nothing of consequence has changed at *The Long House* except that all but one of the rooms now has its own bath. Warm commendations continue to reach us: 'Unreservedly support the entry . . . quite remarkable that the two young owners do *everything* between them and employ no other help. Hence the high standards and extremely good value.' 'Outstanding value for money. During our stay, the number of guests varied from 2 to 10. Large numbers made no difference to the extremely efficient and pleasant service. The set dinner never failed to please and satisfy; quality and quantity unbelievable, sauces and vegetables especially noteworthy, imaginative and well-balanced.' 'Our second visit in six months – this time with an older member of the family who had been somewhat sceptical of our glowing report . . . she loved every minute and was even more spoiled – being somewhat anti-electric blanket, she had a hot-water bottle placed in her bed every night. Food was just as delicious. Can't wait to go back . . . remarkable value.' And so on. *(Charles Cortis, Colonel and Mrs A Harvey; also P D Willis, Dr R Million, Ch J Titulaer and others)*

Open: All year.
Rooms: 6 double, 1 single – 6 with bath.
Facilities: Sitting room/bar, dining room. ½ acre garden.
Location: On S edge of village; parking for 10 cars.
Credit cards: Access/Euro, Barclay/Visa.
Terms: B & B £10.75–15.75; dinner, B & B £17.00–22.00. Set meal: dinner £6.50. Bargain breaks with 12½% discount for 3-night stays May–September; 2-night stays October–April. Weekly reductions available. Reduced rates for children sharing parents' room; special meals provided.

PORT ISAAC, Cornwall — Map 1

Port Gaverne Hotel [GFG]   *Telephone:* Port Isaac (020 888) 244

An enviable location: *Port Gaverne* is at the top of a secluded cove half a mile east of Port Isaac, in an area of special beauty, with the Coastal Path passing its door and the beach no more than 100 yards away. It has been an inn since 1608, and retains many innish features. 'It must be unusual to find a delightful early 17th-century seaside inn run by a soft-spoken American, Frederick Ross, and his wife Marjorie. Very reasonable prices. The *carte du jour* at £6.95 [April 1982] provided three choices for each course. The seafood chowder and coarse-cut game *pâté* were both excellent, and the pork fillet in cider with apple and cream quite delightful. Vegetables well cooked, and a good sweet trolley. Service generally friendly and helpful. The wine waiter knew his business. The hotel is comfortable, warm and clean, and delightfully situated.' *(R V Gillman)*

Open: 19 February–15 January.
Room: 15 double, 3 single, 2 suites – 11 with bath, tea-making facilities. (1 suite with TV, shower and tea-making facilities in annexe.)
Facilities: Residents' lounge, TV room, bar lounge, 4 bars, dining room; small conference/function facilities. Sheltered swimming cove 100 yards with safe bathing, rocky and sandy beach; sea and shore fishing, golf, pony trekking, surfing, sailing within easy reach.
Location: ½ mile E of Port Isaac off the B3314 Delabole–Polzeath road. Car park for 20 cars, covered bay for 2.
Restriction: No dogs in dining room.
Credit card: Diners.
Terms: B & B £12.75–19.50; dinner, B & B £117.25–168 per week. Set meal:

dinner £7.50 (buffet lunch only; packed lunches on request); full *alc* £9. Reduced rates for children sharing parents' room: under 2, 15%; 2–12 years, 50%; over 12, 75%. Special meals provided but not for infants. Bargain rates for 2 nights or more from 1 October.

PORTSCATHO, Truro, Cornwall   Map 1

Gerrans Bay Hotel   *Telephone:* Portscatho (087 258) 338
Gerrans

Anne and Bob Key celebrate their 20th birthday at *Gerrans Bay* this year. The hotel is in the beautiful unspoiled Roseland peninsula, away from the worst seasonal holiday crowds, about half a mile from the beaches. It's an unpretentious family establishment – no special frills in the furnishings or decor – but drawing back regular customers year after year because of the 'home from home' atmosphere, the 'nothing too much trouble' approach to guests' comforts and the fact that the cooking, without being ambitious or elaborate, uses first-class materials well; also, Bob Key is clearly a festive character. *(H A Cohen, H J Challenger, Leonard Elton)*

Open: Easter–October.
Rooms: 12 double, 3 single – 12 with bath, all with tea-making facilities. (Some rooms on ground floor.)
Facilities: TV lounge, lounge, cocktail bar, restaurant. Garden. Sandy beaches and golf courses nearby; boating, sailing, fishing, waterskiing available.
Location: From Tregony follow the signposts to Gerrans, pass Gerrans church on your left and *Gerrans Bay Hotel* is 100 yards further on the right; car park.
Restrictions: No children under 10; no dogs in public rooms.
Credit cards: Access/Euro/Mastercard, American Express, Barclay/Visa.
Terms: B & B £11–15; dinner, B & B £17–21. Set meals: lunch (Sunday only) £5, dinner £8; full *alc* £11. 25% reduction for children sharing parents' room.

ROMALDKIRK, Barnard Castle, Co Durham   Map 4

The Rose and Crown Hotel   *Telephone:* Teesdale (0833) 50213

'This is that mythical find, a genuine old country inn, full of fishermen and Dales folk swapping tall stories, the finest honest plain cooking outside a private house, excellent beer and comfortable, but not luxurious room. All the best ghost and fishing stories begin with a group of yarnsmen sitting round the fire in a place like this. On the banks of the Tees, in one of the finest of the Dales villages, and near High Force Waterfall and the Bowes Museum, it gets full in the grouse season, but is a pleasure all year round.' *(MW)*
   Recent visitors, including the Editor, endorse last year's entry quoted above, though with a few reservations, e.g. bathroom not cleaned daily, not enough hot water, poor and expensive wines (but *excellent* beer). One visitor thought the food well above average, another found it a bit patchy, a third 'very disappointing'. But the consensus is strongly positive: the place has a genuinely welcoming air and Mr Jackson, the innkeeper, to quote one reader, is 'pleasant, positive, welcoming and ambitious, with expansion in train.' The last epithet refers to the fact that the *Rose and Crown* has now eleven double rooms, all but two of which have baths en suite. *(John Hills, E R Fulton, HR)*

Open: All year, except Christmas Day.
Rooms: 11 double, 3 single, 1 suite – 9 with bath, 2 with shower, 3 with colour TV, all with radio, baby-listening and tea-making facilities on request. 1 four-poster bed.
Facilities: 2 lounges (one with TV), 2 bars, 2 dining rooms; fishing, golf, sailing, pony trekking, shooting, etc., nearby. Barnard Castle 6 miles; Raby Castle and Bowes Castle within easy reach.
Location: 6 miles from Barnard Castle on the B6277.
Restriction: No dogs in public rooms.
Credit cards: All major credit cards accepted.
Terms (no fixed service charge): B & B single £15–17, double £28–35. Set meals: lunch £5.75, dinner £8.50. Special winter weekend rates. Reduced rates and special meals for children. Sporting and other activity weekend.

ROSS-ON-WYE, Hereford and Worcester   Map 2

Pengethley [GFG]   *Telephone:* Harewood End (098 987) 211

We hear good things of this small Georgian hotel, four miles from Ross on (but out of earshot of) the A49 in the direction of Hereford. It has 15 acres of its own grounds overlooking the Wye valley in a peaceful unspoiled corner of rural England between the Welsh border and the Malvern Hills. The resident owner is Andrew Sime, who cares about the reputation of his restaurant and wine list. He organizes dinners for bodies like the International Wine and Food Society and has star 'names' to entertain his guests at Burgundy Wine and Dine evenings and suchlike. Comfortable rooms, friendly staff and good value for money are the recurring notes in our file. More reports welcome. *(Nigel Smith, Pamela Harman)*

Open: All year.
Rooms: 20 double – 18 with bath, 2 with shower, all with telephone, radio, TV and baby-listening. (5 rooms in annexe.) 2 rooms on ground floor, specially designed for disabled.
Facilities: Library, bar, restaurant, function room, games room with TV. Jazz every Thursday, Wine & Dine evenings monthly throughout spring, summer and autumn. 15 acres grounds with heated swimming pool; trout fishing lake. &.
Location: 4 miles from Ross on the A49 in the direction of Hereford.
Restriction: No dogs in public rooms.
Credit cards: All major credit cards accepted.
Terms: B & B £23–38; dinner, B & B £25–48; full board £32–55. Set meals: lunch £7, dinner £11.50; full *alc* £22. Reduced rates and special meals for children. Activity weekends, special Christmas package, mini-breaks (2 nights minimum).

RUSHLAKE GREEN, Heathfield, Sussex   Map 2

The Priory Country House Hotel [GFG] *Telephone:* Rushlake Green (0435) 830553

This beautifully restored Augustinian priory in a thousand acres of Sussex countryside, close to the Kent border, has earned many gracious tributes in the past, both for the exceptional tranquillity of the landscape and of the house, and the many little extra thoughtful touches which Jane Dunn has provided for the greater comfort of her guests: the abundance of flowers, the quality of the soap, towels and linen, the taste of the furnishings, the provision of books by the bedside and so forth. The restaurant has also been praised – the imaginative cooking as well as the generous portions. Not quite such an unblemished report this year: it may be that readers had hit a bad period for staff, who have tended in the past to be untrained local girls. Poor breakfast service was mentioned in more than one letter. But one reader, at least, found everything *comme il faut*:

'Everything you had promised: a delightful restful country hotel. They were most kind to nine-year and over children. It is impossible to eat *simply* from the huge choice on the menu, so we ordered the day before plain food for our daughter. Cooked breakfast – superb. Everything here is done to create a restful atmosphere. A real treat – and beautiful countryside, too.' *(Elaine Shear)*

Open: All year, except for 3 weeks at Christmas.
Rooms: 11 double, 1 single – all with bath and TV. 6 rooms in a converted oast house annexe.
Facilities: 2 drawing rooms, 2 dining rooms; small conference facilities, Glyndebourne picnic facilities. 4 acres garden with croquet; 1,000 acres farmland with pheasant shooting and good walking. Brook fishing within 400 yards. Not far from the sea, the Weald, South Downs, Sissinghurst Castle, Glyndebourne, etc.
Location: About 15 miles N of Eastbourne. Turn S off the B2096 at Three Cups Corner which is 4½ miles from Heathfield, 8 miles from Battle.
Restrictions: No children under 9. Dogs by arrangement only.
Terms (no fixed service charge): B & B £21.25–28.18. Set meals: lunch £8.35, dinner £14.10.

RYALL, Whitchurch Canonicorum, Bridport, Dorset **Map 1**

The Butts *Telephone:* Chideock (029 789) 255

We had a particularly tempting first entry last year for this six-bedroomed conversion of a bakehouse and some early 18th-century cottages in a ravishing unspoilt area of the South coast – praising, in the words of a correspondent, 'the gourmet standard' of the four-course candle-lit dinners as well as the comforts of the house. In consequence, Mr Makinson, the owner, tells us that, of the 139 inquiries he received last year, 43 emanated from the Guide. (For those who are interested, the rest derived: 21 from the British Tourist Authority's Commended Scheme; 13 from an article in *The Guardian*; 1 from Ashley Courtenay and 61 from *The Butts'* previous guests.) 'Reluctantly,' Mr Makinson writes, 'I could only book in 16 Guide readers, leaving 27 disappointed.' Our reports this year have, on the whole, confirmed the good opinion we had formed earlier, though the word 'gourmet' (not a word we care for anyway) was felt to be somewhat inappropriate. There were other small details that need to be mentioned to avoid subsequent disappointments. One couple commented that their room, though very comfortable, was a little too small to enable them to sit and enjoy the view; and they would have liked more drawer-space to obviate living out of suitcases. Another reader mentioned that the TV had been taken out for the summer, and with no radio or telephone, she felt a shock of withdrawal. Guests sit together for meals, which doesn't suit everyone; the hotel has as yet no table licence; and there's no choice on the dinner menu, though an omelette was offered as an alternative when a main course was unpopular. None of these drawbacks seriously spoiled the pleasure of the visits for most correspondents. 'For the seeker of utter seclusion, *The Butts* might be close to heaven.' *(Christine Rogers; also Rebecca Foster)*

Open: April–October.
Rooms: 3 double, 1 single – 1 bathroom, 2 showers available.
Facilities: Drawing room, dining room, 1 acre grounds. Sea within 2 miles, farmland walk; riding, fishing, golf, tennis, squash nearby.
Location: Ryall signposted 1 mile W of Chideock on the A35.
Restrictions: No children under 15. Dogs permitted if kept in owners' car.
Terms: Dinner, B & B £17.50. (The hotel is not licensed to supply wines, so bring your own.) The hotel can be taken on an exclusive house party basis.

RYE, East Sussex Map 2

The Old Vicarage Guest House *Telephone:* Rye (079 73) 2119
66 Church Square

'Ruth and Ernest Thompson opened this charming detached residence in August 1981. Mainly Georgian in style, it was formerly the vicarage of St Mary's Church (a vicar cousin of Gladstone lived here in the 1880s). Close to Lamb House (Henry James) and the old town centre, *The Old Vicarage* is secluded and quiet, surrounded on all sides by gracious timbered houses. I stumbled across it by accident, having left it too late to reserve a room at the *Mermaid Inn* nearby, and being reluctant to stay anywhere else less typical of the ancient Cinque Port. I need not have worried as I had the best of both; dinner at the *Mermaid Inn* as well as a thoroughly enjoyable night in this clean, quiet and comfortable well-run guest house, hosted by genial Ernest Thompson. Breakfast is, of course, included and what a breakfast! – admirably cooked by Mrs Thompson in a spotless kitchen. I felt absurdly proud that the young French and Dutch couples, all of whom were visiting Rye (and Britain) for the first time, had been so well introduced to our shores. No dinner but reservations can be made for you elsewhere in Rye. An ideal place to stay for the budget-conscious visitor, who is no less sensitive to ambience and good standards.' *(Paul Hogarth)*

Open: All year, except Christmas.
Rooms: 5 double – 2 with shower, all with mono TV.
Facilities: Sitting room, dining room. Small walled garden. Safe bathing/sandy beach 2 miles; golf courses in locality.
Location: In town centre, near St Mary's Church. No special parking facilities.
Restriction: No dogs.
Terms: B & B £10–15. Packed lunches available. Reduced rates for children sharing parents' room.

ST AUSTELL, Cornwall Map 1

Boscundle Manor [GFG] *Telephone:* Par (072 681) 3557
Tregrehan

We like what we hear of this relatively new hotel in a relatively old building. The Manor is 18th-century, and was acquired and converted by Andrew and Mary Flint into a civilized small country house hotel in 1978. It lies in a bosky setting about a mile from the sea at Carlyon Bay; by the time this Guide appears, it should have its own swimming pool. The Flints were both new to the hotel trade, one having been in marketing and the other in accountancy. Probably that is as good a training as any other since good individual hoteliers rarely come from catering colleges. Mary Flint tells us that a powerful culinary influence on her life was her late husband, a Polish emigré, who had taught her the discipline of French cuisine. 'Something really worth knowing in a food and hotel desert. Beautiful – elegant – intelligent food – highly cultured – low price. A real find.' *(Rita Masseron)*

Open: All year, except 24 December–2nd Monday in February. (Restaurant closed Sundays and Bank Holidays to non-residents.)
Rooms: 4 double, 2 single – 1 with bath, 4 with shower, all with telephone, radio and colour TV.
Facilities: Lounge, cocktail bar, restaurant. 2 acres garden with putting and croquet and heated swimming pool. Beaches 1 and 6 miles; riding, fishing available nearby.
Location: 2 miles E of St Austell, 100 yards off the A390 on road signposted 'Tregrehan'.
Restriction: Dogs allowed 'with reluctance' and not in public rooms.
Credit cards: Access/Euro/Mastercard, American Express, Barclay/Visa.
Terms: B & B £18–24. Full *alc* £14.50. Special meals for children by arrangement.

ST IVES, Cambridgeshire   Map 2

Slepe Hall Hotel   *Telephone:* St Ives (0480) 63122
Ramsey Road

'"Strong men," wrote Rupert Brooke, "have blanched, and shot their wives/rather than send them to St Ives". But this placid Fenland market-town hardly merits such vitriolic whimsy. It has half-timbered houses beside the Ouse, a 15th-century arched stone bridge, and a green statue of Oliver Cromwell who lived and farmed here. Cambridge and Ely are less than 15 miles away. *Slepe Hall* is a Victorian mansion on the edge of town. Our weekend was most civilized. No harm came to *my* wife: in fact, she might have shot *me* if I'd not brought her here with me. Slepe was a boarding school till the 1960s, but you'd never guess it; Peter and Maggie Scott, the present owners, have converted it into a friendly and sophisticated little hotel, its "dorms" now partitioned into modern, comfortable bedrooms. Lounge and dining room are both elegant, with William Morris wallpaper and soothing pink-and-lilac colour schemes. Here James Edwards' *cuisine* is reputedly better than any in Cambridge itself, sometimes even luring dons from their high tables. We were not disappointed. From the shortish, inventive menu we chose shellfish mousse, fluffy mushroom flan (a daring combination of piquant sauce and egg-white soufflé), steak-and-venison pie, poached salmon – all good. Veg. were above average for England, the creamy desserts were delicious, and the wines well chosen though pricey (the house red is best value). Skilled and smiling service by Luigi, the maître d', and his team of fresh-faced local girls. In summer, meals and drinks are served in the small garden. A good range of superior bar snacks, such as Chicken Maryland.' *(JA)*

Open: All year except Christmas.
Rooms: 12 double, 2 single – 9 with bath, all with telephone, radio, colour TV and baby-listening.
Facilities: Residents' lounge, bar/lounge, restaurant; Brunel suite for functions; small garden. River 200 yards; boating, fishing available.

Location: 10 minutes' walk from town centre; parking. Continue round St Ives Bypass, follow signs to St Ivo Recreation Centre. Hotel is on Ramsey Road opposite turning to Recreation Centre.
Restriction: No dogs in public rooms.
Credit cards: All major credit cards accepted.
Terms (excluding service): B & B £18.50–27.50; dinner, B & B (minimum 2 days) £20–30; full board £125–165 per week. Set meals: lunch £7.65, dinner £8.50; full *alc* £13.75. Reduced rates and special meals for children.

SALCOMBE, South Devon   Map 1

The Marine Hotel   *Telephone:* Salcombe (054 884) 2251
                                                              Telex: 45185

This sophisticated modern hotel is magnificently sited right on the water's edge, offering a ringside seat on one of Devon's most colourful and busy sailing estuaries.

Paul Grotrian writes to put in his annual good word: 'Comes the year when my wife and I do not spend a week in the early spring at the *Marine*, it will mean we are insolvent or dead or both. Taking all in all, this is the best hotel I know: service and efficiency at their very best. The *Marine* is the sort of hotel where, when they know you, you do not have to ask for anything, it just arrives. If you do have to ask for anything, you do not have to ask twice. The standard of service in the buttery and the restaurant is as good as the service elsewhere, but some quite stupefying things go on in the kitchen. The establishment buys very high-class materials which are sometimes rendered unrecognizable. One evening we had scollops and another some turbot; both delicately flavoured things but murdered in violent sauces. Yet the scollops were just *au point* and they are so easy to overcook. Another evening, with some trepidation, we ordered guinea fowl. It arrived cooked quite beautifully. The veg. have always been odd at the *Marine*: good fresh veg. but either mucked about or not cooked at all and yet, one evening, we had a delicious dish of salsify with a sauce on it which was just right.' A first-time visitor fully endorses Mr Grotrian's views, while echoing his warnings about the food. 'Provided you choose the less pretentious items on the menu you eat well. We had an excellent lobster thermidor and lovely fresh fruit salad, but the sauce on the scollops was dreadful. My husband spent two happy hours in the sauna, solarium, indoor dip pool and jacuzzi. Our bedroom, with private balcony, overlooked the hotel's waterfront gardens and swimming pools, and Salcombe's animated harbour. Breakfasts were delicious. We were prepared to pay for a comfortable weekend with good service and food and that was what we got.' *(Paul Grotrian, J Sebag-Montefiore)*

Open: 1 March–1 December.
Rooms: 41 double, 9 single, 1 suite – 51 with bath, all with telephone, radio and colour TV.
Facilities: Lift, lounge, bar, buttery, games room, conference rooms in off-season, solarium – all with panoramic views; dancing once a week in high season. Indoor and outdoor heated swimming pools; poolside bar. Garden of ½ acre with lawn; cliff railway from driveway to lawn level; hotel grounds lead to the water's edge, private launching and landing facilities. Sandy beach at Small's Cove across the estuary reached by local passenger ferry; fishing, tennis, golf and riding nearby. &.
Restrictions: No children under 7. No dogs.

Location: Central; parking for 60 cars.
Credit cards: All major credit cards accepted.
Terms: B & B £28.50–34.50; dinner, B & B (minimum 3 nights) £38.50–44.50.
Set meals: lunch £4.95; dinner from £10.50; full *alc* about £16.95. Reduced terms
for midweek and one-week stays in autumn, spring and early summer. Family rates
available in high and low seasons.

SHEFFIELD, South Yorkshire   Map 2

Hotel St George   *Telephone:* Sheffield (0742) 583691
Kenwood Road   *Telex:* 547030

Modern industrial cities never lack modern hotels to cater for the business
visitor. The *St George*, 1½ miles from the city centre, has all that you
would expect in the way of amenities. Its 77 rooms all have bathrooms *en
suite*, colour TV, telephones, automatic call-systems, 24-hour service,
etc. The restaurant is adequate rather than stimulating. But its special
attraction is its ten-acre well-maintained garden, complete with lake and
putting green. 'An unusual find for a convenient city hotel.' *(J E A
Samuels)*

Open: All year.
Rooms: 28 double, 48 single, 1 suite – all with bath, telephone, radio, TV and
tea-making facilities. (Some rooms on ground floor.)
Facilities: Lift, lounge, garden lounge, bar, dining room, patio. Conference/
function facilities. 10 acres grounds with putting green and lake with coarse fishing;
golf nearby. &.
Location: 1½ miles SW of town centre in the Nether Edge area; car park for 80
cars.
Restriction: No dogs in public rooms.
Credit cards: All major credit cards accepted.
Terms: B & B £16–29.50. Set meals: lunch £4.75, dinner £6; full *alc* £11.50.
Bargain weekend breaks. Reduced rates and special meals for children.

SHERBORNE, Dorset   Map 1

Eastbury Hotel   *Telephone:* Sherborne (093 581) 3387
Long Street

Sherborne is a beautiful old stone-built town, with hardly an ugly building
to be seen. Its fine old Benedictine Abbey – or what is left of it – now
houses Sherborne School. The *Eastbury* is in one of the oldest streets in
the place, and close to the Abbey and Castle. It has a fine Georgian
facade, but parts date back to the 16th century. It has old-world charm:
not a place for gastronomic experiences, but sympathetically furnished
and with caring resident owners. A special attraction is its large well-kept
walled garden, with clipped yews and hedges forming secluded arbours.
(R M Sinclair and others)

Open: All year.
Rooms: 7 double, 3 family, 5 single – 5 with bath, all with radio and baby-
listening.
Facilities: Lounge, TV room, bar, 3 dining rooms. 1 acre old walled garden with
croquet. Golf nearby.

Location: 5 minutes' walk from town centre and from Sherborne Abbey and New Castle; parking.
Restriction: No dogs in public rooms.
Terms: B & B £11.50–14. (£2 private bath supplement); dinner, B & B £17–20; full board £20.50–23.80. Set meals: lunch £3.80, dinner £6. Reduced rates for children sharing parents' room; special meals provided.

SHURDINGTON, Cheltenham, Gloucestershire   Map 2

The Greenway Hotel   [GFG]   *Telephone:* Cheltenham (0242) 862352
                                                           Telex: 437216

Tony and Maryan Elliott have been engaged in a major two-year facelift of their Cotswold stone manor house three miles out of Cheltenham and handy for the race meetings and other sporting events in the area. The hotel now has its own helipad, and is delighted to welcome helicopters at any time, given 15 minutes' warning. The Elliotts have not only expensively refurbished their twelve double bedrooms and public rooms, but have also invested in a superior restaurant. Not everyone, though, is equally enthusiastic about this place: there have been minor reservations about the heating and the lighting, but perhaps the warmth of welcome is what is in question. It could be that, as we have seen elsewhere, a place that gears itself up to meet the needs of business executives does not find it easy to adapt to the more relaxed requirements of the non-business customer. More reports welcome.

Open: All year except 28 December–10 January. Restaurant closed Saturday lunch.
Rooms: 12 double – all with bath, telephone, radio and colour TV.
Facilities: Lounge hall, large drawing room, cocktail bar, restaurant; room for private functions. 37 acres grounds with garden, parkland and croquet.
Location: On A46 2½ miles S of Cheltenham. Parking.
Restrictions: No children under 7. No dogs.
Credit cards: All major credit cards accepted.
Terms (excluding service): B & B £30–50. Set meals: lunch £8.50–9, dinner £12.50–13. Summer and winter weekend breaks. 4-day Christmas holiday.

SIDMOUTH, Devon   Map 1

The Royal Glen Hotel   *Telephone:* Sidmouth (039 55) 3221
Glen Road

A house of character, facing south and overlooking the sea, in one of the more charming and least spoilt of South Coast resorts. We are grateful to the hotel's brochure for the following information: 'In October 1819, the Duke of Kent came to Devonshire to look for a suitable house for his family. Sidmouth proved most satisfactory and Woolbrook Cottage was chosen and described as the Glen, a 'large cottage orné'. Here the Princess Victoria celebrated her first Christmas. The visit was not without incident. On 28th December a young apprentice shooting at small birds smashed the nursery window (this window is marked by a coloured pane of glass); fortunately the shot, which passed near to the infant's head, missed her. The Royal baby was carried about the grounds for her daily airing and watched with great interest by the inhabitants of Sidmouth who realized that they were possibly seeing their future Sovereign. The Duke of Kent had constantly quoted to his friends his faith in Victoria's destiny with the words "Take care of her for she will be Queen of England". The Hotel is justly proud of its Royal history, you may find yourself residing in the Duchess of Kent's boudoir, the Duke of Kent's bedroom or even in the Princess Victoria's nursery.'

And here is a tribute from a grateful guest: 'This hotel is a real bargain. £13 [in 1982] dinner, bed and breakfast in a house where Queen Victoria lived as a baby. I slept in her nursery. Mr Crane, the resident owner, inherited it from his mother and has been in the hotel business all his life. All rooms have nice Victorian furniture. Only some of the rooms have baths. Some single rooms small and no telephone. But look at the price. A beautifully cooked five-course dinner, but at the set time of seven o'clock which is why Mr Crane can charge only £4 if you have a guest. I have stayed at this hotel for the past six years and am always amazed at the price of what I receive.' *(Mrs M D Prodgers)*

Open: All year.
Rooms: 27 double, 10 single – 17 with bath, 8 with shower, 25 with TV.
Facilities: TV room, drawing room, lounge bar, restaurant. 1-acre garden. Golf course nearby.
Location: 5 minutes from town centre; parking, some under cover.
Restrictions: No children under 8. No dogs in public rooms.
Credit card: Barclay/Visa.
Terms (no fixed service charge): B & B £9.65–19.45; dinner, B & B £10.90–22; full board £12–23.50. (Packed lunches available.) Set meals: lunch/dinner £4; full *alc* £5.36. Reduced rates for children. Special bargain breaks (min. 3 nights).

SOUTHMOOR, Nr Abingdon, Oxfordshire   **Map 2**

Fallowfields   *Telephone:* Longworth (0865) 820416

Fallowfields is one of those hard-to-categorize places. It belongs to an association called Wolsey Lodges which exists to promote small country homes whose owners wish to enter the bed-and-breakfast business – or, to quote their brochure 'an Englishman's home where you are welcome to stay as a guest for a night or more'. But *Fallowfields*, in a rather nondescript village ten miles SW of Oxford, is something more than a B & B. The house itself, to drop a name, used to belong to the Begum Aga Khan before her marriage to the Aga Khan. It stands in 12 acres, has a swimming pool as well as a croquet lawn, and serves four-course dinners. Mrs Alison Crowther is your hostess here and plainly a character. We note from her brochure the following: 'At the change of seasons the house will not be found to be overheated (a blessing to some); electric fires are available for use if necessary.' Note: there are also electric blankets in the rooms, and 'every effort is made to keep the heated outdoor pool at a temperature over 70F by the end of May.' From a guest information sheet, we read: 'Mrs Crowther is very deaf, so please don't hesitate to shout at her.' These disarming admissions may put off some, but we have the impression of a civilized house, full of books, with good cooking and, by today's prices, exceptional value. *(A and S Downs, Norah Gladwell)*

Open: Easter, and 1 May–1 October.
Rooms: 3 double, 1 single – 1 with shower, all with radio and tea-making facilities. 1 four-poster bed.

Facilities: TV room, sitting room, dining room. Library facilities. 12 acres grounds with croquet and heated swimming pool.
Location: 9 miles from Oxford on the A420; parking.
Restrictions: No children under 10; dogs at management's discretion and not in public rooms.
Terms: B & B £10–12.75; dinner, B & B £17–19.75. Set meal: dinner £7. Children of 10–14 years, 50% reduction.

SOUTH ZEAL, Okehampton, Devon   Map 1

Poltimore Guest House   *Telephone:* Sticklepath (083 784) 209

A sympathetic modest alternative to plush and pricey country-house hotels. *Poltimore Guest House*, in the Dartmoor National Park, is an old thatched cottage on the side of a hill, with views of farmlands and woods. It is one of the few guest houses in the West Country to receive the British Tourist Authority's award for outstanding hospitality, service, food and value for money. Since last year, four of the double rooms have been given their own bathrooms. 'Mr and Mrs Harbridge score on all points. Nothing pretentious here, but an instant sense of relaxed well-being. Central heating, a log-fire in the huge granite fireplace. Bedrooms are simple, spruce, strong on essentials – good bedside lights, somewhere to stand your case, razor point, sound plumbing. And Mrs Harbridge offers superlative home cooking – English dishes with a Devonshire accent.' *(Roger Smithells; warmly endorsed by G K Dodger)*

Open: All year.
Rooms: 5 double, 2 single – 4 with bath. 4 rooms in annexe.
Facilities: Lounge, TV lounge, dining room. 3 acres garden. Direct access to Dartmoor: horse riding, fishing, golf.
Location: The hotel is near the *Rising Sun Inn*, 17 miles from Exeter along the A30 towards Okehampton. Coming from Exeter ignore the turning to South Zeal and continue along the A30 for another ¼ mile. Turn left when you see *Poltimore*'s black and white signpost.
Restrictions: No children under 7. No dogs in dining room.
Terms: B & B £9.50–10.50; dinner, B & B £14.50–15.50. Set meal: dinner £5. 10% reduction on above rates for minimum stay of 2 days. Winter breaks. 70% reduction for children sharing parents' room.

SPARSHOLT, Winchester, Hants   Map 2

Lainston House   *Telephone:* Winchester (0962) 63588
                               Telex: 477375

'Very impressive country house hotel in a park. Decorated and conducted with style so it's not at all cheap. Service very friendly and pleasant. Bedroom comfortable, well-equipped. Nice new bathrooms. Good, Swiss-inspired menu for dinner. Almost London prices. An excellent addition to hotels in the area. Vastly superior to anything in Winchester or thereabouts.' *(P A Rosenthal)*
  'Everything is perfect – surroundings, service, food. . . . The price of dinner is astonishingly low for such a good meal. . . . Superlatives fail me – the beautiful gardens, and the mile-long avenue of lime trees; the civilized atmosphere; the bar with its cedar panelling; the well-judged

pastel decor; the beautiful presentation of the bill (even!). Service was very good, with apologies for the one delay – they sounded sincere, too. Searching for criticism, all I can manage is that, on our first visit, on a wet wintry evening, the gravel drive was very muddy, and the car park a long way from the house. Result – muddy shoes and an initial lukewarm impression, which was quickly dispelled once inside. In summer, even that did not mar the utter perfection.' *(S C Nash)*

Thus our first reports on what must be one of the grandest new hotels to have opened its doors this past year. *Lainston House* is two miles north-west of Winchester. It has records dating back to the 14th century, but the present building is essentially a 17th-century manor house in 63 acres of parkland, including an impressive avenue of limes. After various vicissitudes, including a decade in the 19th century when it became a lunatic asylum, it was acquired in 1980 by the former managing director of the *Dorchester*, Robin Oldland, and his wife Marie-José, who is a member of the Seiler family, the famous Swiss dynasty of hotelkeepers. The Oldlands have undertaken a major job of renovation, as well as building an entire new wing on the site of old garages. From a visit we made before the hotel was formally open, we can testify to the sumptuousness of the furnishings and fittings. Further reports welcome.

Open: All year.
Rooms: 21 double, 7 single, 1 suite – 27 with bath, 1 with shower, all with telephone, radio and colour TV. 14 rooms in annexe. (Some rooms on ground floor.)
Facilities: Drawing room, 2 bars, restaurant. 63 acres grounds with children's play area; trout fishing, golf, riding nearby. &.
Location: On A272 Stockbridge Road 2½ miles outside Winchester.
Restriction: Dogs in grounds only.
Credit cards: All major credit cards accepted.
Terms: B & B £27.80–40.80. Full *alc* £15. Winter weekend package (October–April) £78 inc. 2 nights, room with bath, dinner, breakfast, lunch, dinner.

STAMFORD, Lincolnshire   **Map 2**

The George of Stamford   [GFG]   *Telephone:* Stamford (0780) 55171
High Street, St Martins   *Telex:* 32578

The George may well be the oldest inn in England: there is said to have been a hostelry for pilgrims here in Norman times. The present building, however, dates from Elizabethan times, built by Lord Burghley, and was greatly extended in the 18th century when it became a notable coaching inn, with 40 coaches, '20 up and 20 down', passing through each day. Today, it still maintains that Christmas-card image of a fine old coaching inn, only there is no gap between appearance and reality. '*The George* is everything *splendid* in the English tradition,' exclaims one enthusiast. Another writes: 'One of the few hotels we have visited where the atmosphere was positively friendly, and where each member of the staff was courteous, pleasant and efficient. The menu in the dining room was such as to create immediate interest and was extensive for this size of hotel. The food was faultlessly cooked and served and the wine very good value. With the prospect of a full English breakfast, including Lincolnshire sausage, a bit of traffic noise at night palls into insignificance.' *(Diane Latham, Keith and Jane Matthewman; also John Timpson, Margery Myers, Sue Riches)*

Open: All year.
Rooms: 35 double, 10 single, 2 suites, 3 triple – 39 with bath, all with telephone and colour TV.
Facilities: Lounge, garden lounge, cocktail lounge and bars, restaurant, sun room; 5 function rooms. Grounds ½ acre – Monastery Garden with gravel walks and sunken lawn. Golf 1 mile, fishing at Rutland Water 5 miles.
Location: In town centre (front rooms tend to be noisy); parking for 150 cars.
Restriction: No dogs in public rooms.
Credit cards: All major credit cards accepted.
Terms: B & B £23–37.50. Set meal: buffet lunch £5.75; full *alc* £15. Reduced rates for children sharing parents' room; special meals provided. No charge for cots. Much reduced weekend rates: bridge weekends, March and November; antique weekends, March; special Christmas programme; New Year's Eve festivities.

STON EASTON, Bath, Somerset   Map 2

Ston Easton Park   [GFG]   *Telephone:* Chewton Mendip (076 121) 631
                                                      Telex: 444738

Yet another de-luxe hotel in or around Bath – to add to *The Priory, Royal Crescent, Hunstrete, Homewood Park, Thornbury Castle*, et al. Can the area sustain so many at the high table? *Ston Easton*, a Grade One Georgian country house, opened its door on 1 June 1982. Our first report, from a much-travelled correspondent, arrived two weeks later. This watcher of the hotel skies had no doubt that a new plant had swum into her ken. We look forward to hearing more.

'Saved from demolition a quarter of a century ago, *Ston Easton* must surely now be the epitome of the English "stately home". It has been beautifully restored by the Smedley family who bought it five years ago, and further embellished by Peter Wilson, former director of the *Lygon Arms* in Broadway, who is now a partner in this venture. The house is a mixture of sophistication and charm, pretty cottons and four-posters, luxurious fittings and rolling views over the lush Somerset countryside. The drawing room is all Georgian elegance, the dining room, a cosier converted parlour, is decorated in white bamboo with floor-length table-cloths, and as pretty as a Liberty print. The food, a mixture of French and English, is absolutely delicious, and unusual. The sorbets were as light as a Parisian chef can achieve. The staff are *Ston Easton*'s crowning glory. £65 was the most I've ever paid for a room, but I reckoned that the *à la carte* dinner was a bargain. If this hotel continues as it started, it will have a queue outside in no time. It's quite lovely.' *(Diane Latham)*. STOP PRESS. *As we go to press, we learn that Peter Wilson is leaving.*

Open: All year, except January.
Rooms: 14 double – all with bath, direct-dial telephone, radio and colour TV. (Several four-poster beds.)
Facilities: Salon, library, sitting room, drawing room, dining room, restaurant, billiard room; functions facilities. 26 acres grounds with croquet; fishing available.
Location: On the A37 from Bristol to Shepton Mallet, 11 miles from Bath and Bristol.
Restriction: No dogs in bedrooms or public rooms; kennels available.
Credit cards: Access/Euro/Mastercard, American Express, Diners.
Terms: B & B £27.50–45; dinner, B & B £35–60. Set meal: lunch £9.25; full *alc* £23. Special meals for children by arrangement.

Little Thakeham   *Telephone:* Storrington (090 66) 4416
Merrywood Lane

Little Thakeham has an architectural head-start over most of its competitors in the Guide. It is a handsome manor house on the South Downs, designed by Edwin Lutyens at the peak of his manor-house period, set in six acres of formal gardens designed by the great Gertrude Jekyll. Both house and garden are lovingly maintained by Timothy and Pauline Ratcliff, who started this small hotel – seven bedrooms only – early in 1980. One couple this year particularly appreciated the friendly welcome they got from the owner when they arrived just before midnight, and liked all the fittings in their small but attractive room, including the provision of bathrobes for visits to *Little Thakeham*'s heated swimming pool. They also wrote warmly about delicious seafood sandwiches in their packed lunch. They weren't quite so enthusiastic about breakfast: some reluctance to serve them at 9.30 a.m., and they suspected the coffee was of the instant sort. The poor quality of coffee featured in another report which specified other weaknesses – in particular inadequate heating and bedroom lighting. A third correspondent summed up her impressions: 'the hotel had a feeling of "good taste" (horrid words, but so descriptive in this case!) – everything underplayed and most comfortable, particularly the bed. Good lighting to read by. Peaceful gardens (not yet quite back to their former Jekyll glory) but lovely to wander round. Food very well presented and cooked to perfection.' More reports please. *(Diana Baird, Patricia Roberts, Elisabeth Lambert Ortiz)*

Open: All year, except February and Christmas. Restaurant closed Sunday evening and Monday.
Rooms: 7 double – 6 with bath, 1 with shower, all with telephone, radio, colour TV and baby-listening. (1 room on ground floor.)
Facilities: Lounge, bar, restaurant. 6 acres formal garden. Heated swimming pool, grass tennis court, croquet lawn. Riding, pony-trekking, golf available nearby. Within easy reach of Goodwood, Plumpton, Fontwell, Cowdray Park and Chichester Theatre.
Location: A24 to Worthing from London. About 1½ miles after Ashington village, turn right and follow lane for 1 mile. Turn right into Merrywood Lane. *Little Thakeham* is 400 yards on left.
Restriction: No dogs.
Credit cards: All major credit cards accepted.
Terms (excluding 12% service charge): B & B £27.50–40. Full *alc* £18. Reduced rates and special meals for children. Special winter breaks.

Stratford House   *Telephone:* Stratford-upon-Avon (0789) 68288
Sheep Street

Peter Wade's unpretentiously sympathetic bed-and-breakfast hotel 100 yards from the Memorial Theatre continues to attract good notices from our readers as well as enjoying the patronage of some of the visiting actors. The rooms – which face a quiet alley – may be on the small side for some tastes, and we think the Wades' boast to provide 'the best English breakfast in the Heart of England' is pitching it high. But there is no doubting the sincerity of our correspondents' compliments. 'I only wish,' writes a typical report, 'that on my travels both on business and as a tourist, there were more of these hotels around, where personal service and quality of life are maintained to such a high standard by the owner/proprietors.' *(B A Bernstein; also Marcia Humphries and Heulwen Pritchard, Philip Evans, Jacqueline and Melvin Lipson, E S Surma)*

Open: All year, except one week at Christmas.
Rooms: 10 double – 8 with bath *en suite*, 1 4-bedded with private bathroom, all with colour TV and tea-making facilities, most with telephone; all available as singles if required. (1 room on ground floor.)
Facilities: Lounge, no bar but residential licence; some small conference facilities. Attractive walled courtyard. &.
Location: In town centre; no private parking but public car parks within a few hundred yards. 100 yards from The Royal Shakespeare Theatre.
Restrictions: Not really suitable for children, though they are not excluded. Dogs allowed if small.
Credit cards: All major credit cards accepted.
Terms (excluding service): B & B £14–28. 2- and 3-night winter breaks.

STUDLAND, Swanage, Dorset   **Map 1**

Knoll House Hotel   *Telephone:* Studland (092 944) 251

Somewhat of a rarity in this book, *Knoll House* is what would be called in the States a resort hotel concentrating on providing holidays for people with children. We had a long entry in our first edition, contributed by Claire Rayner, a keen supporter of the place, who wrote: 'It's one of those places at which departing guests make their bookings for next year as they check out, and part from staff and fellow guests with ardent promises of frequent contacts in the grey winter months and heartfelt assurances of "see you next summer". So newcomers in the high season (that is, the school summer holidays), may find a certain cliqueishness among guests at first. But not for long: most of the regulars are civilized people who welcome new blood to their annual house-party.'

We left the entry out in 1979, because it didn't seem like anything else in the Guide. Perhaps we made a mistake. If readers would like more *Knoll Houses*, we hope they will let us know. But we should add that the place has its detractors as well as its admirers. One reader complained of the food and called *Knoll House* a middle-class Butlins; we don't think people will go to this sort of hotel for the cooking anyway, and a certain amount of regimentation is probably inevitable when catering for children in these numbers. But we should welcome further reports. Meanwhile, here is a recent commendation:

'A perfect family hotel, catering for all ages. It has the most wonderful facilities for children which include: a children's dining-room for under-eights serving a full range of the foods children like from tinned purée to fish fingers; a playroom, supervised between 1 and 2 p.m. for children whose parents wish to lunch in peace; a games room fully equipped with Space Invaders, slot machines, pool table and table tennis; an adventure playground complete with spectacular full-scale pirate ship and plank; a large swimming pool and a small children's paddling pool (my only criticism is that the pool isn't heated – which is necessary in England). There is a well equipped area beside the pool for spectators and sun-bathers and a refreshment kiosk serving drinks, ices and snacks. There are also a nine-hole golf course, tennis courts and a putting green adjacent to the hotel. The beach is five minutes' walk from the hotel; it is sandy, but somewhat crowded in summer. Other activities include family quizzes on Monday – great fun – and discos for teenagers. Spacious lounges, TV rooms and cocktail bar add to the atmosphere, and tea on the front lawn overlooking the sea is a particularly agreeable part of the day. Rooms are small but adequate, and service (mostly students on vacation) is friendly and helpful. The food is adequate; excellent salads at lunch and a splendid spread of puddings in the evening.' *(Gillian Hawser)*

Open: 28 March–17 October.
Rooms: 54 double, 57 single – 83 with bath, all with telephone and baby-listening. (7 rooms in annexe; 48 rooms on ground floor.)
Facilities: 6 lounges, including TV room and bridge room, 3 games rooms, bar, main restaurant, junior restaurant; function facilities; weekly discos in high season, Easter, bank holidays. 100 acres grounds with children's playground, 9-acre golf course, putting green, 2 hard tennis courts, swimming pool; riding, squash nearby; direct access to 3-mile beach with sand, safe bathing, sailing, windsurfing, pedalos and beach huts. &.
Location: Take the A351 via Wareham (10 miles), then the B3351 to Studland. Knoll House is on the road leading from Studland to Sandbanks Ferry.
Restriction: No dogs in restaurant.
Terms: B & B £19–33; dinner, B & B £23–37; full board £27–41. Set meals: lunch/dinner £7. Reductions for children according to age. Special 5-day breaks.

STURMINSTER NEWTON, Dorset   **Map 1**

Plumber Manor [GFG]   *Telephone:* Sturminster Newton (0258) 72507

'For those interested in the Michelin Book of Records,' we wrote in the 1980 Guide, 'this is the only establishment in the British Isles to earn two red knives and forks as well as a red rocking-chair.' If you are unfamiliar with the Michelin classifications, these insignia indicate a specially pleasant restaurant with rooms, in a peaceful secluded position. At the time of writing, that unique claim to Michelin distinction still holds, but perhaps not for much longer. For in March 1983, Richard Prideaux-Brune is doubling the accommodation at his ancestral home and working farm – it has been in the family since the 17th century – with a six-bedroom annexe converted from an adjoining barn. The question of what constitutes a restaurant with rooms is a moot one: what is quite certain is that, notwithstanding the 76 covers in the dining rooms, residents at Plumber Manor have always felt themselves more than adequately catered for in the hotel sense as well as being remarkably well fed at mealtimes. There's nothing fawlty towers about the Prideaux-Brune brand of hospitality (Richard is front of house, brother Brian is in charge of the kitchens) – they just provide their guests with the amenities to enjoy themselves. The report below catches the atmosphere well:
  'It claims to be only a restaurant with rooms, and the rooms are spacious and perfectly adequate – no great artistry, but practical with very comfortable beds and a welcome bottle of Malvern Water for night drinkers. It wasn't until we had dined that we settled down to enjoy our stay. I have so much admiration for excellent food presented without excessive fuss. The garnishes, the herbs, the sauces were all there and quite perfect – but taken as a matter of course rather than affecting the chi-chi of, say, ——. The owners were refreshingly down-to-earth and full

of humour – very English! For me one of the exciting items that will draw me back was the lovely fish – particularly lobster (at only £1.50 extra) and on the menu every night. My husband insisted I try his Dover sole which was quite the best I have ever tasted. Definitely full marks for cuisine and that certain touch of English hospitality.' *(Patricia Roberts; also HR, Mr and Mrs R Langford, J M Chandler, T M Wilson, S M Gillotti)*

Open: All year, except January and February. Restaurant closed Mondays. March/April, November/December; buffet dinner on Monday, May–October.
Rooms: 12 double – all with bath. (6 in annexe.)
Facilities: Drawing room, bar, restaurant. 3 acres garden with a trout stream running through; 400-acre farm. Several golf courses, fishing on the river Stour, and riding nearby; coast 30 miles; within easy motoring range of Bath, Salisbury, Dorchester, Longleat, Stourhead, Wilton, etc.
Location: 2 miles SW of Sturminster Newton, on the Hazelbury–Bryan road, which is a southward turn off the A357 (about halfway between Sherborne and Blandford).
Restrictions: No children under 12. No dogs.
Terms: B & B £17.50–25; dinner, B & B £29–36.50. Set meal (service at guests' discretion): dinner £11.50. 10% discount for weekly stays of 2 days or more October–December (excluding Christmas) and March.

TAUNTON, Somerset   **Map 1**

The Castle Hotel   [GFG]   *Telephone:* Taunton (0823) 72671
Castle Green   *Telex:* 46488

Taunton is fortunate in its *Castle*: few provincial cities can boast a hotel of such general excellence (though the main lounge needs a facelift). Its success owes something to its rich historical associations (with Perkin Warbeck, Cromwell and Judge Jeffreys, to name but three) and its good fortune in being surrounded by its original moat and Norman keep – it is rare to find a hotel providing a beautiful secluded garden in a city centre. But it owes much more to the personal drive of its managing director, Christopher Chapman, who for many years past has been busy improving this feature or that of his hotel and equally energetic in its promotion. We are regularly informed throughout the year about special Festival Weekends, programmes on Fine Wines, Music, Theatre and Heritage, Gala Dinners for the Royal Wedding and so forth. But the most interesting recent development has been the appointment of John Hornsby, formerly executive *sous-chef* at the *Dorchester* under Anton Mosimann, as the hotel's chef de cuisine. Hornsby, aged 30, belongs to a small elite group of young British chefs, Country Chefs Seven, and first reports of his cooking at Taunton have all been encouraging. But we were glad to hear from an elderly lady travelling by herself and a vegetarian, who, she tells us, is not an easy customer, and particularly notes how she is received, whether ignored or welcomed. She met with immediate kindness at *The Castle*, and appreciated the thoughtful way in which her vegetarian needs were catered for. *(Mrs M D Prodgers; E R Graham-Wood)*

Open: All year.
Rooms: 22 double, 18 single, 1 suite – all with bath and telephone, radio, TV and baby-listening. (Road-facing rooms are double-glazed.)
Facilities: Lift, drawing room, 2 bars, restaurant, coffee shop; some rooms for

functions and conferences. 1½ acres grounds with Norman moat, keep and square Norman well. &.
Location: Central; parking for 40 cars.
Restriction: Dogs by arrangement.
Credit cards: All major credit cards accepted.
Terms (no fixed service charge): B & B (continental) £30.20–37.20. Set meals: lunch from £7.50, dinner from £12; full *alc* from £20. Reduced rates at weekends and midweek (min. 2 nights) throughout the year and special weekend programmes of fine wines, music, theatre and heritage. Reduced rates for children at weekends only; special meals provided. 4-day Christmas programme.

TEMPLE SOWERBY, Nr Penrith, Cumbria   Map 4

Temple Sowerby House   [GFG]   *Telephone:* Kirkby Thore (0930) 61578

There have been mixed reports this year for the Georgian hotel on the A66 between Penrith and Appleby (front rooms double-glazed), started a few years ago by Joseph Armstrong (chef) and John Kennedy (front of house). The well-furnished and equipped bedrooms are generally appreciated, also the 'glorious' two-acre walled garden. At least one reader considered his meal 'memorable' and the service faultless. Another reader took a very different view: he had detailed criticism of the dishes, and in general felt both the menu and the wines over-priced; and the service, when he was there, had been far from adequate. But here is confirmation of its virtues from someone who, as the catch-phrase puts it, will 'call again': 'We consider *Temple Sowerby House* an excellent place for a weekend break or longer stay, within easy travelling distance of the Lake District but away from the hubbub. It is on one of the main roads to Scotland, but the impression is one of being "away from it all" without having to travel miles to achieve it. Our bedroom, though quite small, was prettily decorated with a colour scheme of lemon, orange and brown. The curtains matched the bedspread and hangings on the four-poster. Fresh flowers were arranged in the public rooms, which are comfortable and welcoming. We were impressed with the food. The service perhaps was slow, if judged by that in many hotel dining rooms; however, I believe that it was deliberately so and the price of the meal was, to my mind, about right. We left next morning after a generous English breakfast, with the firm intention of making a return visit.' *(Rosamund Hebdon)*

Open: 11 March–22 December.
Rooms: 10 double, 2 single – 10 with bath and radio; 2 four-poster beds. 4 rooms in the Coach House annexe. (2 rooms on ground floor.)
Facilities: 3 lounges, sun lounge, TV room; small conference facilities out of season. 2 acres walled Georgian garden. &.
Location: 6 miles from the M6 (Junction 40) on the A66 Penrith–Scotch Corner road, 6 miles NW of Appleby.
Restrictions: No children under 5. Dogs by arrangement.
Credit cards: Access/Euro, Barclay/Visa.
Terms (service optional): B & B £16–20. Set meal: dinner £11. 20% reduction for 2 or more nights mid October–end March.

> If you consider any entry incorrect, inadequate or misleading, you would be doing us and your fellow travellers a service by letting us know as soon as possible.

THORNBURY, Bristol, Avon   **Map 2**

Thornbury Castle [GFG]   *Telephone:* Thornbury (0454) 412647
                                            Telex: 449986 CASTLE G

When one of the more lustrous English country restaurants decides to
offer bed and breakfast as well as lunch and dinner, it inevitably attracts
the attention of hotel connoisseurs, especially when the location is as
atmospheric as this partially ruined 16th-century castle. There are not
many genuine castle hotels in Britain, and *Thornbury Castle* will appeal to
those who like to sleep as well as eat like a lord. Kenneth Bell has
approached the task of conversion with taste and flair. At the end of this
year there should be ten bedrooms open, and more may follow in the next
year or two. The rooms at present available include one amazing octagonal chamber, and another high up with five bay windows. The provision of
bathrooms has been managed with as little offence to the fabric as
possible. Inevitably, however, some rooms work better than others: you
don't expect perfect proportions here, only skilful compromises.

How does the place work as a hotel? We think that Michelin's decision
to rate the Castle as a restaurant with rooms is correct. The meals are
likely to be memorable – if dear, even by London standards; and the same
goes for the remarkable tome that goes by the name of a wine list – though
there is a useful short list of wines, including some interesting Californian
ones, at reasonable prices. (Warning: there is a resident pianist in the
evenings; if, like the Editor, you mind the intrusion of music at mealtimes,
you should make sure that you ask for a table in the unmusical dining
room.) Whether the Castle will seem attractive enough to persuade
people to stay more than a night is uncertain. A test inspection, a month
after the accommodation side had started, revealed a fair measure of
teething troubles – including some snags with heating, ventilation and
plumbing. Despite the lavish attention given to the decor, a castle is not,
in essence, a cosy place. We admire Kenneth Bell's enterprise in deciding
to extend his hugely successful restaurant activities, and wish him well.
But we should be glad to hear from other visitors how they find the new
rooms. *(HR)*

Open: All year, except 3 weeks over Christmas and some bank holidays.
Rooms: 8 double, 2 single – all with bath, telephone, radio and colour TV.
Facilities: Residents' lounge, bar, 2 dining rooms. 10 acres grounds.
Location: At the N side of Thornbury, just off the B4061; the lodge gate is beside
the parish church (St Marys).
Restrictions: No children under 13. No dogs.
Credit cards: Access/Euro/Mastercard, American Express, Barclay/Visa.
Terms: B & B £25–38. Full *alc* £21.

THORNTON-LE-FYLDE, Nr Blackpool, Lancashire   **Map 2**

The River House [GFG]   *Telephone:* Poulton (0253) 883497
Skippool Creek

There are plenty of Blackpool regulars who would never dream of staying
anywhere but in the centre of this gaudy resort. Ministers have to be on
show, journalists would hate to miss the fun by staying outside. But there
are others – a former Prime Minister for instance – for whom the *River*

House, a gentleman's residence *circa* 1830, four miles outside the city on the River Wyre, is a godsend, not least because it boasts a first-class restaurant, the best for many miles around. 'An oasis for delegates seeking quiet surroundings and good food. Its four bedrooms, overlooking the gardens and the river, are colourful but otherwise reasonably comfortable. There is a good deal of mahogany surrounding the Victorian sanitary fittings. Bill Scott, the owner, is also the cook, and likes to know your choice of menu before you arrive. There is usually fresh fish from Fleetwood and a large selection of game. The service is efficient and there is an attractive lounge for your coffee.' *(BH)*

Open: All year. Restaurant closed Monday to non-residents.
Rooms: 4 double – 1 with bath, all with telephone, radio and TV.
Facilities: Sitting room with TV, bar, restaurant. Function facilities. Small garden on river. Beach 3 miles; fishing, golf, boating nearby.
Location: From S, take M6, then M55; turn off at 1st exit (No. 3) on to the A585 to Fleetwood. From N, leave the M6 at Exit No. 33. Join the A6 going S; turn right on to the A586 to Blackpool (9 miles), then the A585 to Fleetwood. Hotel is 4 miles from Blackpool; parking for 20 cars.
Credit card: American Express.
Terms (no fixed service charge): B & B £17.50–20. Packed lunches available. Set meal: dinner £8; full *alc* £15. Reduced rates for children sharing parents' room; small meal portions. Special weekend breaks.

THORVERTON, Exeter, Devon **Map 1**

Berribridge House *Telephone:* Exeter (0392) 860259

An unpretentiously agreeable small hotel half a mile outside the village on a quiet country lane converted from a terrace of thatched cottages dating from the 17th century, with those hallmarks of an old English country hotel – oak beams, log fires and suchlike. 'We stayed there for three nights – and it was like heaven. The owners welcomed us warmly, the rooms were beautifully decorated and furnished, and we much enjoyed the cooking. It's all very peaceful. The small garden in front is a mass of blooms and at the rear there is an acre of lawns and rock gardens. It's a wonderful find.' (R J Harrison-Church)

Our entry last year, reproduced above, has been endorsed by subsequent visitors, though 'like heaven' seemed a bit much for two correspondents who didn't altogether care for the Sandersons' ultra-modern decor and furnishings. But all our readers have agreed about 'the unassuming but warm welcome', and the 'ridiculously modest cost' of the excellent dinner, bed and breakfast. *(Anne Morris, Roy and Edith Johnston, Mrs E K Driver)*

Open: All year.
Rooms: 6 double – 2 with shower.
Facilities: Reception, lounge, TV lounge, bar. 1 acre grounds.
Location: Drive to top of village of Thorverton, take left fork, carry on for ⅔ mile on this country lane.
Restrictions: Children over 12 preferred, younger ones accepted by arrangement. No dogs in dining room.
Terms (no service charge): B & B £13–15. Set menu (lunch and dinner) £6.75. Full *alc* £10. Special rates for 2, 5 or 7 days' stay 1 October–30 June. £3 each for children sharing parents' room; no charge if in cot; special meals provided.

TREBARWITHSTRAND, Tintagel, North Cornwall   Map 1

The Old Millfloor   *Telephone:* Tintagel (084 0770) 234

No hotel, but a tiny guest house – just three rooms – with a couple of self-catering chalet bungalows nearby. At £8 (the estimated price for B & B in 1982), it must rank among the cheapest entries in the book. 'Total silence and you are left in peace. Deep valley with millstream, dark peaceful house. Excellent cooking. One mile from beach – rocks, surf – and near cliff path. Take your own wine.' (John Broadbent)

Thus last year's entry. Tiny budget-priced guest-houses are often hard to evaluate, and few bedrooms usually means few reports. Having had no feedback on the *Millfloor*, we sent an inspector down, who filled in more of the picture: 'So small and so hidden in the glen that one would easily miss it without the signboards. Definitely not for the disabled as there's a steep path down from the road. A perfect place for families: lots of pets, an interesting garden to explore with steep banks and a millstream for children, and cheap prices and good food for parents. We had a large room and access to an equally large bathroom, shared by guests and family alike. Slight dinginess compensated for by the very reasonable price, windows overlooking the garden and letting in the noise of the stream, adequate hanging space, extra blankets, magazines and books (mostly old and a bit low-key), and – a nice touch – a large bottle of Perrier. Dinner was far beyond our expectations: mushrooms in garlic, pork fillet slices and raspberry sorbet were particularly good, all served with nicely cooked vegetables (apart from mushy peas). Excellent value for £5 odd a head. Early morning coffee was promptly served. Excellent breakfast, except for weak coffee. Lovely walk after dinner to cove with gorgeous sandy beach and rocky shale cliffs. The cove itself has souvenir shops and other hotels; one of the best things about the *Millfloor* is its complete seclusion and distance from this crowded spot. Verdict: excellent value in a most attractive setting.'

Open: 15 March–15 December.
Rooms: 3 double with tea-making facilities on request; also 2 self-catering bungalows.
Facilities: Lounge. 14 acres grounds with stream and orchard. Sandy beach 10 minutes' walk.
Terms (no tax or service charge): B & B £9. Set meal: dinner from £9 (bring your own wine). Bungalow £63–97 per week. Children under 12 half price; special meals on request.

TRESCO, Isles of Scilly, Cornwall   Map 1

The Island Hotel   *Telephone:* Scillonia (0720) 22883

For garden lovers, the name of Tresco will be associated with the Tresco Abbey Sub Tropical Gardens, but for others it may well just mean *The Island Hotel* which has been for several decades a dependable retreat for those who want to get a little farther away from it all. The island itself, two miles by one, is a private one and *The Island Hotel* has five acres of grounds beside the sea, with its own private beach. Our entry last year was written shortly after the arrival of new managers, John and Wendy Pyatt (the hotel itself belongs to the Prestige group), and they have been busy with redecorations and other improvements, including, unusually, the provision of more single rooms in the better parts of the hotel. Not everyone cares for the new decor in the public rooms, and we have also had a complaint about poor insulation in some of the bedrooms. But in general the special qualities of this exceptionally tranquil hotel have continued to be warmly appreciated.

'The views from bedrooms, dining room and lounges are enchanting – plenty of comfortable sitting room, and the staff were without exception delightful – friendly, smiling and helpful. We particularly liked the many thoughtful extras which we found in our bedroom. The standard bedclothes are rather heavy continental quilts, but these were replaced by conventional linen instantly on request. (Intending guests with any feelings on the subject might do well to mention it when booking.) The food was good and occasionally exceptional: a seafood mousse was memorable, and the spectacular setpiece of the Sunday evening cold buffet a sight to remember. Lobster on the *table d'hôte* is not something one expects, nor excellent crab that appeared quite often. The dessert table is a daily feature with a fine choice of rich-looking puddings etc., but also – during our stay – strawberries daily as well as other fruit. Breakfast had the standard wide selection, but often for those that wanted it included cheese and a big bowl of fresh fruit. Soups and sauces not really a strong point, however. Arrangements for the somewhat complicated connections from helicopter to launch to hotel worked with admirable efficiency and the welcome from the management was most warm.' *(Mrs R B Richards; also S B, T M Wilson)*

Open: Mid-March–mid October.
Rooms: 28 double, 7 single, 1 suite – all with telephone, baby-listening and radio, most with colour TV; some rooms arranged in groups of 1 double and 1 single, sharing a bathroom. (3 rooms on ground floor.)
Facilities: Lounge, sun lounge, TV room, cocktail bar, dining room, games room for adults with table tennis and bar billiards, children's playroom, laundry facilities. 5 acres grounds with heated swimming pool, bowls and croquet; private beach with safe bathing; guests have use of motor sailing and rowing boats.
Location: There are boats and helicopters daily except Sundays from Penzance to St Mary's Airport, and Brymon Airways run a service to St Mary's from Exeter, Plymouth and Newquay. Island guests are met by launch from St Mary's. (Booking for flights is essential.)
Restriction: No dogs.
Credit cards: All major credit cards accepted.
Terms (no fixed service charge): Dinner, B & B from £31.50. Set meal: dinner £14; *alc* lunch from £3. Tresco gardeners' holidays in spring and autumn. Reduced rates for children in bunk beds or cots; special meals provided.

ULLINGSWICK, Nr Hereford, Hereford and Worcester   **Map 2**

"The Steppes" Country House Hotel   *Telephone:* Burley Gate (043 278) 424

There are hotels that make their name through conventional channels – Michelin, Ronay and the like – and others which, because they don't fit the mould, have to find a different route to public recognition. *The Steppes* belongs to the latter category. It is a 17th-century country house in a tiny hamlet, deep in the Herefordshire countryside. There are only three bedrooms – six beds in all – fitted with showers and WC. The house is owned and run by Tricia and Henry Howland, who do everything themselves, and, as Tricia Howland puts it, 'are able to offer personal help on the ratio 1:3'. The house itself is full of good period furniture, the rooms are individually furnished, and the cooking is of a piece with the general style: thoroughly imaginative four-course menus, often with neglected local recipes, always using fresh local produce, cooked with flair. Not a hotel in the accepted sense of the term – dinner is at 7 p.m., and it's a no-choice menu – but very much a place for this Guide. *(Roger Smithells and others)*

Open: All year except Christmas and New Year. Restaurant closed to non-residents. Bar lunches only.
Rooms: 3 double – all with shower, radio, TV and tea-making facilities. (1 room on ground floor.)
Facilities: Lounge/bar, dining room. 1½ acres garden; riding, fishing nearby. ♿.
Location: Off the A417 Gloucester to Leominster road.
Restrictions: No children under 12.
Terms: B & B £10–12; dinner, B & B £18–23. Set meal: dinner £7.50; bar lunches available. Bargain breaks, 1 November–31 March.

ULLSWATER, Penrith, Cumbria   Map 4

Howtown Hotel   *Telephone:* Pooley Bridge (085 36) 514

Howtown calls itself a hotel, though maybe guest house would suit it better. It couldn't be more unlike *Sharrow Bay*, our other hotel on Ullswater, though both are excellent in their different ways. *Howtown* is a long low building among the peaks of the Eastern Fells, a few hundred yards from the shore of Ullswater at the end of the eastern road from Pooley Bridge. It has been owned by generations of the Baldry family, who farm the land around. Michael Baldry is the farmer and runs the bar, and his wife Jacquie does the cooking. The house is full of antiques – old pewter ware, carved sideboards, Regency tables, grandfather clocks, etc. – as well as a fine collection of paintings, both Victorian and contemporary. Guests are summoned for a set meal with a traditional gong. Some share tables. It is the kind of place where people talk to each other rather than stick to their nuclear units – at table or in the lounges. Limited-choice menu, and the food is good plain country cooking – in the complimentary sense – but with no attempt at fancy foreign fare. Bedrooms are on the first floor of the hotel and in a terrace of old cottages nearby. Rooms vary in size, and some are more simply furnished than others. One French visitor called *Howtown très anglais et très pittoresque.* It certainly wouldn't be everyone's choice, and those in pursuit of sybaritic comforts would be advised to try the establishment below, two miles up the road. But the place has always attracted loyal supporters who wouldn't dream of staying anywhere else in the Lakes. Here is testimony from a new convert:
'Unbounded gratitude to the *Good Hotel Guide* for introducing this, the hotel of our dreams, to my husband and me. Everything you say is true. Our whole stay marvellous value. And they are not listed in the AA book because, forsooth, they do not display printed menus or have locks on the bedroom doors – just like home!' *(Isabel S Jacobs)*

Open: End March–1 November.
Rooms: 13 double, 3 single; 2 cottages for renting. 4 rooms in annexe.
Facilities: 4 lounges, 2 bars, dining room. Garden of ½ acre. 300 yards from the

lake with own private foreshore; yachting, boating, water skiing, fishing, walking, climbing.

Terms (no fixed service charge): B & B £10.75; dinner, B & B £16.75 (£14.75 for 4 nights or more). Set meals: lunch from £3.50, dinner £6.30. Reduced rates for children sharing parents' room.

ULLSWATER, Penrith, Cumbria   Map 4

Sharrow Bay Country House Hotel   [GFG]   *Telephone:* Pooley Bridge
                                                              (085 36) 301/483

Whenever two or three hotel connoisseurs are gathered together and exchanging reminiscences, it is more likely than not that the name of *Sharrow Bay* will crop up. The year 1983 is the 35th anniversary of Brian Sack's and Francis Coulson's incumbency, and during that period they have made their hotel on the eastern shore of Lake Ullswater justly famous for the exceptional generosity of their hospitality, and for the attention to the small details of making their guests feel welcome which is the fine tuning of hotelmanship. There is only one criticism that is ever offered about *Sharrow Bay*: that there is just a bit too much of everything. That is a criticism that is levelled most often about the fairly amazing menu: a choice of 23 starters, for instance, then a fish course, followed by a sorbet, then a choice of a dozen or so entrées, followed by a similar *embarras de choix* when it comes to the desserts. And then, for those with really robust appetites, there is a cheese trolley as well. . . . Too much food has been a standing complaint about this hotel for many years, even from discriminating trenchermen who fully appreciate all that is being put before them. Brian Sack points out in a letter to us: 'It is not necessary for clients to feel over-full. They can always ask for small portions. And very few people eat two meals a day here as they nearly always spend the day walking or touring.' Yes, but as one guest points out: 'To give one too much food is not merely wasteful (that's the hotel's business) but oppressive to the guests; one does not like leaving food on one's plate and so eats more than one actually enjoys.' We echo these criticisms, and would like to see *Sharrow Bay* offer smaller menus or an *à la carte* as an alternative to their regular marathons. It needs to be added that the same almost-too-muchness is evident in the fitting-out of the rooms – quite small in the hotel itself, though larger in the annexe of Bank House, a mile further along the shore: lavender spray, soap flakes, trouser press, plants, books, games, etc., and all manner of bric-a-brac in the bedrooms fill the available space – 'we more or less have to dress one at a time'. But the palpable excess is also one of the features of the hotel, we think, which make a stay here memorable, and cause people to call it 'the best hotel of its kind we know' or to say 'It sets the standard against which all other restaurants and hotels are judged.' *(Heather Sharland, Dr and Mrs J Biggs; also Conrad Dehn and others)*

Open: 4 March–5 December.
Rooms: 24 double, 6 single, 2 suites – 20 with bath, 2 with shower, all with telephone, radio, TV, some with tea-making facilities. 17 rooms in cottages and Bank House. (7 rooms on ground floor.)
Facilities: 3 drawing rooms where drinks served as there is no separate bar, elegant restaurant. 12 acres garden and woodlands; ½ mile of lake shore with private jetty and boathouse; lake bathing (cold!) and fishing from the shore; boats for hire nearby; steamer service in season across the lake; magnificent walking/climbing country. &.

Location: On the E shore of Ullswater, 2 miles S of Pooley Bridge. M6 exit 40.
Restrictions: No children under 13. No dogs.
Terms: Dinner, B & B £40–63. Set meals: lunch from £15.50; dinner from £19.50.

UNDERBARROW, Nr Kendal, Cumbria   Map 4

Greenriggs Hotel   [GFG]   *Telephone:* Crosthwaite (044 88) 387

As will be clear from the number of names below, there has been no shortage of readers to endorse the entry for this 18th-century farmhouse at the foot of an escarpment, three miles west of Kendal in a delightfully secluded off-the-beaten-track location. Correspondents have praised – this year as much as ever – the quality of Frank Jackson's cooking, the beauty and peacefulness of the setting, and the very reasonable cost of staying at *Greenriggs*.

However, there have been some critical notes sounded this year, mostly in the minor key and to do with the accommodation. More than one reader has mentioned damp, inadequate heating and/or inadequate hot water; we think it likely that all these criticisms relate to the rooms in the stable-block annexe, which lack central heating, rather than to those in the main house. There is also a familiar niggle about the dining room not being quite big enough when the hotel is full and outside diners are accepted. These carpings apart, *Greenriggs* earns high marks from *F G and G M Sutherland, R C Sim, E R Fulton, E M Riley, Mrs William E Hasker, J H Mitchell, Diana Cowen, P Norris, Angela Evans, B M Newman, Margery Myers.*

Open: All year, except January; weekends only November–mid March.
Rooms: 13 double, 1 single – 10 with bath. 4 rooms in annexe. (2 self-contained family units.)
Facilities: Residents' lounge, coffee lounge, cocktail bar, restaurant; 1½ acres grounds with croquet.
Location: 3 miles W of Kendal. M6 exit 36 or 37.
Terms (no fixed service charge): B & B (Sunday only) £13–15; dinner, B & B £22–24. Set meal: dinner £10.50. Winter week-end breaks from November–end May (excluding January). Reduced rates and special meals for children. 3 night Christmas house party.

UPPER SLAUGHTER, Bourton-on-the-Water,   Map 2
Cheltenham, Gloucestershire

Lords of the Manor   *Telephone:* Bourton-on-the-Water (0451) 20243
Telex: VIA 83147

Another ageless Cotswold manor – in this case dating from the 17th century – in an unspoilt peaceful village, enjoying a fresh lease of life as a well-bred country hotel. The breeding has special point here: the Manor has been the home of the Witts family for 200 years, was converted into a hotel ten years ago, and is still managed by members of the family.

'After a winding, narrow road, it is a delight to come upon this manor house in its extensive grounds, peaceable, remote, yet only a few miles from the hurly-burly of Stow-on-the-Wold and Bourton-on-the-Water. We slept in both the old manor house and some new construction built on a courtyard, with flowers in hanging baskets. Meals were delicious and

121

imaginative, served on small gleaming mahogany tables, each brightened with fresh flowers. A nice touch in the bedrooms, each with private bathroom, was a selection of current magazines. The lounge bar was like the drawing room of a home. In terms of quality, prices were modest. It would be the prospect of a stay at *Lords of the Manor* that would entice us again to the Cotswolds.' *(Mrs J M Evans)*

Open: All year.
Rooms: 14 double, 1 single – 14 with bath, 1 with shower, all with telephone, tea-making facilities and baby-listening. (2 rooms on ground floor; 1 four-poster bed.)
Facilities: Garden room (with TV), drawing room, bar, dining room. 7 acres grounds with croquet, dry fly trout fishing and children's play area.
Location: In village centre; parking. Off the A429 Stow-on-the-Wold–Bourton-on-the-Water road.
Restriction: Dogs in public rooms at management's discretion.
Credit cards: All major credit cards accepted.
Terms: B & B (continental) £29. Set meal: lunch £5.95; full *alc* £11. Reduced rates and special meals for children. Special bargain breaks. Christmas package.

UPPINGHAM, Rutland, Leicestershire   Map 2

The Falcon Hotel   *Telephone:* Uppingham (057 282) 3535
High Street East

A traditional coaching-inn on the main market square of a pleasant unspoilt market town, the inn is 16th-century or even older, though remodelled in Victorian times, and it still preserves its cobbled yard even though the entrance to it has now become the lounge and reception. Two independent correspondents wrote to us about their friendly welcome and had appreciated the comfort and skilful modernization of their rooms which were over the courtyard, and quiet. Both also had enjoyed their dinner. But each mentioned a fall from grace at breakfast. In one case, there had been an invasion of boys from Uppingham School (the hotel, the chief one in town, obviously does a lot of its business with visiting parents) which had caught the staff unprepared. But she would still go again, and felt the place well worth an entry in an area poorly served by recommendable reasonably-priced places to stay. Further reports welcome. *(Clarissa M Turner, N I Cameron)*

Open: All year.
Rooms: 26 – 14 with bath, 2 with shower, all with telephone and colour TV. 3 rooms on ground floor. (1 four-poster bed.)
Facilities: Foyer/lounge, bar lounge, bar, restaurant; conference/function facilities. ½-acre garden. Golf, fishing, sailing, squash, riding available nearby. &.
Location: In market place; parking for 25 cars.
Restriction: No dogs in restaurant.
Credit cards: All major credit cards accepted.
Terms: B & B £13–18. Set meals: lunch £4.50, dinner £6.75; full *alc* £10. Reduced rates and special meals for children. Special weekend breaks.

If you have difficulty in finding hotels because directions given in the Guide are inadequate, please help us to improve them.

WALLCROUCH, Wadhurst, East Sussex   Map 2

Spindlewood Hotel   [GFG]   *Telephone:* Ticehurst (0580) 200430

We had our first entry for *Spindlewood* last year. The house, late 19th-century, in five acres of garden and woodland, had been opened as a hotel two years earlier by Robert Fitzsimmons, a former Michelin inspector. Our reports in the 1982 Guide praised the whole enterprise – the attractiveness of the grounds, the decor and spaciousness of the rooms, the friendly atmosphere as well as the high quality of the cooking. On the whole, the hotel has continued to earn good marks from our readers, though one had struck unlucky with a two-day visit which had coincided with the chef being away – not the first time that a *locum tenens* has let the side down. But the reader had another complaint. She had taken the 'No dogs' restriction in last year's entry to mean that there would be no dogs around, and was disconcerted by the ubiquitous presence of the owner's red setters, and their barking late at night. 'My husband and I,' she writes, 'have to put up with other people's dogs all through the year wherever we go, and see no reason to *pay* to put up with them.' We feel she has a point, and in the case of *Spindlewood* had better warn those with a canine antipathy that 'No dogs' does not in fact mean *no* dogs.

Here, in contrast, is a report from a reader for whom every *Spindlewood* prospect pleased: 'I cannot speak highly enough of this hotel. I went for a week and was immediately charmed by the courtesy and friendliness of the staff. The food was excellent. I enjoyed some quite lyrical soups – carrot and coriander one night and on another, cream of sorrel made from a carefully nurtured plant in the garden. The hotel is not averse to revealing culinary secrets and I returned to London ready to dazzle my future guests with a brilliant pudding containing, among other goodies, pineapple and black pepper. A visit to *Spindlewood* is recommended to find out the rest. The garden is a delight with no sound except that of birdsong. I shall surely be returning for further rejuvenating holidays.' *(Ursula Cheyne; also Mr and Mrs T Gallagher)*

Open: All year except Christmas. Restaurant closed for lunch and to non-residents Sunday/Monday.
Rooms: 8 double, 2 single – 9 with bath, 1 with shower.
Facilities: Library lounge with TV, lounge bar, restaurant. 5 acres grounds with hard tennis court. Bewl Bridge Reservoir with trout fishing 3 miles.
Location: 2¼ miles SE of Wadhurst on the B2099.
Restriction: No dogs.
Credit cards: Access, Barclay/Visa.
Terms (no fixed service charge): B & B £15.50–18.50. Set meal: dinner £7.50; full *alc* £15–16. Bargain breaks October–June. Reduced rates for children sharing parents' room; special meals provided.

WANSFORD, Nr Peterborough, Cambridgeshire   Map 2

Haycock Inn   *Telephone:* Stamford (0780) 782223

A true old inn, stone-built, dating back to 1632, rich in innish things like inglenook fireplaces as well as contemporary equipment like colour TV and trouser presses in the bedrooms. It also has quite a lot of history to boast of: no one has suggested that Queen Elizabeth slept here, but Mary

Queen of Scots may have visited the place on her way to imprisonment at Fotheringhay in 1586, and Queen Victoria visited the inn in 1835 when she was Princess Alexandra Victoria. 'A wonderful inn. Our room was in converted stables. It was modern, well-furnished, immaculate and comfortable. Staff were courteous and friendly. Dinner was excellent.' *(J B Aultmann)*

Open: All year.
Rooms: 18 double, 10 single, 2 suites – 15 with bath, 2 with shower, all with telephone, radio, colour TV and baby-listening; 4 four-poster beds; 7 rooms in annexe.
Facilities: 2 lounges, bar, restaurant; function rooms. 6 acres grounds; pétanque, fishing, cricket. Marquee during summer.
Location: Just off the junction where the A1 meets the A47.
Credit cards: All major credit cards accepted.
Terms: B & B £17–28.00. Buffet lunch from £3.25; bar food dishes from £1.25; full *alc* £14.00. Special weekend breaks. Reduced rates and special meals for children.

WAREHAM, Dorset   **Map 1**

The Priory Hotel   [GFG]   *Telephone:* Wareham (092 95) 2772
Church Green

An exceptionally comfortable hotel, converted sympathetically from the 16th-century Priory of Lady St Mary close to the centre of this small market town, with two acres of attractive gardens on the banks of the River Frome (moorings available for guests arriving by boat). As previously, our files are full of such compliments as 'Deserves every praise for service, comfort, warmth, courtesy and helpfulness of staff. I actually saw the cleaning lady washing paintwork over doors. Everything spotless. Fresh towels every day. *Super* breakfast: everything you could possibly want in any combination and fresh croissants thrown in.' Another reader writes: 'A delightful atmosphere of antiquity and comfort. The decorations and upholstery are charming and much of the furniture is antique. The staff are unfailingly charming and helpful, even to an old buffer like me. As it would not be helpful to suppress niggles, I would add that we deplored the muzak in the main lounge, though admittedly you can find blessed silence in the lounge upstairs.' The only other criticism worth noting refers to the food. Many readers clearly enjoyed their meals as much as they enjoyed every other feature of their stay; but others, more discriminating or pernickety, were disappointed by this dish or that – the more disappointed perhaps because everything else about the place was so strongly to their liking. *(Ian and Francine Walsh, T M Wilson; also Anthony Fletcher, Ivor Hall, G M Denton, J B Stewart)*

Open: All year.
Rooms: 14 double, 1 single – all with bath/shower, all with telephone, radio and colour TV.
Facilities: Lounge, residents' lounge, bar, 2 dining rooms. 6 acres grounds with 2½ acres landscaped gardens – on river with bathing, fishing and sailing; shooting can be arranged.
Location: 150 yards from centre; parking.
Restriction: No dogs.

Credit cards: All major credit cards accepted.
Terms (service at guests' discretion):   B & B £17.50–27.50. Set meals: lunch £5 (Sunday £7); dinner (Sunday–Friday) £10.50, (Saturday) £12.50, full *alc* £12.50. Winter weekend breaks 1 October–30 April except bank holidays. Reduced rates for children sharing parents' room; special meals provided.

WARMINSTER, Wiltshire   Map 2

Bishopstrow House   *Telephone:* Warminster (0985) 212312
Bishopstrow

'Why have you missed out *Bishopstrow*?' we have been asked more than once in the past few years. It is a fair question: this decidedly handsome late Georgian mansion in its 25 acres of beautifully maintained wooded parkland, with its own river frontage, is a quintessential English country-house hotel of the more opulent kind. And its virtues have been signally recognized in other Guides: it has earned a red star in the AA book (denoting warm welcome – 'a firm favourite amongst inspectors and members'), scores 82% on the Egon Ronay scale, gets the red treatment ('pleasant') in Michelin who also add 'tastefully furnished.' Two years ago, it joined the exclusive Relais et Châteaux 'club'.

How do we account for its relative failure in our book? The Guide is dependent on recommendations from the public, and until this year, we had had precisely one report – enthusiastic about the rooms and less than enraptured about the five-course no-choice dinners. Knowing what garlands the hotel was earning elsewhere, we sent inspectors on two separate occasions, and both of them, for similar reasons, came down against inclusion. The reasons were long and detailed; they included tangible weaknesses, like the quality of the food in relation to the cost and pretensions of the establishment, and also unquantifiable features like the general atmosphere of the place. This year, for the first time, we have had reports from readers whom the hotel has clearly succeeded in pleasing in an unambivalent way: e.g. 'Gave the feeling of visiting royalty', 'the most beautiful hotel I have ever seen' and 'A first-class and lovely hotel (private house really) to stay in surrounded by antiques and lovely things everywhere. Deserves all the merits it has already won.' It is clear from these reports – as indeed it was already clear from its star treatment in other guides – that the hotel is able to enchant some of its visitors. As with *Inverlochy Castle* at Fort William (q.v.) there will, we imagine, continue to be others who will find the formal 'swank' of the place not to their liking and will raise again that most tricky question of value for money. We should welcome more reports. *(Patricia Roberts, T M Wilson, Janet Lowy, Mrs R Gromb)*

Open: All year, except end December and January.
Rooms: 13 double, 1 single – all with bath, telephone and colour TV.
Facilities: Reception room, morning room, drawing room, dining room, conservatory. 25 acres grounds with river, Doric temple and summerhouse. Fishing on River Wylye, tennis.
Location: 1½ miles E of Warminster on the A36 Salisbury road; parking.
Restrictions: No children under 7; dogs by special arrangement only, and not in bedrooms or public rooms.
Credit cards: Access/Euro/Mastercard, American Express, Barclay/Visa.
Terms (no service charge):   B & B (continental) £18–42. Set meals: lunch £15, dinner £16–18. Special meals for children on request.

Holdfast Cottage Hotel   *Telephone:* Hanley Swan (0684) 310288

'For those seeking a peaceful holiday walking in the Malvern Hills or exploring charming small unknown unspoilt towns like Upton-upon-Severn or Bewdley, this is an ideal place. It is situated in two acres of gardens amid orchard and farmland at the foot of the Hills – a delightful and marvellously quiet place to stay. The house, originally 17th-century, was enlarged during the last century. It now has nine bedrooms, mostly with private bathrooms. Dennis and Diana Beetlestone, who moved here with their small children as a retreat from the city, have extensively redecorated the rooms with a mixture of Laura Ashley and old English chintz, which may be too floral and florid for some tastes. The food is traditional English, and is all home-grown or locally reared. The hotel is hidden away, difficult to find and no good without a car. Also, it is no use calling on spec. as faithful patrons seem to book up from one year to the next.' *(Dennis and Madeleine Simms; also Roger Smithells)*

Open: All year.
Rooms: 7 double, 2 single – 4 with bath, 2 with shower.
Facilities: Lounge (with TV), lounge bar, dining room, terrace. 2 acres grounds.
Location: 4 miles from town centre. On the A4104 midway between Little Malvern and Welland. Accessible from the M5 via the M50, leaving at Exit 1. Follow the A38 N, then turn left on to the A4104 through Upton-upon-Severn and Welland. Parking.
Restriction: Dogs allowed in public rooms with agreement of other guests.
Terms: B & B £12.50–15; dinner, B & B £20.50–23. Set meal: dinner £8.50; full *alc* £11.40. Reduced rates for children sharing parents' room; special meals provided. Bargain winter, summer and Christmas breaks.

WHIMPLE, Nr Exeter, Devon   **Map 1**

Woodhayes   *Telephone:* Whimple (0404) 822237

This small Georgian country house in an apple orchard village, nine miles east of Exeter and about four miles from the M5, had had for several years a specially warm entry in the Guide under its previous management of David and Barbara Townsend. The hotel changed hands a year ago, just as we were going to press, and opened again, after extensive redecoration, in March 1982. We knew that the Townsend act would be hard to follow, but are glad that our first reports of the regime of John Allan, a graduate of Grosvenor House, and Graham Hartley, formerly a Michelin inspector, are thoroughly encouraging – not to say glowing. One couple, who announced their engagement while spending a few days at *Woodhayes*, were chuffed to find a complimentary half-bottle of champagne with their breakfast the following morning. Another mentioned with awe that their car windows were cleaned every day. A third couple warmly approved of the decor throughout, spoke enthusiastically about the quality of the meals, and mentioned a number of details that had particularly appealed to them: the quality of the towels and the soap, the changing of all linen every day, home-made biscuits and China tea with the tea tray brought to them on arrival, the hot flaky croissants and home-made jams for breakfast, the imaginative wine list with nine or ten house wines at £5.50 a bottle as well as a comprehensive selection of American and European wines. All correspondents spoke enthusiastically about the unobtrusive attentiveness of the proprietors and the excellent value for money. Finally, a tribute from across the Atlantic: 'The best value and most pleasureful stay we had during three weeks in England.' *(S E C Dean, JR, Kathleen Balkman, Mrs M E C Scott, N M P Crooke, Robert W Allen)*

Open: All year, except January; restaurant closed to non-residents Sunday and Monday.
Rooms: 5 double, 1 single – all with bath, telephone, radio and colour TV.
Facilities: 2 lounges, dining room. 1½ acres garden and 1½ acres paddock with lawns, aboretum, gazebo and kitchen garden.
Location: On the edge of Whimple village, which is just N of the A30 Exeter–Honiton road, 9 miles E of Exeter.
Restrictions: Dogs and children by arrangement.
Credit cards: American Express, Access, Barclay/Visa, Diners.
Terms: B & B £15–25. Set meals: lunch £10, dinner £12. Reduced rates for winter breaks and longer holidays.

WHITWELL ON THE HILL, York   Map 4

Whitwell Hall Country House Hotel   *Telephone:* Whitwell on the Hill
                                                  (065 381) 551

Whitwell on the Hill is 12 miles north-east of York on the way to Malton, but what may interest 1983 tourists more than the proximity to York or the North Yorkshire Moors is its even greater proximity to Castle Howard, made newly famous by *Brideshead* on TV. Anthony Andrews slept here, is the proud boast of *Whitwell Hall*, and, they add intriguingly, 'he made quite an impression on the staff'. The hotel is a fairly recent conversion of an ornate creepered Tudor Gothic mansion, *circa* 1835, set in 18 acres of park and woodland. Commander and Mrs Peter Milnes opened it as a country-house hotel of the grander sort six years ago. Our reporters speak enthusiastically about the restaurant. 'The best we encountered during a week's touring,' writes one. 'Nearly unfailing good results on four consecutive evenings,' writes another. But there have been grumbles about the bedrooms. Some of the rooms are in the main house, and others, including some large ones, are in a converted coach house. From our correspondence, it is clear that the rooms vary considerably in quality of furnishing as well as in size. There has been some extensive refurbishing of rooms this past year, but it would be prudent to discuss what rooms are available at the time of booking. We have also had a complaint about off-hand reception. Further reports welcome.

Open: All year.
Rooms: 18 double, 2 single – 10 with bath, 10 with shower, all with telephone, radio, TV on request, and tea-making facilities. 9 rooms in annexe.
Facilities: Large entrance hall with bar, lounge, dining room; conference facilities. 18 acres grounds with views over Vale of York. Tennis, croquet; bicycles provided; golf, shooting and fishing nearby. &.
Location: 12 miles from York. Follow the A64 from York; hotel is signposted to the left.
Restriction: No children under 12.
Credit cards: All major credit cards accepted. (Warning: you may expect a surcharge if you pay by credit card.)

Terms (excluding service): B & B £16–23; dinner, B & B £26–36. Set meal: dinner £13. 2-day or weekend breaks; 4-day Christmas package. Reduced rates for children sharing parents' room.

WILLITON, Somerset   Map 1

The White House Hotel   [GFG]   *Telephone:* Williton (0984) 32306

'Delightful. Despite its main road position, we felt wonderfully relaxed, sleeping well in a back room. The hotel is imaginatively and delightfully decorated and furnished with Laura Ashley linens and wallpapers, modern and antique furniture in juxtaposition and some lovely old prints on the walls. Our room did not have TV, but there is a large comfortable TV lounge and another lounge-bar. We thought this an ideal family-run hotel, with many personal touches, a warm welcome and friendly, comradely atmosphere. Nothing but praise for the food and drink. Breakfasts, too, were highlights with croissants, herrings in oatmeal and a different breakfast menu every day. Barefoot and slightly punk daughter/waitress shouldn't put anyone off: she is charming and polite.' *(Anne M Boustred)*
  A characteristic tribute to the hospitality offered by Kay and Dick Smith at their Georgian house on the A39. We heard from one dissatisfied customer, a disabled man, who had been offered no help with his luggage on arrival or departure and who also felt let down by the portion of his evening meal. But his was a lone voice of dissent: all our other correspondents have spoken warmly and gratefully of *The White House*'s restaurant, quite a number have mentioned the barefootedness of the Smiths' two daughters (if they had been topless, our mail would have come in a sack!) and several have referred to the hotel being on the A39. There are in fact three front rooms, six somewhat austere rooms in an annexe facing the back, and five further rooms in the main (Georgian) building, away from any road noise, and generously proportioned. No doubt these are the ones to reserve if available.

Open: Mid May–end October.
Rooms: 14 – 4 with bath. (6 rooms in annexe on ground floor.)
Facilities: Lounge with TV, lounge-bar, dining room; small conference facilities. Sea 2 miles. &.
Location: On the A39 in village centre; parking for 20 cars.
Restriction: Dogs by prior arrangement.
Terms (no fixed service charge): B & B £14–17.20; dinner, B & B £21–24.20. Set meal: dinner £9.50. Bargain breaks May–31 July. Reduced rates for children sharing parents' room; special meals on request.

WINDERMERE, Cumbria   Map 4

Miller Howe   [GFG]   *Telephone:* Windermere (096 62) 2536
Rayrigg Road

We must declare a personal interest: John Tovey, the host of *Miller Howe*, is a personal friend. But that should not be allowed to disqualify his hotel from a place in the Guide, for he is in fact a paradigm of hosts, who has the enviable gift of making friends wherever he goes. His is an ebullient personality, and, as with all good hoteliers, his house abundantly reflects his personality. Staying at *Miller Howe*, like a visit to the theatre, is an occasion. The location itself is theatrical: on a bluff overlooking Windermere, with a spectacular backdrop of famous peaks across the water. Meals here are an experience too – with the curtain rising punctually at 8.30. Those familiar with John Tovey's books will know the titillation of the palate to be expected from his five-course dinners, with a plethora of vegetables accompanying the entrée, and a constant bombardment of original tastes.

As we have noticed in previous years, fame often carries with it too high expectations. Not all our postbag is equally complimentary. Some readers have been disappointed with the size of the rooms. Others have felt that the place isn't quite the same when Tovey himself is abroad on one of his not-infrequent travels – though most pay tribute to the warmth of welcome conveyed by all who work here. Again the food – and the lack of choice until the dessert – doesn't suit everyone. But the consensus, eloquently conveyed in the report below, is clear: a visit to *Miller Howe*, with or without a few reservations, is something to write home or dine out on. Would that the claim could be made about all our entries!

'*Miller Howe* is a classic target for the English disease . . . petty criticism of the original and brilliant. It's a delightful hotel, with the kindest of staff and its standards never waver from the quality of the soap (which I can't afford in real life) to the blend of the tea. In spite of its deserved international reputation, it's not intimidating; and it's not full of gourmets picking at meals but ordinary people who can afford £15 a head for food. Even if it is a set meal, there's such variety within it that there's something to every taste . . . even a vegetarian was suited whilst I was there. With such a breathtaking setting it's a sheer delight to visit and extraordinary value for money in over-priced Britain. *(Diane Latham)*

Open: 3 March–8 December.
Rooms: 13 double – 11 with bath, 2 with shower, all with radio; TV available.
Facilities: 4 drawing rooms (drinks served here, as no separate bar), 2 dining rooms, sun-lounge terrace; conferences possible out of season. 4 acres grounds with landscaped garden and views over Windermere and the skyline of high fells. Quick access to walking and climbing country; tennis nearby; easy access to Windermere with sailing and fishing and water sports; lake steamer service and cruises.
Location: On the A592 N of Bowness.
Restriction: No children under 12.
Credit cards: American Express, Diners.
Terms (not including 12½% service charge): Dinner, B & B £40–65. Set meal: dinner £16. Cookery courses in off-season. Special weekend spring and autumn breaks.

WITHERSLACK, Grange-over-Sands, Cumbria **Map 4**

The Old Vicarage [GFG] *Telephone:* Witherslack (044 852) 381

This little Georgian hotel is situated in beautiful walking country south of Lake Windermere, and, though only 15 minutes from the M6, it is quiet and secluded, away from the heart of the village. Mrs Brown and Mrs Reeve run the hotel informally as a joint family enterprise. The rooms are pleasantly furnished – William Morris curtains, Heals' lampshades, lots of pine and cane in the bedroom, ample reading light. The emphasis is on quality – a few rooms beautifully equipped and furnished; nothing flash, but first-rate and imaginative. The hotel's cooking is warmly commended.

Home-made bread and rolls are a speciality. There is a five-course set menu dinner – no choice except at the dessert stage where a hot and a cold sweet are offered, and you can have both.

'It is difficult to fault the surroundings or the food and its presentation,' writes one recent visitor. Another expresses her appreciation as follows: 'Drive through a sleepy village of about ten houses. Arrive at *Old Vicarage*. Greeted by elderly retriever called Venus and owner called Jill, who did not know who I was, but was on her way to my bedroom with some fresh-cut daffs from the garden. Room was delightful, large and comfortable, and with attached bathroom. Dinner was divine. Enormous breakfast next morning. The owners need all the encouragement they can get as they are applying the highest standard in a gastronomic wasteland. Next time I am going back with my husband: it is a perfect place for a honeymoon, first or second.' *(John Scott, Mrs S Chait; also Dr R L Marks)*

Open: All year, except Dec 24–26 inclusive.
Rooms: 7 double – all with bath, TV, tea-making facilities and baby-listening.
Facilities: Sitting room, coffee lounge, 3 dining rooms; musical evenings. Garden. Sea 4 miles, Lake Windermere 5 miles, river fishing 6 miles. Fell walking. Weekend cookery courses.
Location: Take exit 36 from the M6: follow route to Barrow-in-Furness. Turn off the A590 signposted Witherslack and take first turning left past 'phone box. Hotel is ½ mile along this lane on the left, just before the church.
Credit cards: Access/Euro/Mastercard, American Express, Barclay/Visa.
Terms (no fixed service charge): B & B £12.75–17; dinner, B & B £21.75–26. Set meal: dinner £10 (£11.50 to non-residents). Reduced rates for children sharing parents' room; special meals provided.

WIVELISCOMBE, Somerset   **Map 1**

Langley House   [GFG]   *Telephone:* Wiveliscombe (0984) 23318
Langley Marsh

Some take naturally to country-house hotelkeeping, and others, however decorative the setting, can never quite bring it off. Francis and Rosalind McCulloch have been the hosts at this stylish Georgian house in the folds of the Brendon Hills – not a touristy part of Somerset, though the Quantocks, Exmoor and Dartmoor are all within touring distance – for little more than five years, but it is clear, from the exceptional number and warmth of expression of our 1982 correspondence, that they are 'to the manor born'. We had one thoroughly disgruntled account of a visit where nothing seemed to go right, but this was an isolated case. Other correspondents did indeed raise the odd niggle or two – one would have liked a radio and telephone in his room, another would have preferred Francis McCulloch, serving at dinner in warm weather, to have kept his jacket on – but a hotel is fortunate if it elicits such trivial grumbles to set against such responses as 'A memorable stay. I had despaired ever of finding a small hotel in the UK of this quality. It was almost like being in France with the super food and reasonable prices' or 'I read the brochure with a little scepticism as brochures do tend to paint exaggerated pictures, but I can say without reservation that it was even better than the brochure's description. It is totally unlike a hotel at all, just a very elegant private manor house. . . . One of the very best holidays I have ever had' or 'I endorse everything that has been said about the delightful couple and the service they provide. . . . We stayed at six Guide-recommended hotels, and by a long head the cuisine at *Langley House* was outstandingly the best and far from the dearest.' *(W Giller, Mrs M Edgar, Dr R Million; also LoRae Fletcher-Trebas, Mr and Mrs R Rogers, B Sapseid, Roy and Norah Hill)*

Open: March–October. Restaurant open Friday and Saturday, October–March.
Rooms: 5 double, 3 single – 5 with bath, 1 with shower; 1 four-poster bed.
Facilities: Drawing room with small bar, lounge, sun room, beamed dining room, separate TV room; small conference facilities. 3 acres landscaped grounds, stabling for 8 horses; kitchen garden. The surrounding Brendon Hills border Exmoor; riding a few minutes' away; trout fishing 2 miles. Fine walking country.
Location: On the A361 between Taunton and Bampton.
Restrictions: No children under 7.
Terms (no fixed service charge): B & B £16.50–18.50; dinner, B & B £25.50–32. Set meal: dinner £9–13; Special gourmet weekends; special 3-day breaks; reduced rates for children sharing parents' room; special meals provided.

WOOLACOMBE, North Devon   Map 1

Little Beach Hotel   [GFG]   *Telephone:* Woolacombe (0271) 870398
The Esplanade

The small resort of Woolacombe has one great natural advantage – the three-mile stretch of Woolacombe Sands that frame Morte Bay. *The Little Beach Hotel* is an Edwardian residence, restored in character, which offers its guests that stupendous view across the sands. It's a newish enterprise of two young men, Nic Lowes and Alan Bradley, neither trained hoteliers – one describes himself as an ex-multinational jetsetter and the other was formerly a film editor with the BBC. They offer, they say, 'something different by the sea!'

'Mr Lowes runs the hotel, efficiently, with efficiency unobtrusive; Mr Bradley cooks. Appointments of hotel comfortable and tasteful (no jazzy carpets). Food is exceptional. Good proper breakfast, five-course dinner, with many unusual dishes, the highlight of the day even after the glorious Devon countryside. There is a lovely friendly atmosphere in the hotel because the owners work so hard and love their hotel, and it has the advantage of being small. The only hotels we have visited with this service and quality were in Switzerland and Jamaica.' *(Mr and Mrs C J Swift)*

Open: February–end October.
Rooms: 8 double, 2 single – 4 with bath, 4 with shower, all with radio and baby-listening.
Facilities: TV lounge, sun lounge, drawing room, bar, dining room; sauna, solarium; small garden with sun terraces; swimming, surfing, safe sandy beach; riding, fishing, golf within five miles.
Location: 200 yards from Woolacombe along sea front; parking.
Reduction: No dogs in dining room.
Credit cards: Access/Euro/Mastercard, Barclay/Visa.
Terms: B & B £11.30–17.25; dinner, B & B £17.60–23.25. Bar or packed lunches only. Set meal: dinner £7.50. Reduced rates for children.

Don't rely on our printed tariffs! Check before booking.

The Butchers Arms   [GFG]   *Telephone:* Fownhope (043 277) 281

An example of that disappearing species, an honest old-fashioned country inn. Woolhope is a small village, equidistant (eight miles each) from Hereford, Ross and Ledbury, and three miles from the River Wye. The *Butchers Arms*, a black-and-white half-timbered building, dating from the 14th century, is a popular village pub, with low beams and log fires in the bars (good bar snacks), but it also has three small but comfortable rooms, and an enterprising *à la carte* menu in its restaurant. Mary Bailey is the welcoming innkeeper. *(Roger Smithells)*

Open: All year. Restaurant closed Sunday–Tuesday, but bar meals and snacks available.
Rooms: 3 double – all with tea-making facilities and mono TV.
Facilities: Lounge bar, public bar, restaurant; patio garden beside stream.
Location: From Hereford take B4224; at Mordiford turn left to Woolhope; at the T-junction in Woolhope take left turn; *Butchers Arms* is ¼ mile outside village.
Restrictions: No children under 14. No dogs.
Terms (no service charge): B & B £10.90. Full *alc* £9.75. Bargain breaks 1 October–31 March (excluding Easter).

WOOLVERTON, Nr Bath, Avon   **Map 1**

Woolverton House   *Telephone:* Frome (0373) 830415

Another of those solid stone-built early-Victorian rectories that have been given fresh life converted for the use of touring laity. It is on the A36, roughly halfway between Bath and Warminster, and with plenty of rewarding things to see in the near vicinity: the Rode Tropical Bird Gardens is just two fields away. It has been a small country-house hotel for many years, but had the misfortune, in the late Seventies, to change hands twice within a short period. Last year, we gave our first encouraging interim entry on the regime of John and Jean Fairfax-Ross, and are glad to say – in the language of school reports – that progress has been well maintained this past year. 'Now back to a good standard – attentive and unobtrusive service. Marvellous family room, relaxing lounge and good food.' *(F H Saint)* 'The hotel is as comfortable as you say in the Guide. The Fairfax-Rosses made us feel much more like guests in a private house than customers. And the food is quite marvellous! Real Cordon Bleu fare – very rich but just what is wanted for a break weekend.' *(Colonel R W H Crawford)*

Open: All year. Restaurant closed Sunday evenings.
Rooms: 7 double, 1 single – all with bath, colour TV and tea-making facilities. 3 rooms in annexe.
Facilities: Lounge, bar, restaurant. 2 acres garden. ♿.
Location: Just off the A36, 10 miles S of Bath.
Restriction: Dogs at owners' discretion, in bedrooms only.
Credit cards: All major credit cards accepted.
Terms: B & B (continental) £14–25; dinner, B & B £25–30. Set meals: English breakfast £2.75; full *alc* lunch £8.50, dinner £12. Bargain winter/spring breaks and special rates for 2 days or more. Reduced rates and special meals for children.

WORLESTON, Nr Nantwich, Cheshire   **Map 2**

Rookery Hall [GFG]   *Telephone:* Nantwich (0270) 626 866

This Victorian Gothic château is set in 28 acres of garden and parkland, with fountains and statuary and a natural pool stocked with ornamental fowl. Inside is of a piece, with splendid panelling, plasterwork ceilings and marble chimneypieces. Happily, a showplace of a house has, as its chatelain, a suitably flamboyant personality in Harry Norton, who has no hangups about dubbing his house 'The English Château'. Without question, he is a superb natural hotelier, and every department of his hotel is attended to devotedly: the service is impeccable, the rooms are delightfully elegant, and the kitchens, under the supervision of Harry's wife Jean, produce six-course dinners that are as dependably delicious in content as they are pretty in presentation. For some readers, this is an ultimate experience – 'the most excellent of all hotels', to quote one unreserved enthusiast. It isn't going to be to everyone's taste of course. There is a minority view that finds the whole place a little oppressive: 'The insistence on comfort, and Harry and Jean popping round corners to ask if all is well rather stifled me – maybe that's just the ascetic bit of my soul. But others loved it, even to having rooms called after months; one very pretty grandmother with a sense of humour said, "They've been kind enough to give me May". So I don't want to be harsh. A great deal of care has been lavished on the hotel, and if you want to be sure you will be looked after thoughtfully by polite and good-natured management and staff, head for *Rookery Hall.*' *(R Bennett, Gillian Vincent and others)*

Open: All year, except last week July, first week August, one week at Christmas. Restaurant closed to non-residents on Sunday/Monday and bank holidays.
Rooms: 6 double, 3 single, 3 suites (1 four-poster double bed) – all with bath, direct-dial telephone, radio and colour TV. (Another double room and a suite will be ready soon.)
Facilities: 2 sitting rooms, 2 dining rooms, 28 acres garden and park with croquet, putting, hard tennis court, riverside and woodland walks, fishing.
Location: If possible avoid Nantwich town centre. *Rookery Hall* is 1½ miles along the B5074 towards Winsford. This road is off the B5073 (the 'Barony' – the Chester by-pass road around the town).
Restrictions: No children under 10. No dogs.
Credit cards: Access/Mastercard, American Express, Barclay/Visa, Diners, Carte Blanche.
Terms (service at guests' discretion): B & B £33.18–49.45; dinner, B & B £51.13–£67.90; full board £57.33–74.10 (four-poster suites extra). Set meals: businessmen's lunch £5.50, gourmet lunch £12, dinner £17.95. Bargain breaks in and out of season.

YORK   **Map 4**

The Judges Lodging   *Telephone:* York (0904) 38733
9 Lendal

A magnificent Georgian town house in the centre of the city, within a couple of hundred yards of the Minster, run with some panache by Gerald Mason and his French wife. Just 13 rooms, all with colour TV, are attractively furnished, and are made more welcoming with complimentary sherry and bowl of fruit. 'The most delightful hotel I have met,' writes one appreciative guest. 'Friendly welcome. Mrs Mason even mended my cassette player. Wonderful antiques and silver everywhere. Silver teapot for tea and flowered china. I had a four-poster bed with crisp clean curtains and lovely embroidered sheets; I even had a view of the Minster lit up by night from my bed.' *The Judge's Lodging* would seem like the answer to the prayers of many cathedral city pilgrims. The only drawback, according to the reports on file, is that the restaurant does not at present live up to the pretensions of the setting.

Open: All year.
Rooms: 9 double, 4 single, 1 suite – 7 with bath, all with telephone, TV and baby-listening. (Some four-poster beds.)
Facilities: Lounge, cocktail bar, 2 dining rooms. 1-acre garden, with tables for lunch when fine.
Location: In town centre; parking.
Restriction: No dogs in public rooms.
Credit cards: Barclay/Visa, Diners.
Terms (no fixed service charge): B & B £27.50–28.75; dinner, B & B (winter rates) £24.50–28.75. Set meals: bar lunches 45p–£2.75; full *alc* £12.75. Reduced rates and special meals for children.

YORK   Map 4

Mount Royale Hotel   *Telephone:* York (0904) 28856
The Mount

'We have visited *Mount Royale* many times. The welcome we receive is always warm, the staff friendly and the rooms now are beautifully furnished and extremely comfortable; the food is consistently good.' This was the latest – and largely typical – report to reach us before the 1983 edition was put to bed. *Mount Royale* has long been a popular place to stay in York for those who want a less bland experience than that provided by the big tourist hotels. It's a building of character, built in 1832 in the Gothic style, and the owners, Richard and Christine Oxtoby, are hotel-keepers of character and calibre too; Richard Oxtoby's cooking is consistently singled out for appreciation. The hotel is near the racecourse, a few minutes walk from Micklegate and ¾ mile from the Minster. One of its chief attractions is its 2-acre garden with heated swimming pool. Its major drawback is the noise of traffic in front rooms, made worse by there being traffic lights on a hill outside; double-glazing helps, but not every one cares to keep the windows sealed at night. The hotel had a major extension two years ago, and we had some mutters during the building that the rooms in the original house had become a bit down-at-heel. We are glad to learn from the owner that most of the bedrooms have now been upgraded to the standard of those in the new house. *(Gillian Andrews; also Anthony Benger and others)*

Open: All year, except 24 December–7 January approx. Dining room closed for lunch (light refreshments available to residents) and for Sunday dinner.
Rooms: 20 double, 2 suites – all with bath, 2 with shower, all with telephone, radio, colour TV, baby-listening, tea-making facilities. (1 room on ground floor.)
Facilities: Residents' lounge, bar, bar lounge, dining room. 2 acres grounds with heated swimming pool.
Location: On A64 from Tadcaster (front rooms have double-glazed windows).

Hotel is on right just before traffic lights at junction with Albemarle Road opposite sign to Harrogate (A59). Parking for 24 cars.

Credit cards: All major credit cards accepted.

Terms (excluding service): B & B £16.50–30. Set meal: dinner £10.75. 2-day breaks £50 per person. York heritage breaks. Reduced rates and special meals for children.

Lake Vyrnwy Hotel, Llanwddyn

Wales

Crowfield   *Telephone:* Abergavenny (0873) 5048
                                                          Ross Road

'We stayed at this small guest house in order to dine at the famous *Walnut Tree* restaurant at Llandewi Skirrid, three-quarters of a mile up the road. It has only recently opened, but the Crabbs spent the four previous years lovingly and tastefully restoring what was originally a virtually derelict Welsh farmhouse. Our delightful bedroom and bathroom were in one of the outbuildings which they are still working on, and it couldn't have been more comfortable. What's more we were supplied with proper-size bath-towels, and even more of a rarity, large bars of bath soap. We dined at the *Walnut Tree* so I can't give you an opinion on the standard of Mrs Crabb's cooking, but from the conversation I had with her, I got the feeling that the standard is fairly high. Very sensibly she doesn't try to compete with the *Walnut Tree*, but concentrates mostly on good roasts with perfectly cooked fresh vegetables. While we were dining out, she poached a salmon caught by one of the guests, and we were told the next morning that it had been superb. The bar is their very elegant drawing room and a tray of drinks is kept there with pad and pen – one helps oneself. The hotel is in the Brecon Beacons National Park and very quiet.' (*Christine Chapman*)

Open: All year, except Christmas.
Rooms: 4 double, 1 single – 4 with bath, 1 with shower; TV on request. (All rooms in annexe.)

Facilities: Sitting room, bar lounge, bar, dining room. 2 acres garden. Salmon/trout fishing by arrangement; golf, pony trekking available nearby.
Location: 2 miles from town centre; on the B4521 Abergavenny–Ross road via Skenfrith; parking.
Restrictions: No children under 12. No dogs.
Credit card: Access/Euro/Mastercard.
Terms: B & B £14–18. Set meal: dinner £7.50.

ABERSOCH, Gwynedd   Map 3

Porth Tocyn Hotel   [GFG]   *Telephone:* Abersoch (075 881) 2966

When a hotel is given a particularly warm endorsement in these pages, we worry whether the place can sustain the high expectations that our compliments will have aroused. *Porth Tocyn*, a beautifully-sited house on a headland overlooking Cardigan Bay and Snowdonia, has been receiving perfumed bouquets from our readers from almost our first issue. No sign of retribution yet! The house, which has a heated swimming pool and tennis court, and is surrounded by its own 25-acre farm sloping down to the shore and golf links, has been owned and run for many years past by Barbara Fletcher-Brewer and her son Nick. In the past year, Nick has married the cook – we should mention in passing that the hotel's reputation for fine cooking is of a piece with everything else – but he tells us that his wife is also a dab hand with wallpaper and upholstery. Major renovation of the rooms in the old wing has been taking place, as well as fresh landscaping of the pool area. It is the kind of place in which improvements of one sort or another are going on most of the time.

Last year, we quoted from readers who felt that, in staying at *Porth Tocyn*, they had been admitted to 'an exclusive Eden uncontaminated by the misdemeanours of the outside world'. No single report this year reached that peak of eloquent appreciation, but the message was the same. One reader returned after a gap of eighteen years and found it every bit as good as she had remembered it. Another wrote gratefully about the hotel's willingness to cater for special dietary needs. A third mentioned the help given with the caring of a small daughter. Not a niggle in the woodpile! (*Mrs D S Hazel, SHH, Mrs C Hampson, Pat and Jeremy Temple, Dr T J David*)

Open: Easter–end October.
Rooms: 15 double, 2 single – 15 with bath; TV on request. (3 rooms on ground floor.)
Facilities: 2 lounges, TV room, library. Garden with tennis court and swimming pool, set within the hotel's 25-acre farm; 5 minutes' walk from sea; sailing, bathing, water skiing, fishing; golf and riding nearby. &.
Location: The hotel is about 2½ miles S of Abersoch. Drive through Abersoch, passing the Sarn Bach crossroads, bear left at the next fork, then turn left at the signpost for *Porth Tocyn*, and follow the road to the very end; look for signs saying 'hotel/gwesty'.
Restrictions: Dogs at management's discretion and in bedrooms only.
Credit cards: Access/Euro, American Express.
Terms (service at guests' discretion): B & B £16–25; dinner, B & B £24.70–38.20; full board £30.20–43.70. Set meals: lunch £5.50, dinner (2 courses) £8.70, (5 courses) £13.20. Bargain breaks out of season. 4-day Christmas break.

Procrastination is the thief of the next edition.

Bontddu Hall   *Telephone:* Bontddu (034 149) 661
                                           Telex: 35142

This imposing example of Victorian Gothic, a style more common in Scotland than in Wales, celebrates its 110th birthday this year, and for a third of that span it has been personally run as a hotel by Bill Hall. Few hotelkeepers can boast such a long and successful innings. The *Hall* has a spectacular position, looking out over well-landscaped gardens to the Mawddach estuary and the Cader Idris range of mountains: a large terrace provides an agreeable position from which to admire the view while fortifying oneself with drinks, bar snacks, and lunch, when the weather allows. It has consistently earned appreciative comments from our readers for its friendly and efficient service. Last year, we referred to a grateful German television crew who had arrived late expecting a surly reception and found the reverse. We don't know whether the hotel has any special appeal to the media, but the only adverse comment this year was from a visitor who found, during a five-day visit, that the prevailing harmony was disturbed by a noisy invasion of a BBC Radio Road Show, followed immediately by a Yorkshire TV team. Otherwise, no complaints. Since last year, Bill Hall has opened a 'really charming' Princess of Wales Bar, and, to combat recession, is offering specially tempting autumn and winter bargain breaks; you don't have to spend more than a night to qualify, and, included in the price [£19.45 in 1982] is not only a four-course Bistro dinner but also – presumably to combat deflation – an 'Eat and Eat' buffet lunch.

Open: All year, except Christmas and New Year.
Rooms: 20 double, 2 single, 4 suites – 21 with bath, 5 with shower, all with telephone and colour TV, 8 rooms in annexe. (2 rooms on ground floor.)
Facilities: 2 lounges, cocktail bar, restaurant. Well-kept garden, private path to estuary. Beautiful walks to estuary or up the mountains behind. Quiet sandy beaches nearby, also trout, salmon and sea fishing, golf, pony-trekking.
Location: Just off the A496, E of Barmouth.
Restrictions: No children under 3. Dogs at management's discretion.
Credit cards: Access, Barclay/Visa.
Terms: B & B £7.50–19.50; dinner, B & B £15–25; full board £19.45–29.50. Set meals: lunch £3.45; dinner £9.50. No charge for children sharing parents' room; special meals provided.

Rhyd-Garn-Wen   [GFG]   *Telephone:* Cardigan (0239) 612742

The last hotel we had in this fairly remote stretch of southern Wales was the lamented *Penlan Oleu* at Llanychaer – a small caring *sui generis* establishment, with Ann Carr's remarkable cooking as a memorable plus. *Rhyd-Garn-Wen* is perhaps in a similar mould. It is even smaller than *Penlan Oleu* in the number of its rooms, run by Huw Jones, formerly a BBC TV producer and a keen wine connoisseur, and his wife Susan, whose cooking, she tells us, is on French lines, following Bocuse.

'An attractive gateway opens on to a long curved drive which leads to this delightful secluded Victorian house, set in a very large garden with a stable yard and coach houses to the rear. There is a large comfortable drawing room, its tables replete with a variety of books which spill over into the bedrooms. A most elegant dining room furnished with the taste which is typical of the house provides an excellent setting for the most delectable food and wine, and adjacent to it is a small bar in what was originally the servants' hall. On the first floor there are three very large bedrooms, two with showers *en suite* and the third with a palatial bathroom opposite. From our original welcome, cordial but not effusive, we were made to feel thoroughly at home to enjoy all the good things with which Huw and Susan Jones had surrounded themselves. Susan Jones is a woman of many parts, not least of which is her skill in planning, preparing and presenting her perfectly balanced meals. One is served graciously by Italian Amelia, clad in ankle-length Victorian dress with a smart apron, a cheeky cap and an unfailing *bon appétit*. The wettest week in June, and in the country of rain at that, was made for us by our hosts, whose unfailing and unobtrusive care for our every need made this the most memorable of holidays.' *(Alan Pratt)*

Open: All year, except Christmas and Boxing Day.
Rooms: 3 double – 1 with bath, 2 with shower; mono TV on request.
Facilities: TV room, drawing room, bar, dining room. 18 acres grounds. Hunting, shooting, fishing by arrangement; stabling for visiting horses; excellent walking country; golf, safe swimming, boating; historical sites, lectures and music festivals in vicinity.
Location: 3 miles from Cardigan, 5 miles from Newport (Pemb); at the Croft crossroad on the main A487 between Cardigan and Fishguard; garage and outdoor parking (mechanic available).
Restrictions: Not suitable for small children or disabled; no dogs in public rooms.
Credit card: Access/Euro/Mastercard.
Terms: B & B £11.50–15.50; dinner, B & B £17.50–22.50. Set meals: lunch £3.95, dinner £9.50.

DRUIDSTON HAVEN, Nr Haverfordwest, Dyfed   **Map 3**

Druidstone Hotel   [GFG]   *Telephone:* Broad Haven (043 783) 221

Since we started the Guide, we have constantly been on the lookout for small seaside hotels that really put themselves out for families with children. They are not easy to find, which makes an entry for *Druidstone* all the more welcome. The hotel, with four adjoining self-catering cottages, stands in 20 acres of wild garden, on the Pembrokeshire Coastal Path about halfway between Broad Haven and Nolton. It has two private paths down to a safe sandy beach 200 yards below. We liked the way in which Jane Bell, who runs the place with her husband Rod, described her establishment: 'A very informal holiday hotel catering for families with children of all ages. The intention is to provide an easy-going relaxed atmosphere in complete contrast to City life, with good interesting home-cooked food available. We try to set as few "rules" as possible, providing early and late meals whenever we can, and allowing people as much freedom as we can. Some say it is like going through a time-slip. Our unconventional approach won't be to everyone's liking. But we must be some people's meat as we have 91 families returning to visit us in the next three months – some of them have been back many times.'

'Beautifully situated hotel on a remote clifftop. The atmosphere is warm, friendly and informal. Lunchtime and evening meals in the cellar bar were excellent; the restaurant meals superb. No private bathrooms but unfailing hot water and the public bathrooms never seemed to be crowded!' *(P H and M M A Tattersall)*

Open: All year, except 31 October–3 December approx. (Restaurant closed lunchtime/Sunday evening.)
Rooms: 5 double, 2 single, 1 suite – all with baby-listening on request. 4 self-catering cottages.
Facilities: Reception, sitting room with TV, bar, dining room, terraces. Occasional live music in bar. 20 acres grounds with petanque and croquet, leading to sandy beach with caves; riding, sailing, surfing, diving, waterskiing and squash available nearby.
Location: In Haverfordwest take the B4341 to Broad Haven; 3 miles out of Haverfordwest fork right to Nolton; 1 mile on, the Nolton Road turns right; continue straight on. At T-junction at Haroldston Farm turn right. 150 yards on, by a field gate, take concealed left turn, signposted *Druidston Haven*. Over 2 cattle grids, 500 yards on, the hotel is on the left.
Restriction: No dogs in dining room.
Credit cards: American Express, Barclay/Visa.
Terms (no fixed service charge): B & B £13.50; dinner, B & B £150 per week; cottages: 2 bedrooms, sleep 5 – £110–160; 3 bedrooms, sleep 6–8 – £125–200. Set meal: dinner £10 approx. Reduced rates for children: under 12 months, free; 1–6 years, 33%; 6–10, 50%; 10–14, ⅔ full rate. Reductions for 10 or more people October–March.

EGLWYSFACH, Machynlleth, Powys   **Map 3**

Ynyshir Hall Country House House   *Telephone:* Glandyfi (065 474) 209

A lovely 16th-century manor house (once owned by the Mappin family of Mappin and Webb fame) with a celebrated ten-acre garden, in a beautiful valley on the edge of the estuary of the river Dovey and backed by the Ynyshir Bird Reserve – *Ynyshir Hall* has a lot going for it, quite apart from its proximity to the Snowdonia National Park. And John and Joyce Hughes, ever since they took the hotel over a few years back, have earned plaudits from readers for all the things which make a stay at a country-house hotel an enjoyable experience. But there have been a few reservations, this year as last, about the upkeep of some of the rooms, and also about the quality of the cooking. We are glad to know from Mrs Hughes that most of the bedrooms and bathrooms have been redecorated and refurbished this past year, also that she has been able to add a ground-floor room to accommodate disabled guests. *STOP PRESS We have just learnt that Ynyshir Hall has changed hands. No details yet of the new owners.*

Open: All year, except January.
Rooms: 9 double, 3 single – 7 with bath, 4 with shower. (1 room with 4-poster.)
Facilities: 2 drawing rooms, cocktail bar, dining room. 10 acres garden with flowering shrubs. 5 miles from sea with sandy beach. &.
Location: Just off the A487 6 miles S of Machynlleth.
Restriction: No dogs in public rooms.
Credit cards: All major credit cards accepted.
Terms (no fixed service charge): Dinner, B & B £28–38. Set meals (excluding 10% service charge): lunch £7.50; dinner £12.50. Reduced rates for children under 10; special meals on request.

The Old Black Lion   *Telephone:* Hay-on-Wye (0497) 820 841
Lion Street

We had an entry for this vintage hostelry – dating back to the 13th century, but essentially a coaching inn of the 17th century – in our first edition, but left it out later for lack of feedback. Expect low beams, creaking corridors and semi-mod cons. The Cromwell Room, possibly slept in by the Protector, has a beamed gallery with twin beds, and two more below. Dorothy Adler, the resident owner, is an enthusiastic cook and home-baker. It should suit those who prefer character and companionship to the more prosaic creature comforts. 'An excellent place to stay while visiting the Book Capital of Wales. Service a bit slow, but attractive food and good value.' *(Raymond Harris)*

Open: All year.
Rooms: 6 double, 1 single, 1 family – 6 with shower, all with colour TV and tea-making facilities. (2 rooms in annexe.)
Facilities: Residents' lounge with TV, bar, dining room, patio. Safe river bathing nearby, fishing licences available; pony trekking, riding, guided scenic walks, sailing, hang gliding in vicinity.
Location: 200 yards from town centre; car park.
Credit card: Access/Euro/Mastercard.
Terms: B & B £14.80–16.15. Full *alc* £9.30 (snacks also available).

LLANBERIS, Gwynedd   **Map 3**

Gallt y Glen Hotel   *Telephone:* Llanberis (0286) 870370

Most readers continue to appreciate the hospitality offered by this small unpretentious hotel, ¾ mile outside Llanberis on the Caernarvon road, with good views towards Snowdonia and the Glyders. The hotel has added to its accommodation this past year with two 'Alpine' bunk dormitories, each sleeping six, with their own WC, washbasin and shower, at £3 per bed per night – ideal for families, or the children of families whose parents can then sleep a bit more up-market in the hotel itself, or for groups of hill walkers; three-course breakfast extra at £1.50.
'The food is very good and varied. The service is careful and unobtrusive. What strikes one immediately is the very pleasant relaxed atmosphere which pervades the place. Climbers will find a kindred spirit in the proprietor, Bob Maslen-Jones, who is one of the leading lights in the local mountain rescue service.' *(L B Marley; also H ap R)*

Open: All year. Restaurant closed on Sunday.
Rooms: 6 double, 2 family – 2 with shower, all with radio and baby-listening. 2 bunk dormitories, each sleeping 6, with own WC, basin and shower.
Facilities: Buttery, TV lounge, bar lounge, dining room, table tennis room; 1 acre garden.
Location: ½ mile out of Llanberis on the A4086 road to Caernarvon.
Restriction: No dogs.
Credit cards: All major credit cards accepted.
Terms (no service charge): B & B £11.95–13.95; dinner, B & B £17.95–19.95.
Set meal: dinner £6.50; full *alc* £11. Weekend and midweek breaks. Dormitory

£3, linen extra. Reductions for long stays. Reduced rates for children sharing parents' room; special meals on request. Christmas and New Year programmes.

LLANDUDNO, Gwynedd   Map 3

Bodysgallen Hall   [GFG]   *Telephone:* Deganwy (0492) 84466
                                             Telex: 8951493 MONTEK G

Grand country-house hotels, increasingly part of the English and Scottish hotel scene, have been notable only by their absence in Wales. *Bodysgallen*, therefore, is something of a Welsh first. It is not, however, like most of its breed, owner-occupied, but belongs to a new company called Historic House Hotels, dedicated, we are told, to the rescue and restoration of architecturally important country houses and to turning them into hotels 'that epitomize the spirit of a well-run large private house in its heyday'. Worthy motives, and we shall look forward to hearing more about their activities. *Bodysgallen* is their first venture. It opened its doors in July 1981, and at the turn of the year we suddenly received a rash of letters from new correspondents all saying, in so many words 'elegant, comfortable, excellent, beautiful'. We marked these reports 'collusive?' and waited to learn more. Then a reader wrote: 'It is a long time since I have been able to go into raptures about a hotel, but our faith in the hotel business was restored by *Bodysgallen*.' Since then, other reports have reached us, of which the one below is the most eloquent:

'The gardens alone would make *Bodysgallen* worth visiting. There's a 17th-century knot garden, a walled 18th-century rose garden and even more important a large vegetable garden. Set in seven acres amid ancient trees *Bodysgallen* has a 13th-century tower, Elizabethan and Jacobean rooms and a unique history. It is the first building of architectural merit to be restored and renovated by Historic House Hotels, a private company dedicated to rescuing listed buildings about to collapse due to lack of loving care but above all lack of money. Richard Broyd, the man behind the company, is a private enterprise whizz-person and he is already enthusiastically renovating Middlethorpe Hall, a Queen Anne pile near York which is due to open in the spring of 1983.

'*Bodysgallen* is authentic and full of carefully chosen furniture. The log fires are huge and real; the flowers perennial; the hot water gushes; for those unimpressed by the past there is colour TV, trouser presses and all the marks of the contemporary country house hotel – biscuits by the bedside, foam bath essence, books and magazines. The cooking is in the hands of Peter Jackson, a 25-year-old Scot, Gleneagles-trained and winner of many awards. He is currently North Wales Chef of the Year and in 1980 won the Taste of Scotland competition. He comes from Inverurie and so does his well-hung beef. Food is excellent. A mile or so from the still beautifully preserved seafront of Llandudno, *Bodysgallen* lies on the west of Pydew mountain. From the 13th-century tower you can see Conway Castle and the mirage of Snowdonia. The views are staggering, the house itself impeccably restored. For what you get the prices are remarkably low. Hurry, can they last?' *(Derek and Janet Cooper; also Elisabeth Lumbert Ortiz, J S Williams, Christopher R Hill, Henrietta Bateman, Mrs P D Fairrie)*

Open: All year.
Rooms: 25 double, 7 single – all with bath, telephone, radio and colour TV. 13 rooms in annexe (2 on ground floor).

Facilities: Hall, morning room, drawing room, library with TV, bar, 2 restaurants; conference/function facilities. 7 acres grounds with tennis court and croquet; golf, sea/river fishing, swimming, sailing, riding available nearby.
Location: Take the A55 to roundabout before Conwy Bridge. Take Llandudno road – ½ mile on right-hand side is sign to *Bodysgallen* up the B5115. Sea 2 miles; town centre 1½ miles; parking. (Guests coming by train can be met at Llandudno Junction.)
Restrictions: No children under 6. Small dogs only, and not in public rooms.
Credit cards: All major credit cards accepted.
Terms: B & B £20–35. Set meals (excluding 10% service): lunch £6.80, dinner £10.80; full *alc* £15. 50% reduction for children sharing parents' room. Champagne breaks, special winter rates and Christmas package; 10% discount on room rate for stays of 7 nights or more.

LLANGADOG, Dyfed   Map 3

Glansevin Hotel   *Telephone:* Llangadog (055 03) 238

A qualified entry only this year for Wil and Gwenda Rees's Georgian mansion in the heart of rural South Wales, with its eight large austerely well-furnished rooms. Some people have appreciated *Glansevin* because of the quality of the hotel and its past reputation for good cooking and fine wines (especially from the Loire). But another significant draw has always been the special Welsh feature of the hotel. The Rees are bilingual, and for many years have offered their guests (in a separate building) a *Hwyrnos* or Singing Supper, celebrated Wednesdays to Saturdays in the summer and on Fridays and Saturdays in the winter. On these occasions, a *Cawl Cynhaeaf* or Harvest Stew is served, with a honeyed leg of lamb, which guests carve at table, and a traditional pudding. There's harp music, traditional folk songs, and 'lots of fun'.

There have been several changes this past year. On the plus side, the hotel now has a heated outdoor pool for the use of residents. On the minus, *Glansevin* has now introduced a Taste of Wales Pancake Menu in place of a traditional set dinner. There are seven different kinds of pancakes available so you don't need to repeat one during a week's visit, and, we are told, this innovation has been very popular with guests and reflects the Welsh character of the place since pancakes (or *Crempogs*, to give them their Welsh name) have always featured prominently in Celtic cooking. Well maybe, but a solid week's diet of stuffed *Crempogs* didn't go down too well with at least one of our readers, especially as he felt they varied considerably in quality.

Readers have also commented that the owners are much less around these days, as they are both busy producing programmes for the Welsh TV channel. A great deal is left to their manager, David Thomas, who is said to be delightful and helpful, but overworked. And when he is away, a young lady from Essex stands in. In general, there are signs that *Glansevin* is not as it used to be. But the teas continue to be excellent – 'Fill up on tea and skip dinner,' recommends one reader. And he sums up: 'The *Hwyrnos* is super: the welcome indescribable, the food succulent, the fun unbeatable. I'd go back for that and for the visual charm of the place. But I'd hesitate to return for any length of time with all those pancakes.' More reports please.

Open: All year, except Christmas Day, but advance booking advisable November–Easter.

144

Rooms: 9 double – 3 with bath, 2 with shower. No specific baby-listening service, but staff within earshot.
Facilities: Reception hall/lounge, bar/lounge, dining room. 4 acres grounds, partly wooded, with pleasant walks; heated outdoor swimming pool; children's play area; fishing, shooting. 'Rural silence may well disturb town dwellers,' say the proprietors; the nightlife – Welsh singing suppers – is in a separate wing.
Location: Just off the A40, halfway between Llandovery and Llandeilo. From the village square take the A4069 towards Llandovery (it passes between the Black Lion and the Mace foodstore.) In 100 yards branch right on to minor road to Myddfai. Carry on straight about 1½ miles. *Plas Glansevin* is on right.
Restriction: No dogs.
Credit cards: All major credit cards accepted.
Terms: B & B £11.50–15. Set meals: lunch and dinner (pancakes only) £3.50–9; *Hwyrnos* £8. Reduction for children sharing parents' room; high teas provided.

LLANGOLLEN, Clwyd   Map 3

Ty'n-y-wern Hotel   *Telephone:* Llangollen (0978) 860252
Maesmawr Road

A modest small hotel standing on its own on a hillside (the name means 'House in the Meadow'). It is conveniently near the Eisteddfod town of Llangollen, but two miles distant from it which must be a special blessing when the festivities are in full spate.

'A 17th-century farmhouse converted some time ago into a hotel overlooking the river Dee and the Llangollen valley, which means wonderful views from the rooms in the front. The rooms are all clean and nicely decorated, and Mrs Murphy who runs the place with her husband could not be friendlier. The staff are just as nice and this goes for the restaurant too, where the menu is excellent value, and the food well cooked. There are ten rooms, so booking must be necessary in the holiday season. Too-spoilt Americans ought to be reminded that only two have baths – though all have washbasins, and there are two bathrooms, and further loos, all on the first floor, where the bedrooms are. Thoroughly recommended.' *(Paul Neuburg)*

Open: 1 March–31 December, except Christmas Day.
Rooms: 8 double, 2 single – 2 with bath, all with mono TV and tea-making facilities.
Facilities: Lounge bar, public bar, restaurant; facilities for functions and parties. 1¾ acres grounds. Trout/salmon fishing in river Dee, 200 yards; pony trekking, golf, canoeing available nearby.
Location: On the main A5 Shrewsbury–Holyhead road, just outside Llangollen, coming from Shrewsbury. Ample parking.
Restriction: No dogs in bedrooms or restaurant.
Credit card: Diners.
Terms: B & B £12–15; dinner, B & B £17.50–20. Set meal: dinner £7.50; bar lunches only; full *alc* £9.50. Children under 3, free; 3–12 years, 50%; 12–15, ⅔ adult rate; special meals if required.

Deadlines: nominations for the 1984 edition should reach us not later than 1 June 1983. Latest date for comments on existing entries: 31 July 1983.

Meadowsweet Hotel   [GFG]   *Telephone:* Llanrwst (0492) 640 732
Station Road

John and Joy Evans have for some time been running an excellent
restaurant from their terraced Victorian house on the outskirts of this
market town overlooking bright green sheep-dotted meadows and distant
mountains, but only recently extended their enterprise into a hotel. We
had our first entry on the place last year, with an appreciation of the charm
and taste of the accommodation, as well as of the food – 'imaginative but
never outlandish.' A couple who spent Easter 1982 here echoed these
compliments. They liked everything about the place, but reported, sadly,
that even though it was a Bank Holiday weekend, it was only quarter-full.
We think the Evans's hotel deserves to be better known. *(Pat and Jeremy
Temple, Dr and Mrs Wolfendale, Elisabeth Lambert Ortiz)*

Open: All year.
Rooms: 10 double – all with shower, telephone and mono TV.
Facilities: Bar lounge, residents' lounge, dining room. Salmon fishing, horse-
riding, golf within easy reach; 20 miles from North Wales coast.
Location: ½ mile from town centre; car park.
Restrictions: Dogs by prior arrangement only.
Credit cards: Access/Euro/Mastercard, American Express, Barclay/Visa.
Terms: B & B £11–18; dinner, B & B £20–27. Set meals: lunch £5.95; dinner £9;
full *alc* £13.50. Reduced rates and special meals for children. Christmas/New Year
house parties; out-of-season gourmet weekends for parties of 10 couples – £45 per
person. Discounts for 4, 10 days or more.

LLANTHONY, Abergavenny, Gwent   Map 3

Abbey Hotel   [GFG]   *Telephone:* Crucorney (087 382) 487/559

Three comments from this year's reports: 'Seemingly unchanged since
late 1950s. Utterly magical atmosphere of ruined abbey in bowl of hills.
Food very imaginative and the whole excellent value. Perversely, the
slightly down-at-heel quality contributes to the atmosphere.' 'It *is* a bit
spartan, but also luxurious – the two exist side by side, and there is no
pretentiousness operating in foolish attempts to weld them together.'
'Regret to say that, after a few visits, we are now confirmed Abbey
"freaks".'
   The small unworldly hostelry to which these readers refer is part of the
west range of a now mostly ruined 12th-century Augustinian priory in the
wildly beautiful Black Mountains. There are just four bedrooms, reached
by a Norman spiral staircase – 62 steps to the top and no lift – nor, for that
matter, any H & C or central heating; from the top room, it's a long climb
down to the shared bathroom and loo, but chamber pots (an almost
vanished domestic convenience) are provided. Modest accommodation
perhaps, but the prices (see below) are *exceptionally* modest too. And the
meals, in contrast to the rooms, are anything but spartan. Susan Fancourt
is American, but her cooking is excitingly eclectic, offering a number of
Welsh specialities but also dishes from Morocco, Mexico, Portugal and
Japan – and several vegetarian dishes too.
   In our entry last year, we mentioned that free tea and coffee is available

to residents in the afternoon. The *Abbey* is now open for afternoon teas, but the free tea facility has been exchanged for bowls of sweets in the bedrooms. No other change worth recording, but if you don't care for nylon sheets, make sure you ask for the cotton variety. *(M Saunders and Kris Heinemann, David Penny, Maggie Angeloglou; D C Ward. See also* Report of the Year, *page 558)*

Open: March–end October. Restaurant closed Sunday and Monday night (bar snacks available).
Rooms: 4 double – no H & C, no central heating.
Facilities: Cellar bar, dining room. A place for tranquillity in fine walking country; hill-climbing in the Black Mountains and Brecon Beacons National Park; pony-trekking centres nearby.
Location: 12 miles N of Abergavenny, by the B4423 (off the A465).
Terms (excluding VAT; no service charge): B & B £7.50. Full *alc* £10. 25% reductions for residents who dine in the hotel. Reduced rates for children sharing parents' room; special meals provided.

LLANWDDYN, via Oswestry, Shropshire   Map 3

Lake Vyrnwy Hotel   *Telephone:* Llanwddyn (069 173) 244

'A comfortable old-fashioned sporting hotel that makes no concession to any modern image' is the disarming claim made by Mrs Moir and Colonel Sir John Baynes, about their solidly-built turn-of-the-century Tudor-style mansion standing 150 feet above the lake. (Note: it is in north Powys, despite the misleading postal address.) The claim is true and helpful. Some will find the upper- and middle-class atmosphere a bit oppressive (ties *de rigueur* at dinner, for instance) and seek their pleasures elsewhere. Others will relish the dependable virtues of large well-cooked meals – much above the regional norm, incidentally – the attentive but not obsequious service, the absence of anything gimcrack or gimmicky. It's a hotel that puts itself out for country pursuits, especially for fishing (the hotel has sole fishing rights on the whole lake and gives priority to its residents) and shooting. But, as the testimonial below makes clear, it also attracts other visitors who return year after year.

'We came across this hotel in the summer first of all; my mother had stayed there before the war and I was curious to see a so-called "sporting" hotel, which I knew it was. As we crossed the threshold, we both fell in love with it – a feeling of comfort, and general before-the-war well-run ambience, unusual in this day and age. We determined there and then to try and get up there for the New Year. We could not have determined better. It was like one great big family house party. We were all beautifully looked after, log fires everywhere, hot water bottles in the beds, and delicious food – all very reasonable, too, we thought. We found that many of the people staying there go year after year, they love it so much, so I am not keen on advertising this if it means none of us can ever get in there again! One amazing thing, to me, was that you could not lock your bedroom door from the outside! I wonder how much longer they will be able to do that.' *(Jill Bickerton; also Mr and Mrs N Cowan, Chris and Dorothy Brining)*

Open: 1 March–1 November, 20 December – 3 January, also by arrangement in November/December for parties.
Rooms: 16 double, 14 single, 1 suite – 11 with bath.
Facilities: Lift to first floor, drawing room, smoking lounge with TV, bar, bar

billiards, nursery for small children's supper. 27 acres grounds with hard tennis court and games hut with ping pong. Trout fishing on lake Vyrnwy, walking and bicycling. &.
Location: 10 miles W of Llanfyllin by the B4393, at the southern end of lake Vyrnwy.
Restrictions: Dogs in cars or kennels only, not in hotel.
Terms: B & B £12.50–20; full board £18–28. Set meals: lunch £4.50 (£6 on Sunday); dinner £7. Reduced rates for stays of over 4 days. Children 3–10, half rate; children 10–16, ⅔ rate; babies £2 per night for cot. Nursery supper £1.

ROBESTON WATHEN, Nr Haverfordwest, Pembrokeshire   Map 3

Robeston House   [GFG]   *Telephone:* Narberth (0834) 860 392

This attractive Georgian house in lovely gardens is just off (and out of earshot of) the A40 and some eight miles from the sea at Tenby. It has been for many years past 'under the very personal supervision' (their phrase) of the resident owners, Grahame and Pamela Barrett. The house is full of good furniture and antiques, and, to quote from one of this year's visitors: 'There is a quiet, restrained, civilized and welcoming atmosphere. . . . Very good value for money.' One other crucial detail needs to be mentioned: Robeston House has a first-class restaurant and an exceptional wine list. *(C Hughes; also Sean and Eithne Scallan)*

Open: All year, except Christmas Day, Boxing Day and New Year's Day.
Rooms: 4 double, 2 single, 1 suite – 4 with bath, all with tea-making facilities and colour TV.
Facilities: Lounge, lounge/bar, dining room; heated swimming pool. 5 acres gardens; outdoor service when weather permits. Salmon and trout fishing, boating, golf, riding within easy reach. Sea within 8 miles to the S.
Location: On the A40 2 miles SW of Narberth and 8 miles E of Haverfordwest.
Restrictions: No children under 14. No dogs, but arrangements can be made for them at nearby kennels.
Credit cards: Access/Euro (reluctantly: owners prefer cheque or cash).
Terms (excluding 10% service charge):   B & B £15.50–17.50. Set meals: lunch £6.50; dinner £10; full *alc* about £13.

ST DAVID'S, Dyfed   Map 3

Warpool Court Hotel   *Telephone:* St David's (0437) 720300

The Lloyd brothers, Grahame and David, took over this large early 19th-century house overlooking St Bride's Bay in 1969, and have made it a hotel of unusual quality. Its position on the westernmost tip of Wales is hard to beat: uncrowded roads, spectacular cliff walks, empty beaches. It is wonderful country for the naturalist – three famous offshore bird sanctuaries, and carpets of wild flowers in the spring– and also for the historically-minded (prehistoric remains, Celtic churches, Norman castles); and for the sports people, there's golf, pony-trekking, sailing, fishing (the hotel has its own boat) and surfing. For those who don't want to go far afield, the hotel has nine acres of garden and a heated covered swimming pool. The Lloyds care about food and wine; they grow a lot of local produce in their own kitchen garden, and make good use of locally caught fish including lobster. Throughout the winter, when most remote country hotels either close or carry on at half-cock, *Warpool Court* runs special musical and bird-watching weekends.

Warpool has been popular with readers for many years, but we had two ambivalent reports this past year. One writer had some minor niggles about the food. The other had appreciated his 'excellent' meals, but had found a lot of other small things which had detracted from the pleasure of his visit: service at dinner in July had been very slow; almost every screw to every fitting in his room had been loose; and he had been surprised to find that he had been charged £1.40 for two small peaches – though, he adds, 'when I queried this, I was refunded £1.50 – do study your bill!'

He had one final complaint. He had been on an annual holiday with his mother aged 80, and the only single rooms at *Warpool* were on the second floor without adjoining baths. 'On this basis,' he reasonably says, 'single rooms ought to be cheaper than half a double.' Occasionally they are, but more often singles are treated as second-class hotel citizens, yet expected to pay over the odds. No easy solution, we fear, to that one.

Open: All year, except January.
Rooms: 22 double, 3 single – all with bath or shower, radio, colour TV and baby-listening.
Facilities: 2 lounges, 2 bars, restaurant; conference room. 9 acres grounds with heated covered swimming pool; 6 beaches within 2 miles; excellent sailing; magnificent country and coastal scenery all around.
Location: Overlooking St Bride's Bay, 5 minutes from St David's.
Credit cards: Access, American Express.
Terms: B & B £20–27.15; dinner, B & B £30.75–37.90; full board £34.75–41.90. Set meal: dinner £9.75; full *alc* lunch £1.35–8.15, dinner £14.50. Large range of special-interest weekend and midweek bargain breaks. Children sharing parents' room: under 1, no charge; 1–4, £1.50; 5 and over, 50%.

TALYLLYN, Tywyn, Gwynedd   **Map 3**

Minffordd Hotel   [GFG]   *Telephone:* Corris (065 473) 665

A small family-run hotel, once a coaching inn, at the foot of the Talyllyn pass, with the path to Cader Idris no more than 100 yards from the hotel door. It is run by Bernard Pickles and his wife, with their son Jonathan who is responsible for the admirable *Minffordd* restaurant, catering for local gourmets as well as hotel residents. There have been some improvements or upgradings in the place this past year: four of the bedrooms now have bathrooms *en suite*, and there is a new sun lounge – no doubt welcome to those who found the public space a bit crowded when the hotel was full.

Once again, our *Minffordd* dossier has been filled with letters of appreciation from grateful guests. 'Are the Pickles in business or running an altruistic service?' wrote one reader, who went on to speak of 'the total absence of niggling about cost in money or time'. And here is another eloquent bread-and-butter tribute: 'My husband is not very mobile, and we were in search of suitable accommodation for his disability. We really landed on our feet when we stayed at *Minffordd* for a week in July, and were so comfortable and enjoyed it so much we decided to join the happy Pickles family for a further week in September. We cannot speak too highly of the warm welcome we received and the kind family atmosphere. Our every need was anticipated in a quiet charming manner. The service and food, appetisingly served, were both excellent. The packed lunches were *most* enjoyable. And Jonathan was always on the spot to give my husband a helping hand when needed.' *(Mrs M E Lawrence, Kathleen Webster; also Donald H Shute, F Tait and others)*

Open: All year except January but weekends only from November–March. Also closed New Year. Restaurant closed Sunday to non-residents.
Rooms: 7 double – 5 with bath, 2 with shower (2 rooms on ground floor).
Facilities: Sun lounge, lounge, bar, dining room. Just over 2 acres of paddock with spectacular views of the Cader Idris southern escarpment; river at the bottom of the paddock. Situated at the foot of Talyllyn pass, ½ mile from Talyllyn lake; the peak of Cader Idris rises from here, path to summit 100 yards away. Sea at Tywyn 12 miles; lake fishing by arrangement.
Location: Between Dolgellau (7 miles) and Machynlleth (9 miles) on the A487 at junction with the B4405.
Restrictions: No children under 3. No dogs.
Terms: B & B £12–19; dinner, B & B £18.50–27. Set meal: dinner £8.50 (packed lunches on request). Winter mid-week breaks, including 4-day courses for ladies (health and beauty, flower arranging, cookery, etc.). Children 3–12 years, 50% discount if sharing parents' room, otherwise 25%. Special meals by arrangement. Bargain break weekends October–May; 10% reduction for stays over 3 days June–September.

WHITEBROOK, Nr Monmouth, Gwent   **Map 3**

The Crown   [GFG]   *Telephone:* Monmouth (0600) 860 254

This cosy 17th-century inn in the heart of the Tintern forest a mile from the river Wye has long been a mecca for gourmets, both under its previous owners and in the regime of the brothers Jackson who took the place over a couple of years ago. They run special Wine Weekends in the winter, and what they coyly call Great Little Breaks throughout the year; but we like the fact that the guests on these latter jaunts enjoy a free run of the *à la carte* menu.

'Any hotel which claims to offer "superb French meals" in the Wye valley is immediately a target for cynicism, but I'll go out on a limb to say that with the right kind of customer support the *Crown* could easily become a much sought-after venue. The two Jackson brothers who run the hotel both have international restaurant experience, and John Jackson was *sommelier* at *Le Gavroche*. That makes the *Crown* great fun for the enthusiastic amateur wine-lover; it's a very interesting, personal, and financially reasonable wine-list. The food was also delicate and delicious, even though I found the portions over-generous. It's by far the friendliest restaurant I've found for a long time, probably because its bar trade is as important at the moment and there's a convivial relaxed atmosphere both sides of the partition. The rooms over the restaurant are tiny, very pretty and thoughtfully furnished, and they've abandoned all hope of receiving TV well in the valley so it's quiet. The nearby walks are nothing short of idyllic, and it would be ideal for a stopover or a longer stay. (Note. There's nowhere else similar to stay "down the road", so it's better to book rather than arrive casually.)' *(Di Latham; also Andrew C Garner, Sean and Eithne Scallan)*

Open: All year.
Rooms: 7 double, 1 single – 6 with bath, 2 with shower, all with radio and baby-listening.

Facilities: Bar/lounge, restaurant. 2 acres grounds.
Location: Travel west on the M4, take the first exit after crossing Severn Bridge, follow signs for Monmouth (A466) through Tintern and Llandogo. At Bigsweir Bridge, bear left for Whitebrook. *The Crown* is 2 miles up a narrow country lane.
Credit cards: All major credit cards accepted.
Terms: B & B £17–18; dinner, B & B £25.50–30. Full *alc* £14. Winter breaks available October–April. Lecture/wine tasting weekends arranged during winter.

WOLFSCASTLE, Nr Haverfordwest, Pembrokeshire   Map 3

Wolfscastle Country Hotel   [GFG]   *Telephone:* Treffgarne (043 787) 225

Halfway between Haverfordwest and Fishguard, and thus very near the end of the long winding A40, Wolfscastle would be a good centre for touring the south-east corner of Wales if you didn't mind staying about eight miles inland from the coast. 'We aim at attracting, hopefully, everyone,' writes the resident director, Andrew Stirling, but particularly, he adds, 'people who have good eating and drinking in mind and possibly take advantage of our sporting facilities.' The latter refers to the hotel's two squash courts as well as a tennis court, which can be used free of charge by hotel guests. Andrew Stirling himself is a qualified coach who is always willing to play a guest in the absence of another partner. 'Quiet, despite main road, well-appointed, friendly, with good service. Food particularly good and house wine smooth but of strength. In a week's tour of places, this was the best value for money – and incidentally the cheapest.' *(S W Burden)*

Open: All year, except 4 days at Christmas.
Rooms: 7 double, 2 single, 2 suites – 7 with bath, all with colour TV.
Facilities: Lounge, bar lounge, dining room. Garden, tennis court, 2 squash courts. Good area for windsurfing, riding, walking, bird watching, sailing, fishing and golf.
Location: Midway between Fishguard and Haverfordwest, just off the A40.
Credit cards: Access, Barclay/Visa.
Terms (excluding service):   B & B £13–19; dinner, B & B £21.50–£27.50. Set meal: dinner £8.50. Full *alc* £12.50. 10% discount for stays of over 3 days or for parties of 4 or over. Prices negotiable for winter weekends. Reduced rates for children; special meals on request. Occasional squash weekends: coaching, exhibitions and competitions.

Cringletie House Hotel, Peebles

Scotland

Summer Isles Hotel   [GFG]   *Telephone:* Achiltibuie (085 482) 282

Some 25 miles north and west of Ullapool, with the last 15 miles being on a single-track road, the *Summer Isles* ranks as one of the most remote hotels in the Guide. It is surrounded by spectacular mountain- and sea-scapes – wonderful country for walkers, climbers, deer-stalkers and bird-watchers. But though the scenery is rugged, the hospitality of the hotel is the reverse: the *Summer Isles* is a highly individual but thoroughly sophisticated hostelry, with a reputation for many years past for the quality of its cooking. Almost everything is produced locally: the hotel has its own smokehouse, shortly to be enlarged, providing smoked salmon and many other smoked specialities; it also grows nearly all its vegetables and produces its own dairy products, quails, ducks, sucking pigs, veal-calves and rabbits. In this past year, Robert Irvine, the highly individual resident owner of this unusual establishment, has introduced a no-choice four-course dinner menu, but he tells us that he always has standbys for those who have an aversion to, say, shellfish or venison.

Most visitors to *Summer Isles* speak enthusiastically about their stay, and many are regulars who find the combination of an exceptionally wild exterior with a highly civilized interior much to their liking. But there have been a few grumbles: some of the log cabin bedrooms are poorly insulated, and their bathrooms cramped; helpings are said to have been a bit small for hungry day-long walkers; and two readers felt their host differentiated between those who in his mind 'fitted' and those who didn't. But all our reports have endorsed the entry – an uncommonly agreeable hotel in an incomparable location. *(J A Matheson, B M Newman, Kevin Myers, Mary Lindsay, Carole Brown)*

Open: April–October.
Rooms: 11 double, 3 single, 1 suite – 7 with bath.
Facilities: Lounge with bar, library/TV lounge, small cocktail bar. 24,000 acres mountain behind the hotel; shingle beach with boats nearby; bathing beaches 2 and 3 miles away. Walking, climbing, birdwatching, sea trout and brown trout fishing, sea angling.
Location: Take the A835 N of Ullapool for 10 miles, then turn left along single-track road skirting Lochs Lurgain, Badagyle and Oscaig; 15 miles later you reach Achiltibuie.
Restrictions: No children under 8. No dogs in public rooms.
Terms: B & B £15–25. Set meal: dinner £14. Reductions for stays of 6 nights or longer.

ARDUAINE, by Oban, Argyll (Strathclyde) **Map 5**

Loch Melfort Hotel *Telephone:* Kimelford (085 22) 233

Jane and Colin Tindal have been 15 years at this highly successful lochside house just off the coast road between Oban (19 miles) and Lochgilphead (18 miles). Most of the rooms are in a modern annexe, with picture-windows and balconies looking south across the many islands of the archipelago, including Jura and Scarba. Colin Tindal is Vice-Commodore of the Highland Yacht Club, and the hotel is a favourite anchorage for the sailing community; the hotel's own yacht is available to guests for day-trips either with a skipper or on a self-sail basis. 'Spectacular setting indeed, marred only on our visit by appalling West Coast weather – but one must remember that if the weather were always good, this place would become like Benidorm. A spirit of genuine friendliness throughout. Comfortable room, very pleasant bar. Good breakfast served in the bedroom. Wonderfully peaceful.' *(D N Whyte; also Derek Cooper, B M Newman)*

Open: Easter–late October.
Rooms: 27 double, 1 single – 23 with bath. 20 rooms in annexe. (Some rooms on ground floor.) 4 self-catering cottages.
Facilities: Lounge, 2 bars, restaurant. 50 acres grounds on the loch. Yacht for charter. &.
Location: On A816 18 miles N of Lochgilphead, towards Oban.
Credit cards: Access/Euro, American Express.
Terms (no fixed service charge): B & B (continental) £18.50–20. Set meals: English breakfast £2; dinner from £10.50. Reduced rates for children sharing parents' room; special meals provided.

B & B prices, unless otherwise specified, are per person. Where two figures are given, they indicate the range of prices. The lower figure is for one person sharing a double room in the low season, the higher figure is for one person occupying a room alone in the high season. We have also given full- and half-board prices when available.

ARISAIG, Inverness-shire (Highland)   Map 5

Arisaig House   [GFG]   *Telephone:* Arisaig (068 75) 622
Beasdale

Another magnificent Scottish mansion, in a location of outstanding
beauty, is reincarnated as a country hotel in the hyper-comfortable class.
It is also the third case in as many years of a Michelin inspector abandon-
ing his role as critic and becoming a performer – the other two, for the
curious, being *Spindlewood* at Wallcrouch and *Woodhayes* at Whimple
(both q.v.). *Arisaig House* is on the famous 'Road to the Isles' to the west
of Fort William. It has a sheltered position in exceptionally luscious
19-acre grounds, about ten minutes' walk from the shore.

'This must be the most unusual pad in the Highlands. The exterior is
traditional country house Victorian; the interior a perfect Thirties period
piece. Built in 1864 to the designs of Philip Webb, *Arisaig* took fire in the
mid-Thirties and was almost completely rebuilt in 1937. Many of the
original Thirties' light fittings are still extant and the house has the feel of
Munich and *The Thirty Nine Steps*. It was recently purchased by a London
surveyor, John Smither, and his family. Alison, the catering-trained
daughter, attends the reception; David, the chef son-in-law and former
Michelin inspector, cooks, and son Andrew who worked as a waiter in the
Chesterfield Hotel in London runs the restaurant. *Arisaig House* is both
expensive and exclusive. It excludes dogs not only from the house but
from the grounds. Passing trade is discouraged and if you are not staying
you may only dine (jackets and ties preferred) by appointment. Even the
sign at the top of the drive – 'Arisaig House' – does not mention that a
hotel is in the vicinity.

'The gardens are a particular delight; a mini-Inverewe of giant rhododendrons, azaleas, oak and larch and ash. The house itself lies close to
the spectacular Mallaig-Fort William railway line and has its own private
station of Beasdale at which the West Highland line will stop its trains by
request. The views from the bedroom windows and the gravelled terraces
towards the Sound of Arisaig and the small islands which dot the mouth of
Loch nan Uamh are among the finest on the west coast. Total peace and
isolation, disturbed by the occasional click of a croquet ball or the turning
pages of *Country Life*, are about all that *Arisaig* offers. Television sets can
be provided on request but with views like that the small box looks mean.

'Food, nourished by a large and well tended vegetable garden, is
outstandingly good. The Smithers try to provide the kind of atmosphere they would like to find in a Scottish country house. Newly-curtained
and carpetted principally from John Lewis (never knowingly undersold),
Arisaig, alas, lacks the grace and flavour of a traditional Highland home.
Where *Inverlochy* is all oil paintings and period pieces, *Arisaig* is contemporary water colours and fitted carpets. We paid £104 [1982] for the best
bedroom-cum-drawing room in the house – windows on three sides with
staggering aspects – a sum which included afternoon and early morning
tea and an unfaultably good dinner – spinach roulade, salmon and brill
mousseline, rack of lamb, redcurrant and gooseberry tart and cheese. The
wines, a big bonus this, are not over-priced and come from that excellent
merchant Lay & Wheeler of Colchester. If it rains there is a billiards
room.' *(Derek and Janet Cooper; also JREB)*

Open: End March–end October.
Rooms: 11 double, 1 single, 2 suites – all with bath, telephone and colour TV.
Facilities: 3 lounges, restaurant, billiard room, terraces. 19 acres grounds with

croquet and jetty for small landing craft. 10-minute walk to loch shore; sandy/rocky beach, safe bathing.

Location: 3¼ miles SE of Arisaig on the A830; parking.
Restrictions: No children under 10. Dogs by special arrangement only.
Credit cards: Access/Mastercard, Barclay/Visa, Diners.
Terms: B & B £27.50–39.50; dinner, B & B £35–52. Set meal: dinner £12.50 (lunches by arrangement only). Reduced rates for children sharing parents' room. Reductions for stays of 7 nights or more.

AUCHENCAIRN, by Castle Douglas, Dumfries and Galloway   Map 5

Balcary Bay Hotel   *Telephone:* Auchencairn (055 664) 217

'A much modernized smuggler's house built right on (i.e. 20 feet from) the Solway Firth. Everything shows the touch of a professional, but that does not mean the hotel is impersonal. Everyone is very friendly and they do their best to make sure the guests want for nothing. There is a magnificent billiard table. But the scenery is really what makes this hotel so special. It is at the very end of a road that leads nowhere and is surrounded on three sides by hills and on the fourth by the sea. The restaurant is good but could be much better. The general impression is that the cook tries to do more things than he ought and the result is that nothing is done as well as it could be. But the fish is good – a local fisherman brings in whatever he can get every morning.' *(Michael Ridout)*

Open: 1 February–end November.
Rooms: 8 double, 2 single, 1 suite – 4 with bath, 1 with shower, all with telephone, tea-making facilities and TV on request.
Facilities: Large oak-beamed lounge, smaller lounge with TV, cocktail bar, cellar lounge bar, dining room, billiard room. 4 acres grounds. On Balcary Bay, rocky beach with some sandy areas; boating trips arranged; golf courses nearby.
Location: Auchencairn is a small village off the A711 (Dalbeattie–Kirkcudbright). Hotel is 2 miles from village.
Restriction: No dogs in public rooms.
Credit cards: All major credit cards accepted.
Terms: B & B £16–24; full board £28.50–35.50. Set meals: lunch £4 (picnic lunches available), dinner £8.50; full *alc* £12. Special winter rates November–March: 5% discount for stays longer than 3 days. Reduced rates and special meals for children.

BALLATER, Aberdeenshire (Grampian)   Map 5

Tullich Lodge   [GFG]   *Telephone:* Ballater (0338) 55406

Hector Macdonald and Neil Bannister acquired this late 19th-century baronial mansion on a commanding site overlooking Deeside and the Grampians in 1968, renovated it in High Victorian style, and have been running it as a highly personal – not to say idiosyncratic – hotel ever since. We had had an entry for *Tullich Lodge* since our first edition, but omitted it from the 1982 Guide after a long detailed report from one of our regular correspondents suggested some fall from previously high standards. Perhaps this guest was singularly unfortunate, but we had also had mixed reports on the hotel's no-choice menus – some feeling that they had dined exceptionally well, and others only so-so. We think it easier to make mistakes with an out-of-the-ordinary-run establishment, and certainly felt that we had done the hotel an injustice when we received the report below from the owner of the admirable *Scarista House* on Harris (q.v.). But we should be glad to hear from other recent lodgers.

'This is without doubt the best place we have ever stayed, and we had here the two best dinners. It's highly individual. The proprietors are themselves, and don't put on faces, but we liked them all the more for it. We could have suspected their friendliness and indeed kindness were assumed because we're in the same line of business but the general satisfaction obvious in the demeanour of all the other guests entirely belied this. Our room was superb – elegant antiques with fabrics and fittings most carefully chosen to match. Roger et Gallet soap in the bathroom. I don't usually like help-yourself breakfasts, but theirs was really good – absolutely fresh at 9 o'clock. So many different good points. Lovingly polished silver and mahogany panelling in the dining room, good coffee, speed and enthusiasm of Hector Macdonald, dashing from plant-watering to tap-mending to bag-carrying. Astonishingly reasonable bill. Not reasonable – underpriced.' *(Alison Johnson)*

Open: April–November.
Rooms: 7 double, 3 single – 8 with bath, some with telephone.
Facilities: Drawing room, sitting room, bar, dining room. 5 acres woodland garden.
Location: 1½ miles E of Ballater on A93 Braemar/Aberdeen road.
Restriction: No dogs in public rooms.
Credit card: American Express.
Terms: B & B £27–30; dinner, B & B £33–37; full board £238–259 per week. Set meals: lunch £8.50, dinner £9.50. Reduced rates for children sharing parents' room or during quiet periods; high tea served in kitchen.

BALQUHIDDER, Perthshire (Central) Map 5

Ledcreich [GFG] *Telephone:* Strathyre (087 74) 230

There are plenty of hotels run by a husband and wife, but enterprises in which other members of the family participate are relatively uncommon in Britain, though common enough in France. Harry and Olive Hilditch bought *Ledcreich* five years ago, having previously had a larger hotel on Skye, and having been in the hotel business all their working lives. It is more a restaurant with rooms than a hotel proper – four bedrooms but 40 covers. The house is early 18th-century in a secluded glen on Loch Voil on which the hotel has private fishing rights (salmon, trout and char). 'The whole operation is based on "The Family",' writes Harry Hilditch. 'We try to give our visitors the feeling of being a guest at a Scottish country house of more leisured days. Chef Duncan Hilditch buys with care and cooks with speed and imagination. His wife Anne looks after the dining room. Wine buyer Daniel looks after the small bar, is reasonably knowledgeable on the wine-list and our 30-odd malt whisky selection. My wife and I are moving (gracefully, we hope!) towards retirement, but keep a supervisory eye and ear on the entire performance, trying to ensure that the efforts of the cast get over the footlights at all times. We enjoy our work, and so long as our guests also enjoy our efforts, we are happy!'

'This small but beautifully situated hotel is miles up the road to nowhere overlooking loch Voil. There are only four bedrooms, but they are delightfully furnished. The food at dinner and breakfast was splendid. A

game casserole was particularly memorable. Definitely worth an entry.'
(A R Campbell)

Open: All year, except a few days at Easter and in October. Restaurant closed Tuesday in winter.
Rooms: 3 double, 1 single – 2 with bath, 2 with shower, all with tea-making facilities.
Facilities: Residents' lounge with TV, coffee lounge, bar, restaurant; conference room. 20 acres grounds; sandy beach adjoins hotel, private fishing rights (trout, char, salmon) on Loch Voil. Golf, tennis, squash, waterskiing and sailing available nearby; deer-stalking by arrangement.
Location: Just off the A84 between Strathyre and Lochearnhead; turn off at the Kingshouse Hotel, following sign 'to the Braes o' Balquhidder'; by village hall go up 'no through road' with Loch Voil on left; *Ledcreich* is just beyond forestry car park.
Restriction: No dogs.
Credit cards: All major credit cards accepted.
Terms (service optional): B & B £15–17; dinner, B & B £24.50–27.50. Set meals: lunch £8, dinner £12.50; full *alc* £16. Reduced rates and special meals for children. Greek/Sicilian evenings, etc.

BANCHORY, Kincardine and Deeside (Grampian)   **Map 5**

Banchory Lodge Hotel   *Telephone:* Banchory (033 02) 2625

A well-bred Georgian building in a felicitous position, close to the confluence of the Dee and the Water of Feugh, and with fishing rights in the water directly opposite the hotel. It's naturally popular with the fishing fraternity, but there are also three good golf courses within easy reach, and magnificent walking and climbing to be had in the vicinity of Deeside. And the house itself, full of Victorian and Edwardian furniture and bric-à-brac lovingly collected over the years by the resident owners, Mr and Mrs Jaffrays, is a friendly place – with flower arrangements and open fires and other signs of welcome to guests. There has been some criticism this past year of details of the catering: an unsuccessful fruit salad and 'abysmal' packed lunches. But in general the food is commended – especially local products like Dee salmon, and good quality beef – and most particularly an enormous and celebrated Sunday evening cold buffet. *(Lady Mocatta and others)*

Open: 1 February–14 December.
Rooms: 30 double, 3 single – 27 with bath, 1 with shower, 8 with TV, all with radio, tea-making facilities and baby-listening. 6 rooms with bath in annexe. (1 room on ground floor.)
Facilities: 2 large lounges (1 with colour TV) overlooking the river, bar, dining room. 12 acres grounds; salmon and trout fishing on the river Dee. Golf courses at Banchory, Aboyne and Ballater; tennis, putting, bowling at Banchory; Glenshee ski slopes an hour's drive west.
Location: On the A93 east of Aboyne.
Credit cards: American Express, Barclay/Visa.
Terms (excluding service): B & B £22–25.30; dinner, B & B £30–34.75; full board (minimum 3 nights) £36.80. Set meals: lunch £5; dinner £9.50–10.95. Reduced rates and special meals for children.

158

BANFF, Banffshire (Grampian)   **Map 5**

The County Hotel   [GFG]   *Telephone:* Banff (026 12) 5353
High Street

'When John Wesley visited Banff, he described it as "one of the neatest and most elegant towns that I have seen in Scotland". It still has some remarkable Georgian architecture; don't miss Duff House, built after a design by William Adam and modelled on the Villa Borghese. If you are looking for Georgian elegance and comfort, you should make for the *County Hotel* on the banks of the river Deveron, looking across the river to Macduff. The proprietors, Michael MacKenzie and Frederic Symonds, bought the hotel in the spring of 1981, and have refurbished it pleasantly. Particular attention is paid to the food which relies to a praiseworthy extent on the excellent local fish and meat. Those who travel with a dog will be pleased to hear that the garden room which opens on to a small walled garden, can be reserved for themselves and their pet(s). Elsewhere in the hotel, dogs are not particularly welcome. Banff is an ideal centre for golf and fishing. There are excellent beats for salmon and sea trout on the Deveron, and the hotel has its own rod rack and drying room. It is also a good centre for exploring the Moray coast and the sea towns of Cullen, Buckie, Portknockie, Pennan and Portsoy.' *(Derek Cooper)*

Open: All year, except last 3 weeks of January.
Rooms: 4 double, 2 single – all with bath, telephone, radio, mono TV and tea-making facilities.
Facilities: Drawing room, dining room. ½-acre garden with patio. Fishing on river Deveron (advance booking for rods); tennis, golf, sea angling, shooting, swimming, ponytrekking available nearby.
Location: In town centre; car park, 1 covered garage.
Restrictions: No children under 10. Dogs allowed by prior arrangement, but not in public rooms.
Credit cards: All major credit cards accepted.
Terms: B & B £17–24; dinner, B & B £22–30. Set meal: dinner £11.75; full *alc* (lunch only) £7.25. Bargain breaks (minimum 2 days); Golfing, Exploring, Fishing breaks, Christmas/New Year package.

BEATTOCK, Moffat, Dumfries and Galloway   **Map 5**

Auchen Castle Hotel   *Telephone:* Beattock (068 33) 407
                                                      Telex: 777205 Auchen

'A slightly stern-looking greystone mansion' was how, in last year's entry, we described this 1849 castle a mile north of the village of Beattock, and with direct access to the A74. We had been misled by the brochure, and the owner, Mr Beckh, in a very civil letter, corrects us: 'The hotel may be forbidding, but it certainly isn't grey stone, but a rather pretty pinkish sandstone which is indeed rare.' Whatever its appearance, the *Auchen Castle*, in its 17 acres of gardens and grounds overlooking the upper Annandale, clearly has qualities which endear it to its guests. Mr Beckh says that he hopes 'we are acceptably informal and without pretensions'. Here is how one loyal subject gives his verdict:
    'I stay at this hotel very frequently, perhaps 20 times per annum. It is ideally situated for easy drives to Glasgow, Carlisle or even Edinburgh.

159

The owners and their staff are always helpful and courteous. The accommodation is most satisfactory and the food is exceptional. I am never able to understand how such a small hotel can provide such a wide range of dishes and wines. The fishing in the hotel loch is superb, although the shooting is variable.' *(R S White; also R D Maclagan)*
(Note: The chef at the time of Mr White's visit, who had been trained at Sharrow Bay, left in the spring of 1982. We should be glad to hear readers' reactions to his successor.)

Open: 1 February–30 November.
Rooms: 28 – 16 with bath, 12 with shower, all with radio, colour TV and baby-listening. 10 of the rooms with shower are in the annexe, Cedar Lodge.
Facilities: Lounge, TV lounge, bar, dining room; private party dining room/conference room; Saturday dinner-dance October–March. 17 acres grounds with trout-stocked loch with boat. River Annan provides fishing for salmon, trout, sea trout. Golf, riding, tennis, sailing nearby.
Location: 1 mile N of Beattock village with signed access from the A74.
Credit cards: All major credit cards accepted.
Terms (no fixed service charge): B & B £10–23.50. Set meal: dinner £7 and £9.50. (Bar lunches available.) Special 'Border Breaks' and 'Dine, Dance and Stay-the-Night' rates; also a Golf holiday. Reduced rates and special meals for children.

BRIDGE OF ORCHY, Argyll (Strathclyde) Map 5

Inveroran Hotel *Telephone:* Tyndrum (083 84) 220

Inveroran is a modest but sympathetic coaching inn set on the edge of Loch Tulla, and surrounded by high hills – marvellous walking and climbing country, and quite populous now that it is on the West Highway Way; there is also fishing in river and loch, swimming in loch and burn, and bird-watching. Last year, we printed two glowing testimonials to the place. Some readers this year have felt that the testifiers' glasses had been rose-tinted: we should have mentioned that the standard of decor was no more than moderate, that you had to be punctual for dinner, that portions at meals for robust hill-walkers could have been larger, and that post-prandial public sector accommodation was limited. We pass these details on, but would also add that other readers have consistently praised the welcome of Margaret Gravell and the outstanding value of her dinner, B & B – £14 in 1982. 'It is difficult to believe,' writes one reader, 'that the price includes a five-course meal including, for example, lentil soup with excellent home-made bread, trout fillet, roast pork with broccoli, roast potatoes and french beans, a choice of gooseberry fool, strawberry shortcake or fresh fruit salad and a decent cheese board. All good Scottish "plain" cooking. . . .' Meanwhile, one of last year's rose-tinted reporters has written again about the delights of the place, extolling both the generosity of the breakfasts as well as the dinners, and concluding: 'We take coffee in one of the two lounges where we all enjoy comparing our hill-walking adventures and observations until we retire filled with joy to our simple little bedrooms – soon to be lulled to sleep by the sound of the Orain burn.' *(Pippa Norris, P and J Gillett; also Dr and Mrs H J Denton)*

Open: March–end November; also 4 days at New Year and other times in winter depending on availability of water (it is sometimes frozen).
Rooms: 6 double, 2 single – all with tea-making facilities. (1 room on ground floor.)

Facilities: 2 lounges, bar, dining room. Spontaneous *ceilidhs* (Scottish song and dance). 1 acre garden. Safe bathing in the loch, boats for fishing; salmon and trout on the river Orchy, and several hill lochs; splendid scenery – fine walking and climbing country; skiing nearby in winter. &

Location: 3 miles from Bridge of Orchy (railway station).

Restriction: No children under 5.

Terms (excluding VAT and service): B & B £9.50; dinner, B & B £16; full board £98 per week. Set meal: dinner £7.50. Reduced rates for children sharing parents' room; special meals provided.

BUNESSAN, Isle of Mull (Strathclyde)   **Map 5**

Ardfenaig House [GFG]   *Telephone:* Fionnphort (068 17) 210

'The house stands at the head of a small loch and is approached by a very long lane so the feeling of peace and remoteness is complete. The house is not distinguished architecturally, but is set in a delightful garden and inside is furnished and decorated with exquisite taste and lovely old furniture and paintings, obviously from the family homes of the two owners, Robin Drummond-Hay and Ian Bowles. There are only five rooms for guests who share three bathrooms, and it all felt more like a house party than a hotel. We were reminded of childhood visits to grandparents, in an age before inflation had made such luxurious living impossible. Our bedroom was so beautifully and comfortably furnished (with a rocking chair and books too) that it was almost a wrench to go downstairs to the small bar and delightful drawing room (complete with grand piano, all possible magazines and newspapers). The whole ambience of luxury, good taste and charm was amply supported by the *wonderful* food. There was no choice at dinner (though we were asked if we had any strong dislikes or diet requirements) and none really was necessary. This is the way people can no longer afford to live, except on a very large income or by opening their home. We've never before felt so thoroughly at home – it was almost decadent, though naturally in the very best taste.' *(Lt-Cdr and Mrs R Kirby Harris)*

Last year's report, slightly truncated, is reproduced above. A recent visitor writes: 'Just returned from annual treat. Top-notch standard marvellously maintained . . . everyone leaves purring loudly!' *(Mary Lindsay; also D J Ironside)*

Open: 1 May–30 September.

Rooms: 4 double, 1 single (but max. 6 guests at a time) – all with tea-making facilities.

Facilities: Lounge, music room, dining room. 16 acres grounds sloping down to loch which has shingle beach, but plenty of sandy beaches nearby. Fishing; safe bathing.

Location: 3 miles from Bunessan on the Iona ferry road. The hotel's long drive is on the right.

Restrictions: No children under 13. No dogs in public rooms.

Terms (excluding VAT and 10% service charge): Dinner, B & B £30. Set meal: dinner £10.50. 10% reduction for 6 days or more.

'Full *alc*', unless otherwise stated, means the hotel's own estimate of the price per person for a three-course dinner with half a bottle of house wine, service and taxes included.

161

The Roman Camp Hotel   [GFG]   *Telephone:* Callander (0877) 30003

This picturesque 17th-century hunting lodge in 20 acres of grounds – it was built for the Dukes of Perth in 1625, and looks rather like a modest château – is full of touches of unusual quality. There are splendid formal gardens with natural woodland leading down to the river Teith (specially recommended for rhododendrons end May and early June). Inside, the house has its original panelling in the entrance, there's a painted ceiling in the dining room and a panelled library. It's about 50 miles from Edinburgh and Glasgow, and also makes a good base for exploring the Trossachs.

We had an entry for *The Roman Camp* in earlier editions, but had to leave it out when its virtues deteriorated. We were delighted to learn that Mr and Mrs Denzler, formerly of the well-esteemed *Denzlers* restaurant in Edinburgh, had taken it over. Here is a first report of the new regime: 'As an hotel one would find it hard to name a disappointment. The setting amongst well kept gardens full of rhododendrons and beside the lovely river Teith is superb. Fresh biscuits from the kitchens, fruit and flowers replenished daily in rooms are an imaginative touch. If one must offer constructive comment, mention might be made of low-power light bulbs. The food deserves special praise. As vegetarians we approach even high-class hotels with apprehension. For short stays vegetarians should have no fears here. The crisp, well-displayed and numerous types of vegetables with equally varied sauces, and especially the aubergine fritters were sufficient to defeat us before we could reach the delights of the apfelstrudels. While the rest of the hotel is 17th-century with beautiful and well-furnished rooms, some with log fires, the dining room is modern and comfortable, and is supervised in very individualistic style by an Italian head waiter who helps his customers with an ease belonging more to the age of the *Orient Express.*' *(B C McDermott)*

Open: All year, except for a short winter period yet to be arranged.
Rooms: 10 double, 4 single, 1 suite – 10 with bath, all with telephone, colour TV and tea-making facilities. 5 rooms in annexe. (3 rooms on ground floor.)
Facilities: Lounge, sun lounge, panelled library with small chapel, bar, dining room. 20 acres grounds with free fishing on river Teith; golf courses nearby.
Location: Enter drive to hotel directly from Callander main street (narrow entrance between two pink cottages at hotel sign); parking.
Restriction: No dogs in public rooms.
Terms: B & B £15–25; dinner, B & B (minimum 2 days) £22–33. Full *alc* £14 (no fixed service charge). Reduced rates for stays over 5 nights. Special rates for children on request.

Riverside Inn   [GFG]   *Telephone:* Canonbie (054 15) 295

Rather more sophisticated than the word 'inn' might suggest, this small 17th-century hotel is well-placed for touring Hadrian's Wall, the Solway Coast and other attractive areas in the vicinity. It is on the A7, but there is little traffic after 6 p.m. and Canonbie is due to be by-passed in the winter of 1983–84.

'An old fisherman's retreat on the banks of the Esk which has been considerably updated in traditional style representing a surprisingly sophisticated venture in such a quiet out-of-the-way place, the only intrusion being through traffic during peak hours. The atmosphere is one of comfortable lightness; there is a small lounge/foyer, a much larger split-level bar with pale wood and traditional furniture and a very pleasant dining room. Accommodation is limited to four pleasant double rooms with bathrooms. The policy for dinner is a small menu but considerable attention to detail. There is not much to do except walk by the river, which is extremely picturesque, so I recommend retiring to the attractive bar and sampling real ale or a tot from the range of malt whiskies. Breakfast was also good with quality coffee served.' *(R A Nisbet)*

Last year's entry, quoted above, is 'thoroughly endorsed' by recent visitors: 'Excellent room, far larger than expected, well-equipped with all the extras normally found only in much larger establishments. All spotlessly clean. Super dinner from small menu for £8.25 [1982] plus short interesting wine list. Enormous breakfast included in room price. No smoking in dining room means an enjoyable meal. Excellent value in an attractive area.' *(Jeremy Temple)*

Open: All year, except Christmas and two weeks in January.
Rooms: 4 double – 3 with bath, 1 with shower, all with radio, mono TV and tea-making facilities.
Facilities: Residents' lounge with TV, lounge bar, dining room. Garden. Park with children's play area and tennis courts nearby; fishing permits available from hotel. A good centre for visiting Hadrian's Wall.
Location: On the A7 Carlisle to Langholm road.
Restriction: No dogs.
Terms (no service charge): B & B £16–20; full board £160 per week (including packed lunch). Set meal: dinner £8.75. Special off-peak breaks. Reduced rates for children; special meals provided.

CRINAN, by Lochgilphead, Argyll (Strathclyde)   **Map 5**

Crinan Hotel   *Telephone:* Crinan (054 683) 235/243

The *Crinan* is one of those fortunate hotels that can attract custom by virtue of an incomparable location: it lies at the seaward end of the eight-mile Crinan Canal looking across to the mountains of Mull and the Isle of Jura. At closer quarters, it has a ringside seat over a yacht basin and the constant movement of craft, big and small, bound for the Inner and Outer Hebrides. A major fire gutted much of the original Victorian building, so the present hotel offers all the 1980s mod cons, including a lift; and the Ryans have gone to much time and trouble to produce rooms that are in their decor a match for the views outside. The hotel also prides itself on its restaurants: relatively conventional in the main dining room, and a more expensive seafood restaurant called *Lock 16* on the top floor. In our entry last year, we mentioned a reader's disappointment at finding *Lock 16* closed; we gather this is a rare occurrence when there is absolutely no fresh seafood to be had from the local fishing boats.

'I came to Crinan one April afternoon, driving aimlessly westward, determined on a cheap bed and breakfast trip. The moment I came round the corner and down the hill, however, I was immediately seduced by the purple prose panorama of Loch Crinan laid out before me, and checked into the *Crinan Hotel* forthwith. I stood on my balcony, facing the bay and a ruined castle, and I knew I had made the right decision. I ate an excellent dinner watching the matchless sunset over the distant mountains of Scarba. Coffee was do-it-yourself in the lounge next door – open log fire and such dim lighting that I almost had to crawl under the lampshade in order to write this report! Comfortable night in brown floral bedroom and boiling hot bath in brown bathwater (peat), good coffee for breakfast. *I shall return!' (Caroline Currie; also A Derville, P W D Roberts)*

Open: Mid March–end October.

Rooms: 20 double, 2 single – 20 with bath, 2 with shower, 9 with private balconies, all with telephone, radio and baby-listening.

Facilities: Lift, 2 lounges (1 with TV), cocktail bar, roof bar, dining room, roof-top restaurant – *Lock 16* – specializing in seafood; sauna. 1 acre grounds with well-kept garden on the loch side; fishing, sailing, waterskiing.

Location: NW of Lochgilphead by the A816, then take the A841 which skirts the Crinan Canal, 9 miles long and flowing into the Sound of Jura.

Restriction: Dogs at management's discretion; own bedding required.

Credit cards: Access/Euro, American Express, Diners, Visa.

Terms (no fixed service charge): B & B (continental) £15.50–22.50. Set meals: lunch from £1.50 (*à la carte* buffet); dinner in dining room £10.50; dinner in *Lock 16* £16.50. Reduced rates for children sharing parents' room; early dinners provided. Special rates mid March–1 May.

DALRY, Castle-Douglas, Kirkcudbrightshire (Strathclyde)   **Map 5**

Milton Park Hotel   *Telephone:* Dalry (064 43) 286

Scottish house of circa 1860, not beautiful but solid (doors well-made, etc.). Large garden. Overlooks the waters of the Ken valley. Superb views of hills, moorland, etc. Pleasantly furnished in a rather old-fashioned manner. Our bedroom had attractive art nouveau furniture and splendid Maples beds, blankets slightly worn but gave impression of staying in a private house rather than a Hilton. The Graysons who run the hotel – he does bar, she cooking – extremely pleasant. Staff delightful and willing. Food simple but excellent; no lapses, but no attempts at elaborate sauces, etc. Coffee very good. Clean damask napkins at every meal. China new and pleasant – Royal Doulton for breakfast, Spode for dinner. Other guests included several amiable fishermen (great centre for fishing) plus North-country middle-aged and some young. Atmosphere remarkably pleasant. Marvellous value for money compared with all other hotels we stayed at in Scotland.' (Christina Bewley)

We repeat our original entry (above) because we believe it faithfully records nearly all the important features of *Milton Park*. It clearly isn't one of those soulless immaculately maintained hotels, and several readers have pointed out minor defects or inconveniences – such as a collapsed sofa in the lounge or the absence of a shelf above the wash-basin. Dinner punctually served at 7 p.m. is 'maddeningly early' for some. The food, we gather, is a bit patchy, but very good indeed at times – even if not every one has appreciated the after-dinner coffee. Having got their various grumbles off their chests, however, readers have invariably gone on to appreciate the many good qualities of the house, also its attractive garden and – universally commended – its amazingly reasonable prices. A particular vote of thanks was recorded by one correspondent who had been with a party of ornithologists, one of whose members had suffered a slight heart attack; Mrs Grayson had driven him and his wife to Glasgow the following day rather than let them suffer the journey on a bus. (*L N Cartwright, Antony Derville, J & J W, R M Sinclair*)

Open: End March–end October. Also open over Christmas and New Year if sufficient demand.
Rooms: 15 double, 2 single.
Facilities: Residents' lounge, TV, bar lounge, 2 dining rooms. 4–5 acres extensive landscaped garden overlooking the waters of the Ken valley. Boats available for excellent fishing on 5 nearby lochs (brown trout, rainbow trout, pike and perch); river and sea fishing close by. Tennis court; golf 3 miles.
Location: NW of St John's town of Dalry, which is on the A713, near Earlston loch.
Restriction: No dogs in public rooms.
Terms (no fixed service charge): B & B £12; dinner, B & B £20 (weekly £125). Set meal: dinner £9. Reduced rates and special meals for children.

DRUMNADROCHIT, Inverness-shire (Highland)   Map 5

Polmaily House   *Telephone:* Drumnadrochit (045 62) 343

Many owners of country-house hotels aspire to create that staying-in-a-private home atmosphere even if there has to be a reckoning at the end of the day. Successful practitioners are not so common, though we rate Veronica Brown, now in her 18th year at *Polmaily House*, of that company. Her rambling Edwardian mansion in its 22 secluded peaceful acres, a short distance from Loch Ness (a visit to the Loch Ness Monster museum is recommended), is full of unusual and beautiful things. One appreciative reader writes: 'Miss Brown displays her household treasures very freely. None has ever been removed by passing guests and we are inclined to believe that this happy state of affairs has been promoted by the domestic serenity, warm homeliness and glowing surroundings which seem to bring out the best in visitors.' Attracting the right kind of guests is of course of the essence of this sort of hotel. We were amused by a note to us from Miss Brown: 'Have met some lovely people – from hitch-hikers to Rolls Roycers – who seem to appreciate our personal style very much, all faithfully clutching your Guide.' In fairness, we have to say that at least one of those clutching faithful failed to be enchanted and moved on – finding the house disagreeably cold in a wet May, and not caring for the fact that the house regularly offers a curry as one of two main-course options at dinner. His was, however, an isolated case. More typical was this reaction:

'We found the house charming, and completely free from the twin scourges of designer and contract furnisher. Every piece of furniture and every curtain or bedspread looks like the owner's own choice, and the place is full of fascinating nooks and crevices containing collections of this and that.' (*Alison Johnson; also George and Trudie Mair*). *STOP PRESS. As we go to press we learn that the hotel has been sold.*

Open: Beginning May–end October.
Rooms: 9 – 5 with bath, all with telephone and radio. (1 with four-poster bed.)
Facilities: Drawing room, residents' lounge, bar, dining room, reading room. 22 acres garden with tennis, unheated swimming pool, putting, clay pigeon shooting; ponytrekking and fishing nearby.

Location: 17 miles from Inverness W of Drumnadrochit on the road to Cannich.
Restrictions: No children under 8. Dogs at the management's discretion.
Credit cards: Access/Euro, American Express, Barclay/Visa.
Terms (excluding VAT; no service charge): Dinner, B & B £23–26.50. Set meals:
bar lunch from £1.50; dinner £10. Special breaks, holiday courses.

DUNBLANE, Perthshire (Central)   Map 5

Cromlix House [GFG]   *Telephone:* Dunblane (0786) 822125

A new star is born in the hotel firmament, possibly a rival to *Inverlochy* at
Fort William, though at more moderate prices. *Cromlix House* opened its
gates in May 1981. Here is a first report:
'The Eden family know something about entertaining. For a hundred
years they have held large house parties for the annual slaughter on the
moors. In its heyday, when Edward VII came to annihilate the grouse,
huge and rambling *Cromlix* required ten indoor servants and ten gardeners to keep it in trim. It was a very self-contained place, with its own fruit
and vegetable gardens, even its own private chapel and minister. Last
year the Hon Ronald Eden (author of that excellent anatomy of grouse,
Going to the Moors), whose family have owned the 5,000 acres of *Cromlix*
for four centuries, decided to turn the house into a hotel. He and his
advisers have carved out eleven rooms, seven of them suites, each with its
own drawing room, bedroom and bathroom. Some of the baths at
Cromlix are freestanding and attended by finely wrought brass fittings –
baths fit of course for a king. Everywhere are oil paintings, prints,
watercolours, portraits and tapestries scattered with the profusion that
comes from four centuries of possessions. The rooms are elegant, the
conservatory large enough for a Palm Court orchestra which is happily
absent. There are huge armchairs for sleeping off elaborate Edwardian
meals, blazing fires fed by seacoal from one of the few independent mines
left in Scotland and the perfect peace you only get in the depths of the
countryside. So absolute that a Californian endured one night and then
fled up the road to the more bustling ambience of *Gleneagles*. Currently
the chef is 22-year-old Andrew Murray who came to *Cromlix* by way of
the *Malmaison* in Glasgow and *Inverlochy Castle*. His cooking is of star
quality – all the produce fresh. Were I to select the top five country-house
hotels in Scotland, *Cromlix* would be among them.' *(Derek Cooper; also
BI)*
*Note: as we go to press, we learn that Andrew Murray has left. His
successor is Mark Napper, who has been head chef at Warpool Court, St
David's (q.v.) for the past 7 years. From a visit we made to* Cromlix *in
September 1982, we would award Mark Napper a similar accolade and in
general share Derek Cooper's enthusiasm for an outstanding hotel and an
exceptionally sympathetic staff.*

Open: All year (except some days between Christmas and New Year).
Rooms: 4 double, 7 suites – 10 with bath, 1 with shower, 7 (suites) with colour TV,
all with telephone and baby-listening.
Facilities: Lobby, morning room, drawing room, conservatory, restaurant. 5,000
acres grounds with fishing, tennis, shooting (advance booking advisable).
Location: ½ mile N of Kinbuck, 4 miles S of Braco; take the A9 to Dunblane,
then the B8033 to Kinbuck; parking.
Credit cards: Access, American Express, Barclay/Visa, Diners.
Terms: B & B £30–45; dinner, B & B £45–60; full board £52.50–67.50. Set meals

(there is no formal menu): lunch from £7.50, dinner from £17. Reduced rates for children.

DUNKELD, Perthshire (Tayside)   Map 5

The Atholl Arms Hotel   *Telephone:* Dunkeld (035 02) 219

A well-run traditional hotel in the centre of town (though village would be the more appropriate, despite Dunkeld's cathedral), overlooking the 5-arched bridge over the river Tay which Telford built in 1809.

'The view in autumn across the wide fast-flowing Tay towards Birnam Woods is quite superb. The hotel has a most attractive entrance hall which is always full of quiet activity. At dinner the bar was a bit bare Scottish-style, so we carried our sherry through to the hall. Dinner was a pleasant surprise. Friendly and efficient waitresses of mature years knew their job and had probably been with the hotel for some time: very much in character with the clean quiet atmosphere of the whole place: not out of date but undisturbed by life. The bedroom was a little small but nice enough, and the bathroom, though not *en suite*, was very handy. The baths had lovely big taps and were big enough to lie down in. (My son's single room was more spacious with armchair and gas fire.)' *(M L Ferrar)*

Open: All year.
Rooms: 14 double, 6 single, 1 triple (quiet rooms at back of house) – 4 with bath.
Facilities: Lounge, residents' lounge with TV, bar. Grounds of ½ acre on river bank, overlooking river Tay; fishing available in the area.
Location: In town centre; parking for 20 cars.
Restriction: No dogs in dining room.
Credit cards: All major credit cards accepted.
Terms (no fixed service charge): B & B £11.50–13.50; dinner B & B £18.50–20.50. Weekly B & B £70, half board £120. Set meal: dinner £7. Reduced rates for children and special meals on request.

DUROR, Appin, Argyll (Strathclyde)   Map 5

The Stewart Hotel   *Telephone:* Duror (063 174) 268
                                        Telex: 778866

'The setting is beautiful and unspoilt (the view from our bedroom window, westwards over the blue water of Loch Linnhe and the stark Morvern mountains beyond, was as good as anything in Greece), and there are wonderful walks to be had in the hills just behind the hotel. The hotel, which faces west, gets the full benefit of any sun that's around (you can sit outside on a terrace above the delightfully lush garden, to read or have a drink). Inside, it has none of the musty baronial gloom of so many Scottish houses: the rooms are cheerfully furnished, à la Habitat, with lots of yellow and orange (the dining room is yellow and green, cleverly spotlit none of those ghastly overhead chandeliers). The lounge is much more welcoming than the usual morgue. The bedrooms, in the neatly-designed modern wing, are small but comfortable, and spotlessly clean.

'*Food.* Obviously a lot of care has gone into the planning of the sophisticated dinner menus. It was delicious to look at as well as to eat, but the portions were very small: perhaps there's a bit too much *minceur* in this cuisine? Otherwise, we had no complaints. The young couple who run the place have a young family of their own, which helps create a relaxed atmosphere. In short, a pleasant family hotel in an exceptionally beautiful part of the British Isles.' *(Sally Sampson)*

Recent reports endorse last year's entry (extracts above), and David Assenti, the resident owner, seems to have taken to heart the reference to mean portions: no complaints on that score this year. One reader did complain of his dinner being served too fast; he felt the meal deserved more leisurely enjoyment. But there is no doubt that this family hotel is in general continuing to give solid satisfaction. *(Sir Patrick Reilly, M D A Jamieson)*

Open: End March–end October/November.

Rooms: 26 double, 3 family suites – all with bath, radio, tea-making facilities, baby-listening and TV on request. (16 rooms on ground floor.)

Facilities: Lounge, TV room, bar, restaurant. Folk singing group most weekends. 15 acres woodlands and terraced garden with many rare shrubs and plants, which leads down to the river Duror at the bottom of the garden; hotel overlooks loch Linnhe; rock beach, safe bathing 2 miles; fishing available, also riding and pony-trekking; sailing, boating, hill walking, rock climbing, skiing.

Restriction: Dogs in bedroom only, at the management's discretion.

Location: 5 miles S of Ballachulish Bridge on the A828 to Oban. Oban 30 miles S, Fort William 17 miles N.

Credit cards: All major credit cards accepted.

Terms (service at guest's discretion): B & B £14.75–23.75; dinner, B & B £20.50–35.50 (2 nights minimum). Set meals: lunch £1.90 (packed lunches also available), dinner £9.50. Special breaks in April, May, September and October. Children free if sharing parents' room; special meals provided.

ERISKA, Ledaig, Connel, Argyll (Strathclyde)   Map 5

Isle of Eriska Hotel   [GFG]   *Telephone:* Ledaig (063 172) 371
Telex: 727897 DOOCOT-G attn ERISKA

There are very few private island hotels in Britain, and only one *Isle of Eriska*. The island itself is not extensive – only one mile by half a mile, joined to the mainland by a private bridge, 12 miles north of Oban. The house is confident Victorian baronial – like so many hotels scattered throughout Scotland. What makes the hotel special is the warmth of hospitality offered by Robin and Sheena Buchanan Smith. In the last decade, *Eriska* has become one of the small band of exclusive top country-house hotels – to be mentioned in the same breath as, say, *Sharrow Bay* on Ullswater, *Miller Howe* on Windermere, *Gravetye* at East Grinstead or *Inverlochy Castle* at Fort William. And, like these other chosen few, it has its detractors. Our entry for the hotel last year was one of the longest in the book – offering two strongly contrasting views about the place. Some of the bedrooms certainly lack elegance, and some of the beds and bedding should be put out to grass, but this year, we are glad to report, the ayes clearly have it. Whatever the opposition may say – and not everyone is enthusiastic about the cooking, which in our personal view falls some way short of distinction – there is no doubting the case for *Eriska* as put by the report below:

'Without hesitation, this is the best country house hotel we have stayed in in the British Isles and we have stayed in many. Expensive yes, but worth every penny. We spent four absolutely delightful days, cossetted by the more than helpful staff. My children's filthy track suits happily washed each night, our enquiries about excursions – ferry times, opening times, decent restaurants, etc., suggested and always checked out without our asking. Our bedroom was large and airy – I slept like a log each night! There was a bowl of fruit in each room, hair-dryer, trouser press, radio, beautiful soaps and bubble bath in the bathroom as well as soap flakes and rack for clothes drying.

But really it was the food – simple but simply outstanding. Such a change from the precious, French-apeing variety found in most English country-house hotels and exactly what should be offered. The breakfasts changed each day – fresh orange juice on the table and then "help yourself" to a vast selection of stewed fruits, home-made yogurt with a tart blackcurrant sauce, porridge and then . . . silver dishes on the sideboard offering maybe kippers, scrambled eggs, kidneys, sausages, mushrooms etc., etc. One day they had pancakes, herrings in oatmeal. Never the same choice twice running. It was a pleasure. At morning coffee and tea time you help yourself from the side board by a roaring fire. The coffee biscuits were gingery and wonderful, both china and Indian tea and a mouth-watering selection of goodies – perhaps griddle scones, fudge shortbread and fruit cake. Each meal was a delight and it was so encouraging to eat simple food perfectly prepared (by Mrs Buchanan Smith and two young helpers). Why oh why don't more English restaurateurs stop stuffing chicken legs with crab meat and get back to delicious basics? Judging by the contented looks in the *Isle of Eriska* dining room I'm sure it would be appreciated – and Guides like yours should do more to encourage the trend.

'My children were welcomed, fussed over and made to feel completely at home. They scrambled about all over the little island, rode the ponies and we only saw them at meal times. They made no fuss about having high tea – I think they were exhausted by then, and we enjoyed our dinner all the more knowing they were snoring happily upstairs. This hotel is a gem. I must just add that I've never written to any Guide before nor do I generally "rave", but then I've never stayed anywhere quite as special as the *Isle of Eriska*.' *(Mrs J Blackburn; also D R G Philip, George B Mair, Esme Walker, Kathryn A Milne, HR)*

Open: Mid-March–mid-November.
Rooms: 16 double, 6 single, 1 suite, 1 family – all with bath, telephone, radio and baby-listening. (2 rooms on ground floor; ramp into house for wheelchairs.)
Facilities: Hall, outer hall, drawing room, dining room, library. Private bridge to mainland; 270 acres grounds with formal garden, park and moorland; croquet, hard tennis court, bathing from shingle beach, sea fishing, anchorage, pony-trekking. Yacht with skipper for charter. &.
Location: 12 miles N of Oban, 4 miles W of the A828.
Restrictions: No children at dinner – high tea at 5.45 p.m. Dogs at management's discretion.
Credit card: American Express.
Terms (excluding VAT): Dinner, B & B £42–54. Set meals: lunch (cold table)£7.15; dinner £15. Special weekly rates. Reduced rates and special meals for children.

Are there no good hotels in Edinburgh? Write *now* if you have suggestions.

Inverlochy Castle   [GFG]   *Telephone:* Fort William (0397) 2177/8

This full-blown example of Victorian Scottish baronial on the lower slopes of Ben Nevis is more than a hotel: it is an institution. By a considerable margin the most expensive place in the Guide outside London, it has become for some on both sides of the Atlantic a once-in-a-lifetime experience, the hotel-lover's equivalent of Glyndebourne, the Taj Mahal or the Grand Canyon. Incidentally, it is the only hotel in Britain where you could find yourself sharing a room with the ghost of Queen Victoria: she stayed a week at *Inverlochy* exactly 110 years ago. The public rooms are magnificent and immaculately maintained. There is no doubt that the hotel can and has delivered the goods. Alas, it is hard for hoteliers to please all-comers – perhaps particularly hard when expectations of an elysium have been aroused and the entrance fee is so high. Some visitors this past year have expressed qualified disappointment – though not, happily, about the cooking. Mary Shaw, herself something of an institution, retired at the end of the 1981 season and Francois Huguet, formerly *sous-chef* at the *Connaught* and later at the Roux brothers' *Waterside Inn* at Bray, assumed the toque at *Inverlochy* at Easter, 1982. First reports of the dinner menus are encouraging, though one reader felt the cheese-board very inadequate. Breakfasts were less appreciated. The juices, one complainant assures us, were not (as declared) fresh, and the marmalade was fresh from the shop – not the first time by any means that a hotel that prides itself on its cuisine at night lets the show down the following morning. Another source of criticism was the service: inadequately trained staff, inattentive at times and over-matey at others. One reader summed up philosophically: 'I felt like a child after staying the night with a rather grand elderly relative. But maybe it's a matter of horses for courses.'

It would be wrong to suggest that all our reports were niggling. Here, for instance, is an American visitor who pulls out all the stops:

'The standard from which all quality hotels in the UK (and elsewhere) can be measured. A remark in the 1982 edition mentioned canned music: nonsense! Each time we stay I play some records of beautiful classical music on the hi-fi after dinner. There is *no* canned music. The owner, Mrs Hobbs and Manager Michael Leonard have put together a staff which nearly approximates the perfection so sadly lacking in some of the major hotels in the UK and on the Continent. Perhaps they ought to send their managers to *Inverlochy* for a few days to see how a hotel in the grand manner is run. One always feels as if one is a guest in a magnificent country home – which one is at *Inverlochy*, as *nowhere else*.' (*Matthew J Ellenhorn, MD; also Kevin Myers*)

Open: April–November.
Rooms: 11 double, 1 single, 2 suites – all with bath, telephone, colour TV and baby-listening; 24-hour room service.
Facilities: Great hall, drawing room, restaurant, billiards room, table-tennis room; facilities for small (25) conferences out of season. 50 acres grounds with all-weather tennis court; trout fishing on nearby private loch; several golf courses within easy driving distance; pony-trekking; chauffeur-driven limousines can be hired.
Location: Take turning to NW off the A82, 3½ miles N of Fort William. Guests met by arrangement at railway station or airport.
Restriction: No dogs.

Credit cards: Access, Barclay/Visa.
Terms: B & B £49–70; dinner, B & B £66–86. Set meal: dinner £21; light lunch available on request. Children half price; special meals provided.

GIGHA, Isle of, Argyll (Strathclyde)   Map 5

Gigha Hotel   *Telephone:* Gigha (058 35) 254

If you have a taste for small islands off the main holiday routes, then Gigha, three miles off the Argyll peninsula (regular ferry service from Tayinloan) may well suit your needs. It is 6 miles long by 1½ miles wide, and has a mild climate. There are plenty of beaches and coves, but the most notable tourist attraction is the 50-acre garden of Achamore House, specially famous for its rhododendron collection. The *Gigha Hotel* is the old inn, but enlarged and thoroughly spruced up (it won a Design Award a few years back), and offers a civilized setting for an island holiday. Rooms have attractive views over Ardminish Bay where the ferry comes in.

Open: All year, except Christmas and New Year.
Rooms: 9 double – 3 with bath. 2 rooms in cottages.
Facilities: 2 lounges (1 with TV), public bar, restaurant; some conference facilities. ¼ acre garden. 300 yards from the sea with white sand and rocks and safe bathing; sea fishing arranged with local fishermen. Achamore Gardens (open April–September) 1 mile.
Location: A83 to Loch Fyne, through Tarbert; S for 17 miles to Tayinloan, and turn right for Gigha Ferry.
Restriction: Dogs allowed 'if well-behaved'.
Terms (service at guests' discretion): B & B £15.50; dinner, B & B £25.50; full board (minimum 4 nights) £25.50. Set meals: lunch £5.50, dinner £10. Reduced rates and special meals for children.

GLENCOE, Argyll (Strathclyde)   Map 5

Kings House Hotel   *Telephone:* Kings House (085 56) 259

Said to be the oldest licensed inn in Scotland, the *Kings House* stands in an exceptionally isolated position on Rannoch Moor on one of the ancient cattle-droving routes from Skye, and a mile from the nearest main road, the A82. It makes a convenient stopover en route between Stirling or the South and the North-west. It is a low-slung building in the Scottish vernacular manner (e.g. with small windows on the bedroom floors) and is set against a background of formidable hills and famous mountain ridges. The recently added lounge displays the views to advantage. The hotel makes a good centre for the active – skiing (it is close to the Glencoe Ski Centre), walking, climbing and fishing – are all to hand. For the less active, only those dedicated to solitude in comfort will stay more than a night or two. 'Scotland is short of good roadside hotels; most of them are frankly tatty. The *Kings House*, with its singularly magnificent situation, is enthusiastically managed by the owner's welcoming elder son. Our room was comfortable and well-equipped, and with a spacious bathroom adjoining. The food is good average fresh food. Hotels ebb and flow: this one flows sweetly.' *(Neil Hunter; also George B Mair)*

Open: March–October.
Rooms: 17 double, 5 single – 10 with bath. (6 ground-floor rooms with 2 steps only.)
Facilities: 2 lounges, 2 bars, restaurant; live Highland music every Saturday in lounge bar. 100 acres grounds. Climbing instruction, trout fishing, skiing available.
Location: On the bank of Moorland river at the E end of Glencoe; 25 miles from Fort William, 1 mile off the A82 Glasgow–Inverness road.
Restriction: No dogs in public rooms.
Credit cards: Access/Euro/Mastercard, American Express.
Terms (no fixed service charge): B & B £10–15; dinner, B & B £16 (off-season only). Set meal: dinner £6 (off-season only); full *alc* £9.25 (high-season only). Reduced rates for children; high teas provided. Bargain breaks (min. 2 days).

GULLANE, East Lothian (Lothian)   Map 5

Greywalls Hotel   *Telephone:* Gullane (0620) 842144
Telex: PREHTL 727396 (Attention Greywalls)

A stylish rural alternative to staying in Edinburgh, especially for golfers. There's a tennis court and a croquet lawn at *Greywalls*, but the chief outdoor attraction of the hotel is the four acres of beautiful formal walled garden and the adjoining Muirfield golf course. The house itself is one of those thoroughly satisfactory Lutyens country houses, built at the turn of the century in a kind of quiet good taste that continues to be respected whatever the vagaries of architectural fashion. The furnishings are all of a piece with the house.

'It is rare to find a place where, from the time your luggage is put in your room until the moment you depart, you experience complete satisfaction and happiness. It is reassuring that such a place exists. *Greywalls* seems to "absorb" you rather than receive you. The public rooms are of the kind you find only as a rule in a private home. Log fires always burning brightly, comfort and quiet, good food. Bedrooms and bathrooms are equipped with all you could wish for. Books that you really want to read are at hand. Fresh fruit by your bedside. The house and garden were designed by the master hands of Lutyens and Gertrude Jekyll. The hotel staff are always available but unobtrusive. Fellow guests seem, in some strange way, to belong to this relaxed and happy place. To recall the time spent in this house is like a shaft of sun on a grey day!' (Richard Webb)

Open: Early March–late December.
Rooms: 16 double, 8 single – 19 with bath, all with telephone. 4 rooms in annexe. (Some rooms on ground floor.)
Facilities: 4 lounges, cocktail bar, restaurant; conference facilities. 4 acres formal walled garden with tennis and croquet. Sea and golf within easy reach. &.
Location: 19 miles E of Edinburgh; 1 mile inland from the sea.
Credit cards: Access/Euro, American Express, Barclay/Visa, Diners.
Terms (no service charge): B & B £20–35. Set meals: lunch £6.75; dinner £13.50. Reduced rates for children under 10 and special meals.

Are there no good hotels in Glasgow? Write *now* if you have suggestions.

INVERGARRY, Inverness-shire (Highland)　　　　　　　Map 5

The Inn on the Garry　　　　　　　　*Telephone:* Invergarry (080 93) 206

A Victorian gabled inn, overlooking the Garry salmon river, roughly halfway between Inverness and the Kyle of Lochalsh. Formerly known as the Invergarry Hotel, it has been given a thorough refitting as well as a change of name by new owners, Iain and Fiona Maclean.

'This was the find of our Scottish holidays. The young couple who have taken over the place have put in private bathrooms, refurbished the rooms, and provide an excellent cuisine. The venison and salmon, and the more elaborate dishes were all delicious. Nicest feature was the personal welcome and attentiveness of Iain Maclean. Although we were at one stage the only guests in the hotel, he made a point of lighting a magnificent fire in the lounge just for our benefit. The rooms have pleasant views across the river (though the main road may be a little noisy in high season), and he is in the process of restoring the garden. Invergarry village itself is uninspiring, but there is magnificent country all around.' *(John Timpson; also M Bowditch)*

Open:　Beginning April–end October.
Rooms:　7 double, 1 single – 3 with bath, all with radio, and tea-making facilities.
Facilities:　Lounge, 3 bar lounges, 3 dining rooms. 1 acre garden. River/loch fishing, boating available.
Location:　On the A82 between Fort William and Inverness; parking.
Restriction:　No dogs in dining room.
Terms (no fixed service charge):　B & B £16; dinner, B & B £25. Set meals: lunch about £3, dinner £9. Special meals for children. Bargain breaks (min. 3, 5 nights).

INVERNESS (Highland)　　　　　　　　　　　　　　Map 5

Culloden House　　　　　　　　*Telephone:* Inverness (0463) 790461
　　　　　　　　　　　　　　　　　　　Telex: Cloden 75402

An 18th-century house, two miles east of Inverness, converted into a 20-bedroom luxury hotel. It has a handsome Georgian facade, magnificent when floodlit, and backs on to the Moray Firth. The interior is Adam-style. With its 40 acres of parkland, its spacious public rooms filled with antiques, and its expensively furnished bedrooms (even though sometimes a bit shabby) it is very much a place for those who like a hotel in the grand manner.

'The McKenzies who run *Culloden House* take their responsibilities with gravity and unfailing politeness. Ian McKenzie is kilted by night and wears the black jacket and dark striped trousers of his profession by day. The house itself set in substantial acres on the outskirts of Inverness is but a claymore's throw from the battlefield where the Jacobite cause died in damp and depressing circumstances. Mr McKenzie put us in Room 11: "The one where we think Bonnie Prince Charlie slept on the eve of his defeat." He would have done better today than then. Colour TV, radio, private bathrooms, the luxury of large towels, trouser presses, Badedas and the feel of country house hospitality.

'It is a pleasant and harmless conceit that Charlie may have slept in Room 11, for *Culloden House* itself, with its imposing classical facade, was built by the Forbeses of Culloden over thirty years after the Prince fled from Scotland. The original castle where Butcher Cumberland and the Prince stayed in turn was destroyed by fire in 1772. All that remains of the castle are the vaults which were incorporated into the new house and a small dungeon where a group of Jacobite officers lay hidden after the battle. They were discovered and shot in the nearby woods on the Duke of Cumberland's order. The dungeon now houses a sauna and solarium. The 20 bedrooms, many with reproduction four-posters, are spotless. This is the sort of hotel where the orange juice is freshly squeezed at breakfast and the coffee freshly made. The dinner menu is three courses or six depending on your appetite and nobody goes hungry at lunchtime.' *(Derek Cooper; also Fiona and Charlie Glass)*

Open: All year.
Rooms: 18 double, 1 single, 1 suite – all with bath and shower, telephone, radio, colour TV and baby-listening. (Some four-poster beds.)
Facilities: Morning room, drawing room, cocktail bar, dining room; live bar entertainment Friday/Saturday. Sauna, solarium. 40 acres grounds with tennis court; fishing, shooting, golf can be arranged; airplane trips, boat/cruiser hire. Culloden battlefield 2 miles away.
Location: 5 miles from airport, 3 miles from town centre. If approaching on the A9 drive to the roundabout and turn right on to the A96. 1 mile along, take minor road to the right, signpost Smithton, Culloden and Balloch. *Culloden House* Hotel is 1 mile along this road. If approaching by Loch Ness, go straight through Inverness on the A96 (signpost Aberdeen). 2 miles from town turn right on to minor road, signpost Smithton, etc.
Restriction: No dogs in public rooms.
Credit cards: All major credit cards accepted.
Terms: B & B £32.50–45. Set meals: lunch £8.50, dinner £15. Sepcial meals provided for children.

Dunain Park   [GFG]   *Telephone:* Inverness (0463) 30512

Michael and Judith Bulger bought Dunain Park (2½ miles south-west of the Highlands capital), in 1974 and converted the solid virtuous largely 19th-century building into a highly personal country house hotel. There are six acres of garden and woodland overlooking the Caledonian canal (good walking along its banks). The Bulgers are proud of their near self-sufficiency: they keep cows, goats, pigs and sheep, grow 90% of their vegetables and their own wood for the log fires; and they make, among other things, their own sausages, jams and pickles. The bedrooms – there are only six in all – are beautifully furnished and decorated and well provided with creature comforts. The two public rooms downstairs – one with TV and the other with periodicals – are similarly sybaritic: log fires, very comfortable armchairs and settees, and a high standard of decor. And the quality of food in the dining room is of a piece with everything else. Judith Bulger is a highly talented cook: there is a short four-course dinner which has won a deservedly high reputation in the locality – as well as in other guides. But it must be said that not everyone enjoys their stay at Dunain Park. *It's very much the Bulgers' own home as well as a hotel. Some visitors, while acknowledging all the agreeable attributes described above, have found the place a little self-conscious and lacking in welcome.*

The above is quoted from the 1981 Guide. We omitted an entry last year after several people had echoed the reservations expressed in the last sentence. We are restoring it this year, being satisfied that if the Bulgers

174

can't please all-comers, they can please some to an uncommon degree, e.g. 'Luxuriously comfortable house, grounds delightful even on a sleety March evening, Mr Bulger, goat and geese all welcoming. We were impressed by the helpfulness of the young staff to cope with our tiresome requests regarding our dog and small child. Delicious dinner.' *(Alison Johnson; also R Bennon, Esme Walker, Beverly M Martinoli)*

On the subject of satisfying guests, Mr Bulger writes: 'We cannot really improve upon our 1981 entry, which presents a very reasonable picture of the way we are. It is true, however, that some guests may *be* a little self-conscious. Please remember that 12 guests constitute a house full, and it may be fair to say that those to whom a "house party" is anathema may feel out of place. There are nooks and crannies – and 6 acres – in which to hide and we do not run a holiday camp by any means, but the whole thing hangs together best if our guests are either gregarious or adequately absorbed in their own conversation. It is very easy to please guests who stay for more than one night, because we can serve the food they enjoy, heat their rooms appropriately, organize their breakfast in bed, remove the flowers from their room if they suffer from hay fever, or perform whatever services they may normally or peculiarly require within our reason and physical capacity (which is well exercised).'

Open: Mid March–end October.

Rooms: 6 double – 4 with bath (1 four-poster bed). 2 self-catering cottages with 1 and 2 bedrooms.

Facilities: TV room, drawing room, dining room. 6 acres grounds with badminton and croquet. Fishing for salmon and brown trout, boating, shooting, stalking, ponytrekking and golf nearby.

Location: On the A82 Inverness–Fort William road, 3 miles SW of Inverness.

Terms (service at guests' discretion): B & B £16.50–27.50. Set meal: dinner £14. 5% discount for dinner, B & B (4, 5 or 6 nights), 10% discount for 7 nights or more. 50% reduction for children sharing parents' room; high tea provided.

INVERSHIN, Lairg, Sutherland (Highland)　　　　　　　　　**Map 5**

Invershin Hotel　　　　　　　　*Telephone:* Invershin (054 982) 202

We had a long entry for Invershin last year, from a contributor who extolled the amazing value for money offered by this family hotel facing the Kyle of Sutherland. It is owned by Major Hedley and run by various members of his family. The writer had enjoyed, over ten evenings, splendid four-course dinners plus coffee for £5, VAT included, and had also appreciated the quality of service in the hotel and the rooms, with their colour TV, carpeted shower and loo. Only serious snags: you had to expect a certain amount of road and train noise at night, and the lounge was a bit too small for comfort when the hotel was busy. We see that Major Hedley, in giving us his estimated prices for lunch and dinner in 1983, continues to offer, hopefully, lunch at £3 and dinner at £5. Here is a recent report:

'The Hedley family are a delightful lot and they do make great efforts to ensure you have all you need in the way of comfort, food and bonhomie. The rooms are small but have every device for your comfort, from tea-kettles to heated towel-rails and electric blankets – and the water is so hot we hardly dared use the shower! The menu is a little too lengthy to be cordon bleu throughout – they might do better to concentrate on fewer dishes – but it is well served and there is plenty of it. Breakfast is really a marathon, with scones and hot rolls as well as toast, quite apart from the three main courses. And what a treat to find somewhere in Scotland which has facilities for sitting and drinking *outside*. Admittedly the weather rarely allows it, but on a fine day the scenery is so marvellous almost everywhere it is a shame not to be able to enjoy it.' *(John Timpson; also Joan M Marr)*

Open: All year, except 1–4 January.
Rooms: 17 double, 7 single – 8 with bath, 8 with shower, 2 with telephone, all with radio, TV, tea-making facilities and baby-listening. 6 rooms in annexe. (Some rooms on ground floor.)
Facilities: 2 bars, 2 lounges. 25 acres grounds with riding by arrangement. The river Kyle is in front of the hotel with free fishing for hotel guests.
Location: Central, parking.
Restriction: No dogs in dining room.
Terms (no service charge): B & B £9–11; dinner, B & B £11–16; full board £67.50–70 per week. Set meals: lunch £3, dinner £5; full *alc* £5. Reduced rates and special meals for children.

KENTALLEN OF APPIN, Argyll (Highland) Map 5

Ardsheal House [GFG] *Telephone:* Duror (063 174) 227

'Passing by a few years ago, American banker Bob Taylor and his advertising account executive wife Jane clapped eyes on Ardsheal House at Kentallen of Appin on the shores of Loch Linnhe. Historic, superbly sited, surrounded by noble trees, it was for sale. They agonized all night and bought it. Now they winter in New York and run Ardsheal in the summer months. Much of the furniture comes from their Manhattan brownstone house, the rest is equally old and fascinating. The house rambles, many of the rooms have splendid views. There are lots of books, a billiard table, a tennis court. But this is walking and rambling country, fishing too if you want it. The Taylors are enthusiasts with taste. The food is excellent, the welcome unpretentious. Ardsheal achieves what so many "country house" hotels conspicuously fail to achieve – a feeling of being lived in. The Taylors are obviously infatuated with their enviable house but they don't make a bore of it. A place to relax in, secure in the knowledge that when you come back at night the salmon and prawns will be fresh from loch Linnhe, the beef will be Aberdeen Angus, the lamb local and the vegetables out of the garden. One of the three top country house hotels in Scotland to our mind.' *(Janet and Derek Cooper; warmly endorsed by HR)*

Open: Easter–mid October.
Rooms: 12 double – 6 with bath, 2 with shower.
Facilities: Reception lounge, TV lounge, lounge overlooking loch, dining room, billiard room. 990 acres grounds with tennis court; rocky beach behind hotel, trout stream nearby, coarse fishing from dinghies on loch; riding, hill-walking.
Location: Take the A82 to Ballachulish, then the A828 towards Oban at the Ballachulish roundabout; the hotel is 4 miles from the roundabout on the right. Parking for 18 cars.
Restriction: No dogs in dining room.
Terms: B & B £15–32. Set meals: lunch £4–5, dinner £11–12. Children: £6 for cot or folding bed in parents' room; high tea on request. Discounts for long stays.

KILCHRENAN, by Taynuilt, Argyll (Strathclyde)   Map 5

Taychreggan Hotel   [GFG]   *Telephone:* Kilchrenan (086 63) 211

A remote and beautiful inn, 16 miles east of Oban on what used to be the main ferry point across loch Awe from Oban to Inverary. The loch, never more than a mile wide, is 24 miles long – the longest freshwater loch in Scotland – and fishing is a leading activity here, though there's good riding and walking to be had as well, and some shooting. The hotel owes everything to the personalities of John Taylor and his Danish wife Tove. The conversion to a modern hotel, though it predates the Taylors' arrival has a Scandinavian feel with its good modern furniture and wood-burning stoves; the lunch is always a *koldt bord*: the staff are quite likely to be Danish students too. The hotel is at present being upgraded, and by 1983 all but two of the double rooms will have their own bathrooms. We are glad to know that John Taylor is happy to let his doubles as a single and only charge a single price.

As for several years past, our reports on *Taychreggan* have been unanimously warm in praise of the Taylors' hospitality: 'A delightful hotel. The old building has been absorbed into a complex of large light rooms looking out on to the garden and the water. There is now a large inner courtyard where guests can enjoy the sun and are sheltered from the wind. The owners take a close personal interest in the welfare of their guests, the service and the excellent food. The Scandinavian influence is strong in the decor and general atmosphere. This fits in well with the loch and island environment. The wood fires, fresh flowers and good service create a feeling of quiet efficiency and comfort.' *(Mrs Richard Webb; also Antony Derville, P W D Roberts, J A Matheson)*

Open: Approx. April–October.
Rooms: 17 double – 14 with bath, and a children's room, all with radio and baby-listening.
Facilities: 2 lounges, hall-lounge, TV lounge, all with log fires; bar overlooking courtyard, dining room. 25 acres grounds on the loch side, with fishing, bathing, boating. Riding, shooting, walking; fine scenery, gardens and historic sites within easy reach.
Location: Northern shore of loch Awe, about 16 miles E of Oban by the A85, turning S just beyond Taynuilt to reach Loch Awe and the hotel.
Credit cards: All major credit cards accepted.
Terms (excluding service):   B & B £16–26; dinner, B & B £26–36. Set meals: buffet lunch £5.50, dinner £10 (excluding 10% service charge). Reduced rates for children sharing parents' room: 50% if under 8 and taking high tea; 20% if over 8 and taking dinner.

KINCRAIG, by Kingussie, Inverness-shire (Highland)   .   Map 5

Ossian Hotel   *Telephone:* Kincraig (054 04) 242

One of those small family-run hotels where the owners really put themselves out to make their guests feel cared for, and also cater generously, but at modest prices, for the most robust appetites. The hotel is run by Mr and Mrs Ramage, with the assistance of their daughter and her chef husband, Mr and Mrs Rainbow. The Aviemore Centre is just up the line by rail, the hotel has fishing rights on the Spey, and Loch Insh, with its windsurfing and sailing, is three minutes' walk away. Here are two testimonials which convey the same message: 'I have enjoyed annual stays here for the last four years. It is run by the very friendly Ramage family, who operate it with splendid efficiency on a totally informal basis. Rooms are comfortable and meals gargantuan. And the real test of any hotel – they do not in the least mind laying on a full-scale breakfast at 7.30 a.m. All this at prices which are very modest.' *(Esler Crawford)* 'You immediately feel you belong here, and the food is the greatest strain on my 25-inch waist that I have ever encountered.' *(Katharine Whitehorn)*

Open: Mid February–1 January.
Rooms: 5 double, 1 single. 4 rooms in annexe.
Facilities: TV lounge, cocktail lounge, restaurant. ½ acre garden; Loch Insh, River Spey 3 minutes' walk; fishing, canoeing, sailing, ponytrekking, riding, skiing, golf, gliding, windsurfing facilities nearby.
Location: Just off the A9 from Perth to Inverness; 6 miles from Aviemore. Turn off the A9 at Kingussie (travelling north) or Aviemore (travelling south) on to scenic route. The Inverness railway runs nearby and might affect light sleepers.
Restriction: No dogs in dining room.
Credit cards: Barclay/Visa.
Terms: B & B £12; dinner, B & B from £18. Set meal: lunch from £3; full *alc* £8. Children: 2–8 years, 50%; 9–12, 75%; special meals provided. Christmas and New Year festivities.

KINGUSSIE, Inverness-shire (Highland)   **Map 5**

The Osprey Hotel   [GFG]   *Telephone:* Kingussie (054 02) 510

We have had an entry for this friendly informal family hotel since 1979. Last year, Duncan Reeves, who runs *The Osprey* with his wife Pauline, wrote: 'Your Guide sends some of our nicest people. You are obviously hitting the button.' As we had lacked feedback that year, we ended our 1982 entry with the plea: 'Could some of those to whom we are hitting the button kindly reciprocate?'

Enthusiasts for the Reeves' brand of hospitality have responded vigorously. We did have one complaint – about the presence of the Reeves' dog and cat at mealtimes, and another reader, referring to a previous entry, remarked that the hot water was *not* everlasting. Otherwise compliments were unqualified and unrestrained: 'Just lovely. Duncan Reeves was a most welcoming host, more than tolerant of the children, full of good advice for my slipped disc. Did you know that this complaint responds to good food, wine and fresh air? For those with troubles in the lumbar region, try to make it to Inverness-shire and let Mr Reeves treat the symptoms.' 'Our stay was one of the most pleasant ever. Some may be reluctant to share tables, but I thought guests were placed judiciously. I was pleased that wholefoods and regional dishes were prominent.' 'Due to travel problems, we didn't get there till 10.50 p.m., but were given drinks and a full four-course meal without any trouble – most unusual these days. . . . Glad I don't live too close: in three days managed to put on 8 lbs.' 'In your next edition, please give more emphasis to the quality of the cuisine. Each dish has been imaginatively created and perfected. There is one main dish each night to which one looks forward eagerly. The first course is an array of gourmet delights and the sweets present similarly tempting choices. Most important, you must correct the impression that the coffee is below-standard. It is in fact the best coffee we have ever had outside Kenya.' *(Shelley Cranshaw, W R Wootton, Jennifer Douglas, Dorothy and Jerome Preston, Dr Michael Denton, Conrad Dehn QC, R J Bryant)*

Open: All year except 1 November–1 January.
Rooms: 7 double, 1 single, 1 family.
Facilities: Lounge, TV room, dining room. Small front garden with herbs and rockery. Most sports within easy reach: golf, salmon and trout fishing on the river Spey ¼ mile, loch fishing for trout 1 mile; wind-surfing; gliding at Glen Feshie nearby, sailing and canoeing 6 miles; all sports facilities at the Aviemore Centre 12 miles; fine country all around for birdwatching, walking and hill-climbing. Skiing in the Cairngorms, usually December–May, 30 minutes by car.
Location: Near the A9, about 10 miles SW of Aviemore and 200 yards from the village centre; parking for 10 cars.
Restriction: No dogs in public rooms.
Credit cards: Access, American Express, Barclay/Visa.
Terms (no service charge): B & B £9–12; dinner, B & B £15–19.50. Set meal: dinner £6.50–7.50. Reduced rates and adjusted meals for children. Special ski packages 1 January–30 April.

KYLE OF LOCHALSH, Ross-shire (Highland)   **Map 5**

The Lochalsh Hotel   *Telephone:* Kyle (0599) 4202
Ferry Road

A well-run British Rail hotel in a magnificent setting beside the ferry to Skye. We had an entry for it in earlier editions, but dropped it last year for lack of feedback. But recent readers have found it a thoroughly comfortable as well as a convenient place to stay, and the location specially attractive, with all the rooms having a ringside view of the comings and goings of the ferry. One reader, while endorsing the entry, complained of a slight *déja vu* air to the place: 'Inevitably the furnishing is reminiscent of all such hotels, very adequate and comfortable, but you feel you have experienced it all before. The food and service fall into the same category, likewise the waiters and the hot water in the bathrooms – a bit intermittent in their warmth and efficiency.' But another reader recommended it without reservation, finding it better value for money than six other Highland hotels visited in the same trip. *(H Mortimer, Richard Webb)*

Open: All year, except 20–30 December.
Rooms: 29 double, 13 single, 3 suites – 29 with bath, 1 with shower, all with telephone, radio, colour TV, tea-making facilities and baby-listening. (Some rooms on ground floor.)
Facilities: Lifts, cocktail bar, lounge, TV lounge, restaurant; ramps for disabled; occasional Scottish evenings. 2 acres garden. Loch/sea fishing available. &.
Location: On the outskirts of Kyle of Lochalsh; parking.
Restriction: No dogs in public rooms.
Credit cards: All major credit cards accepted.
Terms: B & B £13.50–29. Set meals (no fixed service charge): lunch £3.95, dinner £8.50; full *alc* £15.50. Reduced rates and special meals for children.

If you consider any entry inadequate or misleading, please let us know *now*.

Beechwood Country House Hotel   [GFG]   *Telephone:* Moffat (0683) 20210

An unassumingly pleasant old country house just outside the centre of Moffat, in 12 acres of beech trees overlooking the Annan valley. *Beechwood* cares particularly for the reputation of its kitchen and its cellars. Sheila McIlwrick personally supervises the cooking, and her husband Keith oversees the front of house. We are glad to know that, since last year, telephones have been installed in the bedrooms, answering last year's complaints about long private conversations in the outer hall. 'A very good centre for touring Galloway and Dumfries. Really extraordinarily comfortable, although, as the house is small, the sitting rooms are slightly cramped. There was a faint air of knowing what's good for you, perhaps because the house used to be a girls' school, but the staff seem genuinely to want to supply your requirements. Dinner was *excellent.* Breakfast also was more than adequate. Our room was small, but very comfortable and well-equipped and nicely decorated. Only inadequacy was the bedside lights – hotels never seem to expect you to read in bed.' *(Anne Viney; also Mr and Mrs K C Twist, Kevin Myers)*

Open: All year, except January.
Rooms: 6 double, 2 single – 4 with bath, 2 with shower, 6 with telephone, all with radio and tea-making facilities.
Facilities: 2 lounges (1 with bar, 1 with colour TV), dining room. 1 acre garden. Fishing in river Annan; golf, tennis and riding nearby.
Location: Turn off the A701 at St Mary's church into Harthope Place. Then left and up track to *Beechwood.*
Restriction: No dogs.
Credit cards: All major credit cards accepted.
Terms (no fixed service charge): B & B £13–16.50. Set meal: dinner £8; full *alc* about £11; bar lunches available. Weekend and midweek breaks in autumn and spring. 10% reduction for children; high tea provided.

Clifton Hotel   [GFG]   *Telephone:* Nairn (0667) 53119
Viewfield Street

There are some hotels which appeal by their quiet good taste, and others whose attraction is – well, rather different. Staying at *Clifton* is a dramatic experience in more senses than one. *Clifton* is a creeper-clad Victorian house a stone's throw from the sea, overlooking the Moray Firth, with the Ross-shire and Sutherland hills beyond. Gordon Macintyre is the *patron* or perhaps the impresario. It has been the Macintyre family house for a century or more, and the place is filled with his and his family's collections of everything under the sun – paintings, sculptures, *objets trouvés*, loot from a hundred salerooms. Apart from his addiction to auctions, Gordon Macintyre also loves to stage plays, concerts, recitals and other events in the hotel from October to May. 'A sense of the theatrical, backed up by cleanliness, really good food and masses of hot water' is the claim, wholly justified we believe, in the hotel's brochure. *(Nadine Gordimer, S C Whittle and others)*

Open: 1 March–end November.

Rooms: 17 – all with bath. (2 rooms on ground floor.) Beds have continental quilts, but conventional bedding is available on request.

Facilities: Large lounge, drawing room, TV room, bar, restaurant, writing room; plays, concerts, recitals October–May. 1 acre grounds. Fishing, shooting, riding available; beach, tennis courts, swimming pools 2 minutes away. 2 golf courses close by.

Location: 500 yards from town centre; parking for 20 cars.

Credit card: All major credit cards accepted.

Terms (excluding service): B & B £21–25; full board £180–190 per week. Full *alc* £10–12. Reduced rates for children by arrangement; special meals provided.

PEEBLES (Borders)   Map 5

Cringletie House Hotel [GFG]   *Telephone:* Eddleston (072 13) 233

A noble example of Scottish baronial which stands in 28 acres of gardens and woodland close to the village of Eddleston, two miles north of Peebles on the Edinburgh road (A703). *Cringletie* has a distinguished pedigree: it was formerly the home of the Wolfe Murray family, and it was Colonel Alexander Murray from *Cringletie* who accepted the surrender of Quebec after General Wolfe had been killed. But it has been a renowned hotel for many years now, and has been enjoying a particularly halcyon phase under the present ownership of Mr and Mrs Maguire.

'One of the best small hotels we have found – surrounded in April by thousands of daffodils in well-kept grounds. The hotel is beautifully managed and obviously cherished. There were coal fires burning from early morning until late at night. We arrived unannounced and were warmly greeted by Elizabeth Temple, the receptionist. Mr Maguire carried our bags up to an enchanting bedroom and bathroom. No TV, radio or telephone, we are glad to report. Complete relaxation is guaranteed. We were offered bargain-break terms which we thought an excellent buy. The food (limited choice menu) was absolutely delicious, cooked by Mrs Maguire. All the staff were willing and pleasant. We really can recommend a long stay here with great confidence.' *(Eve Webb; also Harry and May McIver, Mrs C Smith, John Timpson, R J Bryant, Anne Viney)*

Open: Early March until after Christmas.

Rooms: 12 double, 4 single – 10 with bath, 1 with shower and WC.

Facilities: Lift, lounge, TV lounge, bar, dining room; occasional small conferences (8–15 people), central heating. 28 acres of gardens and woodlands with hard tennis court, croquet and putting. Golf and trout and salmon fishing nearby.

Location: Off the A703, 2 miles N of Peebles.

Restriction: No dogs in public rooms or unaccompanied in bedrooms.

Terms (service at guests' discretion): B & B £16.50–19.50. Set meals: lunch £7, dinner £11. Reduced rates for children sharing parents' room; high teas provided.

POOLEWE, by Achnasheen, Ross-shire (Highland)   Map 5

Pool House Hotel   *Telephone:* Poolewe (044 586) 272

'Having gone to Poolewe to visit Inverewe Gardens we were attracted to the *Pool House Hotel* by its commanding position at the head of loch Ewe, and we were so charmed by the high standards of comfort and service and simply delectable food (at a very reasonable price) that we spent the remainder of our holiday there.'

So ran the opening lines of the entry last year for the Hughes's unassumingly pleasant family hotel, old-fashioned in the complimentary sense. A reader this year also picked this hotel by chance from a Scottish Tourist Board list, and wrote: 'What a lucky dip it was! We loved it and wish we could have stayed longer. Our dinner table in the picture window of the dining-room was special. My husband ate a large helping of home-made treacle pudding smothered with cream while I watched a gannet catching his supper in the sea loch. Nothing was too much trouble. I asked for a kipper from the breakfast menu. There weren't any, but a smiling waitress was pleased to offer me a pair, if I wished, next day. Cheerful fire in the sitting-room along with a bottomless coffee-pot on the sideboard. What could be nicer on a chilly evening?' *(Eileen Broadbent; also Lt Cdr and Mrs R Kirby Harris)*

Open: 1 April–14 October.
Rooms: 10 double, 4 single – 3 with bath, 2 with shower; tea-making facilities on request.
Facilities: Lounge with TV, 2 bars, dining room.
Location: ½ mile from Inverewe Gardens between Gairloch and Aultbea.
Restriction: No dogs in public rooms.
Credit card: Barclay/Visa.
Terms: B & B from £12; dinner, B & B from £19. Set meal: dinner £7. Weekly breaks, 5-night stays and weekly terms on application. Reduced rates for children; special meals provided.

PORT APPIN, Argyll (Strathclyde)   **Map 5**

The Airds Hotel   [GFG]   *Telephone:* Appin (063 173) 236

Another good year for this early 18th-century ferry inn overlooking loch Linnhe, the island of Lismore and the mountains of Morvern – both for the comforts of the house and the remarkably good cooking. One reader wrote: 'We've been going for years. It keeps getting better and better under Mr and Mrs Allen. This time I feel I really must *rave* about it! The Allens keep doing improvements; this year they have replaced the lattice windows which slightly impeded the wonderful view of loch Linnhe. No dish is ever a disappointment. It is the only hotel in Scotland we feel this way about.' Another view: 'Evidence of the Allens' supervision and meticulous attention to detail are everywhere, without the slightest hint of becoming overbearing. The food was superb. Mr Allen shows a genuine interest in wine and maintains an excellent cellar. Service was good. Our meal moved at exactly the right pace, and it was pleasing to see that little things like linen napkins, which are so often neglected in British hotels are not overlooked here. The *Airds* will be a "must" on all our trips north in the future.' *(Jean Dundas, Rosamund V Hebdon, Nathan and Sarah Joseph)*

Open: 28 March–23 October.
Rooms: 14 double, 2 single – 6 with bath, 6 with shower. (2 rooms in annexe.)
Facilities: 2 residents' lounges, cocktail lounge, public bar, dining room. Small garden. Near rock beach with safe bathing, fishing, boating, pony-trekking, forest walks.
Location: 2 miles off the A828, 25 miles from Fort William and from Oban.

Restriction: Dogs at management's discretion.
Terms (no fixed service charge): B & B from £14.50; dinner, B & B £25–29; full board £28–31.50. Set meals: snack lunch £3, dinner £11. Reduced rates in spring; reduced rates and special meals for children.

PORTPATRICK, Dumfries and Galloway   Map 5

Knockinaam Lodge Hotel   *Telephone:* Portpatrick (077 681) 471

A characteristic Scottish Victorian lodge on the west coast of the Mull of Galloway, three miles south of Portpatrick. The hotel is set in 30 acres, with lawns that run down to a sandy cove. Because of its remote position, it was chosen in World War II for secret meetings between Churchill and Eisenhower. A few years ago, the hotel was acquired by the present resident owners, Simon and Caroline Pilkington, who have done a lot of refurbishing of the bedrooms, all of which have garden or sea views. 'The setting', say the owners, 'is outstandingly beautiful and very secluded; the hotel is ideally suited for exploring this little-known area, for lovers of peace and country, walking and gardens. It appeals to those who want to come and go as they would at home, and see very little evidence of "hotel".' A view echoed by a correspondent: 'An ideal spot for a quiet getaway weekend where one can relax and look forward to dinner. The food is imaginative and excellently cooked. The service is both friendly and personal.' *(John and Rona Greene)*

Open: All year, except 4 January–end February.
Rooms: 9 double, 1 single – 7 with bath, 1 with shower, all with radio.
Facilities: Lounge/bar, drawing room, dining room. 30 acres grounds with croquet. Sea 50 yards, sandy beach, safe bathing, sea fishing, slipway for boats.
Location: 3 miles S of Portpatrick on minor road. Turn left (coming from Stranraer) on the A77 3 miles after Lochans and 3 miles before Portpatrick.
Restriction: No dogs in public rooms.
Credit cards: American Express, Barclay/Visa.
Terms (service at guests' discretion): B & B £19; dinner, B & B £27–31. Set meal: dinner £11 (bar lunches, picnic hampers only); full *alc* £13.50. Reduced rates and special meals for children. Bargain breaks March–May, October–December (min. 2 nights, excluding Christmas/New Year).

ROCKCLIFFE, by Dalbeattie, Kirkcudbrightshire   Map 5

Baron's Craig Hotel   *Telephone:* Rockcliffe (055 663) 225

A traditional but well-run Scottish baronial hotel in an exceptional and untouristy setting. Rockcliffe is a small village overlooking the mouth of Rough firth as it opens out to the broad reaches of the Solway. *Baron's Craig*, built as a shooting lodge about a century ago, is in wooded country about three minutes from a good sandy beach, safe for children. We had one poor report on the food, and, on the whole, would not recommend *Baron's Craig* for the more serious sort of gourmet; in general, however, the restaurant as well as the accommodation gives satisfaction. 'We fully endorse everything you have written about the comfort and friendliness of this hotel. The staff are young, agreeable and well-trained under obviously good management. Breakfast arrived in our room punctually and dinner could be taken leisurely when we wanted it – within reason. A very agreeable hotel.' *(Sir Patrick Reilly·· also Mr and Mrs W C Twist)*

Open: 1 April–10 October.
Rooms: 19 double, 8 single – 20 with bath, all with radio and baby-listening. (5 rooms with bath on ground floor.)
Facilities: 2 lounges, 1 lounge bar, separate TV room. 11 acres wooded grounds and gardens with 9-hole putting course. 300 yards from safe, sandy beach. Boating, sailing and fishing nearby.
Location: Rockcliffe is a small village off the A710 overlooking the mouth of Rough firth.
Restriction: No dogs in public rooms.
Terms (no fixed service charge): B & B £19.30–31.60; dinner, B & B (minimum 3 days) £27.60–39.50. Set meals: bar lunch from £2.50, dinner £10. Reduced rates and special meals for children. Bargain breaks when space available.

ST ANDREWS, Fife   **Map 5**

Rufflets Hotel   *Telephone:* St Andrews (0334) 72594
Strathkinness Low Road

Not the main hotel in St Andrews – the large modern *Old Course* beside the 17th fairway – but an agreeable family-run 1924 country house alternative, 1½ miles inland. 'This is one of the most pleasant hotels we have stayed in, set in large beautifully kept grounds with a remarkable kitchen garden. Service is excellent. The food we had was consistently good, and not expensive by today's standards. There seemed to be typical Scottish dishes on every menu – at lunch smokies and haggis with neeps, and at dinner we had "Cabbie Claw" – a delicious haddock dish which was on as a main course but available as a fish course at 50p extra. There was a sweet trolley but we chose to follow with Orkney cheeses. There is a good wine list but the red house wine is undistinguished.' *(W Frankland)* More reports welcome.

Open: Mid February–mid January
Rooms: 21 – all with telephone, radio and baby-listening, 3 rooms in cottage.
Facilities: Front hall, residents' lounge, lounge bar, TV room, restaurant, 10 acres grounds with putting, gardens with streams. 1½ miles from beach; fishing, golfing, etc., can be arranged.
Location: On the B939 1 mile W of St Andrews.
Restriction: No dogs.
Credit cards: All major credit cards accepted.
Terms (no service charge): B & B £22–23; dinner, B & B £19–30 (min. 2 nights). Set meals: lunch £4.50, dinner £8.50; full *alc* £18. Special Christmas and New Year packages with entertainment. Short winter breaks. Children free when sharing parents' room; special meals provided.

ST FILLANS, Perthshire (Tayside)   **Map 5**

The Four Seasons Hotel   [GFG]   *Telephone:* St Fillans (076 485) 333

A well-designed modern Scandinavian-style hotel in an exceptional location, looking down the length of Loch Earn from the eastern shore. The hotel prides itself on its Italian cooking (Signor Donetti is *il padrone*), also

HUNTER'S BOOKS
Pasadena

- 9 JAN

$002.98   3
$000.19   TAX
$003.17   TOL

/426

on a wide-ranging wine list. In addition to the accommodation in the main building, there are also six chalets on the hillside above, specially suitable for families. Sailing, waterskiing, golf, fishing, shooting, squash and tennis are all to be had in the immediate vicinity. 'Bedrooms super-comfortable – excellent simple furniture, really adequate lighting for once, well-equipped bathroom, small TV – and a superb view over the loch.' *(Anne Viney; also D J V Murdoch)*

Open: April–end October.
Rooms: 12 double – 11 with bath, 1 with shower, all with telephone, mono TV and baby-listening. Also 6 chalets in hotel grounds, sleeping 2 adults and 2 children or 3 adults.
Facilities: Lounge, writing room, 2 bars, restaurant. Private jetty for use of guests with own boats. Waterskiing, sailing, golf, riding, fishing within easy reach.
Location: Just off the A85 W of Perth.
Credit cards: None now accepted.
Terms: B & B £19.50–28.50. Set meals (excluding 10% service charge): lunch £6; dinner £8.50; full *alc* £14. Reduced rates for stays of 4 days and more. Special rates for chalets if occupied by more than 2 people; high tea 5.45–6.30 p.m.

ST OLA, Nr Kirkwall, Orkney Islands   **Map 5**

Foveran   *Telephone:* Kirkwall (0856) 2389

Our first hotel on the Orkneys, 2½ miles from Kirkwall, the county town, and half a mile inland from the sea.

'An architect-designed welcoming small hotel overlooking Scapa Flow. Owned and managed by Mr and Mrs Hasham, it offers perhaps the most comfortable accommodation in Orkney. The restaurant specializes in well-prepared local dishes and enjoys a strong local following. The bedrooms are Scandinavian in design, with pleasant accents of colour. An ideal centralized location.' *(S M Gillotti)*

Open: All year, except October.
Rooms: 4 double, 3 single – 2 with bath, 1 with shower, all with tea-making facilities. (All rooms on ground floor.)
Facilities: TV room, lounge, dining room. 15 acres grounds; small sandy/pebble/rocky beach. Loch and sea fishing, archaeological sites, bird reserve, swimming, golf and squash nearby.
Location: 2½ miles south-west of Kirkwall.
Restriction: No dogs in public rooms, and in bedrooms by arrangement only.
Credit cards: Access/Euro/Mastercard, American Express, Barclay/Visa.
Terms (service at guests' discretion): B & B £12.50–17.50. Full *alc* £9.50. Reduced rates for children sharing parents' room; special meals provided. Special weekend breaks 26 August–14 June; special rates for stays of 7 nights or more 15 June–25 August.

SALEN, Isle of Mull   **Map 5**

Glenforsa Hotel   *Telephone:* Aros (068 03) 377

'Built in the Norwegian Log Hotel pattern, and you might think you were actually in Norway, so beautiful is the scenery in all parts of Mull. All rooms are on the ground floor, some with bath or shower – and there is plenty of provision for those without. One lounge has TV, and the other observation lounge (the only room not on the ground floor) looks over the adjacent air-landing strip and the Sound of Mull to the mountains of Morvern. The hotel has been run for the past 20 years by Mr and Mrs Howitt, who are helped by their sons and their daughter-in-law Frances, who shares the cooking with her mother-in-law. We much enjoyed the excellent home cooking, both four-course dinners and superb breakfasts. One of the very few hotels where we can honestly say that we could find no fault at all.' *(R J Bateman; also Richard and Rosemary Taylor)*

Open: Late March–late October, Christmas and (if sufficient demand) New Year.
Rooms: 14 double – 7 with bath, all with colour TV. (All rooms on ground floor.)
Facilities: Lounge with TV, lounge/bar, lounge/cocktail bar, dining room, terrace; monthly *Ceilidhs* with dancing. 6½ acres grounds with access to river; shingle beach 250 yards, dinghy available; seatrout/salmon fishing on river Forsa, loch and sea fishing, ponytrekking, 2 golf courses close by. &.
Location: 1¼ miles from Salen village; parking. 10 and 5½ miles respectively from the two Mull ferry terminals of Craignure and Fishnish, then 250 yards off the Craignure–Tobermory road. (All guests given instructions and ferry timetables when booking.) Airstrip adjacent to hotel (open dawn to dusk).
Restrictions: No children under 5; no dogs in public rooms.
Terms: B & B £12–18; dinner, B & B £19–25. (Packed and bar lunches available.) Set meals: lunch £3.75, dinner £7.50; full *alc* £9.50. 10%–50% reduction for children between 5 and 12 years.

SCARISTA, Isle of Harris, Western Isles Map 5

Scarista House Hotel [GFG] *Telephone:* Scarista (085 985) 238

Last year's entry for Andrew and Alison Johnson's Georgian manse overlooking a magnificent stretch of Atlantic beach belonged to the nonpareil order of enthusiasm. Sometimes a rave notice one year is followed by nemesis the next. Happily, we know of nothing likely to diminish the pleasure of a visit to *Scarista*, and what may enhance it for some is that the hotel hopes to have an extra few double bedrooms with bathrooms *en suite* in 1983 as well as, with luck, a restaurant licence. Meanwhile, here is our latest report from Harris:
'This is the nicest hotel I ever stayed in, and between here and Kathmandu, I've stayed in a good many. No need to say any more about Mrs Johnson's superb imaginative cooking, as this has been adequately described in both your Guide and the *Good Food Guide*. But I think I might go on about the breakfasts a little. Two kinds of coffee and two kinds of tea are offered, there are home-made scones, oatcakes and a kind of croissant, both black and white Stornoway puddings, and of course the usual eggs all ways, bacon, sausages, kippers and smokies. *And* no smoking in the dining room. Heavenly bliss.
'There are a lot of small thoughtful things that make a hotel more than just comfortable. Beds are made while guests are having breakfast so you don't have the feeling of getting in the staff's way while you rush about the room trying to tidy up and get ready for the day's outing. Several different kinds of tea bags are provided in the room, and the coffee is also in bags, not the instant kind. Fresh flowers everywhere, charmingly arranged. But in the end perhaps the most important thing of all is the warm welcome and the way the young Johnsons make all their guests feel really wanted.'
(Mary Earle; also Kevin Myers; HR)

186

Open: All year, except usually last 3 weeks November.
Rooms: 4 double – 2 with bath, all with tea-making facilities. More rooms with bath planned for 1983.
Facilities: Drawing room with peat fires (and central heating), well-stocked library, restaurant. 1 acre grounds. Access to miles of sandy beach; sea fishing, trout and salmon fishing.
Location: 15 miles SW of Tarbert on the A859, 50 miles from Stornoway. Regular ferries from Ullapool to Stornoway and Uig to Tarbert; daily flights to Stornoway from Glasgow and Inverness. The hotel will arrange car hire.
Restrictions: No children under 8. Dogs by special arrangement.
Terms (no fixed service charge): B & B £11.50–20.50. Full board £23.50–37. Light or packed lunch £4–6. Set meal: dinner £12.

SCOURIE, Sutherland (Highland) Map 5

Eddrachilles Hotel *Telephone:* (0971) 2080
Badcall Bay

We had our first entry last year for this simple and remote hotel in the far north-western part of wildest Scotland, from readers who commended 'the impeccable haven of comfort and the ample home cooking of Mr and Mrs Wood.' One reader, who visited *Eddrachilles* during a particularly dreadful spell of weather in May thought the food only average and the hotel decidedly too cold for comfort and left. Another wrote:

'A long lonely and narrow road runs north-west from Dornoch or Lairg to a hamlet on the edge of restless waters bedecked by myriads of isles, islets and islands. The country which it crosses lies close to some of the oldest mountains in the world. Not too many travellers have explored this general area and the countryside alone should make any visit rewarding. The narrow road suddenly begins to dip downhill at a dramatic viewpoint (so be prepared to pause) and tiny Scourie lies ahead. *Eddrachilles* lies *beyond* the village and is quite well signposted from the road. Hill-walkers living in the area claim that *Eddrachilles* has interest enough around it for two fully occupied weeks of hill-walking and hill-scrambling. The hotel is also ideally placed for bird-watchers and there is an important bird sanctuary on Handa Island.

'We feel that the 1982 description is essentially accurate, though the furnishings were uninspiring. Another problem: 'home cooking' does not necessarily mean 'especially good or memorable cooking' and eight or nine days later we find that the meals we had have faded into the countless memories of nothing-very-special left by others throughout the years. One thing is certain, however: this hotel has an austere location but it provides bed and board way beyond what any (even experienced) traveller would be likely to expect in such a remote area.' *(George Mair; also David Sprecher and Kym Amps)*

Open: All year except 10–24 November.
Rooms: 11 double, 2 single, 1 suite – 4 with bath, 10 with shower, all with radio, TV (8 mono, 2 colour), tea-making facilities and baby-listening.
Facilities: Lounge, lounge bar, public bar, 2 dining rooms. Hotel stands in its own 320-acre estate at the head of Badcall Bay with woodland paths. Brown trout fishing. Near to sea with rocky shore and boats, and to Handa Island bird sanctuary.
Location: Just off the A894 Kylestrome–Scourie road. The hotel is well signposted from the road.

Restriction: No dogs in public rooms.
Terms (no service charge): B & B £14.30–18.90; dinner, B & B £18.95–24; full board £21.55–27.80. Set meal: dinner £5.10; full *alc* £11.50. Reduced rates available for stays of 3, 6 or 10 nights, and for children; special meals for children.

SLEAT, Isle of Skye, Inverness-shire (Highland)   **Map 5**

Hotel Eilean Iarmain   *Telephone:* Isleornsay (047 13) 266
     Telex: 75252

Eilean Iarmain, in a little fishing harbour overlooking the Sound of Sleat, describes itself as a small old-fashioned Gaelic-speaking Highland inn. A fair description: this small friendly hotel *is* unsophisticated in some respects, and certainly lacks one or two of the conventional late 20th-century mod cons, like bathrooms *en suite* and central heating. But bedrooms do have electric fires and hot water (also hot-water bottles) and Ian Noble, the owner, tells us that he hopes shortly to offer open fires in the bedrooms at an extra charge. Downstairs there are peat fires. The cooking is praised: menus are in Gaelic, but an English translation is provided. In our entry last year, we reported one guest's criticism of the coffee, but we are assured that this matter has been taken care of, and good strong fresh coffee is now provided. Mr Noble also asks us to mention, with reference to the available sport, that 'shooting and stalking (with keeper) are available over 20,000 acres, including grouse, pheasants, woodcock, cormorants, hares and wild fowl, not to mention roe deer.' Shooting is obviously big business hereabouts.

Open: All year.
Rooms: 11 double, 2 single (5 rooms in annexe).
Facilities: Dining room, lounge, bar; occasional dancing; dogs allowed. Boat trips, fishing, shooting, stalking available.
Location: In peninsula of Sleat, at the south of Skye.
Terms (no fixed service charge): B & B £10–14; dinner, B & B £17.50–25; full board £22–29. Set meals: lunch £4–5; dinner £7.50–11. Special winter rates. Reduced rates for children.

SLEAT, Isle of Skye, Inverness-shire (Highland)   **Map 5**

Kinloch Lodge   [GFG]   *Telephone:* Isle Ornsay (047 13) 214
     Telex: 75442 Donald G

Kinloch Lodge presents us with a dilemma. It has many characteristics of a good hotel in the Guide sense: it is a place of character – an old white-painted shooting lodge, attractively sited at the foot of a hill, half a mile from a minor road, with the garden leading directly to a sea loch; there are fine views on two sides of the house. The Lodge is owned and managed by Lord and Lady Macdonald, a thoroughly affable couple, and Lady Macdonald is personally responsible for the food. Most of the food is fresh and home-made from the marmalade at breakfast (of the full Scottish variety) to the after-dinner fudge. The cuisine is not haute and not all the dishes are equally successful, but the standard maintained is high. From a gastronomic point of view, Skye has no hotel to compare with *Kinloch*, and the dining room, despite modest wooden chairs, is a very pleasant place to eat, with gleaming silver, candles and excellent service.

Unfortunately, the hotel, though attractive at night, is less beguiling by day. The rooms vary in size – those towards the back are uncomfortably cramped – but even the larger rooms are spoiled by shoddy furniture and fittings. The lounge and bar, too, are furnished with utterly impersonal institutional tables and chairs. Service, except at mealtimes, is poor. A couple arriving at lunchtime found the place deserted. They were shown to their rooms by a man who promptly disappeared; they only discovered later that the hotel offers bar lunches, but they were offered no refreshments. No fires were lit, despite wretched weather. They felt they had arrived at a motel. From the names at the end of this entry, it is clear that, notwithstanding these shortcomings, the attractive features of *Kinloch Lodge* persuade many guests to overlook its shortcomings. But our files also contain criticisms which go beyond mere niggles. Part of the problem, we suspect, lies in the hotel being under-capitalised: the pockmarks on the drive are symbolic of the interior blemishes. But having visited the hotel ourselves in the autumn of 1982, we also concluded that the hotel lacks a strong controlling hand to oversee the show. Lord and Lady Macdonald supervise, but they do not live above the shop – and it shows. *(Mrs I Webb, Susan Loudon, Anne Viney, Diana and Peter Rudd, S M Gillotti, Mary Earle)*

Open: All year except 31 December and 1 January.
Rooms: 8 double, 2 single – 8 with bath. (Some rooms on ground floor.)
Facilities: Lounge, cocktail bar with TV, dining room. 40 acres grounds; 100 yards from the sea, safe sandy beach below the hotel at low water; fishing available on hotel's own freshwater lochs; splendid walking country. Daily flights from Glasgow to Skye. &.
Location: Off the A851 6 miles S of Broadford between Armadale ferry and Kyle of Lochalsh ferry.
Terms: B & B £12–22; dinner, B & B £21–30: full-board rates depend on length of stay. Set meal: dinner £11.50. Special off-season rates on application. Reduced rates and special meals for children.

SLIGACHAN, Isle of Skye, Inverness-shire (Highland)   **Map 5**

The Sligachan Hotel   *Telephone:* Sligachan (047 852) 204

A famous old inn, centrally placed for exploring Skye, at the head of a sea loch from which it draws its name, and with the Cuillin hills as a theatrical backdrop. It has a particularly hallowed name in the annals of Scottish mountaineering; almost every great 19th-century mountaineer has signed *Sligachan*'s visitor's book. In our entry last year, we reported criticism of the standard of accommodation here, which it was felt had not moved with the times. A loyal supporter rises to its defence:

'We have been to *Sligachan* a number of times and have never been disappointed by the food or the accommodation or by anything else. We have no memories which are not laced with contentment. The architecture is in harmony with the surroundings, which are austere. The Highlands have developed a quite typical style of domestic design which one finds in "great" houses as well as in more minor mansions. There is an emphasis on deeply cosy armchairs and really thick solid wood. Places look as if they had been made to last for several generations. *Sligachan* tends to reflect the character of the people whom it served when character was being moulded. So it is stern, perhaps off-putting at first sight, may appear to be disapproving of frivolity (especially on a Sunday), yet it has its own local way of generating a great deal of fun, and, above all, it seems to be a reliable haven of security among mountains which have taken many lives.' *(George B Mair)*

Open: May–September.
Rooms: 15 double, 8 single – 9 with bath.
Facilities: 2 lounges, cocktail lounge, dining room. ½ acre grounds beside the river (fishing free to residents). Golf 3 miles; boats for hire on local lochs.
Location: Mallaig–Armadale ferry (Sligachan 30 miles); Kyle of Lochalsh–Kyleakin ferry (Sligachan 24 miles). Bus services from both ports to Sligachan.
Restrictions: No children under 8. No dogs in public rooms.
Terms: B & B £17.50–18; dinner, B & B £25–25.50 (4 nights and over). Set meal: dinner £8.50; full *alc* £7. Reduced rates for children.

STRACHUR, Argyll (Strathclyde) Map 5

The Creggans Inn [GFG] *Telephone:* Strachur (036 986) 279
Telex: 727396 att. Creggans

'The hotel lives up to the beauty of its setting – every window is a picture of Loch Fyne and its glorious hills. The food is all we had expected – the constant use of Lady Maclean's famous cookbook shows genius. I was with a convalescent friend, and we were both touched by the unobtrusive care that supported her. Mrs Huggins, the manageress, is tireless in her aim – keeping the hotel the oasis that it is.' A very handsome tribute indeed for this prosperous hostelry – still a local for the locals, but now, with its private telephones in all the bedrooms and baths adjoining most, decidedly more of a hotel than an inn. Sir Fitzroy and Lady Maclean are the owners, but not in residence; Mrs Huggins is the spirit in charge. Some of the rooms are more comfortable than others: we had one negative report, from a guest whose bedroom could only be reached through the lounge and, with a large bathroom carved out, was decidedly too cramped. Another guest complained of slow service at meals. But these were lone voices: most guests have appreciated the comfort of the house as well as the fare – and the view. *(Frances S Perry; also Michael Wareham, Anne Viney)*

Open: All year.
Rooms: 17 double, 5 single – 17 with bath, 2 with shower, all with telephone, radio, TV and baby-listening. (2 rooms on ground floor.)
Facilities: 2 lounges, sun lounge, TV room, restaurant; conference/party facilities. 6 acres grounds with woodland walk. Small beach by loch Fyne for bathing. Sea fishing in loch; trout and salmon fishing can be arranged. &.
Location: On the A815 Dunoon–Strachur road, on the edge of loch Fyne.
Credit cards: Access/Euro/Mastercard, American Express, Barclay/Visa.
Terms: B & B £20–31; dinner, B & B £25–31.50. Full *alc* £16. Reduced rates and special meals for children under 12. Special rates (dinner, B & B) for stays of 3 days or more. Special Christmas/New Year package.

Most hotels have reduced rates out of season and for children, and some British hotels offer 'mini-break' rates throughout the year. For details you should write direct to the hotel.

TWEEDSMUIR, Biggar, Lanarkshire (Borders)　　　　Map 5

The Crook Inn　　　　　　　　*Telephone:* Tweedsmuir (089 97) 272

A modest family-run hotel in the heart of John Buchan country. It also has associations with Sir Walter Scott and Burns; the latter wrote 'Willie Wastle's Wife' in the old kitchen of *Crook*. Good walking and climbing country: Broad Law, the second highest peak in southern Scotland, is five miles from the inn. There are three golf courses within easy reach. As for fishing, hotel guests have the run of 30 miles of trout water on the Tweed; there are also seven miles of private salmon fishing six miles downstream from the hotel available to its guests

'I dropped in for a pub lunch on my way north. Excellent home-made brown bread and *pâté* at the bar, plus a very friendly welcome. So I decided to spend the night on my way south. Spotlessly clean and cheerful room. Most delicious dinner. Choice of first course: again I had *pâté*. One hot main course each day, mine was pork tenderloin in wine with mushrooms – delectable, and lovely fresh vegetables. Choice of good and original cold sweets and cheese and coffee. Most charming waitresses and really good service. Breakfast equally good, with oatcakes and home-made marmalade. I thoroughly recommend this pub in every way. The atmosphere, the friendliness, the comfort, the food and drink. It was like an oasis in the desert when I first found it, as there is nothing else in the area.' *(Lady Holland-Martin)*

Open: All year except Christmas.
Rooms: 7 double, 1 single – 6 with bath, all with tea-making facilities.
Facilities: Residents' lounge with TV, lounge, bar, restaurant, games room. 3 acres garden. Salmon and trout fishing; 3 golf courses nearby.
Location: On the A701 Edinburgh road, 1 mile north of Tweedsmuir; parking.
Restriction: No dogs in public rooms.
Terms: B & B £14–16.50; dinner, B & B £21–24.50. Full *alc* £9. Reduced rates and special meals for children. Special bargain breaks. 3-day New Year package.

ULLAPOOL, Wester Ross (Highland)　　　　Map 5

Altnaharrie Inn　[GFG]　　　　*Telephone:* Dundonnell (085 483) 230

'The *Altnaharrie Inn*, opposite Ullapool across Loch Broom, is tiny, cosy and charming. As *Altnaharrie* is virtually inaccessible by land, you get ferried over the water like Lord Ullin's daughter in the proprietor's excellent wee motor-boat. The house is a centuries-old drovers' inn with just a handful of bedrooms. The furnishing is comfortable and pretty and the food wonderful. I asked the proprietor, Mr Fred Brown, why his brochure promised only "good food" when the reality was a marvel. His reply: the guests might enjoy the nice surprise. I go quite weak when I remember the loch Broom prawns, large as langoustines, local fresh salmon, venison *pâté*, succulent roast lamb and puddings of such creamy lightness as defy gravity. Oh the delight of lying in an *Altnaharrie* bath with a pre-prandial drink, relaxing in that soft Highland water straight off the peat, of a colour somewhere between lager and Guinness, the only noises off being your companion murmuring through the door what's on the evening menu (so that Miss Erikson can cook your choice specially) and loch Broom outside the window gently turning itself over at the edge.

The neighbourhood has splendid walks. We saw deer, seal and all sorts of great northern sea birds. Further, at Ullapool for 20 weeks of the summer, the mackerel catch is landed and it is an entertainment and an education to watch the haul being transferred from ship to shore. Our host Mr Brown was kindness itself. When the car seized up and had to be towed away to Inverness, practical help was offered promptly and sympathetically. In praise of good hotels your subscribers have maintained that their visit was more like staying with friends. In Brown's house it is like staying with a favourite cousin. He is both a yachtsman and a practising vet. In the garden climbing trees is a pair of milk-white goats offered to him as a fee. Their lyrical presence is entirely in keeping with the pleasures of this place – very honeymoony.' *(Shelley Cranshaw; warmly endorsed by HR)*

Open: 1 April–31 October. Also a self-catering chalet.
Rooms: 4 double – 2 with bath.
Facilities: Residents' lounge, bar, dining room. 15-acre garden, pebbled beach. Trout/lobster/deep sea fishing; free canoes/small dinghies.
Location: By water's edge on shore of sea loch. Access to hotel by private launch from Ullapool harbour (10 minutes); private parking in Ullapool; guests requested to telephone for launch on arrival in Ullapool.
Restriction: No dogs in dining room or unaccompanied in bedrooms.
Terms (no fixed service charge): B & B £11.50–14.50. Full *alc* £10.30. Reduced rates and special meals for children.

ULLAPOOL, Wester Ross (Highland)   Map 5

The Ceilidh Place   *Telephone:* Ullapool (0854) 2103
14 West Argyle Street

An informal off-beat establishment, owned and run ('hopefully in an efficiently casual way') by the actor Robert Urquhart and his wife Jean. To quote from their fairly theatrical brochure: 'Come stay with us. Our house and your house. Hotel, restaurant and dining room: art gallery, theatre and concert room: call it any of these if you wish. We call it a *ceilidh* place. We will arrange sea angling for you, skiing tow boats, loch fishing and ponytrekking. We will tell you of and guide you in all manner of strenuous pursuits like mountain climbing and deep sea diving, but we shall also provide you with comfort, music and rest so that you may contemplate the madness of such strenuous activity.'

'Ullapool sits halfway along the eastern shore of loch Broom, which means that it has few rivals in the matter of scenic grandeur. One cannot argue with the booklet on local walking which lauds the peace and tranquillity of Wester Ross, while adding a warning that there is always an element of danger in its solitude "for the unprepared and unwary".' The mountainous country around this fishing village is virtually a wilderness. There are great rewards for just following your nose, but you get more reliable value from a map. Taking pot luck on food and accommodation is also hazardous up here, so it is a joy to find Robert and Jean Urquhart's *Ceilidh Place* providing such comfort and good eating. It is done with a discreet kind of flair. 'Ceilidh' (pronounced 'kaly') is Gaelic for something like get-together, and the ambience of the all-day coffee shop (and bar, open at the usual hours) is intended to cheer, but not too insistently. The taped music is mostly classical; the live shows, frequent in the summer, offer mostly folksong and trad jazz. The very young staff serve excellent light meals – the unconventional salads are particularly good – with the impression of being glad to. The coffee shop was the foundation of the Urquharts' little spread – it grew, in fact, out of the cottage Robert was born in. In more recent years they have added a hotel of really individual character; simply, robustly furnished, with plenty of dark wood and tweedy fabrics; roomy, utterly informal. If you recoil from the thought of a hotel bedroom that overlooks a caravan site (some rooms do) or a council house back garden (others do) then avoid this hotel. More sensibly you will accept the foreground as part of the village life and then lift your eyes to the hills – weather permitting, as it may not. It's that kind of place. The hotel dining room, separate from the coffee shop, does no damage whatever to local salmon, prawns, steak and lamb chops; and, again, the kitchen has a rare way with refreshing salads. The resplendent trolley of puddings is a nightly seducer: thrill, unashamedly, to the apple pie laced with marmalade.' *(Arthur Hopcraft)*

Open: April–November.

Rooms: 12 double, 3 single – 8 with bath, all with baby-listening. 11 extra rooms in club house in annexe.

Facilities: Lounge, games room/bar, coffee shop, dining room; June–August occasional musical evenings and theatre groups. ¼ acre garden; private fishing in Ledmore Lochs, rocky beach, boat trips, sea angling, waterskiing, ponytrekking, climbing, deep-sea diving.

Location: 1st right after Pier at W end of Main Street; large car park.

Restriction: No dogs in public rooms.

Credit card: Diners.

Terms (no fixed service charge): Rooms (annexe only) £6.25 per person; B & B (hotel) £15–16 (annexe) £10. Packed lunches available. Set meals: lunch £1–4, dinner £6–12; full *alc* £14. Children under 2, free; under 9, £6.50 B & B (hotel); special meals provided. Painting, Sailing, Canoeing, Field Study courses. Special rates for 6 days or more.

Dixcart Hotel, Sark

Channel Islands

White House Hotel   *Telephone:* Guernsey (0481) 22159 or Herm 83

'The hotel stands in the most perfect island I have ever clapped my eyes on. It is owned and run by Major Wood, the tenant of Herm, and quite plainly he has revelled in turning this old country house into a superb hotel with spacious dining rooms and lounges overlooking the sea. For island-lovers here is paradise.' *(Christopher Portway)*

Herm Island, 1½ miles long by 1 mile wide, has a native population of 36 including children, though it has to meet an invasion of up to 2,000 day-trippers from Guernsey in August. The *White House* is the only hotel. There is a farm that produces and exports milk to Guernsey, a pub called *The Mermaid*, two beach cottages and 8 self-catering cottages. And that is about it. There is no swimming pool at the *White House*; it doesn't need one as there are 1½ miles of sandy beach. There is no TV either. There are no clocks on any of the buildings, no cars, and, according to the hotel director, Andrew Forbes, 'Herm hasn't developed into a hard-sell commercial island, and the hotel, even in mid-summer, retains its country-house atmosphere: you can sit in total peace in the lounges and the private gardens.'

We should be glad to hear from other visitors to this enchanted isle.

Open: In principle, all year – but check in winter when they sometimes close for short periods.

Rooms: 22 double, 2 single, 10 suites – 31 with bath, all with radio, tea-making facilities and baby-listening. 20 rooms in 3 cottages in the grounds.
Facilities: 2 sea-facing lounges, 2 bars, 2 restaurants. 2 acres garden. Tennis, croquet, table-tennis available.
Location: Direct to Guernsey, then by high-speed launch to harbour where hotel porter will meet guests. (No cars on Herm.)
Credit cards: Barclay/Visa.
Terms (no service charge; no VAT payable in the Channel Islands): Full board £22.50–30. (NB Guests who stayed in 1982 will pay 1982 prices in 1983.) Set meals: lunch £4.20, dinner £6.20. Children under 6 free in family suites (which have 2 bedrooms and a bathroom) April–July inclusive and after mid-September. Special meals provided. Christmas programme.

ST SAVIOUR, Jersey   Map 1

Longueville Manor Hotel   *Telephone:* Jersey (0534) 25501
                                                            Telex: 4192306

For those who like and can afford to live graciously, *Longueville* is, by quite a margin, the most agreeable hotel in the Channel Islands – a view, incidentally, in which Michelin concurs since *Longueville* has been for many years the only hotel in the archipelago to get the red treatment, indicating a specially pleasant place to stay. It is 1½ miles inland from Jersey's capital, St Helier, and 2½ miles from the Royal Jersey Golf Course. The hotel is a family affair, owned by Mr and Mrs Neal Lewis and run by their daughter and son-in-law, Mr and Mrs Simon Duffy. In the past there has been only one fly in *Longueville's* soup: the restaurant, at least in the view of most readers, has not been of the same standard of excellence as the rest of the enterprise. Hopefully, all that has changed. We were delighted to learn that the hotel has now acquired a young new chef from the *Connaught*, London (q.v.), John Dicken, who has been earning high compliments. And every other prospect continues to please. Here is a recent unqualified report from an American visitor: 'Truly excellent unobtrusive service. Excellent food and wine – well deserved four stars. My favourite hotel in our two-week tour of France and England.' *(LoRae Fletcher-Trebas)*

Open: All year.
Rooms: 31 double, 5 single – 34 with bath, 2 with shower, all with telephone, radio and colour TV. (6 rooms on ground floor; one 4-poster bed.)
Facilities: Hall lounge, bar/lounge, reading room, panelled dining room. 15 acres grounds with heated swimming pool, putting green, riding stables. Golf, bowls, squash, tennis within easy reach; coaches call by arrangement for island drives and other excursions. &.
Location: 1½ miles E of St Helier; ¾ mile from the sea; bus stop near main hotel gates.
Restrictions: No children under 7. No dogs in public rooms.
Credit cards: All major credit cards accepted.
Terms (no VAT payable in Channel Islands): B & B £28–36; dinner, B & B £40–46; full board £45.50–52. Set meals (excluding 10% service charge): lunch £7.25; dinner £10.25; full *alc* £15. 40% reduction for children sharing parents' room.

Procrastination is the thief of the next edition.

SARK, via Guernsey   **Map 1**

Aval du Creux Hotel   [GFG]   *Telephone:* Sark (048 183) 2036

Last year's entry for this popular farmhouse hotel, with a remarkably good restaurant, quoted a reader, who had just booked for his seventh year, noting 'the usual compliment of departing guests seen removing the invisible flies from their eyes'. There is no single metaphor in this year's postbag as striking as that, but the sentiments have been the same: 'Our fifth visit. Standards as high as before – a unique blend of efficiency with friendly atmosphere, and the choices on the set menu not repeated once in eleven days.' 'Our fifth stay, and not much I can add to previous reports on this excellent hotel. It astounds me how Peter Hauser and his family keep up their standards in all areas.' *(J H Myring, N E Cooper)*

Open: 1 May–1 October.
Rooms: 2 single, 5 suites – all with shower.
Facilities: Lounge with TV, sun-lounge, bar (with zither music by request), dining room. 1 acre grounds.
Location: Just W of Creux harbour.
Restriction: No dogs.
Credit card: Visa.
Terms (no VAT payable in Channel Islands): Dinner, B & B £18; full board £21. Set meals: lunch £4; dinner £7; full *alc* £10. Reduced rates and special meals for children.

SARK, via Guernsey   **Map 1**

Dixcart Hotel   [GFG]   *Telephone:* (048 183) 2015

Sark, without crowds or cars, is a dependable haven for the jaded urbanite, and a paradise for naturalists. Only 3½ miles long by 1¼ miles wide, it has 40 miles of coastline with many coves and wonderful cliff walks. There are boats every weekday from Guernsey and a couple of hydrofoils operate from Jersey; the *Dixcart* collects your luggage by tractor. It's an early 19th-century building, stone-built and partly creeper-covered. Swinburne and Victor Hugo are among the illustrious names of former residents. It is a flowery and friendly old house, described by one of its grateful guests as possessing 'a unique atmosphere of insouciance and charm'. The rooms, although small and simple, are comfortable. The charges are reasonable, and we are glad to learn from the presiding genius of *Dixcart*, Peggy Ravenshaw – a character and an institution – that she hopes to keep close to the 1982 prices for 1983. There have been some criticisms of the food at *Dixcart* in recent years, but recent visitors have felt that the cooking had returned to previous high standards. 'It makes no attempt,' one writer concludes, 'to reach *Holiday Inn* uniformity. *Dixcart* is like staying with friends, not at a hotel.' *(AM, JR-T)*

Open: Easter–October.
Rooms: 12 double, 6 single – 7 with bath or shower. (8 rooms in wing and annexe.)
Facilities: 2 sitting rooms, lounge, library, bar, restaurant, forecourt. 9 acres grounds. 5 minutes' walk to sea with sandy beach and safe bathing; fishing from rock and sand; fine walks.

Restriction: No dogs in restaurant or bar.

Terms (excluding 10% service charge; no VAT payable in Channel Islands): Dinner, B & B £18–24.05; full board £19.80–25.85. Set meals: lunch £5, dinner £7; full *alc* £12. Reduced rates off-season for children under 10. Special breaks during May, June and September.

SARK, via Guernsey

Map 1

Hotel Petit Champ [GFG] *Telephone:* Sark (048 183) 2046

The *Petit Champ* has the admirable virtue of maintaining its character and quality over a long period of time. It is a pleasant late 19th-century granite building in a secluded part of Sark, well away from the day-trippers, but half-an-hour's walk to any part of the island. Most of its rooms have views over the sea and the neighbouring islands of Guernsey, Herm and Jethou. It has a well-tended garden and a solar-heated swimming pool cleverly excavated from a sun-trapping disused quarry. There is also, *mirabile dictu*, a first-rate restaurant. Mr and Mrs Scott have been the resident owners for many years past. Their hotel is the sort of place where a congenial crowd regather at the same season year after year. Some prefer rooms in the new wing, with bathrooms *en suite*; others like the less ornate but more individual rooms in the old house, even if a bathroom has to be shared. Mealtimes tend to be sharpish – breakfast at 8 a.m., for example – and everyone sits down at the same time. But prices are extremely reasonable, and most guests are happy to accommodate themselves to a well-run system. A first-timer writes: 'In many years of globe-trotting, I have never found a hotel so pleasant – or so difficult to leave.' Only major change reported to us this year is that the Scotts have acquired a new gardener who has improved the garden 'beyond recognition'. Otherwise, all continues placid in the little meadow. *(Margaret Handley, Mr P B Spanoghe, Anthony Fletcher)*

Open: 23 April–8 October.
Rooms: 11 double, 3 single, 2 suites – 11 with bath; tea-making facilities on request.
Facilities: 1 lounge, 3 sun-lounges, bar, 3 dining rooms, TV room. 1 acre garden with heated swimming pool.
Location: 30 minutes from Guernsey to Sark; then carriage to hotel, or lift by Island Transport to the top of the hill and a 20-minute walk.
Restrictions: No children under 8. No dogs.
Credit cards: Access/Euro, Barclay/Visa, Diners (but only for meals).
Terms (no fixed service charge; no VAT payable in Channel Islands): B & B £9.25–13; dinner, B & B £14.50–19.50; full board £16–21. Set meals: lunch from £3.50, dinner from £7; full *alc* lunch £5.50, dinner £8.50. Reduced rates (⅓) for children sharing parents' room.

Northern Ireland

ANNADORN, Downpatrick, Co Down   **Map 6**

Nutgrove   [GFG]   *Telephone:* Seaforde (039 687) 275

'*Nutgrove* lives up to – and exceeds – your commendation. Elegance and comfort in a beautiful house in beautiful surroundings. The food is superb. British, Irish and continental dishes are cooked to perfection. The home-made wheaten bread is delicious and Queen's Pudding is a gourmet's delight! A special diet for one of us was always unobtrusively supplied – just an example of the thoughtfulness and helpfulness of our hosts.' *(Herbert and Dorothy Gallagher).* A typical endorsement, one of many for last year's entry which we reproduce, slightly shortened, below:

Nutgrove is clearly not a hotel in the accepted sense of the term and both more idiosyncratic and also more sophisticated than the term 'guest house' implies. The description in the brochure tells a lot: '*Nutgrove* is an early Victorian Mill House, built about 1836, set in the heart of County Down. It is run by Christopher and Heather Cowdy – helped by Natasha, Jessica and Christopher-Robert – as a romantic revival of older-day living. The house now stands as it was built. The family have been adamant that absolutely no changes should be made to the house at all. The dining room, which seats about 30 people, is open on Wednesdays, Thursdays, Fridays and Saturdays for dinner at 8.30 p.m. If residents would like something to eat on the other evenings, a simple meal can be arranged. The menu, which changes every month, is very short, as everything is cooked that day by Heather Cowdy. 'We don't have any notices or rules and are quite flexible about special diets, etc. The house is definitely rather quiet – no radio, no TV, no piped music and is up a narrow lane. Breakfast is taken on the large landing and we usually

199

provide a log fire and newspapers on Sunday mornings. Most of our visitors come because we are slightly cut off from the outside world.' And here is the view of one grateful guest: 'A delightful blend of old-world grace and sophistication without pretension: delightfully and restfully unique.' *(Rosemary Metcalfe; also J H Sheerin)*

Open: 1 April–30 November.
Rooms: 4 double – 2 with bath.
Facilities: Drawing room, breakfast room. Garden with stream. Golf, fishing, beaches nearby.
Location: From Seaforde village, turn into Seaforde road by the cottages. Take 2nd left and then 1st right.
Restrictions: No children under 10. No dogs in public rooms. Hotel has no licence so guests are asked to bring their own wines and spirits; no corkage charge.
Terms (no fixed service charge): B & B £11–18. Set meal: dinner £10.50–14.

DUNADRY, Templepatrick, Co Antrim   **Map 6**

Dunadry Inn   *Telephone:* Templepatrick (084 94) 32474
                                     Telex: 747245

Not by any means your little old-world country inn, but a large and sophisticated hostelry, with 77 rooms and a restaurant that can take 80 at a sitting, not to mention a ballroom that can dine 300 at a time. Inevitably, a place of this size and tariff carries a certain whiff of the expense account about it – but, as the report below makes clear, it meets a local need.

'The *Dunadry Inn* is in the country about 15 minutes from the airport; an old house with stables linked to it to form a long wing of bedrooms. A lovely arrival: a large entrance hall with polished floors and 'good' rugs, beams rescued, I understand, from an old water mill – and, most important of all, at 10.20 p.m., a friendly and efficient welcome. The restaurant was closed, but in about 10 minutes a tray of excellent, hot, gamey soup, slightly plastic cheese, an apple and a good pot of coffee had been brought to my room. The bedroom was spacious by modern hotel standards, sympathetically furnished, and the bathroom excellent. All the downstairs areas and rooms are huge – and the dining room one of the biggest, looking out over the river surrounded by lush foliage. The breakfast was "good hotel" (butter and marmalade in horrid packs) but the poached eggs had been done in water properly, and the toast was fresh. Altogether a hotel which combines the best of the old and the new, very well-run, convenient and in a pleasant setting. It was expensive, but was certainly streets better than other places I've stayed at at similar prices, and gave a superb first impression of Northern Ireland.' *(Elizabeth Stanton)*

Open: All year except Christmas.
Rooms: 46 double, 31 single, 8 suites – 57 with bath, 20 with shower, all with telephone, radio, colour TV and baby-listening. 2 rooms in annexe.
Facilities: Reception lounge, restaurant, ballroom, banqueting and conference facilities; dinner-dance every Saturday except July; jazz nights. 6 acres garden; river with trout fishing; riding, golf nearby. &.
Location: 3 miles from Antrim; 13 miles from Belfast.
Restriction: No dogs in public rooms except guide dogs.
Terms: B & B £22.50–36. Set meal: buffet lunch £4; full *alc* £12.25–14.25. Weekend breaks. Babies free; children under 12, 50%; special meals on request.

Longueville House, Mallow

Republic of Ireland

Gregan's Castle   *Telephone:* Ballyvaughan 5
                                                         Telex: 28110

Gregan's Castle is the only hotel in the heart of the Burren, that weird 100 square miles of lunar landscape roughly halfway between Galway and Shannon airport. The Burren is full of rare flowers and plants, both alpine and arctic, and is a paradise for botanists, but it is also rich in historic and prehistoric remains, and has a vast underground cave system, so it attracts geologists, archaeologists and spelaeologists too, not to mention ornithologists. Yeats lovers will be attracted to Thor Ballylee, a town of great charm where he lived for a few years near Lady Gregory. But *Gregan's Castle* is not only a base for cultural activity:

'This hotel is a gem. We visited first in 1979 and have been back annually three times since – lured as much by the welcome at *Gregan's Castle* as by the magic of the Burren topography and flora. This is a country-house type of hotel where the atmosphere is calm and leisurely and visitors really feel more like house guests than hotel customers. *Gregan's Castle* is owned and run by Peter and Moira Haden. They make themselves accessible and are eager to ensure their guests' comfort and enjoyment. When they took over *Gregan's Castle* the surrounding trees were dangerously old and had to be felled, so that the grounds seemed raw and bleak for a few years. Each winter the Hadens work hard at improvements outside and inside, and the grounds are beginning to

201

acquire a maturity to match the elegant interior. The furniture in the public rooms is comfortable and stylish; and apt decorations for an hotel set in a botanical Mecca are the orchid paintings by Raymond Piper in the lounge and paintings of other Burren flowers by James Flack in the bedrooms. The staff are mostly local, and obviously hand-picked for their warmth and charm as well as for their ability to anticipate guests' needs. The same staff have been at the hotel each of the four successive years that we have stayed. The dining room looks down a valley to Galway bay and the changing play of evening light on the flanking, grey limestone hills is a scenic pleasure that enhances the gastronomic excellence of the four-course dinner. Delicacy and freshness are the keynotes of the cuisine – no aggressive sauces smother the carefully chosen meat or the beautifully prepared and cooked local fish. Vegetables – generally a sensitive indicator – are superb. There is a full and representative wine list. There is a full Irish breakfast, or a "weight-watchers" alternative. The inexhaustible pleasures of the Burren have beckoned us outdoors irrespective of weather and so lunch cannot be reported on directly – it is served only in the bar, but the menu is the offering of a restaurateur rather than a publican.' *(Drs L and E Perry; also Mr and Mrs J H Carney, Roger Wilsdon, Sheelah R Draper)*

Open: Mid March–late October.
Rooms: 14 double, 2 single – 12 with bath. (2 rooms in annexe on ground floor.)
Facilities: Hall with fireplace, 2 lounges (1 with TV), Corkscrew Bar, dining room with large picture windows overlooking Galway Bay. 14 acres of grounds with parkland and gardens. Safe, sandy beach within 4 miles with excellent shore fishing; surfing farther off at Fanore; boat available June–September for sea fishing and trips to the Aran Islands.
Location: Shannon Airport 37 miles, Limerick 47 miles; 3½ miles from village: entrance is on road between Ballyvaughan and Lisdoonvarna.
Restriction: Dogs allowed, but not in bedrooms, nor public rooms except on lead.
Credit cards: American Express, Barclay/Visa.
Terms (excluding 12½% service charge): B & B IR£14–25. Set meal: dinner IR£12.50; full *alc* (11.0 a.m.–5.0 p.m. only) IR£10. Reduced rates for children; special meals on request.

CASHEL, Co Galway   **Map 6**

Cashel House   *Telephone:* Clifden 252
                                                           Telex: 28812

OF HISTORIC INTEREST, says the brochure: 'It was in Cashel House Hotel that the late General and Madame de Gaulle spent two weeks of their Irish holiday in 1969.' It must be hard for the hotel to forget the instant immortality conferred on it by General de Gaulle making this his highly publicized hide-out on his sudden retirement. The hotel still gets a lot of French visitors, but we are assured that it also entertains British ones too, including a retired Prime Minister. Meanwhile, this handsome white-painted mid 19th-century house, at the head of Cashel Bay, in a well-cared-for 50-acre estate, continues to give satisfaction to lesser mortals. Dermot McEvilly, the owner, tells us that his food has greatly improved recently, and most of our reporters have been enjoying their meals here – 'splendid breakfast; huge platter of smoked salmon in bar for lunch; good mussels, trout and salmon for dinner' – as well as other features of the hotel's hospitality. *(R F V Heuston; also J & A Hartley and others)*

Open: 1 March–1 November.
Rooms: 20 double, 2 single, 9 suites – 30 with bath. (8 rooms on ground floor.)
Facilities: 2 lounges, dining room. 50 acres gardens with flowering shrubs and woodland walks; hard tennis court; small sandy beach private to residents; grounds lead to Cashel Hill. Many other beaches within easy reach; golf, lake and river fishing, birdwatching, riding, deep-sea fishing. &.
Restrictions: No children under 5. No dogs in public rooms.
Credit cards: Access/Euro, Barclay/Visa.
Terms (excluding 12½% service): B & B IR£14.95–21.50; dinner, B & B IR£27.95–35.75. Set meal: lunch IR£10, dinner IR£13; full *alc* IR£14.

CORK   Map 6

Arbutus Lodge Hotel   [GFG]   *Telephone:* Cork (021) 501237
Montenotte   From UK dial 0002 instead of 021
                                                          Telex: 75079

Arbutus Lodge has been a famous Cork hotel for many years – its reputation being as much for the quality of the table (the only Michelin-starred restaurant in the country) as for the welcome of the house. The owner is Sean Ryan, assisted by his two sons, Declan and Michael, both of whom had been trained as chefs at the *Hotel des Frères Troisgros* at Roanne (q.v.). Last year, we reported that Declan and his wife Patsy had left to start the *Cashel Palace Hotel*. Alas, it was a bad year to open a new de-luxe hotel; the *Cashel Palace* has been sold and Declan is once again at *Arbutus.*

As for the *Lodge*, it is a merchant's house, circa 1802, built on the north scarp of the river Lee in one of the fashionable suburbs of Cork, Montenotte, 15 minutes' walk or 5 minutes' drive from the city centre. There are fine views over the city, especially at night. One of the features of the hotel is its splendid terraced garden, with many fine trees including *Arbutus unedo* from which it gets its name. Another is a notable collection of modern paintings. The entrance floor has a large and comfortable bar, a residents' lounge and the restaurant, with its large bay window and reassuringly solid Victorian appearance – starched white table-cloths, good china and glasses, flowers, candles, etc. Bedrooms are on the upper floor, and there are reception rooms for weddings and suchlike on the lower floor; disco noises will sometimes percolate to the public rooms, but not to the bedrooms, which are thoughtfully equipped with good-quality furniture and the usual range of mod cons. Everything about the place reflects the caring hand of the owners – not least the service.

Open: All year, except 1 week at Christmas. Restaurant closed Sunday except to residents.
Rooms: 12 double, 8 single – 15 with bath, 5 with shower, all with telephone, radio and colour TV.
Facilities: Lounge, bar, restaurant. Small garden with patio for eating out in summer.
Location: 5 minutes by car from town centre; parking.
Restriction: No dogs.
Credit cards: All major credit cards accepted.
Terms: B & B IR£26–35. Set meals: lunch IR£13, dinner IR£15; full *alc* IR£18.50.

Buswells Hotel   *Telephone:* Dublin (01) 764013
Molesworth Street   (from UK dial 001 instead of 01)
                                                          Telex: 24858

In the first edition of the Guide, we had entries for two famous old Dublin hotels, *The Shelbourne* and *Royal Hibernian*, now both part of the Trust House Forte chain. We have long wanted a smaller, more personal hotel to recommend, and hope that *Buswells*, which calls itself the oldest family hotel in the city, may fit the bill. It is close to St Stephen's Green, the Dáil and the main shopping centres, and prices are reasonable. Some rooms are small, but all are decently appointed. 'It is not what one would call elegant, nor is the restaurant anything to shout about. But the hotel itself has excellent service, and good and friendly attention to guests' whims and needs. If you linger in *Buswells* attractive bar, you cannot but meet an expansive and friendly Irish MP who will tell you all about his country and its politics. But above all, *Buswells* is a comfortable place to stay in.' *(Cesar Ortiz; also Mark Barty-King)*

Open: All year.
Rooms: 41 double, 16 single – all with bath, telephone, radio, colour TV and hair-dryer; baby-sitters on request.
Facilities: Lift, residents' lounge with TV, bar/lounge, restaurant; conference facilities.
Location: In St Stephen's Green area; public car park close by.
Restriction: Dogs allowed in bedroom only.
Credit cards: Access/Euro/Mastercard, American Express, Barclay/Visa.
Terms: B & B £28.80–34.70. Set meal: lunch £3.85–6.60; full *alc* £11.50 (excluding 12½% service charge). Winter weekend breaks November–April; 3-day Christmas package. 50% reduction for children under 12 sharing parents' room; special meals provided.

Marlfield House   [GFG]   *Telephone:* Gorey (055) 21124
                                       (Code only applicable within Ireland)

Mary Bowe, the owner, herself converted this noble three-storey Regency house, formerly the dower house of the Courtown estate, into a peaceful country-house hotel. The comforts of the house, its position – a mile from the sea with sandy beaches, close to a golf-course and with plenty of the beauty spots of Co Wicklow and the south-east within easy touring distance, not to mention the cooking which is taken seriously here and has a substantial non-resident following (strong emphasis on locally caught fish, home-grown vegetables and fresh herbs) – all are reasons why people return here regularly.

Our entry last year, while substantially favourable, did comment on the overcrowding and slow service in the restaurant when full, also some blemishes in the cooking. We are glad to learn from Mary Bowe that she has been carrying out major structural changes, especially in the restaurant and reckons to have made major improvements in the standard of service and the quality of food – more particularly following a course she took with Roger Vergé in France, and another that her head chef took with Robert Carrier. One recent reporter much enjoyed his stay, but found his meal a little curate's-eggy – some parts masterly and others fumbled. Others were unqualified in their enthusiasm: 'The new extension to the dining room is magnificent. Excellent food and value for money. All in all, a gourmet's delight.' *(Athacta Quinn)* 'This hotel must – after the addition of their garden restaurant – be the most beautiful in Ireland. The meals are not only exquisite in their taste but visually a delight.' *(Anne Lewis-Smith)*

Open: All year, except Christmas.
Rooms: 12 double – 11 with bath, 1 with shower, all with telephone.
Facilities: Lounge, TV room, restaurant. 36 acres woodland with river, duck pond, pheasantry; shooting available. Sandy beaches with safe bathing and fishing 1 mile; golf club nearby. &.
Location: On the Gorey Courtown road, 55 miles from Dublin, 28 miles from Wexford.
Restrictions: No children under 6. No dogs.
Terms (no fixed service charge): B & B IR£20.45–24.50; dinner, B & B IR£36–40; full board IR£44–48. Set meal: dinner IR14.50; full *alc* lunch IR£13. Reduced meal rates for children. Bargain breaks November–April.

KILLARNEY, Co Kerry   **Map 6**

Aghadoe Heights   *Telephone:* Killarney (064) 31766
(Code only applicable within Ireland)
Telex: 26942

'In spite of all the hoo-ha, Killarney is almost unbelievably beautiful outside the scruffy market-cum-tourist town. *Aghadoe Heights* is a modern hotel overlooking the lakes just over three miles outside the town and adjoining the ruins of Aghadoe Cathedral, dating from the 7th century (car recommended). Half the bedrooms (and the dining room) have a view over the lakes and mountains that no possible travel brochure could excel. W B Yeats wrote that it was not the green land of Ireland that was so wonderful, but the clouds and skies over it. I have spent whole mornings after breakfast just lying in bed looking at the changing colours and sky patterns on lakes and mountains. There is a little too much muzak in the public area, and the food in the restaurant is international and willing rather than gastronomic. The proprietor, Louis O'Hara, has ties with France, whence come many professional people to play golf, enjoy the superb scenery – and the peace.' *(Thomas Annesley)*. More reports welcome.

Open: All year except 20 December–20 January.
Rooms: 55 – most with bath, all with telephone and TV.
Facilities: Lounge, restaurant; conference facilities. Garden; tennis court; salmon and trout fishing from hotel's 22 km stretch of river bank.
Location: 3 miles from town centre; parking.
Credit cards: All major credit cards accepted.
Terms (excluding service charge): B & B IR£14.40–30.50. Set meals: lunch IR£6.25, dinner IR£11.75; full *alc* IR£16.50. Special weekend, 2-day and weekly rates.

Perryville House Hotel   *Telephone:* Kinsale (021) 72731
                                          (Code only applicable within Ireland)

An 18th-century house of striking character, now a quayside family hotel.
Please note that the nominator has not tried out the *Perryville*'s restaurant, *The Four Seasons*. Further reports, especially on that aspect,
would be appreciated.

'With its Regency facade and Spanish wrought-iron, *Perryville House*
resembles one's ideal(!) of a New Orleans bordello from the outside.
Inside, the public rooms and *Four Seasons* restaurant (unsampled in a
town that calls itself Ireland's gourmet capital) are elegant. The hotel is
family-run. The "son" of the house – John Costello – is manager and
omnipresent, ensuring that guests have precisely what they want. There
are mini suites overlooking the harbour, with comfortable cane furniture;
in the bathroom are packets of Alka Seltzer and Anadin (sensible in
Kinsale) and large sachets of shampoo. The breakfasts, with fresh soda
bread, are huge. There for the annual wine festival, we – five of us – were
spoiled rotten for three days. Phone messages were, in our absence,
transmitted around the town by bush telegraph; and in general the
Costellos could not do enough to make us feel at home. A real find in a
notorious don't-care country. Can't wait to go back.' *(Hugh Leonard)*

Open: Easter–end October.
Rooms: 11 – 7 of which are suites with bath, all with shower, telephone and
tea-making facilities.
Facilities: Lounge/foyer, bar, restaurant, courtyard; weekend discos, dinner
dances. ½-acre garden being landscaped; fishing, bathing close by.
Location: In town centre, overlooking Kinsale harbour; parking.
Restriction: No dogs in bedrooms or public rooms.
Credit cards: All major credit cards accepted.
Terms: B & B £13.50–20; dinner, B & B £23–29.50. Bar lunches only. Set meal
(no fixed service charge): dinner £10; full *alc* £15. Reduced rates and special meals
for children. Midweek breaks all year, except July/August.

Rosleague Manor Hotel [GFG]   *Telephone:* Moyard 7

'A Georgian house with a modern bedroom wing situated among the
scenic grandeur of Connemara, with an exquisite view across Bearnaderg
bay. It is one mile from the Connemara National Park. The public rooms
are comfortable, and there is an air of tranquillity about the place. It is
spotlessly clean and well-run by Patrick and Anne Foyle, who are brother
and sister. The food is superb; one night we had a sea trout caught that day
by the chef himself. We look forward to another visit. *(N and E Cowper)*
The above recommendation, from the 1982 edition, has been endorsed
by others, though with reservations about the food. We should be glad of
further reports.

Open: Easter–November.
Rooms: 15 double, 1 single, 1 suite – 15 with bath, all with baby-listening.
Facilities: 2 lounges, bar, dining room. 40 acres grounds with paths to sea through

woods. Fly fishing and clay pigeon shooting tuition by hotel chef; painting courses; good local sea trout, salmon, etc. Sauna.
Location: 7 miles north of Clifden.
Restrictions: Dogs, if small, by arrangement, but not in public rooms.
Credit card: Visa.
Terms (excluding 10% service charge): B & B IR£15–16.20; dinner, B & B IR£25.80–27; weekly IR£151–156. Set meal: dinner IR£10–12. Reduced rates and special meals for children.

MALLOW, Co Cork   Map 6

Longueville House   *Telephone:* Mallow (022) 27156
(Code only applicable within Ireland)

A very noble house indeed – early Georgian in its central part, with two wings added later, and a showpiece of a Victorian conservatory, full of graceful ironwork, added later still. Its position is noble too, in the centre of a 500-acre wooded estate overlooking the Blackwater river, sometimes called the Irish Rhine, famous for its salmon and trout. The house originally belonged to the O'Callaghans, but Cromwell confiscated their lands and demolished their castle. After three centuries, the estate is once more back in the family, and Michael and Jane O'Callaghan are the present owners and, far from being absentee landlords, very much the present hosts. Beautiful houses in glamorous settings are often content to settle for mediocrity in their kitchens, but *Longueville* has won accolades both for its cooking, under the supervision of Jane O'Callaghan, and for its extensive and reasonably-priced wine list.

In previous issues we have carried long and fulsome compliments from grateful guests of the O'Callaghans. We have not had a bad one yet. But for the past year, we have not heard from a single *residential* visitor. Such reports would be welcome. In the meantime, a diner-only writes: 'This gorgeous place well deserves its reputation in every respect. . . . The whole evening lived up to our expectations.' *(Rhona Kilcoyne)*

Open: Easter–mid October. Restaurant closed Sunday/Monday to non-residents.
Rooms: 14 double, 4 single – 15 with bath, 3 with shower. 3 rooms in annexe.
Facilities: Drawing room, TV room, cocktail bar, President's dining room, library, conservatory; billiards, table tennis, darts. Situated in 500 acres wooded estate, with garden and 3 miles of salmon and trout fishing on the river Blackwater which flows through the estate. Riding nearby and free golf on the Mallow course. &.
Location: 4 miles W of Mallow on the Killarney road.
Restrictions: No children under 10. No dogs.
Terms: B & B IR£20; full board (weekly) IR£210. Set meal: dinner approx. IR£15.50; full *alc* IR£18.

MARLFIELD, Clonmel, Co Tipperary   Map 6

Inislounaght Country House   *Telephone:* (052) 22847
(Code only applicable within Ireland)

A characteristically Irish thoroughbred Georgian house standing in large grounds, with gardens and wooded walks. The house is owned by the Reilly family, who grow their own fruit and vegetables. Fly fishing for trout is available on the river Suir, which is a field away from the house. 'A beautiful quiet country house of distinction. Breakfast included home-made marmalade – the acid test of a first-rate establishment.' *(Brian Scott-McCarthy)*

Open: April–October.
Rooms: 6 double, 1 single – 5 with bath, 1 with shower.
Facilities: 2 lounges, dining room. 15 acres grounds with gardens and croquet lawns. Fishing and golf available nearby. Waterford Glass Factory, Kilkenny Design Centre within reach – also Rock of Cashel, Cahir Castle, Mitchelstown Caves.
Location: 1 mile W of Clonmel, in village of Marlfield; parking.
Terms (no service charge): B & B IR£18; dinner, B & B IR£30; full board (weekly) IR£180. Set meal: dinner IR£12. Reduced rates for stays over 3 days. Reduced rates and special meals for children.

NEWPORT, Co Mayo   **Map 6**

Newport House   *Telephone:* Newport (098) 41222 and 41154
                                   (Code only applicable within Ireland)
                                          Telex: 33740

Our first hotel in County Mayo: a marvellous centre for fishing, though the championship course at Westport close by will attract keen golfers too; and it's also sensational walking country. We stayed at *Newport House* ourselves many years ago, and are delighted to learn from the report below that it has changed little over the years. 'Medium-sized very attractive Georgian house, with the garden running down to the river. Much original furniture. Ramshackle in best Irish style. Fishermen and French tourists patronize it. Not cheap, but very good value for money. Near Clew Bay, which is magnificent. Superb major domo, very good food: vegetables from the garden, salmon, steak, fish in excellent sauces, good soup, only fresh fruit lacking. Authentic (unselfconscious) Irish (shabby) atmosphere.' *(Christina Bewley)*

Open: 1 April–30 September.
Rooms: 16 double, 4 single, 2 suites – 18 with bath, 2 with shower, some with telephone; radio and TV available on request. (8 rooms in annexe.)
Facilities: Inner and outer hall, TV room, lounge, drawing room, lounge bar, restaurant, billiards room, games room with ping-pong. Musical evenings and youth choral group. 20 acres park with walled garden, leading to river and private quay. Fishing, shooting, golf, swimming, hang-gliding, riding. &.
Location: Entrance near town centre and clearly visible from Westport/Achill road; parking for 40 cars.
Restriction: No dogs in public rooms and only in certain bedrooms.
Credit cards: All major credit cards accepted.
Terms: B & B IR£17–22; dinner, B & B IR£27–32; full board IR£32–37. Set meals (no fixed service charge): lunch IR£6, IR£8; dinner IR£9, IR£12.50; full *alc* IR£11. Reduced rates and special meals for children.

The length of an entry does not necessarily reflect the merit of a hotel. The more interesting the report or the more unusual or controversial the hotel, the longer the entry.

OUGHTERARD, Co Galway   **Map 6**

Currarevagh House   [GFG]   *Telephone:* Galway (091) 82313
(Code only applicable within Ireland)

'The Hodgson family have been living in this mid-Victorian country house on the banks of lough Corrib for five generations, and June and Harry Hodgson now run it as an unstuffy, personal hotel. It is set in 150 acres of its own grounds, and there is beautiful wild country around for walks and golf and riding nearby, but it is particularly popular with fishermen. There's a book in the hall where you can enter the number of fish caught, and that is a characteristic of the "private house" approach of the owners. There are no keys to the bedrooms – not that one would be likely to take one's diamonds to this remote spot. The decor hasn't changed much since 1900: the beds are marvellously capacious, with heavy linen sheets; splendid bathroom fittings, lots of Edwardian furniture. There are huge baskets of turf and large open fires in the two reception rooms – and the public rooms and hall are so spacious that it is easy enough to be on one's own. The food is good home cooking, such as one would get if one were lucky as a weekend guest in the country. Excellent home-made brown bread for breakfast, for instance, and first-rate coffee, kept hot over individual spirit lamps. Trout from the lough for dinner, simply cooked with melted butter.'

The above is quoted from the first edition of the Guide, published in 1978. We republish it in 1983 because it is clear that this is one of those blessed spots that maintains its character from decade to decade and, with any luck, from generation to generation. There have been changes in the past five years – there are six more rooms with their own baths or showers, for instance – but the essential elements remain the same. 'Our fifth visit this Easter,' to quote from the most recent letter in our files, 'and the same outstanding welcome. The Hodgsons combine unobtrusive efficiency, friendliness and good humour. The rooms maintain their style and comfort: the private bathroom built within our large bedroom had the same solid skirting-board as the rest of the room – attention to detail which is typical of the place. Hot-water bottles automatically put in our beds. We know of no place remotely like *Currarevagh* and cannot speak too highly of it.' *(VW and others)*

Open: Easter–early October.
Rooms: 11 double, 5 single – 11 with bath or shower. 4 rooms in annexe.
Facilities: 2 sitting rooms, TV room. 150 acres park and woodland; 100 yards from lough Corrib, 2 miles of foreshore belonging to the hotel; trout fishing, grilse in June/July; the hotel owns several boats. The lough is unpolluted and safe for bathing; much other fishing in the vicinity. Sporting rights over 5,000 acres moors near the house for grouse, woodcock and snipe in season; golf and riding nearby. &.
Location: 4 miles NW of Oughterard on lake shore road; Galway 20 miles.
Restrictions: 'Children are tolerated but not encouraged. Consequently parents wanting to bring children will have an agreed reduced rate only if children share parents' room. No listening service or games.' Dogs by arrangement.
Terms (excluding 10% service charge): B & B IR£18 20–21; dinner, B & B IR£28–31; full board IR£31.75–34.55. Set meals: lunch IR£5.85; dinner IR£11.75. Reduced rates for children by advance agreement, if children share parents' room; special meals 'if necessary'.

Coopershill Farmhouse   *Telephone:* Sligo (071) 75108
(Code only applicable within Ireland)

Coopershill calls itself a Holiday Farmhouse. It is no sense a hotel, and the prices are extremely modest, but it is also more civilized and elegant than the term 'farmhouse' might suggests. It has a spectacular position, with the Bricklieve mountains and vast peat bogs to the south, and the town of Sligo and the sea to the north. This is Yeats country, and the poet himself is buried at Drumcliff not far from Riverstown.

'An extraordinary spell of weather enhanced the beauty and calm of the setting, but the spaciousness of this fine four-square 18th-century house, the friendliness, comfort and ease of the O'Haras' hospitality, and the evening fire in the drawing-room after dinner, would make this a worthy entrant in any weather for "the finest farmhouse hotel in the book". The food is extremely good and graciously served. It's remarkable value. The whole place has a charming simplicity and feeling of tradition: a special place with special people.' *(John and Eileen Spencer)*

Open: Easter–30 September.
Rooms: 5 double, 1 suite – 1 with bath; most rooms with four-poster beds.
Facilities: Drawing room, dining room, playroom for children with TV, piano, record-player, table tennis, etc. Large garden within 500 acres of farmland; a donkey and cart. A river runs through the grounds, with fishing for pike and perch; trout fishing nearby; sandy beach at Sligo, also golf.
Location: 2 miles from Riverstown; on road from Dublin to Sligo, take second right turn towards Riverstown. After about 1 mile, by black post and rail fence, turn left; turn right by ruined lodge, cross stone bridge and two cattle grids.
Terms (excluding 10% service charge): B & B IR£15–16. Set meal: dinner IR£10. Reduced rates and special meals for children.

Ballymaloe House   [GFG]   *Telephone:* Cork (021) 652531
(from Britain dial 0002 instead of 021)
Telex: 75208 BHI

What a pleasure to write an entry for a hotel that consistently, year after year, elicits so many expressions of satisfaction from grateful guests. Not that *Ballymaloe* is, strictly speaking, a hotel: it is classified by the Irish Tourist Board as a Grade A guest house and by Michelin as a restaurant with rooms. But the distinction is irrelevant – *Ballymaloe* by any name would smell as sweet. It's a mainly 17th-century house, in the middle of a 400-acre farm, 20 miles east of Cork, and for many years past Myrtle Allen and her family have been dispensing here a very special brand of relaxed hospitality, which seems to work equally well with adults on their own and families with small children. The sea is 2½ miles away, and there are lots of lovely walks in the vicinity, but there is also a lot going on in and around the house – including a swimming pool, a tennis court, and a mildly improved nine-hole 'bush' golf course. Fifteen of the rooms are in the main house; others are in the Old Coachyard, the Gate Lodge and a 16th-century Gatehouse. No mention of *Ballymaloe* would be complete if it didn't mention the restaurant, which has long enjoyed a reputation for its fine cooking. Indeed, one reader this year wrote specially from Australia to express his awed delight: 'I regularly eat out in Sydney and, although not an expert, I certainly appreciate good food. At *Ballymaloe* I had what I consider the best meal I have ever enjoyed. It disappointed me as an Australian meat-eater to have to admit I never had such sweet and tender lamb.' Another, a first-timer, though she did raise an eyebrow at the lack of cosiness of the bar/lounge, summed up: 'I couldn't have enjoyed it more; all the nice things I have been hearing about it for so many years are absolutely substantiated.' *(John Supple, Uli Lloyd Pack; Charles Acton, Ronald T Horton, D J M Tregear)*

Open: All year, except 24–27 December.

Rooms: 23 double, 3 single – 20 with bath, 3 with shower, all with telephone and baby-listening. 9 rooms in annexe. (4 ground floor rooms with bathrooms suitable for wheelchairs in annexe.)

Facilities: 3 sitting rooms (1 with TV), restaurant, playroom. 400-acre farm and grounds with tennis court, swimming pool, 9-hole golf course, trout pond, children's play area. Horses and ponies available for guests. Sea 2½ miles, with safe sandy beaches; sea and river fishing by arrangement. The Shanagarry pottery is a mile down the road, with Mr Pearse's pots (cheaper than in the shops) and his son's glass. Irish craft shop in the grounds, selling tweeds, woollens, pictures, also fresh produce. &.

Location: 20 miles E of Cork.

Restriction: No dogs in bedrooms.

Terms (excluding 10% service charge): B & B (continental) IR£13.20–21.85, (English) IR£15.20–24.40; dinner, B & B £27.70–38.75; full board IR£33.90–45.60. Set meals: lunch IR£6, dinner IR£12.50. November–February 10% of all stays of 3 nights or more. Reduced meal prices for children under 10; high tea IR£3.

Part Two

AUSTRIA
BELGIUM
DENMARK
FINLAND
FRANCE
GERMANY
GREECE
HOLLAND
HUNGARY
ITALY
LUXEMBOURG
MALTA (including Gozo)
NORWAY
PORTUGAL (including Madeira)
SPAIN (including Andorra, the Balearics
and the Canaries)
SWEDEN
SWITZERLAND (including Liechtenstein)
YUGOSLAVIA

Hotel im Palais Schwarzenberg, Vienna

Austria

BEZAU, 649M Vorarlberg   **Map 12**

Hotel Gams   *Telephone:* (05514) 2220
                                             Telex: 59144

'*The Vorarlberg, Austria's most westerly province, carries at least its fair
share of tourist traffic. But even in the height of summer it is possible to
escape the buzz of the cars around Lake Constance and take refuge in the
Bregenz Forest, where cattle and not combustion engines provide most of
the sound. Bezau is literally the end of the line. A tiny train drawn three
times a week by a steam engine chugs up from Bregenz through the hills.
Beyond Bezau, the mountains take over: the Klein Walserthal, the other
side of the range, is a part of Austria accessible only from Germany.*

'*The* Hotel Gams *looks like an old coaching inn that might have had
songs composed by Robert Stolz. Petunias cascade down from the balconies; the public rooms are numerous; the mountains provide the view. I'm
not sure that I like my outlook broken by tennis courts and swimming pool,
but some people cannot resist keeping fit on holiday. The more sensible will
discuss the cellar with the owner and if they show themselves sufficiently
informed, they will soon find themselves sharing a bottle with him, but not
one from the Vorarlberg itself which is now reduced to two vineyards, both
of them indifferent. Ask for a room with a balcony and take your breakfast
with a gulp of the Bregenzer Wald air.*' *(John Higgins)*

A recent visitor endorses our 1982 entry, adding: 'The public rooms are
large, and the breakfast room vast (and almost magnificent). We had

demi-pension, and were always asked whether the set menu was acceptable (it was!) and invariably second helpings were offered. On Tuesday evenings, instead of the usual dinner, one can participate if one wishes in a barbecue on the terrace. Although quite a large establishment, the owner always seemed to be at hand and the rest of the staff were equally keen on ensuring the guests' comfort.' *(B W Ribbons)*

Open: All year.
Rooms: 70 beds – 14 rooms with bath, 12 with shower, some with balcony.
Facilities: Lift, lounge, dining room; sauna, swimming pool, tennis courts.
Location: 37 km NW of Lech.
Terms: B & B 285–470 Sch; full board 450–640 Sch.

DRASSBURG, A7021, Burgenland **Map 12**

Schloss Drassburg *Telephone:* (02686) 2220

A castle hotel of the grander kind accommodated in what was once the summer residence of the Esterhazys: the present owner is the fifth generation of the family that succeeded them. There are 25 acres of grounds laid out by Le Nôtre of Versailles fame. And there are a lot of special facilities – see below. One visitor this past year was ambivalent about our previous entry, feeling the place had a somewhat musty air and objecting to being summoned to Madame's room to book in. Another reader took a more positive view, even though he had communication problems, as no one spoke much English: 'A splendid hotel, even if slightly frayed at the edges. Absolutely magnificent grounds including formal garden, fountains, orchard, woods, lake, terraces and stream. Good for wildlife and fungi and interesting birds. Whole place very quiet and restful. Good food and service – and good value too,' Another couple were even more enthusiastic: 'Our idea of a perfect hotel in every way.' *(Pamela and Norman Dutson)*

Open: 1 April–30 November.
Rooms: 25 double, 11 single, 1 suite – 22 with bath, 8 with shower; radio and TV on request. (Some rooms on ground floor.)
Facilities: Large hall with fireplace, salon, glassed-in veranda; baroque dining room; conference facilities; indoor swimming pool. 25 acres of grounds with swimming pool, sauna, tennis courts, ice-skating rink, riding course. English spoken.
Location: Between Eisenstadt and Mattersburg; 11 km from Eisenstadt; private landing strip 6 km; bus connections from all directions; guests can be met at Wiener Neustadt railway station; Schwechat airport is about 1 hour away.
Terms: B & B 504–725 Sch; dinner, B & B 620–840 Sch. Set meals: lunch/dinner 270 Sch.

DÜRNSTEIN, A 3601, Lower Austria **Map 12**

Richard Löwenherz *Telephone:* (02711) 222

Dürnstein is on the northern bank of a particularly luscious stretch of the Danube, about 50 miles east of Vienna. The whole area, known as the Wachau, is steeped in the history of central Europe from the Stone and

Roman Ages onwards. Richard the Lionheart was imprisoned in the town in 1192 – hence the name of the hotel. Many of the finest buildings of the Austrian Baroque are close at hand. 'You find this entirely delightful hotel at the end of a narrow side street in this romantic village. The main road now passes beneath the village in a tunnel, so all is quiet. The hotel is built on the site of an old abbey and incorporates some of the old buildings; there are flower-filled gardens and a shady bar-terrace on top of a cliff looking across one of the most beautiful stretches of the Danube. Comfortable rooms, good food and wine from the hotel's own vineyard.' *(William Goodhart)*

Open: Mid March–31 October.
Rooms: 34 double, 4 single – 10 with bath or shower, most with telephone.
Facilities: Hall, TV room, bar/terrace, dining room. Large garden with heated swimming pool. English spoken.
Location: 15 minutes' drive from the nearest large town; parking.
Terms: B & B 450–950 Sch; full board 600–1300 Sch.

DÜRNSTEIN, A3601, Lower Austria   **Map 12**

Schloss Dürnstein   *Telephone:* (02711) 212
3601 Dürnstein/Donau   *Telex:* 071147

Schloss Dürnstein was built in 1630. The Emperor Leopold I, escaping from the Turks during the Siege of Vienna in 1683, took refuge here. For centuries it belonged to one of the great aristocratic families, the Princes Starhemberg, before being reincarnated as a luxurious hotel. Lovely antique furniture is in evidence both in the public rooms and in the bedrooms, which vary in size between large and huge; most have a spectacular Danube view, some have balconies. The restaurant terrace is a specially agreeable place to eat – for the view as well as for the fine cooking. Meals tend to be as substantial as everything else at the Schloss. The wine comes from the castle's own vineyard and is specially recommended. 'Expensive but highly elegant and with a very good restaurant.' *(HC and Elsa Robbins Landon)*

Open: 25 March–30 November.
Rooms: 31 double, 4 single, 2 suites – 35 with bath, 2 with shower, all with telephone, radio and baby-listening; colour TV on request. (Some rooms on ground floor.)
Facilities: Lift, salon, TV room, writing room, bar; restaurant unit includes rooms of all sizes – catering for conferences, weddings and other occasions. Terrace overlooking the Danube for fine-weather refreshments. Large outdoor heated swimming pool, sauna, solarium. English spoken. &.
Location: Central; large parking area.
Credit cards: All major credit cards accepted.
Terms: B & B 340–680 Sch; dinner, B & B 500–800 Sch. Set meals: lunch/dinner 180–220 Sch; full *alc* 350 Sch. Reduced rates for stays of more than 5 days in July. No charge for children under 6 sharing parents' room; special meals available.

We ask hotels to estimate their 1983 tariffs. Not all hotels in Part Two reply, so prices in Part Two are more approximate in some cases than those in Part One.

Hotel Insel *Telephone:* (04254) 2145

'A charming anachronism: the *Insel* sits at the edge of an island, half a
mile by a quarter-mile, which, apart from the hotel, contains a superb
old-fashioned bathing establishment, some tennis courts, and a dense
wood. The island itself is in the middle of the small Faaker See, said to be
the warmest of the Carinthian lakes. The mainland is reached by a gently
purring motorboat (1925 model) driven by a naval person with peaked
cap. The food is superb, the service efficient and cheerful; shoes left
outside the room-door are back early next morning, cleaned and polished
– an anachronism indeed. The whole is presided over by Herr and Frau
Bartosch, who personify Austrian charm at its best. This is the second
time we have been at the *Insel*, and we will come again.' *(Rudolf and
Hanna Strauss)*

Open: End May to end September.
Rooms: 29 double, 7 single – 24 with bath, 4 with shower, most with telephone,
many with balcony. (9 rooms in annexe.)
Facilities: TV room, three intercommunicating salons with bar, restaurant,
terrace; dancing and other entertainments, conference facilities in off-season.
Situated on island with private sandy beach; sailing, windsurfing and fishing; 3
tennis courts.
Location: On island in the lake; hotel has private motorboat (garages and car
park at the jetty).
Terms: B & B 420–970 Sch; dinner, B & B 450–1000 Sch; full board 480–1030
Sch. Set meals: lunch 120–140 Sch, dinner 160–190 Sch; full *alc* 250–450 Sch.
Reduced rates for children under 4.

FUSCHL-AM-SEE, A 5330, Salzburg **Map 12**

Seewinkel Hotel *Telephone:* (062 26) 344

'Herr and Frau Ferstl make one very welcome in their beautiful, new
hotel, situated at the end of the village in a quiet spot beside lake Fuschl.
Although only recently erected, the hotel is built in the traditional style
with splendid wood and wrought-ironwork. All the rooms have bath and
toilet as well as balconies, the majority of which are overlooking the lake.
There are chairs and a table on the balconies. There is also a television
lounge. A small private beach connects the hotel with the lake. Only
breakfast is served, but Frau Ferstl allows guests to leave food in her
fridge which is useful if you take picnics or have snack meals on your
balcony. There are several hotels in Fuschl where you can get an excellent
meal. Being less than 15 miles from Salzburg, Fuschl is an ideal place to
explore that city and at the same time to enjoy a quiet stay in the beautiful
countryside.' *(Mr and Mrs P E Roland; endorsed by J Dixey)*

Open: All year.
Rooms: 26 double, 3 single – 18 with bath, 11 with shower, all with balcony, most
with lake view.
Facilities: Lounge/hall, TV lounge, library. Musical evening once a week. Garden with playground, private sandy beach. Mini-golf, fishing, boating, sailing,
riding, tennis, swimming, walking, cycling, winter sports. English spoken.

Location: 15 km from Salzburg on the edge of the village; garage parking.
Credit card: American Express.
Terms: B & B 160–300 Sch; dinner, B & B 240–380 Sch. Set meal: dinner 85 Sch; full *alc* 130 Sch. Reduced rates and special meals for children.

GMUNDEN, A 4810, Salzkammergut   Map 12

Schlosshotel Freisitz Roith   *Telephone:* (076 12) 4905/6081
Traunsteinstrasse 87

Gmunden is a colourful small resort town on the Traunsee in the Salzkammergut, with one of the best-equipped lake beaches on the north slopes of the Alps. The *Freisitz Roith* is a traditional balconied turn-of-the-century hotel, a few minutes from the centre of Gmunden at the foot of the Gruenberg, and with panoramic views across the Traunsee. In addition to the restaurant, there is an attractive terraced café and a vaulted bar. 'The building seems quite old, but the rooms and bathrooms have been modernized with care and were entirely suitable to our needs. The views were beautiful. Our reception was cordial, there was help with our luggage, and our host was agreeably attentive and helpful on the two evenings of our visit. The food was very good and well-presented. We shall return.' *(J Dixey)*

Open: 15 April–15 October.
Rooms: 20 double, 7 single, 1 suite (in annexe) – 19 with bath, 7 with shower, all with telephone.
Facilities: Lift, lounges, TV room, bar, restaurant, café. Private beach. English spoken.
Location: SW of Linz on the N145; on E bank of Traunsee.
Credit cards: American Express, Euro.
Terms: B & B 350–400 Sch; dinner, B & B 450–500 Sch; full board 550–600 Sch; full *alc* 230 Sch. It is advisable to make reservations for weekends.

HALLSTATT, A 4830, Upper Austria   Map 12

Seehotel Gruener Baum   *Telephone:* (061 34) 263

'In 1978, I saw a picture of Hallstatt on a calendar: it showed a lake, a cluster of wooden houses overlooking the water and snowcapped mountains rising very steeply behind. The scenery was so perfect that I wondered whether the photograph could be genuine. But in fact Hallstatt *is* so perfect. The village, which lies to the south-east of Salzburg, is small and is at the end of a turning off a minor road. It can't take coaches, and only a few cars can be accommodated since all the houses in the narrow main street overhang. There are car parks at both ends of the village, and the hotel has its own special parking area. The village lies along the Hallstatter See, and the *Seehotel Gruener Baum* is the only hotel. It dates back to 1670, and has been in the hands of the Lissbauer family for six generations. It is currently managed by Frau Lissbauer and her daughter, Doris Werner, who speaks perfect English.

Many of the rooms overlook the lake which comes right up to the terrace, where meals and drinks can be taken – breakfast, too, unless you have it in your room. Most of the lakeside rooms have balconies with

219

geraniums in baskets; on first-floor balconies, there is room to sunbathe. Rooms on the other side face the delightful Market Square: there is a fountain surrounded by wooden houses, again with the customary balconies covered in flowers. A waterfall cascades down behind the houses, and the mountain rises steeply behind. The staff, many of whom spoke excellent English, were all very courteous. The rooms were spotless, with a small vase of flowers renewed daily. The food was well-prepared local Austrian food, with the speciality being fish from the lake: particularly fine was the local trout; also recommended is the veal. There were a couple of American families staying there, who were from the New York Met, and who had been staying regularly at the *Gruener Baum* for many years before the Salzburg Festival.

'My wife and I have always taken a holiday on our wedding anniversary, with the provision that on the actual day we should be "on water and drinking champagne" (we had had our wedding reception on a boat on the Thames). We have spent our anniversary in Paris, Venice, Amsterdam, Bangkok, Hong Kong and the Greek Islands. Hallstatt and the *Gruener Baum* has some competition. But my wife and I agree that our brief stay at this lovely hotel in a delightful village was the finest yet.' *(David Whittaker)*

Open: April–end September.
Rooms: 20 double, 1 single – 11 with bath, 6 with shower, 6 with telephone.
Facilities: TV lounge, bar (live music once a week), 2 restaurants, terrace, children's playroom. Tennis, table-tennis, bowling, sauna, fishing, rowing, platform for bathing in lake, steamer trips, barbecues available in vicinity. English spoken.
Location: 50 km SE of Salzburg; parking in centre of village, in market square.
Terms: B & B 190–360 Sch; full board 390–570 Sch. 10% reduction in low season.

HEILIGENBLUT, am Grossglockner, A 9844, Carinthia   **Map 12**

Hotel Senger   *Telephone:* (0484) 2215

'The Grossglocknerstrasse is surely one of the most spectacular mountain highways in Europe. Far too many people just drive over it, and go on to the Carinthian lakes, to Italy or Yugoslavia. But skiers who want to get off the most beaten tracks in Austria, and summer walkers know that Heiligenblut, at the Carinthian end of the Grossglocknerstrasse, is ideal, beautiful, adventurous territory. Just above the village, there happens to be one of those rare family hotels that offer comfort, excellent food, and the kind of personal attention that makes everyone feel relaxed and good-humoured. At any time, more than half the guests in the *Haus Senger* are people who have come again and again. It looks like a typical, large mountain chalet – in fact it's an old one with a new house skilfully added. Most of the rooms have balconies – two of them have large terraces. The telephones have the direct-dialling system normally found only in luxury hotels. The food is so copious that almost everyone opts for breakfast and dinner, and skips lunch – though the cook bakes fresh cheesecakes, and Sachertorte and Apfelstrudel almost every day, and there is always the temptation to try it still warm from the oven for afternoon coffee after a day out on the mountains. They are happy to work there; and guests are happy to meet them. This is not just Austrian *Gemütlichkeit* – it's a place that you are always sad to leave, and where you know that you will return.' *(Hella Pick)*

Open: June–September; December–April.
Rooms: 16 double, 7 single, 2 suites – 4 with bath, 12 with shower, 2 with terrace, most with balcony, all with telephone. TV on request.
Facilities: Salon, bar, TV room, restaurant; sauna, table tennis. Garden. Walking and winter sports. English spoken.
Location: On the 107 N of Lienz; 10 minutes from centre. Parking.
Terms: B & B 190–330 Sch; dinner, B & B 250–450 Sch. Set meals: lunch 90 Sch, dinner 120 Sch; full *alc* 140 Sch. Reduced rates for children sharing parents' room; special meals provided.

IGLS, A 6080 Innsbruck, Tyrol   **Map 12**

Sporthotel Igls   *Telephone:* (052 22) 77241
                                                     Telex: 05-3314

Igls is 20 minutes by car above Innsbruck. It is on a sunny plateau, with masses of sporting activities, both winter and summer. The cable car which takes you to Patscherkofel at 2,200 metres is 300 yards from the *Sporthotel*. For those who like lively resort hotels, it has much to recommend it (see 'Facilities' below).
   'Superb, friendly, welcoming service. Very good food. Attractive pool. The hotel has a real flair and vitality. The staff were obviously enjoying themselves, and so did everyone else. Plenty of life and conversation between different nationalities. The Beck family, always in evidence, also own the much more expensive, smaller, more exclusive *Schlosshotel* in Igls. It is supposed to be much more luxurious, but it wasn't nearly as lively as the *Sporthotel*.' *(B J Whittaker)*

Open: All year.
Rooms: 80 – all with bath or shower, telephone and radio, some with TV.
Facilities: Lounge, bar, restaurant, conference facilities, sauna, solarium; terrace and garden. Near Sport Centre with indoor swimming pool, beauty treatment, tennis; 2 golf courses nearby.
Location: In centre of village; underground parking.
Terms: Half board 430–745 Sch. Full board 63 Sch added to room price. Set meals: lunch/dinner 160 Sch. Reduced rates for children sharing parents' room. Special off-season rates; summer golf and tennis holidays.

KITZBÜHEL, Tyrol A-6370   **Map 12**

Hotel Montana   *Telephone:* (053 56) 2526
Hahnenkammstrasse 5

'We came here on a package tour for a week's skiing and found the standard of this hotel well above what we had expected. It has been recently refurbished with all rooms having private bathrooms as well as being large and well-furnished. The hotel is particularly well equipped with saunas, solarium and indoor swimming pool, all available at no extra charge to guests. It is right by the ski-school, close to the main cable car and only a few minutes' walk from the town centre. It is family-owned and run with very friendly staff – and our arrival, delayed by snow and ice from midday to midnight, was greeted with great warmth and efficiency; a hot meal was ready for us – and it was good! There is a cheerful and friendly atmosphere, the food is varied and the buffet breakfast outstanding with an enormous choice of cold meats, cereals, fruit juices and cheeses. *(Angela and David Stewart)*

Open: All year, except April, October and November.
Rooms: 40 double – all with bath and telephone, most with balcony; baby-listening on request.
Facilities: Lift, TV room, salon, dining room, terrace; nightly entertainment in bar; sauna, solarium, heated indoor swimming pool; table tennis. &.
Location: 5 minutes from town centre, beside ski-school and close to cable car; parking.
Terms: B & B 300–640 Sch; dinner, B & B 350–690 Sch. Set meal: dinner 90–140 Sch. 25% reduction for children under 12.

LANS, Nr Innsbruck, A 6072, Tyrol   **Map 12**

Gasthof 'Zur Traube'   *Telephone:* (052 22) 77.2.61

This characteristic Austrian *Gasthof*, decidedly Tyrolean both in its furnishings and its style of cooking, dating from the 14th century, is in the centre of the village of Lans, which is in the hills to the south of Innsbruck, about 20 minutes' distance by car. The hotel has been in the hands of the Raitmayr family for fifteen generations! 'Absolutely fantastic scenery, both in summer and winter. The friendliness of Herr Raitmayr and his staff is typically Tyrolean, and I recommend the local dishes on the menu.' *(P R Cockman)*

Open: 1 May–10 October, 20 December–15 March. Restaurant open all year.
Rooms: 23 double, 7 single – 3 with bath, 11 with shower.
Facilities: Hall with TV, dining room. Occasional Tyrolean evenings with local band. Large lawn with deck chairs, children's play area. 10 minutes from lake with safe bathing; golf, tennis, riding, winter sports nearby. English spoken.
Location: 10 minutes' drive from Innsbruck (6 km). In village centre; parking.
Terms: B & B 220–285 Sch; dinner, B & B 270–370 Sch; full board 385–435 Sch. Set meals: lunch/dinner 100 Sch; full *alc* 170 Sch. Reductions out of season. Reduced rates for children sharing parents' room 2–6 years, 50% discount; 6–10 years, 30%; special meals on request.

MUTTERS, A-6162, Tyrol   **Map 12**

Haus Rossmann   *Telephone:* (052 22) 272502
Schulgasse 13

'When visiting Innsbruck we decided to stay in the small village of Mutters, overlooking Innsbruck. We found Frau Rossmann's beautiful guest-house/home to be immaculately clean, and her hospitality to be truly gracious. The rooms have thick feather quilts and open onto a balcony overflowing with geraniums, and what a view! Breakfast included warm rolls, creamy butter, jam, coffee, tea and hot chocolate – couldn't be better to wake up to. In Mutters there are hiking trails, frequent trains to Innsbruck and the Mutterbaum (chairlift). Friday evenings there is an open-air concert which you can see and listen to from the balcony.

Our trip to Mutters and *Haus Rossman* was the highlight of our European tour.' *(Richard M Boyle)*

Open: All year.
Rooms: 4 double, 1 single – no private baths, but bath and shower on each floor – all with balcony.
Facilities: Reception room, terrace, lawn.
Location: 4 km from Innsbruck.
Terms: B & B 110–140 Sch. (No restaurant.)

SALZBURG, A5020 — Map 12

Hotel Elefant
Sigmund-Haffnergasse 4

Telephone: (062 22) 43.3.97/43.4.09
Telex: 63 2725

A reasonably-priced (even in mid-Festival) central (in the middle of the old town and about three minutes' walk from the Opera House and concert halls), moderately quiet (it is in a pedestrian precinct though the pedestrians can be noisy) old (there's a beam on the third floor with 1259 carved on it, though the house has been renovated over the centuries) and friendly hotel. Breakfast is served in a charming Biedermeierish dining room. One reader complained that the hotel would not serve him a drink after 11 p.m.; but there are plenty of places to drink in the locality after hours. One warning: the precinct is not too easy to find and is a five-minute walk from a large underground car park.

Open: All year. Restaurant closed Tuesday.
Rooms: 19 double, 13 single, 4 suites – 13 with bath, 25 with shower, all with telephone and radio. TV in the suites.
Facilities: Lift, hall with bar, cellar bar, lounge, breakfast room, dining room. English spoken. &.
Location: Central, but located in pedestrian precinct; 5 minutes from municipal parking. Drive along Hauptstrasse, follow Rudolfskai, go round Mozart-Platz and Alter Markt.
Credit cards: All major credit cards accepted.
Terms: B & B 250–315 Sch. Set meals: lunch/dinner 110–120 Sch. Reduced rates for children under 10 sharing parents' room; special menus.

SALZBURG, A-5021 — Map 12

Hotel Markus Sittikus
Markus Sittikus Str 20

Telephone: (062 22) 71.1.21 and 71.3.26

Last year's entry for this caring and well-tended bed-and-breakfast hotel has been endorsed by recent visitors: 'A useful small hotel, well-placed and inexpensive in a city where accommodation can be difficult. We found the staff helpful and friendly. Our room with bathroom was pleasing and comfortable.' *(John and Rosemarie Williamson)*

Open: All year.
Rooms: 23 double, 17 single – 10 with bath, 21 with shower, all with telephone and colour TV.
Facilities: Lift, hall, TV room, breakfast room. English spoken. &.
Location: Central; parking.
Credit cards: Access/Euro/Mastercard, American Express, Barclay/Visa.
Terms: B & B 230–460 Sch. (No restaurant.)

Hotel Schloss Mönchstein   *Telephone:* (062 22) 41363/41366
Mönchsberg   *Telex:* 632080

'By a happy chance, on my first-ever visit to Salzburg, I found myself
staying at this most delightful hotel. From what I saw of other establishments, apart from the famous (and expensive) *Schloss Fuschl* they were
mostly situated in the town centre, and though convenient for sight-seeing
and opera-going I imagine they could be somewhat noisy. Not so the
Schloss Mönchstein. Here is a hotel that is not more than 15 minutes by
foot from the Festspielhaus and yet it so remote from the tourist hurly-
burly that you might be staying in, say, *Gravetye Manor* outside East
Grinstead (q.v.). The back of the Festspielhaus is built into the Mön-
chberg which overlooks the city, and thanks to an efficient lift service
which runs until two in the morning, you can be whisked to the top of the
mountain in a mere 30 seconds from where a short walk through a wooded
park leads you to the *Schloss Mönchstein*. It is beautifully quiet and the air
is fresher than down in town.
   'The hotel has only 14 rooms, and is most pleasantly and efficiently run.
Though by no means "de luxe" in the generally accepted sense of the
word, it caters for your every need in a rather understated and well-
mannered way. The lady receptionists are smiling and helpful, the young
girl who brought breakfast to the room laid it out prettily on a table by the
window, the manager was solicitous without being obsequious. They all
spoke excellent English. Naturally everything was spotlessly clean, sheets
and towels were changed daily, breakfast arrived punctually and direct-
dial telephoning was a boon. I cannot speak for the restaurant as we were
seduced by the ambience in the old town, and perhaps we would have
been more tempted to try it had a menu been somewhere in evidence.'
(Geoffrey Sharp)

Open: All year.
Rooms: 4 double, 3 single, 7 suites – 11 with bath, 1 with shower, all with
telephone and radio, TV on request. (Some rooms on ground floor.)
Facilities: Lift, hall, 2 salons, bar, restaurant, chapel for weddings, terrace with
café; situated in large garden with tennis court. English spoken. &.
Location: Above Salzburg on Mönchsberg Hill; 3 minutes by car to the city
centre, 7 minutes by the Mönchsberg lift. Outdoor parking and garages.
Credit cards: All major credit cards accepted.
Terms: B & B 600–1300 Sch. Set meals: lunch 200–300 Sch, dinner 250, 300 and
350 Sch; full *alc* 350 Sch. 3-day 'Winterdream Package' including tour of Salzburg.
Reduced rates for children sharing parents' bedroom; special meals available.

Hotel Weisses Rössl   *Telephone:* (052 72) 6206

Steinach is an attractive little alpine resort on the Austrian side of the
Brenner Pass, a skiing centre in the winter and a good base for walking in
the summer. The *Weisses Rössl*, one of the larger hotels in town, is on the
narrow main street opposite the church, with no forecourt. But the toll
motorway over the Brenner keeps most of the traffic at bay. The hotel has
plenty of *pension* guests, and there is nightly dancing in the Rosskeller

(well-insulated from the bedroom floors) and a busy dining room for residents as well as a more intimate one for the non-*pension* visitors. A couple who have been using it regularly for several years as a welcoming nightstop write: 'This year we had an exceptionally pleasant room in the old part of the building, with an enclosed balcony, at the back away from the traffic, but with a glimpse of the river, then the railway (far enough away not to be disturbing), and beyond that again the steeply rising and brilliantly green meadows and woodlands. We had a good evening meal in the *à la carte* restaurant, a quiet and comfortable night and a decent breakfast before resuming our journey.' *(Charles and Margaret Baker)*

Open: 20 December–20 October.
Rooms: 34 double, 10 single – 13 with bath, 27 with shower and *sitzbad*, some with radio, all with telephone; TV on request.
Facilities: Lift, 2 bars, hotel dining room, smaller intimate restaurant; indoor swimming pool, sauna. Mountain climbing, good walks, winter sports.
Location: Central, but not much noise at night; garage.
Terms: B & B 285–330 Sch; full board 410–470 Sch.

VIENNA, A 1010   **Map 12**

Pension Elite   *Telephone:* (0222) 63.25.18
Wipplingerstrasse 32

'Our favourite hotel in Europe. This A-class pension is on the third floor of a centrally located office building near the Graben. Our room (with bath) was very reasonable, and authentically furnished even to the goose-down filled red satin quilts. There is a charming breakfast room and lounge and – most important – the staff are very friendly and helpful. Breakfasts featured excellent coffee and wonderful rolls.' *(Martin and Deborah Zehr)*

Open: All year.
Rooms: 22 double, 12 single – 10 with bath, 12 with shower, all with telephone.
Facilities: Lift, lounge, breakfast room. English spoken.
Location: Central.
Terms: B & B 370–450 Sch. (No restaurant.)

VIENNA, A 1015   **Map 12**

Hotel Europa   *Telephone:* (0222) 52.15.94
Neuer Markt 3   *Telex:* 112292 hoeuw a

In contrast to the ornate baroque of the *Sacher*, the *Imperial* and many other of the traditional Viennese grand hotels, the *Europa* is spanking modern – but carried out with quiet panache. Its entrance is in the Neuer Markt, with its fine Donnerbrunnen fountain; its back faces the smart shops of Kärtnerstrasse, halfway between the Opera and St Stephen's Cathedral. Everything about the *Europa* works well – not excepting the quality of the restaurant and coffee house. (Warning: although the Kärtnerstrasse is a pedestrian precinct, revelry at night can disturb light sleepers as much as traffic on the Neuer Markt. But rooms are double-glazed and air-conditioned.) *(HR; also Hella Pick, C H Cole)*

Open: All year.
Room: 90 double, 10 single – all with shower, telephone, radio, mini-bar and air-conditioning; colour TV on request.
Facilities: Hall, café, bar, restaurant; zither music daily at dinner, except Monday; conference facilities. English spoken. &.
Location: Central – go to centre of city, near Opera; left on Kärntnerstrasse, then right; garage parking.
Credit cards: All major credit cards accepted.
Terms: B & B 635–980 Sch. Set meals: lunch/dinner 240 Sch; full *alc* 350–400 Sch. Children under 12 accepted free of charge.

VIENNA, A 1010 **Map 12**

Hotel Kaiserin Elisabeth *Telephone:* (0222) 52.26.26
Weihburggasse 3 *Telex:* 112422

A thoroughly traditional Viennese hotel – perhaps a little on the genteel side – on the edge of the pedestrianized Kärntnerstrasse and within a few yards of St Stephen's Cathedral; the entire Inner City is within a few minutes' walk. The public rooms, though large and comfortable, face inwards – not a major drawback, however, if one is out all day sightseeing. Rooms vary in size and price. Few of the single rooms have private bathrooms, and some rooms are a little claustrophobic. But the *Kaiserin Elisabeth* has many loyal followers:

'My fifth visit to this delightful and pleasantly old-fashioned hotel in the quiet centre of Vienna has only strengthened me in my view that it is one of the best small hotels in Europe. It continues to attract the Austrian nobility and gentry, as well as an increasing number of discerning foreigners. The hotel is being discreetly modernized, but in a way which adds to its attractions. Prices are slightly up on last year, but they are ''inclusive''; no-one expects anything but verbal thanks except the porter who handles one's luggage. The staff are charm and courtesy personified and the comfort very much more than adequate, though single rooms tend to be a bit small. But the hotel has that now fast-disappearing quality, style.'
(E George Maddocks)

Open: All year.
Rooms: 51 double, 21 single, 2 suites – 59 with bath, all with telephone and air-conditioning.
Facilities: Lift, hall, salon, breakfast room. English spoken. &.
Location: Central, near St Stephen's Cathedral; public parking nearby.
Terms: B & B 420–693 Sch.

VIENNA, A 1030 **Map 12**

Hotel im Palais Schwarzenberg *Telephone:* (0222) 78.45.15
Schwarzenbergplatz 9 *Telex:* 136124

The *Palais Schwarzenberg* is 10 minutes' walk to the Opera and the main shopping area, but has formidable compensations. It is discreet, quiet, impeccably elegant in all its furnishings, and it is housed in one wing of the very grand and handsome palace which the Schwarzenbergs have lived in since the early 18th century; it was bombed during the war, but has been faithfully reconstructed. Most of the rooms are in fact in what was once the servants' quarters and stables, but there is nothing menial in its present incarnation. Antique furniture and original oil paintings abound, and quality is apparent in every aspect, not least in the restaurant which is one of the best in Vienna. An additional pleasure for the guests is the 20-acre park of the Palace.

'Certainly one of the pleasantest hotels we have ever had the good fortune to stay in. Our bedroom was large and elegantly furnished, with all necessary facilities, and had an extensive view over the old city. Although it was cold and windy during our visit, meals were still served on the terrace facing the park, glazed in but occasionally somewhat draughty. The food was excellent and efficiently served. By November the statues in the garden were covered to protect them from the weather, and the further part of the park was closed, but it was nevertheless pleasant to be able to walk in the garden itself. The staff were without exception friendly and helpful; indeed one of the waiters volunteered to take us on a conducted tour of the rest of the *Palais* which is, of course, not usually open to hotel visitors.' *(Kenneth Garside)*

Open: All year.
Rooms: 36 double, 3 single, 3 suites (1 with kitchenette) – all with bath, telephone, radio; TV on request. (Some rooms on ground floor.)
Facilities: Lift, hall, bar, restaurant with summer and winter terraces; conference facilities. 18 acres private park with tennis courts, swimming pool and sauna. English spoken. &.
Location: Close to centre; despite its address entrance is at bottom of Prinz-Eugen-Strasse; unlimited parking.
Credit cards: All major credit cards accepted.
Terms: B & B 800–1180 Sch. Full *alc* approx. 600 Sch. Special meals for children on request.

VIENNA, A 1010   **Map 12**

Hotel Sacher   *Telephone:* (0222) 52.55.75
Philharmonikerstrasse 4   *Telex:* 01/12520

'At the height of Imperial grandeur in this most baroque of all cities, the *Hotel Sacher* became the premier hostelry of the Austro–Hungarian Empire. It maintains its position inside Vienna's Ring opposite the Opera House. Go here to be pampered de luxe, and remember to sample the sybaritic *Sacher Torte* from the original pastry kitchen – which tastes quite different from the exported examples.' *(George Herzog)*

Open: All year.
Rooms: 83 double, 38 single, 3 suites – 115 with bath, 3 with shower, all with telephone, radio and colour TV.
Facilities: Lobby, lift, Blue Bar, Red Bar, Marble Room, restaurant, coffee shop, coffee bar; piano and sometimes zither music in evening; conference and banqueting facilities. English spoken. &.
Location: Off the Ringstrasse, behind the Opera; parking.
Terms: B & B 875–1200 Sch; full board 700 Sch per person added. Full *alc* 800 Sch. Children under 6 free; special meals provided.

Don't rely on our printed tariffs! Check before booking.

Pension Suzanne   *Telephone:* (0222) 52.74.15
Walfischgasse 4

Probably the first hotel in the Guide that has its rooms above a sex-shop.
Don't be put off! The Walfischgasse is no sleazy Soho alley, but a
respectable thoroughfare, 100 yards from the Opera House and the start
of the pedestrianized Kärntnerstrasse. Like other Viennese pensions, the
entrance is unimpressive: the bedrooms are on the second and third
floors, some facing the street (double-glazing) and some a parking lot in
the rear. No public rooms: breakfasts are served in your own bedroom.
What distinguishes the *Suzanne* is its agreeable Viennese furnishings – no
ticky-tacky stuff, but handsome beds, chairs and tables, fine mirrors,
decent pictures – that, and friendly efficiency on the part of the English-
speaking staff. *(HR)*

Open: All year.
Rooms: 43 beds – 18 double rooms with bath, 5 with shower.
Facilities: Lift. English spoken.
Location: Central.
Terms: B & B 305–440 Sch.

Hotel Post   *Telephone:* (042 42) 26.1.01/2
Hauptplatz 26   *Telex:* 45-723

Villach, close to the Italian border, was a busy trading centre in the 16th
and 17th centuries, and the town still has many fine Renaissance buildings. The *Post* itself was a 16th-century palace, but has been a hotel for the
past 250 years, and has included among its former VIPs both the Emperor
Charles V and the Empress Maria Thérèse. 'It has an excellent dining
room and a first-class wine list. Rooms are comfortable, and the town
itself is fascinating and beautiful.' *(HC and Elsa Robbins Landon)*

Open: All year.
Rooms: 150 beds – 49 rooms with bath, 10 with shower, all with telephone.
Facilities: Lift; hall, bar, salons, 2 dining rooms; facilities for conferences and
private parties; courtyard with outdoor meals in fine weather. The hotel has a
bathing beach at the Ossiachersee. Winter sports. &.
Location: Central; 8 minutes' walk to station.
Terms: B & B 252–500 Sch; full board 440–690 Sch.

Hotel-Gasthof Moawirt   *Telephone:* (064 13) 30.6.08
Schwaighof 123

Wagrain is an all-the-year-round resort, 25 miles south of Salzburg, just
off the Salzburg–Villach *autobahn*. 'We first visited *Moawirt* in 1981 for a
night stop. We were very impressed with the rooms and restaurant, and

promised ourselves a return visit in 1982. We were delighted. The hotel is just the same; excellent food, beautiful large rooms with balconies and every facility, and everyone is so kind and helpful. The hotel, which is three years old, is owned and run by the Familie Maurer who are delightful. We must quote details of the hotel as written by the son: "We are a family hotel, my mother Antonie Maurer runs the hotel, keeps a sharp eye on all the things happen in our house. Casually we have a small agriculture which brings us many products for our business. My father Michael is agriculture and butcher. My sister Michaela and I, I am Ernst the son of the owners, are working in the service." Broken English, but we feel it portrays the full flavour of this hotel. The surrounding country-side is lovely, perfect for relaxing or walking in the summer in peace and quiet, and an excellent resort for winter skiing, a chair lift being opposite the hotel.' *(Hugh and Elsie Pryor)*

Open: All year.
Rooms: 24 double, 4 single – 10 with bath, 18 with shower, many with balcony. (3 rooms in annexe.)
Facilities: Lift; salon, dining room; ramps for disabled; garden. Winter sports. English spoken. ⅃.
Location: About 25 miles S of Salzburg, just off the Salzburg–Villach autobahn.
Credit card: Access/Euro/Mastercard.
Terms: B & B 220–290 Sch; dinner, B & B 270–340 Sch. Set meals: lunch 110 Sch, dinner 120 Sch; full *alc* 180–210 Sch.

WINDISCHGARSTEN, A 4580 Upper Austria   Map 12

Hotel-Pension Schwarzes-Rössl   *Telephone:* (075 62) 311

We spent a week at this warmly hospitable old family inn set in a pleasant village of the Teichl valley in 1978, and an entry written by us appeared in the 1979 edition. The hotel dates from the 15th century. It is in the centre of the village: there is traffic noise but thick walls and double-glazing mitigate the nuisance. The owners, the Baumschlagers (Frau Baumschlager speaks good English) were – and clearly still are – model innkeepers. But because Upper Austria isn't one of the more touristy parts of Austria (and all the more pleasant in consequence), feedback has been slow coming. We would not have kept the entry in had we not been sure from other sources that the hotel was maintaining its form. In the past year, however, two reports have reached us fully confirming our own good opinion. The first correspondent wrote: 'After an annual visit to many areas of Austria for 15 years, I discovered that *Gasthof Grab* and *Hotel Ripoff* had taken over: that rolls were cotton wool and coffee was instant, and service was grudging. I vowed never to go again. However, I was tempted by the description of Windischgarsten given by a well-known Senior Citizens' brochure. In great trepidation I went, and, joy of joys, it was the Austria I had known and loved for so long. So I stayed a whole month. Frau Baumschlager is always available for advice cheerfully given. No eight-hour day for her. She superintends everything, does most of the cooking and still finds time for a swim or a display of yodelling in the evening. The staff take their cue from her. I have rarely met such kindness and helpfulness even in Austria. She catered for the whims, fancies and disabilities of an elderly group, and freely gave water with all meals without a hint of disapproval. This is rare nowadays; a brusque "Kein Wasser!" is the usual reply.' *(Mrs R H Godfrey)*

Here is how the hotel struck someone of a young generation: 'My family have just returned from an excellent holiday in the *Schwarzes-Rössl*. We still find it difficult to accept how inexpensive it was. Windischgarsten and the surrounding countryside are lovely. The hotel for us was ideal. I thought it more like a pub than I had expected, with local people in the "bar" in the evenings and particularly full on Sunday at lunchtime which seems to indicate that it was good value. The bar served very appetizing food. The rooms were clean and exceptionally spacious. The food was not *haute cuisine* but it was never less than interesting to us and ample. The evening meal was always looked forward to, particularly after a day's walk in the mountains. Meals for us consisted of a substantial continental breakfast and a four-course evening meal. The Baumschlagers and staff were very friendly. Altogether one of our best holidays and most certainly the best value.' *(Robert Barratt)*

Open: All year, except November. (Restaurant closed Monday out of season.)
Rooms: 16 double, 5 single, 2 suites – 12 with bath, 13 with shower.
Facilities: Reading room, TV/playroom for children, restaurants. Entertainment (zither and concertina playing, etc.) can be arranged on request. Indoor and outdoor games for children. The facilities of the nearby *Sport Hotel* are all available to guests at the *Schwarzes-Rössl*. They include large grounds, tennis court, heated outdoor swimming pool and terrace where coffee, cakes and pastries are served. Mountains, skiing, fishing, alpine flowers nearby. English spoken.
Location: Central; parking.
Terms: B & B 210–240 Sch; dinner, B & B 260–280 Sch; full board 280–300 Sch. Set meals: lunch 88 Sch, supper 75 Sch; full *alc* 145 Sch.

Belgium

Hôtel St Jorishof, Gent

Hôtel Duc de Bourgogne   *Telephone:* (050) 33.20.38
Huidenvettersplein 12

A beautifully sited hotel or restaurant with rooms at the junction of two canals: you look out over banks of scarlet geraniums to a backcloth of immaculately preserved Renaissance buildings. Very expensive, but the interior decor is of a piece with the view outside. Specially recommended: Table 5, right by the window, but you have to book months ahead. To one visitor, a regular, the *Duc de Bourgogne* this last year was 'as splendid as ever – both the hotel room and the restaurant'. Only complaint: 'the mosquitoes were a bit hungry.' Another guest was slightly less enchanted, chiefly becauase his room was a second-floor attic, with no view of the canal or the town because of a high window. Perhaps the moral is to book well in advance for a room with a view, as well as for Table 5. *(Mrs R B Richards, W H Baily)*

Open: All year, except January and July.
Rooms: 8 double, 1 single – all with bath and telephone.
Facilities: Salon, dining room. English spoken.
Location: Central. Make for Grand Place after Philipsstockstraat by the Place du Bourg, where you park – from there 2 minutes' walk.
Credit cards: All major credit cards accepted.
Terms: B & B 860–1100 Bfrs. Full *alc* 1800 Bfrs.

Groeninghe   *Telephone:* (050) 33.64.95
29 Kurte Vuldersstraat

'A B & B hotel, built in the mid-19th century, with the feel of a beautifully furnished and maintained family home. Run by a young (early twenties) brother and sister, who combine friendliness, attentiveness, and unobtrusiveness. Each bedroom decorated individually and spotlessly clean. Beds very comfortable. Shower, toilet, etc., *en suite*. Super breakfast: freshly pressed orange juice, delicious rolls, boiled egg on offer, large jug of excellent coffee – more if wanted. Very close to cathedral, and the myriad of buildings worth seeing in this marvellous city; and yet quiet. And the cost? Just £16 [1981], everything included, for the two of us, per night – i.e. £8 each. How do they do it? (Or why can't the English do it?)' *(D G Randall)*

Open: All year.
Rooms: 8 double – all with bath or shower, telephone and radio.
Facilities: Bar (no restaurant).
Location: Central, near cathedral.
Credit card: Euro.
Terms: Rooms with breakfast (single) 1210 Bfrs; (double) 1430 Bfrs.

L Hôtel Amigo   *Telephone:* (02) 511 5910
1–3 rue de l'Amigo   *Telex:* 21618

Medium-priced (by capital-city prices) and medium-sized, the *Amigo* is the first choice in Brussels for many visiting diplomats and marketeers. It's a post-war construction of a Belgian builder, who is also responsible for two other recommended *Amigo* hotels in Verviers and Masnuy-Saint-Jean – all possessing similar virtues of good design inside and out. There's no special chic about the Brussels *Amigo*, and the restaurant is wholesome rather than enterprising. There are far more exciting meals to be had in dozens of places within strolling distance of the hotel, and one of the best restaurants in the city, the *Maison du Cygne*, is fifty yards up the street. What commends the *Amigo* is its dependable efficiency and welcome, and its close proximity to one of the supreme joys of Brussels, the *Grand Place*. It is the only hotel of 'class' close to the square. *(HR; also Graham W Greene, Peter Allsop)*

Open: All year.
Rooms: 157 double, 26 single, 11 suites – 173 with bath, 10 with shower, all with telephone, radio and colour TV.
Facilities: Lift, various salons, TV room, restaurant. English spoken.
Location: Central, behind the Grand Place; garage.
Credit cards: All major credit cards accepted.
Terms: B & B 1300–3300 Bfrs. Set meals: lunch/dinner 730 Bfrs; full *alc* 1200 Bfrs. Children accepted free of charge if under 12 years; special meals available.

> Please don't just leave the feedback to others.

DURBUY, 5480 Luxembourg   Map 8

Hostellerie Le Sanglier des Ardennes   *Telephone:* (086) 21.10.88
and **Hôtel Au Vieux Durbuy**   *Telephone:* (086) 21.20.23

*'The little village of Durbuy is in the beautiful sheltered valley of the river
Ourthe, and is a centre for walks along the river and in the unspoilt forest of
the Ardennes. The vast car park in the village square could probably take a
charabanc for every inhabitant, but they come and go in daytime; at night
Durbuy is calmness itself. Nevertheless, choose to go before the high season
– May is green and lovely, autumn sees the Ardennes clothed in red and
golden splendour. The main hotel for a gastronomic treat is the* Sanglier des
Ardennes. *Only the brave or starving would tackle the six-course* menu
gastronomique, *but any smaller meal taken in the dining room overlooking
the tumbling Ourthe and the flowering lilacs on its bank in the spring, is still
a pleasure. The table service is impeccable, white linen cloths and napkins.
The* Hôtel Au Vieux Durbuy *(same owners) is used as an annexe when the*
Sanglier *is full and is much preferred for a quiet night. Opt for rooms
overlooking the river and with views to the medieval witch-hatted castle.* Au
Vieux Durby *provides excellent accommodation, breakfast is served in the
room, and there are luxurious bathrooms to every bedroom.' (Valerie
Ferguson)*

One couple, who recently visited the *Sanglier* out of season, felt the
hotel failed to live up to our previous description reproduced above. The
place was cold and depressing, and the bedroom too basic for their liking.
But it was chiefly the food that had disappointed. Perhaps the *Sanglier*
isn't somewhere to go out of season. Two months later, other visitors
reported quite differently (see below). Further reports welcome.

'Valerie Ferguson's description cannot be bettered. The hotel is
pleasant in a rather old-fashioned way, with some attractive period
pieces. There is a large comfortable lounge, with many inviting (unusual,
this!) private corners to sit in. Upstairs, maintenance perhaps not all that
it might be in paintwork and wallpaper. Obviously many people in the
dining room were, to quote Ferguson, either "brave or starving" or quite
simply Belgian as most of them were opting for the huge gourmet menu.
Not being Belgian, we ate on a more modest scale, but still extremely
well. We will long cherish the memory of an asparagus dish which was
superbly cooked and a feast for the eye as well. The staff are friendly and
helpful, and some of them speak English.' *(Ian and Agathe Lewin)*

Open: All year, except 1 January–10 February. Restaurant closed Thursday.
Rooms: 36 double – 13 with bath, all with telephone. 14 rooms in annexe.
Facilities: Salon, TV room, 2 restaurants; 2 banqueting/conference rooms; children's play area; terrace on the river, boating. English spoken.
Location: 45 km south of Liège; parking.
Credit cards: Access/Euro/Mastercard, American Express, Diners.
Terms: Rooms (single) 755–1135 Bfrs, (double) 1025–1405 Bfrs; dinner, B & B 1565–1780 Bfrs. Set meals: breakfast 160 Bfrs; lunch/dinner 965–1400 Bfrs; full *alc* 1300 Bfrs. *Weekends gastronomiques* and *Soirées évasions* – special terms. Reduced rates for children under 10.

We should like to be able to recommend a budget-priced hotel in
Brussels.

Hôtel St Jorishof   *Telephone:* (091) 23.67.91
Botermarkt 2

The capital of the province of East Flanders is an important industrial complex, but it also possesses, as a tourist mecca, a famous medieval quarter, with many historical buildings and museums and the splendid cathedral of Saint Bavon, with Van Eyck's masterpiece 'The Adoration of the Mystic Lamb'. The *Hôtel St Jorishof* is in the centre of the old town, and dates from the 13th century. It claims – we can't remember how many other claimants there are – to be the oldest hotel in Europe. But it is certain that many renowned personages, such as Charles V and the Emperor Napoleon, stayed here, and the hotel, while adding modern accommodation in an annexe, has maintained in fine order many of the original rooms, including a spacious Gothic Hall. There's no residents' lounge, but the rooms, with or without baths *en suite*, are comfortable; and the restaurant, much patronized by the local gentry, offers 'enormous amounts of food – cooked richly and well.' *(The Bishop of Edmonton and others)*

Open: All year, except 20 December–5 January. Restaurant closed Sunday and public holidays.
Rooms: 60 double, 6 single, 2 suites – 44 with bath and shower, all with telephone; 2 with colour TV. (30 rooms in annexe.)
Facilities: Lift; bar, restaurant; conference facilities. &.
Location: Central; garage and car park.
Credit cards: All major credit cards accepted.
Terms: Rooms with breakfast, 990–1800 Bfrs. Set meals: lunch/dinner 770–990 Bfrs.

KORTRIJK (Courtrai), 8500 West Flanders   **Map 8**

Hôtel du Damier   *Telephone:* (056) 22.15.47
Grote Markt 41

A Roman town, close to the French border, and 14 km north of Lille, Kortrijk (or Courtrai) is now a lively commercial and industrial centre. 'An old coaching inn on the market square, but my enormous room at the back was totally quiet. The bar, alongside the arched entrance, is a lively spot, much frequented by local businessmen. The huge inside lounge is comfortable and peaceful. The dining room opens off it, and whilst at first sight it looks fairly ordinary, the food (not expensive) more than makes up for lack of pretty decor, and the place is always packed.' *(Tony Morris)*

Open: All year.
Rooms: 25 double, 15 single, 3 suites – 20 with bath, all with telephone.
Facilities: Lift, hall, TV room, lounge, bar, 2 restaurants; conference facilities.
Location: In town centre; no private parking.
Credit cards: Access/Euro/Mastercard, American Express, Diners.
Terms: Rooms: 500–1100 Bfrs. Set meals: breakfast 160–260 Bfrs; lunch 600 Bfrs; dinner 700–950 Bfrs; full *alc* 1200 Bfrs.

LO, 8180 West Flanders   **Map 8**

Oude Abdij   *Telephone:* (058) 28.82.65
Noordstraat 3

A quiet old inn tucked behind the church in a small town in West
Flanders, ten miles south of the coast and just west of the Veurne–Ieper
motorway. Lo is a place of some antiquity: Caesar is said to have tethered
his horse to an ancient yew still to be found beside the 14th-century
Westpoort, one of Lo's several fine medieval buildings.
   'My husband and I discovered this hotel three years ago and have
returned a number of times with our family. It is run by a young couple
(Jan and Nelly Clement-Wittevrongel) – the husband/owner being a chef
of the highest order. The bedrooms are comfortable, well furnished and
spotlessly maintained. The restaurant is, without exception, excellent –
fish their speciality. Highly recommended for food and hospitality. Marvellous cocktails!' *(Mrs J L Andrews)*

Open: All year. (Restaurant closed Sunday evening and Monday.)
Rooms: 6 double, 1 suite – 6 with bath and shower, all with telephone, mono TV
and baby-listening.
Facilities: Salon, bar, restaurant, solarium. Small garden; small lake (with fishing
for eels); beach 15 km. English spoken.
Location: 15 km S of Veurne, just off the Veurne–Ieper motorway.
Credit cards: American Express, Diners.
Terms: B & B 1250–2000 Bfrs. Set meals: lunch/dinner 975, 1250, 1450 Bfrs; full
alc 1500 Bfrs. Special meals for children.

NOIREFONTAINE, 6831 Luxembourg Belge   **Map 8**

Auberge du Moulin Hideux   *Telephone:* (061) 46.70.15
                                                         Telex: 41989 Hideux B

One of the higher pleasures of the practising hedonist is to enjoy a
supremely good dinner and then be able to retire to a bedroom which is in
every way as sympathetic as the meal. Perfection on both scores is not so
easily found: often the double- or treble-starred restaurants have no
rooms, or if they provide accommodation, it isn't quite as exquisite as the
cuisine. It is the rare achievement of Monsieur and Madame Lahire, a
young couple but both descended from a line of hoteliers, to score equally
on both counts. *Le Moulin Hideux*, a venerably creepered 18th-century
mill in a secluded corner of the Ardennes forest just north of the French
border near Sedan, has only thirteen rooms, but this is a true hotel not just
a restaurant with rooms. Unassumingly impeccable elegance is the
keynote. You would need a strong constitution, if you were to make a
protracted stay here and engage yourself nightly on the wonderful *table
d'hôte*, but the hotel is much patronized by active ramblers who presum
ably are able to walk off during the day the gastronomic exercises of the
night before. 'Hugely expensive,' we quoted a reader as saying in the 1981
Guide. A correspondent challenges this comment, which he fears would
put people off: 'You only get what you pay for. If you accept their set
meals, you will find perfection at the right price.' *(J Wilkinson; also HR)*

Open: Mid March–December. Restaurant closed Wednesday.
Rooms: 11 double, 2 suites – all with bath, telephone and mono TV.
Facilities: Sitting room, loggia, restaurant; garden with tennis court; golf 40 km, riding 10 km. Fine walking country. English spoken.
Location: 22 km N of Sedan, 8 km N of Bouillon.
Credit card: American Express.
Terms: Rooms 2000–2160 Bfrs (single), 2400–2600 Bfrs (double). Suites 2700–2920 Bfrs. Full board (min. 3 days) 4500 Bfrs daily for 2. Set meals: breakfast 200 Bfrs, lunch 1500 Bfrs, dinner 1800 Bfrs; full *alc* 2600 Bfrs.

OOSTKAMP, 8020   Map 8

Château des Brides   *Telephone:* (050) 82.20.01
Breidelstraat 1   *Telex:* 81.412 (aero)

'Very little can be found to put in the "minus column" for the *Château des Brides*. The multilingual amiability and helpfulness of the owners, together with a faint air of amateurism, creates a relaxed and familial atmosphere. Our suite (the "Versailles") was mildly surreal – worn at the edges (but marvellously comfortable beds), an outrageously *chinois* sitting room and huge Edwardian bathroom, all three rooms with superb views over the park. On chilly spring days, heating can be temperamental. The breakfast room (no other meals – the only visible staff being the owners' daughter and an aged gardener) has an air of faded elegance and provides a delicious if basic foundation for the day's gastronomic delights. An oasis of tranquillity with formal gardens, ponds and innumerable rabbits, ten minutes' drive from Bruges.' *(Don and Di Harley)*

Open: All year.
Rooms: 11 – 6 with bath.
Facilities: Entrance hall, salon, breakfast room; conference facilities. Large garden and woods. English spoken.
Location: 7 km from Bruges; 25 km from the exit Oostkamp on the Ostend–Brussels motorway.
Credit cards: All major credit cards accepted.
Terms: Rooms with breakfast 800–2300 Bfrs (single), 1400–3080 Bfrs (double).

ROCHEHAUT SUR SEMOIS, 6849   Map 8

Hostellerie Un Balcon En Forêt   *Telephone:* (061) 46.65.30

We visited the *Hostellerie* ourselves in 1981, and wrote the entry in the 1982 edition. Our own view corresponded with the one below, except in respect of the food which we felt lacked distinction. But perhaps we had just been unlucky.
'This small hotel hotel clings to the rock face of a steep hill overlooking the Semois where it embraces Frahan hundreds of feet below. It is an enchanting view, somewhat degraded by a caravan site on the river bank. The whole area, however, is most beautiful, deep in the Ardennes forest, where the Semois loops for mile after mile expressly, it would seem, to provide nesting places for villages and viewpoints for breath-taken tourists. It is also within a stone's throw of France. It is probable that the hotel was once a hunting lodge, old enough to have atmosphere, cleverly enough modernized and extended for comfort. Like other Belgian hotels

it has a passion for wallpaper and drapes which suggest rather than provide four-poster canopies over bed and bath. It has a touch of the courtesan about it – except for the pillows which are indescribably awful. Downstairs the accommodation is sturdier, with large, enveloping, most uncontinental chairs in a bar lounge leading into a glass-walled restaurant overlooking that famous view. Here one eats very well indeed without pomposity, advised and served by the patron. One could be lucky enough to light on one of his gastronomic weekends, as for example one I just missed based on products *de la chasse*. Stopping here only overnight I greatly wished I could have stayed longer cocooned in comfort and friendliness.' *(Frances Howell)*

Open: 1 April–15 November. Weekends only 15 November–1 March. Closed Sunday evening and Monday.
Rooms: 14 double – all with bath and telephone. TV on request.
Facilities: Lounge with bar, restaurant; conference facilities; indoor heated swimming pool; sauna, solarium, ping pong; garden with terrace.
Location: 26 km N of Sedan. Hotel is 300 metres outside Rochehaut on the Alle road opposite Frahan viewpoint.
Credit card: American Express.
Terms: Dinner, B & B 1210–1650 Bfrs; full board 1430–1870 Bfrs. Set meals; lunch 485 and 600 Bfrs, dinner 600, 980 and 1200 Bfrs; full *alc* 1300 Bfrs. Special gastronomic weekends September–Easter. Reduced rates for children sharing parents' room; special meals provided.

RONSE, 9681 Maarkedal   Map 8

Hostellerie Shamrock   *Telephone:* (055) 21.55.29
Ommegangstraat 148, Nukerke

'If you think that something called a *Hostellerie* is going to be jolly and a bit rustic, in this case you are totally wrong. *Hostellerie Shamrock* is like a private country house and oozes with dignity, quiet elegance and comfort. It is set in its own beautiful grounds with woods behind the house and a rhododendron avenue, immaculately groomed lawns and mixed borders in front. There are only a few guest rooms. Ours was spacious and well furnished, with a large equally well-equipped bathroom. But the *Shamrock* is obviously chiefly visited for its gourmet food which is served in the dark and dignified dining room and the adjacent (not very cosy) hall. The head waiter is like a high priest performing his holy task, lighting a candle, decanting the red wine over another candle, or whatever. Our charming hostess glided from table to table checking that everything was done to the liking of her guests. It certainly was to ours, because the cooking is superb, although we could not have tackled the long gourmet menu – far too much. But the Belgians love their food and don't seem to hesitate. Only by the fourth or fifth course the Belgian ladies take on a slightly glazed look but, loyal to their menfolk, valiantly carry on eating. An interesting detail – new to us, but we may be very inexperienced – was that instead of being given a plate vulgarly groaning with food, our main course (of lamb, as it happened) was served in two smaller, delicately arranged lots, each time with fresh plates and cutlery, and with a variation in the accompanying vegetables. "We always do this, because the food would not stay hot otherwise," was the explanation. There is a small elegant lounge, but everyone seemed to make for the door for some fresh air and exercise after the two-hour session of concentrated eating.' *(Agathe Lewin)*

Open: All year, except Sunday evening. Monday, the last 2 weeks in July and Christmas.

Rooms: 5 double, 1 single – 5 with bath, 1 with shower, all with telephone and radio.

Facilities: Salon, bar, restaurant. Shady gardens of 5 acres. Swimming pool and tennis 4 km; golf 15 km; fine walking country. English spoken.

Location: Ronse 4 km. The hotel is best reached from the north, whether you are coming from Ostende or Brussels. Take the E3 and E5, then the N58 via Oudenaarde. On the Ronse–Oudenaarde road, take the direction of Muziekbos. The hotel is not *in* Nukerke, but close to the tiny villages of Louise-Marie and Muziekbos.

Credit cards: American Express, Diners.

Terms: B & B 1040–1390 Bfrs. Set meals: lunch 1100–1700 Bfrs, dinner 1700 Bfrs; full *alc* 1700 Bfrs. Reduced rates for children.

Denmark

Steensgaard Herregårdspension, Millinge

---

71 Nyhavn Hotel   *Telephone:* 01-11.85.85
Nyhavn 71   *Telex:* 27558 nyhhot dk

Not exactly a wonderful little inn in this beautiful capital city – we should love to have one recommended to us – but a place of some character nevertheless. It is in the heart of the old city, on the waterfront opposite the hydrofoil boats for Malmø.

'This comfortable and friendly hotel at the end of an inlet looking over the harbour was converted from an 1804 warehouse, retaining the thick walls and beams, imposing some constraints on room space, but giving much character. The restaurant provides excellent food (including a splendid buffet lunch) if you want to stay in: but shopping, royal palace and museums are within easy walking distance. The staff are helpful and welcoming, and it is not so big as to be impersonal.' *(Denys Watson)*

Open: All year. Restaurant open for breakfast buffet only on 24–26 December.
Rooms: 37 double, 38 single, 6 suites – 13 with bath, 68 with shower, 16 with TV, all with telephone and radio; baby-listening can be arranged.
Facilities: Lift, bar, restaurant, 2 conference/function rooms, nightly entertainment in bar. English spoken.
Location: In town centre, facing the Nyhavn Canal and the harbour; parking.
Credit cards: All major credit cards accepted.
Terms: B & B, 330–515 Dkr.

239

Store Kro *Telephone:* (03) 28.00.47
Slotsgade 6

Store Kro is close to Fredensborg Castle, the Queen's spring and autumn residence. It was built by Frederik IV in 1723 at the same time as he was putting up his royal palace next door. He was in fact, we are told, the first innkeeper here, and one of the original buildings is still in use as an annexe. The main building, however, is much more modern, and is constantly being extended. The modest inn is now quite a grand sort of hotel, but still retains an intimate atmosphere. It caters for the overflow from the Royal Palace, but you can dine quietly not aware that there is a party of 100 also dining. The rooms are individually furnished. Opinions differ about the food – some finding it 'superb', others not really worthy of the setting.

Open: All year.
Rooms: 15 double, 31 single, 3 suites – all with bath and baby-listening. 16 rooms in annexe.
Facilities: Lift, lounges, dining room; banqueting rooms, conference facilities. Riding and tennis nearby; near Esrum lake with fishing and bathing; sea at Hornbaek 15 km. English spoken. &.
Location: 9 km NE of Hillerød. Hotel is in centre of Fredensborg; parking for 20 cars.
Credit cards: All major credit cards accepted.
Terms: B & B 235–310 Dkr; dinner, B & B 380–430 Dkr; full board 460–500 Dkr. Set meals: lunch 110 Dkr, dinner 180 Dkr. Special weekend rates.

Steensgaard Herregårdspension *Telephone:* (09) 61.94.90

'*Steensgaard* is a stunning, three-winged half-timbered manor house set in a 27-acre park on the island of Funen (or Fyn). The oldest part of the house dates from around 1535, the rest from the 17th century. We were told it belongs to a Count who lives in Switzerland, but it is run by two young people, Kirsten Lund and Bent Lillemark, who obviously know what they're doing. The service is informal and friendly, guests are able to do very much what they please. We were there in the spring and the gardens were beautiful with a profusion of flowers and shrubs. There is a tennis court and riding, and obviously lovely walks. The bedrooms (just 15) are comfortable, the public rooms exquisitely decorated and filled with antiques. The dining room is particularly elegant. Breakfast is a splendid buffet, dinner a three-course set meal (one night we had wild boar). The food was excellent. The house sometimes caters for large parties – one when we were there was pretty noisy into the wee hours. But we considered this a minor matter for *Steensgard* was certainly the highlight of our stay in Denmark.' *(Cynthia Vartan)*

Open: 14 February–31 December.
Rooms: 13 double, 2 single – 8 with bath, 2 with shower, all with telephone and TV.

Facilities: Hall, 5 salons, library, dining room; billiards, chess; large park with lake (fishing), tennis and riding. Rocky beach 5 km. English spoken.
Location: NW of Millinge, off road to Middelfart.
Terms: B & B 154–314 Dkr; dinner, B & B 278–450 Dkr; full board, 349–450 Dkr. Set meals: lunch (buffet) 98 Dkr, dinner 138 Dkr. Half-price meals for children under 10.

RIBE, 6760 Jutland **Map 7**

Hotel Dagmar *Telephone:* (05) 42.00.33
Torvet 1

Once the nation's capital, Ribe is one of Denmark's oldest and best preserved towns. It's on the windy west coast of Jutland, in typically flat Danish countryside. The town itself has great charm, with its 800-year-old cathedral, its cobbled narrow streets and many listed buildings. In the spring, you can see the celebrated storks' nests on the rooftops. The *Dagmar* is in the central square. It was built in 1581, and is well in keeping with the rest of the town. The public rooms are of various shapes and sizes, rather ornately gilded in places, mostly old-fashioned and full of character, with low ceilings and chintzy armchairs. Some bedrooms are in the atmospheric old part, but there is also a new wing with thickly carpeted, net-curtained comfortable rooms with modern bathrooms. There are two restaurants – a posh one, with a considerable reputation for its cooking, and a livelier cheaper one in a cellar. 'Olde-worlde in the nicest sense (i.e. genuine), with the management equally so.' *(Tony Morris)*

Open: All year.
Rooms: 35 double, 7 single – 20 with bath or shower, all with telephone and radio.
Facilities: 2 salons (1 with TV), 2 restaurants; fishing, riding, swimming pool nearby.
Location: Central; parking.
Terms: Rooms 160–460 Dkr. Set meals: lunch 90 Dkr, dinner 140 Dkr; full *alc* 180 Dkr. Children under 12 half price when sharing parents' room.

VEJLE, 7100 **Map 7**

Munkebjerg Hotel *Telephone:* (05) 82.75.00
Telex: Munken 61103

A large resort hotel, 5 km out of Vejle, in a particularly lovely setting of beechwoods, 90 metres above Vejle fjord.
'We stayed over Easter when they have a special offer which is extremely good value. The food was very good. There is much more staff than one has become used to when staying in Danish hotels, all willing and capable. The rooms (there are also suites) were small but adequate. The wine list looked extremely impressive – a very unusual list of old vintages for those with that sort of money. But the really important point about the hotel is the service and, certainly if one gets a special offer, the excellent (well, almost: the peas the first night were perfect, the beans the next terrible) value for money in the restaurant. If one has to pay the full price it is better than the norm in Danish provincial hotels. There is dancing in

241

the cellar bar at times, but teenagers won't like it, as the music is rather trad. Small children seem to be very welcome. To sum it up: if anybody can afford to spend a holiday in Denmark, this is a very good hotel situated near-perfectly for touring Jutland.' *(Dr and Mrs W N Brown)*

Open: 7 January–20 December.

Rooms: 108 double, 16 single, 2 suites – 62 with bath, 62 with shower, all with telephone, radio, colour TV and baby-listening.

Facilities: Lounge, TV room, bar with live music, restaurant, banqueting rooms; nightclub open nightly except Sunday; billiard room; heated indoor swimming pool, sauna, solarium; large grounds with tennis court and children's playground; bicycles; beach ½ km, golf 1 km. English spoken. &.

Location: 6 km from town centre; limited parking facilities. To reach hotel drive along S side of the Vejle fjord; from Vejle follow serpentine road up the hill.

Credit cards: All major credit cards accepted.

Terms: B & B 217.50–310 Dkr; full board (weekly) 400 Dkr. Set meals: lunch 100 Dkr, dinner 160 Dkr. 50% reduction for children under 12 sharing parents' room; special meals provided.

Hotel Torni, Helsinki

Finland

Kalastajatorppa
Kalastajatorpantie 1, Fiskatorpsvågen

Telephone: 90-488 011
Telex: 121571

'*Kalastajatorppa* – the name simply means "Fisherman's Cottage", and this must be the most sophisticated cottage I've ever seen. For, in reality, it is a de-luxe hotel offering a high degree of sophistication coupled with a magnificent setting by the sea, yet only minutes away from the city centre. The rooms are modern with all the facilities one expects, and many of them have the superb sea view. The main restaurant carries the shield of the Chaîne des Rôtisseurs and offers an international floor-show with dinner and dancing nearly every night. There is an intimate nightspot for those who want to enjoy themselves into the small hours. And one can freshen up in the hotel's keep-fit, sauna bath and swimming pool complex. I found the staff very friendly, and the standard of service high, but I especially enjoyed the magnificent view of the setting sun reddening the sea as it slowly crossed the sky at midsummer.' *(Michael J Fitzpatrick; also Tony Morris, Marja-Leena Rautalin)*

Open: All year.
Rooms: 217 double, 10 single, 8 suites – 149 with bath, 78 with shower, all with telephone, radio and colour TV.
Facilities: Lifts; lobbies, bar, café, restaurant; conference facilities; hairdresser,

243

night-club; keep-fit room, swimming pool, sauna; tennis, boating, fishing and winter sports nearby.
Location: 5 km from town centre, on the Baltic; garage parking.
Credit cards: All major credit cards accepted.
Terms: Rooms 300–510 FM. Set meals: breakfast 32 FM, lunch 60–90 FM, dinner 100–180 FM (excluding 14% service charge); full *alc* 215 FM.

HELSINKI 26, 00260   Map 7

Hotel Mercur   *Telephone:* (90) 407 313
Ruusulankatu 5

'This is what Finns call a "summer hotel", meaning that for most of the year it is a students' hostel but is open as an ordinary hotel from the beginning of June until late August. For anyone who would rather spend money on other things and is prepared to accept fairly simple standards, this place can be recommended. It is centrally situated – eight minutes by tram from the middle of the city and about ten minutes' walk from the Sibelius monument or the well-known church hewn out of the rock. The rooms, if not exactly spartan, are certainly not lavishly furnished: two beds (not particularly soft), two chairs, a table and a telephone. But there is any amount of cupboard space, a huge window running from end to end of the room with an equally long writing-desk in front of it and a private loo and washroom (rather shabby). There are two showers and a bathroom in the corridor. Everything was spotlessly clean and of good quality, though well used. The situation is quiet and we could not hear any traffic at all even though it was Monday morning. The restaurant was another kettle of fish altogether. Dinner was excellent – good food well served, though the menu was not a large one. Breakfast, included in the price of the room, is of the help-yourself type. There are no other public rooms, but in the basement there is an enormous, 16-lane skittle alley where you can also buy refreshments, etc. We enjoyed our stay here, and it was certainly good value for the money. The staff are mostly students and are a very helpful lot.' *(Stephen Howard)*

Open: 1 June–31 August.
Rooms: 39 double, 10 single – all with WC, 1 with TV.
Facilities: Lift, restaurant; conference rooms; nightclub, dancing, disco. Sauna. 25-lane bowling alley with cafeteria.
Location: 8 minutes by tram from town centre; 10 minutes' walk from the Sibelius monument; parking.
Terms: Rooms with breakfast 123 FM (single), 160 FM (double). Set meals: lunch 16–26 FM, dinner 21–42 FM.

HELSINKI 10, 00100   Map 7

Hotel Torni   *Telephone:* (90) 644 611
Yrjönkatu 26   *Telex:* 125153 turni sf

The *Torni* is a fifty-year-old hotel that was completely renovated in 1981. It combines the spaciousness of a good traditional hotel with all the comfort one hopes to find in a modern one. It is very central and fairly easy to find if one drives into Helsinki down Mannerheimintie, the main avenue. Although right in the middle of the city, near the big shops, the

244

railway station and the port, it is nevertheless quiet, being in a small street just off the main avenue. Our room was large and comfortable, with a bow-window that let in plenty of fresh air, three good armchairs, a table, a big writing-desk, and ample cupboard space. I don't think we have ever been in a hotel room where we have felt so little crowded – one of our nicest surprises. The bathroom was equally spacious. There are a lot of public rooms of one sort or another. The food was excellent and the service good, but oh, the wines! It is not the fault of the hotel but official Finnish policy: the price of wines is out of all proportion to the quality. We liked the hotel very much and felt thoroughly at home there. Apart from the spaciousness of the room and the sterling solidity of everything, we found the atmosphere congenial and relaxing. Smiles everywhere and, incidentally, quite good English too, even from the cleaning staff.'
(Michael and Marit Stevens)

Open: All year.
Rooms: 95 doubles, 18 de-luxe doubles, 45 singles – 33 with bath, 125 with shower, all with telephone and radio.
Facilities: Lift, salons, bars, restaurants; conference room; dancing and disco; sauna, casino.
Location: In city centre, just off the main Avenue, Mannerheimintie.
Terms: B & B 320 FM (single), 440–600 FM (double). Set meals: lunch 66 FM, dinner 77 FM.

MESSILÄ, SF-15980   **Map 7**

Messilä Manor Hotel   *Telephone:* (918) 531 666
                                                   Telex: 16286 messi sf

'On the slopes of a ridge with a fine view of lake Vesijärvi. The heart of the hotel is the old manor house, which has been in the possession of the same family for two hundred years. This building, is now the restaurant and bar, is furnished with great taste and has real charm. The reception and a number of bedrooms are among the trees behind this small manor in a modern annexe which, despite the fact that it is made mostly of glass and steel, somehow melts into its surroundings. Rather remarkable. The other rooms are in little red wooden cottages, fully modern inside, about fifty yards away from the restaurant. Our room was in the annexe, not particularly large but very comfortable and well-equipped, looking through the trees to the manor and the lake. The shower-room was unusual: one wall was made of glass and another was a mirror, which made it immensely light and airy. The restaurant serves a good set dinner at reasonable prices. Excellent buffet-type breakfast. The real joy of the hotel, however, are all the facilities available for recreation. Firstly there are the stables – 12 horses for hire – and miles of well-prepared rides through the countryside, which is rather attractive here being quite hilly. Then there is a tennis court, a mini-golf course and a long "summer" bobsleigh run. There are unlimited opportunities for walking and the hotel supplies you with a map showing all the tracks in the neighbourhood. The lake also has a great deal to offer: besides rowing boats, which visitors may borrow free, there is a wind-surfing school with boards for hire. There is also an indoor swimming pool and, of course, the saunas. As *Messilä* consists only of the hotel and one or two private houses, these facilities are to all intents and purposes just for those staying at the hotel. An ideal place for anyone who would like to spend a few days really away from it all. We should have liked to stay longer and go for long rides. And how good the air smells here!' *(Michael and Marit Stevens)*

Open: All year.
Rooms: 31 double, 5 single – 5 with bath, 31 with shower, 33 with telephone, 18 with radio; TV for hire. (18 rooms in 4 annexes.)
Facilities: Lounge, bar, café-restaurant, restaurant; conference/function facilities. Dance on Saturdays in restaurant, 1900s Gala Dinner every Thursday, chamber music concerts; art and costume exhibitions. Heated indoor swimming pool, sauna; handicraft workshops. Garden. Tennis court, mini-golf, riding, skiing, 'summer' bobsleigh run, windsurfing, rowing, children's play centre. English spoken.
Location: 8 km from town centre; parking.
Credit cards: Access/Euro/Mastercard, American Express, Barclay/Visa.
Terms: Rooms with breakfast 150 FM (single), 210 FM (double). Set meals: lunch 42–49 FM, dinner 49 FM. Christmas, Easter, skiing packages. Reduced rates for children sharing parents' room.

SAARIJÄRVI, SF-43140   Map 7

Rantasipi Summassaari Hotel   *Telephone:* (944) 21311
431 40 Summassaari   *Telex:* 28222 summa sf

'If you would like to stay at an extremely comfortable hotel in bold modern Finnish design, you will enjoy *Summassaari*. We did not think the front of the hotel looked particularly beautiful – austere might have been a better word – but we were totally unprepared for our bedroom – a large fan-shaped room the far wall of which was glass. Right outside the window was the pine forest through which we caught a glimpse of the blue lake: a breathtaking prospect. The room itself was modern, with severe lines and forms, but not in any way forbidding. Both the bedroom itself and the shower-room (with an excellent thermostat-controlled shower) were well designed and the furniture was comfortable. At first we thought that the price – 380 marks – was a bit high, but then we found that we had been given two fifty-mark coupons which we could use either as payment for the set dinner or as part-payment for an *à la carte* meal. Breakfast is included in the price of the room as usual. The hotel has a lot to offer. It is beautifully situated on a wooded island just outside Saarijärvi. Down by the lake there is a swimming pool and large sauna, free for hotel guests. There is tennis, mini-golf and badminton, and you can hire canoes, rowing-boats, motor-boats, sailing-boats, wind-surfing boards, fishing equipment and bicycles. Once a week there is a barbecue evening and for the adventurous the hotel organizes half-day, one-day or two-day canoe safaris with or without rapids to negotiate. There are also twenty-five self-contained bungalows down by the lake.' *(Stephen Howard)*

Open: All year.
Rooms: 41 double, 16 single, 2 suites – all with shower, telephone and radio; baby-listening on request. (Most rooms in 23 bungalows, each with 2 bedrooms and a sitting room.)
Facilities: TV lounge, bar, restaurant; conference room. Dancing 6 nights a week, disco 3 evenings. Sauna, swimming pool. Large grounds with lake, tennis, mini-golf and badminton; canoes, rowing-boats, motor-boats, sailing-boats, windsurfing boards, fishing equipment, bicycles for hire. Weekly barbecue evenings; ½–2 day canoe safaris. Sandy beach 200 metres; fishing rights. English spoken.
Location: 8 km from Saarijärvi; 65 km from Jyväskylä, direction Kokkola.

Credit cards: All major credit cards accepted.
Terms: Rooms with breakfast 230 FM (single), 310 FM (double); bungalows 440 FM (excluding breakfast), 520 FM (with sauna). Set meals: lunch/dinner 55 FM; full *alc* about 120 FM. Children under 4, free; 4–14 years, 50% reduction; special meals provided. Special weekend rates.

SAVONLINNA 31 Map 7

Rauhalinna Hotel   *Telephone:* 1/6-31/8 (957) 53119
Lehtiniemi 57310   1/9-31/5 (957) 22864

'Of all the hotels we have seen and stayed at in Finland, this is the one we really fell in love with. The building itself is unique, the rooms delightful, the food excellent and the staff unusually nice; and you feel that you are not staying at a hotel at all, but rather at a private house whose owner has left instructions that you are expected and are to be well looked after. *Rauhalinna* (which means "Castle of Peace") was commissioned in 1897 by General Nils Weckman, the officer in charge of the Czar's fortifications. He obviously intended the house to be as different as possible from his military works and for three years he had a small army of craftsmen working on the exterior and interior decorations. The result is this fantastic building, well-known to art historians. If you are lucky, you will be given Room 201, the general's own beautiful octagonal room just under the tower. It is spacious and comfortably furnished with a fine view over the lawn and down the drive to the lake. There is a magnificent dining room, once the scene of banquets and balls, which serves an excellent dinner. It is such a peaceful spot and it can never be crowded, for there are only eight rooms. Paying the bill is a pleasant surprise: this was one of the cheapest nights we spent in Finland, as well as probably the most memorable. Are there really no disadvantages? Yes, of course there are – no reading lamps or washing facilities in the bedroom and a bathroom/shower in the corridor. But neither worried us in the least.' *(Michael and Marit Stevens)*

Open: 1 June–30 September.
Rooms: 7 double, 1 single, 1 with hot and cold water, 1 with shower, 1 with WC.
Facilities: Salon, cafeteria, dining room; grounds with lake, swimming, sauna and fishing.
Location: To get to Rauhalinna, turn off road No. 14 (Punkaharju–Savonlinna) 4 km east of Savonlinna on to road No. 471 running north to Enonkoski and Heinävesi. There is a Union petrol station at the road junction. From here, the road to Rauhalinna is clearly marked.
Terms: Rooms with breakfast 150–182 FM (single), 192–235 FM (double). Set meals: lunch 47–53 FM, dinner 55–62 FM.

Parc Hôtel, La Croix-Valmer

France

Hostellerie des Trois Mousquetaires   *Telephone:* (21) 39.01.11

This small late 19th-century château, 60 km south-east of Calais, 70 km east of Boulogne, and close to the motorway, is popular with readers as a night-stop on the way to or from the ports. It is very clean, and the rooms are comfortable and full of little extras such as sewing equipment. There is a lounge for coffee, also a garden and small playground for children. Philippe Venet, the chef and son of the *patron*, has recently married the energetic head waitress, and has since put on weight – 'always a good sign'. Everyone praises the food (e.g. *escargots en brioche, truite au poivre rose*) and the reasonable prices. The Venets have only eight rooms, often booked out long in advance, and they demand a deposit. This has sometimes led to mistakes and confusions, so it is as well to explain very clearly what you want. *(Paul Dyer, K and R Burglass, Mrs C Smith, Dr M B Matthews, Eileen Broadbent and others)*

Open: All year, except 15 January–15 February; closed Sunday evening and all day Monday.
Rooms: 8 double – 6 with bath, 2 with shower – all with telephone and TV.
Facilities: Salon, TV lounge, 2 restaurants. 7 acres garden with lawns leading to a river. English spoken.
Location: Between Calais and Arras, 2 km from centre of Aire on the Arras side; private parking; 50 km from the sea.

249

Terms (excluding 15% service charge):   Rooms 50–160 frs. Set meals: breakfast 15 frs; lunch/dinner 50–115 frs. Special meals for children.

AIRVAULT, 79600 Deux-Sèvres   Map 8

Auberge du Vieux Relais   *Telephone:* (49) 64.70.31

Airvault is north-west of Poitiers and not far south of the Loire. The *Auberge* is an old coaching inn in the centre of the town which has an imposing 12th-century abbey. It's a simple, casual sort of place, with nowhere except the bar and a courtyard to sit in the evenings, and the noise hazards of a mini-aviary full of vociferous canaries and the town band practising with open windows. One fastidious traveller thinks it best suited for an overnight stop. The plusses are the really good local cooking at fair prices, the good selection of interesting local Vendée wines, and the comfortable, inexpensive bedrooms – 'lovely quietness, disturbed only by half-Burmese cat Chloe coming off the roof on to our bed in the early morning, just like home.' *(Charles Shepherd and others)*

Open: All year, except 1–15 October. Closed Monday.
Rooms: 8 double, 4 single – 3 with bath, 4 with shower.
Facilities: Bar with TV, restaurant; courtyard and garden; river and swimming pool nearby; fishing and hunting. English spoken.
Location: Just off the N138 about halfway between Saumur and Niort – about 30 km from either. In the town centre near the church. Parking.
Terms: B & B 53–115 frs; full board 115–160 frs. Set meals: breakfast 15 frs; lunch/dinner 44–145 frs; full *alc* 87 frs. Reduced rates and special meals for children.

AIX-EN-OTHE, 10160 Aube   Map 8

Auberge de la Scierie   *Telephone:* (25) 46.71.26

In the heart of the undulating Othe country, 31 km west of Troyes and a little farther from the cathedral towns of Sens and Auxerre. This unusual auberge, just outside the little town of Aix, has a special idyllic quality all its own. It consists of four farmhouse-type buildings, two of them 18th- and 19th-century converted (one a former sawmill, as the name implies) and two modern, scattered around a big garden beside a stream. One reader has now been there five times and is firmly in love with the place. Here is the gist of her 1981 and 1982 reports: 'The inn is in attractive grounds with a river containing delectable trout: there are ducks, geese, peacocks, a donkey and two dogs. We always receive a warm welcome, and the staff are most helpful. The rooms are in chalets in the garden, round a small unheated swimming pool: light and airy, and prettily decorated with flowery paper. There is an attractive rustic bar with wooden beams, horse brasses, woodcutters' tools, sheepskins, bellows, etc. The dining room reflects the same mood. The wine list is good, apart from a limited choice of white wines, which is surprising being near Chablis. The food is excellent with generous portions. On a summer evening in 1982 we dined out in the charming gardens: local cured ham; rabbit *pâté*; fresh salmon marinaded in herbs and oil, very succulent; a sorbet served before the main course; steak in a rich red wine sauce and sweetbreads in a white wine and cream sauce. Cheeseboard immense and in good condition; fresh strawberries for dessert.' Another 1982 visitor concurs with this praise. Rooms, he says, are remarkable value, though meals are rather more pricey. He wonders why Padi Howard did not mention the three gentle horses which can be hired by guests. *(Padi Howard; also JA)*

Open: 1 April–1 December.
Rooms: 10 double – 6 with bath, 4 with shower, all with telephone and radio. (5 rooms on ground floor in chalets.)
Facilities: Salon, TV room, bar, restaurant. Garden and river; unheated swimming pool. English spoken.
Location: On the RN374 between Troyes and Sens, 2 km S of Aix-en-Othe. Parking.
Credit cards: American Express, Diners.
Terms: Rooms 180 frs; half-board 185–200 frs. Set meals: breakfast 25 frs; lunch/dinner 83–150 frs; full *alc* 180 frs.

AIX-EN-PROVENCE, 13090 Bouches-du-Rhône, Provence   Map 9

Hotel Le Pigonnet *Telephone:* (42) 59.02.90
Avenue du Pigonnet *Telex:* 410629

'*Le Pigonnet* is a stately creeper-covered mansion about 1 km south of the city's historic centre, in a quiet side-street. It has a sober elegance that goes well with Aix, and we did not mind paying such high prices for so much quality. Our large bedroom had real antique furniture, cheerful wallpaper, and a balcony with views of Cézanne's Mont Ste-Victoire. We enjoyed playing *boules*, watching the antics of the squirrels in a cage in the garden, and lazing by the swimming pool which is set amid flowers. The garden itself is most unusual, all rose-bowers, fountains and ornamental pools – more like the garden of some romantic *fin-de-siècle* villa than of a chic hotel. Service was courteous, though a little impersonal; and we found the dining room too a little formal for our tastes. But we enjoyed lunching out under the chestnut trees. The food was mostly very good, especially the fish, though on some days we found the quality erratic and service slow.' *(Peter and Sarah Abbott)*

Open: All year. (Restaurant closed Sunday evening 1 November–31 March.)
Rooms: 44 double, 6 single, 1 suite – 39 with bath, 11 with shower, all with telephone and TV; baby-sitting by arrangement. (14 rooms in annexe.)
Facilities: Lift, lounge, bar, restaurant, terrace. Garden with heated swimming pool and *boules*. Rocky and sandy beach 25 km. English spoken.
Location: Coming from Nice or Toulon, leave the autoroute at the Aix-Est exit; coming from Lyon or Paris, leave it at the Aix–Sud exit. The hotel is 800 m from the city centre, in a quiet side street; parking.
Credit cards: All major credit cards accepted.
Terms: B & B 165–330 frs; dinner, B & B 275–445 frs; full board 390–560 frs. Set meals: lunch/dinner 124 frs; full *alc* 140 frs. Free bed for children under 6; special meals on request.

In the case of many continental hotels, especially French ones, we have adopted the local habit of quoting a price for the room whether it is occupied by one or more persons. Rates for B & B, half board, etc., are per person unless otherwise stated.

251

La Réserve   *Telephone:* (63) 60.79.79
Route de Cordes   *Telex:* 520850 F

A smart modern *Relais et Château*, 3 km out of town on the north side, owned by the Rieux family who have also been running Albi's celebrated *Hostellerie Saint-Antoine* (see below) for five generations. There are some who like to stay in the centre, but: 'We prefer *La Réserve*. It has a superb setting on the Tarn, with a sweeping lawn, tennis court and swimming pool. The dining is first class, in a handsome inside room or on the terrace overlooking the river. Bedrooms are well appointed with lovely fabrics.' *(S M Gillotti)*

Open: 1 March–30 November.
Rooms: 15 double, 5 single – 16 with bath, 4 with shower, all with telephone.
Facilities: Salons, one with TV, bar, restaurant, banquet/conference facilities. Set in a large park with tennis court and heated swimming pool. Near river. English spoken.
Location: 3 km from town centre on the road from Albi to Cordes; parking.
Credit cards: American Express, Barclay/Visa, Diners.
Terms: Rooms 250–440 frs; dinner, B & B 270–430 frs, full board 370–530 frs. Set meals: breakfast 30 frs, lunch/dinner 110–180 frs; full *alc* 200 frs.

Hostellerie Saint-Antoine   *Telephone:* (63) 54.04.04
      Telex: 520850 MAPALBI

This former monastery, its rooms built round a lovely inner garden, lies in the town centre yet is quiet, and is only 500 metres from Albi's two glories – its stunning red-brick cathedral and the adjacent Toulouse-Lautrec museum. A hostelry since 1734, the hotel provides elegance and comfort ('charmingly pretty rooms') as well as 'notably obliging service' and above-average *cuisine* (remarkable desserts). Guests are free to use the swimming-pool and tennis courts of *La Réserve* (see above). For what it is worth, Michelin puts *La Réserve* in red (the *Saint-Antoine* is merely the standard black), but Gault-Millau thinks the *Saint-Antoine*'s food is slightly better (13 points against 12). More verdicts, please, on this Rieux family competition. *(R S Ryder, David Ballard)*

Open: All year.
Rooms: 44 double, 12 single – 40 with bath, 16 with shower, all with telephone, 25 with colour TV.
Facilities: Lift, salon, TV room, bar, restaurant; banquet/conference facilities. Delightful inner garden. Free tennis and swimming 3 km, at *La Réserve*. English spoken.
Location: In the centre of Albi; very quiet; parking.
Credit cards: All major credit cards accepted.
Terms: Rooms 180–380 frs; dinner, B & B 230–360 frs; full board 310–440 frs. Set meals: breakfast 25 frs; lunch/dinner 100–160 frs; full *alc* 180 frs. Children free in parents' room; special meals provided.

ANDUZE, 30140 Gard, Languedoc   Map 8

Les Trois Barbus   *Telephone:* (66) 61.72.12
Générargues

Anduze is in the wooded southern foothills of the Cévennes, 47 km from
Nîmes. 'This place was a real find, in the middle of nowhere in the
Cévennes. A breathtaking situation, overlooking a gorge and a branch of
the river Gardon. Lovely views in all directions. It is on a steep slope, a
series of terraced gardens, with an excellent swimming pool on the lowest
– a great joy after a long hot drive. It is a family-run affair: when I asked
the presiding matriarch who the "three bearded gentlemen" were, she
said simply: "Ce sont mes fils."
'Our room was comfortable, if not spacious. Very quiet, the only sound
at night being a waterfall down in the gorge. But almost the best of all was
the restaurant. I cannot understand why it has no rosette in Michelin.
Marvellous sauces, light and original, and the menus well balanced.
Charming Limoges china.' *(Mrs R B Richards)*

Open: 20 March–30 October, except Monday. (Restaurant closed Monday,
except July/August.)
Rooms: 36 double – 34 with bath, 2 with shower, all with telephone, many with
balconies. (5 rooms on ground floor.)
Facilities: TV room, bar lounge, bar, grill room, restaurant, terraces; seminar
room; discothèque. Small garden with unheated swimming pool and *boules*.
English spoken.
Location: 6 km N of Anduze on D50 at Le Roucan-Générargues.
Terms: Rooms 190 frs; dinner, B & B 220 frs; full board 280 frs. Set meals:
breakfast 20 frs, lunch/dinner 100 frs; full *alc* 180 frs. Reduced rates and special
meals for children.

ANNOT, 04240 Alpes de Haute-Provence   Map 9

Grand Hôtel Grac   *Telephone:* (92) 83.20.02
Place des Platanes

*'An old country inn with real character in the shady main square of a very
pretty little town in a relatively unknown corner of inland Provence. We
found much of interest nearby – Alps and gorges, and the amazing walled
medieval village of Entrevaux. The Hôtel Grac is furnished in the local
style, and has a garden with swings which our small daughter enjoyed. The
Provençal food is really super, copious and amazing value. No wonder the
dining room seemed always packed out with locals and tourists.' (John and
Ludmila Berry)*
So ran last year's entry, but recent visitors disagree: 'Disappointing.
Reasonable value, but nothing exceptional. Room badly needed redecorating.' Further reports welcome.

Open: 1 April–30 October.
Rooms: 26 – some with bath or shower.
Facilities: Restaurant; garden.
Location: NW of Vence on the D908; parking.
Terms: Rooms 60–110 frs; full board 120–160 frs. Set meals: breakfast 13 frs;
lunch/dinner 80–105 frs.

Hôtel Royal   *Telephone:* (93) 34.03.09 and 34.29.89
Boulevard du Maréchal-Leclerc

On the front, across the road from the sea, and about 500 metres from the Vieille Ville and Picasso museum. 'An excellent three-star family hotel, owned and run by the Duhart family, supported by a friendly and efficient staff. Rooms are charming and comfortable; the front balcony ones, which may be noisy in summer, face the bay and the hotel's small private beach. The attractive restaurant provides good food in generous portions, and the coffee and croissants for breakfast are outstanding. Warmly recommended.' *(Eve and Ben Perrick)*

Open: 21 December–end October. Restaurant closed Wednesday out of season.
Rooms: 39 double, 4 single – 16 with bath, 21 with shower, all with telephone, some with balcony overlooking sea. Baby-sitting can be arranged.
Facilities: Lift, salon, TV room, bar, restaurant, terrace restaurant. Terrace with snack bar overlooking private beach; windsurfing, waterskiing.
Location: On the front, 500 metres from town centre, in the direction of Antibes; sandy beach close by.
Credit cards: American Express, Diners.
Terms: Half board 190–265 frs; full board 265–335 frs. Set meals: breakfast 22 frs, lunch/dinner 90–100 frs.

Grand Hôtel Clément   *Telephone:* (21) 35.40.66
91 Esp. du Maréchal Leclerc   *Telex:* 130886 F (Res. Clement)

The 'typical Frenchness' (whatever that means) of the *Clément* has long held a strong appeal for hordes of British visitors who regularly make it their first or last stop of a Continental holiday: it is a sedate little country hotel on the edge of a small town only 17 km from Calais, on the road to the Paris *autoroute*. In the past, reports on the quality of the cooking and of the bedroom furnishing have varied, but this year's crop are uniformly favourable. 'Many bedrooms are being redecorated. We had a delightful room with lovely furniture and heavenly bathroom. Personally I don't enjoy the heavy sauces of Flanders cooking, but I'd go back simply for the escargots with walnuts.' 'Room at front in lovely pink colours, hand-carved furniture, lovely garden, all staff polite and helpful. Recommend the 200-franc [1982] nine-course menu.' Quantity goes hand-in-hand with reasonable quality in the cooking of Paul Coolen, *patron/chef*; he and his wife Monique offer their guests a warm welcome; and their quiet hotel is a member of the *Relais du Silence*. *(Di Latham, W Georgiadis, Dr and Mrs G Collingham, W Frank, Diana Weir)*

Open: All year, except 15 January–15 February. Restaurant closed Monday and Tuesday, also midday out of season.
Rooms: 17 double, 1 single – 12 with bath, 4 with shower, all with direct-dial telephone.
Facilities: Salons, bar, 2 dining rooms; conference facilities in winter. Garden with swings, terrace; ping pong. 1 km from lake. English spoken.

Location: 17 km from Calais on the N43 to St Omer and Lillers, whence autoroute to Paris.
Credit cards: Access/Euro/Mastercard, Barclay/Visa.
Terms: Rooms 120–200 frs. Set meals: breakfast 18 frs; lunch/dinner 120–230 frs.

ARDRES, 62610 Pas de Calais   Map 8

Le Relais   *Telephone:* (21) 35.42.00

Recommended as a slightly cheaper alternative to the often crowded *Grand Clément*, in a reasonably quiet situation with a pleasant garden, and first-class French home cooking, though if you are thinking of more than a night's stay you need to be warned that the menus do not change from day to day. The dining room, to quote a previous reader, is 'attractive French olde-worlde, phoney but tasteful.' 'Ideal for a first night stop after arriving at Calais. Easy to find and parking convenient. Pleasant decor in bedroom. Enjoyable evening meal and most attentive service. Good value for money.' *(Mr and Mrs B Dawkins; also C and C Orio)*

Open: January–October. Restaurant closed Friday evening and midday Saturday.
Rooms: 11 double – 3 with bath, 8 with shower, all with telephone.
Facilities: Bar/restaurant; party/conference facilities. Garden. English spoken.
Location: Central; parking.
Credit cards: Barclay/Visa.
Terms: Rooms 130–215 frs; full board 190–215 frs. Set meals: breakfast 15 frs; lunch/dinner 55–90 frs.

ARLES, 13200 Bouches-du-Rhône, Provence   Map 9

Hôtel d'Arlatan   *Telephone:* (90) 93.56.66
26 rue du Sauvage   *Telex:* SI Arles 440096

A hotel of exceptional charm and character, even by Provençal standards. The building, dating from the 15th century, was the ancestral home of the Counts of Arlatan; it fronts a quiet street in the heart of old Arles, and has a very special secretive quality. Its idyllic little garden is enclosed on one side by the high wall of the palace of Constantine. Numerous visitors have raved about the place: 'One of the loveliest hotels I have ever visited,' writes one enthusiast; 'one passes through an arched gateway into a courtyard with a lone palm . . . a cool place to sit and sip on a hot day. The interiors are done with great taste and care, with lovely antiques and fabrics. Service is excellent, and the owner and all the staff are charming and helpful.' Indeed, there has usually been nothing but praise for the cultivated Desjardin family who run the place with so much pride. However, one recent visitor has reported an unpleasant squabble over money when settling the bill, and has spoken of mosquitoes in his room (common enough in this area in August). No restaurant, but you can eat well in town at the *Jules César* (expensive), *Le Vaccarès* (medium priced) and the *Hostellerie des Arènes* (cheap). *(HR)*

Open: All year.
Rooms: 40 double, 6 single – 37 with bath or shower, all with telephone. (5 rooms in annexe).

Facilities: Reading room and library, Louis XIII lounge with TV; conference room. Garden with courtyard patio decked with trees and shrubs for outdoor refreshments.
Location: Central, near the place du Forum; garage parking.
Credit cards: American Express, Diners.
Terms: Rooms 140–320 frs. Set meals: breakfast 25 frs.

ARPAILLARGUES, 30700 Uzès, Provence   Map 9

Château d'Arpaillargues   *Telephone:* (66) 22.14.48
                                                     Telex: 490730

Uzès is one of the most lovely and fascinating old towns in Provence: do not miss the Duché, the Tour Fenestrelle and the Place aux Herbes. About 5 km to the west, on the edge of the village of Arpaillargues, stands this 18th-century château, formerly the home of the d'Agoult family (Liszt was the lover of Marie d'Agoult). It has been stylishly converted, and is maintained impeccably, with cool and spacious rooms furnished with antiques. There are tennis courts, a large swimming pool, a library, a park, and views over the rolling hills. On fine days, you can dine out by the pool, or on a beautiful terrace by the garden; when it is cooler, a log-fire burns in the baronial banqueting-hall. The cooking is always interesting, and as ambitious as the setting, though the chef does have his off-days.
(Antony Vestrey, R W G Wilson)

Open: 15 March–15 October. Restaurant closed Wednesday out of season.
Rooms: 25 – all with bath or shower and telephone. Some rooms in annexe.
Facilities: Salon, library, restaurant, courtyard; conference facilities. Park, tennis courts, swimming pool. &.
Location: 5 km W of Uzès; parking.
Credit cards: Barclay/Visa, Euro.
Terms: Rooms 275–350 frs; full board 365–470 frs. Set meals: breakfast 25 frs; lunch/dinner 125 frs.

AUXERRE, 89000 Yonne, Burgundy   Map 8

Hôtel Le Maxime   *Telephone:* (86) 52.14.19
2 quai de la Marine

The historical city of Auxerre stands at the entrance to Burgundy, 168 km down the autoroute from Paris, and is worth a visit if only for the frescoes in the 11th-century crypt of its cathedral. *Le Maxime*, new to the Guide, is a three-star hotel overlooking the river Yonne, near the cathedral. Its decor is hardly beautiful, but it has other virtues – 'bedrooms are comfortable, with good bathrooms and, if facing the river as mine was, light. When I got up to collect the car, someone had washed the windscreen and cleaned it perfectly. No restaurant; but the one next door, also called *Le Maxime*, has good fresh fish.' Another visitor found 'a frosty reception at the desk – perhaps Madame had had a rough day, or perhaps I myself looked rather rough', but otherwise enjoyed his stay. *(GK, James Shorrocks)*

Open: All year.
Rooms: 25 double – most with bath or shower, some overlooking river.

Facilities: Lift, salons (no restaurant, but *Le Maxime* next door).
Location: In town centre, near the cathedral; garage parking.
Credit cards: All major credit cards accepted.
Terms: Rooms 200–300 frs. Set meal: breakfast 22 frs. Set lunch or dinner at *Le Maxime* restaurant 160 frs.

AUXERRE, 89000 Yonne, Burgundy   **Map 8**

Hotel de Seignelay   *Telephone:* (86) 52.03.48
2 rue du Pont

'A modest hotel in the town centre, quietly run by middle-aged Burgundian professionals. It has given us much pleasure for over 12 years. Set around a courtyard, it has a charming setting through an arch, with contrasting cream walls and red roofs. Pleasant sitting room with open fire for cold days; some modern bedrooms with baths, the others with washing only. The usual array of menus, including two with five and seven courses; strictly traditional food, and excellent choice. In a week, I can eat my way through all the Burgundian specialities and expect to see different *tartes* each evening. Good house red.' *(John Thirwell)*

Open: All year, except early January–early February and Mondays, October–mid June.
Rooms: 24, mostly double – some with bath or shower, most with telephone.
Facilities: Salon, restaurant, courtyard; conference facilities for 80 people.
Location: Near centre of old town; garage parking.
Terms: Rooms 70–175 frs. Set meals: breakfast 14 frs, lunch/dinner 65–115 frs.

AVALLON, 89200 Yonne, Burgundy   **Map 8**

Hostellerie du Moulin des Ruats   *Telephone:* (86) 34.07.14
Vallée du Cousin

The medieval fortified town of Avallon is only 15 km from Vézelay with its glorious hilltop basilica, and not far from the rolling wooded country of the Morvan. 'The *Moulin* is a very special hotel in an idyllic green valley two miles west of Avallon. One can be lulled to sleep by the murmurs of a brook running under this hotel which was once a mill. One can also enjoy a superb bottle of wine from nearby Chablis while sitting in the grounds. The food I thought outstanding. The rooms are fairly small and not overly elegant, but comfortable.' Another reader, however, while agreeing about the idyllic setting, found the food conventional and over-priced, and the large dining room a little dull and formal. A third, who appreciated the hotel, warns of the need to book for dinner even if a resident, to avoid a long wait. More reports please. *(Caroline D Hamburger, James Joll and others)*

Open: 1 March–31 October.
Rooms: 21 13 with bath, 1 with shower, all with telephone.
Facilities: Restaurant. English spoken.
Location: 3 km W of Avallon in the direction of Vézelay; parking.
Credit cards: All major credit cards accepted.
Terms: Rooms 100–230 frs. Set meals: breakfast 26 frs, lunch 140 frs. *Alc* dinner (excluding wine) 135–210 frs.

Hostellerie de la Poste   *Telephone:* (86) 34.06.12
13 place Vauban

A famous and dignified old hostelry, with a flower-decked cobbled courtyard: Napoleon spent a night here on his way back from Elba. One reader was delighted to find stylish service in the grand old manner: uniformed porters and chambermaids leapt to attend to his needs, without a trace of servility. He praises 'the warm and professional atmosphere felt throughout this hotel. It is well-maintained and furnished, beautifully warm and well-lit, and has a superb restaurant (two Michelin rosettes). Search as I did, my only cavil (and how petty can one get?) was the oversweetness of the commercially produced jams at breakfast. If only they'd been home-made! If you are going to run a hotel to the highest of standards in which the cost of employing a large and professional staff must be a major expense then it cannot be cheap. The prices at *La Poste* are elevated but justified. A cheaper alternative could be *Le Relais Fleurie* 4 km up the road: but don't expect it to be in the same class as *La Poste*.' *(Geoffrey Sharp)*

Open: All year, December–beginning January.
Rooms: 17 double, 3 single, 5 suites – 22 with bath, 2 with shower, all with telephone.
Facilities: Lounge, bar, restaurant. Courtyard. English spoken.
Location: In town centre; parking.
Credit cards: American Express, Barclay/Visa, Diners.
Terms (excluding 15% service charge): B & B 220–310 frs. Set meals: lunch 150 frs, dinner 275 frs; full *alc* 350 frs. Reduced rates and special meals for children.

Le Moulin des Templiers   *Telephone:* (86) 34.10.80
Vallée du Cousin

The setting could not be more idyllic: an old watermill, attractively converted into a comfortable and tranquil little hotel beside the quiet-flowing Cousin, little more than a stream. 'The gardens stretch along the river, and there is a beautiful terrace at the water's edge where breakfast is served. Reception and service were friendly and efficient.' 'Quite enchanted with the setting, the peace, and our pretty though very tiny room. One grumble: the water was cold in the shower at 10 p.m.' No restaurant: but nearby Avallon and Vezelay (q.v.) have several excellent ones. *(Warren Bagust, Eileen M Broadbent; also JA)*

Open: March–November.
Rooms: 14 – most with shower, all with telephone.
Facilities: Breakfast terrace. Garden, river.
Location: 3 km W of Avallon in the direction of Vézelay; parking.
Terms: Rooms 110–178 frs. Set meal: breakfast 17 frs. (No restaurant.)

Please write and confirm an entry when it is deserved. If you think that a hotel is not as good as we say, please write and tell us.

AVIGNON, 84000 Vaucluse, Provence   Map 9

Hôtel d'Europe   *Telephone:* (90) 82.66.92
12 place Crillon   *Telex:* 431965

The *Europe* stands in a small square just inside the old city walls, a mere 300 metres from the Papal Palace. Whereas most Avignon hotels are modern and functional, this one has classic character: it is a former 16th-century aristocrat's house, and was already an inn when Napoleon stayed here in 1799. One visitor finds it 'a splendid building, cool, spacious and elegant. Beautifully decorated rooms with Nobilis wallpapers. The furniture on the stairs and in the public rooms would make an antique dealer salivate, as would the period mirrors.' According to this report, the *Europe* is 'unobtrusively well run' and 'quiet at night', but not all readers agree. One has complained of 'motorcycles racing outside our window all night' (best ask for a room facing the back), while another found his bedroom 'small and poky' and the service offhand to the point of incompetence. More reports, please.

There is less dissent about the quality of the classic *cuisine* in the hotel's *Vieille Fontaine* restaurant. You can eat in a rather formal dining room or – preferably – under the plane trees beside a fountain in the graceful courtyard. At night, lamps are lit on each table. Good choice of Côtes du Rhône and other wines. *(Anthony Vestrey, S M Gillotti)*

Open: All year. Restaurant open evenings only, and closed 1 January–8 February and Sunday.
Rooms: 50 double, 9 single, 6 suites – 47 with bath, 13 with shower, all with telephone.
Facilities: Lift, 2 salons, restaurant, conference facilities. Courtyard. 5 minutes' walk from Palace. English spoken.
Location: Leave autoroute A9 at exit Avignon Nord. Cross pont de l'Europe and turn left. Enter city by porte de l'Oulle; place Crillon is just inside. Private garage.
Credit cards: American Express, Diners.
Terms: Rooms 230–305 frs (single), 350–460 frs (double). Set meals: breakfast 28 frs, dinner 90 frs; full *alc* 110 frs. Special meals for children; cots free.

BANDOL, 83150 Var, Provence   Map 9

Hôtel de l'Île Rousse   *Telephone:* (94) 29.46.86
Bvd Louis-Lumière   *Telex:* 400372 Ilerous

Bandol is the largest and most sophisticated resort between Marseille and Toulon, lively and popular all summer. There is plenty going on around the beach and yacht port: regattas, waterskiing, sand sports, and a casino and dancing. Offshore (seven minutes by boat) is the tiny island of Bendor, with a sailing and diving school, art galleries, and a remarkable museum of wines. The *Ile Rousse*, on the edge of the resort, facing out across a bay, is Bandol's de-luxe hotel – very modern, with its own sandy beach and heated swimming pool with lido. The bedrooms are decked out in 'period' style, with attractive tiled floors, and most have sea views from their balconies. There are three restaurants – two unpretentious ones by the beach, and a third indoors, much more formal and gastronomically ambitious, but uneven in quality. The hotel is part of the streamlined PLM chain, and one reader feels that it thereby lacks the personal charm of a family-run place. Maybe: but it does have one special asset in the form of the talented and irrespressible Charles Roux, who doubles as *maître d'hôtel* and resident comedian/conjuror, putting on shows in the bar after dinner. Most guests, if not all, find him hilarious. *(Martin Gilbert, Peter and Sarah Abbott)*

Open: All year.
Rooms: 53 double, 2 suites – all with bath, telephone, radio, and air-conditioning; some with colour TV.
Facilities: Lift, large lounge overlooking the beach, TV room, bar, 3 restaurants, terraces, night club; 4 conference rooms. Heated swimming pool; solarium; direct access to private sandy beach with café; water sports and safe bathing. Tennis courts, riding, sailing, casino nearby. English spoken.
Location: 5 minutes from town centre; garage parking.
Terms: B & B 165–705 frs; dinner, B & B 285–830 frs; full board 410–960 frs. Set meals: lunch/dinner 140 frs; full *alc* 160 frs. Free extra bed for child in parents' room; special meals for children.

BANDOL, 83150 Var, Provence   **Map 9**

Hôtel La Ker Mocotte   *Telephone:* (94) 29.46.53
Rue Raimu   *Telex:* 400383

On a low cliff above the beach, 200 metres round the bay from the *l'Ile Rousse*. 'We were quite beguiled by this unusual beach-hotel, which is run with verve and imagination by a smart couple from Alsace, the Goetzes. Once a week or so, they hold get-together *soirées* for residents, with charades, dancing and singing – yes, it could have been awful, but they managed it with style. Our bedroom was nothing special, but it had a good view of the sea, and we took breakfast under the pines in the garden. There is a private sandy beach, where we could wind-surf, as well as leave our eight-year-old with a *moniteur*. The food was quite good, notably the help-yourself buffet of *hors d'oeuvres*. The hotel was originally the private villa of the Provençal actor Raimu, who lived here till he died in 1946. His wife was from Brittany, and the name 'Ker Mocotte' was their private joke, for *ker* means 'house' in Breton, and *mocotte* is Provençal slang for *toulonnaise* (Raimu's home town). In the foyer the Goetzes have put up a poster of Pagnol's *Fanny*, one of Raimu's best-known films.' *(Gerald and Mary Prescott)*

Open: February–October.
Rooms: 18 double, 1 suite – 8 with bath, 10 with shower, all with telephone, radio and colour TV.
Facilities: 2 salons, restaurant; weekly soirées. Garden, private sandy beach; windsurfing. English spoken.
Location: 200 metres round the bay from the *Hotel L'Ile Rousse* (q.v.); limited parking.
Credit card: Barclay/Visa (restaurant only).
Terms: Rooms 180–235 frs; full board 227–293 frs. Set meals: breakfast 20 frs, dinner 82 frs.

> The length of an entry does not necessarily reflect the merit of a hotel. The more interesting the report or the more unusual or controversial the hotel, the longer the entry.

BARBIZON, 77630 Seine-et-Marne, Île de France   Map 8

Hostellerie de la Clé d'Or   *Telephone:* (6) 066.40.96
73 Grande-Rue

Barbizon, much frequented by Millet, Théodore Rousseau and other 19th-century painters, is in the heart of the forest of Fontainebleau, 10 km from the town of Fontainebleau and about 45 minutes' drive from Paris. The *Clé d'Or* is the oldest inn in the village, and is known in the area for its food as well as its pleasant service. Spacious rooms all open on to a small garden with geraniums, an atmosphere which reminded one reader of some of Mexico's more personable village hotels. Meals are served in the garden on fine days. The furniture is agreeably old, the plumbing – most of the time! – agreeably modern. *(P R Harrison, Nancy Foy, and others)*

Open: 18 December–15 November. Closed Sunday evening and Monday.
Rooms: 14 double, 1 single – 8 with bath and WC, 7 with shower and WC. (8 ground-floor rooms in annexe.)
Facilities: Salon, bar, restaurant; rooms for receptions, banquets, etc.; interior patio. Garden. English spoken. &.
Location: Central, just off the D64; parking.
Credit cards: Access/Euro/Mastercard, American Express, Barclay/Visa.
Terms: Rooms 150–220 frs. Set meals: breakfast 23 frs; lunch/dinner 130 frs; full *alc* 190 frs. Special meals for children.

BAR-SUR-AUBE, 10200 Aube   Map 8

Hôtel du Commerce   *Telephone:* (25) 27.08.76
38 rue Nationale

'Bar-sur-Aube is one of those unexpected but delightful small French towns. It is near the upper Marne valley, halfway between Champagne and Burgundy. All the centre is lined with old, picturesque houses; there is a mill race. Right in the middle of the main road is the *Hôtel du Commerce*, with its courtyard, when you can park your car for the night. Bedrooms are splendidly over-decorated; bathrooms excellent; and the dining room delightful in the worst possible French taste. The restaurant regularly earns one rosette (in Michelin) and is indeed very good. Service is efficient and helpful.' A leading speciality is *écrevisses au whisky* – fancy that, so near to Champagne and Burgundy! *(Martyn Goff)*

Open: All year, except Christmas and Sunday evening and Monday 1 October–30 May.
Rooms: 15 double, 3 apartments – 8 with bath, 4 with shower, all with telephone and colour TV.
Facilities: Salon, TV room, restaurant. English spoken.
Location: In town centre; parking.
Credit cards: American Express, Diners.
Terms: Rooms 85–200 frs. Set meals: breakfast 20 frs, lunch 85 frs, dinner 120 frs; full *alc* 180 frs.

> Sterling and dollar equivalents of foreign currencies at the date of going to press will be found under Exchange Rates on page 566.

Oustau de Baumanière   *Telephone:* (90) 97.33.07
                                            Telex: 420 203

The ruined village and castle of Les Baux, on a high spur of the Alpilles, has become one of the show-places of Provence. Formerly the seat of an ancient and powerful feudal house, it has had a long, romantic, often bloodthirsty history. The original dynasty died out in the 15th century, it fell into the hands of Protestants, and Richelieu had the castle and ramparts – 'the eagle's nest' he called it – demolished in 1632. Now it is a ghost city, and coachloads from Arles and Avignon daily pick their way across the grey jagged rocks of bauxite (hence the name) and through the spooky remains of medieval grandeur.

You can stay, if you wish, in the old town, but the connoisseurs of high living will make for the *Baumanière*, one of the great restaurants of France. The *Baumanière* should, properly speaking, be called a restaurant with some rooms, in view of the extensive non-residential trade, and is so designated by Michelin which gives it their top five red knives-and-forks and three-star treatment. The Queen and Prince Philip dined here on their last State visit to France in 1972 – it's that sort of place. It is also one of the few top restaurants in France still to stick rigorously to classic cuisine and to eschew the modish *nouvelle cuisine*. Not all our correspondents, it has to be said, are enthusiastic about the food – some have found its standards uneven. But here are the comments of a reader who fell totally under its spell: '*Superb!* Lived up to our expectations, particularly dinner. Excellent wine list with many local specialities very reasonably priced. Very comfortable room with four-poster, not quite as lavishly furnished as it could be. Well-equipped bathroom, etc. Good breakfast and friendly, efficient staff. And our car had been washed and polished when we came to leave the next morning!' *(Pat and Jeremy Temple)*

Open: All year, except 15 January–1 March, Wednesday lunchtime and Tuesday 15 October–31 March.
Rooms: 15 double, 11 suites – all with bath, telephone, TV and air-conditioning. 16 rooms in 3 annexes. (10 rooms on ground floor.)
Facilities: Salon, arcaded restaurant. Garden, swimming pool, tennis courts, riding stables. English spoken. &.
Location: 19 km SW of Arles; 60 km NW of Marseilles.
Credit cards: American Express, Barclay/Visa, Diners.
Terms: Rooms 480 frs. Set meal: breakfast 40 frs. *Alc* 205–280 frs (excluding wine).

BAYEUX, 14400 Calvados, Normandy   **Map 8**

Lion d'Or   *Telephone:* (31) 92.06.90
71 rue St Jean

Few visitors are likely to be unimpressed by Bayeux, one of the most fascinating old towns in Normandy, and by its famous tapestry. Nearby are the Normandy invasion beaches, and the remarkable D-Day museum at Arromanches.

The *Lion d'Or*, an old coaching inn, is very quiet (a *Relais du Silence*, in fact) though in the town centre: its rooms are set back from the street, round a paved courtyard. In past years, readers' reactions to the hotel have been mixed: some have been delighted, others have grumbled about the decor, the service, the pricing. But this year criticisms are very few. 'Most satisfactory: a very well-run hotel giving value for money. The bedrooms are comfortably and attractively furnished. But one word of warning: there is no lift, and the third floor could cause difficulty. The fixed menus are interesting.' The dining room wins a Michelin rosette and a Gault-Millau *toque* for its regional cooking (e.g. *andouille chaude à la Bovary*). *(I F Somerville)*

Open: 20 January–20 December.
Rooms: 31 double – 24 with bath or shower, all with telephone.
Facilities: Large dining room. Garden.
Location: Central; parking.
Credit cards: Barclay/Visa.
Terms: Rooms 105–215 frs; full board 205–330 frs. Set meals: breakfast 20 frs; lunch/dinner 70–155 frs.

BAZAS, 33430 Gironde, Aquitaine   **Map 8**

Relais de Fompeyre   *Telephone:* (56) 25.04.60
Route Mont-de-Marsan

On the eastern fringe of the huge Landes forest, just outside the small town of Bazas, 58 km south-east of Bordeaux and close to the Sauternes country. Would make a good overnight stop on the way to or from the Pyrenees. The *Relais de Fompeyre* is a very reasonably-priced three-star hotel. 'We hadn't booked; there were four of us, and there was room only for two. But the manager and his staff were exceedingly helpful and found a folding double bed. The children enjoyed the pool. The gardens were pleasant, the room comfortable and quiet, the surroundings tranquil. But the main reason for including the *Relais de Fompeyre* is its restaurant (rosette in Michelin). We had a superlative meal, served with friendliness and intelligence, and the wines were excellent.' *(James Price)*

Two recent visitors agree – one whole-heartedly, and the other with the warning that, despite its large garden, you will need ear-plugs if you sleep with your window open as lorries grind all night up the long hill on the main road outside. *(B J Woolf, Angela and David Stewart)*

Open: 15 March–15 October.
Rooms: 31 plus 4 suites – some with bath or shower.
Facilities: Lift, restaurant, covered terrace for meals and refreshments; some conference facilities. Large park and garden. 2 swimming pools (1 for children), tennis court.
Location: About 35 miles S of Bordeaux on the D932; parking.
Credit cards: American Express, Barclay/Visa.
Terms: Rooms 145–180 frs; suites 435 frs; full board 275–290 frs. Set meals: breakfast 20 frs; lunch/dinner 86–150 frs.

Deadlines: nominations for the 1984 edition should reach us not later than 1 June 1983. Latest date for comments on existing entries: 31 July 1983.

Le Métropole   *Telephone:* (93) 01.00.08
15 Boulevard Maréchal Leclerc   *Telex:* 470304

Beaulieu with its floodlit palms is still sedately elegant, though no longer madly fashionable as in pre-war days. There is a casino, and much of interest close by: e.g. the Ephrussi de Rothschild museum at Cap Ferrat.
'For once a luxury hotel of the old style that has not been over-modernized but simply kept in immaculate order. It is in no way pretentious. Set back from the road, overlooking the sea and Cap Ferrat and Italy, surrounded by a pretty garden and terrace, *Le Métropole* enjoys absolute quiet except for the occasional speed boat or the more relaxing "chug-chug" of a tiny fishing boat. It is right on the shore (shingle and concrete like all this part of the coast). For swimming and sunning you can choose between the pleasant pool or a generous concrete area below with direct access to the sea. In either case, once installed, your table, chairs, towels, etc., will all be laid out for you in the same spot each day. Bar service in both these areas. Use of swimming facilities at modest fee. Lovely restaurant on a large terrace outside the dining room. Sitting under the enormous white awning and enjoying the stunning view gives genuine pleasure. Food and service excellent and you are never hurried. From the five-course menus, *grilled scampi with rouille, tranche de gigot aux herbes* and a *coupe* composed of vanilla ice cream with *crème anglaise* and a chocolate sauce were a few of the highlights. Particularly good-value out-of-season terms.' *(Geoffrey Sharp)*

Open: 20 December–20 October.
Rooms: 40 double, 10 single, 3 suites – all with bath or shower and telephone.
Facilities: Lift, bar, terrace restaurant, dining room, air-conditioning. Garden with terrace, swimming pool, private beach. English spoken.
Location: 10 km from Nice on the N559; parking.
Terms: Half board: 350–965 frs; full board 415–1030 frs.

La Réserve   *Telephone:* (93) 01.00.01
Boulevard Maréchal Leclerc   *Telex:* 470301

One of the Riviera's most famous, most refined and – not surprisingly – most expensive hotels. 'This relatively small hotel is a gem. Most of the rooms open onto the Mediterranean, and the views, from Nice to the Italian border, are staggering. Like the *Ritz* in Paris, there are almost as many staff as there are guests. There is a magnificent pool, with glassed-in walls, so that when the wind blows off the sea you don't get cold. The rooms are delightful, and the place is quiet as the only road goes by the front of the hotel; most of the rooms face the back or the sea. The restaurant has had one Michelin star for years and is first-rate. You can and should have lunch by the pool. Anything you want. Jean Potfer, who ran this place for years, was sensational, and his successor has retained the refinement of *La Réserve*. You feel, as the bartender at the *Ritz* once said to me, *"Vous êtes chez vous"*.' *(Alfred Knopf Jr)*

Open: All year except 1 December–10 January.
Rooms: 50, mostly double, 3 suites – all with bath or shower.

Facilities: Lift; salon, restaurant, garden with swimming pool.
Location: On the seafront near the Rade de Beaulieu; parking.
Terms: Rooms 470–1000 frs. Set meals: breakfast 37 frs; lunch/dinner 200–280 frs.

BEAUNE, 21200 Côte-d'Or, Burgundy   **Map 8**

Hôtel Le Cep   *Telephone:* (80) 22.35.48
27 rue Maufoux

'The *Le Cep* is a charming 17th-century house a few minutes' walk from the centre of this pleasant little town, the capital of the Burgundy wine region where the famous wine auctions, banquets and festivities take place every November. Parking is available in a large private garage to the rear. The entrance hall, which also serves as a lounge, is welcoming, beautifully furnished with antiques and offers a most civilized atmosphere. The bedrooms, again comfortably furnished in antique style (but most have pretty, modern bathrooms), are named after the wines of the regions. At breakfast, really fresh orange juice followed by Earl Grey tea were bonuses. The proprietor is most friendly, and while he speaks no English, staff are at hand who do.' *(Rosamund V Hebdon)*

Open: 1 March–30 November. Closed Wednesday in low season.
Rooms: 19 double, 2 single – 17 with bath, 3 with shower, all with telephone.
Facilities: Reception lounge, conference facilities; courtyard. English spoken.
Location: In town centre; garage parking.
Credit cards: American Express, Diners.
Terms: Rooms 185–460 frs. Breakfast 26 frs. (No restaurant.)

BELFORT, 90000 Jura   **Map 8**

Hostellerie du Château Servin   *Telephone:* (84) 21.41.85
9 rue Général Négrier
7 rue Heim

Belfort, 65 km west of Basle, is on one of the main routes from Paris to Switzerland. Well worth a visit is the famous statue of the Lion of Belfort, at the foot of the Vauban castle. This huge monument was erected to commemorate the heroism of the Belfort garrison in fighting off the Prussians in 1870.

'Weary from long hours on the French motorways, we sought a good meal and a quiet, restful night: we could hardly have improved upon the Hostellerie. A 19th-century town house in its garden, surrounded by high walls and tall wrought-iron gates: inside, a slightly cluttered Victorian reception hall, not very well lit: but the dining room was beautiful, with walls and curtains elegantly draped in tawny velvet, lamps and a flower arrangement on every table, and the food all that one believes the French are capable of, with a devotion to detail and presentation that clearly showed why this restaurant bore two rosettes from the Michelin Guide. There are only ten rooms, and the family are patently involved at every stage (we glimpsed at least four generations having their own meal at one long table in another room, as we arrived). We occupied the Louis XV room, charmingly furnished in period style with deep rose velvet, and the most comfortable bed and utter quiet that we had met for a long time. As one would expect, not cheap – but we felt fair value for money. Definitely a place we would plan to fit into our next touring holiday!' *(Angela and David Stewart)*

Open: All year, except August. Restaurant closed Fridays and Christmas Day evening.
Rooms: 10 – all with bath or shower and telephone.
Facilities: Reception, dining rooms, air-conditioning; conference facilities. Garden. English spoken.
Location: Hotel has two entrances (see above) 50 m E of Faubourg de Montbeliard; parking.
Credit cards: American Express, Diners.
Terms: Rooms 200–260 frs; Set meals: breakfast 30 frs; lunch/dinner 160–260 frs.

BESSE-EN-CHANDESSE, 63610 Puy-de-Dôme, Auvergne   **Map 8**

Les Mouflons   *Telephone:* (73) 79.51.31
Route de Super-Besse

High up in the volcanic Monts-Dore area of central Auvergne, Besse is a medieval village, some of its old houses made of black lava rock. In summer there are glorious mountain walks, and in winter good skiing at the new resort of Super-Besse, 7 km away. 'The casualties caused by the development of modern skiing do not include Besse, a delightful little town which remains virtually unaffected: its inhabitants tend to be surly to downright rude. The meadows around were a paradise of flowers, including yellow gentians, pink campion. And the skiing has brought a bonus – *Les Mouflons*, a typical modern chalet-type skiing hotel of no obvious charm at first sight, but everything there was in its own way right. It is just outside and above the town. We had a very nice dinner in this reasonable, unpretentious place: dining room a bit barn-like, but there was plenty of space between tables. Most if not all the bedrooms (many would consider them cramped in the inevitable modern way) face out across the meadows. Above all there was a delightful friendly atmosphere.' Michelin rosette, and Gault Millau *toque*, for good Auvergnat *cuisine*. *(John Hills)*

Open: End May–end September, end December–Easter.
Rooms: 50 double – most with bath or shower.
Facilities: Restaurant. Garden. Skiing 7 km.
Location: 51 km SW of Clermont-Ferrand; hotel is just outside village on road to Super-Besse.
Credit card: Barclay/Visa.
Terms: Rooms 205–220 frs; full board 195–250. Set meals: breakfast 20 frs, lunch/dinner 65–185 frs.

BEYNAC ET CAZENAC, 24220 St-Cyprien, Dordogne   **Map 8**

Hôtel Bonnet   *Telephone:* (53) 29.50.01

Not far from Domme and Sarlat, the village of Beynac is one of the classic tourist centres of the lovely Dordogne valley. It dominates a curve in the river, with four medieval castles in full view, including the Château de

Beynac itself which frequently changed hands in Anglo-French battles. Much more recently, and more peacefully, the *Bonnet* too has seen regular invasions by British visitors, and has been in our own Guide since our first edition. 'A wide staircase leads up to the entrance beneath the terrace which is attractively arranged with tables and umbrellas. The welcome was friendly; all the staff were most charming and helpful. The bedroom was small but attractively furnished; the bathroom shone with care and cleanliness.,' ran one report on this traditional family-run inn. More recent visitors continue to enthuse over the 'delicious' food, the good value for money, the friendly ambience, and the view of the river. However, one snag is that the hotel is on a busy main road, and front rooms facing the river can be noisy: if you want quiet, you might be advised to forego the view and ask for a room at the back. *(Ian and Francine Walsh, Ray and Angela Evans, and others)*

Open: After Easter–15 October.
Rooms: 20 double, 2 single – 17 with bath, 3 with shower, all with telephone.
Facilities: Salon, bar, restaurant, creeper-covered terrace for meals above the river; garden. The hotel overlooks the Dordogne, with beach and bathing nearby; also boating, canoeing, fishing, tennis and riding. English spoken.
Location: 9 km W of Sarlat; free garage and outdoor parking.
Terms: Rooms 80–170 frs (single), 105–170 frs (double); dinner, B & B 175–195 frs. Set meals: breakfast 18 frs, lunch/dinner 70–135 frs.

LES BÉZARDS, 45290 Nogent-sur-Vernisson, Loiret Map 8

Auberge des Templiers *Telephone:* (38) 31.80.01
Telex: 780998 F TEMPLIE

'An old posting house on the N7 about 1½ hours drive south from Paris, luxuriously renovated and with about 20 rooms and apartments scattered around the grounds at the rear in various (new) buildings. Our room, with an enormous bathroom, was like a small bungalow. Beautifully furnished and spotlessly clean. The restaurant boasts two Michelin rosettes and three Gault Millau *toques*, and the cooking was excellent. Breakfast can be taken in the room or the lounge bar in the main building. There is an outdoor swimming pool and tennis courts and in summer the gardens would be most attractive. A good base for the upper Loire, though very expensive. Owners and staff most welcoming and friendly.' The chef, Jean-Claude Rigollet, combines classic *cuisine* with *nouvelle* (e.g. *salade de navets tièdes au foie gras*). A new terrace/dining-room, just opened, allows all tables to have a view of the garden. *(Pat and Jeremy Temple)*

Open: All year, except mid January–mid February.
Rooms: 20 double, 7 suites – 25 with bath, 2 with shower, all with telephone and TV.
Facilities: Lounge bar, 2 restaurants; conference facilities. Garden; heated swimming pool; tennis court. English spoken. &.
Location: On the N7, 138 km S of Paris and 69 km E of Orléans.
Credit cards: Barclay/Visa, Diners.
Terms: Rooms 240–590 frs, suites 850–1100 frs. Set meals (excluding 12% service charge): breakfast 35 frs; lunch/dinner 190–280 frs. Special meals for children.

Procrastination is the thief of the next edition.

Café des Arcades   *Telephone:* (93) 65.01.04
16 Place des Arcades

'Here's a real oddity for you – but *il vaut le détour*, as they say. It's in a small arcaded square in the old hill-village of Biot, just inland from Antibes: the superb Fernand Léger museum is just down the road. This "café" *is* in part just that: a noisy café where the villagers drink, chatter and play chess. But it's also rather more: a 15th-century inn of great character, *and* believe it or not, an art gallery. This is due to its *patron*, André Brothier, an engaging, bohemian type, who lines the inn's dining room with Braques and Miros and is a friend of Vasarely and his son Yvaral, painters whom I happen to adore. The bedrooms are too, too olde worlde, but the plumbing, happily, is not. The inn has a hyper-relaxed ambience which may not suit all tastes, and it can be trying to have loud pop music resounding from the café while you eat your *tian provençal* or *tripes niçoises*. Nonetheless, at least for a day or two's visit, this eccentric and endearing place is exhilarating fun.' *(Jenny Towndrow)*

Open: All year, except November; restaurant closed Sunday evening and Monday.
Rooms: 10 double – 5 with bath, 5 with shower, all with internal telephone.
Facilities: Restaurant, art gallery. Beaches nearby.
Location: 8 km from Antibes.
Terms: Rooms 100–150 frs. Set meals: breakfast 15 frs; lunch/dinner 85 frs; full *alc* 110 frs.

Hôtel L'Aiguebrun   *Telephone:* (90) 74.04.14

In a narrow upland valley of the lovely and curious Luberon hills, due north of Aix. The church at Bonnieux village, 6 km from the hotel, has fascinating 15th-century German paintings. 'This could be just the place for anyone seeking a civilized rural retreat, and we loved it. Roger Chastel, a gentle and reserved Parisian, artist and former couturier, has taken over this little 19th-century manor house beside a stream which he runs more like a private home than a hotel: modern paintings, period furniture, cosy sitting room with log fire – and no TV. We had a large bedroom, 'rustic' but comfortable, with a view of the wooded hills. We were quite inspired by the setting of poplar-lined meadows beside an old mill, where only the birdsong broke the silence, and we found that several fellow-guests had come here to paint or write. You can eat out in the garden. Food is very good, though expensive (*à la carte* only), with *nouvelle-cuisine* flourishes such as *figues fraiches à la crème de fenouil*.' *(Nicholas Osmond)* Red *toque* in Gault Millau.

Open: All year, except mid-November–early February. Restaurant closed Monday midday.
Rooms: 8 double – most with bath and telephone.
Facilities: Salon, restaurant, garden.
Location: Just off the D943, 6 km SE of Bonnieux which is 48 km N of Aix, 47 km SE of Avignon.

Credit cards: Access/Euro/Mastercard, Barclay/Visa, Diners.
Terms: Rooms 250–275 frs. Set meal: breakfast 23 frs; *alc* 115–185 frs.

BORMES-LES-MIMOSAS, 83230 Var, Provence   Map 9

Safari Hôtel   *Telephone:* (94) 71.09.83
Route du Stade

'Bormes, just inland from Le Lavandou, is one of the showpiece hill-villages of Provence. And whereas most of the others, such as Èze and St-Paul-de-Vence, are built of severe grey stone, Bormes is all in pastel shades, pink, blue and ochre, and makes a cheerful contrast. The vogue for smart *résidences secondaires* has brought it a new lease of life, without spoiling its quality. The *Safari* is on a hill above the sea, a mile east of the village. At first sight, we were dismayed by this modern white rectangular block – like something in Benidorm. But soon we warmed to the breezy ambience and friendly service, and we spent a happy week here, playing tennis, swimming in the big heated pool or lazing at the bar beside it, and gazing at the beautiful Iles d'Hyères from our wide bedroom balcony. Whereas so many hotel gardens in Provence are just flower-beds and gravel paths, this one has a real grass lawn. The restaurant only serves grills but we ate well at the *Tonnelle des Délices* and the *Belle-Vue* in Bormes and, down in Le Lavandou, at the *Vieux Port* (expensive but first-class, and English-owned).' *(Gillian and Peter Clark)*

Open: 1 April–15 October. Restaurant closed Sunday evening.
Rooms: 33 double – all with bath and telephone.
Facilities: Salon, bar, breakfast room, restaurant, terrace; conference/function facilities. Night clubs nearby. Garden with boules, 2 tennis courts, heated swimming pool. Near sandy beach; waterskiing, sailing, boating, riding: golf 10 km. English spoken.
Location: 1 km E of Bormes, and 4 km NW of Le Lavandou, on a hillside. Car park.
Credit cards: Access/Euro/Mastercard, Barclay/Visa, Diners.
Terms: Rooms with breakfast 300–330 frs. Full *alc* 70 frs.

BOULOGNE-SUR-MER, 62200 Pas-de-Calais   Map 8

Hôtel de la Plage   *Telephone:* (21) 31.45.35
124 boulevard Sainte-Beuve

'Preferable to all the other hotels we have tried in Boulogne. A simple, clean, cheerful family-run place opposite the casino and very near the beach. Helpful staff and family and very good food. Mainly local custom and French businessmen.' *(Hugh and Anne Pitt)*

Open: All year, except Christmas and New Year. (Restaurant closed Sunday evening and Monday.)
Rooms: 10 double – 2 with bath, 6 with shower.
Facilities: Restaurant. Beach, casino nearby. English spoken.
Location: Near casino and beach; about 1 km from town centre and ferry port; parking.
Terms: B & B 87.50–122 frs. Set meals: lunch 52 frs, dinner 65 frs; full *alc* 110 frs.

Hôtel Ombremont   *Telephone:* (79) 25.00.23

Le Bourget is a smart resort at the southern end of the lovely lac du Bourget, with a pleasant *plage* and a fine Carolingian church. The *Ombremont*, a country-house style hotel, stands secluded in its own big garden by the lake, 2 km north of the town. New owners, the Carlos, with new young chef trying his hand at *nouvelle cuisine*, arrived early in 1982. They have already won praise: 'We were most impressed with this elegantly furnished, very peaceful hotel. The setting is lovely, with magnificent views across the lake to Aix-les-Bains and the mountains beyond. The dining room has large windows opening onto a terrace for meals in warm weather, and seldom have we taken dinner in such a delightful situation. The food was delicious and service attentive, though wines were pricey. Our bedroom was spacious, comfortable, with lake view. We were made most welcome by the new young proprietors, Pierre-Yves and Monique Carlo.' *(Rosamund V Hebdon; also James Joll)*

Open: All year, except end November–early February. Restaurant closed Monday except July and August.
Rooms: 18 double – all with bath and telephone.
Facilities: Salon, restaurant, terrace. Garden leading down to lake, with swimming pool. English spoken. &.
Location: 2 km N of Le Bourget on the N504.
Credit cards: American Express, Barclay/Visa, Diners.
Terms: Rooms 210–315 frs. Set meals: breakfast 35 frs; lunch/dinner 100–225 frs.

Auberge La Solognote   *Telephone:* (48) 58.50.29
Grande Rue

Brinon is a small pleasant village a few miles east of the N20 between Bourges and Orléans. It is in the heart of the strange haunting forests and marshlands of the Sologne, i.e. at the centre of the Alain-Fournier country, near to his birthplace at La Chapelle d'Angillon and to the château which inspired him to write *Le Grand Meaulnes*. 'The inn is close to the centre, but we had a peaceful night, with practically no traffic noise. Modest bedroom, clean and comfy. Bar-cum-seating area adjacent to small shingle patio, with tubs and pots of flowers and umbrellas. Attractive dining room in country style: tiled floor, pottery plates and local artists' pictures on the walls; thick damask table linen and flowers on each table. Monsieur and Madame were very welcoming. Good food. We had the second most expensive menu. The *mousseline d'homard* was really memorable with chunks of lobster in it – we had succulent steaks and a dish of fried aubergines and cheesy potato cakes, and for dessert *tarte aux fraises du bois* – locally picked. The overall impression was of efficient, professional, friendly, caring people. The inn is really worth a visit for a comfortable quiet night en route north or south.' *(Maureen A Montague)*

Open: All year except 2 weeks in May, 2 weeks in September, and Wednesday.
Rooms: 10 double – all with bath or shower, all with telephone. (2 rooms on ground floor.)

Facilities: Salon, bar, dining room, patio. Tennis 200 metres; bathing and sailing in nearby lake. English spoken. &.
Location: SE of Orléans.
Terms: Rooms 150 frs. Set meals: breakfast 15 frs; lunch/dinner 72, 100, 150 frs.

BRIOUDE, 43100 Haute Loire, Auvergne   **Map 8**

Hôtel de la Poste et Champanne   *Telephone:* (71) 50.14.62
1 boulevard Dr Devins

Halfway between Clermont-Ferrand and Le Puy, Brioude is a good centre for touring the Massif Central. It is a medieval town of narrow streets, most famous for its 12th-century romanesque basilica of St-Julien. The *Poste et Champanne* is a family hotel presided over by Madame Albertine Barge, assisted by her granddaughter. It is in two parts: the restaurant, with a bar, is in an old house on the main road, and serves excellent food at modest prices; it caters a lot for local groups and also for coach tours, who are put in a separate dining room. Residents stay in a modern and relatively noise-free annexe in a garden behind the main building. 'Good, substantial, plain French provincial cooking, very willing staff, most reasonable prices and a happy-go-lucky atmosphere.' *(B W Ribbons; also M W Hardwick, E H Platt)*

Open: All year.
Rooms: 10 double – all with bath. (All rooms in annexe.)
Facilities: TV room, bar, 2 restaurants. Small garden. English spoken.
Location: On the N102, halfway between Clermont-Ferrand and Le Puy.
Terms: Rooms 60 frs (single), 120 frs (double); dinner, B & B 95–120 frs; full board 130–150 frs. Set meals: breakfast 12 frs, lunch/dinner 50, 60, 80 frs.

CABRERETS, 46330 Lot   **Map 8**

Hôtel des Grottes   *Telephone:* (65) 31.27.02

Cabrerets is a picturesque village with two castles in the valley of the river Célé, close to the lovely valley of the Lot. It is near local beauty spots such as St Cirq-Lalopie; Cahors is 35 km to the west.

The *Grottes*, on the edge of the village, offers a cheaper and simpler alternative to *La Pescalerie* (below). 'The hotel is in a beautiful and tranquil setting. Our room in the annexe was comfortable: little touches like the provision of toothpaste and a sewing-kit were appreciated. Housekeeping is fastidious: Madame is reserved, courteous, efficient. Meals are served on a lovely terrace overlooking the river with its limestone cliffs and hanging willows: they were varied, well cooked, attractively served, and good value.' (Five-course meal for 62 francs in 1982.) *(Rebecca Foster)*

Open: Easter week–11 November. Restaurant closed midday one day a week (not fixed at the time of going to press), Easter–15 June, 15 September–1 November.
Rooms: 17 double – 3 with bath, 2 with shower, all with telephone. 5 rooms in annexe. (Some rooms on ground floor.)

Facilities: Salon, dining room, terraces overlooking river where meals are served. Swimming pool. English spoken.
Location: 35 km E of Cahors, on the edge of the village; parking.
Terms: Rooms 83–150 frs; dinner, B & B 106–205 frs (min. 3 days). Set meals: lunch/dinner 50–98 frs; full *alc* about 115 frs.

CABRERETS 46330 Lot   Map 8

La Pescalerie   *Telephone:* (65) 31.22.55

The hotel stands alone in the countryside, at the foot of a rocky hill, 2.5 km outside the village. 'This quiet and very special hotel is run with true charm and kindness. It opened in 1980 after four years of restoration – an 18th-century Quercy country house, decorated with the most exquisite and restrained taste. There is a large semi-formal garden which stretches away to the wooded banks of the Lot where jays call and kingfishers arrow through the shadows. Our meal was good but unambitious. There is no lift, and the beautiful wooden staircase is rather steep for the less youthful. But the luxury of the bedrooms was almost sinful, the elegance of breakfast on the terrace under a huge magnolia tree, with oleanders in bloom, was unforgettable.' The hotel is owned by a practising local surgeon, Roger Belcour, who amazingly spends part of his time actually running the place, including helping to serve in the dining room. His manageress/chef, the charming Hélène Combette, wins a *toque* and laurel leaves in Gault Millau for her regional cooking using fresh local produce including vegetables from the garden. She too once practised as a doctor. *(Don and Maureen Montague; also Margaret Lewis)*

Open: 1 April–1 November.
Rooms: 10 double – all with bath and telephone, and colour TV on request.
Facilities: Lounge with TV, bar, dining room. Garden running to the river with swimming, fishing, boating. English spoken.
Location: 35 km from Cahors, 2.5 km after Cabrerets on D19 to Figeac.
Credit cards: American Express, Barclay/Visa, Diners.
Terms: Rooms 225–385 frs; dinner, B & B (min. 3 days) 300–460 frs. Set meals: breakfast 30 frs, lunch 160 frs, dinner 160–190 frs; full *alc* 250 frs. Reduced rates for children.

CABRIS, 06530 Peymeinade, Alpes-Mar., Provence   Map 9

Hôtel L'Horizon   *Telephone:* (93) 60.51.69

Gide and Marcuse are among the many intellectuals and artists who have lived in the hill village of Cabris, drawn here by its superb situation above a verdant valley west of Grasse. It still has a sophisticated residential colony. '*L'Horizon* is an unassuming little country hotel, neatly modernized, on the edge of the village facing across the valley. Our bedroom was smallish and rather ordinary, but we had a superb view from the balcony, and it was quiet at night – the place is a *Relais du Silence*. There is a delightful little walled garden, full of creepers and red flowers. Food was varied, and as meals are rarely served to non-residents the place has something of the air of a superior *pension* – but none the worse for that. Jean Roustan, the young owner, is a lively and unusual man, an active local councillor and a lover of books and music; we had long talks with him in his more-or-less fluent English. He told us that Camus, Sartre and St-Exupéry used to stay in this hotel, and that more recent guests have included Leonard Bernstein, who even composed here, in the garden. Amazing! Surely *he* could afford three times the prices of this modest place where full *pension* in 1982 was a mere 160 frs.' *(John and Ludmila Berry)*

Open:　5 February–15 October. Restaurant closed Thursday.
Rooms:　18 double – 9 with bath, all with telephone, some with balcony.
Facilities:　Salon with TV, restaurant, functions room. Garden. English spoken.
Location:　On edge of village which is 5 km W of Grasse.
Terms:　Rooms 95 frs; dinner, B & B 122–170 frs; full board 160–200 frs. Set meals: breakfast 15 frs, lunch/dinner 60 frs.

LA CADIÈRE D'AZUR, 83740 Var, Provence　　　　　　**Map 9**

Hostellerie Bérard　　　　　　　　　*Telephone:* (94) 29.31.43
　　　　　　　　　　　　　　　　　　　　　　　Telex: 400509

'La Cadière, though only 9 km from the hectic coast at Bandol, is a still-unspoilt hill village. In its main street, perched above the valley below, we were delighted to find this 19th-century auberge of real character, with white vaulted ceilings and red-tiled floors, run most sympathetically by René and Danielle Bérard. It is snug and spruce, but not trying to be "fashionable". Attractive swimming pool, and modern bedrooms – ours was in an annexe converted from an old monastery. The *patron/chef* provides real Provençal cooking, such as *bourride*. We took lunch on the terrace, gazing dreamily over the valley, while at night the dining room is prettily lit with wicker lanterns, and suffused with the aroma of the log fire used for spit-roasts. We'll be back.' *(John and Ludmila Berry)*

Open:　All year.
Rooms:　35 double, 5 single, 2 suites – 27 with bath, 13 with shower, all with telephone. (18, 11 rooms in 2 annexes.)
Facilities:　Salon with TV, bar, dining room, conference room, terrace. Small garden with heated swimming pool. Sandy/rocky beaches 7 km. English spoken.
Location:　9 km N of Bandol, just off the Marseille–Toulon autoroute (exit St-Cyr/Bandol). Garage parking.
Credit card: Barclay/Visa.
Terms:　B & B 125–295 frs. Set meals: lunch 70 frs, dinner 90–130 frs; full *alc* 130 frs. Special meals for children.

CAGNES-SUR-MER, Haut-de-Cagnes, 06800 Alpes-Maritimes　　**Map 9**

Le Cagnard　　　　　　*Telephone:* (93) 20.73.21 and 20.73.22
Rue du Pontis-Long

The sizeable town of Cagnes-sur-Mer is divided, like Caesar's Gaul, into three parts: the ugly sprawling resort of Cros-de-Cagnes; just inland, Cagnes-Ville, unremarkable save for the inspiring Renoir museum in its outskirts; and, higher up, Haut-de-Cagnes, one of the region's most sophisticated hill-villages (fascinating museum in the château). Here *Le*

Cagnard, a well-known and very *soigné* little hotel, has been artfully converted out of some 13th-century houses by the ramparts and virtually clings to the side of a cliff. 'An oasis of medieval tranquillity', 'highly romantic', 'splendid views of the sea', are some comments, though one visitor found the setting 'a trifle claustrophobic'. Rooms vary in size and comfort – some are small suites – but the conversions have been carefully done to harmonize new with old, while also offering such mod cons as a small fridge. (*Warning*: the hotel is accessible only by a narrow tortuous alley, impassable to large cars.)

You eat either on the terrace – stunning views over the village to the sea – or in a graceful candle-lit room, formerly the guardroom of the Château Grimaldi. Here for the past 20 years Louis Barel has supervised a *cuisine* that is both classic and ambitious, with prices to match. Standards are usually high, though both food and service can be erratic in high season, when *Le Cagnard* bulges at the seams with *le beau monde*. (*Pat and Jeremy Temple, James Burt, AL*)

Open: All year, except 1 November–15 December. (Restaurant closed for lunch on Thursday.)
Rooms: 10 double, 2 single, 7 suites – 18 with bath, 1 with shower, all with telephone. (7 rooms in annexe.)
Facilities: Bar, restaurant, crêperie, terrace. Night club, discothèque. Small garden. English spoken.
Location: On the ramparts, 2 minutes from the château.
Credit cards: American Express, Diners, Barclay/Visa.
Terms: Rooms with breakfast 200–300 frs. Set meal: lunch/dinner 190 frs.

CALAIS, 62100 Pas-de-Calais   **Map 8**

Hôtel Meurice   [GFG]   *Telephone:* (21) 34.57.03
5 rue E-Roche

Calais' hotels are a humdrum lot: the *Meurice* is the one with a touch of class, though we had one complaint of staff discourtesy. 'Big, old midtown hotel, rebuilt in original style after war damage. Quiet and very spacious, with huge rooms (some smaller ones in an annexe) comfortably furnished with antiques and neo-antiques. An excellent breakfast, with *fresh* orange juice, is served in a neatly converted corridor. The city museum is opposite the hotel and Cap Blanc (Beachy Head plus-plus-plus) is just down the coast road in the direction of Boulogne.' (*Frank and Joan Harrison*)

Open: All year.
Rooms: 40 – all with bath or shower and telephone; TV available (15 frs). Some rooms in annexe (some on ground floor).
Facilities: Lift, bar, breakfast area. Garden. There is a restaurant in the building, but under separate management.
Location: In town centre; garage parking.
Credit cards: American Express, Barclay/Visa, Diners.
Terms: Rooms 135–175 frs. Set meal: breakfast 16 frs.

'Full *alc*', unless otherwise stated, means the hotel's own estimate of the price per person for a three-course dinner with half a bottle of house wine, service and taxes included.

CANNES, 06400 Alpes-Maritimes   Map 9

Chalet de l'Isère   *Telephone:* (93) 38.50.80
42 avenue de Grasse

It would be hard to find a more striking contrast to the swanky palaces of La Croisette than this small and very personal *pension*, which stands on a hillside in the Cannes residential suburbs about 400 metres from the harbour. The house belonged to de Maupassant shortly before his death, and from here he would gaze out at the sea and the rocky Esterel coast. An enterprising reader reports on her *trouvaille:* 'The hotel/pension has room only for eight, and the *patronne* gave us the meals which she cooked for her own family, and very good they were, but she was always anxious to know if we had any special likes or dislikes and did her best to fit in with them. Her great gift was cooking, and we had many chats in the kitchen about recipes and I learned several useful dishes from her. The *patron* and *patronne* had their meals with us in the dining room which served as salon as well: conversation was general and centred round the television which was switched on at meal times. My French improved 100 per cent. The *patron,* though he had lost an arm in a sawing accident, still did the marketing himself: fish was his speciality. The *patronne* had been a hairdresser, and she did my hair for me one day and wouldn't hear of being paid for it. They couldn't have been kinder or more concerned for my well-being. I mustn't forget Katy, their ebullient teenage daughter, who bounced about giving us sweets.' More reports welcome on this exceptional home-from-home. *(Dorothy Morland)*

Open: All year, except November.
Rooms: 7 double, 1 single – 5 with shower. (2 rooms on ground floor.)
Facilities: Salon/dining room. Large garden.
Location: 700 metres from town centre; parking at the hotel opposite.
Terms: B & B 95–130; full board 100–160 frs. Set meals: lunch/dinner 45 frs. Reduced rates for children.

CASSIS, 13260 Bouches-du-Rhône, Provence   Map 9

Hôtel Roches Blanches   *Telephone:* (42) 01.09.30
Route de Port-Miou

'Despite the recent overbuilding and the trippery overcrowding, the old fishing-port of Cassis has still kept the picturesque charm that once drew Dufy and Matisse to paint here. It's a less garish St-Tropez – with the plus of a very swish modern casino, very lively, packed with Marseillais who are great gamblers. The *Roches Blanches* is well away from the hubbub, a mile west of the town, alone on a rocky, pinewoody promontory, facing out across the bay – and in this lovely setting we spent a happy week. The Dellacase family are civilized hosts, and they seem to attract an equally civilized kind of guest. Their hotel is a handsome creeper-covered villa with a big garden that rambles down to the rocky shore (no sand). Here they have built a spacious stone terrace that is good for sun-bathing – and the sea-bathing too is good, if you don't mind deep water. We had two gripes. First, the restaurant serves just grills and snacks (you must go down-town for a proper meal). Second, though our room was comfort-able, with a balcony facing the sea, its utility modern furnishing was hardly in keeping with the hotel's otherwise graceful tone.' *(Anthony Hildesley; also A G Don)*

Open: March–November.
Rooms: 35 double – 27 with bath, 8 with shower, 15 with colour TV, all with telephone. (10 rooms suitable for disabled.)
Facilities: Salon with TV, salon, bar, restaurant, terraces. Solarium. Large garden leading to rocky shore; children's play area, boules. English spoken. &.
Location: 1 mile W of Cassis; hotel signs in the town; parking.
Credit cards: American Express, Diners.
Terms: Rooms 85.50–276 frs. Set meal: breakfast 15 frs. Full *alc* 50–90 frs.

CAUDEBEC-EN-CAUX, 76490 Seine-Maritime, Normandy　　　　Map 8

Manoir de Rétival　　　　　　　　　　*Telephone:* (35) 96.11.22
Rue St Clair

Caudebec stands above a great loop of the Seine, midway between Le Havre and Rouen. Burned down in 1940, it has been rebuilt with far more elegance than most of the war-wrecked towns of northern France (e.g. hideous Le Havre itself). The interesting 15th-century Gothic church of Notre-Dame survived the holocaust. The *Manoir de Rétival* is quiet and secluded – 'a mostly 19th-century hunting lodge, tastefully furnished and decorated, run by nice people, and (the real pull) with a marvellous terrace overlooking the Seine, near the graceful new Pont de Brotonne. I can sit there for hours, watching the boats going up to Rouen. No restaurant, but one can eat in Caudebec, at the *Normandie*.' *(M and A Wolf)*

Open: 1 April–15 October.
Rooms: 12 double – 8 with bath, 4 with shower, all with telephone. (4 rooms in annexe, 1 on ground floor.)
Facilities: 2 salons, breakfast room, conference room; terrace, garden.
Location: 50 km E of Le Havre, 32 km NW of Rouen on D982. 500 metres from town centre; parking.
Credit cards: American Express, Diners.
Terms: Rooms 150–290 frs. Set meal: breakfast 28 frs. (No restaurant.)

CÉAUX, 50220 Ducey, Manche, Normandy　　　　　　　　　　Map 8

Au P'tit Quinquin　　　　　　　　　　*Telephone:* (33) 58.13.46

'A very modest but pleasant hotel for an overnight stop en route to Cherbourg from Brittany or south-west France. It's in a quiet village, 3 km from Pontaubault and 18 km from Mont-St-Michel. We had quite the best meal of our entire holiday. Monsieur Barbier, the owner, does the cooking, and drives to Granville to buy the fish straight off the trawlers. We had tender little *crevettes au naturel* then *praires farcies*, served in their shells with parsley and garlic butter. For main course we chose *sole meunière* and were each given two small plump fish – creamy and succulent. One astonishing note: the sheets on our beds were linen and hemstitched by hand – and dazzling white: we saw line on line hanging to dry in the orchard.' A place that clearly merits its red 'R' in Michelin for 'good food at moderate prices'. *(A S Kyrle Pope)*

Open: 19 March–9 October. Restaurant closed Tuesday except July and August.
Rooms: 17 double – 6 with bath, 2 with shower, all with telephone.
Facilities: Restaurant.
Location: 11 km SE of Avranches, 3 km from Pontanbault on the D43, on main road: back rooms advisable for light sleepers; parking.
Terms: Rooms 80 frs; half board 125–160 frs. Set meals: breakfast 13.50 frs; lunch/dinner 45–82 frs; full *alc* 90 frs.

CHABLIS, 89800 Yonne, Burgundy   Map 8

Hôtel de l'Etoile-Bergerand   *Telephone:* (86) 42.10.50
4 rue des Moulins

The late Robert Speaight, in his *Companion Guide to Burgundy* (1975), described the *Etoile* as having 'a deserved reputation for *cuisine* and hospitality', where the traveller 'will not get better value for his money in Burgundy'. Strange praise, maybe, for such a simple little place: but a recent visitor says that he finds Speaight's judgment still valid, on balance: 'The old-fashioned virtues of hospitality are apparent. A young woman employee wearing a uniform not quite of the present day greeted us with forthright energy. There was nothing cossetting about our bedroom; rather, a hint of that spartan atmosphere which was common to almost every ordinary hotel in France years ago. A well-trained staff brought breakfast to our bedroom on the dot.' The report praises the cheaper 40-franc menu (1981): '*terrine* in chablis, *quenelles* in chablis, and outstandingly good fillets of *rascasse*', washed down with the town's famous dry white wine and 'a smooth red house wine at 10 francs the half carafe'. *(Norman Brangham)*

Open: 15 February–15 December, except Monday.
Rooms: 13 double, 2 single – 3 with bath, 7 with shower.
Facilities: Restaurant.
Location: In centre; parking.
Terms: Rooms 55–140 frs; dinner, B & B 110–130 frs. Set meals: breakfast 12 frs, lunch 49 frs, dinner 50 frs. Full *alc* 120 frs.

CHAGNY, 71150 Saône et Loire, Burgundy   Map 8

Hôtel Lameloise   *Telephone:* (85) 87.08.85
36 Place d'Armes

The little town of Chagny lies amid woods and vineyards in the heart of Burgundy, between Beaune and Chalon-sur-Saône. The *Lameloise*, in its main street, is a 15th-century mansion, elegantly converted, and is renowned for its *cuisine*, probably the best in Burgundy (three Michelin rosettes and Gault-Millau *toques*). 'The hotel is very comfortable, with large well-equipped rooms and bathrooms, fresh flowers and bowls of sweets. The food is superb (more or less *nouvelle cuisine*) though expensive. Breakfasts too are excellent.' The visitors who reported thus in 1981 have since returned a year later: 'Very late arriving but still a friendly welcome in the restaurant which seems even to have improved, if this is possible, and the service seemed warmer and less formal.' *(Pat and Jeremy Temple)*

Open: All year, except 27 April–13 May, 30 November–17 December, Thursday midday and Wednesday.
Rooms: 25 – 23 with bath or shower, all with telephone and TV.
Facilities: Restaurant.
Location: Central; parking.
Credit card: Barclay/Visa.
Terms: Rooms 160–345 frs. Set meals: breakfast 28 frs; *alc* 195–265 frs (exc. wine).

CHAMBORD, 41 Loir-er-Cher, Loire Valley   **Map 8**

Hôtel du Grand Saint-Michel   *Telephone:* (54) 46.31.31

Directly opposite the largest and grandest of the Loire Valley châteaux (8 bedrooms overlook it). After dinner in summer you can stroll over to the *son et lumière*, and before breakfast you can drive out to see the wild boar and deer of Chambord forest feeding. This privileged setting is the hotel's chief attraction. Visitors praise its comfort, too: but there have been criticisms of food, service and ambience. One reader enjoyed the 'attractive salons, designed to resemble a hunting lodge' and found her room 'large and comfortable, with early 19th-century decor', but thought the restaurant 'rather like a cafeteria in atmosphere and menu: service was rushed and casual, the food unimaginative.' She sums up: 'In order to enjoy Chambord to the full, the hotel's the place to stay: but it can't be recommended for an extended visit or as a base for exploring the Loire.' Another visitor found the food good, but the ambience 'rather like a boarding school'. More reports please. *(Anne Abel-Smith; also Mrs M K Nelles)*

Open: All year, except 14 November–23 December. Restaurant closed Monday evening and Tuesday 15 October–1 April except public holidays.
Rooms: 38 double, 2 suites – 17 with bath, 3 with shower, all with telephone. (1 suite on ground floor.)
Facilities: Restaurant; conference facilities; terrace, grounds with tennis court. English spoken.
Location: Just S of the Loire valley, 18 km from Blois; opposite the château; parking.
Credit card: Barclay/Visa.
Terms: Rooms: 90–260 frs. Set meals: breakfast 18 frs; lunch/dinner 70–120 frs.

CHAMONIX, 74400 Haute-Savoie   **Map 8**

Hôtel Albert Premier et Milan   *Telephone:* (50) 53.05.09
119 Impasse du Montenvers

'Fleeing from dreadful Milan into glorious France, we heaved a sigh of relief as we drove through the Mont Blanc tunnel, and picked this hotel (despite its ominous Milanese name) from the French guidebooks. It proved to be splendid – a big chalet-type place, roomy and comfortable, full of well-heeled skiers enjoying their *après-ski*. Friendly informal service by young people; log fire and piano in the salon; huge bedrooms, with views from their windows of the toothy white peaks all round. A large sophisticated dining room, and ambitious, interesting cooking by the son of the *patron*, Pierre Carrier; *nouvelle cuisine* influences, but not too much so, and lavish helpings – skiers no doubt wouldn't tolerate the customary *n.c.* stinginess. Some *savoyard* dishes on the cheaper menus. We splashed on the dearer *carte* – delicious local trout, *magret de canard*, succulent scallops with lobster sauce, enterprising desserts. Good *savoyard* white wines. The hotel is set in its own big garden (*piscine*, tennis, etc.) near the middle of the resort. When fine, it's well worth taking the *téléphérique* (the world's highest, they claim) to a point just below the summit of Mont Blanc, for a roof-of-the-world view.' *(J and JA)*

Open: All year, except 25 April–19 May and 3 October–10 November.
Rooms: 31 double, 1 single, 2 suites – all with bath, telephone, TV and mini-bar.
Facilities: Lift, 2 salons, 3 dining rooms. Garden with tennis court, swimming pool (heated in summer), and children's play area. Winter sports, good walking. English spoken.
Location: In a side road, 150 metres from station and 500 from town centre; parking.
Credit cards: American Express, Barclay/Visa, Diners.
Terms: Rooms 165–245 frs; dinner, B & B 185–260 frs; full board 225–300 frs. Set meals: breakfast 20 frs, lunch/dinner 75–140 frs. Full *alc* 170 frs. Reduced rates and special meals for children.

CHAMPAGNAC DE BELAIR, 24530 Dordogne — Map 8

Moulin du Roc   *Telephone:* (53) 54.80.36
Telex: 570335 CHACOM

A village in northern Périgord, 6 km north-east of the beautiful little town of Brantôme. The *Moulin* is a gracefully-converted 17th-century walnut mill, in a quiet pastoral setting beside a stream; a *Relais et Château* establishment, but prices are reasonable. Michelin (two rosettes) and Gault-Millau (two *toques*) both consider that the *cuisine* of the owner's wife, Solange Gardillou, is as brilliant as any in the region: her *forte* is variations on local dishes, e.g. *foie gras poêlé à la ciboulette*. 'Tiny hotel, small rooms, small garden, everywhere cluttered with flowers, *objets*, old walnut-mill equipment turning by electric motors or just lying about. Small sitting areas amid the museum pieces. Our room with four-poster bed, dim lights. Dinner, with tables squeezed in, comfortable service, lots of small courses, even an extra pudding; and M. Gardillou's smiling presence. Friendly atmosphere, and tables could speak to each other without inhibition. Silver-tray breakfast: strawberries, home-made jams. View from our window of maids and waiters crossing yard with plates and trays and chairs; rinsing a bin in the mill stream. . . .' An idyll to make the heart swoon. *(Anne Carr and Martin McKeown)*

Open: 1 April–1 November. Restaurant closed Tuesday.
Rooms: 8 double, 2 suites – all with bath, telephone, radio and colour TV.
Facilities: Salons, restaurant. Small garden. English spoken.
Location: 6 km NE of Brantôme; parking.
Credit cards: All major credit cards accepted.
Terms: Rooms: 240–300 frs; dinner, B & B 290–320 frs; full board 380–420 frs. Set meals: breakfast 32 frs, lunch/dinner 90, 150, 220 frs; full *alc* 180 frs.

Hôtel Royal Champagne   *Telephone:* (26) 51.25.06

Standing 6 km out of Épernay on the Reims road, this 18th-century coaching inn had a grand restaurant on the main road, and also offers sophisticated accommodation in little chalets in its grounds, each room having its own veranda overlooking the famous vineyards of the area. 'It is casual and formal, all rolled into one, which only the French can achieve with perfection', says one visitor. About the cooking (Michelin rosette, Gault-Millau *toque*) there is equal enthusiasm: one reader speaks with awe about his *Menu de Champagne*, where every course has been created to be enhanced by the champagne with which its is served. Other readers, too, reach for their superlatives: 'Superb', 'Gastronomic delights', 'Wonderful wine list' and so forth. As for the bedrooms, there were some grumbles a year or two ago about the state of repair, but happily these have now ceased, and latest reports are of pleasant newly decorated rooms. *(Robert Grice, M Cookson, Robert Heller and others)*

Open: All year.
Rooms: 16 double, 2 suites – 16 with bath, 2 with shower, all with telephone, radio and private veranda, 1 with television. (14 rooms on ground floor.)
Facilities: Salon, TV room, bar, restaurant; facilities for functions. Park and garden. Tennis, riding in the forest, swimming pool and golf in vicinity. English spoken. &.
Location: On the N51 between Rheims and Épernay.
Credit cards: American Express, Barclay/Visa, Diners.
Terms: B & B 205–375 frs. Set meals: breakfast 25 frs, lunch/dinner 130–260 frs; full *alc* (with champagne) 250 frs. Reduced rates and special meals for children.

Hôtel Moderne   *Telephone:* (85) 24.07.02
Avenue de la Gare

A small town on the Moulins–Mâcon road, and on a secondary route from Paris to Lyon. 'True, the *Moderne* looks out on the drab, disused railway station: but it is quiet, a little outside the cramped town centre, and suitable for a night's stop. In a small garden at the side is a swimming pool. The restaurant has a Michelin star, but we found it wore none of the smug airs common to places thus elevated. The 52-franc (1981) menu began with disappointing *crudités*, but the main dishes and desserts were of high quality, while the house Beaujolais was young, lively and fair value. Our bedroom was large and furnished with that odd combination of modern bed and light-fittings and a brontosaurus of a wardrobe.' *(Norman Brangham)*

Open: All year, except 23 December–1 February. (Restaurant closed Monday midday.)
Rooms: 18 double – 11 with bath, 3 with shower, all with telephone. (7 rooms in annexe; 3 rooms on ground floor.)
Facilities: Salon with TV, restaurant. Small garden with unheated swimming pool. English spoken. &.

Location: On the Mâcon–Moulins road (N79), 59 km NE of Roanne; garage parking (charged).
Credit card: Barclay/Visa.
Terms: Rooms 180–200 frs. Set meals: breakfast 18 frs, lunch/dinner from 70 frs. Special meals for children.

CHARTRES, 28000 Eure-et-Loir   Map 8

Le Grand Monarque   *Telephone:* (37) 21.00.72
22, Place des Epars   *Telex:* 760777

The best hotel in Chartres, formerly a coaching inn and now a more sophisticated hostelry, with one of the town's best restaurants. 'A five-minute walk from the greatest of all Gothic cathedrals, *Le Grand Monarque* offers quiet elegance, fine cuisine, and a staff both polite and helpful and also thoroughly comfortable in English. Rooms in the back are quieter and simply furnished. Those facing the town's main circle include antiques and tasteful appointments. If you have not stopped in *Le Madrigal* bar for a nightcap, try it for continental breakfast. There you sink into green plush seats surrounded by rich panelling and are pampered with good croissants, fruit and first-class coffee.' *(George Herzog)*

Open: All year, except February. Restaurant closed Sunday evening and Monday 1 November–1 April.
Rooms: 42 double – 34 with bath, 8 with shower, all with telephone and colour TV.
Facilities: Lift, salons, bar, restaurant; conference facilities; courtyard.
Location: Central, near the cathedral; garage parking.
Credit cards: All major credit cards accepted.
Terms: B & B 105–265 frs; half board 230–390 frs. Set meals: breakfast 23 frs, lunch/dinner 127–187 frs; full *alc* 180 frs.

CHÂTEAU-ARNOUX, 04160 Alpes-de-Haute-Provence   Map 9

La Bonne Étape   *Telephone:* (92) 64.00.09
Chemin du Lac   *Telex:* ESIDIGN 430605 BONETAP

'A marvellous place, though you might not think so from outside. The little town is nothing special, in an ugly part of the Durance valley, and the *auberge* stands on the main road, though it looks onto open fields and hills at the back. It's a 17th-century coaching inn, now transformed into a stylish and very comfortable little hotel, owned and run by the delightful Gleize family who are strongly anglophile – father created the restaurant at the *Capital* Hotel in London, while son Jany worked at the *Connaught* (he also trained with Chapel, Troigros, etc.). They now provide some of the best cooking in Provence. We're not always sold on so-called *nouvelle cuisine*, but were fully won over by the Gleize's *gâteau de mostèle, lapereau farci,* and the local speciality, Sisteron lamb, whose subtle aromatic flavour comes from its being reared on the herbs of Provençal upland pastures. Breakfasts, too, were excellent. We had an attractive bedroom in Louis XV style, with a balcony facing the hills; and we enjoyed lazing on the pretty patio beside the swimming pool. We were lucky to get a room at the last moment (due to a cancellation), for the 11 bedrooms are usually booked out months in advance in season: the hotel

281

is on the main route down via Grenoble into Provence.' *(Peter and Sarah Abbott)* Two Michelin rosettes and three red Gault Millau *toques*.

Open: All year, except 5 January–15 February and 20–30 November. Restaurant closed Sunday evening and Monday out of season.
Rooms: 18 double, 5 suites – all with bath, telephone, radio and colour TV, some with balcony.
Facilities: Salons, bar, 2 dining rooms. Garden with heated swimming pool and patio. Lake 200 metres. English spoken.
Location: Near centre of town, which is 14 km S of Sisteron; garage and outside parking.
Credit cards: All major credit cards accepted.
Terms: Rooms: 200–420 frs. Set meals: breakfast 36 frs, lunch/dinner 135, 230, 260 frs; full *alc* 200–280 frs.

CHÂTEAUNEUF-EN-AUXOIS, 21320 Pouilly-en-Auxois, Côte d'Or, Burgundy
Map 8

Hostellerie du Château　　　　　　　　　　*Telephone:* (80) 33.00.23

A picturesque Burgundy hill village of old fortified farms dating from the 14th and 15th centuries, clearly visible on the east side of the A6 autoroute, some 10 km south of Pouilly. Next to the château is the *Hostellerie*, a very small and simple country hotel, well modernized from an old building, still with flagged stairs down to a sitting room. Visitors tend to find that the quality of the cooking compensates for the smallness of the bedrooms, 'too cramped for a long stay'. 'For those who do not mind a room which is mostly bed, this delightful ancient village and the ambience of the hotel should prove an attraction. The menu is imaginative and some of it inspired: do not miss the mousseline of pike.' Fine range of vintage burgundies on the wine list. *(Dr M B Matthews, C T Bailhache, and others)*

Open: 15 March–15 November. Closed Monday evening and Tuesday out of season.
Rooms: 11 double – 4 with bath, 7 with shower, all with telephone.
Facilities: Sitting room, 2 restaurants, banqueting room. Small garden with games for children; sailing on reservoir 3 km. A little English spoken.
Location: 7 km from Pouilly-en-Auxois. *Note:* Although the château is visible to the east of the motorway, one must go *west* from the Pouilly exit, along the road to Arnay-le-Duc; there is a signpost to Châteauneuf after a short distance.
Credit cards: All major credit cards accepted.
Terms: Rooms 80–180 frs. Set meals: breakfast 17 frs; lunch/dinner 90–180 frs; full *alc* 165 frs. Extra bed for child in parents' room 32 frs; special meals by arrangement.

CHÂTEAUNEUF-LES-BAINS, 63390 St Gervais d'Auvergne, Puy-de-Dôme
Map 8

Hôtel du Château　　　　　　　　　　　*Telephone:* (73) 86.67.01

Well off the tourist track, and 30 miles north-west of Clermont-Ferrand, Châteauneuf is 'a tiny, charmingly derelict spa set in the narrow, wooded valley of the Sioule'; its waters are said to be good for rheumatism and neuralgia. This spruce modern hotel by the river is 'a good example of the unpretentious friendly type of French country inn. Mod-cons a little lacking by today's standards but good food and excellent value for money.' *(William Goodhart; also W H Bruton)*

Open: 1 May–30 September.
Rooms: 33 double, 5 single – 21 with bath, 9 with shower. 18 rooms in annexe.
Facilities: Reception, salon, bar, 2 restaurants; terrace; garden with play area for children. Near river with bathing and fishing. English spoken.
Location: On the D109, off the N143 between Riom and Montlucon; parking.
Credit card: Barclay/Visa.
Terms: B & B 65–135 frs; full board 86–150 frs. Set meals: lunch/dinner 45–80 frs; full *alc* 90 frs. Reduced rates for children, depending on age; special meals on request.

CHÂTEAUNEUF-SUR-SARTHE, 49330 Maine et Loire   Map 8

La Sarthe   *Telephone:* (41) 42.11.30

Unanimous praise for the riverside setting of this modest small hotel on the edge of a little town north of Angers – 'the stretch of river is one of the loveliest I have seen for a long time, complete with old mill, medieval church and a weir.' When fine, meals and drinks are served on a terrace by this river. 'A friendly family hotel, idyllically peaceful, clean and comfortable.' *(Norman Swallow)* 'A lovely little place built at the turn of the century, furnished in 17th-century style. Dinner was excellent.' *(Anne Abel Smith)*. However, one recent report has complained of 'surly, offhand service', also an offhand smell coming through the bedroom window.

Open: All year, except October. Restaurant closed Sunday evenings and Monday in winter.
Rooms: 7 double – 2 with bath, 2 with shower.
Facilities: Salon, bar, rustic dining room overlooking river; terrace overlooking river. Public swimming pool 1 km; tennis courts 200 m. English spoken.
Location: 31 km north of Angers; parking.
Terms: Rooms 60 frs; dinner, B & B 95 frs; full board 135 frs. Set meals: breakfast 13 frs; lunch/dinner 45–125 frs; full *alc* 120 frs. Reductions for children.

CHÂTEAU-RENAULT, 37110 Indre et Loire, Loire Valley   Map 8

L'Écu de France   *Telephone:* (47) 56.50.72
37 Place J Jaurès

The town, between Blois and Tours, is well placed for visiting the Loire châteaux. 'This old inn on the large market square has been modernized without losing character. Our spacious room was quiet except when late-night motor-bike yobboes used the deserted square for a race-track. The ruined château was floodlit in the evening with lovely music, and there is an interesting tannery museum.' *(Jane Foulsham)*. 'Our meal was excellent. The food and the good local wines were more than enough to offset the fox-pelts and weapons on the wall and the medieval television room. Some of the proprietor's efforts to create the right historical ambience have been a little over-energetic, but the hotel offers good value: it is quiet, clean, comfortable. Parts are said to be 14th-century. An archway leads to a rose-filled coachyard where you can park.' *(Paul Vaughan)*

Open: All year, except Christmas. Restaurant closed Monday lunchtime.
Rooms: 6 double, 6 single, 1 suite – 6 with bath, 6 with shower, all with telephone.
Facilities: Lounge, TV room, dining room. Swimming pool 500 m; walks in the forest. English spoken.
Location: Central; parking.
Credit cards: American Express, Barclay/Visa, Diners.
Terms: Rooms 110–195 frs. Set meals (excluding service): breakfast 12.70 frs; lunch/dinner 50 and 100 frs; full *alc* 65 frs. Special meals for children.

CHAUMONT-SUR-THARONNE, 41600 Loir-et-Cher   Map 8

La Croix Blanche   *Telephone:* (54) 88.55.12
5 place Mottu

Chaumont-sur-Tharonne is deep in the Sologne, a strange flat region of wide forests and little marshy lakes. *La Croix Blanche* (a member of the *Relais de Silence* association) is a well-modernized creeper-covered old building in the central square, with a flowered courtyard where you can eat or drink in sunny weather. A convent in the days of Charlemagne, it has been the village inn for the last 300 years, with a distinguished, exclusively feminine gastronomic tradition for the past two centuries. Gisèle Crouzier, Vice-President of the *Association des Restauratrices Cuisinières*, has been in charge of the kitchens for the past 35 years. 'Comfortable beds were good for sleeping off the *fabulous* meal. Guests walk through a large kitchen, all oak beams, scrubbed tables and gleaming pottery tiles, to the dining room. Madame Crouzier is one of the best cooks in France and a very original one. (Books which include some of her recipes are set out on a sideboard in the breakfast room; and she has high accolades in French hotel guides.) The service was friendly and professional, with the family very much in charge of a skilled staff.' Michelin rosette, two Gault-Millau *toques*. *(Sheila and Uwe Kitzinger, also W H Bruton)*

Open: All year except 12 January–18 February and 29 June–9 July. Also closed on Wednesdays.
Rooms: 11 double, 4 single, 1 suite – 9 with bath, 7 with shower, all with telephone. (9 rooms in annexe; 5 rooms on ground floor.)
Facilities: Hall, salon, 3 restaurants. Courtyard for refreshments; garden with ping pong and boules. Handy for Loire châteaux. English spoken.
Location: Midway between Romorantin and Orléans (Orléans 34 km) S of La Ferté St-Aubin by the D922. In centre of village; parking.
Credit cards: All major credit cards accepted.
Terms: Rooms 130–345 frs. Set meals: breakfast 25 frs; lunch/dinner 140–320 frs; full *alc* 250 frs. Special meals for children.

Don't keep your favourite hotel to yourself. Hotels are *glad* to be in the Guide. Good hotels need all the support they can get.

CHEFFES, 49330 Châteauneuf-sur-Sarthe　　　　　　　　Map 8

Château de Teildras　　　　　　　　*Telephone:* (41) 42.61.08
　　　　　　　　　　　　　　　　　Telex: 720910 Public Angers F

The village of Cheffes lies in the rich farming country of the Sarthe valley,
24 km north of historic Angers. Some ten years ago the Comte de
Bernard du Breuil inherited this graceful little 16th-century château,
white-walled, grey-roofed, and decided that the only way to preserve his
family estate was to turn it into a small hotel. This he has done,
meticulously. You can ride, fish or go for walks in the large park, and
enjoy the Comtesse's light and subtle cooking, e.g. *pigeonneau à l'ail en
chemise*. 'All is to the highest standard. Two charming daughters variously serve and help with everything. The Comte produces the wine, including their own house *blanc*, which is delicious. Comfortable, quiet, unhur-
ried, the best of family atmospheres. We revelled in it.' *(Timothy Benn;
also Adam and Caroline Raphael)*

Open:　1 March–15 November. Restaurant closed Tuesday lunchtime.
Rooms:　11 double – all with bath and telephone; TV on request.
Facilities:　2 salons, 2 dining rooms. Wooded park, river within 500 metres;
fishing, riding. English spoken.
Location:　24 km N of Angers; Château is well sign-posted; turn out of Cheffes
towards Juvardeil; parking.
Credit cards:　All major credit cards accepted.
Terms:　Rooms: 400–540 frs (single rate 300–390 frs); half board 485–550 frs; full
board 610–700 frs. Set meals: breakfast 32 frs, lunch/dinner 150 frs. Full *alc*
200–240 frs. Reduced rates and special meals for children.

CHENEHUTTE-LES-TUFFEAUX, 49350 Gennes,
Maine-et-Loire　　　　　　　　　　　　　　　　　　　Map 8

Hostellerie du Prieuré　　　　　　　*Telephone:* (41) 50.15.31
　　　　　　　　　　　　　　　　　Telex: 720183

This famous hostelry which, in its former incarnation as a priory, dates
back to the 12th century, has an awesome position on a bluff overlooking
the Loire near Saumur. It's a *Relais et Château*, and, as you would expect,
luxurious in all its appointments. There is a large heated swimming pool in
the grounds, and 60 acres of private wooded park. The restaurant of the
Prieuré (Michelin rosette) is as elevated as its location – and its prices.
　One recent visitor registered a slight disappointment: the food was as
excellent as he had expected, but the service had been on the cool side;
although some of the rooms are in the château itself, others are in
bungalows in the grounds – a long walk through a garden which, he felt,
could have done with some attention. Another reader, though not
without a few reservations, was more positive: 'We booked one night and
stayed three. A lovely modern room the first night, spotlessly clean with
everything in luxury you could think of – bath robes, bath oil, perfumed
soap. The second and third nights we had a smaller older room in a turret
overlooking the Loire. We really felt that we were defending it. The
bathroom, well that was loo and wash-basin in one cupboard, and nip out
and into another cupboard for bathing! Not quite so luxurious, but
beautifully furnished. A lovely terrace for drinks, and a beautiful salon in

285

which you dared hardly breathe. Why are French lounges like this?'
(Heather Sharland; also Raymond Harris)

Open: All year, except 5 January–1 March.
Rooms: 30 double, 5 single, 1 suite – 33 with bath, 2 with shower, all with telephone; (15 ground-floor rooms in bungalows in the grounds.)
Facilities: 2 salons, TV room, bar, dining room. 60 acres grounds with heated swimming pool, mini-golf and tennis courts. English spoken.
Location: Overlooking the Loire; 7 km W of Saumur off the D751.
Credit card: American Express.
Terms (excluding 15% service charge): Rooms 290–600 frs. Set meals: breakfast 35 frs, lunch/dinner 160–220 frs. Reduced rates for children; special meals provided.

CHINON, 37500 Indre-et-Loire, Loire Valley   **Map 8**

Hôtel Diderot   *Telephone:* (47) 93.18.87
7 rue Diderot

Chinon, near the Loire, is a lovely old town with a half-ruined fortified castle on a hilltop. Here Joan of Arc first met the Dauphin. Praise continues to reach us for the *Diderot*, a sympathetic bed-and-breakfast hotel run by the friendly Cypriot M. Kazamias and his French wife. 'The rooms are large, cheerfully light and clean, and mine had a fine modern bathroom. Be careful not to run over the proprietor's kids, and be grateful for the seemingly endless number of jars of home-made *confitures* (including elderberry and rhubarb, apricot and myrtle) which will be offered you at breakfast. Incredibly cheap. Minimum of fuss: they make you welcome, then leave you alone.' A more recent visitor tells us that the jams also include banana, and that M. Kazamias is now extending the hotel and improving the late-night parking facilities for his guests. 'He has a rather ambitious programme which involves the creation of a reading room: could be ominous, but on the other hand what he has done so far with the hotel (built around 1780) is splendid – his restoration has been done with good taste and discretion. An exceptionally helpful and agreeable man.'
(Charles Osborne, Paul Vaughan, RCA, and others)

Open: All year, except 15 February–31 March.
Rooms: 15 double, 5 single – 10 with bath, 10 with shower, all with telephone. (4 rooms with bath on ground floor.)
Facilities: Salon, TV room, breakfast room; limited conference facilities. Courtyard. English spoken. ♿.
Location: Near Place Jeanne d'Arc; hotel is well sign-posted; private parking.
Credit cards: Access/Euro/Mastercard, Barclay/Visa.
Terms: B & B 55–149 frs. (No restaurant.)

CLUNY, 71250 Saône-et-Loire, Burgundy   **Map 8**

Hôtel de Bourgogne   *Telephone:* (85) 59.00.58
Place Abbaye

The old town of Cluny contains the remains of a mighty Romanesque abbey that in the Middle Ages was one of Europe's leading religious, artistic and intellectual centres. Built in the early 12th century, it was the largest church in Christendom, larger even than St Peter's, Rome. Today little of it remains; but the medieval town of narrow streets and pink tiles is still well worth a visit. Here the *Bourgogne* stands in the main square facing the abbey – a dignified old mansion that has been an inn since the 18th century (Lamartine often stayed here, and guests can still sleep in his bed). Our readers continue to praise the 'friendly welcome', 'discreetly elegant furnishings' and 'delicious meals'. We quote from an earlier report:

'Monsieur Gosse's well-run hotel has a special charm. Most of the bedrooms look out either onto green hills or the towers of the abbey buildings; they are all papered with intricate designs. The dining room, with black and white tiled floor and a wide fireplace, provides many pleasures. Our *feuilleté de coquelet* was delicious and light; the cheese-board is large, even by French standards, and the 'chariot' groans with peaches and nectarines in wine and *millefeuilles*. Sadly (as so often in good French hotels, especially in Burgundy) even the cheapest wine, an unexciting Mercurey, is horribly expensive. The personal attention that M. Gosse and his wife give to small details is what makes this a very special hotel. It is wise to reserve a room well in advance.' *(Bryan Stevens; also Mrs M D Prodgers and others)*

Open: February–15 November, except Tuesday and Wednesday midday.
Rooms: 18 double – 13 with bath or shower, all with telephone.
Facilities: Salon with TV, bar, restaurant. Courtyard.
Location: On the N79, 27 km from Mâcon. Hotel is opposite the abbey; garage parking.
Credit cards: American Express, Barclay/Visa, Diners.
Terms: Rooms 180–220 frs. Dinner, B & B 360–380 frs. Set meals: breakfast 22 frs; lunch/dinner 110–200 frs. Special meals for children.

CLUNY, 71250 Saône-et-Loire, Burgundy　　　　　　**Map 8**

Hôtel Moderne　　　　　　　　　　　　*Telephone:* (85) 59.05.65
Le Pont de l'Etang

The *Moderne* has new owners and a new chef in his mid-twenties, Patrick Descamps, who must be a proud man: not only has he won the accolade of a *toque* in the Gault-Millau guide for his inventive cooking, but President Mitterrand came to dine here on a private visit soon after taking office in 1981. He is said to have been satisfied, as was our reporter: 'Less attractive externally than the *Bourgogne* (see above), and in a less central position, being on the river a kilometre out of town, everything else makes the *Moderne* the only place to stay. Not all the bedrooms are well-decorated, but one can always enjoy the pretty terrace over the river, and the staff make a special effort to be welcoming. Prices are very reasonable, notably the dinner menus – our dinner was *memorably* better than at our two-star restaurant later in the trip. The best chocolate gâteau I've ever eaten.' *(Caroline Hamburger)*

Open: All year, except 15–30 November and 1 February 10 March. Restaurant closed Sunday evening and Monday.
Rooms: 15 double, 3 single – 9 with bath, 2 with shower, all with telephone, some with TV.
Facilities: Dining room; banqueting room for up to 90. English spoken.
Location: 1 km from centre in the direction of Mâcon; parking for 6 cars.

Credit card: Barclay/Visa.
Terms: Rooms 75–180 frs. Dinner, B & B 141–296 frs; full board 191–396 frs. Set meals: breakfast 16 frs; lunch/dinner 55–140 frs; full *alc* 160 frs.

COGNAC, 16100 Charente   Map 8

Hostellerie Les Pigeons Blancs   *Telephone:* (45) 82.16.36
110 rue Jules-Brisson

Cognac savours tradition, so it is fitting that this old coaching-inn should have been owned and run by the same family, the Tachets, since the 17th century. 'Delightful hotel with dull facade on a grim steep street across the river from town. Very small: six rooms, beautifully decorated with antiques, flowers, old prints, and that precisely chosen and applied decoration you see in superior private houses in France. Charming small sitting room for residents and a large restaurant, beautifully furnished in a sophisticated pastoral style. The old house is surrounded by a little *parc*, in this case a roughly cut meadow with fruit trees and old roses. Two terraces occupied by fantailed doves and no-tailed Siamese cat. Incredibly good food – especially a hot eel mousse with lemon sauce; chicken cooked with vinegar, hare in port, on 60-franc menu. Every detail in bedroom and bathroom was lovingly thought out. And the warm home-made croissants and jam made a delicious breakfast.' *(Maggie and Christopher Angeloglou).*

Open: All year, but closed Sunday.
Rooms: 6 double – 4 with bath, 2 with shower, all with telephone. (1 room on ground floor.)
Facilities: TV room, salon, 3 dining rooms. Small garden with terraces (meals served outside in fine weather). Tennis court and swimming pool 1 km. English spoken.
Location: 1 km from town centre, off route St Jean d'Angély; midway between Saintes and Angoulême (25 km).
Credit cards: American Express, Diners, Visa.
Terms: B & B 97–212 frs; full board 257–302 frs. Set meals: lunch/dinner 80 frs (including wine); full *alc* 140 frs. Reduced rates for children: 55 frs for a small bed.

COLROY-LA-ROCHE, 67420 Saales, Bas-Rhin, Alsace   Map 8

Hostellerie La Cheneaudière   *Telephone:* (88) 97.61.64

This smart modern hostelry, one of the *Relais et Châteaux*, lies peacefully amid the wooded uplands of the Vosges. 'A great location, in the midst of flowery Alsatian villages; breathing the mountain air was a treat. Despite the hairpin curves, the descent to the valley doesn't take long, and one can easily manage a day trip to Riquewihr and Kayserberg. *Extraordinary* comfort in the new part of the hotel. I felt a bit guilty staying in a rather Holiday Inn ambience instead of in a place with more "character", but we did enjoy it. The rooms in the old part of the hotel might have had more flavour, but the view from *my* part of the hotel was splendid. The menu is

---

Hotels are dropped if we lack positive feedback.

limited, poor in the way of starters (all outrageously expensive), but we enjoyed the best venison we have ever eaten, and the desserts are superior.' The *cuisine* is starred in the French guides; one of them stresses the copious help-yourself breakfasts – quite a revolution for France. *(Caroline D Hamburger)*

Open: All year, except 15 January–15 March.
Rooms: 28 double, 1 suite – 21 with bath, 3 with shower, all with telephone and TV.
Facilities: Salon, restaurant. Garden with tennis court. English spoken. &.
Location: 62 km SW of Strasbourg on the N420; parking.
Credit card: American Express.
Terms: Rooms 275–390 frs. Set meals: breakfast 28 frs; lunch/dinner 185–205 frs. Reduced rates for children.

COMPS-SUR-ARTUBY 83840 Var, Provence   Map 9

Grand Hôtel Bain   *Telephone:* (94) 76.90.06

The village lies on a bare plateau, circled by rocky hills, just east of the stunning Gorges du Verdon, the deepest in France. 'From the name, we half expected some palatial spa hotel. In fact it's a modest country inn, which the friendly Bain family have owned and run since 1737. They are true local people, who know the meaning of hospitality. Our bedroom, though adequate, was simple, and I'd rate this more a place for an overnight halt than a full holiday. The big dining room is no beauty, but has fine panoramic views, and we enjoyed the lavish local *cuisine* – good *daube provençale*. We were also amused by the Provençal mottoes round the wall, while the coachload of chattery old-age pensioners added to the informal ambience. Monsieur Bain's brother runs a hotel at Monterey, California.' *(Anthony Day)*

Open: All year.
Rooms: 14 double, 3 single – 6 with bath, 2 with shower.
Facilities: Salon, bar, restaurant, terrace. River Artuby 2 km. English spoken.
Location: On the D955 32 km N of Draguignan; parking.
Terms: Rooms 65–80 frs (single), 80–110 frs (double). Full board 188–220 frs. Set meals: breakfast 12 frs, lunch/dinner 40–90 frs; full *alc* 110 frs.

CONQUES, 12 Aveyron, Massif Central   Map 8

Hôtel Sainte-Foy   *Telephone:* (65) 69.84.03

Conques is halfway between Figeac and Rodez, and makes a good halt on the way from the Dordogne to the Languedoc coast. It was one of the famous staging points on the pilgrimage to Santiago de Compostela. Amazingly, this tiny village on a steep wooded hillside above a gorge has kept the air of a sacred place and is wholly of the Middle Ages: its slate-roofed houses and cobbled streets surround a massive and awesome abbey church, famous for the masterly Romanesque stone carving on the west doorway and for its very rich gold and silver treasure. The *Sainte-Foy*, the only hotel, is called after the martyred girl whose weird gold relic is still to be seen in the abbey museum. It's a fine medieval house, facing the great abbey, with a shaded courtyard in the rear and handsome old furniture in the public rooms. The hotel has for many years enjoyed a well-merited Michelin rating for good meals at modest price (no lunches): try the local Rouergue dishes, such as *feuilleté au roquefort*. Service is very friendly. It isn't a place for an extended stay, but Conques itself is so remarkable, especially in the evening when the abbey is floodlit and the sightseers have gone, that it is well worth a special visit. Among recent enthusiastic reports, one referred to the great forests of sweet chestnuts all around. Another – 'a delightful hotel in a splendid place' – offered a warning to light sleepers: two sets of church clocks tell the time at half-hourly intervals all night. *(Peter Fraenkel, Angela and David Stewart, John Hills)*

Open: 1 April–3 November.
Rooms: 18 double, 2 single – 12 with bath, 8 with shower, all with telephone.
Facilities: 2 reading rooms, TV room, dining room; small patio. English spoken.
Location: Off the D601 and not far from the N662 between Figeac (54 km) and Rodez (37 km). Hotel is central, opposite cathedral; garage and car park.
Terms: Rooms 100–300 frs; dinner, B & B about 200 frs. Set meals: breakfast 20 frs, dinner 75 frs; full *alc* 90 frs. 10–20% reductions out of season. Special meals for children on request.

CORDON, Par Sallanches, 74700 Haute-Savoie   **Map 8**

Hôtel les Roches Fleuries   *Telephone:* (50) 58.06.71

'*Roches Fleuries* has a grandstand view of the permanently snow-covered Mont Blanc and its neighbouring peaks. It is a sight you will never forget; especially if you watch the snow turn pink in the sunset as you take your *apéritif* on your balcony and later see the full moon come up over the ridge while you are having a splendid dinner. The hotel, a big Alpine chalet, is attractive, quiet and very comfortable. Food and service are excellent. There are spacious terraces and then fields between this and neighbouring hotels. There is a separate chalet bar in the garden. An ideal base for a walking or skiing holiday. Sallanches, 4 km away on the road to Chamonix (28 km), has one of the best markets we have seen.' *(Warren Bagust)*

Open: All year, except 10 October–20 December.
Rooms: 29 – 23 with bath, 1 with shower, all with telephone and balcony; TV on request. 5 rooms in 2 annexes. (1 small suite on ground floor.)
Facilities: TV room, salon with log fire, bar, dining room, terraces; fondue evenings, soirées; conference facilities. Ping pong. Garden with bar; lake 4 km with bathing, windsurfing and boating. English spoken.
Location: 4 km from Sallanches on the D1113; parking.
Terms: B & B 200 frs; full board 230–280 frs. Set meals: lunch/dinner 75 frs. Reduced rates for children according to age; special meals provided.

B & B prices, unless otherwise specified, are per person. Where two figures are given, they indicate the range of prices. The lower figure is for one person sharing a double room in the low season, the higher figure is for one person occupying a room alone in the high season. We have also given full- and half-board prices when available.

COTIGNAC, 83850 Var   Map 9

Hostellerie Lou Calen   *Telephone:* (94) 04.60.40
1 Cours Gambetta

Cotignac is a genial village nestling in the hills of the Haut Var. It calls itself *Village des Artisans, Le Saint Tropez du Haut Var*, which is stretching things a lot, but arts and crafts abound in the region, and the local craft shop does have a superior display. *Lou Calen* (the Provençal name means 'place of the oil lamp') is *the* hotel – an admirable family-run establishment. Rooms are simply but pleasantly furnished, with modern plumbing. You eat well (classic Provençal cooking) on a beautiful terrace facing a wide view. There is a large swimming pool. Nothing outstanding, but everything as it should be – including a warm welcome. Only minor drawback: though the hotel faces sideways to the road, there is some traffic noise – revving and gear-changing at night. P.S. Do visit the château at Entrecasteaux, 8 km away: a wonderful reconstruction by the Scottish surrealist artist/diplomat, the late Ian MacGarvie-Munn. *(HR; also C H Cole)*

Open: April–31 December, except Thursday. Restaurant also closed Thursday out of season.
Rooms: 5 double, 11 suites – 15 with bath, 1 with shower, all with telephone, 5 with TV.
Facilities: Salon, TV room, bar, restaurant, terrace. Garden with swimming pool. Tennis 1 km. English spoken.
Location: On Route des Gorges du Verdon. For Cotignac take exit Brignoles or Le Luc – Toulon off the N7.
Terms: Rooms 140–220 frs; half board 165–230 frs; full board 240–305 frs. Set meals: breakfast 20 frs; lunch/dinner 75 frs.

COULANDON, 03000 Moulins, Allier   Map 9

Le Chalet   *Telephone:* (70) 44.50.08

Coulandon is a small village in the very centre of France, 6 km west of the busy market town of Moulins (do not miss the Gothic cathedral with its splendid stained-glass and choir) and 6 km east of Souvigny, noted for its priory church. *Le Chalet*, just outside the village, is a former hunting lodge set in total tranquillity (it is a *Relais du Silence*) in its own spacious park with pond full of fish. 'Very pretty clean room in converted stable in very pretty grounds,' says one reader. Another adds, 'The rooms are de-luxe with superb fabric wall covering – too sophisticated for the country. The food was good but not spectacular. One could stay for a week in a sleepy drowse. Most expensive hotels have rooms in which one would have no room to swing a cat. This hotel could take several cats.' Indeed, 'The hotel cat will escort you on your evening walk' (preferably to the fish-pond, one supposes). *(Gerald Campion, C S Nelles)*

Open: 15 January–15 December. Restaurant closed midday, and evenings 1 October–28 February.
Rooms: 21 double – 7 with bath, 9 with shower, all with telephone.
Facilities: Reading lounge, restaurant, seminar room.

Location: Well sign-posted: outside the village, down a side-road just N of the main N145.
Credit card: Access/Euro/Mastercard.
Terms: B & B 65–165 frs; full board 135–230 frs. Set meals: lunch/dinner 50 and 85 frs; full *alc* 85 frs.

COURRY, 30500 St-Ambroix, Gard   **Map 8**

Auberge Croquembouche   *Telephone:* (66) 24.13.30

A quietly secluded little inn, in the eastern foothills of the Cévennes. 'It was in the proverbial middle of nowhere when we suddenly saw a sign pointing down a narrow lane indicating the *Auberge Croquembouche*. We decided to investigate and came upon a true haven for the weary traveller. A smiling welcome from Madame Labrosse, who spoke good English, and invited us into her delightful *Auberge* which had been converted by her husband from a ruin. The public rooms are small, interconnecting and cellar-like, whilst the bedrooms, all complete with bathrooms, are of the highest standard. Outside is a small swimming pool and plenty of ground for the children to tire themselves out in. However the best treat was still to come when we went down to dinner. The cooking, which is done by the Labrosses' son, is superb. A *terrine de poissons à la menthe fraîche* was followed by *grenadin de veau à l'estragon*, delightful pats of cheese from the local village and fresh fruit. An ideal place to rest for the night when travelling to or returning from the Mediterranean resorts.' *(Ann and Michael Lisamer)*

Open: All year, except 15 February–15 March, and Wednesdays except between Easter and end September.
Rooms: 5 double, 1 suite for 4 people – all with bath and telephone.
Facilities: Reception, salon, bar, restaurant. Garden with swimming pool. English spoken.
Location: Off the D904 from Alès to Aubenas, 6 km N of St-Ambroix, opposite Grotte de la Cocalière.
Credit card: Access/Euro/Mastercard.
Terms: Rooms 178 frs; half board 150 frs; full board 235 frs. Set meals: breakfast 19 frs, lunch/dinner 57 frs; full *alc* 80–115 frs.

LA CROIX-VALMER, 83420 Var, Provence   **Map 9**

Parc Hôtel   *Telephone:* (94) 79.64.04
Avenue Georges Sellier

The dullish village of La Croix-Valmer lies at the far side of the glorious Ramatuelle peninsula from St-Tropez, not far from the charming hill-villages of Gassin and Ramatuelle, and near to good beaches too. The *Parc* is on the outskirts, two miles from the sea, set back from the road behind formal gardens. Though this imposing white mansion looks like a former stately home, it was in fact built in 1903 as a girls' school; it has now been converted, with huge bedrooms which used to be the dorms.

'A pleasant base for a holiday in the area, yet avoiding the expensive razzmatazz of the coast. The hotel stands in large gardens with beautiful views of the sea and the Hyères islands. Inside all is cool and spacious with lofty ceilings, chandeliers, marble floors, and spotlessly clean. It is all so large and airy that one is unaware of anyone else staying there and it would be a good place to hide away and write a book for example. There is a bar but no restaurant. The staff were pleasant and helpful.' Other readers have confirmed this report. One commented on the 'unfailingly obliging young staff', but found them a little disorganized. *(Ray and Angela Evans, Mrs R B Richards)*

Open: Easter–1 October.
Rooms: 24 double, 1 single, 8 suites – 14 with bath, 19 with shower, all with telephone.
Facilities: Lift, 2 salons (1 with TV), bar. Attractive grounds and terrace; beaches nearby with sailing and underwater fishing. English spoken.
Location: 500 metres from town centre; parking; off the N559 Toulon–Nice road on the D93, travelling E.
Credit cards: Barclay/Visa, Diners.
Terms: Rooms 105–245 frs. Set meal: breakfast 19 frs. (No restaurant.) Reduced rates out of season.

DIEPPE, 76200 Seine-Maritime, Normandy　　　　　　　　**Map 8**

Hôtel de L'Univers　　　　　　　　*Telephone:* (35) 84.12.55
10 Boulevard de Verdun　　　　　　　　*Telex:* 770741

The *Univers*, facing Dieppe's elegant esplanade, has many British devotees, who make it a regular night-stop on their way to or from the south, or who come over specially from Newhaven for a weekend break. It is a middle-class hotel with old-fashioned virtues, run by professionals who know their business. Food, furnishings, service have all been appreciated, with only an occasional dissenting note. *(Heather Sharland, Raymond Harris)*

Open: All year except 6 December–1 February.
Rooms: 30 – 28 with bath or shower, all with telephone and TV; some with balcony.
Facilities: Lift, restaurant; conference facilities. ᕯ.
Location: Central; parking.
Credit cards: All major credit cards accepted.
Terms: Rooms 160–320 frs; full board 235–320 frs. Set meals: breakfast 23 frs; lunch/dinner 80–115 frs.

DIJON, 21000 Côte d'Or, Burgundy　　　　　　　　**Map 8**

Le Chapeau Rouge　　　　　　　　*Telephone:* (80) 30.28.10
5 rue Michelet　　　　　　　　*Telex:* 350535F

This attractive, classic hotel is very central, close to the cathedral and not far from the splendid Beaux-Arts museum. It's a noisy street, but front rooms have double-glazing; back ones may be quieter, but some are darker and less comfortable. Parking can be hellish. The hotel is the only one in Dijon with a Michelin star for its food and a high Gault-Millau rating too; outstanding wines. 'The restaurant is the most elegant I have ever encountered, and the food fine.' This earlier report has now been warmly endorsed: 'The perfect small hotel, at reasonable prices; lovely restaurant, with marvellous food, service and ambience.' *(Arnold Howell; Christine Brownlie)*

Open: 10 January–20 December.
Rooms: 29 double, 4 single, 2 suites – all with bath, radio, colour TV, air-conditioning and refrigerated mini-bar. Baby-listening on request.
Facilities: Lift, hall, salon, bar, elegant restaurant; conference facilities. English spoken.
Location: Central, near cathedral; parking for 15 cars.
Credit cards: All major credit cards accepted.
Terms: Rooms with breakfast 235–390 frs. Set meals: lunch 110 frs, dinner 120 frs; full *alc* 220 frs. Reduced rates and special meals for children.

DIJON, 21000 Côte-d'Or, Burgundy   Map 8

Hôtel du Nord   *Telephone:* (80) 30.55.20
Place Darcy

Recommended as a good middle-priced hotel, centrally placed for exploring the city. 'We had a spacious bedroom with nice solid old furniture, heavy brocade bedspread and curtains and a large bathroom. The candle-lit dining room is especially inviting, with panelled walls and beamed ceiling, and windows overlooking the Place Darcy. Service was efficient and courteous, and we were offered a good choice of dishes with Burgundian specialities much in evidence. We ate extremely well in a pleasant atmosphere.' *(Rosamund Hebdon)*

Open: 14 January–23 December.
Rooms: 26 double, 2 suites – 16 with bath, 10 with shower, all with telephone.
Facilities: TV room, bar, restaurant, banqueting room. English spoken.
Location: Central; parking in square.
Credit cards: All major credit cards accepted.
Terms: Rooms 80 frs; dinner, B & B 163 frs. Set meals: breakfast 15 frs, lunch/dinner 75 and 100 frs; full *alc* 120 frs. Special meals for children.

DINAN, 22100 Côtes-du-Nord, Brittany   Map 8

Hôtel d'Avaugour   *Telephone:* (96) 39.07.49
1 place du Champ'-Clos

Dinan is a handsome medieval town on a rocky hilltop above the river Rance: it has a beautifully laid-out *jardin anglais*, and a sturdy 14th-century castle where Duchess Anne de Bretagne used to live. The *d'Avaugour* is fully worthy of this setting – a spacious Breton mansion, unusually comfortable and attractive, with a flowery garden beside the summit of the ramparts. One reader extols his 'first-class lunch at this delightful hotel, not exactly cheap but good value'. The French guides, too, rate the *cuisine* very highly, including such exotic dishes as hot oysters with curry and salad of lobster and mango. More reports welcome. *(R S Ryder)*

Open: All year.
Rooms: 27 double – 15 with bath, 2 with shower, all with telephone, 15 with colour TV.

Facilities: Lift, TV room, bar, restaurant, terrace. Garden with children's play area. River Rance 1 km, beach (Dinard) 20 km. English spoken.
Location: In town centre; coming from Rennes, turn left after the viaduct, continue straight until you reach the Place, then left; no private parking.
Credit cards: All major credit cards accepted.
Terms: B & B 116.50–186.50 frs; full board 250–290 frs. Set meals (excluding 12% service charge): lunch/dinner, 60, 100, 150 frs.

DOLANCOURT, Nr Bar-sur-Aube, 10200 Aube   Map 8

Moulin du Landion   *Telephone:* (25) 26.12.17

'An excellent place from which to explore the little-known and most interesting southern part of Champagne,' runs one report on this 'converted mill – the dining room with picture windows is built around the mill stream – in absolutely quiet countryside. The rooms are modern, plain and of good size – a blessing for people who find cramped conditions tiring – and very reasonably priced. The kitchen provides good food, the cellar stocks wines of a fair range, also unreasonably priced. The staff are pleasant and helpful – for example, I wanted a vegetarian meal for dinner, and there was no difficulty about adapting the menu and no extra charge. Recommended for the lover of peace and quiet.' *(Pamela Vandyke Price).* Two more recent visitors concur with this praise. However, two other reports suggest that the hotel's apparent seclusion and tranquillity may be a delusion. One reader was dismayed to discover that the main Paris–Basle railway, hidden behind some trees, was only 100 metres from her bedroom and the trains woke her up. More contributions, please, to this debate on noise *v* peace. The moral may be to book a room facing away from the railway. *(A H H Stow, M H Smye)*

Open: All year, except Christmas and New Year.
Rooms: 16 – all with bath and telephone. (8 rooms on ground floor.)
Facilities: Salon with TV, dining room. Garden with children's play area. River fishing, bathing. English spoken.
Location: 9 km from Bar-sur-Aube, on the N19 between Troyes (52 km) and Chaumont (42 km); parking.
Credit cards: Access/Euro/Mastercard, Barclay/Visa.
Terms: B & B 103–163 frs. Set meals: lunch/dinner 80–150 frs; full *alc* 140 frs. Reduced rates out of season. Special meals for children by arrangement.

DOL-DE-BRETAGNE, 35120 Ille-et-Vilaine, Brittany   Map 8

Logis de la Bresche d'Arthur   *Telephone:* (99) 48.01.44
36 Boulevard Deminiac

Dol-de-Bretagne, roughly halfway between St Malo and Mont-St Michel is a most attractive town, full of fine medieval houses and an imposing cathedral. The 8th-century tidal wave which turned Mont-St Michel into an island, swept up to Dol-de-Bretagne, which is surrounded by fertile marshland. 'The rooms of the *Bresche d'Arthur* are a little spartan, but more than compensated for by a wonderful variety of food – a wide choice all most thoroughly prepared. The proprietor is young and very helpful. Parking is easy, and, despite traffic, the hotel is quiet. It is a useful

staging-post to the morning boat from St Malo, 24 km to the north-west.'
(S W Burden)

Open: All year, except November.
Rooms: 24 – all with bath and telephone. (3 rooms on ground floor.)
Facilities: Salon/bar, TV room, restaurant; conference facilities. Garden 6 km from sea. English spoken.
Location: Between St Malo and Mont-St Michel on the N176; hotel is central; underground garage.
Credit cards: All major credit cards accepted.
Terms: Rooms 150 frs; dinner, B & B 160 frs; full board 210 frs. Set meals: breakfast 20 frs; lunch/dinner 48–140 frs. Reduced rates for children.

DOMME, 24250 Dordogne   **Map 8**

Hôtel l'Esplanade   *Telephone:* (53) 28.31.41

'Domme, overlooking the Dordogne valley, is tastefully restored, in the tradition of Viollet-le-Duc, a stone tribute to the determined orthodoxy of French fine art tradition, and it is full of expensive antique shops and *foie gras*. The caves, to which one may descend by lift in the covered market square, are not very interesting, since no local Abbé Breuil had time to colour them prehistorically, but they are cool on a hot day. The countryside around is varied, hilly, and there is swimming not far away in the river or in a *piscine municipale*.

'Monsieur and Madame Gillard (he the chef, she the front-of-house manager) have refurbished this hotel which always enjoyed a superb view. The rooms are individually decorated in a variety of floral wallpapers in the best tradition of the French country hotel, but they also have private baths or showers. Monsieur Gillard's dishes deserve stellar acknowledgement: the *mousseline de brochet* is particularly delicious. His table can be recommended not only for the skill he brings to it, but also for the size of the dishes in which that skill is revealed. The dining room is large and airy, and the hotel stands at the peak of a town on a peak.' The writers of this account, which they first wrote three years ago, have now endorsed it. They are happy to learn that M. Gillard's *cuisine* has been rewarded, if not with Michelin stars, at least with a *toque* and laurels for 'good local recipes' in Gault-Millau. *(Frederic and Sylvia Raphael)*

Open: All year, except November and February.
Rooms: 14 double – all with bath and telephone.
Facilities: Salon with TV, 2 dining rooms; terrace with panoramic views. River 2 km, swimming pool 10 km. English spoken.
Location: 1 km S of the Dordogne; Sarlat 12 km, Gourdon 26 km.
Credit card: American Express.
Terms: Rooms 95–215 frs; half board 190–230 frs; full board 210–250 frs. Set meals: breakfast 18 frs; lunch/dinner 80–190 frs.

We ask hotels to estimate their 1983 tariffs. Not all hotels in Part Two reply, so prices in Part Two are more approximate in some cases than those in Part One.

EUGÉNIE-LES-BAINS, 40320 Landes, Aquitaine   Map 8

Les Prés d'Eugénie   *Telephone:* (58) 58.19.01
                                          Telex: 420 470F

Michel Guérard's restaurant, 53 km north of Pau, is world-famous as the
home of that purest form of the 'new cooking' known as *cuisine minceur*:
dishes at once gastronomically delicious and low on calories. 'Ancillary to
the restaurant is an excellent hotel, a thermal establishment and, para-
doxically, a health farm where guests pay to reduce on diets devised by a
three-star chef. The casual visitor who has practised consistent self-denial
in order to minimize the effects of advancing years and a liking for good
food and drink, can feel comforted as he looks around him on the sun
terrace or by the pool at those who have been rather less disciplined. The
rooms are individually furnished in lavish French taste, the bathrooms are
large and well-equipped. Needless to say the food is impeccable, its
presentation theatrical and the prices are commensurately high.' That
report from last year's Guide is backed up by newer visitors to this Second
Empire mansion: 'Style is everything in this famous hotel, full of lovely
idiosyncracies. It could almost be too design-conscious – carefully placed
haycocks in the meadow (in October), enchanting chinoiserie bridges,
marvellously romantic colour schemes – but escapes partly because the
staff are so engagingly young and anxious to please. Most guests lunch in
towelling dressing gowns.' Guérard, one of the six winners of Gault-
Millau's 'Best Meal of the Year' award in 1982, today goes from strength
to strength and is more a guru figure than ever. One English writer,
ringing up and asking to speak to him, was told in hushed tones, '*Le
Maître* is holding a seminar.' *(David Wooff, Maggie Angeloglou)*

Open: 1 April–31 October.
Rooms: 35 double, 3 suites – 22 with bath, 11 with shower, 20 with colour TV, 13
with mono TV, all with telephone and radio.
Facilities: Salon, smoking and billiard room, TV room, gallery, dining rooms.
Beauty salon, thermal baths, sauna. 2 tennis courts, bowls, unheated swimming
pool. Garden and river. Golf 25 km. English spoken.
Location: Off the D944 St-Sever–Aubagnan. 50 km from Pau.
Credit card: American Express.
Terms (excluding 15% service):   Rooms 470–760 frs. Set meals: breakfast 40 frs,
lunch/dinner 230–250 frs. Reductions for children under 10 sharing parents' room.

LES EYZIES-DE-TAYAC, 24620 Dordogne   Map 8

Hôtel du Centenaire   *Telephone:* (53) 06.97.18

Les Eyzies with its famous caves has been called 'the capital of prehis-
tory'. The *Centenaire* is a modern hotel in the village centre (in summer,
traffic is heavy during the day, but quiet at night). It has long been
gastronomically notable; and today the chef, Roland Mazère, *fils de la
maison*, has won it two Michelin rosettes and two Gault-Millau *toques* for
his inventive modern-style *cuisine* based on local produce (e.g. *feuilleté
d'escargots et de cèpes*). The somewhat formal dining room was prettily
redecorated in 1982.
   'The *Centenaire* might easily seem just the kind of characterless and
over-priced place to avoid. It is certainly somewhat expensive (though not

by the standards of routine English hotels), but it is not to be missed, especially if food is part of your idea of a good holiday. (If it isn't, what point is there in going to the Dordogne?) The *Centenaire* remains a family affair, now in the hands of the younger generation, with a brilliant *nouveau cuisinier* in the kitchen and his charming, elegant brother-in-law in charge of the front-of-house. Pretentiousness is wholly absent.

'Les Eyzies is dominated by the steep cliffs which are riddled with the most astonishing concatenation of prehistoric caves in Europe. The call of culture can thus be answered honourably, and variously, between meals and, if desired, swims in the rivers (dangerous) or the reliable *piscines municipales* of the region. Les Eyzies is not, perhaps, the prettiest place in the department, but beauties abound in all directions. The *Centenaire* is unashamedly a *bourgeois* hotel; its suitability for family holidays may be questionable, but its courtesies and delights are beyond criticism.' *(Frederic and Sylvia Raphael; also R S Ryder)*

Open: 1 April–3 November.
Rooms: 28 double, 4 single, 2 suites – all with bath or shower and telephone. 10 rooms in annexe. (5 rooms on ground floor.)
Facilities: Lounge, bar, restaurant. Garden, terraces. English spoken. &.
Location: 20 km from Sarlat on the D47; 45 km from Périgueux.
Credit cards: All major credit cards accepted.
Terms: Rooms 150–220 frs; full board 300 frs. Set meals: breakfast 28 frs, lunch/dinner 95–240 frs; full *alc* 220 frs. Special meals for children.

LES EYZIES-DE-TAYAC, 24620 Dordogne   **Map 8**

Hôtel Cro-Magnon   *Telephone:* (53) 06.97.06

Though its cooking is in the same lofty league as that of the *Centenaire* above (similar *nouvelle* variations on classic local dishes), the *Cro-Magnon* is in other respects quite different. It's a creeper-covered, much mansarded building on the outskirts, away from the tourist hubbub, with a delightful garden and swimming pool. It has a rather formal elegant decor, and its special atmosphere comes from the fact that its founder was a pre-historian of the late 19th century who first identified Cro-Magnon Man and discovered the nearby prehistoric sites. Some of the artefacts he dug up are on display in the hotel. 'We stayed here in 1981 and 1982 after a gap of sixteen years. We have always found the hotel excellent, the staff obliging, the food and standards of service high, fully deserving the Michelin rosette, and the prices reasonable. We had a large and airy room in the small annexe in the quiet garden which gives the impression of being in the country.' *(K C Turpin; also C H Cole)*

Open: 1 April–10 October.
Rooms: 25 double, 3 suites – 25 with bath, 2 with shower, all with telephone. (12 rooms in annexe. 1 room on ground floor.)
Facilities: 2 lounges, 2 dining rooms, garden restaurant; 5 acres parkland with heated swimming pool; river at the foot of the grounds. English spoken. &.
Location: 600 m from town centre; garage and parking facilities.
Credit cards: All major credit cards accepted.
Terms: Rooms 100–180 frs; dinner, B & B 230–310 frs; full board 260–340 frs. Set meals: breakfast 30 frs, lunch/dinner 90–210 frs; full *alc* 150–220 frs.

> Don't rely on our printed tariffs! Check before booking.

FÈRE-EN-TARDENOIS, 02130 Aisne **Map 8**

Hostellerie du Château *Telephone:* (23) 82.21.13
Telex: OTELFER 145526F

Visitors with a taste for luxury, and for French *cuisine* at its most brilliant, continue to praise this grand manor house, part-Renaissance, part-19th-century. It is 45 km west of Reims, in its own sizeable park which lies within a forest. 'We picked a perfect day to visit the *Hostellerie*. The room we decided on was quite large and covered with typical French flower design silk wall hangings. Beautiful linen and bedspreads; dainty chairs, bedside tables; a writing desk; a fridge filled with just about every drink one could desire; some fresh fruit, a knife and napkins. The bathroom was huge and well-fitted, including a hair-dryer. The windows opened on to a superb view of the grounds, and in the early morning we watched rabbits playing on the lawns. The service was very formal, but quite faultless. We had drinks on the terrace before dinner while we studied the enormous menu and an equally vast wine list. We finally decided on the tasting menu, which enabled us to try minute portions of three different fish courses: lobster mousse, *goujons* of sole and asparagus and *lotte* poached in wine wrapped in lettuce. All delicate and exquisitely presented. This was followed by a delicious sorbet of marc, and then a very uninteresting rabbit. Excellent cheeseboard. The desserts were masterly; any thoughts of calories must be discarded. The dining room was delightful with elegant furnishings and superb linen and tableware.' This entry from the 1982 Guide has been endorsed by a reader this year: 'Splendid place – the sort where I would feel slightly intimidated but for the universal friendliness. Complete peace in perfect countryside.' *(Padi Howard; also John Hills, Robert Heller and others)*

Open: All year, except January/February.
Rooms: 13 double, 7 suites – all with bath or shower and telephone; 5 with TV, some with frigo-bar. (5 rooms on ground floor.)
Facilities: Salons, restaurant; some conference facilities. Large park and formal gardens within surrounding forest, with tennis court. Fishing, riding 5 km; golf 40 km. &. English spoken.
Location: 3 km N of Fère-en-Tardenois. Take the D967 and the Route Forestière.
Credit cards: American Express, Barclay/Visa.
Terms: Rooms 290–500 frs for 2 people. Set meals: breakfast 30 frs; lunch/dinner 160–250 frs.

FONTAINEBLEAU, 77300 Seine-et-Marne, Île de France **Map 8**

Hôtel Aigle Noir *Telephone:* (6) 422.32.65
27 Place Napoléon Bonaparte *Telex:* 600080

'The best value so far on my trip. A palatial bedroom with lovely antiques, and a real welcome in the dining room where my vegetarian meal was served with pleasure.' 'We found it almost impossible to criticize – they could not have been more helpful.' These accolades go to the grandest hotel in Fontainebleau, in the centre, facing the gardens of Napoleon's favourite palace. *'Ambiance napoléonique'* was how an earlier visitor had summed up the experience. The hotel combines classic Louis XVI and

Empire decor with all the latest mod cons – glass-fibre sound-proofing, etc. – but it also remains a family place, run by Monsieur Duvauchelle and his two sons. Gault-Millau gives it a red *toque* for the 'happy modernism' of its *cuisine*. *(Mrs M D Prodgers; also Mr and Mrs R G Ewen, Dr D M Ainscow)*

Open: All year.
Rooms: 20 double, 6 single, 4 suites – 28 with bath, 2 with shower, all with direct-dial telephone, radio, TV, mini-bar and double-glazing.
Facilities: Salons, bar, restaurant; conference facilities. Garden.
Location: Adjoining palace grounds.
Credit cards: All major credit cards accepted.
Terms: B & B 215–430 frs. Set meals: lunch/dinner 140 frs; full *alc* 200 frs. Children under 12 free in parents' room.

FONTAINEBLEAU, 77300 Seine-et-Marne, Île-de-France   **Map 8**

Legris et Parc   *Telephone:* (6) 422.24.24
36 rue du Parc

'A welcome and unexpected find after a long slog up the Autoroute du Sud. It exudes style as befits its 1659 ownership by Louis d'Oyer, Marquis de Cavoye, a favourite of Louis XIV and friend of Racine. Large bedrooms; plenty of towels in well-appointed bathroom. Furnished in keeping with the general fabric of the building, backing on to the elegant railings of the Palais de Fontainebleau park. A fine dining room looks out over a formal garden in the French style, with flowers and shrubs planted for spring and summer colour. Friendly and discreet service, comfortable public rooms. No traffic noise.' *(Kay and Arthur Woods)*

Open: All year, except 20 December–1 February. Restaurant closed Sunday evening.
Rooms: 19 double, 7 suites – 18 with bath, 7 with shower, all with telephone. (1 room on ground floor.)
Facilities: 3 salons, restaurant; conference facilities. Garden.
Location: Adjoining palace grounds, W of Avenue des Cascades. Parking opposite.
Credit cards: Access/Euro/Mastercard, Barclay/Visa.
Terms: Rooms 125 frs. Set meals: breakfast 16 frs; lunch/dinner 60 and 95 frs; full *alc* 100 frs.

FONTVIEILLE, 13990 Bouches-du-Rhône, Provence   **Map 9**

Auberge La Regalido   *Telephone:* (90) 97.70.17
Rue Frédéric-Mistral

The little town of Fontvieille, in the foothills of the Alpilles, makes a good centre for exploring the Arles and Les Baux areas. On a hill nearby is Daudet's famous windmill. 'No praise is high enough for this jewel of a hotel,' writes one recent visitor to *La Régalido*, a former oil-mill in a side street, now converted into a most welcoming little *auberge*, luxurious yet unpretentious. The flowery garden with its neatly cut lawn is especially attractive. 'Each bedroom, named for a plant (mine was *genévrier* – juniper), has great individual charm. The *Auberge* is run by the Michel family. Madame Michel's hand is evident in the decor of the rooms and bathrooms, and in the flowers which grace all the rooms. The food is memorable. The greatest talent of the Michels, however, is to have created so warmly welcoming an atmosphere.' This report from an earlier edition has since been endorsed by others, one of whom, arriving in October, found 'a fire blazing in the sitting-room fireplace.' Jean-Pierre Michel's cooking wins a Michelin rosette, and a Gault-Millau *toque*, for such dishes as *mousseline de poissons au fenouil. (Elisabeth Lambert Ortiz, Barbara Anderson, Dr J E M Whitehead)*

Open: All year except 30 November–mid January. Restaurant closed Monday, and Tuesday midday.
Rooms: 10 double, 1 suite – 10 with bath, 1 with shower, all with telephone.
Facilities: Large reception room, 3 small salons (1 with TV), restaurant. Garden. Sea 35 km. English spoken.
Location: Arles 8 km W; Avignon 30 km N. Parking.
Credit cards: American Express, Barclay/Visa, Diners.
Terms: Rooms 290–460 frs. Set meals: breakfast 35 frs; lunch/dinner 155–200 frs. Special meals for children.

FLAGY, Nr Montereau-Faut-Yonne Map 8
77156 Thoury-Ferrottes, Seine-et-Marne, Île-de-France

Hôtel-Restaurant au Moulin *Telephone:* (6) 096.67.89
6 rue du Moulin

An enchanting 13th-century mill, beautifully converted and standing beside a stream, in a village 25 km south-east of Fontainebleau and 10 km from Montereau by the D120. It is more restaurant than hotel, but correspondents have appreciated both. 'Rushing water can be seen and heard from the delightful lounge featuring some of the mill-wheels and pulleys. The restaurant also overlooks the same rushing torrent. Our bedroom was on top of the lock gates. The resident cat wakes you in the morning by scratching at the door. Unfortunately our dinner was only average: but everything else made up for it, and we'd certainly go again.' A previous visitor had been more impressed with the food, dubbing it 'a gastronomic experience'. Prices are remarkably modest for the Ile-de-France. *(Peter Marshall, also Janet McWhorter)*

Open: All year, except 19 December–22 January, 11–23 September; also Sunday evening and Monday, except July and August.
Rooms: 10 double – all with bath.
Facilities: Lift; lounge, bar, beamed restaurant. Garden with riverside terrace.
Location: 20 km E of A6 motorway; 10 km SW of Montereau: about 85 km S of Paris.
Credit cards: Barclay/Visa, Diners.
Terms: Rooms with breakfast 135–250 frs; full board 345–365 frs. Set meals: lunch/dinner 80–150 frs.

Important reminder: terms printed must be regarded as a rough guide only to the size of the bill to be expected at the end of your stay. For latest tariffs, check when booking.

Les Résidences du Colombier *Telephone:* (94) 51.45.92
Route de Bagnols *Telex:* 470328

Fréjus' varied attractions include sandy beaches; a superb cathedral complex, with cloisters, archaeological museum and 5th-century baptistry; and some Roman remains from the days when this was a major port. *Les Résidences* lies 3 km north-west of the town, close to two rather scruffy open-air zoos and a curious raspberry-coloured mosque. 'As devotees of the good old Club Méditerranée, we were thrilled to find echoes of it at this high-spirited holiday hotel where the accent is similarly on get-together fun-and-games. Like the Club's newer *villages*, it is a smart, modern place, set spaciously amid lawns and flowers in its wide park. You can bask by the big swimming pool, or play tennis or ping pong. And twice a week we were regaled with a *soirée dansante et folklorique* – one night, Flamenco guitarists; another, a Tahitian folk-group. The bedrooms are in bungalows spread around the garden, each bearing the name of a Mediterranean island (another Club touch): but they are comfortably modern, *not* straw huts! Some have four beds, for this is a hotel for families. Lunch on the terrace was a lavish help-yourself affair, Club-style, while breakfast went one better than Le Club – it was a self-service brunch lasting all morning, most un-French. Dinners were copious, but the food unremarkable.' *(Jill and Peter Clark)*

Open: 1 April–10 October.
Rooms: 20 double, 40 suites – 40 with bath, 20 with shower, all with telephone, radio and colour TV. (Some rooms on ground floor.)
Facilities: Bars, restaurant, terraces. Conference facilities. Special *soirées*. Garden. Swimming pool, tennis, ping pong, billiards, children's playground. Sandy beach 3 km. English spoken. &.
Location: 3 km NW of Fréjus, just N of the N7 (take the D4 road to Bagnols). Parking.
Credit cards: All major credit cards accepted.
Terms: B & B 200–330 frs; dinner, B & B 300–420 frs. Set meals: lunch 80, 100 frs, dinner 120 frs; full *alc* 150 frs. Reduced rates and special meals for children.

GASSIN, 83580 Var, Provence Map 9

Bello Visto *Telephone:* (94) 56.17.30

'A converted 18th-century grange in one of the best-known of Provençal hill-villages, five miles from St-Tropez. We took our meals on a terrace under tall nettle trees, with a sublime panorama before us of the bay of St-Tropez, the Maures mountains, and the vine-clad hills of the lovely Ramatuelle peninsula – *bello visto* indeed. It was pretty at night too, in a kitschy way, with strings of coloured bulbs. And it was fun observing our fellow-diners, a motley, cosmopolitan *Tropézien* crowd of bohemians, would-be trendies, and the more *outré* kind of tourist. Mainly this is a restaurant, but the few rooms are comfortable, or at least ours was. Run by local people, sometimes a bit too rushed to be very friendly. Good Provençal home cooking, especially the *soupe au pistou* and *soupe de poissons*: the *carte* is very pricey, but the *prix fixe* (65 frs in 1982) is fine value. A sympathetic place for a two- or three-day stay, we felt, more than for a full holiday.' *(John and Ludmila Berry)*

Open: 1 April–30 September. Restaurant closed Tuesday.
Rooms: 9 double – most with bath or shower.
Facilities: Restaurant, terrace.
Location: In the village, which is 7.5 km from St-Tropez.
Terms: Rooms 160–200 frs. Set meals: breakfast 19 frs, lunch/dinner 75 frs.

GIENS, 83400 Hyères, Var, Provence   **Map 9**

Hôtel Le Provençal   *Telephone:* (94) 58.20.09
Place de l'Église

The hilltop village of Giens stands on a peninsula of the same name, south of Hyères. At La Tour Fondue, 2 km away, boats leave regularly for the beautiful island of Porquerolles. '*Le Provençal* is a confident, typical four-star seaside hotel, full of confident well-off families enjoying themselves. It's splendidly sited, on a hill, with its own large garden sloping down in front of it to the sea, some 500 yards away. The balcony of our pleasant bedroom had fine views of this lovely part of the coast. There was plenty for us and our children to do – tennis, a kids' playground, a sea-water pool, and a concrete terrace built on the rocks, where we could bathe or sunbathe (alas, no sand). Lunches were served under the pines, down by the sea (we think this happens only in high season). Food was copious and well cooked, though not in the gastronomic league. One warning: our bedroom facing the sea was quiet, but our daughter whose room was on the other side, facing the village, complained of noises from traffic and late revellers.' *(Peter and Jill Clark)*

Open: 10 February–2 November.
Rooms: 50 double – most with bath or shower, some with balconies overlooking sea.
Facilities: Lift, lounges, bar, restaurant, terrace. Garden with swimming pool, tennis court and children's playground.
Location: On edge of village, which is 12 km S of Hyères.
Credit cards: Diners, Euro.
Terms: Rooms with breakfast 245–400 frs; full board 455–520 frs. Set meals: lunch/dinner 100–170 frs.

GIVRY, 71640 Saône-et-Loire, Burgundy   **Map 8**

Hôtel de la Halle   *Telephone:* (85) 44.32.45

On a side road 9 km west of Chalon-sur-Saône, this modest small hotel is in the centre of a pleasant Burgundy village, facing the old market hall (no longer in use) on the other side of the square. It is itself a venerable building with a fine spiral staircase. The hotel's restaurant, warmly recommended, is much used by locals. Christian Renard, the *patron*, is also the chef, and learned his trade on an Atlantic liner. Warning: front rooms are distinctly noisy. *(E Scott, Patrick Gibbs, and others)*

Open: All year. Closed Monday.
Rooms: 10 – 2 with bath, 4 with shower.

Facilities: Salon, restaurant. Garden. Swimming pools 5 and 8 km away, also swimming in nearby river; walks in woods and vineyards. English spoken.
Location: On a minor road (D981) between Chagny and Cluny.
Credit cards: Access, American Express, Diners.
Terms: Rooms 75–125 frs. Set meals: breakfast 20 frs; lunch/dinner 60–100 frs.

GOUMOIS, 25470 Trevillers, Doubs   Map 8

Hôtel Taillard   *Telephone:* (81) 44.20.75

An elegant and spacious chalet, secluded on the slope of a wooded valley, only 300 metres from the Swiss frontier, between Belfort and Neuchâtel. 'It has a beautiful situation overlooking the river Doubs where it separates France and Switzerland. It must be a fisherman's and walker's paradise. There are only 17 rooms; the ones overlooking the valley are particularly attractive, some with small balconies on which one can have evening drinks or breakfast. The rooms are papered with lovely flowery French wallpapers, and have good cupboard space and usually excellent lighting. Bathrooms vary considerably, and some baths are the little sitting-only type. The Taillard family have owned the hotel for more than a century and cater mainly for people wanting peace, quiet and good food. The staff are friendly and helpful. The dining room overlooks the valley; there are usually enormous vases of flowers, and the meals cater for hearty appetites. Specialities include *jambon de montagne, caquelon de morilles à la crème* and *truite belle goumoise.* The wine list is comprehensive, including some lesser known Jura wines – Meursault, Les Tessous 1975 was FABULOUS.' *(Padi Howard)*

Open: 15 February–31 October. Closed Wednesdays in March and October.
Rooms: 17 double, 3 suites – 10 with bath, 7 with shower, all with telephone. Some with mini-bar. (2 rooms on ground floor.)
Facilities: Salon, TV room, bar, 2 dining rooms, terrace; river, trout fishing; riding and winter sports nearby. English spoken.
Location: 50 km from Montbeliard, 18 km from Maiche on the D437A and D437B. Leave autoroute A36 at Montbeliard Sud or Besançon exits. The hotel is near the church; parking.
Credit card: Diners, Barclay/Visa.
Terms: Rooms 80–150 frs; full board 180–220 frs. Set meals: breakfast 16 frs; lunch/dinner 90–150 frs; full *alc* 140–160 frs. Reduced rates and special meals for children.

LA GRAVE, 05320 Hautes-Alpes   Map 8

Hôtel La Meijette   *Telephone:* (76) 80.05.34

La Meijette, 5,000 feet up, is on the N91 Grenoble–Briançon road where it runs above the Romanche torrent on a ledge which just allows a few houses and a car park. The *Restaurant Panoramique*, a modern addition, beautifully constructed in wood, has been cantilevered out over the Romanche and has spectacular views, also shared by the bedrooms, over the Upper Romanche valley and the high snow mountains – La Meije rises almost to another 9,000 feet only 5 km away. One reader, who has been coming to *La Meijette* since 1967, recommends it as a splendid centre for mountain walks of every standard. Another writes:

'This is as near a perfect hotel for us as any we know – for its combination of setting, unostentatious comfort, very good, homely food, friendly family and possibly the best area for wild flowers known to us (our holidays tend to revolve around this interest). There are some older *chambres grand confort*, but most of the bedrooms are chalet-type and very comfortable. There is a five-course meal each evening and there is a different menu on a two-week cycle. The hotel is run by a delightful family, the Juges. Father and mother are behind the scenes cooking and organizing, the eldest daughter, who speaks good English, runs the hotel and the second daughter runs the restaurant with fascinating efficiency and friendliness. We have watched this hotel improve its rooms and its restaurant since 1973, but its friendly welcome has remained the same. The time to go for mountain flowers is between mid June and mid July – the millions (yes millions) of narcissus and violas are expected to be at their best about the end of June.' *(A H H Stow; also Alison Chesshyre)*

Open: 10 February–30 September. Restaurant closed Tuesday out of season.
Rooms: 18 – 15 with bath or shower and telephone.
Facilities: Large sitting room with open fire, bar, restaurant, sun terrace. Winter sports. English spoken.
Location: On the N91 Grenoble–Briançon road. Hotel is in centre of village; parking.
Terms: Rooms 65–280 frs. Set meals: breakfast 17 frs; lunch/dinner 80–100 frs.

GRIMAUD, 83360 Var, Provence   Map 9

Hostellerie du Côteau Fleuri   *Telephone:* (94) 43.20.17
Place des Pénitents

Grimaud, just inland from St-Tropez, is the kind of Provençal hill village that is now very much *à la mode*: that is, many of its old stone houses have been smartly converted as summer homes for Parisians and others. This may have spoilt the place's authenticity, but at least has given it a new lease of life. As for the Grimaldi feudal castle on the hill above, that is still a peaceful ruin, quite unrestored. The *Côteau Fleuri* is on the edge of the village, an attractive 1900-ish *auberge* in local style, with tiled floors, plenty of flowers, and a friendly atmosphere. There is a piano for guests to use, and a log fire for chilly days. Bedrooms are rather small, but modern, with pretty furnishings and Provençal prints. A terrace leads to a delightful rambling garden slope, with olive trees. Bedrooms and dining room alike have fine views over the Maures mountains, but the sea is not visible. Sound local cooking (dinners only) at reasonable prices. *(Lady Redmond, Mary and Gerald Prescott)*

Open: All year, except Christmas and New Year. Restaurant closed November–March.
Rooms: 14 double – 9 with bath, 5 with shower, all with telephone.
Facilities: Salon with TV and piano, bar, 3 dining rooms. Terrace. Small garden with fine views. Beach 3 km. English spoken.
Location: 3 km from Port Grimaud; 10 km from St-Tropez; in village centre, parking.
Credit cards: Barclay/Visa.
Terms: Rooms with breakfast 250–300 frs; dinner, B & B 320–370 frs. Set meals: dinner 58–68 frs; full *alc* 120 frs.

Le Madrid   *Telephone:* (59) 26.52.12
Place Jean-Toulet

For those with simple tastes or slim budgets, *Le Madrid* is recommended
as a spruce and sympathetic little hotel/restaurant in a Basque seaside
village between Biarritz and St-Jean-de-Luz, run by friendly local people.
It has black beams and white walls in the true Basque style and stands in
the village centre a few minutes' walk from the beach. The dining room,
and some bedrooms, have views of the sea. Decent Basque cooking at low
prices. The only drawback: trains hurtle past on the nearby main line.
(Catharine Edwards)

Open: Easter–end September.
Rooms: 6 double, 1 family – 2 with bath.
Facilities: Dining room with terrace overlooking sea. Beach nearby.
Location: On the coast road between Biarritz and St-Jean-de-Luz; in village
centre; no private parking.
Terms: Half board 125–150 frs. Set meals: lunch/dinner 48–80 frs.

La Châtaigneraie   *Telephone:* (97) 65.99.93/65.98.08
Route Saint Maurice

There are hotels that appeal by the warmth of their hospitality. *La
Châtaigneraie* scores in precisely an opposite way. It offers, for those with
a taste for it, a kind of absolute in luxurious privacy. The hotel itself is a
modern purpose-built manor-house hotel in secluded grounds, about 2
km from the small resort town of Guidel, and 5 km from one end of a
spectacular 16-km stretch of sandy beach, in the direction of Lorient. Lots
of campers and caravan sites in the area, but plenty of beach for all. *La
Châtaigneraie* serves no meals except for a lavish breakfast, and fellow
guests are hardly seen or heard. The rooms, small but hyper-elegant, are
thickly carpeted on all six surfaces – the walls and ceiling in velvet. By
each bed is a console (also cloaked in velvet) which provides controls for
the large TV (no need to get out of bed to change the channel), radio and
clock; there is also a panel of buttons to avoid your having to shout out to
the waiter with your breakfast 'Entrez', 'Attendez', or 'Occupé' as the
case may be. It would make a perfect hotel for a honeymoon, though in
the wrong company *La Châtaigneraie* could well seem like a prison of
padded cells. *(HR)*
   A recent visitor, having read our entry, reports on what he calls 'that
carpeted place . . . It *is* all carpeted, and patterned too! And all over the
ceilings and doors. Terribly camp. Rooms rather small, but *clean* and
reasonable. I suppose they Hoover the ceilings. And the doors have bells
because, with all the padding, they can't knock. Charming owner. I must
go back.' *(Gerald Campion)*

Open: All year.
Rooms: 10 double – all with bath, telephone, TV and radio.
Facilities: Breakfast room. Garden. 5 km from beach. &.

Location: On the D162m 10 km from Lorient, 12 km from Quimperlé. Hotel is 1 km from Guidel on the road to Clohors and Carnoët.
Credit card: Barclay/Visa.
Terms: Rooms 250 frs. Set meal: breakfast 25 frs.

LE HAVRE, 76600 Seine-Maritime, Normandy   Map 8

Grand Hôtel de Bordeaux   *Telephone:* (35) 22.69.44
147 rue Louis-Brindeau   *Telex:* 190428 F

In this big Communist-run city, here is a modern utility hotel, close to the port but fairly quiet: it would make a useful stopover for Southampton ferry tourists. 'Service with a smile: a three-star hotel with many four-star facilities – mini-bar, face cloths and facial tissues in bathroom (now *there's* four-star luxury for you!)' *(Palmer Bayer; also Dr T J David)*

Open: All year.
Rooms: 22 double, 9 single – 20 with bath, 11 with shower, all with direct-dial telephone, colour TV and mini-bar.
Facilities: Salon (no restaurant). English spoken.
Location: In town centre; no private parking.
Credit cards: All major credit cards accepted.
Terms: B & B 150–355 frs. 15% reduction for 8 days or more.

HENNEBONT, 56700 Morbihan, Brittany   Map 8

Château de Locguénolé   *Telephone:* (97) 76.29.04
Route de Port Louis   *Telex:* 950636 CHATEL F

On the south coast of Brittany, near Lorient, and 45 km west of Vannes. This château has been the family home of the de la Sablières since the year 1200; and today, rather than sell it, the Comtesse de la Sablière runs it as an exclusive hotel. 'A graceful mansion situated in acres and acres of its own woodland, with a meadow, stretching from the front of the house to the banks of the river Blavet. On a warm, sunny afternoon, such as it was when I was there, it must be one of the most restful places on earth, with only the birds stamping about in the trees or the occasional fly on booster-jets to disturb the tranquillity. Most of the furniture in the public rooms, and some of the bedroom furniture too, is well over a hundred years old (I had an Empire *escritoire* in my room) as are the prints and pictures that adorn the walls. I start to have reservations, however, when this passion for antique furnishings extends to stair carpets. When new, the plain, scarlet carpet must have glowed like a coal against the dark wood of the stairs; today, it is fifty per cent soiled scarlet and fifty per cent hessian backing that shows.

'The glory of the *Château de Locguénolé*, however, radiates with unmistakable brilliance from its *cuisine*: its preparation and presentation, is proud, caring and truly magnificent. The château is both hotel and restaurant; the latter, justifiably, very popular and well worth its two Michelin stars and three Gault-Millau *toques*. Indeed, at meal times, although the dining-room staff are very efficient and perfectly capable, everyone seems to gravitate towards the dining room, receptionists desert switchboards, and seek to share with the kitchen in its finest hours. Some might think it expensive. Personally, for the setting, the square miles of

307

private quiet, the (rather genteel) charm – perhaps a little frayed in places – but, above all, for the deference and imagination which they extend towards the wholesome ingredients of a good meal, I am happy to pay the price.' More recent visitors confirm this report from last year's guide. 'Fish soup out of this world,' says one. *(Jeff Driver; also R S Ryder, JA)*

Open: 1 March–25 November. Restaurant closed Monday, except July–August and bank holidays.
Rooms: 35 double, 3 suites – all with direct-dial telephone; baby-listening on request. 12 rooms in annexe. (10 rooms on ground floor.)
Facilities: Salons, TV room, music room, bar, dining room; banqueting room, conference facilities. 250 acres park; unheated swimming pool. Tennis 3 km, golf 20 km. On river; 9 km from beaches. Riding nearby. 2 night clubs and cabaret 1 km; discos nearby. English spoken.
Location: 3 km from Hennebont. Take the D781 and travel S for 4 km; sign to hotel is on right. On the highway from Vannes, Auray, Nantes and Rennes use the exit Port Louis.
Credit cards: American Express, Barclay/Visa, Diners.
Terms: Rooms 300–500 frs; B & B 210–330 frs; dinner, B & B 365–490 frs; full board 525–650 frs. Set meals: lunch/dinner 160–280 frs; full *alc* 230 frs. Reduced rates for children sharing parents' room.

L'ILE ROUSSE, 20220 Haute-Corse, Corsica   Map 9

Isola Rossa   *Telephone:* (95) 60.01.32

On Corsica's spectacular north-west coast, L'Ile Rousse is a modish resort with yacht harbour, sandy beaches and a mild climate. 'A delightful family-run hotel, scrupulously clean. Noisy by day as it is on the way from the town to the port (15 minutes' walk into centre of town) but dead quiet at night. Our bedroom was large. Breakfast in garden; no restaurant.' *(Dennis Johnson)*

Open: All year.
Rooms: 20 double or triple – all with bath and telephone. (Some rooms on ground floor.)
Facilities: Garden, terraces. Sandy beaches, yacht harbour.
Location: 400 metres from town centre towards the port; parking.
Credit card: American Express.
Terms: Rooms 130 frs (double), 170 frs (triple). Set meal: breakfast 15 frs. (No restaurant.)

ITTERSWILLER, 67140 Bas Rhin, Alsace   Map 8

Hôtel Arnold   *Telephone:* (88) 85.50.58 and 85.51.18

Itterswiller, a typical village on the Alsace *route du vin*, is within easy reach of Strasbourg (41 km) and Colmar (36 km). The *Arnold* is a small modern hotel built in the local black-and-white half-timbered style, and it lies at one end of the village, its windows looking onto a panorama of vineyards. 'They have no restaurant in the hotel, which makes it wonderfully quiet. Almost opposite, in the village street, they have their own *Weinstube* or restaurant, a bar, and a small shop stocking excellent local souvenirs. The restaurant is "Alsace rustic" in style, many regional dishes are on the menu, the wine and liqueur lists are long. Hotel clients use the restaurant as they wish. The staff are friendly and pleasant, and the Alsatians find the place very popular, which is in itself a tribute.' *(Pamela Vandyke Price)*

Open: All year. Restaurant closed 24 January–18 February and 24 June–12 July.
Rooms: 28 double, 1 suite – 16 with bath, 12 with shower, all with telephone, radio and colour TV, most with balconies.
Facilities: Hall, salon, breakfast room; some conference facilities; restaurant, bar and shop opposite. Garden; river nearby. Private pond for trout fishing. English spoken. &.
Location: On the N425, 40 km SW of Strasbourg; parking.
Credit card: Diners.
Terms: Rooms 215–405 frs. Set meals: breakfast 20 frs; full *alc* 120–160 frs.

JOUCAS, 84220 Gordes, Vaucluse, Provence   Map 9

Le Mas des Herbes Blanches   *Telephone:* (90) 72.00.74

The hamlet of Joucas lies midway between the famous (and now very modish) hill villages of Gordes and Roussillon. Both should be visited – Roussillon for its ochre quarries and its multi-coloured old houses, all shades of pink and yellow; Gordes for the Vasarély museum in its château, and for the nearby lovely Cistercian abbey of Sénanque and the ancient and mysterious *trulli*-like conical stone huts known as *bories*. The *Mas des Herbes Blanches*, too, is built of rough local stone, and stands alone on a hillside looking out across the wide valley to the Lubéron range; there is a swimming pool on its broad open terrace. 'A well-restored Provençal farmhouse in a lovely setting. Very professional and comfortable, run by young hoteliers who had trained in Switzerland. My husband found it too "distant" in atmosphere to be really enjoyable, but it was a very good hotel. Our room was lovely – large, air-conditioned, opening onto a big terrace. Furniture French traditional repro. Breakfasts were superb: fresh fruit juices, lots of coffee, home-made jams, local honey and cheeses. The food was not memorable but good: I remember a delicious green and red pepper mousse.' *(Ann Carr)*

Open: All year except December, January and February.
Rooms: 14 double – all with bath, telephone, radio and television. (3 rooms on ground floor.)
Facilities: Salon, restaurant, bar. Garden with swimming pool. English spoken.
Location: 2.5 km N of Joucas, and 7 km NE of Gordes, by the D102A.
Credit cards: American Express, Diners.
Terms: Rooms 360–470 frs; dinner, B & B 360–650 frs. Set meals: breakfast 35 frs, lunch 135 frs, dinner 160 frs; full *alc* 240 frs. Special meals for children.

JOUÉ-LES-TOURS, 37300 Indre-et-Loire, Loire Valley   Map 8

Hôtel du Château de Beaulieu   *Telephone.* (47) 53.20.26
Route de l'Epend

Stanley Kubrick shot scenes for *Barry Lyndon* in the elegant courtyard of this quintessential 18th-century château on the outskirts of Tours – a suitable base for a Loire holiday. There are seven acres of formal gardens, a swimming pool and mini-golf and, inside, a graceful wide staircase, large rooms furnished in style, and well-decorated bedrooms overlooking the park. The owners, Jean-Pierre Lozay and his Scottish wife, win general praise for their 'delightful hotel', even if their modernization has not been 100 per cent proof: 'Apart from the bed, which may also have been "quintessentially 18th-century", we were very comfortable. Service and food were excellent.' 'Staff were efficient and friendly', runs another report. Note: as often occurs in France in high season, overnight guests must also take dinner. *(M J Corner, R W Stumbo, Paul Vaughan)*

Open: All year.
Rooms: 16 double, 1 single – 9 with bath, 7 with shower, all with telephone. (3 rooms on ground floor in annexe.)
Facilities: 2 sitting rooms (1 with TV), 2 dining rooms; conference room. Large garden with ping pong and boules. Tennis, swimming and mini-golf nearby; riding, fishing, golf, sailing a few km away. English spoken. &.
Location: 4 km SW of Tours by the D86 and D207.
Credit card: Barclay/Visa.
Terms: Rooms 90–320 frs; dinner, B & B (for 2 people staying 3 days or more) 420–550 frs; full board (for 2 people staying 3 days or more) 600–750 frs. Set meals: breakfast 22 frs, lunch/dinner 115–220 frs; full *alc* 130–150 frs. 20–30% reduction in rates November–end March; reduced rates for children.

JUAN-LES-PINS, 06160 Alpes-Maritimes, Provence   **Map 9**

Auberge de l'Esterel   *Telephone:* (93) 61.08.67
21 rue des Iles

'Juan in summer is the noisiest resort on the whole Côte d'Azur, a cross between a mini-Blackpool and a less garish St-Tropez. The *Esterel* happily escapes the din: it's in a quiet side-street half a mile from the centre, yet only five minutes' walk from the beach. It's a simple little family-run hotel, comfortable but unexciting, and the main reason for staying here is the food. The restaurant, separately managed, is run by two young brothers who introduced us to *nouvelle cuisine*. Jacques Plumail acts as *Maître d'hotel*, courteously explaining the dishes, while Christian behind the scenes prepares such delights as *salade tiède de cailles* and *lapin en papillote*. All very civilized and pleasantly informal. Prices are unusually modest for this kind of cooking (75 frs set meal in 1982, with good choice). The dining room's a bit ordinary, but when fine you can eat in the flowery garden.' *(Nicholas Osmond)* Red *toque* in Gault Millau.

Open: Mid-January–November.
Rooms: 16 double – most with shower.
Facilities: Restaurant. Garden.
Location: 300 metres from beach; 600 metres from town centre; parking.
Terms: Rooms 155–220 frs; full board 425–450 frs. Set meals: breakfast 17 frs, lunch/dinner 50–100 frs.

In the case of many continental hotels, especially French ones, we have adopted the local habit of quoting a price for the room whether it is occupied by one or more persons. Rates for B & B, half board, etc., are per person unless otherwise stated.

JUAN-LES-PINS, 06160 Alpes-Maritimes, Provence   Map 9

Hôtel Juana   *Telephone:* (93) 61.08.70
Avenue Georges-Gallice   (93) 61.20.37 (restaurant)
    Telex: 470778 JUANA F

'Expensive, but worth it, was our verdict on this small luxury hotel, well modernized but run in the classic style – service by uniformed staff was efficient but never servile. Our top-floor bedroom was rather too heavily furnished for our taste but superbly equipped, air-conditioned, and with a view of the sea. (Lower-floor rooms, incidentally, look onto pine trees, not the sea). The hotel is out of earshot of raucous downtown Juan, and seems to be an oasis of chic sophistication in this nowadays rather down-market resort. It is screened from the sea by a pine grove, but has its private beach 80 metres away, where we could wind-surf and water-ski and have lunch served to us in our swimsuits. The hotel has a very sleek bar, and an even sleeker clientèle, and the open dining terrace facing the palm-shaded garden is romantically lit at night. Probably the best feature of all is the cooking, by Alain Ducasse, a disciple of Vergé and Guérard. We were delighted by such inventions as *râble de lapereau farci* and *ragout de palourdes*. But what prices! Reckon 300 to 400 frs a head per meal, *tout compris.*' *(Sarah and Peter Abbott)* Michelin rosette and two red Gault-Millau *toques.*

Open: 20 March–20 October.
Rooms: 32 double, 10 single, 5 suites – all with bath, telephone, radio, colour television and air conditioning; babysitting.
Facilities: Hall, salon, bar, restaurant, terrace. Garden; 80 metres from private sandy beach with windsurfing. English spoken. &.
Location: 200 metres from sea, 400 metres from town centre; parking.
Terms: Half board 465–865 frs. Reduced rates for children sharing parents' room; special meals provided.

KAYSERSBERG, 68240 Haut Rhin, Alsace   Map 8

Hôtel les Remparts   *Telephone:* (89) 47.12.12

Kaysersberg, one of the loveliest of Alsatian wine villages, was the birthplace of Albert Schweitzer and has a museum devoted to him. *Les Remparts* is a modern hotel on the outskirts: 'The rooms are excellently equipped, complete with tiny balcony looking out towards the vineyards. It is efficient and completely impersonal. Not for those requiring atmosphere, but a haven of comfort.' *(E Newall).*

    This entry has been endorsed by more recent visitors, though one has complained of the 'sonorities of the plumbing', and another of the 'cold hard strip lighting' and the burgeoning of a building-site close by. No restaurant: but the *Auberge du Tonneau d'Or* has good, cheap Alsatian food. *(B W Ribbons; Mrs R B Richards)*

Open: All year.
Rooms: 29 double – all with bath, telephone, radio, mini-bar and balcony, most with black and white TV. (12 rooms on ground floor.) 6 rooms in annexe.
Facilities: Salon, bar, breakfast room. Tennis and swimming pool 1 km. English spoken. &.

Location: 300 metres from town centre; parking. Kaysersberg is 11 km from Colmar.
Terms: Rooms 200 frs. Set meal: breakfast 16 frs.

LAMASTRE, 07270 Ardèche, Massif Central　　　　　　　　　Map 8

Hôtel du Midi　　　　　　　　　　　　　　　*Telephone:* (75) 06.41.50
Place Seignobos

A pleasant little town on the edge of the Rhône valley, 40 km west of Valence on the road to Le Puy. The hotel is in the market square and is recommended 'for a stop of one or two nights in a small town in the heart of ravishing country. The reception is warm, the rooms large, simply furnished and scrupulously clean. It does one's heart good to see the army of local women Hoovering the stairs, arranging the flowers and polishing the glasses for the day ahead – this sort of family-run hotel is, alas, disappearing rapidly in France. But the main *raison d'être* of the *Midi* is its restaurant (rosette in Michelin): dinner was excellent with five inventive menus ranging from 100 to 250 francs [1982].' There is not much in the way of sitting-room space, and front bedrooms are less quiet than those on the courtyard. *(Geoffrey Sharp; also Conrad Dehn)*

Open: 1 March–15 December except Sunday. Restaurant closed Sunday night and Monday lunch except July/August.
Rooms: 18 double, 4 single – 12 with bath, 3 with shower, all with telephone. (1 room on ground floor.)
Facilities: 2 salons, 3 restaurants. Garden.
Location: Central; parking.
Credit card: Barclay/Visa.
Terms: Rooms 70–170 frs; full board 170–250 frs. Set meals: breakfast 20 frs; lunch/dinner 100–250 frs. Special meals for children.

LANGRES, 52200 Haute-Marne　　　　　　　　　　　　　　Map 8

Grand Hôtel de l'Europe　　　　　　　　　　　*Telephone:* (25) 85.10.88
23–25 rue Diderot

A useful *étape* on the way to Switzerland or the French Alps. 'A delightful place to stop overnight,' writes one reader, endorsing earlier reports; 'we had an attractive bedroom overlooking a courtyard. With it came a gleaming new bathroom – total luxury for 100 francs [1981]. The 60-franc menu was superb.' This is one of the few two-turreted hotels in Michelin also to win a red 'R' for a meal offering specially good value – most places with a red 'R' are in the cheaper one-gable class. And Langres is well worth a visit on its own account – largely 17th- and 18th-century in its architecture, it is steeped in earlier history and surrounded by 5 km of ramparts. The main road bypasses the town, which is therefore quiet at night. *(Alex and Rachel Macdonald; also Mary and Rodney Milne-Day and others)*

Open: All year except 1 October–2 November, the first week in May and on Sunday nights. Restaurant closed Sunday evenings and Monday lunchtime.
Rooms: 24 double, 2 single, 2 suites – 8 with bath, 17 with shower and WC, all with telephone. 9 rooms in annexe.

Facilities: Salons (1 with TV), bar, 2 restaurants. Garden. English spoken.
Location: Between Chaumont (35 km) and Dijon (66 km); railway station 3 km. Central (rooms overlooking the garden are quietest); parking.
Credit cards: Access/Euro/Mastercard, American Express, Barclay/Visa.
Terms: Rooms 90–130 frs. Set meals: breakfast 12 frs; lunch/dinner 40–90 frs.

LAON, 02000 Aisne, Picardy   Map 8

Hôtel de la Bannière de France   *Telephone:* (23) 23.21.44
11 rue F Roosevelt

A thousand years ago, Laon was the capital of France, before Hugues Capet, elected king, decided to move his court to Paris in 987 AD. There is little left in Laon of that distant era, but it is a highly atmospheric town with 13th-century ramparts, on a ridge commanding an immense plain, and the old part is full of fine houses in narrow streets clustering around a magnificent 12th-century cathedral. Reims and Compiègne are both fairly near. *La Bannière de France* stands aloft in the old town in a narrow one-way street (some readers have found the front rooms noisy) and has its own garage. The hotel continues to be popular with those looking for a first or last night's stop, some 3 hours' drive from the Channel ports. Most visitors find the bedrooms clean and comfortable, with attractive old-fashioned furniture, and everyone likes the food, which is mainly classic with 'modern' touches such as *salade de saumon cru au mesclun*. However, one or two readers this past year have found the plumbing poor and the service clumsy and offhand, so we should welcome more reports. *(A J A Leys, Rosamund V Hebdon, Dr and Mrs P M Tattershall, and others)*

Open: All year, except 20 December–10 January.
Rooms: 13 double, 5 single – 5 with bath, 7 with shower, all with telephone.
Facilities: Small bar, 2 dining rooms; banqueting room. English spoken.
Location: Central; hotel has garage (small payment); free car park nearby.
Credit cards: All major credit cards accepted.
Terms: Rooms 70–165 frs. Set meals: breakfast 17 frs; lunch/dinner 58–150 frs (including wine); full *alc* 130 frs. Special meals for children.

LECHIAGAT, 29115 Guilvinec, Finistère   Map 8

Hôtel du Port   *Telephone:* (98) 58.10.10

This village is on the coast of south-west Brittany, in the charming Bigouden country where Breton folk traditions survive most strongly. Quimper is 30 km away. 'The *Hôtel du Port* is really a large French pub, with a big dining room and *chambres*. I have stayed here two years running, and it grows on you. Food is normally excellent and copious – especially the *plateau des fruits de mer*, which is colossal and a speciality. However, when it is the chef's night off, things may slip. The hotel looks out over the harbour basin but is quiet.' *(S W Burden)*

Open: 4 January–30 October, 1–31 December except Christmas and New Year. Closed once a week (day not decided at the time of going to press) in winter.
Rooms: 35 – 8 with bath and WC, 27 with shower (22 of which also have WC), all with telephone, most with mono TV.

Facilities: 5 rooms (some of them for functions). Sea fishing, sailing, sandy beach, swimming pool, riding and tennis nearby.
Location: Turn left at the first traffic light on entering Guilvinec.
Credit cards: Access/Euro/Mastercard, Barclay/Visa, Diners.
Terms: B & B 52.50–145 frs; full board 160–210 frs. Set meals: lunch/dinner 60–190 frs.

LESSAY, 50430 Manche, Normandy　　　　　　　　　　　　　　　**Map 8**

Hostellerie de l'Abbaye　　　　　　　　　　*Telephone:* (33) 46.43.88

A modern and functional but pleasant inn, on the main road 54 km south of Cherbourg; it would make a useful overnight stop on the way to or from Brittany or points south. Lessay has a splendid 11th-century abbey, well restored after its 1944 war damage. And if you are there on 9–12 September, you will find the village holding the leading annual fair in Normandy, including the open-air roasting of sheep and geese. More modestly, the *Hostellerie* contents itself with a red 'R' in Michelin for good food at modest prices. Bedrooms are small but charming, and the welcome most friendly. *(C S Nelles)*

Open: All year, except end September–30 November and Monday.
Rooms: 12 double – most with bath or shower and telephone.
Facilities: Restaurant. Garden.
Location: 54 km S of Cherbourg on the D2.
Terms: Rooms 80–185 frs; full board 160–220 frs. Set meals: breakfast 17 frs, lunch/dinner 70–115 frs.

LEVENS, 06 Alpes-Maritimes, Provence　　　　　　　　　　　　**Map 9**

La Vigneraie　　　　　　　　　　　　　　*Telephone:* (93) 91.70.46
Rue Saint-Blaise

'It is hard to believe that the bustle of Nice is a mere fifteen miles away, when you settle into this quiet and very pretty little family-run hotel, just outside the hill-village of Levens. We found it a good centre for exploring the beautiful Alpine country to the north. The bedrooms are simple but comfortable and amazingly cheap – a mere 80 frs for two in 1982. I can't think how they do it. The Bastiens, a local couple, are charming hosts, and we had a happy time, though young people might find the place a little *too* quiet; it seems to attract mainly the old. The Provençal cooking is rather good, and on fine days you eat out in an idyllic creeper-covered patio. We should have liked a little more choice on the menu.' *(Anthony Day)*

Open: All year, except 3 October–12 December.
Rooms: 20 – 10 with bath or shower, all with telephone.
Facilities: Restaurant. Garden, patio.
Location: 23 km from Nice on the D19; parking.
Terms: Rooms 70–115 frs; full board 140–172 frs. Set meals: breakfast 11 frs; lunch/dinner 45–75 frs.

If you have difficulty in finding hotels because directions given in the Guide are inadequate, please help us to improve them.

LOCHES, 37600 Indre-et-Loire　　　　　　　　　　　　Map 8

Hôtel de France　　　　　　　　　　　　*Telephone:* (47) 59.00.32
6 rue Picois

Loches, a small historic town on the Indre, 41 km south of Tours, is a good centre for touring the Loire châteaux, and also itself has many remarkable buildings – notably in the *cité médiévale* with its ramparts, castle and former torture chamber. Loches was where the French kings kept many of their leading prisoners: but today, reports a reader, its main hotel, the *France*, is a most welcoming place, and inexpensive. It is praised in the French guides, too, for the honest food served at low prices in its 'Louis XV rustic style' dining room. More reports welcome. *(John Mainwaring)*

Open:　All year, except 4 January–10 February, Sunday evening and Monday midday.
Rooms:　22 double – 7 with bath, 10 with shower, all with telephone.
Facilities:　TV room, restaurant. Conference facilities. English spoken.
Location:　In town centre; parking.
Terms:　B & B 66 frs. Set meals: lunch/dinner 35, 47, 64 frs.

LOUVIE-JUZON, 64260 Arudy, Pyrénées-Atlantique　　　Map 8

Hôtel Dhérété　　　　　　　　　　　　*Telephone:* (59) 05.61.01

This village, 20 km south of Pau, amid the soft green hills of Béarn, would make a good centre for exploring the western Pyrenees. A mountain road leads south up the Ossau valley, past the towering Pic du Midi d'Ossau (2,885 metres) and over the Col du Pourtalet into Spain. 'The *Dhérété* is on the outskirts of the village, set back in a garden from the main road to Pau. We liked it very much. Slightly geriatric clientèle (they have two dining rooms, and put children and families in one, others in the other). The food is conscientious, and the first night our dinners included as tender a *côte du mouton* as I have tasted anywhere, a good cheese omelette, trout *meunière* properly done, and a home-made Grand Marnier *parfait* with a good taste. A little sitting room, rather grotty basement bar and breakfast room, tables under the trees outside for drinks, excellent double rooms plus or minus shower with firm beds for about 80 francs [1982], and a charming, efficient young manageress. Also, someone there likes and understands claret.' *(Charles Shepherd)*

Open:　All year, except 15 October–15 November and Wednesday out of season.
Rooms:　18 double – most with shower and telephone.
Facilities:　Small salon, bar/breakfast room, 2 dining rooms. Conference facilities for 40 people. Garden.
Location:　20 km S of Pau; on edge of village, on Pau road; garage and outside parking.
Terms:　Rooms 75–140 frs; full board 115–205 frs. Set meals: breakfast 14 frs, lunch/dinner 55–70 frs.

Please write and confirm an entry when it is deserved. If you think that a hotel is not as good as we say, please write and tell us.

Auberge du Moulin de Mombreux   [GFG]   *Telephone:* (21) 39.62.44

Only 45 km from Calais, a very pretty mill-house by a stream amid meadows, and, moreover, with a Michelin rosette for its food – what more, you might think, could the British tourist ask for as he lovingly savours his first or last taste of a French holiday? Small wonder that our mailbag for the *Moulin* is fatter than for any other French hotel. However, not all the latest reports are as enthusiastic as one that we carried last year: 'The sort of place where your spirits rise as you drive in. Plenty of flowers and garden furniture. Spotlessly clean. You can sit in the front and listen to the noise of the mill race. Really a restaurant with six rooms, small, not luxurious, but very French and very pretty: ours overlooked the gardens where chickens scratched about among the flowers, also cockadoodle-dooed at about 4 a.m. Pleasant people.' Other writers agree that the rooms, though small, are pretty, and the beds very comfortable; but there are some complaints of poor soundproofing ('light sleepers are aware of all the creakings and snorings'). It is also pointed out that the idyllic view from the mill carries the blemish of a huge cement works a mile away.

The bar is elegant, and drinks come with a pleasing variety of *amuse-gueules*. The circular first-floor dining room is set round the old mill-wheel. Here service is generally summed up as 'professional rather than friendly'. *Patron/chef* Jean-Marc Gaudry's cooking is ambitious, quite pricey, and while some readers find it delicious ('extraordinary combination of flavours: sea-food with fruit, for example'), some others think it chi-chi and too bland. More reports welcome. *(Heather Sharland, Di Latham, D R and A J Linnell, AH, JA and others)*

Open: All year except 15 December–5 February. Also closed Sunday evening and Monday.
Rooms: 6 double – 4 with bath, all with telephone.
Facilities: Salon, bar, restaurant. Garden, leading to river with fishing. Tennis and swimming nearby. English spoken.
Location: 2 km W of Lumbres; between the N42 from Boulogne to St-Omer and the D202 Nielles–Lumbres.
Crédit cards: American Express, Diners.
Terms: Rooms 70–120 frs. Set meals (excluding 15% service charge): breakfast 12 frs; lunch/dinner 130–170 frs. Special meals for children.

Hôtel le Montaigu   *Telephone:* (62) 92.81.71

Luz is a summer resort in the central Pyrenees, within easy reach of Lourdes and of such beauty spots as the spectacular Cirque de Gavarnie. 'A modern hotel on the outskirts, run with charm and efficiency by a young couple, and very good value for money. The rooms are comfort-

---

We should be glad to hear of good hotels in Lyon.

---

able, most with splendid views of the surrounding peaks. The food is excellent, with a five-course dinner for pensionnaires. It was hard to take the decision to move on.' *(J A F Somerville)*

Open: 15 December–30 April, 1 June–30 September.
Rooms: 20 double, 3 triple – 4 with bath, 12 with shower, all with telephone.
Facilities: Lift, salon, bar, restaurant; discothèque in bar, folk evenings in high season; banqueting/conference facilities. Garden with terraces. Horse trekking, skiing, mountain excursions. Tennis, swimming pool in village. English spoken.
Location: At Esquièze-Sère, in the N outskirts; parking.
Terms: Rooms 120–150 frs; dinner, B & B 130–150 frs; full board 150–180 frs. Set meals: breakfast 15 frs, lunch/dinner 60 frs. 30% reduction for children under 7; special meals provided.

MARSEILLE, 13007 Bouches-du-Rhône   Map 9

Résidence Bompard   *Telephone:* (91) 52.10.93
2 rue des Flots Bleus   *Telex:* 410 777

Up on the steep hill that rises south from the Vieux Port and is crowned by that hideous local landmark, the basilica of Notre-Dame-de-la-Garde. 'In this noisy, congested city the down-town hotels are mostly a dreary lot, so we were amazed and delighted to find the *Bompard*, set quietly in its own seven-acre park yet only a mile from the town centre (La Canebière). You can loll on a broad patio under sophora trees – quite idyllic. The owners, two eager Lebanese brothers, have picked up some motel-type ideas from their American travels: for example, some of the rooms, including ours, are bungalows with kitchenettes, and there are communal washing-lines – decidedly un-French. We could see the sea from our balcony. The hotel is modern and its bedrooms functional, but neat. The attractive panelled bar reminded us of some English pub. Altogether, the *Bompard* is a splendid antidote to the rigours of Marseille, and its prices are startingly low.' *(Mary and Gerald Prescott)*

Open: All year.
Rooms: 46 double (some in bungalows) – all with bath, telephone, mini-bar, radio and mono TV; tea-making facilities in bungalows. (12 rooms on ground floor.)
Facilities: 2 salons, bar, conference room, terrace. 7 acres park. Beach 500 metres. English spoken.
Location: On a winding side-road, 500 metres W of the basilica, and 400 metres above the coast road (corniche); parking.
Credit cards: American Express, Diners.
Terms: B & B 128–213 frs. (No restaurant.)

MARTIN-ÉGLISE, 76370 Neuville Les Dieppe, Normandy   Map 8

Auberge du Clos Normand   *Telephone:* (35) 82.71.01 or 82.71.31
22 rue Henri IV

Six km from Dieppe: an ideal first or last night's stop, but also an easy place to go for a weekend in France without the bother of taking the car. And the point about this restaurant with rooms is that, while very close to a Channel port, it is extremely French. The bedrooms are in a separate rather dilapidated building, perhaps once a stables or a hayloft, with a romantic garden which has a pavilion for eating out in summer, and a stream; it's very quiet except for farmyard noises, emanating from the farm which lies just across the stream. 'There is something Chekhovian about the place,' wrote one reader; 'it is slightly decrepit, but has great charm and is not expensive.' Not all our correspondents have been equally ravished by the Chekhovian charm. Some of the rooms are decidedly modest, and dinner (*à la carte* only) is obligatory. The food is typically Norman: lashings of cream, butter and calvados and no nonsense about *nouvelle cuisine.*

'Six of us went for Bank Holiday weekend, including two small children. The rooms are in an old barn, each with a little balcony and creeper growing up the outside of the building – so very pretty. All our rooms were pleasantly furnished and the beds *really* comfortable. The food – well, it really was lovely. Perhaps the atmosphere contributed a lot to this feeling. The wife takes the orders, fetches the drinks and serves the tables, while the husband-cum-chef does all the cooking at the end of the long room, in full view of everyone. Coffee is made in those rather ancient machines and tastes marvellous! Altogether one feels one has discovered a place that has not been hit by tourism and still remains enchanting and rural. It's a magic place for a weekend away.' That 1981 rave has since been endorsed by another visitor: 'In March our bedroom was splendidly warm, as was Madame's welcome. We would strongly recommend the deliciously garlicky pink lamb.' *(T Brigden Shaw, Val Bethell and others)*

Open: March–November, except Monday evening and Tuesday.
Rooms: 7 double, 1 single – 3 with bath, 1 with shower, 3 with basin and bidet, in separate building in the garden.
Facilities: Lounge, restaurant. Garden with large lawn and stream flowing at the bottom; pavilion for outdoor summer meals. Function ballroom below bedroom annexe.
Location: 6 km from Dieppe; off the D1 to Neufchâtel.
Credit cards: American Express, Barclay/Visa.
Terms: Double rooms 70–140 frs. Set meal: breakfast 14 frs; full *alc* 90–160 frs.

MERCUREY, 71640 Givry, Saône-et-Loire, Burgundy   **Map 8**

Hôtellerie du Val d'Or   *Telephone:* (85) 47.13.70

In a village producing one of the region's great wines, this restaurant-with-rooms is a good centre for touring Burgundy vineyards. It serves excellent local food (rosette in Michelin) to merry cohorts of Burgundians. 'Our bedroom, though tiny, had been recently redecorated, in excellent taste. The restaurant is a cosy room with a fireplace, and the owners were much in evidence during the meal, showing great concern that we enjoyed it. Out of the ten hotels we visited on our holiday this was the only one to offer an outstanding soup. My *coq au vin* was ordinary, but a replacement was offered; my husband's Charolais beef was excellent.' *(Caroline D Hamburger)*

Open: All year, except 15 September, 15 December–8 January. Closed Sunday evening November–15 March and Monday, except public holidays. Restaurant also closed Tuesday midday 15 March–15 November.
Rooms: 11 double, 1 single – 5 with bath, 5 with shower. 5 with colour TV, all with telephone.

Facilities: Reception, salon, bar, 2 restaurants. Garden. English spoken.
Location: 13 km from Chalon-sur-Saône. Leave the autoroute at the Chalon exit and take the D978 Autun–Nevers road, then a turning to the right to Mercurey; parking.
Terms: Rooms 75–190 frs. Set meals: breakfast 18 frs; lunch/dinner 65, 100 and 180 frs; full *alc* 200 frs.

MEXIMIEUX, 01800 Ain   Map 8

Hôtel Claude Lutz   *Telephone:* (74) 61.06.78
17 rue de Lyon

A town just west of the Jura foothills, on the old main road from Lyon to Geneva. The *Claude Lutz*, a classic small-town *auberge*, has a high reputation locally for the quality and copiousness of its *cuisine bressane* (rosette in Michelin), and its dining room is often packed out. 'Anyone going near this hotel who enjoys *superb* food should visit it. My wife had *fricassée de volaille de Bresse à la crème*; I had sliced breast of duck, and it was beautiful. The hotel is in need of decoration, and the restaurant might be considered drab, but the reception and service were most friendly and welcoming – particularly creditable as there was a large wedding reception in the hotel the night we dined. We stayed there because we wanted to visit the bird sanctuary at Villars-les-Dombes (France's Slimbridge). It was sad to see all the eagles caged (though they are obviously well looked after for they are in splendid condition), but the large *étang* has a huge range of free duck and geese.' *(A H H Stow)*

Open: All year, except 16 October–8 November, and 1 week in February.
Rooms: 17 double – 5 with bath, 10 with shower, all with telephone.
Facilities: TV room, bar, restaurant; conference facilities. Garden. English spoken.
Location: 36 km NE of Lyon on the N84. In village centre; private parking. There could be some noise from the autoroute.
Terms: Rooms 70–140 frs. Set meals: breakfast 16 frs; lunch/dinner 50–160 frs; full *alc* 160 frs. Special meals for children.

MEYRONNE, Nr Souillac, 46200 Lot   Map 8

Hôtel La Terrasse   *Telephone:* (65) 32.21.60

A modest and very cheap but highly *sympathique* hotel housed in an old monastery above the Dordogne river, run by a hard-working lady and her nephew. The food is excellent, accommodation on the basic side. 'One of the secret sanctuaries in our life, and should never have been revealed to the tourist world. Is nothing sacred?' was an anguished cry from a reader. Since then, we have had grateful letters from those who have benefitted from the generosity of our correspondents. As we have said before, highly individual establishments like this one need all the encouragement they can get: they thrive on recommendations and die from neglect.

We think the report below catches the character of *La Terrasse* pretty well: 'We started badly, cold and tired, and wanted above all else a soothing hot bath, which of course there wasn't. A dribbling shower and handkerchief towel didn't help, nor did the cold lino. But the warmth of the welcome more than compensated. Log fires were lit and free drinks offered. Our first three courses for dinner by the fire were vegetable soup, *pâté de fois gras truffé*, and surprisingly a pink grapefruit. For one awful moment we thought this must be starters, meat and dessert, but no, along came in bewildering succession: *jambon cru, veau aux champignons, haricots verts,* cheese and oranges flambéd in rum. I had admired the first *muguets du bois* (lilies of the valley) on the tables. When we left, they were wrapped up and left in the car. Perhaps April was too early. We loved every minute of our three days there, but it would have been pleasant to have sat on that terrace overlooking the Dordogne, and to have been a bit warmer in bed (extra blankets hastily provided when discomfort discovered). Next time we shall go later and for longer.' A more recent visitor adds: 'Our spacious room was furnished with antiques, including armchairs, delightful for enjoying the views down the river – the best 90 francs' worth of bedroom we experienced.' *(Patricia Fenn; also Rebecca Foster and others)*

Open: 1 March–1 December.
Rooms: 16 double (6 in annexe).
Facilities: Dining room; also meals on terrace overlooking the Dordogne. Small garden.
Location: Between Souillac and Rocamadour, 12 km from both.
Restriction: No children under 5.
Credit card: American Express.
Terms: Rooms 50–90 frs; dinner, B & B 80–90 frs; full board 100–120 frs. Set meals: breakfast 10 frs; lunch/dinner 50–80 frs. Reduced rates for children.

MEYRUEIS, 48150 Lozère, Massif Central   **Map 8**

Château d'Ayres   *Telephone:* (66) 45.60.10

Originally a 12th-century monastery, this old château (much rebuilt) stands in open country 1½ km from Meyrueis, on the edge of the Cévennes National Park and the upland limestone *causses*, and not far from the gorges of the Jonte and the Tarn. 'The landscape, described by Stevenson in his *Travels with a Donkey*, is really superb, and the hotel is a real discovery, run with great professional skill by Chantal and Jean-François de Montjou. Large rooms overlook a park of giant sequoia, chestnuts, cedars. There is an air of total calm (occasionally disturbed by music from the distant village) and the service is of impeccable courtesy and friendliness. A *table d'hôte* at 89 frs [1982] which is always good (especially the soups and roast meats) and a good wine list. Very good value indeed. We shall return.' *(Prof. Robert Cahn)*

Open: 1 January–15 October.
Rooms: 23 double, 1 single, 3 suites – 20 with bath, 4 with shower, all with telephone.
Facilities: 3 salons, restaurant. Park.
Location: 1 km SE of Meyrueis.
Terms: B & B 125–205 frs; dinner, B & B 200–300 frs; full board 260–360 frs. Set meals: lunch/dinner 98 frs; full *alc* 135 frs.

We should be glad to hear of more good hotels in Corsica.

MIOMO, 20200 Bastia, Haute-Corse, Corsica

Map 9

Hôtel les Sablettes   *Telephone:* (95) 33.26.13

Miomo is a seaside village 5 km north of Bastia, Corsica's largest and busiest town (the Vieux Port should be visited, also the Genoese citadel with its museum and hanging gardens). Northwards stretches the beautiful wild peninsular of Cap Corse, where old villages perch up in the hills. 'On the main road, on a narrow strip of land between it and the sea, *Les Sablettes* is a kind of motel with restaurant. We ate outside on the large dining terrace under a network of vines with lights strung from pillar to pillar – a very popular eating place for locals – and here we enjoyed one of the best meals we had in Corsica, with half a lobster as just one course on the 4-course 75-franc menu [1982]! But in the hotel we felt the lack of a woman's touch – unswept litter, stained carpet, very basic bedroom furnishings, no flowers anywhere. However, worth visiting for the meal alone.' *(Angela and David Stewart)*

Open: February–November.
Rooms: 48 double – most with bath or shower and telephone.
Facilities: Restaurant, terrace.
Location: 5 km N of Bastia; garage and outside parking.
Terms: Rooms 115–285 frs; full board 265–330 frs. Set meals: breakfast 17 frs, lunch/dinner 60–95 frs.

MIONNAY, 01390, near Lyon

Map 8

Alain Chapel   *Telephone:* (7) 891.82.02

Alain Chapel was chosen *'premier cuisinier'* of France in 1980, and Gault-Millau in 1982 were still awarding his cooking their top rating of 19 out of 20. His restaurant, in an otherwise undistinguished village, has long carried Michelin's three rosettes, as well as four red knives and forks. He is a great innovator, and changes his menu regularly according to the season and what is available in the market. His is a light imaginative style of cooking – *nouvelle cuisine*-ish. Some, no doubt, would vote him the greatest chef in the world, though how any judge could survive such arbitration is difficult to imagine. But *Alain Chapel* also has 13 bedrooms (usually booked out weeks ahead). They are in the best of good taste, though, for one reader, *much* too expensive, and lacking certain contemporary refinements such as a mini-bar and a television set. On the question of food, there is no equivocation: 'The best food I have ever eaten – with *crise de foie* to match, the next day.' *(Paul Levy; endorsed by the Editor, with no reservations, no complaints, no* crise de foie*)*

Open: All year, except January, Monday (except public holidays) and Tuesday lunch.
Rooms: 13 double – all with bath and telephone, 1 with colour TV.
Facilities: Salon/bar with TV, restaurant, private dining rooms. Garden. Swimming pool nearby. English spoken.
Location: 20 km N of Lyon on N83. Coming from Paris on the autoroute A6 take first exit after Villefranche and take the D51 S.
Credit cards: American Express, Diners.
Terms: Rooms 300–420 frs. Set meals: breakfast 41 frs; lunch/dinner 275 frs (excluding service). Special meals for children.

Tour d'Esquillon *Telephone:* (93) 75.41.51

Within easy reach of Cannes and St-Raphaël, Miramar is a small but
select resort on the astonishing Esterel coast with its rugged red rocks.
Close by is the bizarre new holiday village of Port la Galère, a Mediterranean fantasy in Guadiesque style. 'We enjoyed our stay at this smart
modern holiday hotel, set high on a cliff facing Cannes across the bay. Our
bedroom was not large, but had a spectacular sea view from its balcony.
The hotel's own funicular leads down to its private beach just below – alas,
no more than a concrete platform, for there is no sand here. But it was
good to be able to eat lunch down *on* the beach. We found the food a little
unremarkable for the fairly high prices charged. But the main dining room
is really glamorous, with cheerful decor and big picture-windows. The
manager and his staff speak English.' *(Anthony Hildesley)*

Open: 1 February–15 October.
Rooms: 20 double, 4 single, 4 suites – all with bath and shower, telephone and
colour TV.
Facilities: Salon, dining room. 2-acre garden; funicular to beach platform where
lunches served. English spoken.
Location: 15 km from Cannes.
Restriction: No children under 5.
Terms: Rooms 300 frs; dinner, B & B 450 frs; full board 550 frs. Set meal:
breakfast 30 frs.

MOLINES-EN-QUEYRAS, 05390 Hautes-Alpes Map 8

Hôtel L'Équipe *Telephone:* (92) 45.83.20
Route St-Véran

Amid the ski-slopes of the snowy Alps, south-east of Briançon. Nearby is
the 13th-century fortress of Château-Queyras, and the isolated village of
St-Véran, which at 2,040 metres claims to be the highest in Europe. Here
a rough narrow road runs into Italy via the Col Agnel. 'A Belgian couple
were at the hotel for the 18th time, and said they never tired of the walks
around this hotel where the tourist brochures claim over 2,000 different
flowers. The friendly reception and the simple, wholesome food – with
more than a touch of flair – greatly pleased us (menus at 39, 62 and 84
francs in 1982). A new annexe was being completed when we were there.'
(A H H Stow)
   This recommendation, which appeared in the 1982 edition, has been
strongly endorsed by a more recent visitor: 'Our fourth visit to the
Queyras and the first time that we had been comfortably lodged. Both M.
and Mme Catalin are charming and really welcoming to their guests. Our
room was delightful, with views of mountains, a sofa (!) and an excellent
bathroom.' *(Alison Chesshyre)*

Open: 11 June–11 September, 18 December–20 April.
Rooms: 13 double, 2 single – 10 with bath, 2 with shower, all with telephone. 7
rooms in annexe.
Facilities: TV room, bar, restaurant; fondue party with dancing once a week.
Good walks in area and winter sports: skiing holidays.

Location: 1 km from the village of Molines on the road to St-Véran.
Terms: Rooms 45–81 frs; dinner, B & B 115–165 frs; full board 150–205 frs. Set meals: breakfast 18 frs; lunch/dinner 39–84 frs; full *alc* 74 frs. Special meals for children.

MONTBAZON, 37250 Indre-et-Loire   Map 8

Château d'Artigny   *Telephone:* (47) 26.24.24
                                         Telex: 750900

For those who like their hotels grand in the old style, the *Château d'Artigny* would be an obvious place to recommend as a base for touring the châteaux of the Loire. It is 13 km from Tours, and stands in its own park above the valley of the Indre. It looks like a peerless 18th-century château itself, but appearances deceive; it was in fact built in the 18th-century style just before the First World War by the famous parfumier, François Coty. He didn't spare much in the way of expenses; there is a huge staircase in polished limestone, an imposing gallery, a brass-inlaid marble floor in the dining room, delicate wood-carving in the library and so on. There are plenty of trimmings outside too: swimming pool, tennis, 50 acres of lawns and wooded walks. Sophisticated Parisian clientèle. Chamber music concerts are held from October to March. 'Elegant, expensive but well worth it. Everything you would want for the high-life including a restaurant which is much admired by Michelin and, more to the point in my opinion, Gault-Millau.' *(Charles Osborne)*

Open: All year except 1 December–10 January.
Rooms: 46 double, 4 single, 6 suites – 54 with bath, 2 with shower, all with telephone; baby-sitting facilities. 20 rooms in 3 annexes.
Facilities: Lifts; 3 salons, TV room, bar, 2 dining rooms; conference facilities. Large garden with 2 tennis courts, heated swimming pool, ping pong; fishing, riding, rowing; golf 12 km away. English spoken.
Location: Leave the N10 at Montbazon, 10 km S of Tours. At Montbazon turn right on the D17 towards Azay-le-Rideau. 2 km on left is private road leading to Château.
Credit card: Barclay/Visa.
Terms (excluding service):   Rooms 170–500 frs; dinner, B & B 340–840 frs; full board 435–940 frs. Set meals: breakfast 32 frs; lunch/dinner 130–250 frs; full *alc* 300 frs. Reduced rates and special meals for children.

MONTBAZON, 37250 Indre-et-Loire   Map 8

La Domaine de la Tortinière   *Telephone:* (47) 26.00.19
                                         Telex: BOY 750806 162Y

The *Tortinière* may be slightly less grand, and gastronomically less outstanding, than its larger rival 3 km away, the *d'Artigny* (see above). But its credentials as a Loire château are more genuine: it is real Second Empire, and no mere 20th-century pastiche. White-walled and grey-towered, it stands amid lovely trees in a 37-acre park above the valley of the Indre. Its *patronne*, Madame Olivereau-Capron, has been known to go to fantastic pains to satisfy her guests' caprices, and today she is still winning their praises: 'A marvellous château with a wonderful view despite modern structures in the valley. The staff were the best we found on our 10-day trip, and the dinner was out of this world. My parents had a turret room, well worth asking for. The *large* bathroom was an added luxury.' *(Marilee Thompson Duer; also Mrs C Smith)*

Open: 1 March–15 November. Restaurant closed Monday, and Tuesday midday. 1 March–1 April and 1 October–15 November.
Rooms: 21 double, 7 suites – 20 with bath. 1 with shower, all with telephone, 3 with colour TV; baby-sitting on request. (5 rooms on ground floor.)
Facilities: Salon, TV room, 2 dining rooms; conference facilities. 100 acres grounds bordering on the river Indre with fishing, boating, swimming pool.
Location: 1.5 km N of Montbazon; Tours 13 km; Azay-le-Rideau 26 km; Chenonceaux 34 km; Loches 40 km.
Credit cards: Access/Euro/Mastercard, Barclay/Visa.
Terms: Rooms 205–485 frs; suites 590–690 frs; dinner, B & B 285–590 frs. Set meals: breakfast 30 frs; full *alc* 150 frs.

MONTE CARLO, Principality of Monaco   **Map 9**

Monte Carlo Beach Hôtel   *Telephone:* (93) 78.21.40
St-Roman, 06190 Roquebrune-Cap-Martin   in UK ring (01) 491 7431
           in USA ring (800) 221 4708

The address of this hotel may look confusing, for in fact it is just inside France, in the commune of Roquebrune. But in all other ways it really belongs to Monaco: it is at the eastern end of Monte Carlo Beach, and its owners are the mighty Société des Bains de Mers, the Monegasque State giant that seems to own nearly everything in the tiny Principality. So we list it under Monte Carlo.

'This delightful place is much smaller than the other luxury hotels in Monte Carlo and in many ways is pleasanter for a true seaside holiday, in this brash city of skyscrapers and big business. The hotel stands quietly on its own at the end of a beach (imported sand), and is right next to a lido and beach club which is free to hotel guests – we could walk from our bedroom in swimming-clothes to go bathing. The lido has a heated swimming pool and a massage-parlour; it will teach you waterskiing, and will even look after your children all day if you wish. We were delighted with our bedroom, newly-decorated in pale green, supremely comfortable, and with a wide balcony facing the sea. Service was most attentive. The hotel and the lido have three restaurants. We chose *Le Rivage*, which is right on the beach: everyone was bronzed and near-naked, and at the next table was the American Negress singing-star from the Casino's cabaret. The food, mainly fish, was nothing special, but the setting was certainly glamorous.' *(Jenny Towndrow)*

Open: April–October. Restaurant open June–September.
Rooms: 46 – all with direct-dial telephone, air-conditioning, TV and mini-bar.
Facilities: Lift, 3 restaurants. Adjacent lido and beach club with heated swimming pool, massage, waterskiing, screened-off sun-terrace for nudist (if desired) sunbathing; tennis and golf nearby.
Location: At E end of Monte Carlo beach, about 1 mile NE of Casino.
Credit cards: All major credit cards accepted.
Terms: Rooms 630–860 frs. No *pension* terms. Set meal: breakfast 40 frs. All restaurant meals *à la carte*, about 170–230 frs (excluding wine).

Procrastination is the thief of the next edition.

MONTICELLO, 20220 l'Ile Rousse, Corsica   Map 9

Hôtel A Pastorella   *Telephone:* (95) 60.05.65

Monticello is a medieval clump of dwellings on a hill, 180 metres high above the port and beaches of L'Ile Rousse, one of the island's smartest resorts. Frank Muir first introduced us to the Corsican idyll of the modest *A Pastorella*: 'It was built about 20 years ago, so the walls are thin and it can be a bit noisy, but it is clean, bright and happy. The food is plentiful and cheap, usually beginning with a real soup, then moving on to something small and interesting like something stuffed with something else. . . .' Since then, other praise has flowed in. 'A winner – we toasted Frank Muir. A cool white dining room with polished dark furniture, bright daisies on the tables and glorious views from the windows and balcony. M. Martini is a cheerful and gentle host who murmurs the menu of the day confidentially to the diners, no menu appearing on paper. The children and their cousins work efficiently in the dining room and Grandfather Martini grows the vegetables, besides minding his sheep. Clearly the family are a local institution. And the silence at night was lovely – no luxury here, but a perfect base for the hill-walker.'

Another couple add: 'The bar is the focal point of the village for all the locals and the whole place bustles with activity. The rooms were slightly old-fashioned, the plumbing likewise, but the food was simple country cuisine, delicious and ample.' Some rooms are very small, and those in the converted cellar annexe can be stuffy: it is best to book early and get a room which 'opens on a stupendous view'. *(Sean and Eithne Scallan, Angela and David Stewart, Frank Muir, and others)*

Open: 1 March–30 October.
Rooms: 15 – all with shower. (5 rooms in annexe.)
Facilities: Salon with TV, bar, restaurant. Garden. Beach 4 km.
Location: Ile-Rousse 3 km.
Terms: Rooms 100–135 frs; dinner, B & B 185–190 frs; full board 195–390 frs. Set meals (excluding service charge): breakfast 18 frs; lunch/dinner 65 frs; full *alc* 137 frs.

MONTPELLIER, 34000 Hérault, Languedoc   Map 9

Demeure des Brousses   *Telephone:* (67) 65.77.66
Route de Vauguières

An 18th-century Languedocian *mas* (country house), set in a 6-acre park with tall, majestic old trees. The elegant interior furnishings are mostly Louis XV and XVI in style. It is just off the A9 autoroute, 3 km from Montpellier and 6 km from sandy beaches. One visitor was irked by the constant low hum from the motorway, but other reports have been entirely positive. 'From the moment we arrived, we felt as though someone had turned the clock back 50 years. What a pleasure it was – faded opulence maybe, but we enjoyed the whole scene. Donkey sitting outside the front door, a horse strolling outside our bedroom window at the back. A lovely place to unwind quietly, away from the rush of life, and good value. The hotel's restaurant, *Le Mas*, is run as a separate business: we had a good set meal [100 frs in 1982] and good local wine.' The large restaurant faces onto gardens, and its much-praised *cuisine* has more than a touch of the *nouvelle*: one speciality is pigeon soup with oysters. *(Peter Marshall)*

Open: April–October. Restaurant closed 15–31 January, Sunday evening and Monday out of season.
Rooms: 13 double, 5 single – 17 with bath, 1 with shower, all with telephone. (1 room on ground floor.)
Facilities: Hall, 2 salons (1 with TV), restaurant adjoining. Park with orangery. 5 km from sandy beach with safe bathing, sailing and watersports; riding, tennis, bowling 10 minutes away. English spoken.
Location: 3 km E of centre of Montpellier, off the A9. Leave the A9 at exit Montpellier Est. Go towards Fréjorgues. After 1 km, at crossing, go towards Boirargues, after 80 m go towards Montpellier for about 1 km.
Credit cards: American Express, Diners.
Terms: B & B 130–220 frs. Set meals: breakfast 20 frs; lunch/dinner at *Le Mas* 120–180 frs.

MONTPELLIER, 34000 Hérault, Languedoc   Map 9

Hôtel de Noailles   *Telephone:* (67) 60.49.80
2 rue des Ecoles-Centrales

The *Noailles* is in the *vieille ville*, a network of quiet alleyways, some now closed to traffic, that forms the kernel of this, one of the most graceful of southern French cities. Near the interesting Fabre museum, and 500 metres from the elegant Peyrou gardens, the hotel is a converted 17th-century mansion, tastefully if rather severely furnished. A couple exult in its contrast with modernism: 'After Frantels [a sophisticated French hôtel chain], etc., the bliss and bargain of the year. Quiet. Excellently decorated, really large bedroom and bathroom, individually furnished. Particularly caring staff. No restaurant.' *(R G and E Tennant)*

Open: All year, except approx. 20 December–5 January.
Rooms: 27 double, 3 single – 18 with bath, 12 with shower, all with telephone. (1 room on ground floor.)
Facilities: Salon.
Location: Central. Nearby parking not easy: the hotel advises guests to use the underground car park in the place de la Comédie (300 metres to south), and will refund the cost of entry if you keep your car-park receipt.
Credit cards: All major credit cards accepted.
Terms: B & B 179–229 frs. (No restaurant.)

MONTREUIL, 62170 Pas-de-Calais   Map 8

Château de Montreuil   [GFG]   *Telephone:* (21) 81.53.04
4 chaussée des Capucins

This hotel, 38 km south of Boulogne, just off the N1 to Paris, has long been a favourite first or last halt in France for British holidaymakers, who have relished its comfort, style and fine cuisine. It is a large old house set in a walled garden, close to the ruined citadel in a quiet part of the medieval hilltop town of Montreuil. The rooms are furnished in a variety of styles: they have polished tiled floors with rugs – some have panelled walls and fireplaces – and one even has plaster monkeys as a wall decoration over the bed. The large bedrooms with baths set in mirrored alcoves have a faded Thirties glitter. Drinks and snacks can be taken in the garden; there is a swimming pool for fine weather.

In 1982 the hotel came under a new ownership already very familiar to gourmets (and the *beau monde*) in the London area. The new resident owners are *protéges* of the famous Roux brothers – they of *Le Gavroche* and the *Waterside Inn* at Bray. Christian Germain, hitherto *chef de cuisine* at Bray, is now *patron/chef* at Montreuil, running the hotel with his wife Lindsay, in business partnership with the Roux. The Germains tell us they are renovating, and their specialities are *mousseline d'huîtres au vinaigre de framboises* and *magret de canard à l'ail doux* – very Roux-ish. First reports on the new regime suggest that standards are being maintained, though service is said to be slow. More verdicts, please, on this bid by the Roux empire to sponsor a barony on their native French soil.

Open: Mid February–end December, except Christmas Day.
Rooms: 10 double, 2 single, 1 suite – 10 with bath, 2 with shower, all with telephone. (Suite in annexe. 1 ground floor room.)
Facilities: Bar, salon, restaurant, conference facilities. Garden with swimming pool. 18 km from sandy beach at Le Touquet. English spoken.
Location: 38 km S of Boulogne, just off the N1; hotel is opposite the citadel; parking.
Credit cards: American Express, Barclay/Visa, Diners.
Terms: Rooms (including breakfast) 250–450 frs. Set meals: lunch 100 frs, dinner 160 frs. Full *alc* 160 frs. Special meals for children.

MONT-ST-MICHEL, 50116 Manche, Normandy   Map 8

Hôtel La Mère Poulard   *Telephone:* (33) 60.14.01

Mont-St-Michel, that spectacular outcrop of pyramidal granite rising out of the sea at high tide – at once a fortress, a town and one of the great Benedictine monasteries of France – is inevitably a mecca for pilgrims, both religious and lay. A visit is rewarding even if made in the company of a milling throng, but there is a lot to be said for an overnight stay: you can appreciate the aura of the place when the crowds have left in the evening and the amazing abbey can be visited early the following morning before the crowds arrive. *La Mère Poulard* is *the* hotel of the town, facing you as soon as you pass through the rampart gates. It isn't the only hotel (the *Mouton Blanc* has been recommended to us as a decent cheaper alternative), but *Mère Poulard* is the place with character and tradition, and also with a restaurant long famous for its omelettes and now renowned too for its *nouvelle cuisine* (3 prized red *toques* in Gault Millau). 'Very comfortable, well-run, excellent food.' 'We had a large and beautiful bedroom. . . . To the large party of Americans staying that night, the ritual beating of the eggs in a copper bowl was as a cabaret, and cameras clicked and flashed.' *(William Goodhart; David and Daphne Marshall; and others)*

Open: 1 April–1 October.
Rooms: 24 double, 3 triple – 14 with bath, 8 with shower, all with telephone.
Facilities: Salon with TV, restaurant, omelette room. English spoken.
Location: 54 km from Dinan.
Restriction: No babies in restaurant.
Credit cards: American Express, Diners.
Terms: Dinner, B & B 224–372 frs. Set meals: lunch/dinner 130–350 frs; full *alc* 200–250 frs.

Hôtel du Tribunal   *Telephone:* (33) 25.04.77
6 place du Palais

The Perche area of Normandy is quite distinctive: an undulating landscape of wooded hills and wide green valleys, full of charming villages.
The manor houses of the district have their own character too, being in
effect small castles, complete with watch-towers and turrets. Montagne-
au-Perche, still partly fortified, is the former capital, with a fine
flamboyant Gothic church. The *Hôtel du Tribunal* was first recommended
to us by the late David Garnett. It is an unpretentious old-fashioned inn
on the site of the old law courts. Prices are exceptionally low. More than
one couple this year found the place altogether too basic – a bed with no
springs, rickety furniture, etc. But the hotel has its supporters:

'From the minute we arrived this was a delightful and charming place
with lots of character. To be led through the beautiful dining room, across
a lovely little courtyard to our room overlooking the courtyard was
breathtaking. The room was lovely (simple) and the only problem was a
missing door handle to the adjacent WC/bathroom. It was a really
romantic experience! We had a good meal, and the *patronne* who gave us
breakfast was very kind and friendly. Very good value.' *(Dr T J David)*

Open: All year, except 3–23 January.
Rooms: 15 double, 1 suite – 8 with bath, 1 with shower, all with direct-dial
telephone. (1 room on ground floor.)
Facilities: Salon with TV, salon with fireplace, bar, dining room, courtyard.
Gardens. English spoken. &.
Location: In centre of old fortified town; parking for 60 cars, garage parking for 8.
Mortagne is on the D391 at the junction with the D398, 17 km N of Bellême.
Credit cards: Access/Euro/Mastercard, Barclay/Visa.
Terms: Rooms 90–150 frs; dinner, B & B 156 frs. Set meals: breakfast 15 frs,
lunch/dinner 54–135 frs; full *alc* 150 frs. Special meals for children.

MOUGINS, 06250 Alpes-Maritimes, Provence   **Map 9**

Le Mas Candille   *Telephone:* (93) 90.00.85

'The posh hilltop village of Mougins, just inland from Cannes, has more
good restaurants per square metre (including Vergé's mighty *Moulin*)
than any other in France, but few good hotels. So we were delighted to
stumble on this graceful yet unsnooty *auberge*, lined with cypresses,
converted from a white-walled 17th-century farmhouse. It stands peacefully in its own flowery park, on a wooded hillside, looking out across the
valley – a blessed retreat from the tumult of the Côte, so near yet so far. Its
swimming pool is just up the hill, in a grove of firs and olive trees. Our
bedroom had a balcony with a fine view, old beams, and a fireplace where
a log fire burns in winter, so we were told: it was definitely "rural" in style
and a bit cramped, but comfortable. We would eat either in the cool
dining room or out in the flower garden above the valley where at night
the mood was wistfully poetic, helped by the rosy light from the red
candles on a huge candelabrum (*candille* in Provençal – hence the hotel's
name). The *cuisine* tended to the *nouvelle* and was usually good, though
with some failures, and the wine list could have been more interesting.

But we warmed to the owner, Jean Moëns, a shy young Belgian widower whose gentle personality seems to suffuse his hotel. I don't know how he manages to offer such comfort and grace at such reasonable prices. A real find.' *(Anthony Day; also Sir Peter and Lady Ramsbotham)*

Open: 1 March–31 October.
Rooms: 23 double, 2 single – 23 with bath, 2 with shower, all with telephone. (Some rooms on ground floor.)
Facilities: 3 salons (1 with TV), 2 dining rooms. Unheated swimming pool. Garden; tennis court planned for 1983. English spoken.
Location: 800 metres W of the village, which is 6 km N of Cannes; parking.
Credit cards: American Express, Diners.
Terms: B & B 190 frs; dinner, B & B 300 frs; full board 400 frs; full *alc* 170 frs.

MOYE, 74150 Rumilly, Haute Savoie   Map 8

Relais du Clergeon   *Telephone:* (50) 01.23.80/01.32.29

Amid the lush green hills of Savoy, in a hamlet near the town of Rumilly, 17 km south-west of Annecy, the *Relais du Clergeon* is once again recommended by readers as a small, quiet hotel, ideal for a relaxing holiday in one of the loveliest regions of France. 'We had a well-appointed modern room, with a small balcony overlooking a lovely view. The staff were extremely welcoming, and the food well cooked. The *demi-pension* menu had a small choice which was open to suggestions if we happened to fancy something else. One night included a party for residents, providing us with our introduction to *raclette*' [a version of cheese *fondue*] – 'a memorable evening with a wonderful atmosphere.' 'The hotel, like the food, is unpretentious but very pleasant, and the Chal family are the most courteous and helpful hoteliers we have ever met. The *demi-pension* at 109 francs each [1981] was a remarkable bargain, *and* we were given a bottle of wine on leaving.' *(Dr and Mrs G Collingham, Mrs Patricia Solomon)*

Open: All year except Monday, January, and the beginning of February, 1 week in June and 2 weeks at the beginning of September. Restaurant closed Monday, and Tuesday lunchtime from April to September.
Rooms: 24 double (2 pairs of communicating rooms), 1 single – 7 with bath, 9 with shower, all with telephone, 4 with balcony. (4 rooms on ground floor.)
Facilities: Hall, salon, TV room, bar, breakfast room, dining room. Garden with children's play area and boules. Peaceful country; walks, tennis, swimming nearby. English spoken. &.
Location: Access from autoroute A41 at Alby-sur-Cheran; 4 km from Rumilly by the D231.
Terms: Rooms 40–140 frs; full board (minimum 3 days) 140–210 frs. Set meals: breakfast 13–14 frs; lunch/dinner 44–120 frs; full *alc* 78 frs.

MUROL, 63790 Puy-de-Dôme, Auvergne   Map 8

Hôtel du Parc   *Telephone:* (73) 88.60.08/88.65.14

Murol lies amid some of the loveliest scenery of central Auvergne, full of knobbly green hills. It is also in the spa belt, with St-Nectaire (kidney treatment) to the east, and Le Mont-Dore (asthma) and La Bourboule (skin diseases) to the west. The *Parc*, a correspondent said last year, is 'a family-run hotel, strongly recommended for an Auvergne holiday, in the centre of an attractive village complete with floodlit castle. . . . One of the best French hotels we have visited – we booked for three days and stayed for 12.' A recent guest writes: 'Murol, a grey granite and slated little town, appeared uninviting after the charming villages and towns of the Dordogne and the hotel itself hardly came up to the description in the GHG at first glance. However, the rose-coloured spectacles soon returned. Our room overlooked a courtyard with severely pruned chestnuts and the dining room had lustred chandeliers to add to its elegance. The meal was excellent and restored one's flagging faith in French cuisine. No choice (*pension* rates) but all the better for that. Then a walk in the afterglow leaving behind a jolly party of French senior citizens wrestling with fondue.' *(W H Bruton; also Elizabeth Pelkie)*

Open: Easter–end September. Open in winter for groups, conferences and skiing weekends.
Rooms: 38 double, 2 single, 5 suites – 12 with bath, 31 with shower, all with telephone. 5 rooms in annexe.
Facilities: Lounge, reading room, 'bar-pub', TV lounge, restaurant, large room for conferences and parties. Large garden with children's play area, boules, tennis and heated swimming pool; terrace for sunbathing, meals or refreshments. Close to Lac Chambon, with beach, swimming and boating; winter sports. Some English spoken.
Location: In village centre; parking. Murol is 37 km SW of Clermont-Ferrand.
Terms: B & B 140–150 frs; half board 125–150 frs; full board 175 frs. Set meals: lunch 55 frs, dinner 55–70 frs; full *alc* 100 frs. Reduced rates and special meals for children.

NAJAC, 12270 Aveyron, Massif Central   Map 8

Hôtel Restaurant Belle-Rive   *Telephone:* (65) 65.74.20
Au Roc du Pont, Route 039

Najac, though it is in an off-the-beaten-track region of France, affords a good overnight stop if one is motoring down from the valley of the Lot towards Albi (48 km south) and Spain. It is a beautiful medieval village on the river Aveyron, with a fairy-tale medieval castle high up on a hill overlooking the river. *La Belle-Rive* has a choice traffic-free position by the bridge; it is a friendly family hotel, run by Louis Mazières, and especially popular for the quality and reasonable price of its meals (local regional dishes, copiously served). In a letter to us, Monsieur Mazières says of his hotel: 'It is surrounded by verdant green on the banks of the river, a very tranquil environment, swimming pool reserved exclusively for our guests, a large shaded terrace opposite the château which is illuminated at night. Meals are served on the terrace, highly recommended for a restful stay.' Our readers agree. Good reports continue to reach us. 'A lovely and quiet place, with excellent, reasonably priced food.' *(Jeff Driver; also SB)*

Open: 1 April–15 October.
Rooms: 39 double – 21 with bath, 10 with shower, all with telephone. (9 rooms in annexe; 4 on ground floor.)
Facilities: 2 salons (1 with TV), 3 dining rooms, bar. Shady terrace with view of castle and river. Garden with heated swimming pool, tennis, ping pong, boules,

children's play area. Bathing, fishing and boating in the river; tennis nearby. English spoken. &.

Location: 2 km from the centre of Najac, on the banks of the Aveyron; very quiet. At top of Najac take D39 to Parisot.

Terms: Rooms 70–130 frs. Set meals: breakfast 14 frs, lunch/dinner 50–120 frs; full *alc* 100–120 frs.

NAJAC, 12270 Aveyron, Massif Central   Map 8

L'Oustal del Barry: Hôtel Miquel   *Telephone:* (65) 65.70.80
Place du Bourg

'Our favourite typically French hotel', one reader wrote of this simple family-run inn, in the village: its *patron/chef*, Jean-Marie Miquel, is the son of the retired local butcher. 'Remarkably good value, and very efficient except for the breakfasts which were unbelievably slow. Food good. One splendid feature is the large terraced garden, which could be a benefit to families needing somewhere safe for children to play.' 'The rooms are lovely as well as cheap', adds another report. But one reader feels that transient one-night visitors are less welcome, and less well catered-for, than longer-term *en pension* guests. *(David Ballard, Mr and Mrs M Zinkin, R L Mobbs)*

Open: 1 March–31 October.

Rooms: 23 double, 1 single – 9 with bath, 11 with shower, all with telephone.

Facilities: Lift, 3 restaurants, TV room. Large garden with children's play area and boules; lake 10 km. English spoken.

Location: On outskirts of village; parking.

Credit card: Barclay/Visa.

Terms: Rooms 82 frs; dinner, B & B 115–120 frs; full board 146–152 frs. Set meals: breakfast 16.50 frs, lunch/dinner 48–140 frs; full *alc* 100 frs. Reduced rates and special meals for children.

NANTILLY, 70100 Gray, Haute-Saône, Jura   Map 8

Le Relais de Nantilly   *Telephone:* (84) 65.20.12

This elegant *Relais et Château* stands quietly in its own wooded park, 4 km west of the town of Gray which is midway between Dijon and Besançon. Gray is on a useful cross-country route from the Channel ports to Switzerland. 'The highlight of our 1981 holiday. *Le Relais* was marked by largesse, both in the accommodation offered by the beautiful 19th-century country house, and in the hospitality we received. Our room was furnished with the sort of interesting old pieces that seem so plentiful in France. The hotel has a tranquil rural setting, the trees of its gardens busy with birds and the slow stream running along its boundary. Our dinner, which left nothing to be desired, was served in a happy, relaxed atmosphere.' The food is traditional and copious, but not cheap. *(Michael and Shirley Pugh)*

Open: All year, except November, and Sunday end November–end March.

Rooms: 23 double – most with bath or shower, telephone and TV.

Facilities: Salons, restaurant. Conference facilities. Garden with outdoor swimming pool.
Location: 4 km W of Gray, by the D2; parking.
Credit cards: American Express, Barclay/Visa, Diners.
Terms: Rooms 240–345 frs. Set meals: breakfast 28 frs, lunch/dinner 110–185 frs.

NANTUA, 01130 Ain Map 8

Hôtel de France *Telephone:* (74) 75.00.55
44 rue du Dr-Mercier

A small, charming town at the end of a beautiful lake, with tree-lined promenades, flowery gardens and lovely views of the Jura hills. The family-owned *Hôtel de France* stands on the main road, in the town centre: but the traffic of Euro-lorries has thinned considerably since the recent completion of the Lyon-to-Geneva *autoroute*.
'Excellent. The rooms were all one could wish for, and the double-glazing ensured a peaceful night's sleep. Breakfast was good, with limitless coffee. But all paled into obscurity when remembering the dinner. We were told that every dish was a speciality of the house – and what specialities! We had French cooking at its best. The artichokes and the terrine were superb. We had to have *quenelles* and cannot imagine them better. And the wine list ranged from our reasonably priced *vin maison* to wines about which we have only read. Excellent value for money.' The hotel has a rosette in Michelin. *(John M Sidwick)*

Open: 20 December–31 October. Closed Friday, except during school holidays.
Rooms: 15 double, 4 single – all with bath, telephone, and colour TV.
Facilities: Salon, bar, restaurant. Garden; lake close by, with beach, sailing, etc. English spoken.
Location: 50 metres from town centre; garage.
Credit cards: Barclay/Visa, Diners.
Terms: Rooms 140–225 frs. Set meals: breakfast 20 frs; lunch/dinner 100–170 frs; *alc* (excluding wine) 165 frs.

LA NAPOULE-PLAGE, 06210 Mandelieu, Alpes-Maritimes Map 9

Hôtel Parisiana *Telephone:* (93) 49.93.02
Rue Argentière

'La Napoule, just west of Cannes, is a middle-sized resort with good sandy beaches and – for sailors – one of the best-equipped marinas on the Côte. The local oddity is the Henry Clews museum in the château on the seafront, full of the sculptured grotesques of the eccentric American artist who owned the place and worked there till his death in 1937. The *Parisiana*, in a quiet side-street a few yards from the beach, has no frills but is spick and span, very comfortable, and run by a charming *patronne*. We breakfasted on a patio under vine creepers. No restaurant: but you can eat quite well and cheaply at the *Pomme d'Amour*, just up the hill, or enjoy the sublimities of Outhier's three-rosette *Oasis*, just across the road.' *(Nicholas Osmond)*

Open: 1 April–1 October.
Rooms: 12 double – most with bath or shower and telephone.

Facilities: Breakfast room with patio. Sandy beaches, marina nearby.
Location: 8 km W of Cannes; hotel is central; no private parking.
Terms: Rooms 160–205 frs. Set meal: breakfast 17 frs. (No restaurant.)

NARBONNE, 11100 Aude, Languedoc   Map 8

Hôtel La Résidence   *Telephone:* (68) 32.19.41
6 rue du Premier Mai   *Telex:* 500 441 SOMARES

In the heart of this ancient Roman city, three minutes' walk from its
famous palace and cathedral, *La Résidence* is a most unusual little hotel,
ornately decorated and furnished in a Victorian style that some might find
a little *too* precious. But the comfort is remarkable and prices not too
high. No restaurant; but you can eat well at the *Alsace* and *Floride*
restaurants, both near the station. 'The room was quiet and delightful, the
breakfast good and the atmosphere very pleasant.' *(Mr and Mrs M
Zinkin; also JA)*

Open: All year, except 4 January–8 February.
Rooms: 26 double – all with bath and telephone. (4 rooms on ground floor.)
Facilities: 3 lounges (1 with TV). Breakfast only served (no restaurant). English
spoken.
Location: Central; parking.
Credit cards: Access/Euro/Mastercard, Barclay/Visa.
Terms: B & B 150–175 frs.

NICE, 06100 Alpes-Maritimes, Provence   Map 9

Le Gourmet Lorrain   *Telephone:* (93) 84.90.78
7 avenue Santa Fior

Down-town, sea-front Nice is full of predictable hotels: so, if you want
somewhere 'different', go 2 km inland to the quiet suburbs, to this lively
and informal little place that is more like a modern rural inn or restaurant
with rooms. The decor, previously criticized for its tattiness, has now been
renovated. 'The Leloups, the eager young owners, manage to create a
family party spirit. We were the only English-speaking guests but were
fully drawn into the fun, and Madame would also baby-sit for us when we
went down-town. It's by no means a smart place but has an array of
facilities, such as ping pong, sunbathing on the roof, and a shallow *piscine*
for kids which our six-year-old enjoyed. Our bedroom's amenities included an alarm clock. The Leloups also offer the bonus of video-cassettes
of 50 classic films (all French) which they lend free of charge for one's
bedroom TV.' (A first – at least in this book.) 'Above all, we enjoyed the
food. Alain Leloup, from Lorraine (hence the name), is indeed a gourmet
and has won prizes for his cooking, which is mostly classic French rather
than Niçois. His menu includes one rarity, based on imported Australian
ostrich meat, *filet d'autruche aux cèpes*. The list of 900 wines and *digestifs*
is amazing, including for example an 1864 calvados.' *(Gerald and Mary
Prescott; also Mr and Mrs M Zinkin)*

> Please don't just leave the feedback to others.

Open: All year. Restaurant closed Sunday night and all October.
Rooms: 15 double – 5 with bath, all with air-conditioning, telephone, radio and mono TV.
Facilities: Salon with TV, bar/terrace, restaurant; some conference facilities; roof solarium, children's swimming pool, ping pong; beach 3 km, tennis and swimming pool for adults nearby. English spoken.
Location: 1 km N of main station: from there, go up avenue Malaussene and avenue Borriglione, then turn left.
Credit card: American Express.
Terms: (excluding 15% service charge): Rooms 100–150 frs; dinner, B & B 90–130 frs per person; full board 110–140 frs. Set meals: breakfast 12 frs; lunch/dinner 60–120 frs; full *alc* 150 frs.

NICE, 06300 Alpes-Maritimes, Provence   **Map 9**

La Pérouse   *Telephone:* (93) 62.34.63
11 Quai Rauba-Capeu   *Telex:* 461 411

'I have been coming to Nice for thirty years, and though I like the place, I find nearly all the hotels are utilitarian bores – except for a luxury palace like the *Negresco*, which I can't afford. So what a delight to come across this medium (well, upper-medium) priced hotel that has some character and, above all, a superb setting. It is perched halfway up the castle rock, at the east end of the promenade, and from our bedroom balcony we had a stunning view of the town and the Baie des Anges. Our room had a kitchenette, too, which is useful, as the hotel has no restaurant (but they serve you a light lunch by the heated swimming pool in summer). The hotel is modern, but not cold or impersonal: they even have a pretty patio with lemon trees where you can take breakfast or a drink. The staff are very friendly.' *(Anthony Hildesley; also James Joll)*

Open: All year.
Rooms: 58 double, 4 single, 3 suites – 56 with bath, 9 with shower, all with telephone, colour TV and baby-listening. Some with cooking facilities in low season.
Facilities: Lift; lounge, bar, snack bar (open in summer); conference facilities. Garden with patio and heated swimming pool, sauna; beach 20 metres. English spoken.
Location: Central; at E end of Promenade des Anglais, by the château; garage.
Credit cards: American Express, Barclay/Visa, Diners.
Terms: B & B 185–355 frs. (No restaurant.)

NIEUIL, 16270 Roumazières-Loubert, Charente   **Map 8**

Le Château de Nieuil   *Telephone:* (45) 71.36.38

Midway between Angoulême and Limoges, this Renaissance château in a 350-acre wooded park is a former hunting-lodge of François 1er. Not surprisingly, it's a *Relais et Château*, and not cheap. 'A real château complete with moat, claiming to be one of the first in France to have been turned into a hotel (in 1937). Full of antiques and old tapestries (Aubusson) and with an imposing marble staircase. The owner, Madame Bodineaud, speaks English and really cares about the comfort of her guests: there are pleasant touches like a single rose in the bedroom. The food is superb, justifying its Michelin rosette and two Gault-Millau *toques*. Guests on *pension* terms are given free choice on the *à la carte* menu. A collection of 200 old brandies, none of them produced commercially, is another attraction – as is the new open-air swimming pool. This hotel is away from tourist attractions and is a haven of peace. On the debit side, there is no comfortable sitting room, but you spend such happy hours in the dining room it doesn't really matter.' *Cuisine* frankly *nouvelle: filets de pintade au parfum de framboises* sounds bold. *(Elizabeth Pelkie)*

Open: All year, except 15 November–20 December and 5 January–5 February. Restaurant closed Tuesday midday and Wednesday to non-residents.
Rooms: 10 double, 3 suites – most with bath or shower.
Facilities: Bar, restaurant; conference facilities for 40 people. Garden with swimming pool and tennis court. English spoken. &.
Location: Off the D739, between Nieuil and Fontafie, 42 km NE of Angoulême.
Credit cards: American Express, Barclay/Visa.
Terms: Rooms with breakfast 270–425 frs; full board 390–565 frs. Set meals: lunch/dinner 115–145 frs.

NOVES, 13550 Bouches-du-Rhône, Provence   **Map 9**

Auberge de Noves   *Telephone:* (90) 94.19.21
Telex: 431312

'This luxurious *Relais et Château* hotel, famous for its *cuisine*, is a 19th-century manor amid lovely open country south-east of Avignon. We had a large and stylish bedroom with pretty decor and a bathroom with every modern gadget including movable, dimmable lights; a balcony with a pastoral view, too. The lounge with its unusual green decor is far more snug and inviting than is usual in French hotels, and we found all the staff most helpful, as was the kindly *patron*, André Lallemand, whose English is excellent. There are neat new tennis courts, but the sprawling garden is somewhat ill cared-for. Meals, served in a cheerful flower-filled room, were delicious though pricey: interesting mint-flavoured mussel soup, and delectable gâteau of wild strawberries.' *(Peter and Jill Clark)*. Two Michelin rosettes.

Open: All year, except January–mid February. Restaurant closed Wednesday 15 October–1 July.
Rooms: 20 double – most with bath or shower and telephone, some with balcony.
Facilities: Salon, dining room. Conference facilities. Garden with swimming pool and tennis courts. &.
Location: Off the D28, 2 km NW of Noves, which is 13 km SE of Avignon.
Credit card: Barclay/Visa.
Terms: Rooms 300–700 frs. Set meals: breakfast 35 frs, lunch/dinner 160–240 frs.

ORNANS, 25290 Doubs, Jura   **Map 8**

Hôtel de France   *Telephone:* (81) 62.24.44
Rue Pierre Vernier

The painter Courbet was born in this small picturesque town on the river Loue, and his birthplace is now a Courbet museum. The lovely Loue valley, nearby, inspired much of his work. The *France* is recommended as 'a delightful old coaching inn in the town centre, at the foot of a famous 14th-century pack bridge. At night the medieval houses along the fast-flowing river are illuminated, and the bridge becomes a haunt for photographers as well as moths. For the size of the hotel, staff were plentiful, with a young boy to carry our cases. On the *à la carte* the local ham was an excellent starter, though expensive; the fresh salmon with sorrel was cooked with skill. Coffee at breakfast was strong, hot and plentiful. In 1981, complete redecoration was carried out with excellent taste. But a few points on the debit side: you need a strong nerve and skill to park in the overcrowded old stable area; and they have timed light switches on the corridors and the time allowed to beat it from the stairs to the bedrooms is, as always, inadequate.' *(Vivien Warrington)*

Open: All year, except Christmas, New Year, February, Sunday evenings and Monday.
Rooms: 27 double, 4 single – 6 with bath, 5 with shower, all with telephone.
Facilities: Restaurant. English spoken.
Location: Ornans is 26 km S of Besançon on the D67; the hotel is central; parking.
Credit cards: Access/Euro/Mastercard, Barclay/Visa.
Terms: B & B 88–113 frs; full board 200–220 frs. Set meals: lunch/dinner 60–160 frs; full *alc* 165 frs. 20% reduction for children.

PARIS   Map 8

Hôtel de l'Abbaye St-Germain   *Telephone:* (1) 544.38.11
10 rue Cassette, 75006, 6e

A delightfully restored 18th-century residence (formerly a monastery) tucked between St-Germain-des-Prés and Montparnasse, furnished and decorated with simple elegance. Wide windows open on to a lovely little flagged courtyard with palms, pot plants and flowers, where breakfast or refreshments can be taken at ease (no other meals served). It belongs to the *Relais du Silence*, and the quietness of its central position, as well as its reasonable prices, have made it highly popular. Early booking essential. *(André Schiffrin and others)*

Open: All year.
Rooms: 45 double – all with bath and telephone. Baby-sitting by arrangement.
Facilities: Lift; 2 salons (1 with TV), bar, breakfast room; interior courtyard/garden for fine-weather breakfast and refreshments. English spoken.
Location: Central, near St-Sulpice Church; parking.
Terms: Rooms with breakfast 300–720 frs. (No restaurant.)

PARIS   Map 8

Hôtel des Deux Iles   *Telephone:* (1) 326.13.35
59 rue St-Louis-en-l'Ile, 75004, 4e

This graceful 17th-century house has a small flower-filled inner courtyard and a hall decorated with bamboo. 'A tiny, very prettily designed hotel in the middle of the Ile St-Louis (so no lovely views of the Seine). Our bedroom was charming, furnished with Provençal fabrics; its smallness was amply compensated for by the generous bathroom – apparently this is a deliberate policy of the designer, who believes in sleeping in the bedrooms and having room to move around in the bathrooms – which was equally attractively decorated, with Portuguese blue and white tiles. Breakfast, which included freshly-squeezed orange juice, was delicious and prettily served in blue and white china. A most agreeable contrast to the mass-production feeling in the design of larger hotels.' *(Sophie Macindoe)* This entry has since met with 'heartfelt agreement' from more recent visitors. 'Excellent value for such a central position. The very attractive cellar bar should also be mentioned.' *(Dr and Mrs P H Tattershall)* 'What a find! Such mastery in interior planning – the cosiness, the good taste in everything!' *(Katie Plowden)*

Open: All year.
Rooms: 12 double, 5 single – 8 with bath, 9 with shower, all with telephone. (1 room on ground floor.)
Facilities: Bar, salons. English spoken. &.
Location: Central; no parking facilities.
Terms: Rooms 270 frs (single with shower), 330 frs (double with bath or shower). Set meal: breakfast 25 frs. (No restaurant.)

PARIS **Map 8**

Hôtel Gavarni
5 rue Gavarni, 75016, 16e

Telephone: (1) 524.52.82
Telex: Gavarni 612338 F

Between La Muette and the Trocadéro, and 1 km from the Etoile. 'Small and beautifully kept, with very quiet rooms. There is a charming breakfast room and a little lounge, but no restaurant. The proprietor, M Mornand, is a graduate of the Lausanne Hotel School, did his training at the Savoy, and has since run luxury hotels around the world. As a result, the hotel is run to a standard well above what one would expect in Paris at its price. Mme Mornand's heart can always be touched by anybody with an affection for Yorkshire miniature terriers or Persian Blue cats.' *(Maurice and Taya Zinkin)*

Open: All year, except 20 July–18 August.
Rooms: 24 double, 6 single – all with bath, telephone and colour TV.
Facilities: Small lounge, breakfast room. English spoken.
Location: Between La Muette and the Trocadéro, 1 km from the Etoile; parking. (Métro Passy.)
Credit cards: All major credit cards accepted.
Terms: Rooms with breakfast 200–265 frs (single), 280–295 frs (double). (No restaurant.)

PARIS **Map 8**

Hôtel Lancaster
7 rue de Berri, 75008, 8e

Telephone: (1) 359.90.43
Telex: Loyne 640991F
Reservations: in UK ring (01) 568 6841
in USA ring (800) 233 5581

One of the more exclusive of Paris hotels: just off the Champs Elysées and close to the Arc de Triomphe. 67 rooms, and a staff of 82 to attend to their occupants. It is owned by the Savoy group who also own London's

Connaught (q.v.) – and might be called a Paris equivalent, though without the latter's gastronomic distinction. Antique furniture, fine paintings, a profusion of flowers, the best quality linen sheets – changed daily of course. Very quiet for a city hotel: you can listen, we are told, to the birds singing while having a glass of champagne in the flowered courtyard. Excellent service. The management tell us that they would always try to accommodate any request that a client might have – a challenging thought. . . .

Open: All year. Restaurant closed for dinner Saturday, Sunday and throughout August.
Rooms: 43 double, 14 single, 10 suites – all with bath and telephone; radio or TV on request; baby-sitting by arrangement; some air-conditioning.
Facilities: Lift, several salons where drinks are served, small bar; facilities for private dinner parties and small functions. Delightful garden patio which many rooms overlook, used for meals in fine weather. Babysitting. English spoken. &.
Location: Central but quiet, off Champs Elysées and near Arc de Triomphe; parking.
Credit cards: Access/Euro/Mastercard, American Express.
Terms (excluding 15% service charge): Rooms 550–715 frs (single); 850–970 frs (double), suites from 1,300 frs. Set meals: breakfast 40 frs, lunch/dinner 105 frs; full *alc* 250 frs.

PARIS Map 8

Hôtel Lenox *Telephone:* (1) 296.10.95
9 rue de l'Université, 75007, 7e *Telex:* 270 105F

'Rosy table lamps and oriental rugs welcome guests into the little marble foyer of this bed-and-breakfast hotel a stone's throw from the river on the Left Bank. Rooms are simply furnished but with great style – our room had walls the colour of Colette's 'pale mauve of hot chocolate' and the furniture was a good quality light cane. The hotel is run with great care: bath towels are big and fluffy and breakfast china is sparkling white. There is a mirrored bar on the ground floor where you can relax among the plants and eat a croque monsieur *or drink a glass of champagne (the barman popped some fresh popcorn for us in case we were peckish and seemed able to cope with a variety of cocktails for a group of beautifully-dressed Parisians in the other corner). The rooms are a little small – ditto the lift – but, if you don't mind that,* Hôtel Lenox *is a very comfortable and pleasing place to stay in Paris.' (Gillian Vincent)*

Last year's entry, quoted above, is warmly endorsed by recent visitors, who add this gloss: 'The biggest benefit of this really charming little hotel is the staff who go "way out of their way" to make your visit a pleasant one. Roland the barman is an absolute wizard at recommending cosy but outstanding little restaurants which will remain in memory for years to come.' *(Mr and Mrs Steven McGuire)*

Open: All year.
Rooms: 34 double, 2 suites – 25 with bath, 9 with shower, all with telephone, some with TV.
Facilities: Lift, bar; no restaurant but light snacks served in bedrooms until midnight. English spoken.
Location: Central; no parking facilities.
Credit card: Barclay/Visa.
Terms: Rooms 240–290 frs. Set meal: breakfast 22 frs.

Hôtel des Marronniers   *Telephone:* (1) 325.30.60
21 rue Jacob, 75006, 6e

Though in the heart of hectic St-Germain-des-Prés, this small modernized hotel is extremely quiet, since it lies at the back of a courtyard. Elegant period furniture, and vaulted basement lounges. A reader refers to the eponymous chestnut trees: 'There is a small tree-lined garden where one can breakfast on warm days. The staff were all helpful and several spoke English. All the rooms have been recently decorated and have bath or shower. It would be hard to find a Left Bank hotel offering better value for money.' *(T R Erskine)*

Open: All year.
Rooms: 34 double, 3 single, 2 suites – all with bath or shower and telephone.
Facilities: 2 salons (1 with TV), veranda. Garden. English spoken.
Location: In town centre; no special parking facilities. (Métro St-Germain-des-Prés.)
Terms: 180 frs (single), 240–360 frs (double). Set meal: breakfast 18 frs. (No restaurant.)

Hôtel Relais Christine   *Telephone:* (1) 326.71.80
3 rue Christine, 75006, 6e   *Telex:* 202606 F

This expensive luxury hotel, newly converted, was once a 16th-century abbey. It is in a quiet side-street near the river on the Left Bank, a short stroll from the lively food markets and shops of the rue de Buci. The rooms are set round a most attractive courtyard. Breakfast is in the converted chapel in the basement (no restaurant). All rooms have colour television and mini-fridge; and there is a car park in the basement. *(Pat and Jeremy Temple, also Jerry Bick)*

Open: All year.
Rooms: 34 double, 17 single – 47 with bath, 4 with shower, all with telephone, radio, colour TV and mini-bar.
Facilities: Lift, salon, breakfast room (no restaurant); conference room for 20; patio. English spoken.
Location: Central; private parking within hotel.
Credit cards: American Express, Barclay/Visa, Diners.
Terms: Rooms 480–800 frs. Set meal: breakfast 30 frs. Out-of-season reductions.

La Résidence du Bois   *Telephone:* (1) 500.50.59
16 rue Chalgrin, 75116, 16e

This *Relais et Châteaux* hotel, small, *de-luxe* and highly exclusive, is close to the Étoile but in a quiet position, and has an enchanting garden. It does not reckon to serve more than breakfasts, but will produce light meals if

339

asked. It's a Third Empire mansion and the rooms, both the bedrooms and the salons, are exquisitely furnished with period pieces.

Open: All year.
Rooms: 16 double, 1 single, 3 suites – 16 with bath, 4 shower, all with telephone and colour TV. English spoken.
Facilities: 2 salons, bar. No restaurant, but simple meals served to residents on request. Beautiful garden full of trees and flowers for fine-weather refreshments.
Location: Central; parking nearby.
Terms: Rooms including breakfast 380–395 frs (single), 515–660 (double), 690–790 frs (suites).

PARIS   Map 8

Hôtel Scandinavia   *Telephone:* (1) 329.67.20
27 rue de Tournon, 75006, 6e

Very close to the Luxembourg Palace and Gardens, this unusually sympathetic hotel is in a 17th-century building, recently converted. Bedrooms are charmingly decorated, some of them with Louis XIII antiques; pleasant lounge. 'The most comfortable, beautiful place I've stayed at in 20 trips to Paris.' But one gripe: 'They always forget to give you your telephone messages.' *(C and C Orio, E Shear, and others)*

Open: All year, except August.
Rooms: 22 – all with bath and telephone.
Facilities: 2 salons. English spoken.
Location: Central; no parking facilities.
Terms: Rooms 240–260 frs. Set meal: breakfast 15 frs. (No restaurant.)

PAU, 64000 Pyrénées-Atlantiques, Aquitaine   Map 8

Central   *Telephone:* (59) 27.72.75
15 rue Léon-Daran

Pau in the late 19th century had the largest British resident population of any town on the Continent. Today it combines the usual bustle of the Midi with modern industrial throb and a chic that is almost Parisian. Its 11th-century château may be 'boring', as a reader says; but on a clear day the view of the mountains from the Boulevard des Pyrénées is majestic. The *Central* is praised as 'small and comfortable. Although very near the centre it is surprisingly quiet, with rooms at a reasonable rate. It gets very full, even out of season, so booking is a good idea. It is also just round the corner from *Pierre*, one of the best restaurants in this part of France' (and one of the priciest). *(Hugh and Anne Pitt)*

Open: All year.
Rooms: 22 double, 5 single – 5 with bath, 12 with shower, all with telephone.
Facilities: Salon/bar with TV, breakfast room; casino and park nearby. English spoken.
Location: Central; no special parking facilities.
Terms: Rooms 76–150 frs. Set meal: breakfast 13.50 frs. (No restaurant.)

PÉGOMAS, 06580 Alpes-Maritimes, Provence   Map 9

Hôtel Le Bosquet   *Telephone:* (93) 42.22.87
Quartier du Château

'No matter that the Binnses and the Eperons have got here first and that half the cars in *le parking* seem to have GB plates. The ebullient and mesmerizing *patronne*, Simone Bernardi, *vaut le détour*, as they say, and so does her idiosyncratic little country hotel, on the edge of this village in the mimosa country between Cannes and Grasse. We were bowled over by the convivial spirit, the clean and simple comfort, the happy communal breakfasts in the courtyard, enjoying La Bernardi's home-made jams. We enjoyed her *piscine*, too, even though she charges extra for it. The garden, though a bit scruffy, is spacious, and there are nice views of the hills. Our room had a kitchenette, which was useful as there's no restaurant: but we ate well at the *Pomme d'Amour* in nearby Mandelieu.' *(Alan and Elsie Campbell)*

Open: All year, except November.
Rooms: 16 double, 2 single – 15 with shower, all with telephone; also 7 studios with kitchenette.
Facilities: Salon, breakfast room with TV, courtyard. Garden with boules and unheated swimming pool. English spoken.
Location: On the road to Mouans-Sartoux, in northern outskirts of Pégomas which is 11 km NW of Cannes.
Restriction: No children under 3.
Terms: Rooms: 90–145 frs, suites 180–220 frs. Set meal: breakfast 14 frs. (No restaurant.)

PEILLON, 06440 L'Escarène, Alpes-Maritimes, Provence   Map 9

Auberge de la Madone   *Telephone:* (93) 91.91.17

'Only ten or so miles from Nice, yet you seem in the middle of nowhere. This civilized *auberge* is just outside one of the most attractive hill-villages in the area, and has super views of the valley and hills. What we liked best of all is that the young owners, the Millos, manage to create a family atmosphere, without overdoing it. The chef's high-spirited kid sister does the waiting. The food is very good (a well-merited *toque* in Gault-Millau) and quite varied, and includes some oddities such as a kind of chilled *bouillabaisse*. The place seems to attract the nicest kind of Parisian – cultured, but not snooty – and we made several French friends during our stay. If you want a really quiet room, ask for one at the back.' *(A Day)*

Open: 15 December–15 October. Closed Wednesday. Restaurant closed September–end June.
Rooms: 19 double, 2 suites – 15 with bath, 4 with shower, 3 with mono TV, all with telephone.
Facilities: 2 salons, TV room, dining room; conference facilities. Garden; sea 20 km. English spoken.
Location: 19 km NE of Nice on the D21.
Credit card: Access/Euro/Mastercard.
Terms: Rooms 160–260 frs; half board out of season 160–260 per person. Set meals: breakfast 18 frs; lunch 65, 80 frs; dinner 80, 100 frs; full *alc* 140 frs.

Ostellerie du Vieux Pérouges   *Telephone:* (74) 61.00.88

The lovely old medieval hilltop village of Pérouges (40 km north-east of Lyon), with its ramparts, cobbled streets and half-timbered houses, is so perfectly preserved that historical feature films are often shot here. The hotel, converted from some 13th-century buildings, is a worthy part of the decor: 'It forms one side of the village square, dominated by an enormous tree several hundred years old. Hotel rooms are in different houses around the square or in an adjoining manor. Ours was enormous: furnishings were all antiques, with a half-tester bed. And the food is excellent!' *(Pat and Jeremy Temple)*

This entry is warmly endorsed by more recent visitors. 'Large, clean rooms with an exceptional view of the hills. There are mouth-watering antiques everywhere – in the dining room, the bedrooms, and the town. Don't miss the museum, which is full of medieval relics and antiques and has a breathtaking panorama from the top of its spiral staircase. P.S. Brace yourself for the local rooster, which starts doing his thing at 4.30 a.m.' *(Barbara Anderson)* Those who do not salivate at the sight of an antique may well be made to do so by the hotel's Michelin-starred *cuisine*, which includes a celebrated local girdle cake, also *volaille de Bresse rôtie* (is the raucous rooster lamenting his loved ones?).

Open: All year. Restaurant closed Wednesday except July/August.
Rooms: 18 double, 4 single, 3 suites – all with bath and telephone. 10 rooms in annexe. (1 room on ground floor.)
Facilities: 3 lounges, dining room. Gardens. English spoken. &.
Location: In the town square; parking available. For Pérouges take the N84 from Lyon to Geneva; turn off on the D4 at Meximieux.
Credit card: Barclay/Visa.
Terms (excluding 15% service charge): Rooms 270–520 frs. Set meals: breakfast 28 frs; lunch/dinner 105–195 frs; full *alc* 120 frs.

LA PLAINE-SUR-MER, 44770 Loire-Atlantique   **Map 8**

Hôtel Anne de Bretagne   *Telephone:* (40) 21.54.72
au Port de Gravette

'A modern hotel facing the rocky shore and setting sun, 3 km out of La Plaine-sur-Mer. Very clean and comfortable. Lots of activity in the seaweed-covered rock pools as the tide goes out and local people search for shellfish. Eight miles from the picturesque port of Pornic and beaches of the Jade Coast on the south side of the Loire estuary. Very professional cooking and service combine to provide an excellent meal in the attractively furnished restaurant, overlooking the sea. Beware toll on the St-Nazaire bridge on the way to/from La Baule and Brittany!' *(R J Harborne)*

Open: All year.
Rooms: 26 – all with bath or shower and telephone.
Facilities: Restaurant; conference facilities.
Location: 3 km from La Plaine-sur-Mer; 8 km from Pornic; parking.

Terms: Rooms 160–175 frs; full board 215–225 frs. Set meals: breakfast 15 frs; lunch/dinner 55–200 frs.

PLÉHÉDEL, 22290 Lanvollon, Côtes du Nord, Brittany Map 8

Château Hôtel de Coatguelen *Telephone:* (96) 22.31.24

In north Brittany, 7 km from the sea, near to good beaches and to interesting old Breton towns such as Tréguier. The hotel is 2.5 km south-west of Pléhédel on the main Lanvollon–Paimpol road. 'This is a genuine 19th-century château, near an older one still being restored, both owned by the Marquis de Boisgelin (Boisgelin is the gallicized version of the Breton Coatguelen – Coat = Wood and Kelen = holly – so Holly-wood). He is constantly about, but does not impose himself! The hotel is all repro – beautifully done. It must have cost a fortune to restore. We had the Bridal Suite in the tower and it was most comfortable and attractive. The food was excellent. The hotel opened in 1981, and is run by Madame de Morchoven, a really sweet person. The welcome could not be better. There is lovely country about.' *(H ap R; also Rebecca Sadin)*

Open: All year, except 5 January–31 March. Restaurant closed Tuesday, except July/August.
Rooms: 11 double, 2 single, 3 suites – 13 with bath, 3 with shower, all with telephone; babysitters available.
Facilities: Salon with TV, salon/bar, restaurant, children's dining room and playroom; ping pong, bridge tables; 2 conference rooms. Large park with unheated swimming pool, tennis, children's play area, horses and ponies, trout fishing, 9-hole golf course; beach 7 km, sailing, windsurfing and sea fishing 10 km. English spoken.
Location: On the D7 between Lanvollon and Paimpol. (It is not necessary to go to Pléhédel); parking.
Credit cards: Access/Euro/Mastercard, American Express, Diners.
Terms: B & B 190–265 frs; dinner, B & B 270–350 frs; full board 380–460 frs. Set meals: lunch/dinner 120 frs; full *alc* 200 frs. Special rates for 5 days minimum. Reduced rates and special meals for children.

PLÉVEN, 22130 Plancöet, Côtes-du-Nord, Brittany Map 8

Le Manoir de Vaumadeuc *Telephone:* (96) 84.46.17

The Vicomtesse de Pontbriand herself converted her elegant 15th-century manor into a small highly personal hotel. It lies in a substantial park in the forest of Hunaudaye, 18 km from the sea on a side road from Dinan to Plancöet. Being so personal, it may not appeal to all tastes: one reader even found it 'pretentious', with indifferent food. But the general verdict is positive. 'This place made an overpowering impression on us', says one visitor. 'The interiors are stunning; the colours of the furnishings are most beautiful. The food is ordinary though good, and much over-priced were it not that the cost of restoring and maintaining the place so wonderfully must be met somehow. The same applies to the wine prices. The service shows very good training by someone, and is most efficient and charming. There are many fine old pieces of furniture. The seven great fireplaces are modern reproductions made to look ancient – likewise many of the exposed beams. The total effect, however, is unbeatable'.' *(H ap R)*

Open: 1 April–November.
Rooms: 9 double – 7 with bath, 1 with tea-making facilities, all with telephone. 2 rooms in pavilions in the garden. 1 room on ground floor.
Facilities: Lounge, dining room. Park with small lake. Golf, tennis, angling, boating, sailing available. English spoken.
Location: 18 km from the sea, on the road from Dinan to Lamballe (through the forest of Hunaudaye).
Credit cards: Access/Euro/Mastercard, Barclay/Visa, Diners.
Terms (excluding 15% service charge): Rooms 190–360 frs; dinner, B & B 350–540 frs; full board 450–640 frs (half board available for minimum 4-day stay). Set meals: breakfast 20 frs; lunch/dinner 140 frs. Special meals for children.

POLIGNY, 39800 Jura   Map 8

Hostellerie des Monts-de-Vaux   *Telephone:* (84) 37.12.50

In hilly, wooded country beside the main Paris–Geneva road, this former coaching-inn is now a member of the luxurious *Relais et Châteaux* association. 'Despite the fact that the hotel is decorated in excruciatingly bad taste, this was a perfect location in the Jura, 5 km east of Poligny (a lovely, under-rated town), and near Arbois and the *route du vin*, the magnificent *route des sapins* and the *région des lacs* with its waterfall. The view from the hotel is spectacular, and one wakens to the sound of cowbells which adorn all the chubby cows of the area, known for their Comté cheese. We felt the need for a *simple* meal, and enjoyed melon, trout stuffed with rosemary and good raspberry sorbet.' *(Caroline Hamburger)*

Open: All year, except 1 November–31 December. Hotel and restaurant closed from midday Tuesday to Wednesday 18.00 hrs.
Rooms: 7 double, 1 single, 2 suites – all with bath and telephone.
Facilities: Salon, restaurant. Large garden. English spoken.
Location: On N5 5 km from Poligny in the direction of Geneva; parking.
Terms: Dinner, B & B 350–400 frs; (suite 900 frs); full *alc* 140 frs.

PONS, 17800 Charente-Maritime   Map 8

Le Rustica   *Telephone:* (46) 91.25.75

Here, to warm any francophile's heart, is a tale of the rich rewards of picking a simple 'restaurant with rooms' on spec out of Michelin, just because it has a red rocking-chair. *Le Rustica* is in the hamlet of St-Léger, north-west of Pons, just off the main La Rochelle–Bordeaux road. 'We found the hamlet with some difficulty and it seemed miles from civilization in the middle of vineyards. There was nothing outside to suggest that this rectangular old building would be comfortable or produce good food. I was finally persuaded to take a chance, and we booked a room. The bar was very simple, but the dining room was most attractive with large open fireplace, wooden beams, tables with flowers. The dinner was one of the best we have had in that price range [35 frs, 1982!]: first *mouclade* (mussels in cream sauce, delicious), then *steak au poivre* with jacket potatoes filled with butter and chopped bacon, then home made plum tart. We had an enormous, very comfortable bed: the loo and shower were both new. Best night's sleep of the holiday – it was so quiet. Eventually woken up by the

cockerel. Helpful and efficient service, incredible value for money.'
(Catharine Edwards)

Open: All year, except most of October, 5–15 February and Wednesday out of
season.
Rooms: 7 double.
Facilities: Bar, dining room.
Location: In St-Léger, just W of the main N137, 5 km NW of Pons which is 96 km
N of Bordeaux; parking.
Terms: Rooms 65–90 frs; full board 115–140 frs. Set meals: breakfast 12 frs,
lunch/dinner 40–95 frs.

PONT-AUDEMER, 27500 Eure, Normandy **Map 8**

Auberge du Vieux Puits *Telephone:* (32) 41.01.48
6 rue Notre-Dame de Paris

Pont-Audemer lies in a valley only 48 km from Le Havre. The *Vieux Puits*
– mentioned by Flaubert in *Madame Bovary* – has long been a favourite
with our readers, and this year's reports are as eager as ever. 'A perfect
first-night stop. The town is attractive: nicknamed "Venise normande"
because the Seine has been rechannelled through it, it's full of cobbled
streets and tiny bridges. The hotel is a collection of three 17th-century
buildings, originally a tannery. It occupies three sides of a courtyard,
which all eight bedrooms overlook. Inside, every attempt has been made
to retain its original character, despite structural difficulties. The result is
charming – antiques, ancient flagstones, oak beams and large fireplaces.
Our room was prettily decorated with painted wood panelling and fabric
wall coverings, but a bit cramped.
   'Dinner was excellent (Michelin rosette), with efficient friendly service.
The specialities – *truite Bovary* (with champagne), *calvados sorbet* and
canard aux cerises – were a delight. Breakfast was equally good – generous
glasses of fruit juice and freshly potted jams. The hotel is family-run and
we were shown round with obvious pride. Sympathetic conversion presents drawbacks however, so ask for a room with a shower (there are no
public ones and no baths), avoid the ground floor rooms if you want
privacy, and don't go in the heart of winter (the hotel is hard to heat
effectively).' *(Anne Abel-Smith; also Val Bethell, Don and Maureen
Montague)*

Open: All year, except 19 December–19 January and 27 June–6 July. Closed
every week Monday evening to Wednesday morning.
Rooms: 7 double, 2 single – 5 with shower.
Facilities: 2 small salons, 2 restaurants, decorated with antique furniture, china,
etc. Small garden. English spoken.
Location: 300 metres from town centre, but quiet as all rooms overlook garden.
Parking.
Restriction: No young children.
Terms: Rooms 75–95 frs. Set meal: breakfast 18.50 frs; *alc* (excluding wine)
140–170 frs.

We ask hotels to estimate their 1983 tariffs. Not all hotels in Part
Two reply, so prices in Part Two are more approximate in some
cases than those in Part One.

La Métairie Neuve   *Telephone:* (63) 61.23.60 or 61.23.31

A handsomely converted Languedoc farmhouse, set in fine open country about a mile north of Mazamet, and a good centre for exploring Carcassonne, Toulouse and Albi, all within 60 km. 'Marielle Tournier has lovingly restored this complex of 18th-century farm buildings, to provide a quiet rural restaurant with rooms, with an air of spacious comfort and elegance. Upstairs are seven bedrooms of individual character: ours was more like a mini-apartment with separate modern bathroom. Menus range from 54 to 110 francs [1982]: even the least expensive includes *cassoulet*, and we were well satisfied. The restaurant is patronized by diners from Mazamet whom Madame recognized as friends rather than customers.' *(K W George)*

Open: All year, except 15 December–15 January. Restaurant closed Saturday.
Rooms: 7 double – all with bath and telephone.
Facilities: Reception/salon, salon, dining room. Garden. Golf, tennis and swimming pool 1 km; lakes in vicinity with beaches and sailing. English spoken.
Location: 2 km N of Mazamet on the N112 Béziers–Castres road; parking.
Credit cards: Barclay/Visa, Diners.
Terms: B & B 113–186 frs; full board (min. 3 days) 320 frs. Set meals: lunch/dinner 65, 115, 130, 180 frs; full *alc* 150 frs. Special meals for children.

Le Manoir   *Telephone:* (94) 05.90.52

'Port Cros is the middle one of the three famous *Iles d'Hyères* (to the west is Porquerolles, to the east the Ile du Levant, given over to nudism and the Navy) and the most beautiful. It is densely wooded, hilly, and full of lush sub-tropical foliage, rare for the Mediterranean. We thought *Le Manoir* a most unusual and captivating place. There's no sign at the gate to say it's a hotel, and no reception-desk either. This is because the owner, Pierre Buffet, is anxious to keep the atmosphere of a private home. His family have long owned this 18th-century manor, and now to help out his finances he runs it as a hotel – but he and his young wife treat their clients more like friends. Many of them indeed are writers, musicians and actors – including Jean-Louis Barrault and his wife – who come back year after year. The Buffets are delightful, cultured people, and we enjoyed our talks with them. They gave us a large room furnished in country style, and they fed us quite well: the menus had no choice, but eating under the trees was idyllic. You come here for rest and escape from the world's cares. The Buffets don't even have television, but they do hire out windsurfers and motor-boats, and we used one of the latter to explore the nearby coves. The island is a National Park and there are underwater guided tours (with scuba masks) of marine life – a fascinating experience. All in all, this gentle manor in its wooded park has a wistful, mysterious air – as does the whole of Port-Cros.' *(Alan and Elsie Campbell)*

Open: Easter–mid October.
Rooms: 19 double, 7 single, some rooms for 3/4 people – 8 with bath, 6 with shower, 10 with terrace, all with telephone.

Facilities: Salons, restaurant. Garden. Windsurfers, motor-boats for hire; scuba-diving. English spoken.
Location: Port-Cros is about an hour by boat from Le Lavandou or Hyères. No cars allowed on island.
Terms: B & B 145–200 frs; dinner, B & B 265–400 frs; full board 320–460 frs. Set meals: lunch/dinner 140 frs. Reduced rates for children; special meals on request.

PORT-GRIMAUD, 83310 Cogolin, Var, Provence   Map 9

Hôtel Giraglia   *Telephone:* (94) 56.31.33
                                      Telex: 470494

'Architectural folly or work of genius? We don't ourselves share the criticisms sometimes hurled at Port-Grimaud, that pleasure-village for yachting types created since the late 1960s as a pastiche of Venice-cum-Provençal-fishing-port. It's artificial, yes, but not phoney. We wouldn't care to live there, but it's great fun for a visit, and in this respect the *Giraglia* serves well as a glamorous new holiday hotel. It is wedged between the sea and one of the canals, integrated into the overall plan of Port-Grimaud. Our 'Provençal-style' bedroom was sumptuous, with a wide sea view from its balcony. We enjoyed the hotel's bright and breezy decor, its unashamed travel-brochure opulence, and its amenities – the sparkling swimming pool by the open-air bar, the private sandy beach, the windsurfing and waterskiing. Best of all, the food is far more interesting than you might expect in this kind of place: more-or-less *nouvelle cuisine*, e.g. an excellent *émincé de canard au mesclun.* You can eat out by the pool when it's fine. Lovely vistas of the bay of St-Tropez.' *(Peter and Sarah Abbott)*

Open: All year except October–24 December. Restaurant closed Tuesday in winter.
Rooms: 47 – most with bath or shower, telephone, TV and balcony.
Facilities: Salons, restaurant, open-air bar, conference facilities. Swimming pool. Private sandy beach with windsurfing and waterskiing.
Location: On edge of new port; St-Tropez 10 km. Parking fairly close.
Credit cards: American Express, Diners.
Terms: Rooms 390–860 frs; full board 485–730 frs. Set meals: breakfast 23 frs; lunch/dinner 150 frs.

PORTO VECCHIO, 20137 Corse-du-Sud, Corsica   Map 9

Hôtel San Giovanni   *Telephone:* (95) 70.22.94
Route d'Arca

Porto Vecchio, an old harbour town, now quite a fashionable summer resort, lies amid cork forests at the head of a deep gulf. The *San Giovanni* is 3 km to the south-west, just inland. 'A small and delightful two-star family-run hotel in truly rural surroundings. You need a car here, but some beautiful beaches are within ten minutes' drive. We had a very nice bungalow room in a newly built outside block. The only noise in the daytime was the sound of the cuckoo and at night we could hear a nightjar singing. There is a small open-air swimming pool. We did not eat any main meals, but did note that the menu seemed rather limited for 60 francs

[1982] and we think we did better in town for 50 francs.' *(Pam and Len Ratoff)*

Open: Mid March–end October.
Rooms: 26 double – most with bath or shower and telephone. Some rooms in bungalows.
Facilities: Restaurant. Garden with tennis court and swimming pool. Beaches nearby. &.
Location: 3 km SW of Porto Vecchio on D659.
Credit card: Barclay/Visa.
Terms: Rooms with breakfast 160–250 frs; full board 275–305 frs. Set meals: lunch/dinner 65–140 frs.

QUENZA, 20122 Corsica Map 9

Hôtel Sole e Monti *Telephone:* (95) 78.62.53

High up in the wilds of southern Corsica, Quenza is a village of simple charm – a popular base for cross-country skiing in winter and mountain walking in summer. The *Sole e Monti* is a small modern hotel on the outskirts, with balconied bedrooms offering stunning views of the awe-inspiring Aiguilles peaks. It serves honest robust Corsican fare. What earns the hotel its entry is the solicitude of its proprietor, Félicien Balesi, a man of character and a true hotelier. He tells us that among many English visitors who have enjoyed his hospitality are Margaret Thatcher and Denis Healey. In this context, it was disturbing to receive a report this year from readers who felt that standards might be slipping. 'Our room was clean, and the dinner good, but no-one seemed to notice the dead flies clustered on the windows.' More reports, please, before we can dare recommend that the Prime Minister returns. *(HR, Angela and David Stewart)*

Open: 15 May–15 November.
Rooms: 20 – all with bath or shower, most with balcony.
Facilities: Salon, bar, dining room; discotheque. Near river; fishing, hunting. English spoken.
Location: On the D420, 14 km from Aullene towards Zonza; 40 km from the sea via winding mountain roads.
Credit cards: American Express, Barclay/Visa.
Terms: Rooms 115–160 frs. Set meal: breakfast 17 frs. Reduced rates for children under 5.

RAGUENÈS-PLAGE, 29139 Nevez, Finistère, Brittany Map 8

Hôtel Chez Pierre *Telephone:* (98) 06.81.06

Readers continue to write warmly of this friendly unassuming seaside hotel, a few metres from a stretch of unspoilt and usually uncrowded beach, and within easy reach of Concarneau and Pont-Aven (where Gauguin painted). It has been owned and run by the Guillou family for many years. Xavier Guillou's fish dishes, such as *turbot au champagne*, are strongly recommended: he has a well-merited red 'R' in Michelin for 'good food at modest prices', and a Gault-Millau *toque* for his 'honest use of fresh local produce'. A pleasant garden and terrace have recently been added as well as a salon and bar, but prices remain very reasonable. 'We were enchanted. We had one of the new suites for ourselves and daughter, with sea views from all windows. Food first-class. The only snag: meat is served only at lunch, so those on *demi-pension* get only fish.' *(Mr and Mrs S Cowherd; also K C Turpin, H David Segat)*

Open: 1–12 April, 29 April–3 May, 10 May–25 September (approx.). Restaurant closed Wednesday 1 June–14 September.
Rooms: 20 double, 1 single – 10 with bath, 4 with shower, all with telephone.
Facilities: Salon, bar, 2 restaurants; conference and banqueting facilities; terrace. Garden with childrens' play area. Beach with sand and rocks nearby.
Location: 12 km from Pont-Aven.
Terms: B & B 70–110 frs; full board 146–200 frs. Set meals: lunch/dinner 60–70 frs; full *alc* 100–160 frs. Reduced rates for children under 10; special supper at 7 p.m. Reductions for stays of a week or longer.

RAMATUELLE 83350 Var, Provence   Map 9

La Figuière   *Telephone:* (94) 97.18.21
Route de Tahiti

'Notorious Tahiti Beach, where the *beau monde* of St-Tropez have been undressing since the 1960s, is a mere 500 metres away: but *La Figuière* is a very different *monde* – an 18th-century creeper-covered farmhouse with modern villas attached, set in spacious grounds amid vineyards. We found it elegant and comfortable. We liked the large swimming pool and the comfy *chaises longues* beside it, and we enjoyed observing our smart fellow-guests. You can eat a salad or grill by the pool, but for real *cuisine* you must go into town, 4 km away.' *(Charles Hildesley)*

Open: April–end September.
Rooms: 37 double, 1 single, 4 suites – 38 with bath, 3 with shower, all with telephone, 3 with TV. (30 rooms on ground floor, 19 with ramps.)
Facilities: Salon/reception, restaurant. Grounds with swimming pool. &.
Location: 4 km SE of St-Tropez, on road to Tahiti beach.
Terms: Rooms with breakfast: 265–485 frs; *alc* 115 frs.

ROANNE, 42300 Loire   Map 8

Hôtel des Frères Troisgros   *Telephone:* (77) 71.66.97
Place de la Gare

A small hotel opposite the railway station in a busy industrial town – that may seem an improbable setting for one of the most brilliant restaurants on this planet, but then, this is France. Though it has only 19 bedrooms, the luxurious *Troisgros* has four gables in Michelin as a hotel – as well, of course, as three rosettes for its food, plus three red *toques* in Gault-Millau. The famous brothers are, along with Guérard, Chapel, Vergé and others, the leading propagators of the so-called *nouvelle cuisine*. The *Observer*'s food correspondent has sent us this note on what he calls a Christmas binge: 'Excellent big rooms decorated in amazing tastelessness in great contrast to the visual sensitivity of the Troisgros in the presentation of food. But thoroughly comfortable and good value although expensive. And of course one of the world's best restaurants.' *(Paul Levy)*

Open: All year, except January and Tuesday and Wednesday lunch.
Rooms: 19 – 17 with bath, 2 with shower, 1 suite – all with telephone, radio and TV.
Facilities: Lift, restaurant.
Location: 86 km NW of Lyon on the N7; 500 metres from town centre, opposite the station; parking.
Credit cards: American Express, Barclay/Visa, Diners.
Terms: B & B 385 frs. Set meals: lunch/dinner 250–300 frs; full *alc* 300 frs.

LA ROCHELLE, 17000 Charente-Maritime Map 8

Hôtel Les Brises *Telephone:* (46) 34.89.37
Chemin de la Digue de Richelieu

Two eloquent recommendations for this modern hotel in a prime position overlooking the estuary and outer harbour of the town. 'Bed and breakfast only, but what luxury – and the best breakfast I have ever had in France. The hotel is right on the sea-front, with a vast terrace on which one can sun oneself over a drink, and two luxurious lounges where one can get coffee or tea. A very warm welcome. Not cheap, but really excellent value for money. Private underground garage. Utterly quiet, with a park between the hotel and the road.' *(E George Maddocks)*
'Staggering view, charmingly furnished room, with a balcony, and several welcome *petits soins*, including finding that our car's windows had been cleaned in the morning. Three red turrets and red rocking-chair in Michelin well deserved.' *(Jessica Mann)*

Open: All year, except 15 December–15 January.
Rooms: 41 double, 5 single – 39 with bath, 7 with shower, all with telephone.
Facilities: Salon, TV room/library, breakfast room, bar; terrace; panoramic views over Iles d'Aix, d'Oléron and de Ré. English spoken.
Location: On sea front 1½ km from town centre, close to the Parc F Delmas; underground garage and car park.
Credit cards: Barclay/Visa.
Terms: 180–370 frs. Set meal: breakfast 20 frs. (No restaurant.)

LA ROCHELLE, 17000 Charente-Maritime Map 8

Hôtel de France et d'Angleterre *Telephone:* (46) 41.34.66
22 rue Gargoulleau *Telex:* 790717 Fratel Rochl

'A return visit in 1982 confirmed my view that La Rochelle is the most attractive town in France – a kind of maritime Bruges, with echoes too of Dubrovnik and the less absurd aspects of St-Tropez. The narrow streets of this ancient fishing port have been beautifully paved and closed to traffic, and all summer the town is splendidly animated, especially during the avant-garde arts festival in July. The *France et Angleterre* is a hotel worthy of La Rochelle – high praise. Gracefully modernized, it is set round a small flowery garden. Staff are well above the French average for amiability. The hotel's very fine restaurant, the *Richelieu*, successfully combines regional classicism with modern inventiveness. The fish is superbly fresh: returning in 1982, I relished the patron-chef's *bar à la vapeur d'algues*, as well as the local delicacy, *mouclade* (mussels in a spicy sauce).' *(JA)*

'An outstanding find. Modern, but not too modern, highly comfortable, efficient and friendly service, very good value. A bustling market nearby, the stunning *Café de la Paix* round the corner. *JA* catches the charm exactly.' *(Brian MacArthur; also H ap R)*

Open: All year. *Le Richelieu* restaurant closed Sunday and 10–31 December.
Rooms: 74 double, 2 single – 36 with bath, 29 with shower, all with telephone, radio, 36 with mono TV (Some rooms in 2 annexes.)
Facilities: Lift, salon, TV room, breakfast room, restaurant; conference facilities. Interior garden for refreshments or meals.
Location: Central, near place de Verdun; parking in adjacent rue du Minage.
Credit cards: All major credit cards accepted.
Terms: B & B 120–219 frs. Set meals: lunch/dinner in the *Richelieu* 115–200 frs.

ROLLEBOISE, 78270 Yvelines, Île-de-France
Map 8

Château de la Corniche
Telephone: (3) 093.21.24
Telex: 695544

Rolleboise is a village on the Seine, halfway between Paris and Rouen. The Monet museum at Giverny, 12 km to the north-west, is worth a visit. 'The splendid *Château de la Corniche*, built by King Leopold II of Belgium, is perched high above the Seine. Front rooms have a marvellous view of the countryside and river; the barges provide an almost non-stop show as they go through a nearby lock. Bedrooms and public rooms are luxuriously comfortable. Service was faultless during our two-day stay. By French standards expensive, which means that you pay about the same as you would in a smart English country hotel, but get something about five times as good. Recommended unconditionally.' *(Warren Bagust)*

Open: All year except third Sunday in January to first Sunday in March. Restaurant closed Sunday evening and Monday September–April.
Rooms: 22 double, 5 single, 1 suite – 19 with bath, 5 with shower, 11 with mono TV, all with telephone and radio. 6 rooms in annexe.
Facilities: Lift, salon, TV room, games room, 2 bars, restaurant, disco; conference room. 4 acres park with swimming pool, tennis court; sailing and surfing 8 km away. Claude Monet museum at Giverny 12 km.
Location: 3 km from Bonnières exit off the Autoroute de Normandie (A13) between Paris and Rouen, or turn off the RN13.
Credit cards: Access/Euro/Mastercard, Barclay/Visa.
Terms: Rooms 170–600 frs. Set meals: breakfast 29 frs; lunch/dinner 130–200 fr full *alc* 220 frs.

Hôtel Vistaëro
Route de la Grande Corniche

Telephone: (93) 35.01.50
Telex: 461021

'Seen from below, it's hard to believe that this glamorous luxury hotel is not about to fall into the sea, so vertiginously is it built out from the cliff-top, beside the Grande Corniche, a thousand feet directly above Monte Carlo. Alike from the bedroom balconies, from the bar with its big picture windows, and from the outdoor dining-terrace, the views of this spectacular coast are enough to put you off your hot croissants, champagne cocktails or *Jambonnette de caneton aux figues*. The hotel is owned by the German hi-fi firm, Grundig – good for them! – and has a young half-American manager, Mr Boone, who is most cordial, as are all his staff. We enjoyed the ultra-modern decor, both in the bedrooms and the public rooms – marble floors, ornamental indoor pool, and all that. The heated swimming pool below the hotel is fine, but it's a bit of a climb, coming back. We paid through the nose at this place, but felt it was worth it – and it's a good excursion centre too. The hill-village of Roquebrune, right next door, is one of the most attractive we've come across in Provence.' *(Peter and Sarah Abbott)*

Open: 6 February–15 November.
Rooms: 22 double, 2 single 3 suites – all with bath or shower, direct-dial telephone, colour TV and mini-bar; baby-sitting; some with balconies.
Facilities: Lift, 2 salons, bar, dining-terrace, restaurant; conference and banqueting facilities; heated swimming pool. Garden. Beaches and water sports 4 km. English spoken.
Location: 5 km from Monte Carlo on the D2564. Leave Autoroute A8 at exit La Turbie–Monaco.
Credit cards: All major credit cards accepted.
Terms: B & B 250–385 frs; dinner, B & B 395–595 frs; full board 550–745 frs. Set meals: lunch/dinner 160–198 frs. Special meals for children.

La Cathédrale
12 rue St-Romain

Telephone: (35) 71.57.95

There are plenty of smart hotels in Rouen, but *La Cathédrale* is the place for those who appreciate old-world atmosphere and courtesy. It's centrally placed in the old town, on a cobbled pedestrian alleyway that runs alongside the cathedral block. It looks as though it has survived from the age of coaching, with a great pair of wooden doors giving on to a charming flowered courtyard. The back rooms are modern and characterless, but marvellously quiet. The front rooms are well-proportioned and graciously furnished but distinctly noisy at night if you open the double-glazed windows. *La Cathédrale* serves no meals except breakfast, but that's scarcely a hardship in a city as richly endowed with good restaurants Rouen. *(HR; also Tony Morris, Rebecca Sadin)*

Open: All year.
Rooms: 24 – 7 with bath, 14 with shower, all with telephone.
Facilities: Hall. Flower-filled courtyard.

Location: Central; no special parking facilities.
Terms: Rooms 98–139 frs (single), 129–170 frs (double). Set meal: breakfast 13.50 frs. (No restaurant.)

ST-BENOIT, 86280 Vienne, Poitou   Map 8

À l'Orée des Bois   *Telephone:* (49) 57.11.44
13 rue de Naintré

About 4 km south of the old cathedral and university city of Poitiers (don't miss its church of Notre-Dame with its Romanesque façade). The inn is at the remoter end of a new suburb, and not easy to find without a car and an up-to-date map – 'but, once found, extraordinarily quiet, and quietly hospitable.' Recommended for down-to-earth simplicity and good value (four-course meal for only 42 francs in 1982), though one gastronome has found fault with the *truite meunière*. More a place for an overnight halt than a full holiday. *(Alan Cooke, Charles Shepherd)*

Open: All year except first week January, first week August and Sunday evening; restaurant also closed Monday.
Rooms: 15 double – 2 with bath, 4 with shower.
Facilities: Bar, restaurant. English spoken.
Location: Leave Poitiers by the N10 to the S (Angoulême direction), then 2 km from the town centre turn left along the D4 and go through the suburb of Naintré. The inn is just beyond Naintré on the left after a dual carriageway; parking.
Terms: B & B 56–79 frs. Set meal: dinner 35, 47, 85 frs; full *alc* 145 frs.

ST-CLAIR, Le Lavandou 83980 Var, Provence   Map 9

Hôtel Belle-Vue   *Telephone:* (94) 71.01.06
Boulevard du Four des Maures, at St-Clair

'Le Lavandou itself has today swollen hideously, all skyscrapers and snack-bars, and has lost much of its former charm as a resort and fishing-port. But St-Clair, 2 km to the east, is much smaller and quieter; and here the *Belle-Vue* stands on a low hill, 300 metres back from the coast road. We found this small and pretty villa-hotel an almost perfect place for an unpretentious beach holiday, on the beautiful Maures coast. It is well named, for the views of the sea are indeed *belles*; and it is very quiet, deservedly a *Relais du Silence* – rare on the Côte d'Azur today! Madame Claire and her three daughters run the place in a personal, friendly style. Our bedroom was a bit small, but cheerful, and it had a wide balcony, with deckchairs, and a sea view. We took breakfast in the flowery garden, under a blue parasol. There are flowers everywhere, including in the dining room which overlooks the bay. Our only gripe: the food, though sound, was unexciting, and there was little choice on the *menu pension*. If you ask, they will cook a special local dish, such as *bouillabaisse*: ours superb, but very pricey.' *(Gerald and Mary Prescott)*

Open: April–October.
Rooms: 17 double, 2 single – 11 with bath, 8 with shov radio.
Facilities: Salons, TV room, bar, restaurant. Garden. sailing, waterskiing facilities. English spoken.

Location: At St-Clair, 2 km E of Le Lavandou, on a hillside just above the coast road (N559).
Terms: Full board 220–380 frs. Reduced rates for children.

ST-CYPRIEN, 24220 Dordogne   Map 8

Hotel l'Abbaye   *Telephone:* (53) 29.20.48

St-Cyprien is a pleasant village in the Dordogne valley, centrally situated for touring the area: Sarlat and Les Eyzies-de-Tayac are both quite close. *L'Abbaye*, noted locally for its sound Périgord cooking (e.g. *ris de veau aux girólles*), is described as 'a most comfortable three-star hotel. The food and service are excellent, the wines reasonably priced. Madame Schaller who runs the hotel with her husband is very friendly and speaks excellent English. The hotel is well-appointed and has a swimming-pool and garden.' *(Richard O Whiting)*

Open: March–end October. Restaurant closed Wednesday out of season.
Rooms: 19 double – 8 with bath, 11 with shower, all with telephone. 6 rooms in annexe. (2 rooms on ground floor.)
Facilities: 2 salons (1 with TV), restaurant. Garden, terrace, heated swimming pool. English spoken.
Location: 200 metres from town centre on the N703 towards Les Eyzies, 9 km from Beynac, 19 km from Sarlat; parking.
Credit cards: American Express, Diners.
Terms: Rooms 150–300 frs; breakfast 18 frs, dinner, B & B 173–260 frs; full board 415–300 frs. Set meals: breakfast 18 frs, lunch/dinner 42–190 frs; full *alc* 145 frs.

ST-ÉTIENNE-LES-ORGUES, 04230 Alpes de Haute Provence   Map 9

Hôtel St Clair   *Telephone:* (92) 76.07.09

'St-Étienne-les-Orgues sprawls at the foot of the southern flank of the long hump of the Montagne de Lure. This is a less frequented corner of upper Provence, though favoured by walkers, geologists and naturalists. The *St Clair* is 2 km out of St Étienne, standing solid on a knoll. Surrounding its gardens are wide expanses of landscape with a backcloth of distant hills. The hotel is a simple, modern, spotlessly clean, fairly large, honest *logis de France*. Taps and fittings gleam and work. The thirty rooms are spacious, and adequately if simply furnished. The bar is tiny, but the list of drinks is long, interesting and modestly priced. What an excellent dinner there was – *pâté* with prunes and *crudités*; a splendid salmon-trout with pine kernels, creamed spinach and succulent *pommes frites*; cheese; ice-cream; and a house-wine which is Beaujolais red, white or rose. This meal was from the cheaper of the two regular menus, which in 1982 was still only 56 francs. Note: the hotel has a large regular clientele. Booking ahead strongly advised. *(A N Brangham; also Alison Chesshyre)*

n: All year except 15 November–15 December and 5–26 January.
: 27 double – 9 with shower. (1 room on ground floor.)
: Salon with TV, bar, restaurant. Garden with swings; terraces. English

Location: 2 km out of St Étienne. Coming on road from Forcalquier, turn left at entrance to St Étienne. Parking.
Terms: Rooms 80–150 frs; full board 130–240 frs. Set meals: breakfast 13 frs; lunch/dinner 60, 90, 120 frs; full *alc* 90 frs. Reduced rates and special meals for children.

ST-HIPPOLYTE, 68590 Haut-Rhin, Alsace   Map 8

Hôtel Munsch: Aux Ducs de Lorraine   *Telephone:* (89) 73.00.09

A self-assured Alsatian mansion, gabled and half-timbered, on the *route du vin* 20 km north of Colmar. Big parties of local people come here to eat solid Alsatian food in a jolly family atmosphere. 'This old hostelry is just outside a typical Alsace village, adjoining the proprietor's vineyards and facing the Vosges and the Château of Haut-Koenigsbourg. The well-designed modern extension contains beautifully appointed bedrooms with balconies. The demi-pension terms included a 4- to 5-course meal: no choice, but excellent quality.' *(Dr and Mrs N Hodgson)*

Open: All year, except 29 November–13 December, 10 January–1 March. Restaurant closed Monday.
Rooms: 40 double, 4 single – 28 with bath, 5 with shower, all with telephone, radio and mono TV; most with balcony.
Facilities: Lift, 2 dining rooms, breakfast room, conference room. Garden. English spoken.
Location: 6 km from Selestat, 20 km N of Colmar; parking.
Credit cards: American Express, Diners.
Terms: B & B 75–225 frs; dinner, B & B 175–325 frs; full board 225–375 frs. Set meals: breakfast 25 frs, lunch 80 frs, dinner 100 frs; full *alc* 130 frs. Rduced rates for children.

ST-JACUT-DE-LA-MER, 22750 Côtes du Nord, Brittany   Map 8

Le Vieux Moulin   *Telephone:* (96) 27.71.02

'*Le Vieux Moulin* is frequented mainly by French bourgeois families of three generations holidaying together, small children of four applying the same intent concentration as their grandparents to the serious business of eating – lunch (five courses) is the highlight (specially good *moules*, mackerel, *colin*, roast beef and an excellent house wine); supper much simpler for those *en pension*. Madam Papin presides over the dining room, Monsieur Papin over the kitchen. Very good value for a quiet holiday in an old-fashioned atmosphere, rooms adequate, all looking out on to the garden and there is an annexe by the beach. St-Jacut-de-la-Mer, a fishing village, where the locals gather shellfish at low tide, is almost an island, and apart from windsurfing, swimming from the numerous sandy coves, or walking along the headland and the beaches, there is blissfully nothing to do except relax.' *(Michael and Sasha Young)*

Open: March–October.
Rooms: 30 – some with bath, all with telephone.
Facilities: Restaurant, terrace. Garden; beach.
Location: 26 km W of St-Malo; parking.

355

Terms: Rooms 60–150 frs; full board 155–210 frs. Set meals: breakfast 17 frs, lunch/dinner 60–130 frs.

ST-JEAN-CAP-FERRAT, 06230 Alpes-Maritimes, Provence   Map 9

Voile d'Or   *Telephone:* (93) 01.13.13
Port de St Jean   *Telex:* 470317

'A very beautiful modernized luxury hotel, built on a low promontory right beside the harbour, on the edge of the fishing village of St-Jean. We had a very pretty and spacious bedroom, with views of the sea, and we were equally delighted by the rest of the hotel – the pastel-shaded decor, the idyllic garden-terrace where you can eat or take a drink, and the two swimming pools. One is down by the rocks, and they serve lunch there (as well as indoors) so you don't have to come back in and change. The atmosphere is informal, though chic. And the food is outstanding: they prepare local fish in delicious and unusual ways. We also enjoyed exploring beautiful Cap-Ferrat with its pinewoods, its charming zoo and the Rothschild museum. The only snag is the lack of sandy beaches on this part of the coast – but that's hardly the hotel's fault.' This account in the 1982 *Guide* has since been endorsed by a family this year who found its 'praise too faint' and added, 'An American friend, accustomed to travelling the world from one luxurious cushion to another, stayed there and wrote to us, "This is heaven".' *(P and S Abbot; C and J McDowall)*

Open: 1 February–30 October.
Rooms: 44 double, 6 single, 1 suite – all with bath, telephone and TV; baby-sitting on request.
Facilities: Lift, TV room, restaurant, air-conditioning; conference facilities. Garden with terrace; 2 heated swimming pools. English spoken. &.
Location: 10 km from Nice; 1½ km from town centre, by the harbour; parking.
Terms (excluding 15% service charge): Dinner, B & B 350–850 frs.

ST-JEAN-DU-BRUEL, 12230 La Cavalerie, Aveyron, Massif Central   Map 8

Hôtel du Midi   *Telephone:* (65) 62.26.04

St-Jean is an old Cévenol village on the river Doubie, between Millau and Le Vigan, a good centre for walking holidays in the Cévennes, or for visiting the Gorges du Tarn or the Caves at Roquefort; also, suggests a reader, for lunching at the *Buffet Gare* at Millau. The *Midi* has recently had a facelift, with a new salon and bar, and newly modernized bedrooms beside the river. Its official category has risen from one star to two, but it still offers remarkable value, especially its honest country cooking. 'A quite unpretentious place in a delightful village run by the Papillon family who give excellent and very friendly service. The food is good, regional, not over-priced, though with limited choice; the *pension* menus are said to be somewhat monotonous. Good packed lunches available.' *(A G Don; also HR)*

Open: 20 March–15 November.
Rooms: 16 double, 2 single – 11 with bath, all with telephone.
Facilities: Lounge, TV room, bar, dining room; situated on the banks of the river Doubie. English spoken.

Location: SE of Millau (45 km) off the D7; 20 km E of N9.
Terms: Rooms 30–50 frs per person; full board 122–158 frs. Set meals: breakfast 12 frs; lunch/dinner 41–113 frs; full *alc* 120 frs. Reduced rates for children.

ST-JEANNET, 06640 Alpes-Maritimes, Provence   Map 9

Auberge de Saint Jeannet "Chez Antoine"   *Telephone:* (93) 24.90.06
Place Sainte-Barbe

'The old hill-village of St-Jeannet, near Vence, is in a splendid part of the Nice hinterland, with fine views towards the coast and a great tooth-like rock looming up behind (good for rock-climbing, I'm told, though we funked it ourselves). *Chez Antoine* is the kind of down-to-earth French inn that we like, a bit noisy, but full of jollity, and dominated by its rotund and extrovert young owner, Antoine Plutino. He talks good English, having been chef at the Burford Bridge Hotel, in Surrey. He also adores modern paintings, hangs them all over his inn, has many artist friends, and will talk you into the night about e.g. the rival merits of Matisse and Chagall. What's more, he does the cooking himself, rather well, and inventively – he's proud of his "creations" such as *filets de volaille à la ciboulette* and *sole aux oranges*. The bedrooms are OK, but don't expect *grand luxe*.' *(John and Ludmila Berry)*

Open: All year, except Monday and January.
Rooms: 9 double – 2 with bath, 1 with shower.
Facilities: Restaurant, function room, terrace. Garden. English spoken.
Location: 8 km from Vence.
Credit cards: American Express, Barclay/Visa.
Terms: Rooms 90–135 frs; half board 125–160 frs. Set meals (excluding service): breakfast 15 frs, lunch/dinner 65–125 frs. Reduced rates and special meals for children.

ST-JEAN-PIED-DE-PORT, 64220 Pyrénées-Atlantiques   Map 8

Hôtel des Pyrénées   *Telephone:* (59) 37.01.01
Place du Général-de-Gaulle

At the foot of the Roncesvalles pass that leads over into Spain, St-Jean is one of the most picturesque towns of the Basque hinterland (15th-century ramparts, hilltop citadel) and also a capital of Basque folklore (festival and pelota championships every summer). It used to be a major resting-place for pilgrims about to cross the mountains on their way to Santiago de Compostella. The *Pyrénées* is 'the town's main *auberge*, run by father and son Arrambide with all the inventive skill of a long-established hotelier and creative young chef.' Accommodation is not luxurious: there are rather gloomy old-fashioned bedrooms, but the restaurant makes up for everything. One gastronomic pilgrim waxes lyrical about 'the joy of taking a meal on the terrace on a fine day, of relishing M. Arrambide's brilliant cooking, such as *pigeon roti aux raviolis de cèpes*, fully meriting the very high rating of two *toques* in Gault-Millau'. *(Maggie Angeloglou; also JA, John Huw Roberts)*

> Don't rely on our printed tariffs! Check before booking.

Open: All year, except 12 November–22 December; also closed Tuesdays in winter, except bank and school holidays.
Rooms: 31 double – 22 with bath, 4 with shower, all with telephone.
Facilities: Lift, 2 salons (1 with TV), 2 dining rooms, terrace. Tennis, swimming, fishing and the forest of Iraty nearby. English spoken.
Location: 54 km SE of Bayonne on the D933; parking.
Terms: Rooms 80–185 frs; dinner, B & B 160–195 frs; full board 200–235 frs. Set meals: breakfast 16 frs, lunch/dinner 66, 100, 140 frs; full *alc* 150–200 frs.

ST-LATTIER, 38160 Saint-Marcellin, Isère   Map 8

Le Lièvre Amoureux et sa Chêneraie   *Telephone:* (76) 36.50. 67

St-Lattier is a small village in the Isère valley, on the N92, not far from the National Park of the Vercors with its winter and summer resorts and its memorials to Resistance heroism; Grenoble is 70 km away and Valence 32. We offer a modest prize to any reader finding a French hotel with a quainter name than this Amorous Hare and his Oak-Grove. 'A restaurant with rooms, or delightful country hotel. Michelin over-rates the cooking (one rosette) but the ambience of the surrounding maize fields, the proximity of the level crossing (reminding one of the presence of industry on which all the indulgence is based) and the alfresco dining make up for such marginal disappointments. There are fine views of the foothills of the Vercors mountains. An open-air wedding reception with dancing enlivened our evening meal and entranced the children even if it diminished sleep. However, the staff were solicitous the next day.' Our reporter adds, 'rooms cheap, food inexpensive', but as menus in 1982 ranged from 100 to 200 francs, this verdict may seem relative. The hare's oak-grove is a secluded modern annexe with four luxury suites. *(J M Dennis)*

Open: All year, except Monday and January (but open bank holidays).
Rooms: 7 double, 4 suites – all with bath or shower and telephone; TV in suites.
Facilities: Restaurant, air-conditioning. Garden and terrace.
Location: Halfway between St-Marcellin and Romans-sur-Isère on the N92.
Credit cards: American Express, Diners.
Terms: Rooms 115–230 frs; suites 460 frs. Set meals: breakfast 34 frs, lunch/dinner 160–270 frs.

ST-MALO, 35400 Ille-et-Vilaine, Brittany   Map 8

Le Valmarin   *Telephone:* (99) 81.94.76
7 rue Jean XXIII

Le Valmarin is in the suburb of St-Servan, just south of St-Malo's harbour – 'not easy to find, but this hotel is worth the effort. It is an 18th-century house in an attractive garden. Rooms were beautifully decorated (ours in white, green and gold). There is no restaurant, but the amiable owner booked a table for us at the excellent *Métairie de Beauregard* some 5 km away.' In St-Malo itself, and rather cheaper, are two other good restaurants, the *Central* and *La Porte St-Pierre*. *(H ap R)*

Open: All year, except 24 December–2 January and February.
Rooms: 5 double, 5 single – all with bath, telephone and radio, 6 with mono TV.

Facilities: Salon/bar. Garden. 100 metres from safe sandy beach. English spoken.
Location: In the centre of St-Servan; 2 km from old town of St-Malo. Parking in garden.
Credit card: American Express.
Terms: Rooms 220–300 frs; breakfast 22 frs. Reduced rates for children's breakfast. (No restaurant.)

SAINTES-MARIES-DE-LA-MER, 13460 Bouches-du-Rhône, Map 9 Provence

---

L'Étrier Camarguais   *Telephone:* (90) 97.81.14
Chemin bas des Launes, Route d'Arles

'We timed our visit to coincide with Les Saintes-Maries' astonishing gipsy festival, held every 23–27 May. *L'Étrier* ("the stirrup") lies in its own park, 3 km north of the town, and is one of a number of modern ranch-like hotels in this corner of the Camargue that cater for riding enthusiasts like ourselves: it has its own herd of local white horses, which it hires to guests by the hour (at a price!), and we spent a happy week here, riding, watching birds, and exploring the Camargue. It's an excellent holiday hotel, spacious and informal, with log-cabin style decor, a breezy youthful ambience, lots of children, incessant music, and jokey staff – sub-Club Méditerranée, you could say. Our bedroom, simple but serviceable, was in a chalet in the garden. Especially we enjoyed the big swimming pool and sun-terrace, prettily lit at night. Food was copious and straightforward – lots of *crudités* and log-fire grills – and usually we ate out by the pool. The hotel runs a lively disco which we found great fun – and it was just far enough away to avoid keeping us awake.' *(Alan and Elsie Campbell)*

Open: 1 April–15 November. Restaurant closed Monday out of season.
Rooms: 31 double – all with bath, telephone and colour TV. (27 rooms on ground floor.)
Facilities: Bar, 2 dining rooms, terrace; night club/disco. Garden with swimming pool, tennis court and boules; horses for hire. Beach 3 km. English spoken.
Location: 3 km N of the town, just off the N570 to Arles.
Credit cards: All major credit cards accepted.
Terms: B & B 180–340 frs; dinner, B & B 280–440 frs; full board 380–540 frs. Set meals: lunch/dinner 100 frs; full *alc* 130 frs.

SAINTE-MAXIME, 83120 Var, Provence   Map 9

Hôtel Marie-Louise   *Telephone:* (94) 96.06.05
Hameau de Guerre-Vieille, Beauvallon

'This white villa in a flower-filled garden stands quietly on a hillside, 3 km south-west of Ste-Maxime, and is blissfully aloof from the mad bustle of the coast. It is run with great charm by a couple in late middle-age, the Brunets, who give it something of the air of a private house. This serene, snug place is not for the young seeking glamour – they should go to Ste-Maxime itself, or to St-Tropez across the bay. We had a small but pleasant room with its own little patio where we breakfasted, amid the

scent of the pines. There are no sea views, but the garden is lovely.'
(Anthony Day)

Open: All year except November, December and January. Restaurant closed 30 October–15 March.
Rooms: 11 double, 1 single – all with shower (4 rooms on ground floor.)
Facilities: Salon, dining room, TV. Garden; beach 300 metres.
Location: At Guerre-Vieille, up a turning off the coast road, 3 km SW of Ste-Maxime and 1 km NE of Beauvallon; parking.
Terms: Rooms 190 frs; dinner, B & B 380 frs. Set meals: breakfast 20 frs, lunch/dinner 55–85 frs; full *alc* 100 frs.

ST-PAUL-DE-VENCE, 06570 Alpes-Mar, Provence   **Map 9**

La Colombe d'Or   *Telephone:* (93) 32.80.02
Telex: 970 607 F

A *très très chic* small hotel in one of the showplace hill-towns behind Nice, but by no means your usual sort of de-luxe establishment. For one thing, the place is a modest treasure house of modern art. Paintings and sketches by, among others, Picasso, Braque, Matisse, Calder and Miro, many given to the former owner, the late Paul Roux, in payment by artists who have stayed or eaten here, are accommodated in a beautiful old house, along with many fine pieces of old furniture. (A less modest treasure house of modern art, the Foundation Maeght, the finest collection of its kind in the South of France, is only 2 km away). Each room has a distinctive character – some with original beams, others all in white stucco with window-seats overlooking gardens. Many have lovely terraces and outsize bathrooms. There is a splendid flowered veranda, decorated with a fine Léger mural, where lunch is served; dinner is taken indoors in a large sophisticated rustic dining room. There is a swimming pool set in the midst of cypress trees. 'As far as I am concerned, this must be the best hotel in the world,' raves one recent visitor. But let's not lose our heads, please: the place isn't going to suit everyone. Service is emphatically casual, the food is unremarkable, and not everything is maintained in 100% working order. One reader summed up: 'If you appreciate this sort of place, it's splendid and worth every penny. But if (a) you want quiet in the mornings (traffic starts at 7 a.m.), (b) a spick-and-span, spotlessly clean bedroom, (c) polished service, this isn't the place. But it deserves its entry in the Guide: it is unique, quite unlike any other luxury hotel I have ever visited.' *(John Hills, Stephen Bayley and others)*

Open: All year, except November–mid December.
Rooms: 16 double, 8 suites – all with bath, telephone, radio and colour TV; many with terrace. (1 room on ground floor.)
Facilities: Salon, restaurant, terrace for lunch or refreshments, sauna. Garden with swimming pool. 10 km from the sea. English spoken.
Location: 10 km from Nice; take the road to la Colle and the Hauts de St-Paul.
Credit cards: American Express, Diners.
Terms (excluding 15% service charge): Rooms with breakfast 460–530 frs (suites 620–645 frs). *Alc* 175 frs (excluding wine).

Report forms (Freepost in the UK) will be found at the end of the Guide.

ST-PIERRE-DELS-FORCATS, 66210 Mont-Louis, Pyrénées-Orientales

Map 8

Mouli del Riu *Telephone:* (88) 04.20.36

This small hotel is peacefully situated in a pastoral setting in the Cerdagne, a plateau in the eastern foothills of the Pyrenees. It is not far from the Spanish frontier, and nearer still to the large skiing resort of Font-Romeu and to the remarkable experimental solar furnace at Odeillo, the leading one of its kind in Europe (open to visits on special request). 'The hotel is run with quirky charm by a middle-aged couple and is very good value, with an agreeable atmosphere. The main building has an engagingly old-fashioned air (though comfort is modern): there is also a modern annexe. Friendly staff including a bilingual (French and Spanish) parrot. Nice food; beautiful Pyrenean walks in easy range.' *(J A F Somerville)*

Open: 18 December–1 October.
Rooms: 15 double – 5 with bath, 10 with shower. (5 rooms in annexe.)
Facilities: TV room, bar, dining room. Some English spoken.
Location: From Perpignan, take the N116 through Mont Louis.
Credit cards: Barclay/Visa, Diners.
Terms: B & B 115–175 frs; dinner, B & B 135–155 frs; full board 170–190 frs.

ST-PONS-DE-THOMIÈRES, 34220 Hérault, Languedoc

Map 8

Château de Ponderach *Telephone:* (67) 97.02.57

'A superb 17th-century château set in lovely gardens, and a splendid resting place after a long and tiring day. It is in the Haut Languedoc Nature Reserve and has been the owner's family home for some 300 years. St-Pons, a pleasant town with an interesting 12th-century church, lies at the foot of the Montagne Noire and is within easy driving distance of Carcassone, Narbonne and the Languedoc centres. Our room was at the top of the old building up an old stone staircase, and beautifully furnished and equipped. Like most of the hotels in the *Relais et Châteaux* association, it was expensive, particularly the *à la carte*.' *(Angela and David Stewart)*

Open: Easter–15 October.
Rooms: 12 – 9 with bath, all with telephone.
Facilities: 2 sitting rooms (1 with TV), restaurant; conference facilities. Large garden where you can eat in good weather. Small lake nearby. English spoken.
Location: 1.2 km out of town on the Narbonne road.
Credit cards: American Express, Diners.
Terms: Rooms 195–345 frs. Set meals: breakfast 27 frs, lunch/dinner 120–276 frs.

We ask hotels to estimate their 1983 tariffs some time before publication so the rates given here are not necessarily completely accurate. Please *always* check terms with hotels when making bookings.

Hôtel Pastorel   *Telephone:* (94) 95.02.36
54 rue de la Liberté

'I've never cared greatly for St-Raphaël, a large, crowded, middle-class
family bathing-resort, rather predictable – no wonder it's been called "the
Riviera's Bournemouth". But the Templars' church is worth a look, also
the archeology museum next door. Few of the scores of hotels and
restaurants are much good – but I'd always except the *Pastorel*, a
down-to-earth little place on a main street at one end of the town, run with
verve by the delightful Pastorel/Floccia family. Rooms at the back are
quieter. Floccia *fils'* fine cooking (notably his fish dishes) fully merits its
red "R" in Michelin and is served in a big cool patio at the back, under
vine-creepers. You could be in Spain. Here for 55 francs (1982) we
enjoyed lavish hors d'oeuvres and good roast chicken and desserts, served
by courteous local girls.' *(Anthony Day)*

Open: March–October.
Rooms: 28 double – most with bath or shower and telephone.
Facilities: Restaurant with patio.
Location: At back of town, 500 metres from beach and casino; no private
parking.
Terms: Rooms: 65–205 frs; full board 180–205 frs. Set meals: breakfast 12.50 frs,
lunch/dinner 65–100 frs.

La Potinière   *Telephone:* (94) 95.21.43
Avenue des Plaines, Boulouris

'A useful holiday hotel for those who like sport and an up-to-date
club-like atmosphere. It is very spacious – a series of low modern
buildings in its own pinewoody park, some 600 metres from the beach in
the smart suburb of Boulouris, 4 km east of St-Raphaël. We swam in the
big pool, played tennis at the club next to the hotel, and went on sea
cruises in the hotel's own skippered yacht. Evenings were animated, and
fellow guests mostly young, French, and glamorous-looking. But when
the jollity has died down the place is very quiet at night (it's a *Relais du
Silence*). We could park right by the door of our room, which had a large
terrace with deck-chairs, but the decor was utility-modern. We enjoyed
taking meals out under the pine trees, and as a change from the usual
Provençal cuisine we were easily tempted by such dishes as *cassoulet* on
the menu – the chef is from Toulouse.' *(Mary and Gerald Prescott)*

Open: All year, except mid November–Christmas.
Rooms: 21 double, 4 suites – most with bath, telephone and TV, some with
terrace.
Facilities: Restaurant. Garden with swimming pool; tennis, sea cruises available.
Beach 600 metres.
Location: At Boulouris, 4 km E of St-Raphaël.
Credit cards: American Express, Diners.
Terms: Rooms 250–320 frs, suites 390 frs. Set meals: breakfast 24 frs, lunch/
dinner 110–160 frs.

ST-RÉMY-DE-PROVENCE, 13210 Bouches-du-Rhône, Provence   Map 9

Hôtel du Château de Roussan   *Telephone:* (90) 92.11.63

St-Rémy is the quintessential small Provençal town, with the bonus of also possessing some of the most curious Roman remains in France (at Glanum, just to the south); nearby is the mental home of St-Paul-de-Mausole where Van Gogh spent a year as a patient after cutting off his ear in Arles. 'The *Château de Roussan* stands secluded in its own large park, 2 km west of the town, off the Tarascon road. Our week here was a most civilized experience, more like being the house-guests of cultured friends than staying in a hotel. This stately pink 18th-century château has been the country home of the Roussel family for over a century; now that times are hard, they are accepting bed-and-breakfast clients to keep it going. Bathrooms are modern, but in other respects the rooms are in careful period style, with real Louis XV furniture. Old Louis Roussel was a courteous, seigneurial host. As soon as we arrived he took us, walking-stick in hand, on a tour of his realm, told us its history, showed us the 16th-century farmhouse in the grounds where Nostradamus once lived, and invited us to browse in his library. The whole place is steeped in a certain poetic melancholy, especially its sprawling, rather unkempt garden, full of pools and fountains, and streams inhabited by ducks and swans. We shall come again. No restaurant: but the *Arts* in the town, a lively, bohemian place, provides honest local cooking at low prices.' *(Anthony Day)*

Open: 20 March–20 October.
Rooms: 12 double – 10 with bath, 2 with shower, all with telephone.
Facilities: Salons (no restaurant). Large park. English spoken. &.
Location: 2 km W of town centre, off the Tarascon road; parking.
Terms: Rooms 180–300 frs. Set meal: breakfast 23 frs.

ST-RÉMY-DE-PROVENCE, 13210 Bouches-du-Rhône,   Map 9
Provence

Hôtel Van Gogh   *Telephone:* (90) 92.14.02
1, Avenue Jean-Moulin

'A small modern hotel on the eastern outskirts. There is no restaurant, but the rooms are comfortable, the situation is quiet and the prices reasonable. Smallish garden and swimming pool, the latter much appreciated by the cosmopolitan guests. The owners are friendly and helpful, and it makes a good base for those wishing to explore the area.' *(E Newall)*

Open: 1 March–31 October.
Rooms: 18 double – 7 with bath, 11 with shower, all with telephone. (8 rooms on ground floor.)
Facilities: Salon, TV room, terrace. Garden with swimming pool.
Location: On outskirts of St-Rémy-de-Provence, 60 km from Les Saintes Maries-de-la-Mer, parking.
Terms: Rooms 150–175 frs. Set meal: breakfast 15 frs.

> Procrastination is the thief of the next edition.

Lou Troupelen   *Telephone:* (94) 97.44.88
Chemin des Vendanges

'The "road of the grape-harvests" does indeed lead to this charming family-run hotel on the outskirts of town, set amid vines. It's quite new, but built in the style of an old Provençal farmhouse; our room was 'rustic', with red-tiled floors, but comfortable, and with a balcony and a view. There is an attractive salon, and a little garden where you can take breakfast. The owners are most helpful, especially the blonde daughter of the house who has a taste for striking Victorian costumes. All in all, a useful escape-hole from the fairground frenzy of St-Tropez. No restaurant, but downtown we ate well at *Le Girelier* and entertainingly at noisy *Chez Nano*.' *(John and Ludmila Berry)*

Open: 1 April–15 October.
Rooms: 42 double – most with bath or shower and telephone, some with balcony.
Facilities: Salon. Garden. &.
Location: 800 metres SE of harbour and town centre; parking.
Credit cards: Barclay/Visa, Diners.
Terms: Rooms 190–265 frs. Set meal: breakfast 25 frs. (No restaurant.)

Le Mas de Chastelas   *Telephone:* (94) 56.09.11
                                        Telex: 461 516 POSTE 75

This is widely regarded as one of the two or three most charming and tasteful hotels in the St-Tropez area, where tranquil charm and good taste are not always the most evident qualities. It's a converted 17th-century *mas* (farmhouse), once used for silkworm breeding, and it stands secluded amid vines 4 km west of St-Tropez and ½ km from the sea. It is stylishly run by a cultured Parisian couple, Gérard and Dominique Racine, who are very much in evidence. Their guests include many famous names (Deneuve, Belmondo, Sagan, etc.) who like visiting St-Tropez but want to avoid the frenzied port area. 'If you must come to St-Tropez – and to be honest it can be delightful in May, June and late September – here, at last, is the sort of hotel that this unique resort deserves. It is simple yet elegant, sophisticated yet unpretentious. The furnishings are mostly in pine, and there are flowers in the bedrooms. It's a very superior hotel, and very quiet. There is a small dining room (or you can eat out on the terrace) with very refined cooking – a buffet at lunch, and an *à la carte* menu in the evening; the breakfasts are excellent. You can sit outside in the sun or shade round the heated pool or in the charming garden.' *(Geoffrey Sharp)*
   This description from an earlier edition has been warmly endorsed by later visitors: 'A superb place to stay. Owners and staff very helpful.' 'A delightfully informal atmosphere more akin to that of a club than a hotel.' *(Peter Marshall, A Fraser).* M. Racine, who writes in faultless English, tells us that he has just added a children's playground and ten suites to his existing amenities (tennis, jacuzzi, etc.). He says that the *Guide* has brought him many new guests – will some of them write to us, please?

Open: Beginning April–end September. Restaurant closed evenings in April.

Rooms: 21 double, 10 suites – 27 with bath, 4 with shower, all with telephone; colour TV in suites, which are in annexe.

Facilities: Lounge, TV room, bar, restaurant. Gardens with 4 tennis courts, swimming pool, jacuzzi, ping pong, boules and children's playground. Beach close by. English spoken.

Location: 3 km from St-Tropez, just off the Gassin road to the E; parking.

Credit cards: American Express, Barclay/Visa, Diners.

Terms: Rooms 390–670 frs. Set meals: breakfast 35–38 frs; lunch 100 frs; dinner 190 frs.

ST-VALLIER-DE-THIEY, 06460 Alpes-Mar., Provence   Map 9

Hôtel le Préjoly   *Telephone:* (93) 42.60.86
Place Rougière

'This was one of the highlights of our touring holiday in Provence – just the kind of country hotel/restaurant that the French contrive so superbly. St-Vallier is a small summer resort on a plateau up behind Grasse: the air is tingingly fresh, and there's a glorious sense of space, with forests and mountains all round. We went for some good hikes. The hotel is on the main street (the Route Napoléon to Grenoble) and front bedrooms could well be noisy: but ours at the back was quiet, and very spruce, and looked out over the meadows and hills. This family-run hotel's quality derives above all from its *patron*/*chef* and his wife, Georges and Arlette Pallanca, who are hard-working professionals, yet also ebullient and affable. In 1981 they won a top prize at a gastronomic festival in Rome for "authenticity of cuisine and courtesy of service", and I'm not surprised. The food, mainly local dishes with some special touches, is lavish and tasty, and the 70-franc menu [1982] outstanding value – a copious hors d'oeuvre buffet, then an entrée such as *gigot en papillote*, then cheese and home-made sweets. One of M. Pallanca's *trouvailles* is to slip in what he calls a *trou chinois* (rose-flavoured brandy) before the entrée. Small wonder the big rustic-style dining room was always crowded, with locals and tourists – and though all the Pallanca tribe were working like demons, their service was slowish. Once we ate out on the shady terrace, but were put off by the noise of traffic.' *(Anthony Day)*

Open: All year, except December/January, and Tuesday out of season.

Rooms: 20 double – all with telephone, some with terrace. (1 room with bath on ground floor.)

Facilities: Salon with TV, restaurant, terrace restaurant; conference facilities. Garden with tennis courts and children's play area. Swimming pool, riding and fishing nearby. English spoken. &.

Location: On the N85, in the village, which is 12 km NW of Grasse.

Credit cards: All major credit cards accepted.

Terms: Rooms 100–120 frs; dinner, B & B (out of season) 160–200 frs; full board (in season) 180–220 frs. Set meal (excluding 15% service charge): lunch 70–90 frs; full *alc* 120 frs. Special meals for children.

Details of amenities vary according to the information – or lack of it – supplied by hotels in response to our questionnaire. The fact that lounges or bars or gardens are not mentioned must not be taken to mean that a hotel lacks them.

Abbaye de Sainte-Croix   *Telephone:* (90) 56.24.55
Route du Val de Cuech   *Telex:* STECROI 401247

This venerable 12th-century abbey, on a hillside 4 km north-east of Salon by a private road, has been sumptuously and carefully restored after 200 years of neglect. 'The Cistercian monks slept in small cells and enjoyed the space of their gardens, ambulatories and refectories. And this is rather what the hotel offers: small rooms (but a few with terraces), a large wooded park, and a dining room giving onto a terrace with a stunning view south across the plain of Salon. The small bedrooms can be claustrophobic, but one can't have it all ways; and the place is full of character and charm, has not been spoilt in the conversion and is superbly situated. One could do without the muzak at the swimming pool and here the surroundings could do with some tidying up, and the garden furniture needs renewing. But it's a good base for visiting Arles, St-Rémy and Les Baux. Dinner by candlelight under the mulberry trees is an unforgettable experience, especially as the service is *soigné* yet relaxed and the food of a standard worthy of the setting.' Two *toques*, in fact, in Gault-Millau for cooking that is both inventive and classically Provençal, on which another visitor comments: 'The *menu d'enfants*, quite right and ample for them (salami, lamb chops, yogurt and a choice from the *chariot de patisseries*) was an appetite-whetting sight for the splendid main menu to come: home-smoked fish of many kinds, steak in blueberry sauce, pork in a wild mushroom sauce, a battery of cheeses, as well as that chariot of puddings.' *(Geoffrey Sharp; also AL)*

Open: All year, except 15 November–15 January. Restaurant closed Monday.
Rooms: 22 double – 19 with bath, 3 with shower, all with telephone and colour TV, some with terrace. (3 rooms on ground floor.)
Facilities: Salon, bar, 2 dining rooms, room for receptions, covered terrace. Wooded grounds and garden with swimming pool and boules. Tennis 100 metres. Riding 3 km, sea 25 km.
Location: 4 km NE of Salon, off the D16; sign in Salon after exit from the autoroute. Parking.
Credit cards: American Express, Barclay/Visa, Diners.
Terms: B & B 205–360 frs; full board 445–600 frs. Set meals: breakfast 30 frs, lunch 150 frs, dinner 180 frs; full *alc* 180 frs. Reduced rates and special meals for children.

SÉGURET, Vaison-la-Romaine, 84110 Vaucluse, Provence   **Map 9**

La Table du Comtat   *Telephone:* (90) 36.91.49

Terraced on a hillside above the Rhône vineyards, the quaint old village of Séguret is within easy reach of Orange and Vaison-la-Romaine (q.v.) and has a fine view of the strange jagged peaks of the *Dentelles de Montmirail*. There is a German-run summer school for artists. *La Table du Comtat*, a Michelin-rosetted restaurant with rooms, stands above the village at the end of a winding lane. 'The setting is outstanding, with the Rhône valley sweeping away into the distance, and cliff-like rocks up behind. The food was pricey – as one would expect with a rosette: 80 frs [1982] for the cheapest menu, so nondescript they obviously considered it quite beneath them. I can visualize a Bateman cartoon: "The British couple who *dared* to choose the 80 frs dinner!" Our bedroom was quite small and simple, apart from the sexy bit of drapery behind the bed! The bathroom small but adequate, and a *most* comfortable bed. A better-than-usual breakfast with *fresh* orange juice. The service was quite good in a dour sort of way: only Madame herself smiled at us occasionally. I think really the residents are just a less important side-line: the restaurant is what matters here. Nevertheless, a good one-night stop in a very pleasant area.' Some more recent visitors have commented on the fact that the set menus rarely change and have queried whether *La Table's table* quite justifies its Michelin rosette. But the setting is hard to fault. And the curving *piscine* beneath its high rock is a delight. *(Lady Elstub; also Norman Brangham, HR)*

Open: All year, except mid January–end February; closed Tuesday evening and Wednesday (except July and August).
Rooms: 9 double – all with bath and telephone.
Facilities: Lounge, dining room; garden with swimming pool. English spoken.
Location: 9 km SW of Vaison-la-Romaine just off the D977; hotel is signposted in the village; parking.
Credit cards: Access/Euro/Mastercard, Diners.
Terms: Rooms 180–250 frs. Set meals: breakfast 20 frs; lunch/dinner 90–150 frs.

SEILLANS, 83440 Var, Provence **Map 9**

Hôtel des Deux Rocs *Telephone:* (94) 76.05.33

Seillans, today much in vogue with writers, artists and others as a summer residential centre (Max Ernst used to live here), is a delightful old hill village with steep narrow streets, fountains and a ruined 12th-century château. It is in a glorious setting west of Grasse, facing across a wide and verdant valley towards the Esterel range. The *Deux Rocs*, in a small and pretty square just outside the medieval quarter, is an 18th-century mansion now converted into an elegant and very personal little hotel, run with friendly warmth by its *patronne*, Lise Hirsch, who was formerly a bio-chemist in Paris. 'Our favourite hotel in France, very comfortable, charmingly furnished. We have spent two weeks there for the past three years. You can eat outside by the fountain under two huge plane trees with a fantastic view.' So runs a recent report, while other visitors have praised the 'delicious' food, the warmth of welcome, the cosy *salon* off the main dining room, and the cheerful bedrooms 'each decorated in a different way – grande toile de Jouey, little Boussac prints.' One guest had reservations, sharply criticizing the food and service, but this seems to have been an isolated bad experience. *(K P E Benton, James Burt, Diana Weir)*

Open: 1 April–1 November. Restaurant closed Tuesday out of season.
Rooms: 15 double – 6 with bath, 9 with shower, all with telephone.
Facilities: 2 salons (1 with TV), bar, dining room. Terrace by the fountain where meals are served.
Location: Grasse 31 km; St-Raphaël 41 km. Hotel is in the upper part of the village.
Terms: Rooms 130–280 frs; dinner, B & B 180–240 frs; full board 250–300 frs. Set meals: breakfast 25 frs, lunch/dinner 70–150 frs; full *alc* 120 frs.

Hôtel de France   *Telephone:* (94) 76.06.10
Place du Thouron   *Telex:* 97.05.30

A sedate family-run *auberge*, in a panoramic setting at the entrance to the medieval village. It has an especially delightful swimming pool, facing out across the rolling hills. One recent visitor found the hotel comfortable, clean and good value, but a little lacking in warmth. Another guest, who tells us that she spent an idyllic honeymoon here, also commented on the functional furnishings in the bedrooms, housed in a modern annexe. No reservations, however, about the hotel's restaurant, the *Clariond*, the name of the *patron/chef*. In summer you can eat out in a charming square under plane trees beside an old fountain.

'For the whole of our stay, the food was delicious and beautifully presented. The dining room, in the old part of the hotel, was a large airy room decorated with a profusion of plants and flowers and had spectacular views to the south over the hills. Despite our disappointment over our room, which was rather overshadowed by a large hedge outside the window, we had a lovely week and would certainly want to stay there again.' *(Teresa Kennard)*

Open: All year, except 3 weeks in January. Restaurant closed Wednesday out of season.
Rooms: 26 double – 13 with bath, 13 with shower, all with telephone.
Facilities: Salon with TV, restaurant, terrace. Garden with unheated swimming pool. Gliding, tennis available nearby. English spoken.
Location: Leave the autoroute A8 at Les Adrets, and take the N562 to Seillans. Parking.
Terms: B & B 115–285 frs; dinner, B & B 220–320 frs; full board 310–430 frs. Set meals: lunch/dinner 90 frs.

Hôtel du Cheval Blanc   *Telephone:* (26) 61.60.27

Between Reims and Châlons-sur-Marne, on the eastern fringe of the champagne country, this old coaching inn has been run by the Robert family for five generations. The hotel straddles the main road of the tiny village, with on one side a modern motel-like block of bedrooms, and on the other the charming creeper-covered old inn, beside a spacious garden. The *Cheval Blanc* has long been praised by our readers both for its quiet pastoral setting (it is a *Relais du Silence*) and for its food (rosette in Michelin), and this year the reports are more numerous than ever. Most are favourable, but not all. One enthusiast writes: 'We had a pleasant room on the ground floor, prettily papered and carpeted, with large french windows opening onto the gardens. There were nice bedside lamps which gave a good light, very comfortable beds and a well stocked mini-bar. You can play tennis or mini-golf. Across the road there is a pretty courtyard, and garden furniture where on a warm summer evening it is a delight to ponder over the menu with a pre-dinner drink. The dining room is elegant.' The report goes on to wax lyrical over the *grenouilles tièdes, écrevisses au vin de champagne*, fresh salmon in sorrel sauce ('utterly ambrosial!') and other delights. However, even this visitor found the service slow, while some others have been horrified by long waits between courses, and there are criticisms, too, of minor faults in bedroom equipment and of slight smells from the stream running through the garden. The overall verdict is of a beautiful place, more concerned with its *cuisine* than with attention to hotel detail *(Padi Howard; also Di Latham, J Dixey, and others)*

Open: All year, except mid January–mid February.
Rooms: 20 double, 2 suites – 9 with bath, 13 with shower, all with telephone; mono TV in the suites. (Some rooms on ground floor.)
Facilities: Salon, reading room with colour TV, restaurant, 2 function rooms, billiard room. Hotel is situated in large park bordered by the river Vesle; tennis, mini-golf, table tennis, volley ball, fishing. English spoken.
Location: 20 km E of Reims, on the D37 off the N44 in the direction of Châlons.
Credit cards: American Express, Barclay/Visa, Diners.
Terms (excluding 15% service charge): Rooms 130 frs; half board 275 frs, full board 380 frs. Set meals: breakfast 23 frs, lunch/dinner 130 and 190 frs; full *alc* 180–250 frs.

SERRE-CHEVALIER, 05240 Hautes-Alpes   Map 8

La Vieille Ferme   *Telephone:* (92) 24.02.79
Villeneuve La Salle

'Serre-Chevalier, 6 km west of Briançon in the high Alps, is the collective name given to three old hamlets. Essentially it is a family resort, with little night life, where people go to ski in winter and to take part in various other pursuits in summer. By no means can it be said to be smartly elegant, but the French do seem to have a natural flair. *La Vieille Ferme* has considerable rustic charm. It is a 17th-century house that a group of Parisians got together to save some ten years ago. The proprietor and manager did most of the modernization with his own hands, and with help from members of his family and friends. Most nights in the winter he is a *rôtisseur* and his *rôtisserie* is usually full. He is helped in most of his endeavours by his delightful wife, and by a young, friendly and competent staff that don't seem to change much over the years. All is done with considerable *éclat*, much good taste, great comfort and delicious food – and yet remains delightfully *in*formal.' The hotel has the advantage of being set back from the main road where snow-clearing activities and food deliveries take place in the small hours. *(H C Beddington)*

Open: 11 December–1 May, 18 June–11 September.
Rooms: 23 double, 7 suites – 18 with bath, 10 with shower, all with telephone.
Facilities: Salon with TV, bar, restaurant, rotisserie; terrace. 500 metres from river.
Location: Central, but set back from main road. Outdoor parking for 25 cars.
Terms: B & B 53–348 frs; half board 110–306 frs; full board 158–360 frs. Set meals: lunch/dinner 70 frs; full *alc* 100 frs.

If you consider any entry incorrect, inadequate or misleading, you would be doing us and your fellow travellers a service by letting us know as soon as possible.

Hôtel Fifi Moulin *Telephone:* (92) 67.00.01
Route de Nyons

A useful halt in a village on the Route Napoléon, the main road south from Grenoble to Provence. A reader describes his first return visit after fourteen years: 'The hotel is larger now, and improved by a spacious lounge and patio which look onto the hills of the Hautes-Alpes. A young, energetic couple now run the *Fifi Moulin*. Fourteen years ago, its restaurant had a Michelin star, and the meal was not very interesting. Now, it has the far more reliable Michelin red "R" ("good food at moderate prices") and deserves it. The sweet trolley is pretty spectacular. One of our least expensive nights on the road.' 'Unostentatious comfort, a good welcome, excellent food, quiet rooms – and also a real bargain stop.' *(A N Brangham; also A H H Stow)*

Open: February–mid November, except Wednesday October–June.
Rooms: 26 – all with bath or shower and telephone.
Facilities: Lounge, restaurant, patio.
Location: 107 km south of Grenoble, 64 km from Nyons, on the N75.
Credit cards: All major credit cards accepted.
Terms: Rooms: 100–150 frs; full board 175–195 frs. Set meals: breakfast 14 frs; lunch/dinner 46–85 frs.

Hôtel des Étrangers *Telephone:* (93) 04.00.09
7 boulevard de Verdun

'The hinterland behind Menton is surprisingly little known, and the charming old town of Sospel makes an ideal centre for exploring its delights – for example, the hill-village of Saorge, clinging to the side of a cliff, and the Vallée des Merveilles, where a rocky lunar landscape is covered with prehistoric graffiti. The *patron/chef* of the *Hôtel des Étrangers*, Jean-Pierre Domérégo, will tell you about this, and more, for he has written a book about Sospel and adores his region. Having worked in the US and Bermuda, he is both English-speaking and americo-anglophile. With great gusto he runs an unpretentious but comfortable little family hotel, and does all the cooking, rather well. His special dishes even include a bouillabaissse made of local trout. The hotel receives regular English package-tours, of the discreet, up-market kind: the guests we talked to were all pleased with their stay, as we were too.' Last year's report is endorsed this year by a reader who praises the welcome, food, comfort and scenery, but was surprised to find the riverside pergola closed in warm May weather. *(Anthony Day; also H K Wane)*

Open: All year, except 1 December–27 January.
Rooms: 33 double, 2 single – 14 with bath, 13 with shower, all with telephone. 5 rooms with cooking facilities in annexe.
Facilities: Lift, salon, TV room, 3 restaurants; conference facilities; riverside pergola. Municipal swimming pool 1 km. English spoken.
Location: 22 km from Menton on the D2204; parking.

Credit card: Euro/Mastercard.
Terms: Rooms 80–160 frs; full board 150–210 frs. Set meals: breakfast 18 frs, lunch/dinner 52–90 frs; full *alc* 110 frs.

STRASBOURG, 67000 Bas-Rhin, Alsace   Map 8

Nouvel Hôtel Maison Rouge   *Telephone:* (88) 32.08.60
4 rue des Francs-Bourgeois   *Telex:* 880 130 F

'A splendid central hotel, 30 yards from the main square, the Place Kléber. A place of Victorian comfort, with good rooms, most with bath or shower; some very attractive furniture. The hotel is widely used by delegates to the European Parliament and the Council of Europe; it is good for access to them (by taxi or bus) and is close to the exceptional prize-winning shopping-area and the cathedral. The staff are multi-lingual, efficient. It is essential to book.' *(John Thirlwell)*

Open: All year.
Rooms: 60 double, 65 single, 5 suites – 90 with bath, 10 with shower, all with telephone.
Facilities: Lift; TV room, bar, breakfast room. English spoken. &.
Location: In town centre; no private parking, but parking available in the Place Kléber 50 metres away (you have to pay).
Credit cards: American Express, Barclay/Visa, Diners.
Terms: Rooms 240 frs. Set meal: breakfast 20 frs.

TALLOIRES, 74 Haute Savoie   Map 8

Auberge du Père Bise   *Telephone:* (50) 60.72.01
Bord du Lac   *Telex:* 385812

'This beautiful small hotel is located in one of the most beautiful spots in all of France. It is situated literally on lake Annecy, which over the past few years has been completely cleared and cleaned so that the water is a beautiful blue. Almost all the rooms have a view of the lake, and many have small balconies. The service upstairs is perfect; maids pick up laundry and pressing, and little needs are well taken care of. Breakfast is served in your room, or outside on small tables right next to the lake. Lunch is on the terrace between the lakeside and the inn itself, with an awning over it in case the weather is inclement. The road traffic is behind the inn, and the road is a dead end, so that you hear no noise at all. And of course it is a Michelin three-starred restaurant. Gault Millau has down-graded it as François Bise, the proprietor, has been quite ill, and Madame Bise is running the show alone. But I found nothing at all to quibble about. The dining room is magnificent, and the food likewise. Most of the people who come here go for the food, and may only stay overnight, and then move on to another three-starred restaurant the next day. We spent four nights here, dined on something different each night, and enjoyed our entire stay. But the real joy, outside of the food, is the location, the stillness and quiet, and the views of the mountains across the lake. A truly beautiful place.' *(Alfred Knopf Jr)*

Open: 6 May–22 November and 6 February–19 April.
Rooms: 15 double, 9 suites – all with bath or shower, telephone, colour TV and balcony.
Facilities: Salon, restaurant, terrace and garden. &.
Location: On lake Annecy; parking.
Credit cards: American Express, Barclay/Visa, Diners.
Terms: Rooms: 345–520 frs. Set meals: breakfast 46 frs, lunch/dinner 400 frs.

TAVEL, 30126 Gard, Provence   **Map 9**

Auberge de Tavel   *Telephone:* (66) 50.03.41

An old Provençal *mas*, gracefully converted, standing at the edge of the famous wine-village and facing onto open rolling country. One seasoned traveller in France reports: 'The atmosphere tempts the lingerer. Eleven bedrooms are furnished with functional simplicity but with a hint of cosy luxury. A bar looks out onto a small garden and pool; the restaurant, elegant and high-ceilinged, has tables set well apart and its menus have a touch of distinction. The centre table is loaded with *hors d'oeuvres* that could make a complete meal on their own. Tavel wines, of course, head the wine list. The village, surrounded by holm-oak woods, is a hub from which to explore western Provence.' More recent reports praise the 'very friendly staff' and food well deserving its Michelin rosette. But one reader found her bedroom depressingly dim, because of skimping on bulb wattage: a familiar complaint. *(Norman Brangham; also C H Cole, Barbara Anderson)*

Open: All year, except February. Restaurant closed Monday October–June inclusive.
Rooms: 11 double – 6 with bath, 5 with shower, all with telephone.
Facilities: Lounge, bar, restaurant, functions room. Small garden with swimming pool. English spoken.
Location: Avignon 14 km SE; Orange 20 km N. 200 metres from village centre; parking.
Credit cards: American Express, Barclay/Visa, Diners.
Terms: Rooms 185–216 frs. Half board 216–332 frs; full board 332–448 frs. Set meals: breakfast 23 frs; lunch/dinner 83–150 frs; full *alc* 235 frs. Reduced rates and special meals for children.

TONNERRE, 89700 Yonne, Burgundy   **Map 8**

L'Abbaye Saint Michel   *Telephone:* (86) 55.05.99

Tonnerre lies in a valley in the extreme north of Burgundy, quite close to Auxerre with its cathedral and Chablis with its white wines. The château of Tanlay, 8 km from Tonnerre, is worth visiting too. Joan of Arc once came for prayer and retreat to this 13th-century Benedictine abbey, now converted into a sleek hotel *(Relais et Château)*. Its cuisine, mainly classic and fairly rich, has won a Michelin rosette and a Gault-Millau *toque*.

'Apart from the clever use of plate glass in the reception area the exterior has the appearance of a lovingly restored Burgundian farmhouse on a rather grand scale. Ivy clings to the walls, the white shuttered windows are scattered at random along the length of the building and the slate roof is in perfect condition. The situation is ideal – just out of the town on the slope of a gentle hill; it has an attractive view looking back towards Tonnerre and the église St-Pierre and the valley of the Armançon. It is blissfully quiet. Inside the rooms are nicely appointed, though as to their decoration I would have preferred to have seen more of the cleverly hidden beams and less of the rather heavy French fabric. There is a particularly attractive suite over the entrance with original stone floor and traces of original paintings on the wall. The restaurant is half underground and in the evening had a warm and welcoming ambience. Maybe it would be less inviting at midday. The food was excellent. There is an extensive wine list. The hotel is not cheap – but for what it offers it is not over-priced.' *(Geoffrey Sharp; also Patricia Solomon)*

Open: All year, except 4 December–1 February and Monday October–April.
Rooms: 7 doubles, 3 suites – all with bath, telephone, radio and TV.
Facilities: Reception, drawing room, bar, restaurant, terrace. Garden with tennis court, mini-golf, children's games, boules; river nearby. English spoken.
Location: 1 km from Tonnere; take road to la Montée de St Michel between the church and the post office.
Credit cards: American Express, Barclay/Visa, Diners.
Terms: Rooms 330–530 frs. Set meals: breakfast 36 frs; lunch/dinner 160 frs.

TOULON, 83000 Var, Provence   **Map 9**

La Corniche   *Telephone:* (94) 41.39.53 and 41.35.12
1 Littoral Frédéric Mistral, Le Mourillon

'We found France's leading naval base a far more interesting place than we'd expected. It's in a superb natural setting, ringed by bare mountains; and the *vieille ville* still has some charm, despite rebuilding after wartime damage. It's worth going up to the top of Mont Faron, by car or *téléphérique*, for the view of the giant harbour and the museum of the 1944 landings in Provence. *La Corniche* is a small and stylish modern hotel opposite the yacht-harbour in the quiet suburb of Le Mourillon. It's very spruce and clean, though service is a bit impersonal. We had a nice bedroom with a balcony overlooking the port, set back from the road, therefore quiet. There's a pretty flowery patio where you can take breakfast. The dining room, amazingly, has been built round three ancient umbrella pines whose ample trunks fill the centre of the room. The Provençal cooking we found unremarkable, but good value. A useful overnight halt, away from the down-town bustle.' *(Charles Hildesley)*

Open: All year. Restaurant closed February, Sunday evening and Monday.
Rooms: 18 double, 4 suites – all with bath, telephone and mono TV, some with balcony.
Facilities: Lift; salons (1 with TV), bar, breakfast patio, restaurant. Sandy beaches nearby. English spoken.
Location: On the seafront at Le Mourillon, 2 km SE of town centre.
Credit cards: Access/Euro/Mastercard, American Express, Diners.
Terms: Rooms 160–275 frs. Set meals: breakfast 24 frs, lunch 85 frs, dinner 140 frs.

We should be glad to hear of good hotels in Toulouse.

Hôtel La Saône   *Telephone:* (85) 51.03.38
Rive gauche

Tournus, roughly halfway between Chalon and Mâcon, and on the river Saône, makes an admirable breather or night stop for those beating down the A6. Its special glory is the abbey church of St-Philibert, older even than Cluny, and one of the best-preserved Romanesque churches in France. But the town is full of fine old medieval houses in cobbled streets. The *Saône*, on the *rive gauche*, is by no means the smartest hotel in town, nor the most 'gastronomic' eating-place. 'It's in the "plain but adequate" class in Michelin; badly sign-posted, but once there it's really pleasant if very simple. No rooms with baths, but a sympathetic management and very cheap. The restaurant overlooks the river, and has menus at 50 frs (recommended in red in Michelin for good value) and 85 frs [1982]. We had the former, and it proved perfectly adequate and enough for two! There's an attractive garden front and back. An ideal stopping-off place, especially for families with children who need to let off steam.' *(Uli Lloyd Pack)*

Open: February–November. Restaurant closed Thursday.
Rooms: 12 – some with shower.
Facilities: Restaurant. Garden.
Location: On the A6 between Chalon and Mâcon; on the left bank of the river Saône; parking.
Terms: Rooms 63–115 frs. Set meals: breakfast 11 frs; lunch/dinner 57–98 frs.

Hôtel Balzac   *Telephone:* (47) 05.40.87
47 rue de la Scellerie

'In a city crammed with hotels often of dubious quality, we found this bed-and-breakfast hotel modestly priced for the high standard of comfort offered. Welcome from the Breton owner idiosyncratic but helpful – the breakfast provided was superb and he was utterly reliable about phone calls, messages, etc. The hall provides comfortable seats and tables – a boon in France. We recommend it.' *(E Davis; also RCA)*

Open: All year.
Rooms: 18 double, 2 single, 2 suites – 7 with bath, 5 with shower, all with telephone. (2 rooms on ground floor.)
Facilities: Reception room, TV room.
Location: Central, opposite the Theatre. No special parking facilities.
Credit cards: Access/Euro/Mastercard, American Express, Barclay/Visa.
Terms: Rooms 45–180 frs. Set meal: breakfast 15 frs. (No restaurant.)

In the case of many continental hotels, especially French ones, we have adopted the local habit of quoting a price for the room whether it is occupied by one or more persons. Rates for B & B, half board, etc., are per person unless otherwise stated.

TOURTOUR, 83690 Salernes, Var, Provence   Map 9

Auberge Saint-Pierre   *Telephone:*   (94) 70.57.17

'We were entranced by this idiosyncratic country hotel, owned and run by
a dedicated Provençal couple, the Marcellins, who believe in keeping up
local traditions and furthering ecology. It's an 18th-century manor,
standing alone amid splendid rolling country just east of the show-village
of Tourtour. It has nearly 200 acres of farmland, and gazelles and horses
graze in the big meadow beside the solar-heated swimming pool. Inside,
we found the stone floors and low ceilings a little austere, though graceful.
But we were intrigued by such oddities as the chapel turned into a TV
salon, the mossy fountain in the dining room (previously it was the
manor's inner court), and the *tableaux vivants* of Provençal clay dolls
(santons) representing the virtues of agricultural tradition. To pursue his
point, M. Marcellin gets his meat, poultry and cheeses fresh from his
home farm. He provided us with a range of tasty local dishes such as *pieds
et paquets*, as well as his own speciality, *beignets d'escargots*. Meals are not
served outdoors, alas, but the dining room does have a good view.
Cultivated fellow guests, pleasant bedrooms – and the whole thing
amazingly good value for the price. We'll be back.' *(Alan and Elsie
Campbell)*

Open: 1 April–1 November. Restaurant closed Thursday.
Rooms: 15 – most with bath, shower and telephone.
Facilities: Salon, TV room, dining room. Grounds with heated swimming pool
and tennis court.
Location: At St-Pierre-de-Tourtour, 3 km E of Tourtour, which is 20 km NW of
Draguignan.
Terms: Rooms 195–230 frs; full board 240–260 frs. Set meals: breakfast 23 frs,
lunch/dinner 110–140 frs.

TOURTOUR, 83690 Salernes, Var, Provence   Map 9

La Bastide de Tourtour   *Telephone:* (94) 70.57.30

Tourtour is an attractive 'village in the sky' as it picturesquely describes
itself, 2,100 feet up, and situated between Aups to the north-west and
Draguignan to the south-east, in central Provence. A good centre for the
Gorges du Verdon, Lac le Croix and many lovely drives in all directions,
and very pretty in the immediate vicinity. *La Bastide* was custom-built in
the Sixties: rooms are exceptionally large and well-designed with beautiful toile for wall-paper and handsome chairs. Nothing obtrusive – not
even (unusually) TV. One wall of the bedroom is a picture window,
opening out on to a private terrace. As befits a luxury hotel, there's a big
swimming pool and tennis court, and the hotel also enjoys a rosetted
restaurant. What earns *La Bastide* a place in the Guide, however, is not
just its sumptuous fixtures and fittings, but its warm *acceuil* – by no means
always found in expensive hideouts. *(IIR)*

Open: End February–1 November. Restaurant closed Tuesday out of season.
Rooms: 24 double, 2 single, all with bath, WC and telephone – all on ground
floor.
Facilities: Lift, TV room, salon, bar, dining room; conference and banqueting

facilities. Garden with solar-heated swimming pool and tennis court. English spoken. &.
Location: 500 metres from Tourtour on Draguignan road; 20 km NW of Draguignan; parking.
Credit cards: American Express, Barclay/Visa, Diners.
Terms: Rooms 240–330 frs. Set meals: breakfast 35 frs, lunch/dinner 150–200 frs; full *alc* 220 frs.

TOURTOUR, 83690 Salernes, Var, Provence   **Map 9**

Petite Auberge   *Telephone:* (94) 70.57.16

'The *Petite Auberge* (a *Relais du Silence*) looks a small rather unremarkable purpose-built hotel – but it has enough to recommend it to encourage us to return for a second year running. It is built on the steep pine-covered slopes a mile below the village, with magnificent views for miles across undulating country. Rather a windy spot, perhaps a little bleak – but the service and the welcome really compensate, we thought. It is spotlessly clean with comfortable bedrooms. Solid rustic-style furniture. Adventurous wall fabrics (though I wasn't *entirely* sold on this year's Jacobean pattern in ultramarine and mustard!). Lovely bathroom. I'm afraid the bedside lamps were only 40 watt, but that didn't worry us; we've learnt that typical French "meanness" and always carry our own! The food was good and far too generous, so the second night we settled for *à la carte*, and it worked out cheaper. The worst one can say about this little hotel is that it certainly isn't glamorous. But if you want good, friendly service, gorgeous views, and complete tranquillity – this is it.' *(Lady Elstub)*

Open: 1 April–30 September.
Rooms: 15 double – all with bath or shower and telephone.
Facilities: Restaurant, terrace; swimming pool. English spoken.
Location: 1.5 km out of Tourtour on the D77; parking.
Terms: Rooms 160 frs; dinner, B & B 155–235 frs; full board 210–290 frs. Set meals: breakfast 20 frs, lunch/dinner 100 frs. Reduced rates for children.

TRELLY, 50660 Quettreville-sur-Sienne, Manche, Normandy   **Map 8**

Hôtel de la Verte Campagne [GFG]   *Telephone:* (33) 47.65.33

Right in the middle of nowhere, this old 18th-century Normandy farmhouse, converted into a small country restaurant with rooms, makes an ideal first stop from Cherbourg, 80 km to the north, along the Normandy coast on the western side of the Cotentin peninsula. It is not far from Coutances, with its haunting Gothic cathedral, and the popular little resort of Granville (warmly recommended for its Saturday market) is an easy drive south. The former (English) proprietor died a few years ago, but his widow, Madame Meredith, who also speaks English, seeks to maintain the tradition and character of this country hotel. With some reservations recently about the food, the hotel has continued to meet with warm approval from our readers: 'The rooms are charming, all different. The tiny single one is delicately sprigged, the next one is done tastefully in red-and-white checked gingham with exposed beams and ancient wardrobe. There is another one that has an added shower which is a bit of a failure, because the shower seems to ruin the proportions. All the rooms are amazingly well-equipped (for France) with Nina Ricci soap in tiny shell-shaped case. Roses climb up the walls and in at the bedroom windows. More roses in the small paddock. The salons are traditional country-house elegant with beams, wood fires, deep chairs.'

Since our last reports a new young chef has arrived, so it is to be hoped that the *cuisine* will now emerge from its brief bad patch. Reports on this welcome.

Open: All year, except Monday. Restaurant closed Monday, also November and February.
Rooms: 6 double, 2 single – 5 with bath, all with telephone. (1 room on ground floor.)
Facilities: 2 salons, bar, 3 restaurants. Rose garden and paddock. Nearest beach Coutances 12 km. English spoken. &.
Location: At the hamlet of Chevalier. Granville 23 km S. Parking.
Terms: Rooms 95–200 frs. Half board 110 frs per person added to room price; full board 160 frs added. Set meals: breakfast 18 frs, lunch/dinner 60–110 frs.

TREVOU-TRESTEL, 22660 Côtes-du-Nord, Brittany   **Map 8**

Le Charma   *Telephone:* (96) 23.72.21

'Trevou-Trestel is a tiny village on the north-Breton coast, 10 km east of Perros-Guirec. *Le Charma*, essentially a restaurant with rooms, is small and unpretentious, within walking distance of a glorious beach. The owners, the Cathous, are most welcoming and accommodating – providing vacuum flasks, and insisting on lending us their washing machine. We had many enjoyable chats at the bar with them and their local clientèle. The food is excellent if a little repetitive, and each meal includes a delicious seafood course. *Le Charma* depends largely on its lunchtime trade, when it's crowded out with about 150 local workers, served very efficiently by only one or two staff. Our room was small but adequate though the walls were thin, and there's only one bathroom and loo for ten rooms. Light sleepers might find the front rooms a little noisy. But, all in all, this is an ideal place for a *cheap* family holiday – friendly and informal. We booked in for three days and stayed a fortnight.' *(Anne Abel-Smith)*

Open: All year. Restaurant closed evenings in October.
Rooms: 10.
Facilities: Bar, salon with TV, dining room. 1 km from the sea.
Location: On the coast. 10 km E of Perros-Guirec.
Terms: Full board 140 frs.

VAISON-LA-ROMAINE, 84110 Vaucluse, Provence   **Map 9**

Le Beffroi   *Telephone:* (90) 36.04.71
Rue de l'Evêché

Vaison is a pleasant little market town in a wooded valley, between the vineyards of the Côtes du Rhône (Gigondas, etc.) to the west, and the wild massif of Mont Ventoux to the east. It contains some of the most interesting Roman remains in France – not big public buildings as at

Orange or Arles, but patrician villas with their attendant shops and outhouses, for Vaison in Roman days was a smart residential centre. Across the river, a 12th-century château stands on a hill above the steep and narrow streets of the medieval quarter. Here is *Le Beffroi*, a rambling 16th-century mansion with bumpy tiled floors and antique furnishings: conversion into a comfortable little hotel has not destroyed its *cachet*. Informal family ambience and reasonable prices. 'Don't be put off by twee names on the bedrooms,' warns one reader: his was called 'Le Cosy'. When it's fine, you can take breakfast, drinks or meals on a flowery terrace overlooking the town below. A new chef arrived in 1982, and first reports speak well of the top-price 'serious' menu; less well of the cheaper one. Only complaint: loud piped muzak.

Open: 11 March–15 November. Restaurant closed all day Monday and Tuesday midday.
Rooms: 18 double, 2 single, 1 suite – 5 with bath, 8 with shower, all with telephone. (1 room on ground floor, 10 in annexe.)
Facilities: Bar, salon, restaurant, function room. Garden, terrace. English spoken.
Location: 27 km NE of Orange, E of the N7. Hotel is in the upper part of the town; parking.
Credit cards: All major credit cards accepted.
Terms: Rooms 53–195 frs; dinner, B & B 136–360 frs; full board 200–490 frs. Set meals: breakfast 18 frs; lunch/dinner 70–95 frs; full *alc* 150–200 frs. Special meals for children.

VALENCE, 26000 Drôme   Map 8

Restaurant Pic   *Telephone:* (75) 44.15.32
285 avenue Victor-Hugo

Many a gourmet, hurrying up or down the Rhône valley *autoroute*, takes the trouble to turn off into the busy but unexceptional city of Valence, to seek out the exceptional *Pic*. A shady garden, pretty bedrooms above a flowery courtyard; and *nouvelle cuisine* at its least affected. 'Do not be afraid about Pic being possibly the best chef in France (among the top six anyway). Or put off by the prices. Everything is absolutely marvellous – from Jacques Pic and his wife and family to all the helpful staff, incredible (but simple) comfort in the bedrooms and total luxury in the dining room. Food out of this world. But the whole place is so undaunting once you have summoned up the courage (and saved the money) to stay there. A charming and helpful atmosphere pervades all and there is no snootiness by anyone, unlike so many other prestigious places. Breakfast a dream of fresh lemon brioche (warm), etc.' *(Hugh and Anne Pitt)*

Open: All year, except Wednesday, and Sunday evening. Restaurant closed August and some of February.
Rooms: 4 double, 1 suite – 4 with bath, all with telephone.
Facilities: Salon, restaurant. Garden; courtyard. English spoken.
Location: In southern suburbs, on the old N7 (leave autoroute by Valence–Sud exit); garage parking.
Credit cards: American Express, Diners.
Terms: Rooms 200–220 frs, suite 450 frs. Set meals: breakfast 23 frs, lunch 180, 260, 320 frs, dinner 260, 320 frs; full *alc* 300 frs.

VENCE, 06140 Alpes-Maritimes, Provence   Map 9

Hôtel Diana   *Telephone:* (93) 58.28.56
Avenue des Poilus

Do not miss Matisse's lovely Chapel of the Rosary, in Vence; nor the
mountain drive to the north, the *'circuit des clues'*. 'An elegant and
efficient small hotel near the town centre. The rooms, although small, are
beautifully designed and furnished. Ours (and I think many of the others)
had a small *cuisinette*.' A more recent visitor adds, intriguingly: 'The
manager, the quite splendid M Jean-Jaque, spends all his time on the
telephone, but once he knows you, will interrupt his phoning for you.
Very efficient and observant, and utterly charming, he enjoys doing two
or more things at the same time. The great feature is the *cuisinette*,
beautifully arranged and equipped – and they do the washing-up!' There
is some dissent over whether the hotel's underground garage is 'adequate'
or 'by far the worst feature, awkward to enter and leave'; also as to
whether the hotel's breakfasts are 'generous' with 'plenty of really hot
coffee' or merely 'adequate'. The hotel provides no other meals: but
down-town you should try the romantic *Les Portiques* or the more
down-to-earth *Farigoule*. *(Winston and Irene Moses; John Hills, Rosamund Hebdon)*

Open: All year.
Rooms: 25 double – all with bath, telephone; some with cooking facilities.
Facilities: Lift, TV room, library, bar. Garden. English spoken.
Location: 6 km from the beach; 200 metres from town centre; garage.
Credit cards: All major credit cards accepted.
Terms: Rooms 150–170 frs. Set meal: breakfast 15 frs.

VERNET-LES-BAINS, 66500 Pyrénées Orientales   Map 8

Hôtel des Deux Lions et Restaurant Le Thalassa   *Telephone:* (68) 05.55.42
18 Bd Clémenceau

Vernet is in the foothills of the eastern Pyrenees. A 2 km drive to the south
and then a steep 30-minute climb on foot, brings you to the romantic
Abbey of St-Martin-de-Canigou, lost in the lovely wooded hills. Today it
is much used for Catholic retreats. Also strongly recommended is the
Abbey of St-Michel-de-Cuza, near Prades, north-east of Vernet. 'A jolly,
family hotel/restaurant at the entrance to this enchanting mountain
village spa where Kipling once lived and helped found the Anglican
Church of St George. It was also popular with Trollope. Nothing is too
much trouble and the food very good indeed, imaginative and fresh.
Garden and terrace for sunny days, big log fire in dining room in winter,
etc. Rooms cosy, simple and clean. Good cheap wine list. A great find.'
(Hugh and Anne Pitt)

Open: All year.
Rooms: 9 double, 3 single, 2 suites – 4 with bath, 9 with shower.
Facilities: Salon, TV room, restaurant, terrace, solarium. Garden (meals out-
doors in fine weather). Swimming pool, riding, skiing, tennis nearby. English
spoken.
Location: 40 km from Perpignan; 12 km from Prades off the N116.

Credit cards: Access/Euro/Mastercard, Barclay/Visa.
Terms: B & B 102–107 frs. Set meals: lunch/dinner 60–140 frs. Special rate for stay of 10 days for Good Hotel Guide readers. Special rates and meals for children.

VERNEUIL-SUR-AVRE, 27130 Eure, Normandy Map 8

Hostellerie du Clos   *Telephone:* (32) 32.21.81
98 rue de la Ferté-Vidame

This historic Norman town, astride main routes going south from Rouen or west from Paris, was built by Henry I of England. It has two superb churches: the 12th-century Notre Dame, and La Madeleine with its high Gothic tower. 'The hotel is a two-coloured brick château-type building (unusual, but charming) located in its own grounds on the edge of town. Our room, attractively decorated, was moderate in size but crammed full of furniture: two large stuffed chairs and a largish table, a desk and a dresser with a colour telly. We got a little box of chocolates with the room. The bathroom was almost as large as the bedroom, with lots of extras. The best bit was dinner: delicious. Some of the best dishes include a terrine of langoustine, a breast of duck with a cider vinegar sauce, a fillet of beef with pistachio sauce, delicate little potato pancakes and a strawberry mousse with raspberry sauce. A very cheap Sancerre was delightful. Service was excellent. The proprietors were friendly and the bill reasonable.' *(J Gazdak)*

Open: 25 January–15 December. Closed Monday, except public holidays.
Rooms: 9 double, 3 suites – 7 with bath, 5 with shower, all with telephone and TV. 14 rooms in annexe. (3 rooms on ground floor.)
Facilities: Salon, 2 dining rooms; facilities for small conferences. Garden. English spoken.
Location: In town centre, just off the N12; parking.
Credit cards: American Express, Barclay/Visa, Diners.
Terms: Dinner, B & B 360–480 frs. Set meals: lunch/dinner 98 frs.

VERSAILLES, 78000 Yvelines, Ile-de-France Map 8

Trianon Palace Hotel   *Telephone:* (3) 950.34.12
1 boulevard de la Reine   *Telex:* 69.88.63

Versailles' one luxury hotel stands beside the château gardens, and some bedrooms overlook them. The Gault-Millau guide speaks of 'the massive arrogance of the décor of this *fin-de-siècle* palace, its pompous *salons*', but our own reporter is kinder: 'Who could afford a four-star hotel in Britain? Not me, but certainly in France. Our bedroom, though slightly faded, was warm, elegant and peaceful. And although it's one of those hotels with a large dining room, it's worth going not only for the food but to meet the head waiter. He greets and seats every client, chats to an elderly *habituée*, and takes endless photographs of Japanese tourists, all the while making you feel you're the only person in the room. The *Trianon* is a real haven.' *(Di Latham)*

Open: All year.
Rooms: 94 double, 18 single, 8 suites – 86 with bath, 28 with shower, all with telephone and baby-listening; mono TV on request. (1 special bedroom with facilities for disabled.)

Facilities: Lift; salons, bar, restaurant; conference facilities. 6 acres grounds. Bicycles. English spoken. &.
Location: By château gardens; large car park.
Credit cards: All major credit cards accepted.
Terms: B & B 247–574 frs; half board 412–623 frs. Set meals: lunch/dinner 130–180 frs. Children under 14 free if sharing parents' room; special meals provided.

VERVINS, 02140 Aisne, Picardy   **Map 8**

La Tour du Roy   *Telephone:* (23) 98.00.11
45 rue Général Leclerc

The small town of Vervins lies near the Belgian frontier, some 2½ hours' drive south-east from Calais. It is capital of the Thiérache, a pastoral stretch of apple orchards, streams and little green hills that contrasts pleasingly with the dull bare plains covering most of this part of France. *La Tour du Roy* is equally inviting: a converted manor house built on the ramparts, run with personal warmth and professional skill by Claude and Annie Desvignes. One reader extols the attractive courtyard, the views from the bedrooms, the tranquillity and the courteous service, as well as the food which wins a star in Michelin. Annie Desvignes' cooking relies on imaginative use of quality local produce, and she is praised as much for her apple tarts and chicken stews as for more exotic dishes such as *flan de crabe au beurre blanc crémé. (Miss P Watson)*

Open: All year, except 15 January–15 February. (Restaurant closed Sunday evening, Monday midday.)
Rooms: 15 double – 11 with bath, 4 with shower, 7 with TV, all with radio, direct-dial telephone and baby-listening. (1 room on ground floor.)
Facilities: TV room, salon, 4 dining rooms; conference/function facilities. English spoken. &.
Location: On the N2, 36 km N of Laon.
Credit cards: All major credit cards accepted.
Terms: B & B 100–120 frs; dinner, B & B 160–180 frs; full board 220–280 frs. Set meals: lunch/dinner 30 frs; full *alc* 100 frs. Reduced rates and special meals for children.

VÉZAC, 24220 St-Cyprien, Dordogne   **Map 8**

Rochecourbe Manoir-Hôtel   *Telephone:* (53) 29.50.79

'Surpassed our expectations. The peace and tranquillity of its country setting and the comfort of the rooms and bathrooms were superb. A spiral staircase in the tower leads from the peaceful garden (reclining chairs for drinks before and after dinner) to the large dining room, and then up again to the seven bedrooms. From our room we looked across the valley to the château at Beynac, and the loudest noise was the bleating of sheep and singing of birds. Dinner is not provided in the evening, but their *petite carte de soir* consisted of food ordered to our desire – *pâté*, omelette, salad, salmon mayonnaise, cheese, fresh strawberries, etc. We cannot speak too highly of the comfort and kindness provided by Monsieur and Madame Roger.' *(Dr and Mrs P H Tattersall)*

Thus our original entry. Dr and Mrs Tattersall have been back recently, and report: 'Just as good as we remembered it. Peaceful – friendly – beautiful setting – excellent evening meal and breakfast.'

Open: 1 April–1 November.
Rooms: 5 double, 1 single, 1 suite – 6 with bath, 1 with shower, all with telephone (2 rooms in annexe).
Facilities: TV room, dining room. Garden. 2 km from river; riding and swimming nearby; excursions to châteaux, museums, caves, etc.
Location: 8 km from Sarlat. On the D5 between Sarlat and Beynac (Michelin map No. 75).
Restriction: No children under 2.
Credit card: Diners.
Terms: Rooms 100–300 frs. Set meal: breakfast 25 frs; full *alc* 70 frs.

VÉZELAY, 89450 Yonne, Burgundy   **Map 8**

L'Espérance   *Telephone:* (86) 33.20.45
St-Père

Three km east of Vézelay on the Avallon road, this small *Relais et Château* hotel is renowned for serving inventive *nouvelle cuisine* (e.g. *salade chaude de champignons sauvages*) to a very high standard (two Michelin rosettes, three Gault-Millau *toques*) in a gracious but unpretentious setting. Damask and silver in the dining room; antique furniture, strikingly pretty bedrooms. 'We were delighted. The hotel is a beautiful manor house with superb garden and grounds, with a river running through it. The hotel is furnished with taste, but bedrooms are on the small side. Friendly and courteous service; outstanding *cuisine*, and Marc Meneau, the *patron/chef*, calls at your table in the most pleasing manner. Terms are not low, but worth every franc.' *(Sally and Curtis Wilmot-Allistone; also JA)*

Open: All year, except 3 January–5 February and Tuesday.
Rooms: 20 double, 5 suites – 16 with bath, 4 with shower, all with telephone, 10 with TV. 5 rooms in annexe. (3 rooms on ground floor.)
Facilities: Restaurant. Garden with river. English spoken.
Location: 3 km E of Vézelay on the Avallon road; parking.
Credit cards: American Express, Barclay/Visa, Diners.
Terms (excluding 10% service charge): Rooms 150–350 frs; dinner, B & B 130–250 frs. Set meals: breakfast 30 frs, lunch 130–250 frs, dinner 180–250 frs.

VÉZELAY, 89450 Yonne, Burgundy   **Map 8**

Poste et Lion d'Or   *Telephone:* (86) 33.21.23
Place du Champ-de-Foire   *Telex:* 800949

The medieval hill town of Vézelay, 50 km south of Auxerre, is one of the most rewarding night stops for those driving up or down the A6. Its supreme glory is the basilica of Sainte-Madeleine, once one of the great pilgrimage churches of France, and still a place for lay pilgrims in cars and coaches, a splendidly airy Romanesque building, with a wealth of magnificent stone carvings. The *Poste et Lion d'Or* is the chief hotel of the town, with something of the atmosphere of a large handsome country house, at the foot of the hill leading to the cathedral. Bedrooms, which are furnished to a high standard, look out over the countryside.

'A hotel of character, enhanced by beautiful arrangements of fresh flowers in the public rooms.' 'Good beds and linen. Excellent food and service. Beautiful location. Only drawback: thin bedroom walls, however typically French they may be.' Rooms in the hotel itself are probably quieter than those in the annexe across the car park. *(Rosamund V Hebdon, T Crone, and others)*

Open: 10 April–2 November. Restaurant closed Tuesday and Wednesday mid-day.
Rooms: 42 doubles, 5 suites – most with bath, all with telephone.
Facilities: Restaurant. Conference facilities. Garden.
Location: 13 km from Avallon; 50 km S of Auxerre; parking.
Terms: Rooms 207–368 frs, suites 495 frs. Set meals: breakfast 25 frs, lunch/dinner 115–207 frs.

VILLANDRY, 37510 Joué les Tours, Indre et Loire   Map 8

Le Cheval Rouge   *Telephone:* (47) 50.02.07

'Hotel on roadside 100 yards from Château Villandry (with the famous 16th-century formal gardens), in a very small village. Not much in village, but there's a road opposite the hotel leading (half a mile) to a quiet stretch of the Loire. Pleasant "pottering spot". Do not expect a rapturous welcome from Madame – she only smiled when we praised the place on leaving. However, she runs an efficient, small, modern country hotel with pleasant entrance lounge and clean bedrooms. The restaurant was the *feature*. It was spacious, air-conditioned and very clean. The food was "gastronomique" – even on the cheapest menu; it was superbly cooked and presented (Michelin rosette). This hotel was well worth an overnight stop – or would make a good base for visiting other châteaux in the Loire valley.' *(Janet Foulsham)*

A recent visitor adds this footnote: 'Most satisfactory hotel – cookery still deserves the Red Guide rosette. Madame thanked us for our patronage and did not remain silent at our praise.' *(M E Kirk)*

Open: All year, except January and Monday; weekends only November, December and February.
Rooms: 20 – all with bath or shower and telephone.
Facilities: Lounge, restaurant, air-conditioning; conference facilities. Garden.
Location: 10 km from Azay-le-Rideau; 20 km from Tours; parking.
Credit card: Barclay/Visa.
Terms: Rooms 145–210 frs; full board 295–340 frs. Set meals: breakfast 18.50 frs; lunch/dinner 75–180 frs.

VILLEFRANCHE-SUR-MER, 06230 Alpes-Maritimes   Map 9

Hôtel Welcome   *Telephone:* (93) 55.27.27
1 Quai Courbet   *Telex:* 470281

Villefranche is a lively and appealing old fishing-port in a deep bay – remarkably unspoilt, seeing that Nice and Monte Carlo are so close. The

383

Welcome, a classic and dignified hotel, stands on the harbour opposite the tiny fishermen's chapel decorated by Cocteau. 'All rooms have sea views and most have balconies. As the hotel faces south-east, these get the breakfast-time sun. There is the constant spectacle of the comings and goings of boats big and small. Restaurant on the quay level, the *St-Pierre*, is pleasant. A rather boring bar with a narrow balcony on the floor above. Slight noise at night from a few over-revved motorbikes on the quay.' *(Geoffrey Sharp; also Gerald and Mary Prescott)*

Open: All year except 1 November–17 December.
Rooms: 30 double, 3 single – 28 with bath, 1 with shower, all with telephone; some with colour TV.
Facilities: Lift, bar, restaurant, TV room; conference facilities; terrace. Beach and water sports nearby. English spoken.
Location: On the quay, near the port, follow signs for Chapelle Cocteau; garage for 2 cars only.
Credit cards: All major credit cards accepted.
Terms: Rooms 145–325 frs; dinner, B & B 260–445 frs; full board 320–510 frs. Set meals: breakfast 21 frs, lunch/dinner 100 frs, full *alc* 170 frs. Special meals for children.

VILLENEUVE-LES-AVIGNON, 30400 Gard, Provence   **Map 9**

Le Prieuré   *Telephone:* (90) 25.18.20
Place du Chapitre   *Telex:* 431042

Villeneuve contains almost as much of interest as Avignon itself, which lies directly across the Rhône. When the Popes held sway in their Palace, it was a favoured residential suburb for wealthy cardinals and other prelates; earlier, the French kings had used it as a fortress town. Relics of that great age include the gigantic Chartreuse, the Fort St-André, the municipal museum (marvellous painting by Charenton) and the church of Notre-Dame with its remarkable carved ivory statuette of the Virgin. Next to this church, *Le Prieuré* is a 14th-century priory, superbly converted, and stylishly run by the affable Mille family as an elegant and luxurious little hotel. Though on the edge of town, it is very quiet and looks out over fields, the only blemish being a large ugly school building on one side. You can choose between a 'characterful' bedroom in the old building (antique furniture, tiled floors) or a larger, more expensive one in the new annexe (wide balconies, big sofas). Amenities include a lovely garden amid rose-arbours, a tennis court, and a swimming pool and lido amid trees. The food, mainly classic, is expensive but excellent (Michelin rosette), and is served either on the lawn or in the beautiful beamed dining room. A warmly recommended hotel. *(Alfred Knopf Jr, Peter and Sarah Abbott)*

Open: 4 March–1 November. Restaurant also closed 1 May.
Rooms: 18 double, 8 single, 9 suites – all with bath and telephone, 30 with colour TV. (2 annexes with 24 rooms.)
Facilities: Lift, salons, bar. Garden with tennis courts and swimming pool. English spoken.
Location: In town centre, behind the church; parking.
Credit cards: All major credit cards accepted.
Terms: B & B 240–540 frs; dinner, B & B 460–760 frs. Set meals: lunch/dinner 220 frs; full *alc* 250 frs. Special meals for children on request.

VILLERS-COTTERÊTS, 02600 Aisne   Map 8

Hôtel Le Régent   *Telephone:* (23) 96.01.46
26 rue Général-Mangin

Villers-Cotterêts was once a staging-post for travellers going north-east from Paris, say to Reims or Belgium. In the early 19th century it had 32 inns, many of them beautiful buildings with dignified façades and inner courtyards. Most of the buildings are still there, but only one is used for its original purpose: the *Hôtel Le Régent* was operational from 1575 to 1864, but was used thereafter as stables until its present owner, Madame Peytavin, restored it with taste and reopened it in 1970. The hotel is described as 'just the place for people who would like to stay in comfort and at reasonable expense in a quiet country town within 50 miles of Paris. The courtyard is charming and guests are made to feel welcome.' Recent reports suggest that the hotel is in need of some renovating, but most of the bedrooms are 'spacious, elegantly furnished and quiet'. The hotel only provides breakfast; other meals (and drinks – *Le Régent* is 'dry') can usually be had at the *Commerce* across the road. *(Alan and Jane Davidson and others)*

Open: All year, except 1–15 February.
Rooms: 14 double, 1 single, 1 suite – 10 with bath, 7 with shower, all with telephone, TV and radio. (3 rooms on ground floor.)
Facilities: Hall, lounge; some conference facilities. Large garden and courtyard. English spoken.
Location: Paris 70 km SW; Meaux 42 km S; Soissons 23 km NE. Hotel is central near church and château, and has garages.
Credit cards: Barclay/Visa, Diners.
Terms: Rooms: 115–163 frs. Set meals: breakfast 16–18 frs. (No restaurant.)

VONNAS, 01540 Ain   Map 8

La Mère Blanc   *Telephone:* (74) 50.00.10
Telex: 380776 G BLANC

With its three rosettes and four red turrets in Michelin, this is one of the most prestigious of France's small rural hotel/restaurants, to be mentioned in the same breath as *chez Bocuse* or *chez Vergé*. It stands beside the river Veyle on the edge of a quiet *village fleuri* between Mâcon and Bourg-en-Bresse, in a pleasant area of lakes and pretty old villages. 'Extremely comfortable, superb service and exceptional food. The bedrooms overlook the river. There is a swimming pool, gardens and terraces. Georges Blanc, who also owns vineyards, sells his own bottled wine in the hotel and in an adjoining boutique and writes cookery books. He himself advises on the choice of meal and wines before you are led through the large and immaculate kitchens into the dining room, beautifully furnished. The atmosphere is friendly, warm and welcoming, without the pretensions sometimes associated with the "grands chef de France".' The sole complaint: service can be slow. *(Pat and Jeremy Temple; also Raymond Harris, Adrian and Sandy Hamilton)*

Open: All year, except January and first week of February, all day Wednesday, and Thursday until 16.00 hrs.

Rooms: 20 double, 2 single, 4 suites – 21 with bath, 3 with shower, all with telephone and colour TV.
Facilities: Lift, salon, bar, dining room, terraces; on the river Veyle. 2½ acres grounds with garden, heated swimming pool and tennis court. English spoken.
Location: 19 km E of Mâcon, 24 km W of Bourg-en-Bresse.
Credit cards: American Express, Barclay/Visa, Diners.
Terms: Rooms 180–550 frs. Set meals (excluding 15% service charge): breakfast 35 frs, lunch/dinner 180–290 frs; full *alc* 260–320 frs.

WIMEREUX, 62930 Pas-de-Calais   Map 8

Atlantic Hotel [GFG]   *Telephone:* (21) 32.41.01
Digue de la Mer

This hotel/restaurant right by the sea, 6 km north of Boulogne, is well known both to locals and to British tourists for serving some of the very best food in the region – notably fish dishes, such as *bar braisé au champagne*. The dining room with its nautical decor overlooks the sea; and the waves break against your very bedroom walls. One reader titillates with a brief report ('Rooms small but clean and adequate; food and service excellent'): we should welcome more, and fuller. *(Raymond Harris)*

Open: All year, except February. (Restaurant closed Sunday evening and Monday 1 October–1 April.)
Rooms: 10 double – 6 with bath, 4 with shower, all with telephone.
Facilities: Lift, salon with TV, bar, restaurant and terrace overlooking sea; conference rooms. Beach. English spoken.
Location: 6 km N of Boulogne on the D940; parking.
Terms: Rooms 120–200 frs. Set meals (excluding 15% service): breakfast 18 frs, lunch/dinner 100–140 frs; full *alc* 110–250 frs.

Hotel Eisenhut, Rothenburg ob der Tauber

Germany

ASCHHEIM, Nr Munich 8011   **Map 10**

Hotel-Gasthof zur Post   *Telephone:* (089) 903.20.27
Ismaningerstrasse 11

About 13 km east of Munich and 2.5 km from Munich airport. 'Very new
and of an artistic standard I have not experienced anywhere. The rooms
are more like elegant suites than ordinary hotel rooms, so cleverly are
they constructed, furnished and subdivided. The decor, furnishing and
carpeting belong to a super-luxury flat as one sees it in modern films rather
than in normal life. The breakfast room is, in itself, a showpiece and like a
modern museum, though the other dining room is of the local Bavarian
cosy type. There is plenty of choice on the menu, and the service is not
confined to unwilling acceptance of orders, but expanded to advice and
explanation. The only drawback is the absence of a comfortable lounge,
yet the individual rooms are so lavishly appointed that, even if a sitting
room were provided, hardly anyone would prefer it to the rooms.
Altogether, an unexpected gem – and very reasonably priced.' *(P G
Bourne; endorsed by Michael and Eileen Wilkes)*

Open: All year, except Christmas–mid January.
Rooms: 20 double, 30 single – 18 with bath, 22 with shower, most with telephone.
Facilities: Lift; TV room, dining and breakfast rooms. &.
Location: 13 km E of Munich; parking.
Credit cards: None accepted.
Terms: B & B 34–69 DM. *Alc* (excluding wine) 14–40 DM.

Gartenhotel Heusser   *Telephone:* (06322) 2066
Seebacherstrasse 50   *Telex:* 454889

'Bad Dürkheim, a spa with the character of an English market town, is on
the famous Weinstrasse, a few kms south of the motorway leading from
France via Saarbrucken to the German motorway at the Worms, Ludwig-
shafen, Mannheim junction. The *Gartenhotel Heusser* calls itself "an oasis
of calm and peace", and is really just that. About half a mile from the
town centre (towards Seebach), the *Heusser* consists of several buildings,
surrounded by a wonderful garden, and is bordered on one side by a large
vineyard. The hotel has a pleasant open-air pool and a splendid very large
indoor pool, kept crystal clear and clean; bathing-caps and rubber shoes,
both required, are all provided free, also a hair-drier. Service is a model of
efficiency. Breakfast is a self-service buffet in a room overlooking the
flower garden.' *(P G Bourne)*
    A recent visitor, while agreeing with the above, warns that the bed-
rooms are small and unimaginative, but praises the sauna.

Open: All year, except 20 December–20 January.
Rooms: 85 double – all with bath, shower and telephone.
Facilities: Lift, hall with bar, lounge, 3 TV rooms, breakfast room, restaurant;
conference facilities; terrace. Garden, heated indoor and outdoor pools, sauna,
solarium. &.
Location: 1 km from town centre towards Seebach. Garages and large car park.
Coming by the B271 from Neustadt, turn left at Amtsplatz.
Terms: B & B 50–67 DM. Reduced rates for children under 10.

Mönchs Posthotel   *Telephone:* (07083) 2002
Doblerstrasse 2   *Telex:* 07245123

'A traditional old posting-house in an attractive little Black Forest spa
town, really a village. Very peaceful, provided you avoid rooms on the
road, surrounded by forests with a small river running through its gardens
into the village part across the road where one can taste the spa water,
warm or cold (actually rather nasty!). Everywhere there are flowers;
baskets of geraniums in all colours cascading down every house and wall.
The welcome was extremely friendly and the room excellent. Deep pile
carpet everywhere, beautifully fitted bathroom with bathrobe, slippers,
bath essence, shower hat, etc., immaculately clean and very comfortable.
The beds all have duvets which we find a real pleasure. There is a dining
room which appeared to be for guests *en pension* but we ate in the
adjoining restaurant, *Klosterschänke*, very popular locally as well, which
was excellent. It has a well-deserved Michelin star. Breakfast was lavish,
part chosen from a central buffet, part served. The gardens had a
swimming pool, bar area for summer months and, everywhere, flowers.'
(Pat and Jeremy Temple)

Open: All year.
Rooms: 40 double, 10 single, 9 suites – 30 with bath, 20 with shower, all with
telephone, 20 with colour TV.

Facilities: Hall, salon, TV room, bar, restaurant, breakfast terrace. Garden with heated swimming pool; tennis and 9-hole golf course close by. English spoken.
Location: Central, parking. Warning: rooms on the road can be noisy.
Credit cards: American Express, Diners.
Terms: B & B 84–107 DM. Set meals: lunch 35 DM; dinner 40 DM; full *alc* 50 DM. Reduced rates for groups out of season, and for children; special meals for children.

BAMBERG, 8600 Bayern   Map 10

Hotel Garni Alt Bamberg   *Telephone:* (0951) 26.66.7/26.56.9
Habergasse 11

Bamberg is one of the showplace medieval towns of southern Germany, as atmospheric as Rothenburg and Dinkelsbühl, but less commercialized than either. There are many larger and posher hotels than the *Alt Bamberg* but this would be a natural choice if you were seeking the *echt* Bamberg experience. The rooms are pleasant and airy and look out on to a winding old narrow street, full of other houses of the same period. There is very little noise, though you are only a short distance from the high Domplatz, with the town's beautiful cathedral, its world-famous Reiter sculpture and its elegant Residenz. *(Lucy Kitzinger)*

Open: All year. Restaurant closed Sunday.
Rooms: 9 double, 11 single, 1 suite – 5 with bath, 8 with shower, 21 with telephone.
Facilities: Breakfast room which serves as living room, with TV. English spoken.
Location: Central, near Grüner Markt; look for Elefantenhaus when trying to find it.
Terms: B & B 35–40 DM; dinner, B & B 55–100 DM. Set meals: lunch 17.50 DM; supper 15 DM. Full *alc* 22 DM. Reduced rates for children; special meals on request.

BAYREUTH 8580 Bayern   Map 10

Bayerischer Hof   *Telephone:* (0921) 23.06.1
Bahnhofstrasse 14   *Telex:* 642737

'The *Bayerischer Hof* has probably the best facilities of the hotels available in this famous little town in northern Bavaria, formerly Franconia. The staff are always courteous and helpful. I have stayed there in the summer, and in the depths of snowy winter; and have enjoyed comfortable, elegant rooms, an excellent heated indoor swimming pool, and luncheon and dinner menus which include plenty of local dishes. Franconian wine occupies a fairly large section of the wine list, and justifiably so. The hotel is in the centre of the town and one minute's walk from Bayreuth railway station, but the trains are never heard. During the *Wagnerfest* the hotel is likely to be full of visiting notables, but at other times the town resumes its normal quiet rhythm, with music in the old churches and the baroque opera house, its new University, and its surrounding countryside of rolling hills, low mountains and forest slopes and slumbering villages.' *(John Spencer)*

Open: All year. Restaurant closed Sunday out of season.
Rooms: 62 – most with bath or shower, all with telephone and TV.
Facilities: Lift, Hans Sachs Room, TV room, Spanish-style cellar restaurant, roof-garden restaurant, conference room. Indoor swimming pool, sauna. Garden with sun-terrace and small swimming pool. English spoken. &.
Location: Central, near station; garage.
Credit cards: Access/Euro/Mastercard, American Express, Diners.
Terms: B & B 42–84 DM; half board 16 DM added to room price; full board 62 DM added. Reduced rates for children: 30% reduction when sharing parents' room; 10% in own room; special meals provided.

BERLIN 15   Map 10

Hotel Am Zoo   *Telephone:* (030) 88.30.91
Kurfürstendamm 25   *Telex:* 0183835 zooho d

'It's not often one can find a hotel slap in the middle of a famous kind of street-life where one can also get some sleep. We asked for a courtyard or well-facing room. I don't know how much rest one would get in the front rooms; I imagine the penance for a free perpetual circus outside the windows would be a very high noise level. But the courtyard-facing room we got was large, high-ceilinged, airy and quiet. We could surge along the Kurfürstendamm among the buskers and street-café eaters and then duck back to the tranquillity whenever we felt tired. We were within a block or two of theatres, the good bookshops and the station at which one takes the Underground for East Berlin, the obligatory one-day pass that enables one to go and see the Berliner Ensemble. The hotel staff – all English-speaking – were outstandingly helpful. Not a "charming" hotel; but an extremely comfortable and convenient place to stay when what one wants is to experience the honest vulgar centre of the city.' *(Nadine Gordimer)*

Our original entry has been confirmed by a recent visitor: 'Nadine Gordimer says it exactly. Impersonal but efficient, clean and comfortable.' *(Professor O Pick)*

Open: All year.
Rooms: 52 double, 91 single, 2 suites – 115 with bath, 20 with shower, 34 with TV, all with telephone and radio.
Facilities: Lift, salon, TV room, bar, dining room (hotel guests only), 3 conference rooms; courtyard. English spoken.
Location: In city centre; parking.
Credit cards: All major credit cards accepted.
Terms: B & B 85–115 DM; dinner, B & B 105–135 DM; full board 125–150 DM; full *alc* 32 DM. Reduced rates for children under 7.

BERNKASTEL-KUES, 5550 Rheinland-Pfalz   Map 10

Hotel Drei Könige   *Telephone:* (06531) 2327
1 Bahnhofstrasse

'An old-established and spacious hotel alongside the river Mosel on the Kues side of town, with most of the bedrooms offering excellent views of Bernkastel and its castle and vineyards. The ground floor has been let to a clothing store, and the *Drei Könige* operates as a *hotel garni* – bed and breakfast only – on the upper floors. The rooms are well-furnished and spacious, and they serve an ample breakfast. There were many good restaurants nearby. Prices were very reasonable.' *(Bruce I Nathan)*

Open: 15 March–15 November.
Rooms: 36 double, 6 single – 9 with bath, 31 with shower, 25 with telephone, 4 with TV, 40 with radio.
Facilities: Lift, TV room, lounge, bar, breakfast room; wine cellar with dancing each weekend. Garden. English spoken.
Location: 200 m from town centre, on the Mosel; parking.
Credit card: Euro.
Terms: B & B 65–85 DM (single), 95–125 DM (double). (No restaurant.)

BONN 5300 Nordrhein-Westfalen   **Map 10**

Hotel Bristol   *Telephone:* (0228) 2.01.11
Poppelsdorfer Allee   *Telex:* 08869661
Ecke Prinz-Albert Strasse

'A modern grand hotel with 120 rooms, centrally situated. We have stayed over the years at a lot of hotels of this type, and quite frankly you could be anywhere in the world. The *Bristol* was different in as much as the staff were so excellent. Everyone was pleasant, friendly and helpful. Whatever you asked for, the answer was "of course". Information was volunteered. We even had a quick run-down on German politics by a charming young waitress in the café. The hotel has all the usual amenities, including a swimming pool, which some of our party were pleased about as the temperature was nearly 30°C while we were there. Only complaint: the air-conditioning found the struggle to keep up impossible much of the time. The food, both in the coffee bar and the restaurant, was of a very high standard. Expensive of course.' *(Heather Sharland)*

Open: All year.
Rooms: 120 – all with bath or shower, all with telephone, radio and TV.
Facilities: Lift; salon, bar, café and restaurants, conference facilities, terrace; heated indoor swimming pool, sauna, solarium and massage. &.
Location: Central; parking.
Credit cards: Access/Euro/Mastercard, American Express, Diners.
Terms: Rooms with breakfast 147–195 DM (single), 190–275 DM (double). *Alc* (excluding wine) 17.50–82 DM.

BREMEN-HORN   **Map 10**

Landhaus Louisenthal   *Telephone:* (0421) 23.20.76
Leher Heerstrasse 105

'We found this hotel in the suburbs of Bremen outstanding in value and comfort. The building and grounds were beautiful, and the bedrooms had solid comfortable furnishings, plus shower and toilets; the whole place was spotless. At present it is a *hotel garni* (no main meals served), but our breakfast was a generous continental one, more like the Dutch than the German. They plan to open a restaurant in 1982. It was near the motorway and the hotel had a parking area as well as its own garage. Bus and tram services passed the door. The hotel is mainly a family concern, and the staff were friendly and helpful.' *(Miss M Byrne)*

Since last year's report, quoted above, the hotel has begun to serve simple meals. A recent visitor, endorsing our entry for an overnight stop, pays tribute to the quietness of the location, but mentions that none of the staff on his visit spoke English. *(Paul Harris)*

Open: All year.
Rooms: 28 double, 13 single – 2 with bath, with shower and telephone.
Facilities: Salon, TV room, dining room; conference facilities. Garden.
Location: 6 km from centre of Bremen. Garage and car park.
Credit cards: American Express, Diners.
Terms: Single room with breakfast 56 DM, double 81 DM; dinner, B & B 65 DM, full board 80 DM. Set meals: lunch 14–18.50 DM, dinner 13–24 DM; full *alc* 29 DM.

ERLANGEN, 8520 Bayern   **Map 10**

Hotel-Garni Rokokohaus   *Telephone:* (09131) 22.87.1 22.87.8
Theaterplatz 13

'Erlangen is a pleasant town, 20 km from Nürnberg, or 15 minutes by bus or train. It has a large university, is the headquarters of Siemens Electric and also has a fine castle and a beautiful rococo theatre. I found the *Rokokohaus* when all the better hotels in Nürnberg were full because of a trade fair. It was built over 200 years ago, and is the only building in Erlangen with a pure rococo facade. It is said that the Markgräfin Marie Caroline Sophie of Brandenburg-Culmbach used the house as a hunting lodge. It was rebuilt as a bed-and-breakfast hotel 15 years ago, with charm and taste. Excellent bathrooms. There's a park in front, and a large parking lot round the corner. The Opera House-Theatre is just a few steps away (the Nürnberg Opera frequently performs in Erlangen) and many of the guest stars stay here.' *(John J Grenz)*

Open: All year.
Rooms: 8 double, 20 single, 2 suites – 6 with bath, all with shower, telephone, radio and colour TV. 6 rooms in annexe, with kitchenette. (2 rooms on ground floor.)
Facilities: Lift; lobby, salon, 2 breakfast rooms, conference facilities for 6–12 people. Courtyard. English spoken.
Location: In town centre; parking.
Credit cards: Access/Euro/Mastercard, American Express, Diners.
Terms: B & B 55–80 DM. (No restaurant.)

GOSLAR HARZ, 3380 Niedersachsen   **Map 10**

Hotel Kaiser Worth   *Telephone:* (05321) 21.11.1
Markt 3   *Telex:* 095 3874

'When about to cross to the GDR, spend the vigil night not in Hanover or Helmstedt, but in this 15th-century Gothic hotel at the foot of the Harz mountains. This dignified, noble building on the medieval town square is one of those places that, once seen, cannot be passed by for any other hostelry in town. Large, airy rooms with firm comfortable beds, good modern bathrooms or showers, spacious lounges and corridors furnished

with beautiful antiques and paintings, excellent food, either local specialities, or, if you must, international dishes, with a long and fairly distinguished cellar of German wines fairly priced, make this a marvellous place
to fortify yourself for the rigours of the New Order across the man-traps
and barbed wire. There is an open-air café, Gothic cellar evenings,
dancing (German style), and all the delights and activities of the Harz
mountains and nearby resorts to satisfy every whim. Not cheap (rooms
overlooking the square are 25% dearer), but a haven after the Rhine or
Ruhr cities.' *(T J Wiseman)*

A recent visitor challenges last year's report, quoted above, in respect
of the large airy rooms and spacious lounges; he found the opposite. More
reports welcome.

Open: All year.
Rooms: 60 – all with bath or shower, telephone and TV.
Facilities: Salon, TV room, bar, restaurant; conference facilities.
Location: Central, in pedestrian zone; parking.
Credit cards: American Express, Diners, Euro.
Terms: B & B 68–89 DM; full board 124–145 DM. *Alc* 19–55 DM (excluding wine).

HAMBURG 2000   **Map 10**

Hotel Prem   *Telephone:* (040) 24.22.11
An der Alster 9   *Telex:* 2163115

This elegant smallish hotel, one of the few in the medium-price range in
the centre of the city, has had an entry in the Guide since our first edition.
The original nominator, who had first stayed at the *Prem* in 1977, found it
had deteriorated when she stayed there recently, and would not have
recommended it in its present form. Another recent visitor, perhaps
because he hadn't known the hotel in other days, gives it a qualified seal of
approval (see below). More reports please.

'A family of five, we were glad to find this hotel en route to Denmark. It
may not be the best in Hamburg, but it is conveniently situated near the
centre: one can walk from it to the shops along the banks of the Alster
lake, so the setting is particularly pleasant. The hotel itself is not too big,
and the staff are very friendly and efficient. There is a particularly
pleasant garden for drinks and food when the weather permits. Bedrooms
are large and elegantly furnished, and it was possible for us to find plenty
of room for two of the children to sleep on the floor in their sleeping-bags,
and the third child was provided with a comfortable portable bed at a
small extra charge. So it worked out fairly reasonable for a family.
Breakfast was acceptable if uninspired. The dining room was small and
quiet in the evening, so we went elsewhere in search of the *Bierkeller*
atmosphere.' *(John Rowlands)*

Open: All year. Restaurant closed Sunday and holidays.
Rooms: 26 double, 23 single – 42 with bath, all with telephone, radio, TV and babysitting.
Facilities: Lounge, TV room, bar, restaurant; conference facilities. Garden for fine-weather meals or drinks. English spoken. &.
Location: Central; garage.
Credit cards: American Express, Barclay/Visa, Diners, Euro.

Terms: B & B 66–150 DM; half board 39 DM per person added; full board 61 DM added. Special weekend rates. Reduced rates for children sharing parents' room; special meals provided.

HINTERZARTEN, 7824 Baden-Württemberg   **Map 10**

Hotel Weisses Rössle   *Telephone:* (07652) 1411
Freiburgerstrasse 38

'There is a local slogan in this holiday resort – "The guest is our king" – and this is certainly the ambience that pervades this little place set high up in the Black Forest. The best time to visit the area is in the spring or autumn, or in the skiing months – omitting the high summer season when accommodation and roads are very full. In winter, road and forest walks are snow-cleared every morning so that walkers need not be housebound while skiers enjoy the slopes. The *Weisses Rössle* is first-class in every sense of the word. Its most important asset is the attitude of everyone from the owner-proprietor, Heinz Zimmermann, and his wife Urda, through to the attendants at the swimming pool. There are three dining rooms, two mostly used by residents, and the rooms are all extremely well-furnished. They serve a mighty German breakfast which makes lunch almost superfluous.' *(Denis Morris; also Conrad Dehn)*

The above is part of an entry for the *Weisses Rössle* which appeared in the first edition of the Guide, and has been repeated annually since, regularly re-confirmed by successive visitors. We quote from the latest: 'We completely endorse your entry – the best hotel ever. Marvellous facilities and, by our standards, wonderful food. Their Friday night's *Schwarzwald* buffet was superb, and our 6-year-old loved the children's menu. We can't wait to go back – the November game week sounds fantastic. Very reasonably priced.' *(Rodney and Mary Milne-Day)*

As we go to press, a late report tells us that Herr Zimmermann had been missing during a September 1982 visit – 'rather like the Berlin Philharmonic Orchestra with no conductor. Back to the podium, please, Herr Zimmermann'. The same correspondent mentions that you can take a week-long walking holiday through the Black Forest, with the *Weisses Rössle* making a perfect beginning or end-point; you walk 20 or 25 km a day, and your luggage is waiting for you at the next hotel. Tours are arranged through DER Travel Service in London and New York. *(Jonathan Williams)*

Open: All year.
Rooms: 29 double, 15 single, 23 suites – 43 with bath, 13 with shower, some with radio, all with telephone; TV and baby-listening on request.
Facilities: Salon, TV room, games room, 3 restaurants; conference facilities; music daily except Mondays; beauty salon and hairdresser; indoor swimming pool and sauna. Terrace, garden with tennis court, volleyball, children's play area. English spoken. &.
Location: 25 km E of Freiburg on B31. Parking.
Credit card: Euro.
Terms: Rooms with breakfast: 54–120 DM (single), 115–240 DM (double); half board 29 DM per person added, full board 45 DM added. Set meals: lunch/dinner 30 DM; full *alc* 40 DM. Off season reductions. Special meals for children. Tennis, skiing, yoga and fitness holidays.

KETTWIG, 4300 Essen 18   Map 10

Hotel Schloss Hugenpoet   *Telephone:* (02054) 6054
August-Thyssen-strasse 51

'A superb moated castle on the banks of the Ruhr in a wooded valley, yet within easy reach of most of the main cities of industrial Germany. 15 km from Düsseldorf, 22 km from Essen and 60 km from Cologne, which was an easy drive each day to a trade fair. Not surprisingly, the hotel and restaurant cater for meetings and functions but this never seemed to intrude during our stay. The welcome was friendly, the staff always pleasant and helpful and the owner in evidence every evening in the restaurant. Our room was large, well-furnished with antique pieces, a mini-bar, TV etc., and with a large well-equipped bathroom. There is a very grand entrance hall/lounge area with a magnificent black marble staircase. Main attraction is the restaurant – a rosette in Michelin. The food is French, superbly cooked and presented, with excellent efficient service. Breakfasts always promptly served in our room were good, and on Sunday there was a magnificent tea-buffet packed with local ladies enjoying the rich cream pastries, etc. Highly recommended.' *(Pat and Jeremy Temple)*

Open: All year.
Rooms: 20 double, 1 suite – all with bath, telephone and TV, some with mini-bar.
Facilities: Lift; large hall, salon, restaurant, conference facilities; chapel for weddings and christenings; terrace; large grounds with tennis court.
Location: 15 km from Essen off the A52, near A2 and A3 motorways. Parking.
Credit cards: Access/Euro/Mastercard, American Express, Diners.
Terms: Rooms with breakfast 53–157 DM (single), 157–190 DM (double); suites 230–265 DM. Half board 42 DM per person added to B & B rate; full board 63 DM added. *Alc* (excluding wine) 40–90 DM. Reduced rates for children sharing parents' room.

LINZ AM RHEIN, 5460 Rhein   Map 10

Hotel Franz Josef   *Telephone:* (02644) 2332
Rheinstrasse 25

This Gasthaus-cum-hotel in a beautiful showplace small town on the east bank of the Rhine has been popular with readers since our first edition. It has been in the Zimmermann family for more than two centuries. Sadly, as we go to press, we learn that the present Franz Josef Zimmermann, patron *and admirable chef, is thinking of retiring at the end of 1982. Hence this italicized entry. The tariff is an estimate.*

Open: All year, except June and December. Restaurant closed Tuesday.
Rooms: 3 double, 1 single.
Facilities: 2 lounges (1 with TV), dining room. English spoken.
Location: Central; parking.
Credit card: Euro.
Terms: B & B 28.50 DM. Set meals: lunch from 11 DM; dinner from 12.50 DM; full *alc* from 23 DM. Reduced rates and special meals for children.

Hotel-Gasthof Zum Bären   *Telephone:* (07532) 6044
Marktplatz 11

'In our view, Meersburg is the prettiest town on the Bodensee (Lake Constance): romantic old castle, "new" pink baroque castle, crowded together in the Altstadt (old town) on a high bluff above the lake. The *Zum Bären*, which has been an inn since the early 17th century, is on the market square on the right when you enter the city gate from the north. This Marktplatz is one of the glories of the town, with three remarkably handsome old streets leading off it. Large comfortable rooms, some overlooking the square. Alpine furniture, beamed ceilings. We enjoyed just looking out through the lace curtains at the busy market square. Good *Weinstube*.' *(Jane Treat-Baum;* endorsed by *B W Ribbons,* who pays special tribute to the helpfulness and charm of the Family Gilowsky-Karrer, who own the hotel, and all their staff – 'A joy to be there.')

Open: 1 March–mid November; closed Monday.
Rooms: 12 double, 4 single – all with shower, some overlooking the Marktplatz.
Facilities: Dining room, wine bar. English spoken.
Location: In town centre; parking.
Credit card: Euro.
Terms: B & B 42–44 DM. Set meals: lunch/dinner 15–25 DM; full *alc* 30 DM. (No *pension* terms.)

Hotel Biederstein   *Telephone:* (089) 39.50.72
Keferstrasse 18

We should be glad to hear from recent visitors to Countess Harach's small hotel in the Schwabing district, about 1 km from the centre of Munich but close to the city's Englischer Garten, equivalent of Hyde Park. The building is modern (1970), but the house is full of the Countess's own antique furniture. 'A snip in the light of current big city prices,' writes one satisfied visitor. 'Our room was small but well-appointed, excellent bedside reading lamps and remarkably quiet. The staff were affable and efficient.' Another reader mentioned an additional reason for choosing the *Biederstein* – the fact that one's car can be kept in the underground garage. *(Michael and Eileen Wilkes)*

Open: All year.
Rooms: 16 double, 13 single, 3 suites – all with bath and telephone, TV by arrangement.
Facilities: Lift, TV room, breakfast room; some conference facilities. Small garden. English spoken.
Location: Central; underground garage (5 DM).
Credit card: American Express.
Terms: Rooms with breakfast 78 DM (single), 98–120 DM (double). Set meals: lunch 25 DM; supper 18 DM. Reduced rates for children.

Procrastination is the thief of the next edition.

MUNICH, 8000 Bayern   Map 10

Marienbad Hotel   *Telephone:* (089) 59.55.85 and 59.17.03
Barerstrasse 11

'Very friendly and warm in spite of freezing weather. Excellently placed for shopping and seeing Munich as it is so central. Difficult to find, but well worth it.' *(Michael and Eileen Wilkes)*
    Thus the latest endorsement for this family-run bed and breakfast hotel situated near the centre of the city (only a few minutes' walk away from the beautiful traffic-free shopping area), very close to the Karolinenplatz from which you must approach it (access road only) and which, with its tall metal column, is an obvious landmark. It is in a quiet situation at the back of an office block which has replaced the bombed part of a well-known pre-war hotel of the same name. The present hotel is the bedroom annexe of the old one and combines modern amenities with the size of rooms found in old buildings. The rooms are well-furnished and well-kept. There is ample parking space.

Open: All year.
Rooms: 15 double, 9 single, 1 suite – 2 with bath, 19 with shower, all with telephone.
Facilities: Lift, salon with TV. Park behind hotel. English spoken.
Location: Central; approach from Karolinenplatz; parking nearby.
Terms: B & B 50–85 DM. (No restaurant.) Reduced rates for children.

MUNICH, 8000 Bayern   Map 10

Hotel an der Oper   *Telephone:* (089) 22.87.11
2 Falkenturmstrasse 10   *Telex:* 522588

'Unobtrusively tucked away in a small side-street off the famous and beautiful Maximilianstrasse and, as its name suggests, much frequented by members of the Opera House. Don't be surprised to hear (as we did to our delight) a soprano warm up before her performance. Rooms are not large, but have every modern amenity. The hotel is very reasonably priced, but one has to book well in advance. It has, so far as I know, no public rooms apart from a smallish entrance hall with a living room corner. But it has a most excellent though expensive restaurant, *La Bouillabaisse*.' *(Katie Plowden)*
    As city travellers know well, narrow side streets are not necessarily exempt from noise pollution at night. One recent visitor, while appreciating the convenience of the hotel's location, especially for those with tickets for the opera, found it very noisy indeed, with most of the drunks congregating around the various night-clubs appearing to be under the hotel windows. He also complained about slow service at breakfast. More reports please.

Open: All year.
Rooms: 55 – all with bath, telephone and radio.
Facilities: Lift, reception-cum-lounge, TV room, restaurant; conference facilities.
Location: Central.
Credit cards: American Express, Diners, Euro.
Terms: B & B 55–91 DM.

Hotel Eisenhut   *Telephone:* (09861) 2041
Herrngasse 3–7   *Telex:* 61367
Reservations: In UK (01) 629 9792;
In USA (800) 223 5652

'Rothenburg on the river Tauber is the most beautiful and famous of all
the towns on the Romantic Road, a perfectly preserved and living town of
tall gabled houses, old churches and cobbled streets, surrounded by the
ancient city wall. The *Hotel Eisenhut* is very much a part of the past and
present life of Rothenburg. As a hotel it is little more than a hundred years
old, but the four houses which now form the hotel date back to the Middle
Ages. It stands in the Herrngasse, a superb old street leading off the
central market place, and over the years it has been developed as a luxury
hotel in ways which enhance rather than detract from its historic character. All the 85 bedrooms have been beautifully and individually decorated. Almost all have baths. The public rooms are furnished with
antiques and original paintings, and there is as much artistry in the cuisine
as in the decor. Considering the quality of accommodation, food and
service, prices are not exorbitant. The special quality of this hotel is its
personal warmth. The present owner is Frau Georg Pirner who arranges
all the table decorations herself and for special occasions these include
ornaments of exquisite old Meissen. The Hanover-born manager Karl
Prüsse has the sensitivity of a musical conductor for the balance of
clientele and staff. I enjoyed the restful atmosphere, the food and wine,
but even more being made to feel such a welcome guest.' *(Penelope
Turing)*

Recent visitors, who spent 10 days at the *Eisenhut* on a half-board
package holiday, warmly endorsed last year's entry in all respects. 'One of
the best hotels we have stayed in.' *(A and B W Williams)*

Open: 1 March–10 January.
Rooms: 63 double, 19 single, 2 suites – 75 with bath, 10 with shower, all with
telephone, radio and TV on request. 20 rooms in annexe.
Facilities: Lift, salon, TV room, 2 restaurants; conference room. Garden, ter-
race. English spoken. &.
Location: 33 km from Ansbach. Hotel is central; parking.
Credit cards: All major credit cards accepted.
Terms: B & B 82.50–145 DM; full board 84 DM per person added. Full *alc* 50
DM. Reduced rates for children; special meals on request.

RÜDESHEIM-ASSMANNSHAUSEN, 6220 Hessen   **Map 10**

Hotel Krone   *Telephone:* (067 22) 2036
Rheinuferstrasse 10

The *Krone* has been a Rhineside inn since 1541. It was small then, and is
now a substantial hotel with a famous and *soigné* restaurant. There are in
fact two separate buildings facing the river, each with well-furnished
rooms of varying sizes, many with balconies overlooking the attractive
gardens and the changing river scene. The hotel is well-staffed and
has several lounges. One British publisher, returning debilitated from the
Book Fair, calls it his post-Frankfurt haven. But light sleepers should be

warned: there are occasional rumbles of trains passing behind the hotel, and the Rhine traffic in front is noisy too. *(Paul Langridge, Timothy Benn and others)*

Open: 15 March–15 November.
Rooms: 50 double, 30 single, 2 suites – 36 with bath, 12 with shower, all with telephone and colour TV, many with balconies. Some rooms in annexe. (Some rooms on ground floor.)
Facilities: Lift, salons, TV room, bar, restaurant, large terrace/restaurant; conference facilities. Garden with heated swimming pool and bar. English spoken.
Location: 28 km from Wiesbaden; 75 km from Frankfurt airport; central; parking.
Credit cards: All major credit cards accepted.
Terms: B & B 52–112 DM. Full *alc* 47 DM.

TODTNAUBERG, 7868 Baden-Württemberg　　　　　　　　**Map 10**

Hotel Engel　　　　　　　　　　　*Telephone:* (07671) 206
Kurhausstr. 3

'Todtnauberg is a hill resort 6 km above Todtnau in the southern Schwarzwald. We were there in April, when the skiing (which seemed good for the area) was all but over. We found ourselves in a peaceful off-season. Good air, soft water, sound sleep at over 1,000 metres in altitude. The hotel was clean, friendly and not expensive – DM 62 per night for two with breakfast [1982] for a fair-sized room with shower, etc. No trouble with our carry-cot and all the things needed for a baby. The public rooms were typically German–Austrian with a big stove in the corner. The restaurant had gastronomic pretensions, hardly tested out of season, but we ate and drank well, and not expensively. Service erratic, but apologetic when slow.' *(E R Fulton)*

Open: All year except November.
Rooms: 22 double, 6 single – 2 with bar, 15 with shower.
Facilities: Lounge, TV room, bar, large dining room; terrace; garden. Near ski lift.
Location: Central, but quietly situated; garages and parking place.
Credit cards: All major credit cards accepted.
Terms: B & B 25–35 DM; dinner, B & B 38–47 DM; full board 46–60 DM. Set meals: lunch 12–20 DM, dinner 10–25 DM; full *alc* 22 DM.

TRENDELBURG, 3526 Hessen　　　　　　　　**Map 10**

Burghotel　　　　　　　　　*Telephone:* (05675) 1021
　　　　　　　　　　　　　　　　Telex: 0994812

The hills and mountains of Upper Hesse are off the main tourist track, and hotels in this region are poorly represented in the Guide. Trendelburg is in the northern part of the province, near Hofgeismar. 'A not-over-restored medieval castle, with great atmosphere. Most of the staff have some English and all make you most welcome. My room was large, the outlook superb, and (if you don't mind just a shower) most comfortable; they even provided a chaise longue as well as a mini-bar. Peaceful. Good food by German standards. Good centre in delightful countryside.' *(T M Wilson)*. (Warning: some rooms are on the poky side.)

Open: 3 March–4 January.
Rooms: 18 double, 5 single – all with bath or shower, telephone and TV.
Facilities: Salon, TV room, wine bar, restaurant, dining on the ramparts in fine weather; conference facilities. Garden with swimming pool, tennis, riding. English spoken.
Location: 35 km N of Kassel on B83.
Credit cards: American Express, Diners.
Terms: B & B 65–90 DM. Full *alc* 45 DM.

TRIER, 5500 Rheinland-Pfalz **Map 10**

Hotel Petrisberg *Telephone:* (0651) 41.18.1
Sickingenstr. 11

Trier, on the Mosel, is a town rich in historical associations. Under the Emperor Diocletian, it became the capital of Gaul and an imperial residence. It is the native town of Karl Marx, and his house is now a museum. There is an important archaeological museum and any number of fine churches and buildings. It is also the centre of the wine trade for Mosel, Saar and Ruwer wines. The *Petrisberg* is a modern, family-run, breakfast-only hotel (though light meals are served in the evening) above the city, close to the Roman amphitheatre and with fine views over the spires and domes. A wine merchant writes appreciatively: 'Clean well-run with excellent breakfasts and personal service of the proprietor. Rooms are compact – comfortable and well-furnished. Very peaceful position, with fresh air and perfect for relaxation after a hard day's work in Trier.' *(Peter Hallgarten)*

Open: All year.
Rooms: 30 double, 1 single – 2 with bath, 29 with shower – all with telephone, TV on request. (Some rooms on ground floor.)
Facilities: Salon, breakfast room, TV room. English spoken.
Location: 20 minutes from centre of town (near Roman Amphitheatre); parking area and garages.
Terms: B & B 45–65 DM. (No restaurant.)

Hotel Minoa, Tolon

Greece

Saint George Lykabettus Hotel   *Telephone:* Athens (01) 790 711
Kleomenous 2, Platia Dexamenis, Kolonaki   *Telex:* HEAM 214253

A de-luxe hotel in the fashionable Kolonaki section of the city, at the foot
of Lykabettus hill and close to Constitution hill. You can walk downhill to
the centre of activities in ten minutes, but a cab (not expensive in Athens)
is recommended for the return journey. 'High, cool and quiet,' we said
last year, 'with beautiful views.' One visitor disputed the quiet: his room,
he told us, had perhaps the best view over the city and the Acropolis and
also a good view of Lykabettus, but he had had to pay the price with
almost incessant noise of cars taking hair-pin bends with squealing tyres.
A room on the opposite side to Lykabettus would, he thought, be
preferable. The same correspondent also warned of small baths in some of
the rooms, not suiting 200-lb six-footers. Another writer, who seems to
have had the same room, but not minded the noise, adds further notes:
   'If you ask when booking, the "beautiful view" can be right across the
rooftops of Athens to the Acropolis – magical to wake up to in the
morning if it's not a smoggy day. There's a rooftop swimming pool that is
bliss after a hot and dusty day. You can stroll to the top of mount
Lykabettus and have a super meal at an open-air restaurant on the way
back – or take the funicular if you are lazy – or you can eat well at the
hotel. So far as I know, it is the only hotel in Athens with luxury and some
degree of a rural setting. Highly commended.' *(John M Sidwick; also Jack
and Esther Holloway)*

Open: All year.
Rooms: 124 double, 21 single, 5 suites – all with bath, telephone, radio, tea-making facilities and air-conditioning, some with balcony; TV on request. (Some rooms on ground floor.)
Facilities: Lift; residents' lounge, lounges with TV, bars, snack bar, restaurants, grill room, roof garden, swimming pool; nightly entertainment in restaurant; dancing on the roof. English spoken. &.
Location: At the foot of Lykabettus hill; large garage.
Credit cards: All major credit cards accepted.
Terms: Rooms with breakfast: single 2,320–2,837 drs, double 3,447–4,875 drs. Set meals: lunch/dinner 770 drs.

AYIOS NIKOLAOS, Crete   Map 15

Minos Beach   *Telephone:* (0841) 22 345
                                              Telex: 262214

What was once a primitive little Cretan fishing port in the beautiful gulf of Mirabello has become over the years a very popular resort indeed – full of boutiques and chic *tavernas*, and hotels of every class as well as *pensions* and '*Rooms/Chambres/Zimmer*'. As a town, it lacks the appeal of Chania at the other end of the island, but, as one reader puts it: 'The Gulf is a spectacular setting and probably compensates for the less interesting local life.' The *Minos Beach* was once *the* de-luxe hotel in Crete, but it has long since lost that exclusive claim as the tour operators moved in, and smart high-rise hotels followed in their wake. The *Minos Beach* does indeed depend much on its package trade – *Horizon* and *Olympic*, to name but two, use it extensively. But it isn't a typical package hotel: its rooms are not piled, floor on floor, but are mostly a collection of bungalows set in beautiful gardens strung out along the coast. The bungalows are simple in their furnishing, and some are more basic than others. As usual, we have had a mixed bag of reports. One visitor, who went in February, found his room cold and the heating inadequate; he had been reading hyperbolic descriptions of the hotel in travel magazines and had been much disappointed. Another reader visited in mid-summer, and complained of mosquito raids with no mesh on the windows. A third correspondent, who had read the last two fairly critical entries in the Guide, had been agreeably surprised. He had gone in May – an ideal month for a Cretan holiday – and possibly the weather helped to put him in a good humour. He had opted for the de-luxe rather than the standard accommodation and had found little to complain about with regard to the furnishing, though the servicing of the room had been no more than cosmetic. As others before him, he had found the evening meal bland international fare. At lunchtime the hotel serves a generous buffet with local dishes, and is probably a better bet for those on half board. This reader, at any rate, felt the no-better-than-average food was a price one has to pay for staying in a very beautiful hotel, and was planning to return for a longer stay. We certainly consider it deserves an entry in the Guide – even if the de-luxe classification needs to be treated circumspectly.

Open: All year. Restaurant closed 10 January–28 February.
Rooms: 124 double, 2 single, 4 suites – 96 with bath, 30 with shower, all with telephone. Some in main building, many in bungalows.
Facilities: 2 lounges, separate TV room, snack bar, indoor and outdoor restaurants and bars, games room. Spacious gardens with heated swimming pool,

mini-golf, tennis court. Disco 300 metres from hotel. Direct access to private rock and sand sea-bathing and all forms of water sports. English spoken.

Location: 68 km from Heraklion; 800 metres from town centre; parking.
Credit cards: All major credit cards accepted.
Terms: Dinner, B & B 3,100–8,100 drs, full board, 4,000–9,500 drs. Set meals: lunch/dinner, 750 drs; full *alc* 950–1,100 drs. Reduced rates for children sharing parents' room; special meals provided.

CHANIA, Crete   Map 15

Hotel Doma   *Telephone:* Chania (0821) 21 772
124 Venizelos Street

In the view of many Crete-lovers, Chania is by far the most attractive town on the island – a fascinating mixture of Turkish and Venetian architecture, and a cheerful bustling port. The *Doma* is about a kilometre from the centre of town. It is on the coast, though there is a road between it and the sea, and the front rooms, which have good views of the town and the rocky shore, are noisy from 7 a.m. onwards. Poor sleepers should ask for garden-facing rooms.

The *Doma* is a neo-classical house of some breeding – a former British consulate skilfully converted. Balustraded stairs lead to a terrace with fragments of broken statuary. All the rooms have showers; some have balconies overlooking the sea. The public rooms have fine Cretan furniture and antiques, which help to give the *Doma*, personally managed by its owner, Irene Valiraki, something of the feel of a private home. On the top floor there is a long breakfast room which doubles as a bar in the evening. If asked, the owner will serve drinks and hot snacks there during the day. Recent visitors, though they have had odd nits to pick – the house clearly is shabby in places, water isn't always very hot, and one reader reported a smell of drains that developed during his stay – essentially echo the sentiments expressed below:

'Although the rooms are by no means luxurious, and the hotel is showing signs of age, it mysteriously adds up to more than the sum of its parts. It stuck in my mind as few other hotels in Crete did, and I would be inclined to head straight for it if I were in Chania again. The final overriding impression is that it has not only great individuality, but also great charm, and is entirely without pretensions. The personal touches: splendid antique furniture – some with quite a story behind them – the photographs, pictures, ornaments, plants, archaeological fragments, and so on all seem genuinely integral elements of the house. You have the feeling, especially after you have met the owner, that you are visiting a tasteful but well-loved home.' *(LH; also SM, David Wooff)*

Open: All year.
Rooms: 26 double, 2 single, 1 suite – all with shower and telephone, some with balconies overlooking the sea. (Some rooms on ground floor.)
Facilities: Lift, lounge, breakfast room-cum-snack bar, residents' suite. Terrace, garden, small rocky beach. Laundry facilities. English spoken.
Location: 20 minutes' walk from town centre on airport road overlooking sea; main beach 20 minutes' drive. No private car park, but parking space available near hotel. Buses stop directly outside.
Terms: B & B 1,280–1,380 drs (single), 1,850–2,050 drs (double), 2,800–3,350 drs (suites).

Hotel Castello   *Telephone:* (0661) 30 184
Telex: 332136 Cast. Gr.

'In my opinion the *Castello* is the most attractive hotel on Corfu despite not having a pool and possibly being less lush than some of the larger and newer establishments. But what it lacks in facilities – and it is really only the pool that's missing – it more than makes up for in service, general ambience and personal care and trouble taken by the management. It is a mock-Florentine castle, formerly a summer residence of George II of Greece, and now converted into a luxury-class medium-sized hotel about 12 km from the town of Corfu. It's been a labour of love by the owners who, together with other members of the family, subsequently built a large hotel on the other side of the island *(Grand Hotel,* Glyfada). There is a large terrace with a fine view of a pine and cedar-wooded valley and the sea, an open-air restaurant for lunch and dinner, and 25 acres of park and well-tended garden. The public rooms are spacious with period furniture, rather English in feeling. There are two annexes in the grounds: they are modern, and one has a restaurant and dance floor, but both have something of the feel of the older building. There are also tennis courts in the grounds, and the hotel has a stretch of private beach about a kilometre away with aquatic sports facilities and a night club; a minibus plies regularly between hotel and beach where lunch can be taken. The "slightly fusty" air which one visitor commented on is in my view one of the attractions of the place.' *(Uli Lloyd Pack)*

Open: 1 April–31 October.
Rooms: 60 double, 12 single – 59 with bath, all with telephone. About half the rooms in 2 annexes.
Facilities: Lounges, TV room, bar, indoor and outdoor restaurants, terrace, 25 acres quiet parkland and gardens; tennis courts; 500 metres from sand and shingle beach where the hotel has a beach-restaurant, night club and all kinds of water sports – transport by minibus.
Location: 12 km from Corfu town. Garage; parking.
Credit cards: American Express, Diners.
Terms (excluding tax): Rooms 1,750–2,300 (single), 2,200–3,300 drs (double). Set meals: breakfast 180 drs, lunch/dinner 680 drs.

Paola Beach   *Telephone:* (0753) 4.1397

'This C-class hotel, whilst somewhat basic in its structure (the usual Greek concrete construction), has an absolutely delightful location in a sheltered bay of a small fishing village. Although only about 200 metres' walk around the edge of the bay from the village centre, it does stand quietly on its own. It was very pleasant to sit on the terrace in comfortable chairs whilst having breakfast and enjoying fresh pressed orange juice. Breakfast only is served plus snacks, and there is a well-stocked bar. Bed linen and towels were clean, but there was a slightly stale smell in the bathroom – continental plumbing no doubt. Although it is not my idea of a good hotel, I would class it as being useful in the area for anyone wishing to stay perhaps one or two nights while visiting the superb ancient theatre and other remains at Epidauros, which is about 11 km away. A small ancient theatre has also been found in the village and there are other remains in the area not yet fully excavated.' *(R S Millsum)*

Open: May–October.
Rooms: 27 – all with bath.
Facilities: Bar, breakfast room, terrace.
Location: 200 metres from village centre; parking.
Terms: Rooms 885 drs (single), 1,170 drs (double). Set meal: breakfast 123 drs. (No restaurant.)

FALIRAKI, Rhodes   **Map 15**

Lido   *Telephone:* (0241) 8.5226
PO Box 363

'The *Lido* is situated at the southern end of the long sandy Faliraki beach away from the new hotel developments. There are other sandy beaches nearby. It is five minutes' walk from shops, restaurants and bus. Rhodes town is 13 km away. The hotel is right on the shore; from your bedroom veranda you look down on coloured umbrellas, mature green trees on the terrace, the beach and the blue sea beyond. This unpretentious hotel, grade C, without package tour influence, is efficiently run by a Greek and his French wife; the staff are friendly and helpful, and they play cards with Madame when off duty. Our bedroom, although not large, was spotlessly clean and the adjoining bathroom had a shower with hot water. The food in the restaurant is above average (*demi pension* is obligatory). The hotel has a certain beachside charm. Do not be put off by the entrance at the back.' *(Sydney Carpenter)*

Open: 1 April–31 October.
Rooms: 18 double, 2 single – most with shower, all with telephone, some with balcony.
Facilities: Reception, TV room, restaurant; garden; on beach. English spoken.
Location: 13 km from Rhodes; 200 metres from town centre; at end of Faliraki beach.
Terms: B & B 950–1,375 drs; full board 1,650–2,175 drs. Set meals: breakfast 100 drs, lunch/dinner 400 drs; full *alc* 500 drs.

FIRA, Island of Santorini, Cyclades   **Map 15**

Hotel Kavalari   *Telephone:* (0286) 22 455

The volcanic island of Santorini is of striking crescent shape. You sail into a wide bay, thought to be the crater of a volcano which erupted in Minoan times, throwing up the spectacular cliffs of pumice and lava that surround the bay. The white-housed town of Fira is perched on the cliffs, 800 steps up from the harbour: you can ride up by mule or, new since 1982, you can take a cable car (160 drs one way) – 'for those tourists who are afraid to come up by mules', says the *Kavalari* a little scornfully. 'The very pleasant C-class *Kavalari* is dug out of the mountain-side, so that every bedroom or small group of bedrooms is independent. Like many of these small hotels or *pensions* in the Greek islands, it only serves bed and breakfast. It is inexpensive, clean and romantic, and in the morning has the most

beautiful views that I've seen since I lived in Hong Kong 25 years ago.'
(Lord Beaumont)

Open: 1 April–31 October.
Rooms: 10 single, 7 double, 5 triple – 12 with shower.
Facilities: Breakfast room. English spoken. Beaches nearby. (*Warning:* not suitable for the disabled or elderly.)
Location: 100 metres from town centre.
Restriction: No children under 10.
Terms: Rooms 565–1,100 drs. Set meal: breakfast 123 drs.

GYTHION, Peloponnesus   **Map 15**

Hotel Pantheon   *Telephone:* (0733) 2.2284, 2.2289
33 Vassileos Pavlou   and 2.2166

'A very clean and tidy C-grade hotel, situated immediately overlooking the small fishing harbour in this somewhat remote village in the south-eastern Peloponnese, the *Pantheon* makes a good base for anyone wishing to explore the even more remote area of the Mani. There are delightful views from the balconies of the bedrooms at the front of the hotel where you can sit in welcome shade after about 2 p.m. Also, similar views from the breakfast and dining room on the first floor. Breakfast is obligatory, and self-service; you can help yourself to the steaming hot coffee until it comes out of your ears if you wish – a welcome change from so many Greek hotels which serve a jug of hot water and packet of instant coffee. The lounge was quite pleasant with large comfortable armchairs and settees, though the leatherette coverings on some have become worn. There is a bar open all day where you can get beer, spirits, coffee or soft drinks.' *(R S Millsum)*

Open: All year.
Rooms: 53 – all with bath, some with balcony.
Facilities: Lounge, bar, breakfast room.
Location: 46 km S of Sparta on the N39.
Terms: Rooms 800–950 drs (single), 985–1,200 drs (double), 1,725–2,050 drs (suites). Set meal: breakfast 110 drs.

KIFISSIA, Attica   **Map 15**

Hotel Caterina   *Telephone:* (01) 801.8495
2 Myconos Street, Kefalari   and (01) 801.9826

A modest C-class alternative to a city hotel for those who prefer to sleep away from the heat and notorious smog of Athens.
'Kifissia is a small town or suburb of Athens about 10 km to the east in hills overlooking the city at an altitude of about 260 metres. It is where the more wealthy Athenians go to escape the city heat and the sadly polluted Athenian air. The *Caterina* (also spelt *Katerina*) is in the Kefalari district about ten minutes' walk from the centre of Kifissia where there are lots of shady trees, a pleasant park and the houses and villas have lovely gardens and beautifully manicured lawns which are seldom found in Greece, but would not be out of place in England. The whole atmosphere of the area is very relaxing. It has an ideal attraction for the tourist wishing to see the

sights of Athens without having to stay in the city itself: there is a Metro, partly underground, and known as the Electrokis which runs from Kifissia into Athens and through to Piraeus taking about thirty minutes into Athens – fare 10p!

'The *Caterina* was quite good value in an expensive area at just over £9.00 for a double room with bathroom and about £14.00 for a larger double room with bathroom and adjoining lounge area [1982]. The hotel is located in a relatively quiet side road with a lot of trees surrounding, but there are neglected houses around; the site may be re-developed with expensive apartments.

'The bedrooms were adequate in size and furnishings, but nothing very special. The bathrooms were small with a tiny sit-up bath which even my 5 ft 2 in frame would not fit into lying down, but there was also a shower. We were disappointed at the lack of spit and polish on the bathroom taps and basins indicating that management supervision was not the hotel's strong point. There is a quite pleasant lounge with a stone fireplace and big open hearth which appears to burn logs in the colder season. No evening meals are served, only breakfast which is of the standard uninteresting Greek variety. The clientele were mostly quite refined and elderly Greeks. There were Bibles in the bedrooms but no brandy in the bar. *(RSM)*

Open: All year.
Rooms: 37 – all with bath.
Facilities: Lounge, bar, breakfast room. Swimming pool, tennis courts nearby. Beach 25 km.
Location: 10 km E of Athens; 50 metres from Kefalari Square; parking.
Terms: Rooms from 660 drs (single), 825–1,300 drs (double), 1,480–1,950 drs (suites).

LEMNOS   **Map 15**

Hotel Akti Myrina   *Telephone:* (0276) 22681/3
Myrina Beach   *Telex:* 0297173 MYRI GR

The green and unspoiled island of Lemnos is about 8 hours' flying time from London allowing for a change of planes in Athens. The de-luxe *Akti Myrina* is in a beautiful setting overlooking a bay 1 km from the small main town. 'The concept is brilliant: 125 bungalows spread over the hillside, each unit hidden by greenery from its neighbour. The central services (pool, beach, etc.) are all within two minutes' pleasant walk. The design assures absolute privacy from one's neighbours, and most units have a little patio/garden with a view, ideal for breakfast and an evening "happy hour". Breakfast is served in one's room, lunch is from an irresistible garden buffet, and dinner in one of three intimate and cool restaurants. Over three weeks, I was aware of neither repetition nor monotony of dishes. In addition there are beach and poolside bars for snacks and drinks, and a formal outdoor speciality restaurant. There are typical beach sports and daily excursions in the hotel's caique.'

In a previous edition of the Guide, the anonymous contributor of the above description had added a number of criticisms about the maintenance of the place and the set menu which he had thought no more than adequate. It is a *Relais de Campagne* hotel (the only one in Greece), but was not, in his view, up to *Relais* standards elsewhere. The same correspondent has been back since, and reports in a more mellow mood: 'The brilliant concept of individual bungalows separated by luscious gardens and separate central services remains superbly unique. As with any hotel, faults exist, especially those intrinsic to an undeveloped remote Mediterranean island, but whatever the weaknesses of the *Akti Myrina*, they are totally compensated for by its attributes, by far the greatest of which is the overwhelming hospitality of the amicable Greek islanders in general and the hotel staff in particular.'

Open: 6 May–15 October.
Rooms: 110 double, 15 suites – 74 with bath, 51 with shower, all with telephone and fridge.
Facilities: Lounge, separate TV room, 3 dining rooms, disco-club, bridge room, library, hairdresser, boutique. Open-air taverna, evening with Greek dances, etc. 20 acres grounds; 2 tennis courts, heated swimming pool and mini-pool for children, volleyball, table tennis, pétanque, mini-golf, beach racquets. Sandy beach with safe bathing, waterskiing, etc. Sail boats, pedaloes, canoes, snorkelling equipment, etc., for hire. Daily trips round the island in the hotel's caique; weekly cruises to other islands.
Location: 2 km from Myrina Port. Parking.
Credit cards: American Express, Barclay/Visa, Diners.
Terms: Half board (compulsory) 3,000–6,175 drs, full board 4,000–7,175 drs. Set meals: lunch/dinner 1,300. 50% discount for children between 2 and 6 sharing parents' room; special meals available.

NAFPLION, Peloponnesus   **Map 15**

Hotel Helena   *Telephone:* (0752) 23 888 or 23 217
17 Sidiras Merarchias

'A C-class gem – spotless, shining marble floors, glistening porcelain in bathrooms, crisp sheets on comfortable beds, good view of antiquity from balcony, and best of all – the price is right.' So ran last year's commendation of this modest B & B within walking distance (500–600 yards) of the town centre. It does have, at least from the top floor, a splendid view of the Palemedi fortress, but there is a price to be paid: the rooms with a view face the main road. One reader found the traffic noise intolerable – the worst he could remember in a lifetime's travel. Anoher found it quiet at night. *Tot sententiae*. But we think that 'gem' probably overstates the attraction of the *Helena*. (Warning: the sign outside spells it *Elena*.) It is not in a particularly attractive part of town, and the lounge is airportish, with plain but functional seating. On the other hand, to quote a recent visitor: 'It deserves continued recommendation for the spotless condition in which the rooms are kept. It is true that the floors and bathroom fittings absolutely sparkle. The bed linen and towels were impeccable, and our beds were always turned down at night. The owner, Mrs Karnezis, has been at the *Helena* for about four years after spending 30 years in the States. She speaks very good English, with a strong Chicago accent, and we found her to be very helpful.' *(R S Millsum; also A W Gardes, Mr and Mrs C D Harvey-Piper)*

Open: All year.
Rooms: 30 double – all with bath.
Location: 12 km from Argos; 70 km from Corinth.
Terms: Double rooms 1,300 drs. Set meal: breakfast 123 drs. (No restaurant.)

NAFPLION, Peloponnesus   Map 15

King Otto Hotel   *Telephone:* (0752) 27 585
3 Farmakopoulon Street

'Its appearance and location suggest that it is at least a category too low. An elegant 19th-century town house, in a side street close to the harbour and the centre of the town, with cool airy hall and staircase and high-ceilinged bedrooms. Excellently clean showers and lavatories are mostly separate from the bedrooms, which presumably accounts for the low price. First-class breakfast served in leafy courtyard full of songbirds. Friendly front desk. Everything that a modern package-type hotel isn't.' *(William Plowden)*

Open: All year.
Rooms: 7 double, 3 single – 4 with shower.
Facilities: Salon with TV, courtyard, garden; near sea with rocky beach.
Location: Central, near the harbour; parking.
Terms: B & B 570–800 drs. (No restaurant.)

NAFPLION, Peloponnesus   Map 15

Hotel Leto   *Telephone:* (0752) 28 093
28 Zygomala Street

'Nafplion is a most attractive Venetian port, ideally situated for visiting Mycenae and Epidaurus, and the *Leto*, for what it costs, is one of the most pleasant hotels one could ever wish to stay. It is up on the hill with good views over the rooftops of the old town, but only five minutes' walk from the front. The rooms are very simply furnished, beds are clean and comfortable, there are private shower-rooms with hot water, and they are clean too. An important plus in summer is that all the rooms face north or east. A delicious breakfast of coffee, toasted French bread, plenty of butter and home-made marmalade, is served on a lovely terrace surrounded by scented jasmine and honeysuckle. The hotel is run by the friendly Rekoumis family, some members of which speak a sprinkling of English.' *(Anna Waley)*

Open: 15 March–31 October.
Rooms: 8 double, 3 single – 7 with bath or shower.
Facilities: Salon, terrace. Rocky beach nearby. Some English spoken.
Terms: B & B 700–800 drs. (No restaurant.)

TOLON, Nr Nauplion   Map 15

Hotel Minoa   *Telephone:* (0752) 59 207 and 59 416
56 Aktis Street   *Telex:* 0298157 MINO GR

The Minoa is a family business – mother and father Georgidakis and three brothers. They speak English, and their brochure offers a superior example of PR prose – certainly the best we have come across in Greece: 'Imagine a generous sweep of bay and beach, fringed by mountains.

Imagine a small secluded town whose main street is never further than a hundred yards from the water's edge. Imagine intimate tavernas no more than ten yards from the water's edge. Then imagine a quietly situated hotel a mere ten feet (yes, ten feet) from the water's edge. Our hotel. The *Minoa*. Since we're a family concern, it has a family atmosphere. It is luxurious without being ostentatious. For example, you'll find your room simply yet tastefully decorated. With private shower, WC and balcony. A radio. And especially handy for ordering breakfast in bed, a telephone. Downstairs, you can unwind over an "ouzo" [Greek aperitif] in our cosy bar. Watch TV (if you can understand the lingo). Or rediscover the art of relaxation in the comfort of our lounge. The cuisine? Suffice to say, Greeks drive the 2½ hours from Athens just for Sunday lunch. Be their choice *à la carte* or *menu du jour*. To work up your own appetite, you can sail, row, waterski, fish (the more adventurous may prefer underwater fishing) and swim in the sort of calm, clear, aquamarine sea that never rings true on postcards.'

Sadly, Tolon, which is 11 km from Nauplion, and therefore within easy driving or bus distance to Mycenae, Argos and Epidaurus, isn't as paradisical as it used to be: tour operators, British among others, have discovered the place, and it has a host of hotels and tavernas along its narrow beach strip. But our readers have mostly enjoyed their stay at the unpretentiously sympathetic and modestly priced *Minoa*. One snag: you can expect noisy pop from the bar up till 11 p.m. If you prefer a quieter place to stay, we are told that the *Minoa*'s sister hotel, the *Knossos*, 60 yards away, has the same facilities without the sound.

Open: 15 March–7 November.
Rooms: 39 double, 5 single – 7 with bath, 37 with shower and WC, all with telephone and radio. (Some rooms on ground floor in annexe.)
Facilities: Lift, 2 lounges (1 with TV), bar, restaurant; dancing every night; breakfast under large beach awning. Small garden with bar. Sandy beach and safe bathing, sailing, pedalos, boating, fishing. English spoken.
Location: Near old port; parking.
Credit cards: All major credit cards accepted.
Terms: Dinner, B & B 1,115–1,600 drs. Set meals: lunch/dinner 450 drs; full *alc* 500 drs. Reduced rates for children sharing parents' room.

XYLOKASTRON, Corinth   Map 15

Apollon Hotel   *Telephone:* (0743) 22239
105 J. Ioannou

On the Gulf of Corinth, between ancient Corinth (34 km) and the port of Patros (100 km), where ferry boats leave for Brindisi in Italy, so a useful nightstop for some travellers. This B-class bed-and-breakfast hotel, part of which was once a presidential residence, though with a modern annexe, is in the town about 200 metres from the sea front. 'The management was friendly, and the chambermaid also pleasant, clean and well turned-out. The furnishings were somewhat mundane, but there were lovely fine crisp clean sheets on the bed. The bathroom was absolutely immaculate and also contained a bidet. There is a pleasant garden terrace at the front of the hotel and drinks are available.' *(RSM)*

Open: All year.
Rooms: 32 – all with bath and telephone; baby-sitting available.

Facilities: TV room, lounges, snack-bar, restaurant, verandas.
Location: Central, 200 metres from sea front; parking.
Terms: Rooms (excluding 10½% tax) 785–1,130 drs (single), 985–1,850 drs (double). Set meals: breakfast 130 drs, dinner 500 drs.

Hotel de L'Europe, Amsterdam

Holland

ALMEN, Gelderland, 7218 AH **Map 8**

De Hoofdige Boer *Telephone:* (05751) 744
Dorpstraat 38

'An old-established family-run hotel in a small village east of Zutphen in Eastern Holland. Very friendly proprietors with some English spoken. Ideal for a quiet holiday, with tennis, swimming, bicycle-hire in the village, and attractive towns and villages nearby. Modern bedrooms, fully equipped, and comfortable lounge; and tea garden in summer. Outstanding food, the best we had in Holland, and excellent value.' *(P Snowden)*

No confirmation yet from readers on the above entry which appeared in our 1982 edition, but we were glad to hear from the proprietor, Dirk Holtslag, who writes: 'We had two American guests who showed us your Guide. Even if I cannot explain it in good English, I like to say that we believe your book reaches the right clients, for that American couple was so kind, just people we like and are used to work for. Now, as we know about your Guide, we will ask English spoken guests if they come by means of your book, so we can tell you about the result.' We appreciate this kindness, but would also hope to hear from some readers direct.

Open: All year, except New Year and early January.
Rooms: 18 double, 2 single – 14 with bath, 6 with shower, 12 with telephone; TV

can be hired; baby-listening can be arranged. (2 rooms on ground floor.) 2 rooms in annexe.
Facilities: Pub lounge with TV, TV room, function room, dining room. Tea garden. 5 minutes' walk to heated swimming pool. English spoken. &.
Location: Central, near the church; parking. About 1½ hrs drive from Amsterdam via Deventer and Eefde.
Credit card: Diners.
Terms: B & B 45–65 glds; dinner, B & B 60–90 glds. Set meal: lunch 15 glds; dinner 30 glds; full *alc* 50 glds. Reduced rates for children sharing parents' room; special meals provided.

AMSTERDAM, 1016 AZ   Map 8

Hotel Ambassade   *Telephone:* (020) 262.333
Herengracht 341   *Telex:* 10158

The Ambassade, a conversion of four five-storey houses on one of Amsterdam's famous radial canals, made its first appearance in the Guide last year. It is ten minutes' walk to the Rijksmuseum and just round the corner from one of the city's liveliest squares, Spui. 'For those who prefer the small cosy family hotel, the *Ambassade* fits the bill perfectly,' we said. Readers agree, though one had minor reservations: 'Students of Dutch domestic architecture, but not sufferers from vertigo, will like this friendly bed-and-breakfast hotel (though light meals are available throughout the day) which offers fascinating glimpses of life at the top in the 17th century: stairs to attic bedrooms reveal a roof-scape outside and behind that is all terracotta tiles and steep pitched roofs. A room for one, tight for two, was comfortable if a little shabby. Its adjoining bathroom, with hip-bath, was reminiscent of a slit trench, but warmer. Two handsome public rooms on the first floor, with long windows overlooking the canal, are for sitting and eating breakfast, which the welcoming proprietors might look at again. Gouda and ham do not make up for soggy or stale bread. The hotel is centrally sited, quiet with the occasional sound of a late-evening demo.' *(AL)*

Others were unqualified in their praise: 'More special than you say – really one of the "very special" places one finds through the years. The service, efficiency and cleanliness were exceptional.' *(Mr and Mrs D Steven McGuire)*

Open: All year.
Rooms: 35 double, 5 single – 38 with bath, 2 with shower, all with telephone, baby-sitters available. 16 rooms in annexe (9 ground-floor rooms).
Facilities: Lounge, TV lounge, breakfast room. English spoken.
Location: Central; no special parking facilities.
Credit cards: Access/Euro/Mastercard, American Express, Barclay/Visa.
Terms: B & B 45–92 glds. Light meals available throughout the day. Cot for child in parents' room 15 glds.

We ask hotels to estimate their 1983 tariffs. Not all hotels in Part Two reply, so prices in Part Two are more approximate in some cases than those in Part One.

AMSTERDAM, 1012 CP   Map 8

Hotel de L'Europe   *Telephone:* (020) 23.48.36
Nieuwe Doelenstraat 2–4   *Telex:* 12081
                              Reservations: in UK telephone (01) 278 4211
                                   in USA telephone (800) 221 1074

One of the older grander hotels in the city, built in 1895 on the Amstel,
and centrally placed for all the sights. Front rooms can be noisy; rooms at
the back or overlooking the river are to be preferred. The hotel's
restaurant, the *Excelsior*, has an excellent reputation for its cooking and
for an outstanding cellar. *(T Crone)*

Open: All year.
Rooms: 42 double, 37 single, 3 suites – all with bath, telephone, radio and colour
TV; baby-sitting on request.
Facilities: Lift, lounge, bar, 2 restaurants; banqueting, cocktail and conference
facilities. 24-hour room service. English spoken.
Location: Central, opposite the Mint Tower and Flowermarket; limited private
parking, public garage.
Credit cards: All major credit cards accepted.
Terms: B & B 167.50–265 glds; dinner, B & B 200–330 glds; full board 252.50–
382.50 glds. Set meals: lunch 52.50 glds, dinner 65 glds; full *alc* 100 glds. Reduced
rates for children sharing parents' room (free with cot); half-price meals.

DELDEN 7491, Overijssel   Map 8

Carelshaven   *Telephone:* (05407) 1305
30 Hengelosestraat

Not far from the main road between Deventer and Hengelo, surrounded
by woods, *Carelshaven Hotel* was built in 1774 as a hostel for sailors and
later turned into a comfortable hotel and restaurant (rosetted in Michelin)
with a modern annexe. The hotel is a good base for visiting Twickel castle
with its beautiful gardens. 'I highly recommend this hotel, particularly for
travellers to Scandinavia and North Germany, being near the border. The
annexe is very quiet and comfortable; there are lovely walks and the
surroundings are beautiful. Good and attractive food and service. Lots of
charm and memories of the past. Not cheap.' *(Tan Crone)*

Open: All year, except 24 December–2 January.
Rooms: 20 double, 5 single – 22 with bath, 3 with shower, 1 with tea-making
facilities, some with TV, all with telephone. (Some rooms on ground floor.)
Facilities: TV room; salon, bar, restaurant; conference facilities. Garden and
terrace. English spoken. &.
Location: 2 km from the E8 motorway. Delden is reached by the A1. There is a
bus stop 100 metres from the hotel and railway stations at Delden (1 km) and
Hengelo (5 km); front rooms might be noisy; parking, garage.
Credit cards: American Express, Diners.
Terms: B & B 65–120 glds. Set meal: dinner 65 glds. Special rates for long stays,
weekends, etc. Special meals for children on request.

> Please don't just leave the feedback to others.

Hotel Leeuwenbrug   *Telephone:* (015) 123062
Koornmarkt 16   *Telex:* 16443-013

'A small bed-and-breakfast hotel (though there are plans to expand and open a restaurant shortly) on one of the canals in the loveliest part of Delft, run by husband-and-wife team, Mynheer and Mevrouw Wubben, who speak English, with running commentary by their parrot (who doesn't). Rooms are smallish, and not all have private bath, but they are warm, adequately furnished and with comfortable beds. Prices are reasonable, the welcome is friendly, and the buffet-style breakfast is excellent. There is only limited space in the lounge, but there is also a pleasant little bar. The hotel has always been full of satisfied guests when we have been there.' *(E Newall)*

Open: All year.
Rooms: 27 double, 2 single – 5 with bath and shower, 24 with shower, telephone, radio, TV and baby-listening. (6 rooms on ground floor.)
Facilities: Lift, bar, breakfast room. Sandy beach 15 km. English spoken. ♿.
Location: Take the Delft Zuid turning off the Rotterdam/Amsterdam highway, and follow the signs to Centre West; paid parking nearby.
Credit card: Barclay/Visa.
Terms: Rooms with breakfast 100–115 glds (single), 120–135 glds (double). (No restaurant.) Babies free.

Hotel de Zalm   *Telephone:* (01820) 12344
34 Markt

'Gouda is such a beautiful place to visit and there is a great deal to see, not just in the town but in the surrounding countryside. We think this would make an ideal base for trips in Holland, because it is very accessible but delightfully peaceful. Rotterdam is 37 km away, The Hague 48 km and Amsterdam 85 km. The hotel is a very old building (16th-century) and has all the charm and atmosphere associated with such an establishment. The staff are friendly and helpful and the food is good – breakfast provided plenty of decent fresh food. While the accommodation could not be classed as luxury, it was quite adequate. Most rooms have a shower and wash-basin. Ours cost 80 guilders [early 1982] for a double room with breakfast. I would put it in a similar class to the *Franz Josef* in Linz-am-Rhein, Germany [q.v.].' *(Ron and Jan Davidson)*

Open: All year.
Rooms: 22 double, 1 single – 22 with shower, all with telephone.
Facilities: Restaurant. English spoken.
Location: In town centre; parking.
Credit cards: Access/Euro/Mastercard, American Express, Barclay/Visa.
Terms: Rooms 55 glds (single), 85 glds (double). Full *alc* 35 glds.

> Please write and confirm an entry when it is deserved. If you think that a hotel is not as good as we say, please write and tell us.

MAASTRICHT, Limburg, 6211 EN   Map 8

Hotel Maastricht   *Telephone:* (043) 54171
De Ruiterij   *Telex:* 56822
                    Reservations: in UK telephone (01) 940 9766
                                   in USA telephone (212) 247 7950

The *Hotel Maastricht* hit the headlines in March 1981 when the town played host to an EEC summit. A conversion of 15th- and 16th-century buildings adjoining the hotel enabled 23 luxurious suites to be made available to Common Market leaders, and named after them, with a guarantee to future residents that details of decoration and furniture are unchanged. The Margaret Thatcher Room, we are told, is in a converted 16th-century inn called appropriately the 'Weapon of England'.

'Although most modern hotels have little to recommend them, this one is an exception. It is situated on the river bank immediately opposite the old centre of a fascinating town. It is an attractive brick building of interesting design, with almost all the rooms and suites overlooking the Maas (Meuse). As it is on the waterfront, there is hardly any traffic noise, and the only sounds you can hear are the throbbing engines of the huge barges passing by the windows on the river. There is an attractive restaurant and bar, also with river view, and a coffee shop where enormous buffet breakfasts are served. The building also includes a hairdresser's and boutique and exhibition area for paintings, etc. Rooms are large, comfortable, and furnished with top-calibre modern furniture, lights and fitments. The furniture is all by Artifort, a manufacturer whose factory is in the town, and the quality and lack of compromise shows. We found it very refreshing.' *(Pat and Jeremy Temple; also Mrs C Smith)*

Open: All year.
Rooms: 103 double, 6 single, 25 suites – all with bath and shower, telephone, radio and colour TV, some with balconies; baby-sitting by arrangement. 23 suites in annexe with tea-making facilities. (1 special bedroom and WC for the disabled.)
Facilities: Lifts, lobby, coffee shop, bar, restaurant; conference facilities for 10–300 people. English spoken. &.
Location: On the bank of the river Maas (Meuse), 5 minutes from town centre; hotel has its own car park. Coming from out of town use Kennedy Bridge.
Credit cards: All major credit cards accepted.
Terms: B & B 145–195 glds. Set meals: lunch from 15 glds; dinner from 40 glds; full *alc* 65 glds. Special weekend breaks. Reduced rates for children sharing parents' room; special meals available.

OISTERWIJK, North Brabant, 5062 TE   Map 8

Hotel Langoed De Rosep   *Telephone:* (04242) 82481
Oirschotsebaan 15

'Tucked into the National Trust beech and pine woods outside the quiet town of Oisterwijk, it sounds and looks remote. But nowhere is "off the map" in Holland, and Oisterwijk is a handy short drive from Eindhoven, Breda and Tilburg. It's an ideal place to unwind. The woods around are dotted with little lakes and ponds, and it is good walking or bicycling country. The *De Rosep* is modern, single-storeyed, and has recently added a new wing and enlarged its public rooms without sacrificing its

417

inherently Dutch atmosphere. Bar and restaurant have a sun terrace overlooking a small lake. Spacious bedrooms; lavish meals; highly efficient service.' *(Valerie Ferguson; endorsed by J E Davidson)*

Open: All year, except New Year.
Rooms: 25 double – all with bath, telephone and radio and TV. (All rooms on ground floor.)
Facilities: Lounge, restaurant, bar with sun terrace; conference rooms; separate TV room. Close to heated lido, riding school, miniature golf course. English spoken. &.
Location: Off the N93 north-east Tilburg.
Credit cards: All major credit cards accepted.
Terms: B & B 63–90 glds. Set meals: lunch 10.50 glds, dinner 25.50 or 31.50 glds. Reduced rates and special meals for children.

WASSENAAR, 2243 South Holland   Map 8

De Kieviet   *Telephone:* (01751) 79403 or 79203
Stoeplaan 27

'An excellent restaurant with six rooms and a sizeable flowered terrace, set in the Wassenaar woods. Comfortable bedrooms with very super bathrooms. The restaurant, with a huge separate area for pre-dinner drinks etc., is much used by the diplomatic set from The Hague – of which Wassenaar is virtually a suburb – but also by local families. Expensive enough, but a lovely place to relax in after a hard day in art galleries and museums in The Hague, and with much more character than the big new hotels in the city itself.' *(Frank and Joan Harrison)*

Open: All year. Restaurant closed Monday.
Rooms: 6 double – all with bath and telephone.
Facilities: Lounge, restaurant. Garden; beach 5 km; golf, tennis, riding nearby. English spoken.
Location: 8 km from the centre of the Hague; 2 km SW of Wassenaar; parking.
Credit cards: All major credit cards accepted.
Terms: Rooms (including breakfast) 105 glds (single), 165.50 glds (double). Set meals: lunch from 47.50 glds, dinner from 62.50 glds; full *alc* 75 glds.

WELLERLOOI, 5856 Limburg   Map 8

Hostellerie de Hamert   *Telephone:* (04703) 1260
Hamert 2, rte Nijmegen-Venlo

'This is a famous restaurant, used by Germans and Belgians as well as Netherlanders, with four rooms. Situated on a big curve on the bank of the Maas, it has one room with a balcony overlooking the river. Though not on any usual tourist route from Britain (unless you are making the delightful trip following the Maas-Meuse from the delta to the source) it is indeed "worth a detour" for the excellent food and service, and the superb view of the river and its traffic from the balconied bedroom (where you can have breakfast), and from the tables by the window in the dining room (where you can watch the sun go down over the river and the flat green landscape). Not the place for an extended stay but perfect for a self-indulgent one-night stand.' *(Frank and Joan Harrison)*

418

Open: All year. Restaurant closed Tuesday and Wednesday.
Rooms: 4 – most with bath.
Facilities: Restaurant.
Location: 20 km from Venlo.
Terms: Rooms 53 glds (single), 85–106 glds (double).

WITTEM, Nr Gulpen, Limburg, 6286 AA   **Map 8**

Kasteel Wittem   *Telephone:* Wittem (04450) 1208
Wittemeralle 3

'*Kasteel Wittem* really is a castle, with 12-feet-thick walls, ancient trees and roses in the garden; but above all, it has an exceptional cuisine: it's a gourmet's paradise. And more than that, Pieter Ritzen and his family run it like a country house and without any trace of stuffiness. When they took over the castle, they aimed at the highest standards – not only first-class food, but equally first-class comfort. Each room has its own private bathroom, which had to be gouged out of the cyclopean walls. It's the nearest to a stately home both in reception and standards that I've ever encountered in Holland. Situated as it is between Maastricht and Aachen, *Kasteel Wittem* is the perfect place for a weekend of peace and plenty before (or after) a tough business week. There is golf in the vicinity and plenty of other outdoor activities. Best of all, you will be cosseted like a favourite relative.' *(Valerie Ferguson)*

The above report dates from 1979, but subsequent visitors have consistently endorsed Valerie Ferguson's comments. Here is the latest to reach us, dotting some i's on the restaurant front: 'The hotel has a standard of cuisine and service I have never encountered in Britain. Presentation of each course is beautifully done using the food itself, without having to resort to floral decoration as in some restaurants. Despite its grand setting the meals are not expensive, and a reduction of 30 guilders per night on the room rate is given if dinner is taken in the restaurant. Breakfasts, too, offer excellent value: fresh orange juice, a boiled egg, meat, cheese and about ten different types of bread are served each morning (leftovers being fed to the swans and ducks in the castle moat). And the wine list is outstanding as well, with a much less severe mark-up than in most British restaurants. All the wines are French with a good choice in each region; there are rarities, but also a good choice in the £4–8 range. If only this hotel was down the road!' *(Norman and Pamela Dutson: also Marilee Thompson Duer, W Frank)*

Open: All year.
Rooms: 12 double, 1 suite – all with bath and shower and telephone; TV on request; tea-making facilities.
Facilities: Salon, restaurant; conference and banqueting facilities. Garden. Golf, bicycling, walking, tennis and trout fishing nearby.
Location: Between Maastricht (17 km) and Aachen (15 km). 1 km SW of Gulpen on Maastricht road.
Credit cards: All major credit cards accepted.
Terms: Double room with Dutch breakfast 145 glds. Set meals: lunch 45 glds, dinner 65 glds; full *alc* 85 glds. Reduction in room price if guests dine in restaurant. Reduced rates and special meals for children.

Don't rely on our printed tariffs! Check before booking.

Hotel Gellért, Budapest

Hungary

Hotel Astoria
Kossuth Lajos utca 19

Telephone: (1) 173/411
Telex: 22 4205

An historic hotel, built before the First World War, with rooms as comfortable and spacious as you would expect from that more opulent age. It is in the heart of Budapest's Inner City, with the metro at your door and the Danube no more than a block away. Front rooms are noisy, so you need to ask for an interior room if you are a light sleeper. The hotel caters for package tours, mostly from 'socialist' countries, but the management separates sheep from goats; those who travel privately are given a special dining room and far better service. We are not sure in which dining room one correspondent was served 'cow soup' for beef consommé, but it was, he reports, delicious. 'For a last gasp of imperial taste in a slightly provincial manner, nowhere suits better than the *Astoria*. The dining-room is marble surrounding a Beaux-Arts urn and just dripping with crystal. Service is pleasant, with English always possible though not always perfect. Rooms are commodiously furnished in turn-of-the-century pieces and tastefully appointed.' *(George Herzog; also E George Maddocks)*

Open: All year.
Rooms: 150 double, 42 single – 80 with bath, all with telephone and radio.

Facilities: Hall, café, dining room, night club; music and dancing nightly except Monday. English spoken.
Location: Central, near river and air terminal. Some noise in front rooms. Parking.
Credit cards: All major credit cards accepted.
Terms: Rooms 460–850 Ft (single), 870–1,350 Ft (double). No charge for children under 6.

BUDAPEST 1111   Map 14

Hotel Gellért   *Telephone:* (1) 46.07.00
Szt Gellért ter 1   *Telex:* 22-4363

'Better than the *Astoria* for those who like character and graciousness, not to mention the sort of courteous and attentive service more typical of the *Grand* at Eastbourne than Eastern Europe. The *Gellért* was a spa hotel in the "good old days". It retains its baths, though they are open to the public and squalid. But the hotel retains its luxury spa character. The foyer only needs a palm court orchestra to fill the role it was built for – except that the armchairs are now plastic! There is a night-club (didn't try it), a superb dining room with equally superb gypsy band and an excellent list of Hungarian wines, a coffee shop, a dollar shop (hard currency only), and you can buy *The Times*. Excellent room service, comfortable "Victorian" rooms, and all mod cons. Highly recommended. You would never know it was State-owned.' *(John M Sidwick)*

Open: All year.
Rooms: 235 – all with bath and telephone.
Facilities: Large foyer, lounges, bar, coffee shop, dining room, night club, 6 conference rooms; indoor swimming pool.
Location: On Gellért Hill, overlooking city; parking.
Terms: Rooms 1,380 Ft (single), 2,060 Ft (double).

VISEGRÁD, 2025, P.F. 24   Map 14

Hotel Sylvanus   *Telephone:* Visegrad 291
     Vagy 231
     Telex: 22-57-20 PANSY H

'Visegrád is on the Danube Bend, ¾-hour from Budapest by hydrofoil (80p single!) and 2 hours by train and bus (60p). It is a grotty little village. But the *Sylvanus* is above it all – literally. On top of a hill (almost a mountain) near to a super old castle and surrounded by what is nearly enough a National Park – marvellous walks and, I think, hunting. And fantastic views over the Danube bend. Not the most luxurious of hotels. But, ideal for a break from Budapest or, perhaps, for a stopover driving from the city to the country. Adequate bedrooms. Excellent food. Good service. Clean. Eat and/or drink alfresco on the terrace. Prices in May 1982 of the order of £10 a night for both of us in a double room with bath. Idiotically cheap food prices. And it's difficult to pay more than £1.50 for excellent local wine. Probably equivalent to a three-star hotel. Don't expect too much except fantastic value in a rural oasis near enough to the city for a one-night visit.' *(John M Sidwick)*

Open: All year.

Rooms: 66 double, 9 triple, 4 suites – all with bath and balcony, 34 with terrace.

Facilities: TV room, bar, snack bar with summer terrace, restaurant, conference facilities; automatic skittle ground, film club; open-air gymnastic ground, thermal bath, tennis courts, riding school nearby; boat trips on Danube.

Location: 48 km from Budapest on the Danube Bend.

Terms: Double rooms: 882 Ft. Set meal: breakfast 145 Ft.

Grand Hotel Duomo, Milan

Italy

Fonte della Galletta   *Telephone:* (0575) 79.39.25

Definitely not for those who want great comfort and first-class facilities. But it should appeal to people who like going somewhere a bit out of the ordinary, with peace and quiet, lovely views, friendly treatment – and superb and unusual food.' So ran the opening lines of our previous entry, and we think it fair – though perhaps the snags as well as the bonuses of staying here need to be underlined. Alpe Faggeto is 6 km above Caprese Michelangelo (the sculptor's birthplace; the house is now a museum, but, apart from the building, which is a genuine relic, is mostly reproduction – photos and copies). It is often quite literally in the clouds, though when the clouds lift the views are breathtaking. The *Fonte della Galletta* is essentially a restaurant with rooms, and the restaurant side of things comes first. The well-named Signor Boncompagni is extremely friendly (though he does not speak English) and an outstanding cook, specializing in using mushrooms and funghi in a variety of fascinating and original ways. *Boletus edulis* (or *porcini*), it seems, with everything. His cooking prowess has won him many awards, including the *Oscar della cucina Italiana.* Although the accommodation is fairly basic, the restaurant is a sophisticated and popular establishment, often catering for large groups, especially at weekends. Some of the rooms are in the main building; one visitor found her sleep disturbed by an electrical generator and moved the following night to an annexe, which she found damp and cold. The only lounge, off the main dining room, houses the TV. In short, recommended chiefly as a fair-weather hotel – though, at the right time of year, it could provide a memorable experience. *(Ian and Agathe Lewin, BA)*

Open: All year. Restaurant closed Wednesday October–May.
Rooms: 20 double, 3 single, 3 suites – 14 with shower, ali with telephone. 6 rooms in annexe.
Facilities: Lounge with TV, bar, restaurant; banqueting facilities; garden.
Location: 6 km SW of Caprese Michelangelo; 50 km NE of Arezzo.
Credit cards: American Express, Barclay/Visa, Diners.
Terms: B & B 17,000–24,000 L; dinner, B & B 24,000–33,000 L; full board 25,000 L. Set meals: lunch 12,000–20,000 L; dinner 10,000–18,000 L; full *alc* 12,000 L.

ANCONA, 60020   **Map 14**

Hotel Emilia   *Telephone:* (071) 801117
Collina di Portonovo

'For several hundred kilometres south from Venice, the Adriatic is flat and uninteresting: seaside after seaside with rows of nearly identical hotels filled with package tourists. Then, suddenly, immediately south of Ancona, comes Monte Conero, a splendid mountain shielding three holiday resorts. Above one of them, Portonovo, is the *Emilia*, an excellent modern cliff-top hotel surrounded by fields on three sides and a sheer gorse-topped cliff on the other. The air must be getting on for the purest in Italy! The hotel is well-run, the dining-room scores a rosette in Michelin, though this applies to those eating *à la carte* rather than *en pension*. Nevertheless the set menu is still good; the wine, from the owner's vineyard, very drinkable. There's a good large spotlessly clean swimming pool and the Portonovo beach is only a few kilometres down (and I mean down) the road. Fellow guests tend to be slightly trendy Italians, but the whole atmosphere is totally informal. We shall certainly go back.' *(Martyn Goff)*

Open: March–October. Closed Sunday evening and Monday.
Rooms: 33 double – all with shower and telephone.
Facilities: Lounge with TV, restaurant. Garden with swimming pool and tennis court. Rocky beach 2 km by road. English spoken.
Location: 10 km from town centre. From the N take exit Ancona Nord; follow signs for port and station; in front of station follow signs for Riviera del Conero.
Terms: Rooms 29,000–49,000 L. Set meal: breakfast 5,000 L. *Alc* (excluding wine and 10% service charge) 21,850–33,350 L.

ASOLO, 31011 Treviso   **Map 14**

Hotel Villa Cipriani   *Telephone:* (0423) 55.444
Via Canova 298   *Telex:* 411060 CIPRAS I

'Situated in the small town of Asolo with marvellous views of the surrounding hilly countryside, this beautiful villa is a small charming very comfortable hotel. No relation to the *Cipriani* in Venice, it is part of the CIGA Hotel group, although, except for the company logo used on china, menus, stationery, etc., it is run very much as an independent country-house hotel. The manager is extremely pleasant, friendly and always at hand. The situation makes it convenient for visiting the villas of the Veneto, Venice, Padua and the many small interesting towns in the foothills of the Dolomites. Our room was large and comfortable with a beautiful view. The restaurant is superb (rosette in Michelin) and attracts plenty of local custom as well as residents. Prices are very reasonable and the wine list will not draw any gasps! The restaurant and the small bar open on to the terrace and garden where normally one takes breakfast in the sun. We had our after-dinner drinks in the garden in October! The staff are plentiful, friendly, efficient and quiet. One of the most pleasing and comfortable hotels we've visited in Italy.' *(Pat and Jeremy Temple; also Alfred Knopf Jr)*

Open: All year. Restaurant closed Monday October–April.
Rooms: 31 double, 1 single – all with bath and shower, telephone and TV, 2 with terrace. (11 rooms in annexe, some rooms on ground floor.)
Facilities: Lift, TV room, bar, restaurant, terrace, air-conditioning. Garden. English spoken.
Location: 35 km NW of Treviso. 300 yards from town centre; parking.
Credit cards: All major credit cards accepted.
Terms (excluding tax): Rooms 87,000–155,000 L. Set meal: breakfast 9,800 L; *alc* from about 34,000 (excluding wine). Special meals for children.

ASSISI, 06081 Perugia   Map 14

Hotel Umbra   *Telephone:* (075) 81.22.40
Via degli Archi 6

The *Umbra*, so far as the Guide is concerned, is *the* hotel in Assisi. Not that the place isn't teeming with hotels big and small, package and private. But the *Umbra* has several special advantages: it is close to the main square, but in a quiet narrow side street; it has an attractive garden; and it also has the only restaurant in the city which Michelin has considered worthy of a star. Most readers over the years have written enthusiastically, but for the past two years a critical note has crept in to some reports, suggesting a fall in standards. The hotel replies: 'We follow with great attention the comments by some of our guests which you have published. These are very important for us as they give us a guide-line as to how to improve. Last year we read in your guide an unfavourable criticism of the standard of our facilities. We can now assure that several things have changed. Four new complete bathrooms, public rooms have undergone important renovations – new curtains, new armchairs and furniture in style. These innovations that we have made to our house have taken more than four winter months. We mention this to make you understand how difficult it is to improve and modernize some of our rooms which date back as far as the 13th century.'

Meanwhile, a recent visitor reports: 'A delightful hotel and – particularly on *pension* or *demi-pension* terms – excellent value. Odd things happen here. The hot water took at least five minutes to arrive. The WC in Room 9 made extraordinary noises ending with an outstanding coda five minutes after flushing. The food was not so good on Tuesdays when the restaurant is closed to outsiders. But, the hot water did eventually arrive. You don't hear anybody else's plumbing. And the food is excellent on non-Tuesdays and even passable on the chef's day of rest. What makes this hotel a delight is everybody's wish to make your stay enjoyable. From

427

the chambermaid to the front desk, people helped. The rooms were large and pleasant. Most of the staff were multi-lingual and those who were not enjoyed sign language or understood my non-existent Italian. All in all, a wonderful place for a 3–4 day stay. *(Roger Bennett)*

Open: All year except 5 November–5 December. Restaurant closed Wednesday.
Rooms: 21 double, 6 single – 17 with bath, 5 with shower, all with telephone and mono TV. (Some rooms on ground floor.)
Facilities: Lounge, TV room, American Bar, restaurant. Garden with terrace for meals in fine weather. English spoken. &.
Location: In town centre, near main square.
Credit cards: All major credit cards accepted.
Terms: B & B 20,000–40,000 L. Full *alc* 15,000 L. Reduced rates for children.

AVIGLIANA, 10051 Torino   Map 14

Hotel Ristorante Hermitage   *Telephone:* (011) 93.81.50

Twenty-four km W of Turin, the small town of Avigliana lies just off the A13 on its way to the Mont Cenis pass and France. The *Hermitage* is a modern restaurant with rooms built in the Piedmontese Baroque style. 'Very comfortable well-equipped bedrooms, with a terrace commanding fine views over a lake to distant mountains. The food was excellent, the service quiet, friendly and attentive, and the proprietor himself particularly helpful.' *(Warren Bagust)*

Open: All year. Restaurant closed Tuesday.
Rooms: 7 – all with bath and telephone.
Facilities: Restaurant, terrace. Garden.
Location: 24 km W of Turin just off the A13.
Terms: Rooms 23,000–27,600 L. Set meal: breakfast 5,750 L; *alc* 20,700–28,750 L (excluding wine).

BELLAGIO, 22021 Como   Map 14

Hotel du Lac   *Telephone:* (031) 95.03.20

For the budget-conscious, a modest Bellagian alternative to the *Serbelloni*. 'On the lakeside: the bedrooms and the restaurant have glorious views. There is a roof-garden for sitting and sunbathing and tables on the covered terrace outside. The hotel is beautifully run and very comfortable. Welcoming atmosphere. The proprietor's wife (English) is charming and extremely helpful. Only snag is that it is in the brochures for package tours, so other guests tend to be English, and the set meal at dinner is not too adventurous.' *(A G Don)*

Open: April–6 October.
Rooms: 48 double – most with bath and telephone.
Facilities: Lift, restaurant, roof-garden and terrace. English spoken.
Location: On the lakeside.
Credit cards: All major credit cards accepted.
Terms: Rooms 33,500–49,500 L; full board 33,500–44,000 L. Set meals: breakfast, 4,600 L; lunch/dinner 11,500–15,000 L.

BELLAGIO, 22021 Como   Map 14

Grand Hotel Villa Serbelloni   *Telephone:* (031) 95.02.16
Via Roma 1   *Telex:* 380330 SERBOT I

'An oasis of peace and tranquillity. Nothing could be lovelier than dinner
on the terrace, with the sun setting behind the mountains across the lake.'
A characteristic tribute, though 'oasis' may conjure up a picture of a
modest watering-hole quite inappropriate to the outsize grandness of this
former 16th-century villa full of original frescoes and with a spectacular
staircase flanked by gilt *putti* on giant candelabra. Everything is on a large
scale: the public rooms, though some are now showing signs of wear and
tear, are palatial, you could drive a coach and four along the marble
corridors, and the bedrooms, also sometimes a bit shabby-grand, are
suitable for regal *levées*. Chamber concerts are often given in the stately
dining room. There's a private beach, heated outdoor pool and the hotel's
own motor and rowing boats; its position on the lake, near the tip of the
peninsula where Como forks, offers incomparable views for a room on the
lake side. Those at the back overlook a private park. De-luxe hotels are
often obsequious or disdainful towards their guests, depending on their
rank and title. But the *Villa Serbelloni* has the reputation for combining
style and informality. We did have one complaint this year of disin-
terested and slovenly service in the restaurant – but this was a rare black
mark. *(Mrs J E Gibbon, Alfred Knopf Jr, and others)*

Open: April–October.
Rooms: 71 double, 14 single, 11 suites – 75 with bath, 10 with shower, all with
telephone, radio and baby-listening; TV on request. (Some rooms on ground
floor.)
Facilities: Lifts, palatial lounges, TV room, bridge room, writing room, games
room, playroom with table tennis, bar, restaurants; conference facilities; terrace
(also for meals), evening orchestra. Gardens with tennis courts and heated
swimming pool with snack bar, which lead to private beach; boating and waterskiing facilities. English spoken. &.
Location: Bellagio is 30 km from Como. Hotel has parking facilities.
Credit cards: All major credit cards accepted.
Terms: B & B 75,000–100,000 L; dinner, B & B 100,000–125,000 L; full board
115,000–140,000 L. Set meals: lunch 27,000 L, dinner 32,000 L; full *alc* 35,000 L.

BERGAMO, 24100   Map 14

Agnello d'Oro   *Telephone:* (035) 24.98.83
Via Gombito 22

Opinions differ about the *Agnello d'Oro*. It is virtually the only hotel in
the *Città Alta*, which, for those who like to be in the atmospheric centre of
things, is a great draw. It is very cheap, and our readers all agree about the
excellent quality of the meals served in its cosy restaurant, which serves
the *cucina tipica bergamasca*. One reader felt it had no place in the Guide:
her room was far from spotless, the bathroom she felt was sub-standard,
and she also minded the noise outside made worse because the old town is
cobbled. Another reader took a different view: 'It is somewhat basic, and
our room the first night was rather scruffy. The second night we changed
to a pleasant room with a shower and a balcony overlooking the tiny

piazza in front. It is an *albergo* of character and charm – and deserves to stay in the Guide.' More reports would be welcome. *(A G Don)*

Open: All year. Restaurant closed Monday and January.
Rooms: 18 double, 4 single – 4 with bath, 18 with shower.
Facilities: Lift, restaurant. Alfresco meals in fine weather.
Location: Central.
Credit cards: American Express, Barclay/Visa.
Terms: Rooms 20,000 L (single), 34,000 L (double); B & B 22,000–25,000 L; full board 52,000–55,000 L. Set meals: lunch/dinner 25,000 L; full *alc* 25,000 L.

BOLOGNA, 40123   Map 14

Hotel Roma   *Telephone:* (051) 27.44.00
Via Massimo D'Azeglio 9

'Well situated in this interesting and gastronomic city, central yet in a quiet pedestrian street. Pleasantly old-fashioned, comfortable rooms. Stylish furniture. Roof-garden. Covered garage at the rear. The staff were very efficient and helpful. Only criticism was the nasty coffee. I would recommend that breakfast is taken at a café in the piazza, weather permitting.' *(A G Don)*

Open: All year. Restaurant closed Sunday and 1–20 August.
Rooms: 80 – most with bath or shower, telephone and air-conditioning.
Facilities: Lift, restaurant, roof-garden.
Location: Central, covered garage at rear.
Credit cards: American Express, Barclay/Visa, Diners.
Terms: Rooms 37,000–57,500 L; full board 64,500 L. Set meals: breakfast 5,000 L, lunch/dinner 17,000 L.

BRACCIANO, 00062 Roma   Map 14

Casina del Lago   *Telephone:* (06) 902.40.25

Bracciano, with its imposing 15th-century castle overlooking the lake that bears its name, is only 40 km north of Rome, but – unlike, say, Virginia Water – is wholly rural and unspoiled by developments. The lake itself is beautiful and unpolluted, and Bracciano makes a useful base for visiting Etruscan sites around. 'The *Casina del Lago*, 1.5 km out of Bracciano itself, is in Michelin as a "restaurant with rooms". It is certainly not luxurious, but splendidly peaceful, with a view over the lake, very good value, and serves efficiently excellent meals in its restaurant.' *(Shirley and Alan Bailey)*

Open: All year except 15 September–15 October. Restaurant closed Tuesday.
Rooms: 12 – all with shower.
Facilities: Restaurant.
Location: 25 miles N of Rome on the N493. Hotel is 1.5 km NE of Bracciano. Parking.
Terms: Rooms 10,350–20,700 L; full board 25,300–26,450 L. Set meal: breakfast 3,450 L; *alc* (excluding wine) 19,320–23,000 L.

CASTELLINA IN CHIANTI, 53011 Siena   Map 14

Tenuta di Ricavo   *Telephone:* (0577) 74.02.21

A highly civilized and cosmopolitan hotel-cum-*pensione* high up in the Chianti hills, 5 km from the hill village of Castellina in Chianti, 22 km from Siena and 34 km from Florence. The buildings, including a medieval manor dating from the 15th century and before are set in 310 acres of gardens and woods. *Tenuta di Ricavo* is a very special place for many readers. One correspondent, to stress his devotion, has asked that his name be printed in bold italics, and as usual, our mail has been full of compliments. Here is a typical one:

'This year my wife and I stayed yet again at this old friend of ours. There is little we can add to the high praise already voiced by others, except to confirm it, especially in regard to location – it is possible to go for a three or four mile walk through the woods and not meet a soul – and, above all, for the genuine friendliness of everyone about the place, from the proprietors to the domestic and gardening staff. It is perhaps indicative of the quality of the *Ricavo* that one is reduced to looking for trivial slip-ups which would not seem worth complaining about elsewhere – or to criticizing an observable imbalance in the nationalities of the guests! Even on this basis we have nothing adverse to report; our stay was most enjoyable in every way.' *(Charles and Margaret Baker)*

The reference to imbalance of nationalities has been raised before. The *Tenuta di Ricavo* does tend to attract a lot of German–Swiss, and the place has a strong Swiss character to it. We think the report below is fair – in its reservations as well as its praise. 'The style is that of a Swiss hotel, and if one goes expecting a more relaxed Italian style, one could well be disappointed – to an extent, we were. We were expecting to spend the usual two hours over evening meal – instead, after one hour, we were just about the only people left in the dining room! The food was a version of Italian – quite good – presented in a totally Swiss style; the wines were uninspired, as is so often the case in Switzerland – but *here*, in Chianti, to be given a choice of eight or so very similar Chianti Classici but not *one* "riserva", was a bit off, really!! (The "riserva della casa" does not count as such!) Once outside the dining room (often a Swiss failing), things were altogether much better. The place ran very smoothly; the gardens were well tended, as were the rooms; the pools were pleasant; the situation outstandingly relaxing. Our room was large and cool. We were given a warm welcome, as was our seven-month-old daughter. Once we had adjusted to being on holiday in "Switzerland" (but near to Siena), then we felt at home and had a super short break.' *(Ed and Lesley Fulton; also Shirley and Ann Bailey,* **Arnold R Horwell***)*

Note: as we go to press we learn that the Bleulers, who took over the running of the hotel in 1978, are leaving. The Bleulers have clearly been popular. Reports on the new regime would be welcome.

Open: April–October.
Rooms: 23 double, 2 single – all with bath, 10 with telephone. (2 rooms on ground floor.)
Facilities: 3 salons, dining-room. Extensive gardens and woodland. 2 swimming pools; boccia (bowls). English spoken. &.
Location: 34 km from Florence, 22 km from Siena; parking.
Terms (excluding 8% tax): Full board 59,000–76,000 L (min. 3 nights). Reduced rates and special meals for children.

Villa Casalecchi   *Telephone:* (0577) 74.02.40

Until this year, Castellina in Chianti has meant only one Guide entry, the *Tenuta di Ricavo* (see above). We knew, however, that this small town 21 km north of Siena housed another hotel that had received, like the *Tenuta*, Michelin's red rocking-chair insignia. From our correspondent's report, it is clearly an excellent, somewhat cheaper and more Italian alternative to the *Tenuta*, both as a base for exploring all the delights of this part of Tuscany – Volterra, San Gimignano, Pisa, Arezzo, not to mention Florence and Siena – and as an utterly tranquil and agreeable place to relax in when the sight-seeing has to stop. Here are a few extracts from a detailed resumé of the hotel's qualities: 'Our room, with its armchairs and its tiled bathroom *en suite* (proper towels), was a perfect combination of old-fashioned character and charm with modern comforts. It looked out across a terracotta-tiled roof over the hotel's swimming pool and terrace to a field of vines, a meadow and a wooded hill. The only sounds after dark were a dog barking in the distance and a cuckoo that, deceived by the nearly full moon, continued to sing long into the night. We heard nothing of our fellow guests – or their plumbing. They built these old villas pretty solidly, which also means they are cool in the summer heat. There was a lovely little dining room with painted wooden boxed ceiling (as in our bedroom), with its walls and curtains all in shades of honey, walnut and ochre. Dinner was a 5-course affair with a choice of five dishes in the pasta, entrée and pudding courses – all the dishes during our stay were well-balanced, well-cooked and well-served. The price of all this luxury was around £25 a head half-board – pricey by Italian non-urban standards, but very good value by English.' *(BA)*

Open: 20 March–31 October.
Rooms: 14 double – 10 with bath, 4 with shower, all with telephone.
Facilities: Lounge, restaurant. Garden with swimming pool. English spoken.
Location: 45 km from Florence, 18 km from Siena; 1 km from town centre; parking.
Credit cards: American Express, Diners.
Terms: Dinner, B & B 68,000 L; full board 75,000 L. Set meal: breakfast 6,900 L; full *alc* 30,000 L.

Hotel Bahia   *Telephone:* (0565) 98.70.55

'After 20 years of holidays in the Mediterranean, I would recommend this spot to my most discerning friends and not worry. Elba is sheer delight. The tariff at the *Bahia* was almost half of what we pay in southern France, particularly in low season. Private sandy beach, crystal-clear seas, delightful outdoor clifftop restaurant, good service and good food. Cottage-style rooms, with air-conditioning, cool and quiet. Only snag is steep steps down to beach; not for aged or infirm, but most people drive down. A car is essential for touring the island. Better to hire as car ferry crossings can be tedious. Smoothest head-waiter almost anywhere we've been – but *nice*. All staff were willing and friendly.' *(D H Bennett)*

Open: April–September.
Rooms: 40 – all with bath or shower and telephone.
Facilities: Restaurant (closed midday), air-conditioning. Garden, private beach.
Location: On the S coast W of Marina di Campo.
Terms: Dinner, B & B 51,750–67,850 L; full board (off-season) 33,350–36,800 L. Set meal: dinner 20,700 L.

COGNE, 11012 Aosta   Map 14

Hotel Bellevue   *Telephone:* (0165) 74022/74222
Via Rana

'Situated in a quiet position in this resort and winter sports centre, facing the Gran Paradiso massive. We were enchanted with the view from our bedroom and with the comfort and excellent cooking here. It was obviously very popular with all nationalities. No English spoken, however. Menus in Italian were translated by waitresses into French! Sunday lunch was intriguing and delicious, including a succession of specialities – *polenta* amongst them. Lounges and public rooms beautifully furnished. Adequate parking provided. Owner manager takes a keen interest in standards. Pleasant wines of the Aosta region, and others were reasonable.' *(Joan A Powell)*

Open: 1 February–Easter, 1 June–15 September, 20 December–5 January. Restaurant closed Wednesday.
Rooms: 38 double, 7 single, 4 suites in annexe – 34 with bath, 9 with shower, all with telephone, most with balcony; radio and TV in suites.
Facilities: Lift, TV room, lounge, reading room, restaurant. Garden. Hunting and winter sports nearby.
Location: 27 km from Aosta off the N90.
Terms: Rooms 18,000–23,000 L; full board 40,000–48,000 L. Set meals: breakfast 4,000 L; lunch 17,000 L; dinner 16,000 L.

COLONNATA DI SESTO FIORENTINO, 50019 Florence   Map 14

Villa Villoresi   *Telephone:* (055) 44.89.032 and 44.36.92

'I had spent a few days at this Class 1 Pension in 1976, and it always stood as the ultimate in my (albeit then limited) experience of hotels. No disappointment this time round, though it's much more pricey now. Variously 12th-, 14th- and 17th-century (depending on which language you read the leaflet in) the *Villa Villoresi* is run by the Contessa and her daughter who own it. Well signposted in the otherwise dead-as-a-dodo Florentine suburb of Sesto, the hotel feels on arrival more like a private home than many a private home we've encountered. You have to walk down a long "loggia" frescoed and furnished beautifully before so much as seeing a reception desk in a similar frescoed and informal room. The old rooms – ask for one with a bath, since as far as we could make out, showers mean new rooms – are breathtaking, and even the new ones are full of personal and felicitous touches. Most people seem to gather in the bar and lounges to chat quietly before and after dinner – reinforcing the idea of a *genuine* house-party rather than hotel. Easy access to Florence, but there is a swimming pool if you want to stay behind. Cheap rooms, food excellent but quite dear.' *(Peppy and Andrew Hunt)*

Open: All year.

Rooms: 24 double, 4 single, 4 suites – 24 with bath or shower, all with telephone.

Facilities: TV room, reading lounge, library, outdoor and indoor bars, restaurant, terrace. Conference facilities. Garden with ping pong, unheated swimming pool, children's pool and play area.

Location: About 8 km N of Florence and 3 km from Exit No. 19 of the *Autostrada del Sole* in the direction of Sesto Fiorentino; parking.

Terms: B & B 32,000–42,000 L; dinner, B & B 55,000–65,000 L. Set meals: lunch/dinner 25,000 L; full *alc* 25,000 L. 20% reduction for children under 6 sharing parents' room; special meals provided.

COURMAYEUR, 11013 Aosta

Map 14

Lo Bouton d'Or
Superstrada Traforo del Monte Bianco 10

Telephone: (0165) 84.23.80

'Courmayeur is a well-established ski resort – almost the last village on the road from Aosta to France via the Mont Blanc tunnel. It is therefore a useful overnight stopping place for travellers returning from Italy, offering fine mountain scenery and also a last opportunity to take advantage of Italian shopping before crossing the border to more expensive and less enticing prospects. We have used *Lo Bouton d'Or* on a number of occasions. It offers spotlessly clean, very comfortable accommodation at very low cost. Many rooms look across to Mont Blanc, others face across the valley to lesser mountains. Rooms are smallish but tastefully decorated with hessian-lined walls, carpets and stylish bedspreads. The attached bathrooms have bright modern tiles and new fittings – some have baths, others showers only. Corridors and public rooms are again furnished in modern, even luxurious fashion. One imagines that in winter the hotel will be a warm, comforting haven after days spent in the snow. Another advantage is that, although the proprietors own a restaurant in the village, terms are bed and breakfast only. Breakfast is a welcome change from the standard Italian one – perfectly fresh French bread and excellent coffee. We normally stay in September which qualifies as low season, giving a further saving on the already extremely low cost. All in all, marvellous value for money – a very attractive combination of Italian decorative flair and French standards at the breakfast table.' *(David Wooff)*

Open: All year, except October.

Rooms: 21 double, 3 single – 15 with bath, 9 with shower, all with telephone and radio.

Facilities: Lift, bar, lounge, TV room, breakfast room. Solarium, sauna. Garden, terrace. English spoken.

Location: 400 km from town centre; parking.

Credit cards: All major credit cards accepted.

Terms: B & B 25,000–36,000 L. (No restaurant.)

Details of amenities vary according to the information – or lack of it – supplied by hotels in response to our questionnaire. The fact that lounges or bars or gardens are not mentioned must not be taken to mean that a hotel lacks them.

ERBA, 22036 Como   **Map 14**

Castello di Pomerio   *Telephone:* (031) 61.15.16
Via Como 5   *Telex:* POMERI 380463

'We recommend this hotel, 15 minutes by car from Como, but with some small reservations; probably because of its proximity to Milan (about an hour's drive) it is used extensively by business people and companies. However it is such a beautiful building and so well converted, we feel it is worth an entry. The castle has been superbly restored to show its 14th- and 15th-century origins, including some magnificent frescoes. The restaurant overlooks the huge inner courtyard, well floodlit and set with tables and chairs in warm weather. Rooms vary in size, but all have exposed beams and brickwork and antique furnishings. Most have bathroom, mini-bar, TV etc. Ours was on two levels with magnificent full-length windows. The garden has a swimming pool with its own bar, open-air dining area with barbecue and tennis courts. These are also used by the local tennis club. There are also several conference rooms in the castle so in this respect it can be less than peaceful. A pleasant bar/lounge area is popular in the evenings and often special musical events are arranged. Food is good although at times service was very erratic. Breakfast was a "serve yourself" buffet.' *(Pat and Jeremy Temple)*

Open: All year. Restaurant closed Monday to non-residents.
Rooms: 42 double, 4 suites – 30 with bath, 18 with shower, all with telephone, radio and mini-bar; TV on request.
Facilities: Lift; bar, restaurant, courtyard; banquet and conference facilities; piano in bar, concerts in March; sauna, games room. Garden, tennis court, heated swimming pool with bar. English spoken.
Location: Near Albavilla. Between Como and Lecco; parking.
Credit card: American Express.
Terms: Rooms with breakfast 64,400–131,000 L; dinner, B & B 92,000–110,000 L; full board 113,000–133,500 L. Reduced rates and special meals for children.

FIESOLE, 50014 Florence   **Map 14**

Pensione Bencista   *Telephone:* (055) 59 163
San Domenico di Fiesole

The *Bencista* is situated some way down from the top of Fiesole, but still high enough to command a romantic view of Florence, 2 km away. It is a beautiful villa set in its own acres of olive groves, which slope away steeply beneath it. The spacious public rooms are full of the antique furniture and old prints which graced it when it was the Simoni family home. The Simonis live here still, and their ancestral home has been for many years now a much-loved resort for visitors to Florence who prefer to do their sight-seeing by day and relax in tranquil and thoroughly civilized surroundings in the evening. Here is a typical tribute from this year's *Bencista* file: 'A perfect haven to return to after an exhausting and exhilarating day in Florence. Also, it is a joy just to sit on the terrace with its miraculous view, breakfasting or not. We were unable to have a private bathroom, but although the hotel was full, we never had to wait for bathroom or loo. We had a car, but never bothered to take it into the city, as the No. 9 bus was so good, dead on time every 15 minutes. Even if we came home in the rush-hour, the strap-hanging and crush were good-humoured and made us feel more of a Florentine. Only criticism: the lounges were crowded in the evening, and at dusk the terraces obviously midgy. Not *too* important as one's feet mostly said "BED".' *(Alex and Rachel Macdonald; also Mary Ann Hamill)*

Regrettably, just as we were in the last stages of preparing the present edition, we received a long and detailed report from someone who had stayed at the *Bencista* before and found that on this occasion there was a really serious falling-off in the standards of service and cleanliness. Signor and Signora Simoni were away (but should they they have been at peak season?), and their absence may have accounted for the general impression of slovenliness and indifference. Another report (when the Simonis had returned) spoke of unimaginative no-choice meals, and rushed dining-room service. Hence this must be a qualified entry. More reports please.

Open: 15 March–31 October.
Rooms: 30 double, 10 single – 18 with bath.
Facilities: 3 lounges, restaurant. 25 acres gardens with vine-covered terraces for meals or refreshments. English spoken.
Location: 7 km from Florence; parking.
Terms: Dinner, B & B 35,000–45,000 L; full board 45,000–55,000 L. (Note: only full or half-board terms available.) Reduced rates for children.

FIESOLE, 50014 Florence   **Map 14**

Hotel Villa Bonelli   *Telephone:* (055) 59513/598941/598942
Via F. Poeti 1

No lack of endorsements for this modern unpretentious family-run hotel, with an attractive top-floor restaurant, offering a panoramic view of the city, though not (unlike many Fiesole hotels) of the great Duomo itself. The No. 7 bus, frequent and dependable, obviates taking a car into the city. Rooms tend to be on the small side, and there is limited seating space except in the foyer which has TV. But correspondents feel these are small prices to pay for 'the marvellous value'. The hotel prefers guests to be on half-board terms from March to October, and you will need to book ahead in this high season. In our entry last year, we quoted a visitor who wondered whether satisfaction with the food would outlast a week in view of the fairly limited menu. But other guests, and the hotel itself, refer to a remarkably good choice of menu. And every one speaks warmly of the cooking. *(Juliet and David Sebag-Montefiore, Dr I Thé, W Ian Stewart)*

Open: All year. Restaurant closed November–end February.
Rooms: 16 double, 7 single – 1 with bath, 13 with shower, all with telephone, colour TV on request, baby-listening.
Facilities: Lift, hall, TV, bar, roof-restaurant, terrace. English spoken.
Location: 300 metres from town centre, right turn after Piazza Mino; parking. Regular bus service to and from Florence.
Credit card: Access/Euro/Mastercard.
Terms: B & B 24,800–26,200 L; dinner, B & B 39,800–41,200 L; full board 47,800–49,200 L. Set meals (wide choice of menu): lunch/dinner 15,000 L; full *alc* 17,000 L. Between March and October, the hotel prefers guests to be on half-board terms. Reduced rates for children; special meals provided on request.

FIESOLE, 50014 Florence   Map 14

Villa San Michele   *Telephone:* (055) 59451
Via Doccia 4

'Marvellous place. I would not have missed it for worlds. It stands a bit above the *Pensione Bencista*, with the classic view of Florence less panoramic but somehow more vivid. Originally a monastery, with a façade said to have been designed by Michelangelo, it was skilfully restored and converted into a hotel after the last war. It aims at and achieves the highest international standards of luxury, combined with the repose and tranquillity of its situation. My room, discreetly lacking a number on the door, opened off an enormous *salone* on the first floor at one end of the hotel. The hotel has masses of space, with a long loggia (with the classic view) serving as dining room at one end and sitting room at the other, a courtyard for sitting, a writing room with an original fresco of the last supper, a bar and a smallish garden. Furnished throughout with many antiques and seemingly endless bowls of flowers, the whole atmosphere is one of unobtrusive luxury, impeccable taste and total peace and quiet. My bedroom, though small, was beautifully appointed, and fulfilled three of the criteria of the hotel of my dreams: (1) I could not hear the noise of anyone else's plumbing; (2) the windows were fitted with mesh screens and I could therefore sleep with them open without fear of Florence's mosquitoes; (3) I could not hear any evidence of the existence of the other guests. The dining room is perhaps the Achilles' heel of the establishment. The food is of the international grand hotel kind, and as such passable but not outstanding. I also found the service a little lacking in polish. But having travelled rather wearily in many parts of Italy, my stay here was an unforgettable interlude. The hotel is described and illustrated in Harold Acton's *Tuscan Villas*, where he says it is for "travellers of discrimination". That is so; but it must be added that it is also for travellers of means. But it was worth it. Highly recommended to connoisseurs of atmosphere. I am saving up to go back.' *(Alex Liddell)*

Open: 20 March–15 October.
Rooms: 24 double, 7 single, 1 suite – 30 with bath, 1 with shower, all with telephone and air-conditioning.
Facilities: 2 sitting rooms, writing room, bar, restaurant, courtyard; conference and banqueting rooms. English spoken.
Location: 5 km from Florence; parking.
Credit cards: All major credit cards accepted.
Terms: Rooms with breakfast 126,500–225,000 L; full board 176,000–230,000 L. *Alc* 37,000–64,500 L.

FLORENCE, 50124   Map 14

Hotel Villa Belvedere   *Telephone:* (055) 22.25.01/2
Via Benedetto Castelli 3

Signor and Signora Perotto's personally-run hotel on a hill, Poggio Imperiale, on the south side of Florence, continues to be appreciated alike for the comforts of the house, the views, and the advantages of being quiet and cool away from the hurly-burly, but within 40-minutes' walking distance of the centre, or five minutes by car. All the rooms are well-furnished, the public rooms are spacious and welcoming, everything is spotlessly clean and well-maintained, including the large garden, swimming pool and tennis court. Breakfast can be taken in the garden. The hotel has no restaurant as such, but it does provide a limited range of simple dishes, well prepared and served with style both at lunch and in the evening.

'If you can stretch to the price – and of course hotels in and around Florence are more expensive than those in less popular parts of Italy – this is a very comfortable well-run place to stay whether for two nights or two weeks. And there is indeed a beautiful view which takes in the dome of the Duomo by day and the twinkling lights of Fiesole by night. The atmosphere was relaxed, a real family hotel even complete with pet dog – an Alsatian who ambles up as you drive in – and always Signor or Signora Perotto at hand. Signor P. provides an extra service by foretelling the weather: we arrived in rain after five or six days of bad weather, but he assured us that we would wake up next day to sun – and we did!' *(BA)*

Open: March–November (inclusive).
Rooms: 24 double, 3 single – all with bath, telephone, air-conditioning and central heating; some with balconies overlooking the garden.
Facilities: Lift, 3 sitting rooms, separate TV room, bar with veranda. Large garden with swimming pool, tennis court, play area for children. English spoken. &.
Location: Corner of Via Senese, near Porta Romana 2 km from Ponte Vecchio; garage parking.
Terms: B & B 46,500–57,000 L. (No restaurant, but light meals available.) 50% reduction for children under 7 sharing parents' room.

FLORENCE, 50121   **Map 14**

Pensione Monna Lisa   *Telephone:* (055) 21.40.41
Borgo Pinti 27

'The *Pensione Monna Lisa* is in fact a dignified Florentine palazzo set in the very centre of the city yet preserving a soothingly calm and tranquil atmosphere. Stepping gingerly from narrow and tortuous Borgo Pinti, one arrives in a cool spacious entrance hall full of antiques and flowers, and glisteningly clean. All the public rooms are furnished with great elegance and the dining room overlooks a large formal garden. Only breakfast is served here – by smiling friendly ladies who provide lots of coffee with the traditional rolls and preserves. Bedrooms are well furnished and most have private bathrooms. The unexpected quiet in this noisiest of cities is possibly the greatest gift this delightful *pensione* has to offer but there are many others. Memories of its charm, elegance and friendliness will long remain with you.' *(Christine Pevitt)*

Most of our correspondents write about the *Monna Lisa* in similarly appreciative terms. 'As like a private house of a stately kind as it is possible for it to be when it is really a hotel,' writes one. Another mentions the warm welcome given to children, the fact that the pleasant staff speak several languages and a particularly useful feature of the large garden – that part of it is reserved for guests' cars; the garden is locked, with strictly controlled access. But we had one report last year that presented a less favourable picture of the *Monna Lisa*. Cobwebs and dead mosquitoes in bedrooms and bathrooms, disagreeable waitresses and stale rolls. An isolated bad experience? Probably, but we should be glad of further reports. *(Lady Maddocks, Walter V Hall and others)*

Open: All year.
Rooms: 20 double, 7 single, 1 suite – 14 with bath, 5 with shower, all with telephone.
Facilities: Several sitting rooms and reading rooms; American bar with taped music, dining room. Inner courtyard-garden with trees. English spoken. &.
Location: Central; garage.
Credit card: Barclay/Visa.
Terms: Rooms 26,700–33,500 L (single), 41,300–53,000 L (double). Set meal: breakfast 7,000 L. (No restaurant.)

FORTE DEI MARMI, 55042 Lucca   Map 14

Hotel Tirreno   *Telephone:* (0584) 83333
Viale Morin 7

Forte dei Marmi regards itself as the Cannes of the *Riviera della Versilia*, and is a favourite summer resort of well-to-do families from the centre and north of Italy. It is a community of villas with large gardens, rich in trees and flowers, in a general setting of conifers; it also has ample public parks, a spacious traffic-free promenade and a long stretch of sandy beach. There are lots of smart shops around. The *Tirreno*, with a delightful garden, is one of the few hotels that opens in the spring and doesn't close till end October – best to avoid the high season if you can. It is run by two generations of the Baralla family.

A recent visitor offers a comprehensive view of the many pleasures and the minor drawbacks of a stay at the *Tirreno*: '*Room*: Excellent – the marble bathroom as big as a bedroom in some hotels. Very clean throughout. Balcony had side-view of sea. *Public rooms*: Plenty of seats for all. Good bar with attentive service. Quite dreadful Italian TV does sometimes obtrude. *Restaurant*: Food plentiful if not over-exciting. Five courses for lunch, four for dinner! We found that asking for special dishes in advance produced excellent results. *Staff*: Both the family that run the hotel and their staff cannot be faulted. *Prices*: Very reasonable, even if you cannot manage to eat all the food placed in front of you. *Complaints*: Breakfast cannot be served in the room before 8 a.m. We sometimes longed for an early-morning coffee – or tea (but the tea is really awful). *Amenities*: Large inviting garden. No pool, but the sea is nearby. Expect to pay on the beach for cabin, deck chairs and parasol – about £5 a day in the *low* season, but the beach is kept clean and tidy.' *(Shaun Howard)*

Open: Easter–October. Restaurant closed May.
Rooms: 49 double, 10 single – 12 with bath, 47 with shower, all with telephone; TV and baby-listening on request. 20 rooms have balconies with sea views. (21 rooms in annexe.)
Facilities: 2 lounges, 2 TV rooms, bar, dining room. Luxuriant garden set with garden furniture and umbrellas. 50 metres from fine, safe beach with bathing and boat rental. English spoken.
Location: 200 metres from town centre.
Terms: B & B 32,000–41,500 L; dinner, B & B 57,500–66,600 L; full board 62,000–72,500 L. Set meals: lunch/dinner 25,500 L; *alc* 25,500 L (excluding wine). 12% reductions for long stays except July and August. Reduced rates and special meals for children.

We should like to be able to recommend more budget-priced hotels in Florence.

439

Hotel Palombella   *Telephone:* (0775) 87.21.63
Via Maria 234

'On the outskirts of Frosinone (about 3 km from the town centre and the same distance from the autostrada) on the way to the famous Casamari Abbey. It is also a good base for excursions to the National Park of the Abruzzi, Pastena Grotto, Gaeta, Fossanova Abbey, Trisulti Abbey, etc. It is a family-run hotel, and the restaurant is well known in the area for excellent meals, most of them cooked "espresso" to order – you have to wait for them, of course. The helpings are generous and only first-class, genuine ingredients are used in the kitchen. Restaurant and bar prices are quite moderate for the quality served. The hotel rooms are large and comfortable. I stayed there with my family for five days to our entire satisfaction and I wish my fellow readers travelling in this area to share my lucky experience. The hotel although classed 2nd Category is extremely cheap. The staff are very kind and eager to assist, although they probably only speak Italian.' *(Candelovo Minissale)*

Open: All year.
Rooms: 34 – all with shower and telephone.
Facilities: Lifts, bar, restaurant, conference room. Garden. English spoken.
Location: 3 km from town centre; parking.
Terms: B & B 24,000–30,000 L; half board 34,500; full board 44,000 L. Set meals: lunch/dinner 12,500 L; full *alc* 17,000 L.

Grand Hotel   *Telephone:* (0365) 20261
Via Zanardelli 72   *Telex:* 300254

One of the old-fashioned grand hotels, but maintained in great style in an exclusive position on lake Garda, with a private 300-metre lakeside promenade. With its 200 rooms, it is substantially larger than most hotels in the Guide, but, for those who like to live in a lordly way, it has a lot to offer. 'A real winner. It may be a bit pricey by your normal standards, but compared to the *Serbelloni* at Bellagio (q.v.), the cost is as nothing. Though we were only staying one night, we were given a palatial corner room overhanging the lake with two balconies, the most beautiful furniture and bathroom appointments in the grandest style. We were given the choice (for two persons) of bed and breakfast at 82,000 L [1982] or dinner, B & B at 105,000 L. Fortunately, we chose the latter: an excellent dinner matched by perfect table appointments and the best of service. In fact the service could not be faulted anywhere.' *(Jack and Esther Holloway)*

Open: 20 April–10 October.
Rooms: 130 double, 50 single – 143 with bath, 37 with shower, all with telephone, many with balcony.
Facilities: Lounge, bar, restaurant, terraces; conference/function facilities; piano in bar July/August. Private beach on the lake, heated outdoor swimming pool; fishing, waterskiing, boating, golf. English spoken.
Location: In town centre (only 20 rooms face the road); parking.
Credit cards: All major credit cards accepted.

Terms: B & B 35,000–63,000 L; dinner, B & B 29,000–85,000 L; full board 57,000–93,000 L. Set meals: lunch/dinner 24,000; full *alc* 28,000 L. Reduced rates for children.

GIARDINI, 98035 Messina, Sicily　　　　　　　　　　　　　　　**Map 14**

Arathena Rocks　　　　　　　　　　　　　　*Telephone:* (0942) 51349

'I have now been to the *Arathena Rocks* several times and get fonder of it on every visit. The owners, Avv Arcidiacono and his fluently English-speaking wife, really have the best of both worlds: they run a hotel that is, at the same time, their home and presumably make money out of it, too. The 40-odd rooms are all individually styled and furnished in traditional Sicilian ways, which means that much of the furniture and doors are painted with local scenes; the overall result is delightful. The hotel always has an abundance of the most gorgeous fresh flowers, for which the Signora is a stickler, and of which the spacious garden at the rear has a profusion; there is a tennis-court here for the more energetic. Numerous pieces of art are scattered throughout the public rooms, proof of the owners' love of art. The swimming pool is hewn out of the lava-rocks immediately in front and though there is a small private, artificial beach there, the main shingle-beach of Naxos is some 200 metres away.

'The *Arathena Rocks* is amongst the very few hotels in the area enjoying absolute peace as it is at the end of a private road away from traffic, yet near to the centre of this bustling and now rather chaotic resort; Taormina itself is only some 3 km away.' *(R W F Wiersum)*

Open: 29 March–October.
Rooms: 37, mostly double – 27 with bath, 10 with shower, all with telephone.
Facilities: Lift; salons, bar, restaurant; tennis court, swimming pool, private beach. Garden. English spoken. &.
Location: 5 km S of Taormina; parking.
Terms: Rooms with breakfast 18,500 L (single), 34,500 L (double); full board (min. 3 days) 48,000 L.

GUBBIO, 06024 Perugia　　　　　　　　　　　　　　　　**Map 14**

Bosone Palace　　　　　　　　　　　　*Telephone:* (075) 927.20.08
Via 20 Settembre 22

This wonderfully preserved and atmospheric medieval city, full of fine patrician palaces, straddling the side of a steep hill, deserves, if one can find it, a suitable modernized palace hotel to stay in. The *Bosone Palace* is the answer: formerly the Raffaeli Palace, it belonged to the Bosone family one of whom had a sonnet dedicated to him by Petrarch and received Dante. Breakfast only is served, and there's not much in the way of public rooms except for a TV salon. But the town, except when it rains, is itself an open-air lounge of some grandeur. The front rooms face one of the noble but narrow Gubbian streets and would be noisy at night; the best rooms are at the back with a stunning panoramic view over town, the plains and distant hills. Its principal bedrooms are decorated in High Renaissance style, complete with vaulted *trompe l'oeil* ceiling, coy maidens in flimsy negligées, *putti* and all, and grand Renaissance-style double beds. *(HR; also J P H Walker, BA)*

Open: All year.
Rooms: 32 double – most with bath or shower and telephone.
Facilities: Lift, salon with TV, bar, restaurant. &.
Location: 39 km from Perugia; garage.
Credit card: Diners.
Terms: Rooms 28,000–38,000 L; full board 38,000–41,500 L. Set meal: breakfast 4,000 L.

IVREA, Lago di Sirio, 10015 Torino   Map 14

Hotel Sirio   *Telephone:* (0125) 42.36.46
Via Lago Sirio 85

A quiet small modern hotel overlooking lake Sirio, which offers rowing, sailing, swimming and fishing; it is 2 km from Ivrea which lies just off the autostrada from Aosta to Turin, Milan and points south. A very useful place for those who want to stop before or after the Mont Blanc tunnel. The cooking is the big surprise for a hotel of this sort in Italy. Also, as one writer has pointed out, it is situated a decent digestif-length's walk away from the town where you can go for an after-dinner expresso or a delicious post-prandial ice cream. In fact, the hotel lost a Michelin star a few years ago, but its restaurant has continued to receive warm compliments from most readers. One report last year, however, suggested a fall in restaurant and service standards. We should be glad to hear from other recent visitors.

Open: All year. Restaurant closed 2–14 November, closed for lunch Monday off season and Friday October to April.
Rooms: 29 double, 8 single, 1 suite – 12 with bath and WC, 34 with shower and WC, all with telephone, TV, tea-making facilities and baby-sitting.
Facilities: Lift, bar, TV room, breakfast room, 2 dining rooms. Terrace and garden – drinks and meals served there in good weather. English spoken. &.
Location: 2 km N of Ivrea, facing the lake. From Ivrea take viale Monte Stella, then via Lago Sirio.
Credit cards: American Express, Barclay/Visa.
Terms: Rooms 25,300–50,000 L; full board 46,000 L. Set meal: breakfast 3,500 L. *Alc* 16,100–21,850 L (excluding wine).

JESOLO PINETA, 30017 Lido di Jesolo, Venezia   Map 14

Hotel Mediterraneo   *Telephone:* (0421) 96.11.75
Via Oriente 106

The Lido di Jesolo is a modern popular resort at the far eastern end of the Venetian lagoon. 'An excellent family hotel, very quiet, although only 6 km from noisy Lido di Jesolo. Private swimming pool and private fenced beach near a fishing village. Very well managed by owner and his family. Excellent for couples with young children. Good food with extensive choice from *à la carte* menu. Beach chairs, etc., provided free, towels changed daily. More suitable for those with a car, although bus stop quite near.' *(Eric Clyne)*

Open: May–September.
Rooms: 57 – most with bath or shower, telephone and air-conditioning.

Facilities: Restaurant. Garden with heated swimming pool; private beach.
Location: 6 km from Lido di Jesolo; parking.
Terms: Rooms 28,750–53,000 L; full board 41,500–60,000 L. Set meal: breakfast 8,000 L; *alc* 19,550–25,300 L.

MANTUA, 46100   Map 14

Albergo San Lorenzo   *Telephone:* (0376) 32.70.44/32.71.53
Piazza Concordia 14

'The nicest place to stay in this charming city. A small reception area only on the ground floor and no restaurant, but a lift whisks you up to pleasantly furnished rooms most of which have a lovely outlook on to the Piazza della Erbe and the Romanesque Church of San Lorenzo in the form of a Rotunda – the higher up you are the better. It is beautifully central and not noisy. The staff are most pleasant and obliging.' *(Geoffrey Sharp; warmly endorsed by A G Don, Mary Ann Hamill, Roger C Bennett)*

Open: All year.
Rooms: 30 double, 14 single – 30 with bath, 14 with shower.
Facilities: 2 lifts; reception area with sitting areas leading off it, TV, bar, terrace at top of building. English spoken.
Location: Central; in pedestrian precinct; parking.
Terms: Rooms 50,000 L; breakfast 10,000 L. (No restaurant.)

MARINA DI PUOLO, Sorrento   Map 14

Pensione Villa Anna   *Telephone:* (081) 87.82.504

'A gem. Adolfo Acampora, now dead, gave this little hotel, with only 15 rooms, to his wife, Anna, and she takes understandable pride in it and runs it as if it were her own house to which she has invited private friends, for that is the way guests are treated. Here, we are all one family. It's 5 km from Sorrento, but difficult to find. Cars cannot get down the steep little path, so package holiday-makers are blissfully absent, though the little beach tends to get crowded with locals on summer weekends. Rooms are surprisingly spacious and comfortable, all with private bathroom. There is no pool, but the small garden, with many interesting plants and flowers, seems to be all that guests want with the beach just in front. Food is simple but of the best Italian home-cooking, and it is a real pleasure to be able to eat out on the terrace after a drink in the thatched garden-bar where pizzas may also be had.' *(Richard Wiersum)*

Open: 1 April–31 October.
Rooms: 22 double, 1 single – 16 with bath, 7 with shower, all with telephone, mono TV and tea-making facilities.
Facilities: Lounge with TV, bar, restaurant; twice-weekly guitar music. Garden with table tennis, terrace; solarium; on safe sandy/rocky beach; fishing; private bus to town centre, station and harbour. English spoken.
Location: 5 km W of Sorrento; parking.
Terms: B & B 20,000–36,500 L; dinner, B & B 30,000–39,000 L; full board 34,000–44,000 L. 30% reduction for children under 6.

Grand Hotel Duomo   *Telephone:* (02) 8833
Via San Raffaele 1   *Telex:* 312086 Duomo

A big-city hotel, opposite the Duomo, that enjoys the peace of a square closed to all motor traffic. The building itself is listed as an ancient monument which means that the façade cannot be altered. The architects have made a virtue of necessity with the balconied rooms on the first floor which are 18 feet high: they have created split-level suites, with a drawing room at the first level and a bedroom and bathroom above, both enjoying the cathedral view. It is on the opposite side of the cathedral square to the famous Galleria (shopping arcade), and within walking distance of La Scala and most of the art attractions that Milan has to offer. In a previous edition, we had quoted a reader who had said that this was one of the few metropolitan hostelries where she dared ask for a room in the front. One recent visitor, while agreeing that he couldn't fault the friendly service or the food, *had* had a disturbed night, with motorcycles racing outside his window. Otherwise, no complaints. *(S M Gillotti)*

Open: All year.
Rooms: 67 double, 75 single, 18 suites – 135 with bath, 25 with shower, all with telephone and radio, TV on request; some have sitting area and frigo-bar; baby-listening by arrangement.
Facilities: Lifts, reception hall, salon, bar, restaurant; conference rooms. Convention hall. Fully air-conditioned. English spoken. &.
Location: Central; no private parking.
Credit cards: Access/Euro/Mastercard, Barclay/Visa.
Terms: B & B 74,500–108,500 L; dinner, B & B 100,000–134,000 L; full board 125,000–159,000 L. Set meal: breakfast 8,500 L; full *alc* 30,000 L. Special meals for children on request.

Hotel Manzoni   *Telephone:* (02) 70.57.00
Via Santo Spirito 20

A pleasant quiet hotel, rather modern in appearance, located in a small side street a block from the via Manzoni which leads to the Piazza La Scala, the Vittorio Emanuele shopping arcade and the cathedral. 'You would be unlikely to find it unless you were looking for it. Yet it's extremely central, comparatively cheap (hotels in Milan are surprisingly expensive) and perfectly adequate. It seemed like a good deal.' *(Bettina Dudkin)*

Open: All year.
Rooms: 54 – most with bath or shower and telephone.
Facilities: Lift, breakfast room.
Location: In the central zone; garage parking.
Terms: Rooms 46,000–69,000 L. Set meal: breakfast 4,000 L. (No restaurant.)

We should be glad to hear of good hotels in Naples.

Hotel Montebianco   *Telephone:* (02) 46.97.941
Via Monte Rosa 90

'The *Grand Hotel Duomo* (q.v.) is fine, but costly. May I offer a super little hotel four kilometres from the city centre but close to the Metro. Full of atmosphere. Old-fashioned, comfortable, friendly. No restaurant, but good ones in the area. A nice bar in the cellar (breakfast there or in your room). Have stayed many times. Standards remain consistently high. Lots of people agree so must book. Don't expect five-star luxury but I'm fussy and it suits me very well indeed.' *(John M Sidwick)*

Open: All year, except August.
Rooms: 44 double.
Facilities: Bar. Air-conditioning.
Location: Off the viale Migliara, NW of the Sempione Park, near the racecourse.
Credit cards: Access/Euro/Mastercard, American Express, Barclay/Visa.
Terms: Rooms 46,000–69,000 L. Set meal: breakfast 4,600 L. (No restaurant.)

MONDELLO LIDO, Palermo 90100, Sicily   **Map 14**

Piccolo Hotel Villa Esperia   *Telephone:* (091) 45.00.04
Viale Margherita di Savoia 53

'A family hotel a few hundred yards from Mondello beach and only ten minutes drive (11 km) from Palermo itself. The large airy rooms in this pseudo-Renaissance style villa are simply but adequately furnished, with their own bathrooms; and there is a lift. The pleasant shady garden also provides parking space behind locked gates, a necessary precaution in Palermo. The food is exactly what one would expect: good plain Sicilian cooking, with excellent pasta and fish. The *Villa Esperia*'s friendly atmosphere, with the *padrone* and his family very much in evidence, is pleasingly different from the impersonal tour-dominated hotels which prevail in so many parts of Sicily.' *(Anne Weitzman)*

Open: All year.
Rooms: 19 – 8 with bath, 11 with shower, all with telephone.
Facilities: Lift, bar, restaurant; air-conditioning. Garden, private beach. &.
Location: 11 km from Palermo; parking.
Terms: Single rooms: 19,500–21,000 L; double rooms: 29,000–32,200 L; full board 29,900–44,000 L.

ORTA SAN GIULIO, 28016 Novara   **Map 14**

Hotel La Bussola   *Telephone:* (0322) 90 198

The popularity of the *San Rocco* (see below) is such that at certain seasons it is impossible to arrive casually and get a room. The *Bussola* makes an admirable alternative. A modern purpose-built hotel, it is situated on the hill above Orta and has a beautiful panoramic view of the lake. The restaurant has an extensive terrace which enjoys the same view, and in addition there is a swimming pool and a separate sun terrace. The Tesseras took over *La Bussola* in September 1980. It is very much a family concern, run with relaxed efficiency by two brothers and their wives who take turns in the kitchens and front of house. One couple, with a 13-month-old daughter, booked for three days, and found it so congenial that they stayed for ten. Another writes: 'If you are not fortunate enough to get a room at the front overlooking the lake, do not despair: the rooms at the back look out over an orchard to the mountains beyond, with not a single human habitation in sight. As the hotel stands well back from the road there is no traffic noise wherever one is. The ambience of the hotel is rather functional and characterless, but it is very comfortable. English and French are spoken and the food is a cut above the average. Prices are reasonable.' *(Alex Liddell; also Mrs Allen, Judith and David Jenkins)*

Open: All year, except 2 weeks in January.
Rooms: 16 double, 11 with bath, 5 with shower, all with telephone and baby-listening, 7 with refrigerator.
Facilities: Lift, TV room, bar, indoor and outdoor restaurants, banqueting room. Large garden, swimming pool. 5 minutes' walk from the lake with possibility of swimming and all other water sports. English spoken.
Location: Central; garage and ample parking facilities.
Credit cards: American Express, Barclay/Visa.
Terms: B & B 24,000–33,000 L; dinner, B & B 37,000–42,000 L; full board 47,000–52,000 L; full *alc* 22,000 L. Reduced rates for children sharing parents' room or out of season; special meals on request.

ORTA SAN GIULIO, 28016 Novara

Map 14

Hotel San Rocco

Telephone: (0322) 90222

Formerly a 17th-century monastery converted with skill and restraint into 'a very special hotel indeed'. Overhanging the lake and well away from the road, the setting is exquisite. All is calm: lapping waters, flowers and old roofs in the foreground; mountains in the distance. Inside, the service is gracious, rooms spacious and food almost too tempting. The hotel is run by Signor Terxi, an hotelier of the old school, assisted by a young cheerful attractive staff. Access except by car is difficult – which is why hotel, town and lake are still untarnished by tourism. (Jean Robertson, Edward Mace)

This entry, under the names of the Travel Editors of *The Sunday Times* and *The Observer*, appeared in the first edition of the Guide. The *San Rocco*, right on Lake Orta, one of the smaller and least spoiled of Italian Lakes, has never failed to elicit warm compliments from readers. (The monastic origins, incidentally, are hardly apparent except on the top floor where some of the rooms are cell-like in their dimensions though not in their furnishings.) Signor Terxi retired three years ago, but the new regime of Signor Ruga gives equal satisfaction. Plans for a major extension of the hotel happily seem to have been shelved. One grateful reader describes her visit as 'one of the most pleasant few days I have ever spent abroad.' Another writes of a three week visit for the second successive year: 'In every respect, the hotel lives up to my previously expressed high opinion. The cuisine is outstanding, and received many compliments from French as well as English visitors. Put simply, everything good which has been reported to you about this hotel requires repeating and emphasizing.' *(Bettina Dudkin, F C Margetts; also P Marshall)*

Open: April–October.
Rooms: 37 double, 2 single – all with bath and shower, telephone and balcony overlooking the lake; TV on request.

Facilities: Lift, hall, salon, TV room, bar with piano, dining room, 2 banqueting rooms. Garden with bar; boating, water-skiing, tennis and mini-golf nearby.
Location: 5 minutes from centre of town; private parking.
Credit cards: Access/Euro/Mastercard, American Express, Barclay/Visa.
Terms: Rooms with breakfast 36,800–60,000 L; full board 46,000–55,200 L. Full *alc* 20,000–30,000 L.

ORVIETO, 05018 Terni — Map 14

Hotel Maitani — *Telephone:* (0763) 33001/2/3
Via Lorenzo Maitani 5/9

'Very attractive newly-renovated old hotel opposite the cathedral. From our window we could see the façade, illuminated well into the night. Pleasant terrace for breakfast in the summer. At other times, it is served (with the best bread I have ever had in an Italian hotel) in a charming room indoors. Under the same management is the *Morino* restaurant, ten minutes' walk through old streets. Excellent food.' *(Walter V Hall)*

Open: All year.
Rooms: 32 double, 12 single, 6 suites – 26 with bath, 8 with shower, all with telephone and colour TV.
Facilities: Lift, salon, bar, dining room, terrace for breakfast in summer. English spoken. ㅤ.
Location: In town centre, opposite cathedral: garage (fee charged).
Credit cards: American Express, Barclay/Visa, Diners.
Terms: Rooms 44,000 L (single), 62,000–74,000 L (double); full board 67,000–80,500 L. Set meals: breakfast 7,000 L, lunch/dinner 26,000 L. 50% reduction for children.

ORVIETO 05018 — Map 14

Hotel Virgilio — *Telephone:* (0763) 352 52
Piazza Duomo 5–6

'A small, quiet and pleasantly modern hotel overlooking a little square directly facing the magnificent *Duomo*. It is somewhat like being in a private home and looking out of one's living-room windows to see Notre Dame. Breakfast only is served, but there is a small and attractive modern bar where we celebrated the birthday of one of our group. Service was crisp and attentive. You can park directly outside in the cathedral square.' *(Mary Ann Hamill)*

Open: All year.
Rooms: 12 double, 2 single – 4 with bath, 8 with shower, all with telephone and baby-listening. 3 rooms in annexe.
Facilities: Lift, TV room, bar. English spoken.
Location: Central; parking in cathedral square.
Terms: Rooms 30,000 L (single), 43,000 L (double). Set meal: breakfast 6,000 L. (No restaurant.)

All hotel prices are approximate. Italian prices are more approximate than others.

Grand Hotel Villa Igiea   *Telephone:* (091) 54.37.44
Via Belmonte 43   *Telex:* 910092

Two contrasting views of Palermo's grandest hotel:

'Spacious but anonymous rooms, pleasant gardens, pool with comfortable furniture and good service. Good but over-priced food. We managed to book on a room-and-breakfast basis so were able to eat out at Palermo's two Michelin-starred restaurants (*Charleston* and *Gourmand's*). Better food in both at just over half the price. Nevertheless the *Villa Igiea* was a welcome haven, though I am sure most guests will suffer pangs of guilt walking up to this palatial building through the adjacent streets, airily described in the Green Guide as "picturesque alleys festooned with washing hung out to dry" – and in reality squalid hovels.' *(David Wooff)*

'Connoisseurs of *l'art nouveau* come from all over Europe to gaze in awe at the salon in this huge Edwardian hotel – or they would if they knew about it. This masterwork by the Palermo architect Ernesto Basile (1857–1932) dates from 1908 and the convolutions of carving and the murals are in pristine condition. The hotel itself, an essay in the castellated Venetian-Moorish style, isn't in too bad condition either. It was built as a private residence by a resident Englishman of wealth called Whitaker; a few years later it was turned into a watering-hole for the *noblesse* whose photographs now decorate the high and arching corridors. Here portly Edward VII and his court; over there SM le Roi du Siam: facing them King George V and Queen Mary. The *Villa* itself has retained its style; apart from a swimming pool overlooking the sea and awnings to protect those lunching alfresco from the burning sun, time hasn't flawed this stately bougainvillea-clad pile. Of all the hotels in Palermo this is still the finest. Service is impeccable and helpful and cool sea breezes rustle the palms in the several acres of garden. There is only one fly in the ointment. Since the *Villa* was built on its lonely prominence on the edge of the town, industry has crept along the shore. An enormous ship repair yard now obscures the easterly view. Riveting is apt to occur at eight o'clock in the morning. All in all, for the spectacular sunsets, the sublime westerly view, the good food, the occasional eruption of a steam hammer is worth living with.' *(Derek and Janet Cooper)*

Open: All year.
Rooms: 92, mostly double – 90 with bath, 3 with shower, all with telephone, piped music, TV, mini-bar and air-conditioning.
Facilities: Lift; salons, bar, restaurants, facilities for receptions and conferences; disco. Terrace for outdoor meals in fine weather. In large park leading down to sea with salt-water swimming pool and tennis court.
Location: Overlooking sea near Punta Acquasanta; parking.
Credit cards: American Express, Barclay/Visa, Diners.
Terms: Rooms with breakfast 72,450–90,000 L (single), 11,500–14,400 L (double); full board 120,750–150,000 L.

We should be glad to hear of good hotels in Perugia.

PORT' ERCOLE, 58018 Grosseto   Map 14

Il Pellicano   *Telephone:* (0564) 83.38.01
                                        Telex: 500131 Pelican

Il Pellicano is on the coast of Monte Argentario about 4 km from the small fishing village of Port' Ercole, which attracts tourists and yachting visitors, particularly on summer weekends. The coast round the hotel is rocky and wild; the road from the village follows its indentations and gives beautiful views of the sea. It is a small luxury hotel standing in lovely gardens overlooking the sea. The rooms are individually designed and the general atmosphere is of casual elegance. During the day the hotel is quiet and rather like having one's own private villa. Dinner is taken on the terrace overlooking floodlit trees and water.

'*Pellicano* is a dream Mediterranean hotel. Rooms and public areas are furnished with the sort of sophisticated rusticity which unfortunately comes rather expensive (but perhaps not by British standards). One word of warning, however. If you go on holiday to make new friends or if you expect your hotel to provide night life until 3 a.m. you'll hate the place. I wouldn't particularly recommend it to those travelling alone either. But if you want to rest and relax in romantically beautiful surroundings, be served by unobtrusive but very pleasant staff, and don't need to worry overmuch about the cost, then I know of few hotels better suited to provide just the right combination of relaxation and style. For anyone visiting outside the high season (15th June to 15th September) substantial discounts are given and the hotel becomes an absolute bargain.' *(David Wooff)*

Open: April–30 September.
Rooms: 30 double – all with sea or garden view, bath and telephone. 4 luxury suites with TV in cottages in the garden.
Facilities: Lounge, bar, restaurant, conference facilities: dinner-dance Friday nights in high season. Rocky beach with safe bathing; heated swimming pool with barbecue; tennis, ping pong, bowls, boats available; riding, sailing and water-skiing; golf 1 hour's drive; sightseeing to nearby Etruscan and Roman sites. English spoken.
Restriction: No children under 14.
Credit cards: American Express, Barclay/Visa, Diners.
Location: 4 km S of Port' Ercole on the Monte Argentario coast.
Terms: Dinner, B & B 84,000–210,000 L; full board 114,000–240,000 L. Set meals: lunch/dinner 34,500 L.

PORTOFINO, 16034   Map 14

Albergo Splendido   *Telephone:* (0185) 69 551
Viale Baratta 13   *Telex:* 331057 Splend

'The name *Albergo* does not seem to suit this luxurious hotel overlooking the bay around the corner from Portofino, a ten-minute walk away, although *Splendido* does. We stayed in January when it was very quiet, but no doubt it comes into its own more in the summer months, with its enormous terrace, swimming pool and tennis courts. (Portofino must be a nightmare in the summer months – even in January there was a half-mile queue of cars to get into the village!) Our room was large, pleasant, and had a small balcony. Many others, all of which look out over the bay, seemed to have larger terraces. The restaurant also has excellent views, and the menu, although not very large, was interesting and meals well cooked. All the staff were extremely friendly and helpful, and the housekeeping efficient. There are numerous walks from the hotel around the peninsula, visiting small villages inaccessible by car.' *(Pat and Jeremy Temple)*

Not everyone is as enthusiastic as the Temples about this grand hotel (five red turrets in Michelin: they don't come any grander). A visitor in June 1982 felt prices were far too high. 'Dinner at 35,000 L was undoubtedly very good and service pleasant. Swimming pool full of middle-aged well-proportioned ladies. Concierge could have been more helpful. I have reservations and would not return.' More reports please.

Open: 10 March–10 January.
Rooms: 45 double, 9 single, 14 suites – 60 with bath, 7 with shower, all with telephone; colour TV in suites.
Facilities: Salon, bar with piano music May–September, restaurant on terrace; conference facilities; sauna, solarium, beauty salon. Large grounds with gardens, swimming pool and tennis. Beach 20 minutes' walk.
Location: Right turn just before entering Portofino; garage (7,000 L per day) and car park.
Credit cards: Access/Euro/Mastercard, Barclay/Visa.
Terms: Rooms 92,000–155,000 L. Set meals: breakfast 9,200 L; lunch/dinner 40,300 L.

POSITANO, 84017 Salerno   **Map 14**

San Pietro   *Telephone:* (089) 87.54.55
                                                Telex: 770072

'A medium-sized (57-room) hotel built on top of, and within, a cliff 2 km east of Positano. The exterior of the hotel is ramshackle, with unfinished concrete and many external pipes and cables. Apparently the owner has gradually extended the hotel using the staff as building labour in the winter months, and the result is certainly an architectural oddity. Fortunately most of the worst defects in the building only become apparent on close inspection from one's terrace, partly because of the hotel's position on the cliff and also because most of the exterior is covered by a profusion of climbing plants and flowers. Bourgainvillea is everywhere and there is a colourful garden on the main terrace which extends in to the large main lounge.

'Inside, the hotel is a different story. The huge arched lounge is furnished with antiques and comfortable seats. Climbing plants grow indoors from the terrace. The rooms are simply but beautifully furnished – all different – with lovely floor tiles extending to the terrace, hall and bathroom (and up the bathroom walls). Our room was very large with immense walk-in cupboards for storage. We stayed here about five years ago – on that occasion we had a much smaller room, although still a charming one, and no air-conditioning. If you need space therefore it would be best to specify when booking. All rooms have stunning views over the sea and the coast. Service is faultless.

'Bathing is from a small gravelly beach or rocks, reached by a lift. Beach furniture is comfortable and there is a bar from which snacks can be obtained at lunchtime. The owner of the hotel, something of a character, clearly enjoys his hotel and guests. He circulates accompanied by a couple of boisterous dogs. Guests return here year after year.

'Breakfast was excellent. Dinner, however, was dull – ungenerous in quality and quantity, clumsily but amiably served. I can only recommend the *San Pietro* as a room and breakfast hotel (if you can obtain these arrangements). Meals are expensive and by the end of our four nights' stay, dinner had become a tedious prospect. This may be a temporary problem, however; I seem to remember the meals being quite good on our previous visit. Another irritation – when I asked for our bill I discovered that the *demi-pension* price quoted in the hotel's booking confirmation letter had been increased by 20,000 lire per night. It was explained that this was allowed in Italy to cover inflation. Another black mark, but the hotel remains beautiful, colourful, has a splendid situation and a pleasant staff.' *(David Wooff)*

Open: April–October. Restaurant closed to non-residents.
Rooms: 57 double, overlooking sea, with telephone and air-conditioning.
Facilities: Lounge, restaurant, terrace. Rocky beach, reached by lift, with bar for lunchtime snacks. Tennis court, outdoor swimming pool.
Location: 2 km E of Positano; parking. (Guests met at Naples Airport if requested.)
Credit cards: American Express, Barclay/Visa, Diners.
Terms: B & B 138,000–230,000 L; full board 115,000–172,500 L. Set meals: lunch/dinner 32,200–40,250 L.

PUNTA ALA, 58040 Grosseto   **Map 14**

Cala del Porto   *Telephone:* (0564) 92.24.55
Telex: 590652

'On the southern tip of the Gulf of Follonica amidst pine forests and hills, the small new resort of Punta Ala has been created, consisting of carefully landscaped villas and four hotels. Part of Punta Ala is adjacent to a splendid sandy beach, whilst on the headland overlooking the Isle of Elba and a yacht marina is the most attractive *Hotel Cala del Porto*. It is a small, privately owned luxury hotel on three floors with 46 rooms. There is an attractive swimming pool set in carefully tended gardens. The tranquillity was at all times noticeable. Breakfast and lunch can be taken on the terraces. The service and attention were excellent and unobtrusive. All meals were of a high standard – Italian (not international) cooking with plenty of choice. There is free transport to the beach, and the yacht marina with cafés and boutiques is a few minutes' walk away. We found it to be an ideal resting place after touring in Tuscany – and want to return as soon as possible. This is the nearest comparable hotel we have found to the *Ta' Cenc* on Gozo (q.v.). *(Derek W Beale)*

Open: 7 April–10 October.
Rooms: 46 double – all with TV and air-conditioning.
Facilities: Restaurant, terraces. Garden with heated swimming pool; sandy beach, yacht marina.
Location: 18 km from Follonica; parking.
Credit cards: American Express, Diners.
Terms: Rooms 109,000–161,000 L; full board 66,700 (off season)–152,000 L. Set meals: breakfast 9,000 L: lunch/dinner 30,000–33,000 L.

Hotel Caruso Belvedere   *Telephone:* (089) 85.71.11
Via Toro, 52

'It is easy to feel that the *Caruso Belvedere* is suspended "twixt sea and
sky", but it is certainly my paradise on earth – a place where, on the other
hand, earthly problems are left behind.' *(J Whittaker)* 'Outstanding
service not only in a routine way, but at times of emergency, too, as we
discovered when my wife's handbag was stolen near Pompeii and the staff
rallied round magnificently, phoning banks and sending international
telegrams. Wonderful pictures adorn the wall, adding a touch of elegant
past. One would not be in the least surprised to see Lord Marchmain
strolling in! He would be very pleased at his welcome from Signor Caruso,
his family and staff.' *(John and Rosemarie Williamson)*
    Two recent tributes, to add to many in previous years, to the depend-
able qualities of this distinguished old-fashioned (in the wholly complimentary sense) hotel in an enchanting town. Ravello is 20 minutes'
twisting drive up into the hills from the hot screeching corniche road
between Sorrento and Salerno. It is full of noble palaces and two
showplace gardens, with a wide cathedral piazza for nightlife. The *Caruso*
is in the old part of the town, on a steep street, with its rooms commanding
a stunning view over the Gulf of Salerno towards Paestum. Signor Caruso
is the third generation to run the hotel and his nephew now works
alongside him. In summer meals are taken on a terrace, with fabulous
views over the 'hot spots' of the coast. In cooler weather the marble-
pillared dining room is used. The Caruso family wine is strongly recommended. The market square and the historic Villa Rufolo (whose garden
is supposed to have inspired Klingsor's in *Parsifal*) are five minutes' walk
away. The hotel also has a garden and there are many shady walks in the
vicinity.

Open: All year. Restaurant closed on Tuesday.
Rooms: 23 double, 3 single, 2 suites – 20 with bath, 2 with shower, all with
telephone. (Some rooms on ground floor.)
Facilities: 2 lounges, TV room, bar, restaurant. Garden and terrace for summer
meals, with magnificent views. Beach 5 km. English spoken.
Location: 25 km from Salerno, off the Salerno–Sorrento coast road. On Piazza S
Giovanni del Toro. Hotel has garage.
Credit cards: American Express, Barclay/Visa.
Terms: B & B 13,000–41,000 L; dinner, B & B 33,000–60,000 L; full board
40,000–67,000 L. Set meals: lunch/dinner 20,000 L. Reduced rates and special
meals for children.

Hotel Gregoriana   *Telephone:* (06) 67.94.269, 67.97.988
Via Gregoriana 18   and 67.85.912

'It's quite difficult to acquire a room at the *Gregoriana* and even more
difficult to claim it – it's the first time I've ever been waitlisted! However,
it's worth waiting for. Despite being only a minute's walk from the top of
the Spanish steps, this tiny hotel could well claim to be one of the quietest
in Rome. Our room, with two broad windows overlooking a little

courtyard was *silent* from midnight until dawn. It was a generous and comfortable room decorated in a mixture of Erté and American Chinese, with a big, sunny bathroom in blues and mauves. Like most small hotels in continental cities, the only place to perch outside one's room is the reception area and breakfast is the only meal served (those who get fidgety about continental breakfasts could bear in mind that this breakfast tray contained an extra pile of Melba toast). Because it is so small, the *Hotel Gregoriana* might be a bit claustrophobic for a long stay but for a few nights it's probably as near perfect as you will get.' *(Gillian Vincent)*

Open: All year.
Rooms: 16 double, 3 single – 12 with bath, 7 with shower, all with telephone and radio; TV on request. (4 rooms on ground floor.)
Facilities: Lift; hall, breakfast room. English spoken. &.
Location: Central; parking.
Terms: B & B 41,000–56,000 L. (No restaurant.) Reduced rates for children.

ROME, 00187   **Map 14**

Hotel Marcella   *Telephone:* (06) 46.21.70
Via Flavia 104

'About ten minutes' walk from the Via Veneto and slightly north, this comfortable little hotel heralds itself with brown and white awnings. The reception – softly-lit with silk sofas and oil paintings and bar and breakfast rooms, simple but immaculate – leads the way by lift to the fourth and fifth floors where the bedrooms are. The other floors are offices. The rooms open off square landings, all thick-carpeted and beige-sofaed. The rooms themselves are simply furnished and decorated in terracotta white and chocolate with plenty of cupboard-space and well-fitted, if small bathrooms. Most rooms have a small balcony. Despite being on a fairly busy street, the hotel is quiet for Rome and there is a very pretty roof terrace with lovely views over three sides. Breakfast is the only meal served but the coffee and rolls are delicious and it's possible to get well-prepared egg and ham dishes. The boiled eggs were huge and brown and the waiter said they came fresh every day from a local hen-lady nearby. The bedrooms contain a fridge with drinks and a tin of biscuits.' *(Gillian Vincent)*

Open: All year.
Rooms: 55 – all with bath or shower, most with telephone, radio, TV and balcony.
Facilities: Lift, salon, breakfast room. &.
Terms: Single room: 45,000 L; double room 65,500 L. Set meal: breakfast 8,600 L. (No restaurant.)

ROME, 00186   **Map 14**

Hotel Raphaël   *Telephone:* (06) 65.69.051
Largo Febo 2   *Telex:* 680235 RHOTEL

A quiet hotel, unobtrusively hidden behind creepers in a small side street not far from the Piazza Navona, which at night is one of Rome's liveliest piazzas. (*Warning:* the narrow streets behind the hotel are a noted hotbed of petty crime.) Very conveniently situated within easy walking distance of the main sights. The inside is air-conditioned and has an intimate atmosphere. It is very elegantly decorated in true Italian style, with sculptures, paintings, antiques and *objets d'art*. Bedrooms, air-conditioned, are less ornate but for the most part comfortable. The nicest thing about it is the rooftop; a tiny area squashed between the tiled roofs, chimney pots and belfries of the surrounding buildings, with a pretty garden and magnificent views. Tables, chairs and sun umbrellas are set out – a lovely spot to escape the bustle of the city. Restaurant adequate, but there are many eating places in the Piazza Navona. *(A G Don)*

Open: All year.
Rooms: 85 – all with bath or shower, telephone and air-conditioning.
Facilities: Lift, lounge bar, small rooftop garden for refreshments.
Location: Central, near the Piazza Navona.
Terms: Single rooms 57,500 L, double rooms 88,000 L. Set meal: breakfast 5,750 L. (No restaurant.)

ROME, 00187 **Map 14**

Hotel La Residenza *Telephone:* (06) 67.99.592
Via Emilia 22

'This small, centrally placed residential hotel is situated within a stone's throw of the Via Veneto and is an ideal and relatively inexpensive base for the tourist. The rooms are comfortable and quiet provided you have a room at the back of the hotel. The front faces a night club which can be noisy late at night. Breakfast is served, but no other meals; excellent inexpensive restaurants abound in the neighbourhood. The hotel management and staff offer excellent personal service.' *(Roger Schlesinger; warmly endorsed in all respects by P D Scott)*

Open: All year.
Rooms: 23 double, 3 single – 23 with bath, all with telephone.
Facilities: Lift, bar, reading room, breakfast room, air-conditioning; garden.
Location: Central, near the Via Veneto; parking.
Terms: Rooms 60,600–75,900 L; 4,000 L charge for air-conditioning. Set meal: breakfast 6,300 L. (No restaurant.)

ROME, 00185 **Map 14**

Hotel Sitea *Telephone:* (06) 47.43.647
via V Emanuele Orlando 90 *Telex:* 614163 Sitea I

'The *Sitea* was very centrally located, and although unprepossessing on the outside, inside it was first-class in every way. Comfortable rooms, with maid service apparently continuous (every time we returned – from lunch, dinner, walks, whatever – someone had slipped in, hung up our clothes and straightened things). The breakfast room – the hotel has no restaurant – is truly lush, and the pastries were fine. The concierge was extremely helpful and friendly.' *(Martin and Deborah Zehr)*

Open: All year.
Rooms: 37 double, 3 single – 37 with bath, 3 with shower, all with telephone; radio and TV on request.

Facilities: Lounge, bar, TV room, breakfast room, coffee shop, roof garden. English spoken.
Location: In centre with own garage.
Credit card: American Express.
Terms: B & B 50,000–80,000 L. (No restaurant.)

SAN GIMIGNANO, 53037 Siena   Map 14

Bel Soggiorno   *Telephone:* (0577) 94.03.75
Via S. Giovanni 91   *Telex:* 53037

A beautiful 13th-century building a few yards inside the walls of the old town, recommended for its modest prices and its memorable views over the vineyards, olive plantations, cypresses and fortified farmhouses of the Tuscan countryside. Rooms vary in size; some have large balconies. 'This *must* be retained in the Guide! Entry correct in all respects especially the staggeringly low price. The food was indeed excellent, and so was the Pescille wine.' *(B W Ribbons)*

Open: All year. Restaurant closed Monday.
Rooms: 27 double – all with bath.
Facilities: Restaurant, TV room. English spoken.
Location: 30 km from Siena; cars allowed in for loading and unloading only; large car park 400 m away.
Restriction: No children under 8.
Terms: Rooms: 21,000 L (single), 37,000 L (double). Dinner, B & B 32,000 L.

SAN GIMIGNANO, 53037 Siena   Map 14

La Cisterna   *Telephone:* (0577) 94.03.28
Piazza della Cisterna 23

'Even a one-night stop-over at this truly classic hotel in San Gimignano, possibly the most attractive and best preserved Italian hill town, is strongly recommended – the tourist coaches and day trippers leave at about 4 p.m. and the discriminating visitor has the privilege to share and enjoy the life of this medieval "town of the beautiful towers". Even the cathedral, museum and palaces are uncrowded and can be enjoyed until 6 or 7 p.m.; and then the fun really starts – the visitor becomes part and parcel of the town life, the local inhabitants crowding the piazza and the main street (mercifully, pedestrian areas). At dusk you may retire to the comfort of *La Cisterna*, formerly one of the aristocratic palazzi of this town, and to dinner at its restaurant, *Le Terrazze*. This restaurant with its breathtaking view over the Val d'Elsa, maintains a very high standard of cuisine and service. The room prices are remarkably low. *(Arnold Horwell)*

Open: All year. Restaurant closed Tuesday, midday Wednesday, and 1 November–10 March.
Rooms: 41 double, 7 single – 21 with bath, 27 with shower, all with telephone.
Facilities: Lift, 14th-century salon, salon with TV, dining room.
Location: Central; cars allowed in for loading and unloading only; car park 400 metres away. English spoken. &.
Credit cards: Access/Euro/Mastercard, American Express.

Terms: B & B 27,000–29,000 L; dinner, B & B 45,000–47,000 L; full board 63,000–65,000 L. Set meals: lunch/dinner 18,000 L; full *alc* 25,000 L.

SAN MAMETE, Valsolda 22010 Como   **Map 14**

Hotel Stella d'Italia   *Telephone:* (0344) 68139
Piazza Roma 1

'This small hotel and its beautiful garden stand right on lake Lugano a few kilometres on the Italian side of the border and manage to combine a perfect setting with peace, good food and amazing value for money. Signor and Signora Ortelli, who speak good English, obviously care deeply for the welfare of their guests. It was recommended to us by three maiden aunts of mine who stayed there regularly in the Fifties and Sixties, and although we knew it was still run by the Ortelli family, we were afraid that increased traffic might have ruined it – but not at all. The main road runs behind it and there appear to be no rooms on that side; all the bedrooms overlook the lake with their own balcony, whereon one breakfasts, and the summer dining room is under a vine in the garden, with the water lapping beside one. The indoor dining room is very pleasant, also with lake views. We had only telephoned the day before and had the last available room which was small and slightly shabby, but most of the rooms were bigger. We found the food fresh, well cooked and, if not gourmet standard, amazing value. It was beautifully presented by charming girls. One can bathe or climb, but essentially we felt it would be a place for a perfect wind-down rest in late spring. There were people there who had been returning for many years, particularly Dutch. We borrowed the hotel dinghy and rowed across the lake, which was a very peaceful occupation if taken slowly. Or one can take the steamer to another village – it called in at San Mamete several times daily.' *(Alex and Rachel Macdonald)*

Open: April–October.
Rooms: 29 double, 9 single – 24 with bath.
Facilities: Salon, bar, 2 dining rooms. Garden. Lake bathing, boating. English spoken.
Location: 10 km from Lugano between Gandria and Menaggio; parking.
Credit card: Access/ Euro/Mastercard.
Terms: B & B from 25,000 L; full board 33,500–40,000 L. Set meal: lunch/dinner 15,000 L; full *alc* 20,000 L. 20–40% reduction for children.

SAN MARCO DI CASTELLABATE, 84071 Salerno   **Map 14**

Hotel Castelsandra   *Telephone:* (0974) 96.60.21
                                                    Telex: 721651 CASTEL

'70 km south of Salerno and 13 km beyond Agripoli, away from the hurly-burly of the Amalfi coast is the Cilento, an area of gentle hills, clear seas and a coastline still completely unspoiled. It is a marine preservation area and judging by the abundance of wild birds, including nightingales in the pinewoods, a wildlife preservation area as well. Here, perched 600 feet up the gentle lump of Monte Licosa (1,000 feet), is the *Hotel*

Castelsandra. It enjoys superb views of the nearby hill town of Castellabate, with its pleasant twin ports of San Marco and Santa Maria, and, on a
clear day, the whole of the Amalfi coast and Capri. The hotel nestles in a
pine wood 4 km from San Marco so a car is advisable, although the hotel
runs a courtesy bus to the beach. In an area as yet short of good hotels, we
would certainly recommend the *Castelsandra*. The situation is positively
idyllic; the public rooms are elegant and spacious and the grounds
extensive and well laid-out; the large pool terrace (two heated pools)
offers panoramic vistas and masses of new and comfortable poolside
furniture. The hotel is superbly well-maintained and pristinely clean, not
a little due to the presence of a formidable housekeeper of the old school!
We do have a few reservations. The management appears a little vague
and amateurish, and the bedrooms are a shade small for an hotel officially
graded 1st class. However, the bathrooms are most stylish and brilliantly
well-lit (especially for Italy) and all bedrooms have terraces with panoramic views. The food was well-cooked and presented, but rather unimaginative and the menu not very extensive.' *(Peter Hacking and Hugh
Wilson)*

Recent visitors to *Castelsandra* have been less enthusiastic than the
original nominators, whose 1982 report, somewhat abbreviated, appears
above. A new manager, Igino Rossi, arrived last year and we hope he is
able to improve the hotel's efficiency and standards of cooking about
which our correspondents have complained. More reports welcome.

Open: April–October.
Rooms: 61 double, 1 suite – 47 with bath, 14 with shower, all with telephone,
mono TV and air-conditioning. 8 rooms in annexe. (Some rooms on ground floor.)
Facilities: Salon, TV room, bar with music in high season, restaurant, conference
room; terrace. Garden with tennis court and children's play area; 2 swimming
pools (1 heated). Sea 5 km (transport by hotel's mini-bus). English spoken. &.
Location: 70 km S of Salerno, 13 km beyond Agripoli on the slopes of Monte
Licosa. Coming from Naples on the motorway, take exit Battipaglia, then direction
Agropoli/Paestum, then S. Maria and/or S. Marco di Castellabate; hotel is 4 km
from San Marco; parking.
Credit cards: American Express, Barclay/Visa, Diners.
Terms: Rooms: with breakfast 26,500–38,000 L; dinner, B & B 39,000–41,400 L
(not applicable in high season); full board 46,000–59,000 L. Set meals: lunch/
dinner 18,500 L. 25–50% reduction for children (under 2 years, free).

SAN MARTINO AL CIMINO, 01030 Viterbo　　　　　　　　**Map 14**

Balletti Park Hotel　　　　　　　*Telephone:* (0761) 29777

'St Martino al Cimino is a village of great beauty close to Viterbo, and the
Balletti Park is a gem. It is one of the most elegantly furnished ultra-
modern hotels that I know. With Aram-type furniture in the lounges and
very modern large wardrobes in the large bedrooms, it is light, airy and
unfussy. It has a super swimming pool and a good restaurant, *Il Cavaliere*.
(On the other hand, if you want to eat superbly, there is, at La Quercia,
9 km distant, *Aquilanti*, a Michelin-starred restaurant and deservedly so.)
Prices are very reasonable. Service is good. And there is lots to see round
about: Viterbo itself; the fantastic park of the Villa Orsini at Bomarzo;
Lago di Vico (unspoilt) and La Quercia. Ronciglione and Bagnaia (Villa
Lante) are also worth a visit.' *(Martyn Goff; warmly endorsed by P G
Bourne)*

Open: All year. Restaurant closed Wednesday.

Rooms: 44 double, 22 flats – 12 with bath, all with shower and telephone, some with balcony. TV and cooking facilities in flats.

Facilities: Lift; hall, billiards room, bar, 2 restaurants, pizzeria, dancing room, conference and banqueting facilities; children's playroom. Large gardens where you can take refreshments; Olympic-size heated swimming pool, also children's pool; tennis. &.

Location: 5 km from Viterbo, 45 km from Orvieto and from sea, 70 km from Rome. (Warning: sign-posting from Viterbo very inadequate.)

Credit card: American Express.

Terms: B & B 27,000–39,000 L; half board 42,000–58,000 L; full board 56,000–69,000 L. Set meals: lunch/dinner 20,000 L.

SESTRI LEVANTE, 16039 Genova　　　　　　　　　　　Map 14

Hotel Helvetia　　　　　　　　　　　*Telephone:* (0185) 41.175
Via Cappuccini 43

Dante and Petrarch were among the earlier admirers of Sestri Levante on the Gulf of Rapallo, though it wasn't quite the same sort of seaside resort in those days. The *Helvetia* has a pleasant and quiet position on the sea overlooking the Bay of Silence, and away from road and rail disturbance. 'We only stayed for two days at this small family-run hotel but were very impressed by the comfort and friendliness. The hotel has terraced gardens, a private beach and a beautiful view. We were lucky to get a balcony overlooking the bay as it was full (late September). I imagine it would be less pleasant in the high season, but the hotel seemed ideal for an early or late holiday. We recommended it to a Dutch friend a few days later and she gave us a good report. We did not sample the food but most other people were clearly staying *en pension*. For those with cars, parking can be difficult as the hotel is in the older part of the town.' *(Mary Rose Hoare)*

Open: 1 April–30 September.

Rooms: 28 double – 14 with bath, 14 with shower, all with telephone and radio. 8 rooms in annexe.

Facilities: Lift, TV lounge, lounge; restaurant with terrace overlooking sea; solarium; large terraced garden; private beach. English spoken.

Location: 100 metres from the town centre, overlooking the Bay of Silence. Some parking.

Terms: Full board 30,000–41,000 L. Set meals: lunch/dinner, 18,000 L; full *alc* 20,000 L. Special meals for children.

SIENA, 53100　　　　　　　　　　　　　　　　　　Map 14

Palazzo Ravizza　　　　　　　　　　*Telephone:* (0577) 28.04.62
Pian dei Mantellini 34

A 17th-century palace in the old city, within strolling distance of the cathedral and the famous piazza. There is no other hotel of its class so well-placed. It has been in the Grottanelli family for almost two centuries, and they have been faithful to their inheritance, leaving all the antique furniture in place, and doing the minimum of modernization, such as the installation of a number of private bathrooms. Most readers have appreciated the patrician quality of the place – the grand piano in the drawing room and the tea room opening on to the terraced garden – and have cheerfully put up with occasional signs of shabbiness amidst the grandeur. 'We could have given a dance in our bedroom,' writes one awed visitor, 'and the warm temperature prevented it being bleak. No private bathroom to be had, but we had a demurely screened-off corner with two large basins, two portable bidets and plenty of towels. The abiding memory is of our waiter who served us with enormous charm, and with white gloves – heaven! The food was not quite up to the standard, but not to be complained about at the price.' The question of the food has always been a source of contention. The hotel itself says it offers 'Tuscan plain cooking'. Another reader sums up: 'In four days we had two quite good meals, one reasonable and one bad. But it was well worth it for the character of the place and the lovely views.' *(Alex and Rachel Macdonald, Lady Maddocks)*

Open: All year. Restaurant closed 1 November–1 March.
Rooms: 21 double, 7 single, 1 apartment – 10 with bath, 3 with shower, all with telephone, TV and baby-listening.
Facilities: Lift, several sitting rooms (1 with TV, 1 with piano, 1 with library); tea room, bar, restaurant. Very large garden with terrace for breakfast and refreshments. English spoken. &.
Location: 300 metres from centre; parking.
Terms: B & B 24,000–26,000 L; dinner, B & B 36,000–38,000 L. Set meal: dinner 12,000 L. Reduced rates for children.

SPERLONGA, 04029 Latine   **Map 14**

Parkhotel Fiorelle   *Telephone:* (0771) 54 092

'Roughly halfway along the coast between Rome and Naples, Sperlonga is a cliff-top huddle of narrow streets and houses jutting out into the sea, bearing comparison with Portovenere for genuine charm (as against villages like Punta Ala, higher up the coast, which looks and feels fabricated). At the northern foot of the town is a good restaurant, *Laocoonta-da Rocco*. One km along the seafront is the *Parkhotel Fiorelle*, set back in its own lush gardens. There's plenty of parking space. A good sandy beach is enhanced by a first-class swimming pool between it and the hotel. Austrian-born Signora di Mille is always charming and helpful, while her Italian husband looks after the kitchens. Food is simple but good; service pleasant. But for sheer value – 20,000 L a day per person *demi-pension* [July 1981] – the place is unbeatable.' *(Martyn Goff)*
     The same correspondent has been back to the *Fiorelle* in July 1982 and sends us this despatch: 'While prices have advanced only slightly, quality is better than ever this year. This is particularly true of the food. Signora di Mille continues to be as caring as ever about every guest.'

Open: March–October. Restaurant closed Thursday.
Rooms: 33 – 7 with bath, 26 with shower, all with balcony.
Facilities: Salon, bar, restaurant; terrace for refreshments. Garden with swimming pool; private sandy beach nearby. English spoken.
Location: On the coast between Rome (127 km) and Naples (106 km).
Terms: Rooms 19,550–28,750 L; full board 27,600–39,100 L. Set meals: breakfast 2,875 L; lunch/dinner 11,500 L.

Grand Hotel   *Telephone:* (0931) 65 101
Viale Mazzini 12

'A small palazzo converted to a hotel, situated in Ortygia, the ancient harbour of Syracuse, overlooking the fishing boats, the Malta ferry, and the spot where Archimedes by his mastery of classical artillery, helped to destroy the fleet of Marcellus in 214 BC. But don't crane your neck to look around. The hideous pylons of the natural gas installations at Augusta (Sicily's boom industry) are creeping inexorably nearer and will surely soon obliterate the hotel's splendid views. We had a large, cool, white-painted front room with high ceilings and heavy shutters to keep out the dazzling white light. The service was competent, courteous and self-effacing. (A blind broke the first evening and was efficiently repaired almost immediately.) As in most Sicilian hotels that cater for locals not tourists, no food is served, though breakfast can be obtained as an extra in one of the alcoves off the main lounge. We followed local custom and had delicious stand-up breakfast snacks in local bars which are on every corner of the town. Another advantage was that one of Sicily's great fish restaurants, *Da Pippo*, was five minutes' walk away. The hotel's most serious drawback was that when the fishing fleet returned at around 3 a.m. in the morning, a hideous din would break out for half an hour or more. Rooms at the back of the hotel, with less attractive views, would probably be a great deal quieter.' *(Dennis and Madeleine Simms; also Andrew Markus)*

Open: All year.
Rooms: 47, almost all double – all with bath or shower and telephone.
Facilities: Lift, lounge, bar. ⅙.
Location: Near harbour.
Terms: Single rooms 15,500–22,000 L; double room 26,300–34,000 L. (No restaurant.)

Villa Belvedere   *Telephone:* (0942) 23 791
Via Bagnoli Croce 79

Apart from the *Villa Fiorita*, which has no garden or pool, the *Belvedere* is clearly the nicest place to stay in Taormina if one wants to be independent for meals. It offers B & B only, though light snacks can be obtained from the poolside bar. Breakfast is continental, but for once the bread is fresh and the coffee strong and individually made. Monsieur Pecaut comes from France, is married to a ravishing Italian girl, and his ochre-hued villa-hotel offers nicely-appointed new rooms with stupendous views over the flowered garden, the bay and Mount Etna, or more traditional and simpler ones with the same view or rooms towards the back (the latter tend to be a bit noisy). A delightful bar and lounge, library, but, above all, the beautiful gardens and pool, left my party of seasoned and experienced Sicily-travellers ecstatic. Very reasonable rates. A real find!' *(RW)*

Open: 1 March–30 October.
Rooms: 37 double, 3 single, 11 with bath, 29 with shower, all with telephone and baby-listening.
Facilities: Lift, lounge, library, lounge bar, breakfast room. Garden, heated swimming pool with bar. English spoken. &.
Location: Central, near public gardens and tennis court; parking.
Credit cards: Access/Euro/Mastercard, Barclay/Visa.
Terms: B & B 18,750–32,200 L. (No restaurant.) Reduced rates for children sharing parents' room.

TAORMINA, 98039 Sicily   Map 14

Hotel Pensione Villa Paradiso   *Telephone:* (0942) 23 922
Via Roma 6

'La Villa Paradiso è stata sempre preferita dalla sua tradizionale clientela inglese,' say the hotel in their brochure. As if that were not sufficient inducement to English travellers in these parts, we pass on a report from one flabbergasted correspondent of his being presented with a bottle of Sicilian wine on his departure from the *Villa Paradiso*, and some weeks later receiving a rebate of £15.60 from the manager on the grounds that he had been charged more than the rate quoted in the Guide. 'This certainly shows the value of mentioning the name of your Guide!' Since we often get complaints from readers that Italian prices in the Guide bear no relation to what is actually charged, we are delighted to hear of the *Paradiso*'s far-sighted policy. In general, readers have continued to appreciate the hospitality of this first-class *pension* fairly close to the centre of town, though one guest in August, when the temperature was 30°C outside, found that he had frequently to ask for the air-conditioning to be switched on; he also complained that room towels were not changed, and that there was bad traffic noise at night especially at weekends. More reports welcome. *(Dr and Mrs J P G Mailer and others)*

Open: All year, except November–16 December.
Rooms: 30 double, 3 single – 28 with bath, 5 with shower, all with balcony, telephone, radio, air-conditioning and baby-listening. (Some rooms on ground floor.)
Facilities: Lift, TV room, library, bar, restaurant; facilities for small conferences; terrace with tables. Next door to public gardens with tennis courts. English spoken. &.
Location: In town centre; no private parking.
Credit cards: All major credit cards accepted.
Terms: B & B 30,500–38,000 L; half board 41,000–58,000 L; full board 50,000–69,000 L. Set meals: lunch 23,000 L; dinner 25,000 L; full *alc* 25,000–27,000 L.

TELLARO DI LERICI, 19030 La Spezia   Map 14

Il Nido di Fiascherino   *Telephone:* (0187) 96.72.86
Via Fiascherino 75

'This hotel is located in a small village 3 km south-east of Lerici. The environment is very similar to that of the *Villa Dubrovnik* (q.v.). Our rooms, with balconies, overlooked the bay of Tellaro, where waves crashed thrillingly day and night over the rocks below. One climbs downstairs to the modern comfortable reception/bar/dining level. The dining area (only breakfast was served during our out-of-season stay) overlooks the bay, and steps lead down to the water itself with various levels including tables and chairs to read or relax. The service here was impeccable – everyone eager to please. For example, my strung-out laundry was carefully rearranged on special lines by the room maid while we were out for a day of sightseeing. Good place to drive to see the *Cinque Terre*. Quiet, clean, handsome, modern.' *(Mary Ann Hamill)*

Open: 20 March–31 October.
Rooms: 13 double, 3 single, 1 suite – 1 with bath, 15 with shower, all with telephone. (Some rooms in annexe.)
Facilities: TV room, bar, dining room, terraces. Garden. Small private beach. English spoken.
Location: 3 km SE of Lerici; parking.
Credit cards: Access/Euro/Mastercard, American Express.
Terms: B & B 27,800–34,300 L; dinner, B & B 47,800–54,300 L; full board 57,500–70,000 L. Set meals: lunch/dinner 20,000 L; full *alc* 30,000 L.

TORCELLO, 30012 Burano   **Map 14**

Locanda Cipriani   *Telephone:* (041) 73.01.50
Piazza S. Fosca 29

'A unique Venetian experience,' wrote Jan Morris last year. 'After dinner, on a summer evening, there can hardly be a pleasure of travel more innocently sensual than to walk beneath the pergolas with someone you love, a glass of the excellent house wine in your hand, looking at the grand old shape of the cathedral beyond the asparagus beds, and listening to the faint stir of the wind off the lagoon.'
   Torcello, for the uninitiated, is a small low island in the Venetian lagoon, reached by boat, either public or private. On landing, it appears uninhabited, but within walking distance of the landing stage there is a famous 11th-century basilica, with magnificent mosaics at present being restored, an octagonal church of the same period, one or two bars and the *Locanda Cipriani*. This is a simple ochre and rose-washed two-storey building – from the front, a modest inn. A hand-painted sign points *Ingresso* to the side, you follow the path round to the back and see with astonishment a huge modern restaurant complex cleverly built into the original façade. As a restaurant, the *Locanda Cipriani* – no relation to the *Hotel Cipriani*, but under the same ownership as *Harry's Bar* in Venice – is a hugely fashionable gastronomic mecca. As a place to stay, it is much less well-known. There are only six bedrooms, maintained in the same elegant style as the restaurant. The height of sophistication planted in the simplest of settings. *(Angela and David Stewart, Jack Rathbone)*

Open: 19 March–31 October. Restaurant closed on Tuesday.
Rooms: 3 double, 2 single – all with bath, telephone, tea-making facilities and air-conditioning.
Facilities: Restaurant, terrace, garden.
Location: On an island in the Lagoon of Venice, reached by motorboat.
Credit card: American Express.
Terms: Dinner, B & B 130,000 L; full board 170,000 L. Full *alc* 50,000–70,000 L.

462

TORRICELLA SABINA, Rieti   Map 14

Hotel Ristorante Salario   *Telephone:* (0765) 73.50.37
Via Salaria

'As the address implies, this hotel is on the main Rome–Rieti road 64 km from Rome. It is utterly unpretentious and desires to be only itself. Ciani Fernando, the owner, does most of the work and cooking. The rooms are modern and comfortable – some with private bathrooms. The restaurant is unattractive in decor but excellent for food and wine. Outstanding home-made pasta, excellent salads and fruit, regional specialities – prosciutto and salamis – and, of course, wines. The *Salario* was chosen by the President of Italy for a regional visit – which underlines its excellence, but this has in no way changed its attitude, which remains straightforward, uncomplicated and provincial. I had a glorious five-day stay, ate far too much, painted too little and at the end spent, I thought, far too little (about 25,000 lire per day for bed, breakfast and an enormous "no holds barred" evening meal!). Thoroughly recommended. There is a lot more I could say. All positive.' *(Charlie Colchester)*

Open: All year. Closed Monday.
Rooms: 14 – 7 with bath, 1 with shower.
Facilities: Lift, bar.
Location: On the main Rome–Rieti road 64 km from Rome; parking.
Terms: Single room 17,200 L, double room 25,000 L. Set meal: breakfast 4,600 L. (No restaurant.)

TREVISO, 31100   Map 14

Le Beccherie   *Telephone:* (0422) 40 871
Piazza Ancillotto 10

'Treviso is a charming little town, 30 km north of Venice, surrounded by ramparts and intersected by canals. The hotel is situated in the heart of the town, near the Piazza dei Signori. The restaurant is on one side of the *tiny* piazza Ancillotto, and the hotel portion on the other. Our room was not particularly big, but well-equipped with shower and all the usual facilities, and very clean. Very friendly helpful reception. No English spoken, but it is remarkable how this improves one's Italian! The restaurant building is old and pleasantly cluttered inside with gastronomic diplomas, old pottery, pictures and mementoes. The dining room is filled with local families gorging themselves – and we certainly had an excellent and very reasonably priced meal. *Warning:* Treviso is a maze of narrow one-way streets, and one may have several shots at reaching the hotel before actually making it. Once there, the fight for an empty parking slot in the tiny piazza starts, in competition with the locals. One just has to sit it out. The sooner Treviso makes this a traffic-free area the better: it would definitely add to the attraction of this delightful little town.' *(Ian and Agathe Lewin)*

Open: All year. Restaurant closed Thurs eves, also all day Friday 10–31 July.
Rooms: 20 double, 10 single – 16 with shower, all with telephone and radio.
Facilities: TV room, bar, restaurant (opposite), air-conditioning.
Location: 30 km N of Venice; central in one-way street leading from railway station; no special parking facilities.

Credit cards: Access/Euro/Mastercard, Diners.
Terms: B & B 23,000–25,000 L. Set meals: lunch/dinner from 17,000 L.

TRIESTE, 34121   **Map 14**

Hotel Duchi d'Aosta   *Telephone:* (040) 62 081
Via dell' Orologio 2   *Telex:* 460358

'The hotel is extremely well-situated in the huge Piazza Unità d'Italia
fronting the sea, where the evening stroll takes place by glittering gilded
and spun sugar palaces, civic buildings and large cafés. Flagposts and
ornate lamps soar up high into the sky in scale with the tall and ornate
buildings. Our large bedroom overlooked the square and was beautifully
furnished; there was a well-stocked refrigerated drinks cupboard discreetly built into the wall. The walls and ceiling were painted to resemble old
vellum, heavy plush curtains could block out all sound and light; there was
retractable mosquito netting at the windows and spacious bedside tables
held elegant lamps with Venetian glass bases. The bathroom was luxurious, richly tiled and with a tremendous battery of lights over the basin
mirror. Our tiny rented Fiat was put away by the porter with as much
ceremony as he would have extended to a Lamborghini. Dinner was
good. There was no pretentious palaver about a wine list – a large carafe
was put in front of us and we were charged only for what we drank. The
dining room was quietly elegant with especially pretty fluted glassware.
Breakfast was of the continental variety but included some particularly
delicious blood red orange juice. In all, a feeling of discreet luxury. It was,
of course, expensive but a similar standard in England would probably
cost much more. We thought it worth every penny.' *(Ray and Angela
Evans)*

Open: All year. Restaurant closed Sunday.
Rooms: 52 double, 42 single, 8 suites – 51 with bath, all with shower, telephone,
radio, mono TV, frigobar and baby-listening by arrangement.
Facilities: 3 lounges, *Harry's Grill Bar* with terrace restaurant overlooking main
piazza and sea. Very near the sea; all types of water sport available. English
spoken. &.
Location: Central; car park for 30 cars in front of hotel; garage 10 minutes away.
Credit cards: All major credit cards accepted.
Terms: Rooms 87,500–113,000 L. Set meals: breakfast 10,500 L; lunch/dinner
38,000–55,000 L. 20% discount for children; special meals available.

VARENNA, 22050 Como   **Map 14**

Hotel du Lac   *Telephone:* (0341) 83.02.38 and 83.05.88
Via del Prestino 4

Varenna is a village on the eastern side of Lake Como, about 24 km north
of Lecco. The *Hotel du Lac*, a place of simple refinement, is, as its name
suggests, on the lakeside with its own landing stage for swimming or
boating. The hotel is run by youngish owners, Signora and Signor
d'Ippolito, who live on the premises and see to the comfort of the guests.
The rooms look right out on the lake, as does the restaurant. The hotel is
an easy walk to the landing stage where all the ferries go in different
directions across the lake.

'Mrs d'Ippolito speaks English but not Mr d'I; both are most pleasant and helpful. The rooms have showers, only exceptionally a bath; my husband and I are both small but to use the lavatory without either flooring the towels or falling into the shower took all our physical ingenuity. The room itself was tiny, its salvation being a large terrace iwth magnificent views. The public rooms and terraces were spacious, clean and inviting, the situation of the hotel delightful, the food reasonable, adding up to a stay ended with reluctance and, having been shown a larger but still modest room, we plan a longer return visit next year.' *(Patricia Solomon)*

Open: All year.
Rooms: 12 double, 5 single, 2 suites – 3 with bath, 16 with shower, 1 with radio, 1 with colour TV, all with telephone.
Facilities: 3 salons, bar, restaurant (with music or electric organ), TV room, shaded terrace with flowers; swimming from hotel pier. English spoken.
Location: 24 km N of Lecco. At the end of the Church Square, on the lake.
Credit cards: Access/Euro/Mastercard, American Express, Barclay/Visa.
Terms: B & B 35,000–45,000 L; dinner, B & B 45,000–52,000 L; full board 50,000–59,000 L. Set meals: lunch/dinner 18,000 L; full *alc* 25,000 L. 30% reduction for groups.

VENICE, 30123   **Map 14**

Pensione Accademia   *Telephone:* (041) 37.846
Fondamenta Maravegie, Dorsoduro 1058

This delightful old villa, with its cool and pleasant garden, only a few metres from the Grand Canal but facing a relatively quiet side canal, has been known and cherished by a generation of English travellers to Venice. Breakfast only is served these days, and the place has become popular with package tours. It may not be the place it once was, but it still has its tranquil garden – and very reasonable prices. Further reports welcome.

Open: All year.
Rooms: 20 double, 6 single – 9 with bath, 10 with shower, all with telephone.
Facilities: 2 lounges, 1 with TV, bar. Garden overlooking the water. English spoken.
Location: Central, near the Grand Canal.
Credit cards: All major cards accepted.
Terms: B & B 34,000–39,000 L. (No restaurant.)

VENICE, 30123   **Map 14**

Hotel Cipriani   *Telephone:* (041) 70.77.44
Giudecca 10   *Telex:* 410162 CIPRVE
                                           Reservations: In UK: (01) 583 3050
                                                           In USA: (800) 233 6800

A hyper-elegant hotel near the eastern end of the Giudecca, facing the island of San Giorgio and the Lido in the misty distance. The hotel's own motorboat is on constant call to speed you across to the private landing-stage by the Piazzetta of San Marco. The hotel has an Olympic-sized pool – a luxurious plus after a long day's slog round the Venetian sights. Not everyone who can afford the *Cipriani*'s high prices cares for the place; some feel it is a bit out of the Venetian swim. Here, however, is a characteristic tribute from a member of the pro-*Cipriani* faction:

'Built in modern style, with a cool, clean and airy feel: lots of pale marble, tall windows and cherished plants and attractively situated in its gardens on the Giudecca. One of the pleasures of staying here is being taken across the mouth of the Grand Canal towards San Marco in the hotel's own boat, watching the whole incredible unique waterfront stretched out before you as you approach. And at the end of the day, after the heat and the crowds, to return to the cool quiet of the hotel in its green setting only four minutes away from the heart of Venice is a most soothing prospect. Our room was modern, simple, and all-white except the rose-terracotta carpet – if anything, we felt it lacked a Venetian "feel" – but was very comfortable. The bathroom was large, particularly well fitted and lit, and almost totally composed of pale beige marble. The designer of the restaurant and bars had used materials and shapes and mirrors to excellent effect, and the staff here were of the best: wonderfully courteous and cheerful in good English. The food in the restaurant we found to be rather dull and uninspired, but the buffet at breakfast was a delightful meal, with great choice (a brandy goblet of strawberries if you chose) and meats and cheeses as well as the usual Continental breakfast. Expensive – as one would expect – but worth it.' *(Angela and David Stewart)*

Open: All year.
Rooms: 76 double, 4 single, 14 suites – all with bath, telephone, radio and baby-listening; colour TV on request. (Some rooms on ground floor.)
Facilities: 2 restaurants (indoor and outdoor), 2 bars (one with piano, 5 function rooms, TV room. Gardens with Olympic-size swimming pool (heated and domed in winter). Private yacht harbour with 10 berths (up to 23 metres). Lectures, cookery courses and guided tours between April and October. English spoken. &.
Location: 5 minutes by hotel's private motor boat to city centre.
Credit card: American Express.
Terms: Rooms 201,000 L (single), 225,500–287,500 L (double), 495,000–747,500 L (suites). Dinner, B & B 65,600 L added to room rate. Set meal: breakfast, 13,800 L.

VENICE, 30124   **Map 14**

La Fenice et des Artistes   *Telephone:* (041) 32.333
Campiello de la Fenice 1936   *Telex:* 411150

'Apparently the first travellers to arrive on the Orient Express chose to dust off at the *Fenice* and, although not exactly economizing, they were splashing out a lot less on their hotel than they paid for a one-way ticket to it. The *Fenice* is a large, efficient hotel masquerading as a small, intimate one, and happily it fooled me. Centrally stashed behind the Teatro de Fenice in a secluded courtyard backing onto a slim canal, it is convenient for a range of restaurants from the *Colombe* to a humble pizza house. The rooms – elegantly furnished but not large enough to be forbiddingly so – are comfortable and remarkably peaceful, and breakfast is served in a cheerful courtyard, linking the two buildings which go to make up the hotel, where drinks can also be taken in preference perhaps to the rather posh and overstuffed public rooms.' *(Pamela Todd)*

Open: All year.
Rooms: 68 – most with bath or shower; air-conditioning (charge 4,500 L).
Facilities: Lift, large sitting room. Breakfast and drinks served in courtyard. &.
Location: Central, behind the Teatro de Fenice.
Terms: Rooms 52,000–93,000 L. Set meal: breakfast 5,200 L. (No restaurant.)

VENICE, 30124   **Map 14**

Hotel Flora   *Telephone:* (041) 70.58.44
San Marco 2283a

Readers continue to write enthusiastically about this well-placed bed-and-breakfast hotel, just off the main concourse between the Piazza San Marco and the Accadèmia bridge. One of its great attractions is its flowery courtyard garden where breakfast can be taken in the summer. Every one speaks warmly about Signor Romanelli, who has owned and run the hotel for almost two decades, and his happy helpful staff come in for compliments too. Some of the rooms are decidedly small, but cunningly designed to minimize inconvenience. As for restaurants, one correspondent appreciates the *Flora* for its closeness to one of the best restaurants in Venice, the one-star *La Caravella*. Another warmly recommends the less expensive *Il Giglio*. (*W Ian Stewart, C A Jackson, Angela and David Stewart*)

Open: 15 February–15 November.
Rooms: 39 double, 5 single – 30 with bath, 14 with shower, all with telephone. (2 rooms on ground floor.)
Facilities: Lift, lounge, TV room, bar, small breakfast room. Courtyard/garden where breakfast and drinks are served. English spoken. &.
Location: Central, just off the Calle Larga XXII Marzo.
Credit cards: All major credit cards accepted.
Terms: B & B 46,500–60,000 L. (No restaurant.)

VENICE, 30123   **Map 14**

Casa Frollo   *Telephone:* (041) 70.82.99
Giudecca 50

A 16th-century *palazzo* bang on the waterfront of the island of the Giudecca, with uninterrupted views of the Doge's Palace and St Mark's, and with its own peaceful garden in the year – it sounds like the answer to many a Venetian traveller's prayer, especially since its prices are ridiculously modest. For many, the *Casa Frollo* has a touch of magic, but there are others who find the facilities too ascetic or who mind having to take the vaporetto to the mainland for meals (no private launch as with the *Cipriani* below). The case for the *Casa* is put eloquently in the following report:

'If you are prepared to forfeit the busy, bruising delights of a humid Piazza San Marco filled in equal parts with crabby tourists trailing after officious guides and sad pigeons trailing after everything, escape across the water to Guidecca and the elegant calm of the *Casa Frollo*: a terraced 17th-century palace with a soothing, uninterrupted view of the square and the Doge's Palace. To gain entrance to this classical haven, you ring, night or day, a bell signalling Madame Flora – no mean concierge – to set in motion a Heath Robinson system of pulleys which release the catch and spill you into a cool, ordered courtyard, running the whole of the ground floor and leading into a neat, narrow garden. Take the stairs to the right and ascend to a vast room liberally stocked with the kind of polished Renaissance furniture you generally meet behind red ropes. Several dozen minor modern masters' works – personally inscribed to Madame – hang along one wall, while the facing wall props up an older school. This is where breakfast is served in the morning and the interior competes distractingly well with the postcard views of the Palace to be glimpsed through the windows. Seventeenth-century swank, however, does not always spell 20th-century comfort and it is a brisk baronial step down lofty corridors to the nearest, virginia creeper veiled, bathroom if you are not in one of the three rooms favoured with a private bath. Still, it is an historical treat and remarkably reasonable: stay there! You could spend twice as much for the most prosaic room in the centre of Venice with a view of crumbling stucco and your neighbour's bathroom. (It should be said that the penalty for the romantic nocturnal view across the water from the rooms at the front is the gentle revving of vaporettos, which stop not far from the hotel. However, some may find that a companionable plus.)' *(Pamela Todd)*

Open: All year.
Rooms: 26 – 3 with bath.
Facilities: Bar, breakfast room. Garden.
Location: On the waterfront on the island of Giudecca.
Terms: Single rooms 16,000–19,600 L; double rooms 30,000–50,000 L. Set meal: breakfast 3,500 L. (No restaurant.)

VENICE, 30124   **Map 14**

Gritti Palace   *Telephone:* (041) 26 044
Campo Santa Maria del Giglio 2467   *Telex:* 410125 Gritti I

Our previous entries for the *Gritti*, the 15th-century palatial home of Doge Andrea Gritti overlooking the Grand Canal, have tended to be of the drooling kind. The *Gritti*, in its own brochure, modestly describes itself as 'the best-loved hotel in the world'. Certainly some readers would not argue with that description. One reader this year takes us to task for not doing the hotel justice in last year's short but flattering entry: 'The service, the food, the decor and the peace are divine. The corner rooms on the first floor, with balconies overlooking the canal are super. Unlike the *Danieli*, it does not have a sidewalk in front of it, just the Canal, so it is quite quiet except for the gondoliers, and I don't consider them noisy.' Sooner or later, however, so much hyperbole provokes a cool response (see below). We should be glad to hear from other recent visitors.

'We met so many people who spoke of this as the finest hotel in Venice that we felt we had to sample its particularly Venetian flavour. We found not quite the splendour we had expected (and felt we paid for!): immense old spotted mirrors, huge gilt furniture tightly stuffed in brocade, and of course – chandeliers everywhere – even in the bedrooms. Our room was spacious and brocade-hung, but on the side canal, and so rather gloomy (particularly as breakfast had to be taken in the room): the bathroom was completely tiled, modern and well-equipped. We came down the staircase for dinner instead of using the lift, and found the carpet undoubtedly worn and threadbare, and the atmosphere slightly musty and dusty. The restaurant, modernized, was pleasant, but seemed to lack any particular style – and so, unfortunately, did the food. We simply cannot understand why a world-famous hotel should not employ the best of chefs – and be content with a sparse collection of residents in the dining room, while most of the guests go out elsewhere to eat – as we did, the second night we were there. It must seem irreverent and presumptuous of us to comment not very favourably on such as the *Gritti* – but this is how it was – and at such cost! We got the feeling quite strongly that they were resting too comfortably on their laurels.' *(Angela and David Stewart; also Alfred A Knopf, Jr)*

Open: All year.
Rooms: 73 double, 9 of which are suites, 17 single – all with bath and shower, telephone, radio and TV.
Facilities: 3 salons, TV rooms, bar, restaurants; terrace-restaurant overlooking the Grand Canal. Conference/function facilities. Beauty parlour. English spoken.
Location: On the Grand Canal, 10 minutes by boat from the Lido.
Credit cards: All major credit cards accepted.
Terms: B & B 190,000–260,000 L; full board on request. Full *alc* 80,000 L. Special meals for children.

VENICE, 30123 **Map 14**

Pensione Seguso *Telephone:* (041) 22 340 or 86 858
Grand Canal Zattere 779

This modest *pensione* on the Zattere continues to be a popular haunt of English-speaking visitors to the city. (Signora Seguso speaks fluent English.) Its special attraction is the stunning view from the front-facing windows of the Giudecca and of Venetian craft of all sizes, including ocean liners; the side rooms have pleasing views over a small canal. It has the virtues of a high-class, old-fashioned establishment – fine old Venetian furniture, dining room with embroidered silk wall covering, friendly service, honest bourgeois fare. Opinions on the Seguso's food vary: one recent correspondent dubbed it 'particularly good', but others have preferred to stay on B &B rather than *pension* terms.

Open: 1 March–30 November, except Wednesday.
Rooms: 41 double, 18 single – 22 with bath, 16 with shower, 4 with telephone; baby-listening can be arranged.
Facilities: Lift, lounge, 2 dining rooms. Garden. English spoken.
Location: Central, on the Zattere.
Credit card: American Express.
Terms: Dinner, B & B 43,000–54,000 L; full board 61,500–72,500 L. Reduced rates for children under 5; special meals available.

VERONA, 37121 **Map 14**

Colombo d'Oro *Telephone:* (045) 59.53.00
Via C Cattanco 10 *Telex:* 480872 COLOMB

A bed-and-breakfast hotel, two minutes from the centre of the city and within strolling distance of the Arena, in a side street. Double-glazing and air-conditioning ensure quiet. The hotel's own private garage ensures your car is still there in the morning. What readers have consistently appreciated about the *Colombo d'Oro* is its friendly service (delicious breakfasts as late as you wish), its value for money and the fact that the bedrooms are unusually large and well-appointed – *viz:* 'Coming from the cramped rooms of a Venetian hotel, the *Colombo d'Oro*'s spaciousness was doubly welcome – at three-quarters of the cost in Venice.' *(Jack and Esther Holloway)*

Open: All year.
Rooms: 40 double, 18 single, 2 suites – 43 with bath, 17 with shower, all with telephone and air-conditioning.
Facilities: Bar, salon, TV room; conference room. English spoken.
Location: Central, in restricted traffic zone, so quiet. Garage in same building as hotel. Leave autoroute at Verona Sud.
Credit cards: American Express, Barclay/Visa, Diners, Euro.
Terms: B & B 40,000–61,500 L. (No restaurant.)

VERONA, 37122   **Map 14**

De' Capuleti   *Telephone:* (045) 32 970
via del Pontiere 26

The *Hotel De' Capuleti* is round the corner from Juliet's Tomb, near the river Adige and within comfortable walking distance of virtually everything. It is only 300 metres from the Arena. But it is not in a congested part of the city and one can park on the street in front. It is essentially a modest family hotel. Bedrooms are small but clean, most with private showers and toilets and tiny balconies. Choose a room at the back; Italian traffic seems noisier than that of any other European nation. There is no lounge, but a pleasant bar. The staff are friendly and several speak English. At the time of going to press, the hotel's own restaurant is only available to groups, but it is hoped to provide normal restaurant service during 1983. Meanwhile, gourmets may make their way to Verona's best restaurant, the *12 Apostles*, ten minutes' walk away.

Open: All year, except 24 December–10 January.
Rooms: 29 double, 5 single, 2 suites – 1 with bath, 25 with shower, most with balcony, all with telephone.
Facilities: Lift, salon with colour TV, bar, restaurant, breakfast room. English spoken.
Location: Central, near Juliet's Tomb; parking available in Via del Pontiere and other nearby streets.
Credit cards: American Express, Diners.
Terms: Rooms 18,000–37,500 L; dinner, B & B 36,000–40,000 L; full board 48,000–63,000 L. Set meals: breakfast 5,000 L.

La Bonne Auberge, Gaichel

Luxembourg

Hôtel de la Moselle   *Telephone:* 76022 and 76717
131 Route du Vin

Ehnen is a small village on the banks of the Moselle, about six miles from Remich. 'A most delightful hotel overlooking the Moselle and vineyards. It is owned by the Bamberg family, who are exceedingly friendly and attentive; the restaurant on the ground floor of the hotel is called *Restaurant Bamberg.* The cooking is superb. The bedrooms, most with their own bath or shower, are beautifully appointed. There is a car park in front. We have been going to the *Moselle* since we first saw it mentioned in an *Observer Time Off* book in 1968. Unfortunately now not cheap, but worth every penny.' *(B W Ribbons)*

Open: 15 January–1 December, except Tuesday.
Rooms: 16 double, 3 single – 7 with bath, 6 with shower, all with telephone, radio and colour TV.
Facilities: Lift, sitting room with TV, dining room. Large park in front of hotel; near river; sailing, waterskiing. English spoken.
Location: 10 km N of Remich: parking.
Credit cards: Access/Euro/Mastercard, Barclay/Visa.
Terms: Rooms including breakfast, 1,150–1,600 frs. Set meals: lunch/dinner 880 frs. Reductions for stays of 2 and 3 days. Reduced rates for children.

Hotel Simmer *Telephone:* 7.60.30
117 route du Vin

'The *Simmer*, classed by Michelin as a restaurant with rooms, has a 15th-century dining room, with delightful soft lighting and quiet background music. The cooking and service are both exquisite, and the restaurant is in great demand with nearby residents and also foreign nationals attending EEC meetings in Luxembourg. Local wine cheap and very good. But there are also 23 bedrooms of a good size, most with bathroom or shower, and tastefully furnished. A chest-of-drawers would have been useful, but we did take too much clothing. There was a slight disturbance early morning from passing commercial traffic. *Pension* or *demi-pension* terms (minimum three days) provide very good value. The *propriétaire* is no longer young but exudes charm and the desire to provide good service.' *(W H Baily)*

Open: All year except 15 January–5 March.
Rooms: 23 – 19 with bath, 4 with shower, all with telephone.
Facilities: Salon, dining room, banqueting facilities, terrace overlooking the river; garden. Watersports and fishing.
Location: 10 km N of Remich.
Credit card: Euro.
Terms: Rooms with breakfast 1,050–2,150 frs; half board 1,450–1,950 frs; full board 1,600–2,100 frs. Set meals: dinner from 930 frs; full *alc* 1,350 frs.

La Bonne Auberge *Telephone:* 391 40

'Gaichel is hardly a hamlet – just two small hotels and a garage at a road junction, about 30 minutes' drive from Luxembourg city, in pleasant rolling wooded country. First of all, the deficiencies, which are considerable. The hotel entrance is a three-foot passage between the dining room and the tiny bar/office. Waiters dashing frantically across make moving suitcases in almost impossible, and the situation was not helped by a youth doggedly vacuuming the carpet. Secondly, the bedroom and bathroom we had were clearly designed by someone who had never ever travelled. Not one flat surface anywhere or even a hook on a door. The bed however was a masterpiece (to use the phrase of one of your earlier contributors, a perfect working surface). Two good-sized singles linked together and made up as a double with beautiful *linen* sheets. (The hotel did offer to make it up as two singles should we so wish.) The real high-spot of the place was its restaurant. Although we did not take the *menu gastronomique*, one of our courses was hot lobster in one of the best sauces I have ever eaten. Not cheap, of course, but wines and spirits are cheaper in Luxembourg than in its neighbouring countries (as is petrol). I would think twice before staying there again, in spite of the wonderful meal, but if I did, would organize my packing to take the absolute minimum. You must make of this what you will!' *(Mrs R B Richards)*

Open: All year, except December. (Restaurant closed Tuesday.)
Rooms: 12 – all with bath and telephone.

Facilities: Bar, dining room; garden with children's play area. English spoken.
Location: 4 km from Arlon on the road to Mersch; parking.
Credit cards: American Express, Diners.
Terms: Rooms 875–1,350 frs; B & B 800–1,000 frs; dinner, B & B 1,565–1,765 frs; full board from 1,800 frs (min. 3 days). Set meals: lunch/dinner 767–1,375 frs; full *alc* 1,500 frs. 30% reduction for children.

REMICH   Map 8

Hotel St Nicholas   *Telephone:* 69.88.88, 69.83.33
Esplanade 31   *Telex:* 3103 HRNICO

'An attractive, new (1976) hotel – designed to fit the surrounding older buildings. Multi-lingual and friendly staff – most helpful and considerate. Room bright, cheerful, comfortable with a lovely view over the Moselle. Duvets on the beds. Super plumbing – and bathroom heated. Dinner in dining room – again overlooking the Moselle, with good service and excellent food. Fresh bread, cream cheese, jams and spreads and good coffee for breakfast. Touches of luxury, e.g. enormous bath towels and telephone with instructions for world-wide use (and price list) and a surprisingly low bill, even in high season [1981].' *(Joan Davis)*

Open: All year.
Rooms: 22 double, 4 single, 1 suite – 10 with bath, 5 with shower, all with telephone and mono TV; baby-listening on request.
Facilities: Lounge (with TV), bar, sitting room, dining room; terrace; playroom, solarium. English spoken.
Location: From Luxembourg city, take direction Saarbrücken; at the German border, the hotel is located on the Moselle river; no special parking facilities.
Credit cards: All major credit cards accepted.
Terms: B & B 500–1,050 frs; dinner, B & B 750–1,500 frs; full board 950–1,800 frs. Set meals: lunch/dinner 490, 680, 890 frs; full *alc* 900 frs. Special meals for children on request.

Hotel Ta'Cenc, Sannat

Malta (including Gozo)

Hotel Ta' Cenc   *Telephone:* Gozo 55.68.19/55.68.30/55.15.20
                                             Telex: MW479 Refinz

The island of Gozo is one of two small islands off the north-eastern corner
of Malta. 14 km by 6 km, it's roughly a quarter the size of the main island.
The ferry takes half an hour, but a 5 km strip of sea makes a world of
difference. The *Ta' Cenc* is the one luxury hotel on Gozo. For our money,
it is the most sympathetic hotel on Gozo or its mother-island, and one of
the half-dozen best hotels – in our own personal usage of the expression –
we have ever stayed in. Seven years after our one-week visit, we can still
recall many individual moments that made our stay so enjoyable – not a
bad test of a hotel's capacity to please. It was indeed the discovery of the
Ta' Cenc that made us embark on the Guide. The hotel is beautifully sited
on a high promontory, built in the local honey-coloured limestone on a
low-profile principle: it's all one storey and cunningly terraced to blend
into the hillside. The rooms are individually designed bungalows, each
with a private patio for breakfast or sun-worship, ranged round a central
pool, with plenty of space between for oleanders, fig trees, cacti and the
like. The pool itself offers a breathtaking view of the sea and Malta
beyond, and many residents are content to brown and browse there all
day. But for the more adventurous, there is lots to see on Gozo – on foot,

by bus or by cheap rented car. There's plenty of good rock bathing all round the island, but only one first-class sandy beach, 10 km from the hotel.

We have not yet carried a bad report on the *Ta' Cenc*, but last year, in a half-page entry, we did refer to reports of a fall in the high standards of the restaurant and invited further reports. We got them, almost by return and robust reading they made: 'The food is the best we have had in any hotel over a week or so for a very long time. . . . We agree that it must rank among the most captivating hotels in Europe.' 'Under the guidance of the indefatigable Italo Rota, the restaurant has improved tremendously and we consider it one of the most enjoyable we have come across in the Mediterranean.' (And much more in a similar vein from *David Bennett, Albert Mellor, Dr D J Westlake, Sheila Mills, Michael Rubinstein, Mrs G M Beastall, V Bailey)*

LATE NEWS: As we go to press, we learn that Signor Rota, the founding General Manager, has retired, and his place taken by Mr Zammit. First reports speak well of the new regime.

Open: All year except 16 January–28 February.
Rooms: 38 double, 12 suites – all with bath, telephone, radio, TV, frigobar, breakfast patio and baby-listening service. Some small family bungalows in the grounds (self-contained).
Facilities: Lounge, bar, restaurant; billiards and table tennis room; piano and music bar; conference facilities. 3 acres gardens and terrace, with swimming pool, tennis courts (floodlit). Sand and rock beach 2 km (transport by private bus, mornings and afternoons); boating. English spoken.
Location: 7 minutes by car from town centre; parking for 50 cars.
Credit cards: American Express, Barclay/Visa, Diners, Euro.
Terms: Dinner, B & B M£17–25; full board M£20–30. Set meals: lunch M£6.50, dinner M£7; full *alc* M£8. Special reduced rates for long winter stays. 50% reduction for children under 6 sharing parents' room; special meals provided.

XAGHRA, Gozo   **Map 14**

Cornucopia Hotel   *Telephone:* Gozo 556.486 or 553.966
10 Gnien Imri Street

For many Gozitan addicts, the *Cornucopia*, under its recently departed owners, Peter and Deirdre Cope, had become something of an institution. The Copes were clearly ideal hosts, and they ran a refreshingly unstuffy hotel. But the good news is that the new owners, Victor Borg, who has been associated with the hotel for some while past, and his wife Linda, from Newfoundland, together with brother-in-law Teddy Xerri (pronounced Sherry) seem to be maintaining or improving the status quo at still remarkably low rates. 'Tarcisio, like a pantomime Buttons, still presides cheerfully at the bar,' writes one enthusiast for the *ancien régime*, 'and if one misses the Copes themselves, the horse, the donkey and the fully integrated cats and dogs, Mr Borg promises to extend the amenities with clock-golf, riding facilities and more accommodation with enhanced comfort – carpets in all bedrooms, heaters in rooms for the winter months, a TV lounge for residents and a reliable source of electricity.' Another old-timer reports on a week's stay with full board: 'The hotel has been smartened up and painted – not in the process losing any of its original charm. The cats have disappeared – thankfully to my mind. The food is good – fresh strawberries in May and good variety at lunch and dinner.

The service – excellent and *all* staff couldn't have been more pleasant and helpful. One relatively minor point – the bed-linen perhaps should not have been "holy", and the towels could have been slightly more luxurious. All in all, though, a wonderful "bolt-hole" for winter-weary Europeans seeking the genuine and unspoilt.' *(MBR, Sybil Craik)*

Open: All year.
Rooms: 13 double, 2 family suites, 2 single – 16 with bath, 1 with shower. (5 rooms on ground floor.)
Facilities: Lounge/library with TV, bar, restaurant, card and games room, table tennis. Patio and large garden with swimming pool; poolside barbecues. Hire of bike, scooter, car. Boat trips; 1 mile from fine sandy beach at Ramla; sailing, scuba diving and windsurfing. English spoken. &.
Location: Central; from Xaphra square follow signs; parking.
Credit cards: American Express, Barclay/Visa, Diners.
Terms (excluding 10% service charge): B & B M£4–9; dinner, B & B M£4.75–11; full board M£5.85–12.25. Set meal: lunch M£2; full *alc* M£4. Reduced rates and special meals for children. Special winter rates.

Are there no good hotels on the Maltese mainland?

Øystese Fjord Hotel, Øystese

Norway

BERGEN, N-5000 **Map 7**

Hotell Neptun *Telephone:* (05) 23.20.15
Walckendorffsgate 8 *Telex:* 40040

Bergen, founded by King Olav Kym in 1070, is one of Norway's oldest towns, and probably the most rewarding for the first-time visitor. The *Neptun* is a well-equipped, modern hotel in a central position overlooking the harbour and the old market. It is quiet at night, and the restaurant is one of the city's best. 'Excellent "bird of passage" stopover. Comfortable and efficient. After two weeks' good but simple fare on a coastal steamer, we thoroughly enjoyed an *excellent* dinner in the most attractive restaurant. Breakfasts (buffet style) are truly astonishing. What a pity that Norway is in general so expensive and that a civilized bottle of wine to accompany a civilized meal is almost prohibitive.' *(Mrs E Newall; also Karen Brook-Barnett)*

Open: All year.
Rooms: 83 double, 26 single – 64 with bath, 45 with shower, all with radio and colour TV.
Facilities: 2 lifts, lounge, bar, café and restaurant (both open till midnight); conference facilities; English spoken.
Location: Central, near old market; some traffic noise, but quiet at night; garage parking 100 metres.
Credit cards: All major credit cards accepted.
Terms: B & B 275–392 Nkr. Set meals: lunch 100 Nkr; dinner 120 Nkr.

Pensjonat Brekkestranda Fjord *Telephone:* (057) 15100 103

A small village on the south of the Sognefjord, not far from the sea, Brekke has a church, a school, a ferry quay, three small shops and 200 inhabitants. Surrounded by little hill farms, it is 102 km and two ferry crossings from Bergen. *Pensjonat Brekkestranda* is not far from the village in completely peaceful surroundings, and consists of a complex of wooden cottages with green turf-covered roofs strung along the shore of the fjord.

'If you are tired of run-of-the-mill hotels, however luxurious, but would nevertheless like to spend a very comfortable night in beautiful surroundings, then *Brekkestranda* is the place for you. It calls itself a *pensjonat*, i.e. a guest house, but it is to all intents and purposes a hotel. It was built in 1970 by the parents of Mr Björn Brekke, the present manager. They succeeded in finding an architect who was inspired by the same idea as they were – an intense dislike of functionalism – and together planned a building that was to be its exact opposite in every respect. This they achieved not only by avoiding man-made materials wherever they could, but also by having as few straight lines and right-angles in the design as possible. The result is a series of long, low, rambling wooden buildings, each with its traditional old Norwegian grass roof. The buildings have windows of all conceivable shapes and sizes and are joined to each other by cloister-like passages of unworked stone. The hotel is superbly situated right on the southern shore of Sognefjord and all the bedrooms except five on the first floor have a back-door opening directly on to the strip of grass between the hotel and the water's edge. If you feel like a morning swim, there is a diving-board too, and the water is clear and deep (and cold). We were lucky enough to have perfect weather and it was a real joy to sit out there in the early morning where the only sound was literally the occasional cry of a gull and enjoy the incredibly beautiful view.

'If the outside of the hotel is eccentric, the interior is no less peculiar, irregularity being the guiding principle here too. Sometimes it has been carried almost to the point of whimsicality; for example none of the wall-panels in our bedroom was vertical with the result that a picture on the wall looked as though it were hanging at a very odd angle. Let us emphasize that this irregularity in no way detracted from our enjoyment of the room, which was comfortable and well-furnished, though not large. The bathroom was also small, but good with the usual Norwegian refinement of a heated floor. One end of the building is devoted to the reception desk, the restaurant, the TV lounge (small) and another lounge that can also be used for dances. Meal times are set, except for lunch, dinner being only for one hour, from 6.30 to 7.30 after which you have to order *à la carte*. We got a good and typically Norwegian three-course dinner and the usual buffet-breakfast next morning, here too with a large variety of dishes. We thoroughly enjoyed our stay here, not least due to the five-star situation of the hotel, but also because it was so refreshingly different and personal. By Norwegian standards it must be considered good value for money. *(Stephen Howard)*

Open: All year.
Rooms: 18 double, 11 single, 3 suites – all with bath or shower, telephone and radio.
Facilities: Lounge, TV room, dining room, ballroom; occasional disco; bicycles free to guests; swimming in the fjord, sailing and fishing; nearby rock pool on shore for children. English spoken.

Location: 102 km NE of Bergen.
Terms: B & B 165–230 Nkr. Set meal: dinner 80 Nkr; full *alc* 100 Nkr.

HANKØ, Østfold   Map 7

Hankø nye Fjordhotel   *Telephone:* (032) 32 105

'Hankø, a small island on the Oslofjord, is known as the Cowes of
Norway, but it resembles the bustling Isle of Wight resort only in being
Norway's most prestigious yachting centre where the royal family race
and the King entertains at his modest house on the hill. It is ten minutes
from the mainland by passenger ferry, there are blissfully no motor cars
on the island and only two hotels: the *Seilersbro*, the Sailors' Inn, on the
quay with 14 beds, and the *Hankø nye Fjordhotel* tucked into a small
green valley. The *nye (new) Fjordhotel* has some 60 rooms and is
comfortable rather than "luxe" but this is reflected in the reasonable
price. It has tennis, dancing to live music and a splendid heated salt-water
swimming pool. If you write in English you get a lucid and fairly prompt
reply.' *(Anne Bolt)*

Open: 1 March–20 December.
Rooms: 67 doubles, 3 suites – 39 with balcony, all with bath or shower.
Facilities: Lift, lounge, TV room, ballroom-bar, dining room; conference rooms;
dancing to live music. Heated indoor swimming pool, gym, solarium, sauna; 4
tennis courts, yachting school, private beach, fishing. English spoken.
Location: 10 minutes from mainland; 15 km from Fredrikstad.
Terms: Rooms (including breakfast) 288–475 Nkr; dinner, B & B 270 Nkr. Set
meals: lunch 105 Nkr, dinner 140 Nkr.

JELØY, PO Box 236, 1501 Moss   Map 7

Hotell Refsnes Gods   *Telephone:* 032/70411

We are always interested to see how hotels describe themselves. 'The
Refsnes Gods,' says their brochure, 'has introduced a new hotel style in
Norway. The peaceful, elegant and complete house with a special character and atmosphere. Hotels founded on these principles are renowned on
the Continent and in Britain. Rich in tradition – but modern. Efficient and
correct – but friendly.' A line at the end of the questionnaire introduces a
further element: 'The hotel is a family and affairs hotel'. Don't read too
much into this last phrase. The *Refsnes Gods* is owned and run by the
family Christiansen and caters for conferences as well as for individual
guests.
   'Jeløy, one of the largest of the many islands scattered along the east
coast of the Oslofjord, is linked to the mainland and the small industrial
town of Moss by a bridge. Businessmen in the upper echelons have built
imposing houses, there are some six-storey flats and pretty bungalows,
but gardens are spacious and the island is green and leafy with many fields.
The climate allows both vines and maize to grow. Rooms at the *Refsnes
Gods* overlook either the fjord or the large swimming pool. At the bottom
of the garden is a lane leading to the seashore only a hundred metres
away. Locals swim there regularly and assure me the water is unpolluted.

Both bedrooms and the extensive public rooms are very elegantly furnished. The food we enjoyed; but beware – Saturdays and Sundays the dining room closes at 7 p.m. in the high season, and the restaurant doesn't function at all on Sundays from October to the end of May.' *(Mrs Maurice Yates)*

Open: All year except Easter and Christmas; restaurant closed Sunday 1 October–31 May.
Rooms: 26 double, 30 single, 6 suites – 12 with bath, 50 with shower, all with radio and mini-bar.
Facilities: Lift, lounges, 2 dining rooms; banqueting rooms. Park, private bathing and boating, outdoor swimming pool with sauna; bicycles, fishing.
Location: Outside Moss on the W side of Jeløy island.
Credit cards: Access/Euro/Mastercard, American Express.
Terms: Rooms with breakfast 300–400 Nkr (single), 400–550 Nkr (double). Set meals: lunch 65–85 Nkr; dinner 135 Nkr; full *alc* 150–200 Nkr. Reduced rates for children sharing parents' room; special meals provided.

LEIKANGER, N-5842 Map 7

Leikanger Fjord Hotel
Telephone: 056/53622
Telex: 40654 SOGTU-N

'When we came to Norway we hoped to discover a dream hotel to report to you; we feel we have found it in the *Leikanger Fjord*. The hotel stands on the edge of the fjord with a magnificent view of the waters and surrounding mountains. It is not one of the really busy fjords, so the hotel is very peaceful: you can watch the occasional liner pass by, and a few ferries call at the quay by the hotel, including the catamaran to Bergen. The building itself is a pleasant mixture of old and new, with a large modern wing. The bedrooms are spacious and thoroughly comfortable. There are two good lounges and a pleasant dining room. Breakfast which is self-service is excellent. Dinner, although a set menu, is well-cooked and plentiful. The hotel has been run by the family Lie since 1920, and the owners and staff are very friendly and do all they can to make your stay a happy and memorable occasion. Language is no problem.

'The hotel offers various mini-bus excursions, rowing boats are available and there is a windsurfer for hire. The fjord must be a fisherman's paradise. It is within easy reach of the Nigard glacier, amongst other beauty spots. There is a beautiful medieval church, and the vicarage garden boasts several unusual trees including a maidenhair tree *(Gingko biloba)* also described as a live fossil, because it is the only surviving species of the Tertiary period, also the *Sequida giganteum* thrives, believed to be the oldest in the world, 100 years old and six metres round.' *(Hugh and Elsie Pryor)*

Open: All year, except Christmas and New Year.
Rooms: 35 double, 5 single, 2 suites – 25 with bath, 12 with shower, all with baby-listening. (5 rooms in annexe.)
Facilities: TV room, 2 lounges, dining room, terrace. Garden with minigolf. Safe bathing/sandy beach, boats, windsurfing, bicycles, fishing. English spoken. &.
Location: On the edge of Sognefjord; 220 km NE of Bergen. Parking.
Credit cards: Access/Euro/Mastercard.
Terms: B & B 190–300 Nkr; full board (minimum 4 days) 200–350 Nkr. Set meals: lunch 85 Nkr, dinner 100 Nkr. Children under 3 years, 75% reduction; 3–12, 50%; special meals provided.

NORDFJORDEID, N-6771   Map 7

Nordfjord Turisthotell   *Telephone:* Nordfjordeid (057) 6400 605

Nordfjordeid, a small village at the head of the Nordfjord, is about 320 km north of Bergen, and can be reached from there by express boat in about five hours, or in about eight hours by car. It's not at all touristy: a sea inlet edged with wooded cliffs and meadows and high snow-capped peaks in the distance: it's a haven of peace, with the clean, energizing air particular to the far north.

'This is the sort of hotel it is a pleasure to stay at, not so much because of the view or the situation, although both are pleasant, but because of the atmosphere, the comfort and the attention to detail noticeable everywhere. It was built in 1976. It has recently changed hands and is now owned by a young couple who take a personal interest in their guests. We were perhaps unusually lucky to get the room we had. We had written to ask for a double room, but when we arrived we were shown into a small suite. Alarmed, we checked with the receptionist, who explained that they had given us this suite as they would not otherwise have been able to accommodate a later booking for a party from Switzerland; the price would of course be what we had been quoted. The dining room was large, light and attractively designed and the dinner, of the buffet type, beautifully displayed on a central table, consisted of a large variety of excellent dishes. The owner circulated during the meal talking to all the guests in good English and German – language is never a problem in Norway. The buffet breakfast next morning was also good, varied and plentiful. Next to the dining room there was a large TV lounge with plenty of comfortable chairs, and when dinner had been cleared away, there was dancing in the dining room. There is not a lot to do at Nordfjordeid itself, but it is very centrally situated for trips to some of the most beautiful scenery in Norway. We thought it very good value for money.' *(Johanne Suul-Eriksson)*

Open: All year, except 22 December–5 January.
Rooms: 31 double, 22 single, 2 suites – 6 with bath, 49 with shower, all with telephone and radio, colour TV in 21 rooms; baby-listening by arrangement. (13 rooms on ground floor.)
Facilities: Lounges, TV room, bar, restaurant; dancing in the evening; some conference facilities. Sauna. Garden with putting green, children's playground and tennis court. Fjord and lake fishing arranged; sailing. English spoken. &.
Location: 320 km N of Bergen; in village; parking.
Credit cards: Access/Euro/Mastercard, Barclay/Visa.
Terms: B & B 195–310 Nkr; dinner, B & B 245–330 Nkr; full board from 275 Nkr. Set meals: lunch 70 Nkr, dinner 100 Nkr; full *alc* 180 Nkr. Children under 4 free of charge; 4–12 years, 50% reduction on *pension* price; special meals on request.

OS, N-5200   Map 7

Solstrand Fjord Hotel   *Telephone:* (05) 30.00.99
                                   Telex: 42050 Solsh

'A wonderful place, 45 minutes by car from Bergen, on the coast, with panoramic views over the fjord. There is plenty to do for all the family: sea fishing in the hotel's own no-charge rowing boats, tennis courts, riding;

and, if it starts to rain, there is a heated indoor pool overlooking the sea. The hotel has a new and an old part; the latter, which I found cosier, was built 90 years ago by Christian Michelsen, who later became Prime Minister. The place has been run by the same family for the past 30 years. The service was very friendly. The food was plain, but that was a minor drawback in view of all the excellent facilities. There's a cold buffet with Norwegian specialities for lunch and a 3-course dinner in the evenings. We enjoyed walks in the surrounding woodlands, and a visit to Lysekloster Monastery, where herbs that the monks brought with them in 1146 still grow.' *(Karen Brook-Barnett)*

Open: All year, except 19–31 December approx.
Rooms: 88 double, 28 single – 101 with bath, 15 with shower, 100 with radio, all with telephone.
Facilities: Lift, lounges, TV room, bar, restaurant; dancing 6 days a week; table-tennis. Garden with tennis and badminton court, putting green; heated indoor seawater swimming pool; steam baths and keep fit room; private rock beach; sea fishing, free rowing boats, speed-boat, waterskiing. English spoken.
Location: 31 km S of Bergen on the Bergen–Hatvik road; parking.
Credit cards: Access/Euro/Mastercard, American Express, Barclay/Visa.
Terms: B & B 270–450 Nkr; dinner, B & B (min. 3 days) 320–500 Nkr; full board 360–540 Nkr. Set meals: buffet lunch 100 Nkr; dinner 110 Nkr; full *alc* 200–250 Nkr. Reduced rates for children sharing parents' room; special meals on request.

OSLO 1 **Map 7**

Hotel Bristol *Telephone:* (02) 41.58.40
Kristian 4des gt 7 *Telex:* 71668

'By convention, Scandinavia is hardly the homeland of the gourmet. Yet it was at the *Hotel Bristol* in Oslo that I had one of my finest gastronomic experiences. This was fresh trout prepared in sour cream; a combination of ineffable splendour I cannot wait to repeat. It occurred in the same dining room where, next morning, I had a long, long breakfast from a loaded buffet starting with several kinds of pickled herring and ending with limitless coffee. That too was an experience. To eat well in Norway one could do worse than breakfast three times a day. The dining room was dark, old-fashioned, with a little bit of plush and tinted window panes; rather like a set from an Ibsen play. In fact, the same may be said of the hotel, at least the public parts. The room I occupied was standard, international three star, but it had enough space; neat, but not gaudy. I found the dining room staff extremely efficient, forthright and friendly; rather like stewards on one of the now so sadly vanished ocean liners. There is character about the place, if somewhat muted. My only disappointment was the lighting in the bedrooms. Why are all hotels of whatever ilk or nationality so stingy in this respect? But that is a cavil. As befits the noble lord after whom it is named, the *Bristol* has the touch of a true hostelry. It does make the arrival in a strange place a little bit of an occasion – as it should be.' *(Roland Huntford)*

Open: All year.
Rooms: 85 double, 53 single, 5 suites – 81 with bath, 62 with shower, all with telephone, radio and TV; baby-listening on request.
Facilities: Lift; large lobby with winter garden, library/bar, restaurant, grill, TV room, night club. English spoken.

Location: In town centre (front rooms may be noisy); parking nearby.
Credit cards: Access/Euro/Mastercard, American Express, Diners.
Terms: Rooms with breakfast 525–575 Nkr (single), 750–1,100 Nkr (double).
Full *alc* 200 Nkr. Special weekend rates. Reduced rates for children sharing
parents' room; special meals provided.

OSLO 1   Map 7

Hotel Continental   *Telephone:* (02) 41.90.60
Stortingsgaten 24/26   *Telex:* 71012

'Oslo has, more than any other European capital, preserved the traditions
and atmosphere of the 19th century. The *Continental*, centrally situated
opposite the National Theatre, preserves the grave dignity, courtesy and
friendly warmth which visitors to Norway, who are privileged to count
Norwegians as their friends and business associates, so much appreciate.
This ambience is as much represented in restaurants and the famous
Theatercaféen as in the size and comfort of the rooms which however lack
no modern amenities. The Theatercaféen would deserve a star, if such
could be awarded to an establishment of this kind – certainly not "Vienna-
style" as the hotel's brochure will have it, but truly 19th-century Norwegian; many of the regular habitués seem to be Ibsen's contemporaries. A
three-piece "orchestra" led by a nonagenarian pianist/composer, enhances this atmosphere. I could wax even more lyrical in remembering the
breakfast's cold table.' *(Arnold Horwell)*

Open: All year. Restaurant closed Christmas Day.
Rooms: 127 double, 40 single, 12 suites – all with bath, telephone, radio and
colour TV.
Facilities: 2 lifts, TV room, salons, bar, 3 dining rooms; banqueting facilities;
disco 6 evenings a week. English spoken.
Location: Central, near City Hall and National Theatre; private underground
garage.
Terms: Rooms (including breakfast) 550–600 Nkr (single), 750–850 Nkr
(double). Set meals: lunch 92 Nkr, dinner 110 Nkr. Special weekend rates.

OSLO 1   Map 7

Savoy Hotel   *Telephone:* (02) 20.26.55
Universitetsgaten 11

In the centre of the city opposite the National Gallery and close to a large
national car park. 'Fine for a few nights – old-fashioned, but none the
worse for that, with nice rooms and attentive staff. Adequate and good
value.' *(Tony Morris)*

Open: All year, except Easter, Christmas and New Year.
Rooms: 28 double, 37 single – 31 with bath.
Facilities: Lift; reception, lounges, TV room, bar, dining room, breakfast room.
Location: Central; parking nearby.
Credit cards: All major credit cards accepted.
Terms: B & B 245–295 Nkr.

Øystese Fjord Hotel   *Telephone:* (055) 55600

'Situated on a truly magnificent part of the Hardanger Fjord, about an hour and a half's drive from Bergen. The hotel itself is very comfortable, with three attractively furnished lounges, one of which, together with the dining room and many of the bedrooms, face over the fjord to the Folgefonn glacier. Some of the rooms do however overlook a road which carries some fairly heavy lorries quite early in the morning. Breakfast was a magnificent feast with something for every taste; the evening meal was well cooked and attractively served but to my taste inclined to be dull, although my husband enjoyed it. When 20 or more people are in to lunch Mrs Bjorstad puts on a cold table which was really excellent. On other days lunch is similar to the evening meal, but we plumped for a packed lunch. I was very impressed by this charming lady and her method of speaking to each visitor in their own language – at any rate I recognized English, French and German, and perhaps more.' *(Roslyn Kloegman)*

Open: 1 May–30 September.
Rooms: 18 double, 2 single – 8 with bath, 12 with shower, all with baby-listening. (5 extra rooms in annexe.)
Facilities: 3 lounges (1 with TV), dining room, terrace. Garden. Bathing in fjord from private jetty, rowing boats available. English spoken.
Location: 90 km from Bergen on the E68. (Rooms facing the fjord are quiet.)
Credit card: American Express.
Terms: B & B 165–195 Nkr; dinner, B & B 240–270 Nkr; full board 320–350 Nkr. Packed lunches available. Set meals: lunch 80 Nkr, dinner 75 Nkr; full *alc* 130 Nkr. Children under 3 years, 75% reduction; 3–12 years, 50% reduction. Reduced rates for stays of 5 days or more.

Hotel Utne   *Telephone:* Grimo (054) 669 83

'On the Hardangerfjord – small, out of the way and very special. Its setting is splendid: the foot of a steep promontory where the Hardanger branches into two smaller fjords; high blue mountains across the water; sheer cliffs above it; a waterfall plunging down the cliff face and rushing through the village; apple orchards on each side. There are fine walks along the fjord in both directions. You can walk the quiet road or climb paths to the high pastures. The village is small and quiet. It has a folk museum, a collection of old farm buildings in the ancient (at least medieval) style. There's a leisurely coming and going of steamers and ferries, from the port of Kvanndal across the fjord, from Bergen and other towns along the shores. You can drive up from the south, from the north-west, or come in by steamer or by a combination of bus and ferry.

'The *Hotel Utne*, which takes 40–50 guests, has been in the same family for over 250 years. It stands in the centre of the village, opposite the boat landing. Behind it, on the hillside, is a small modern annexe. Inside, the hotel is like a charming country home, with fine old furniture, painted wood, brass and copper. Meals are hearty and excellent. On Sundays you have a magnificent smorgasbord. Fru Aga Blokhus and her staff, wearing the Hardanger costume, look after you with grace and enthusiasm. You take afternoon tea with the hostess, either in the parlour or, in fine weather, on the terrace, with wide views of water and mountains.' *(Edward W Devlin)*

That report dates from 1978, but has been consistently endorsed by guests since, including, among this year's batch, one who concludes with that clinching cliché: 'We will return!!' Aga Blokhus writes to us about the warning to the socially retiring in last year's entry that guests dine communally in tables set for eight people: 'We usually set the tables for eight, but there are also tables for smaller groups. We believe in mixing people with different nationalities so that they may get to know each other, and the different customs from other parts of the world. We feel our guests appreciate this, and several make friends and continue their journey in Norway together. Usually, language is no problem.' *(R N Elderfield, Ray Hassell)*

Open: All year.
Rooms: 21 double, 5 single – 3 with bath, 10 with shower. 8 rooms in nearby annexe on the hillside. (1 room on ground floor.)
Facilities: Sitting rooms, dining room, games room; some off-season conference facilities; badminton. Garden and terrace; safe bathing in the fjord in front of the hotel; fishing, boating, cycling and good walks. English spoken.
Credit cards: Access/Euro/Mastercard, American Express.
Terms: Rooms with breakfast 152 Nkr (single), 295 Nkr (double); half board 215–238 Nkr; full board 230–255 Nkr. Set meals: lunch 61 Nkr; dinner 62 Nkr. Reduced rates for stays of 5 days and over, and for children.

York House, Lisbon

Portugal

ARMAÇÃO DE PÊRA, 8365 Alcantarilha   **Map 13**

Hotel do Garbe
Av Marginal

Telephone: (0082) 321 87
Telex: 18285

'This four-star, family-run hotel overlooks the beach in a small coastal village between Faro and Lagos (about 40 km in each direction). It is comfortable and friendly, with good public rooms and an excellent restaurant. The bedrooms are reasonably equipped. An elderly and particular cousin who stayed here was very pleased with it. The hotel was well-heated in January, which can be quite cold in the Algarve, whatever the travel agents say. When my cousin said she might come back the following year, she was told that it would be best to book immediately as many of the guests reserve their rooms a year ahead, even in January.' *(D S Smith)*

Open: All year.
Rooms: 90 double, 11 suites, 2 studios – many with bath.
Facilities: Salons, bar, restaurant, air-conditioning; outdoor swimming pool, mini-golf.
Location: Between Faro and Lagos just off the N125.
Credit cards: Barclay/Visa, Eurocard.
Terms: Rooms (including breakfast) 3,500–5,500 esc.

Estalagem Quinta das Torres   *Telephone:* Azeitão (19) 20.80.001

'Azeitão, consisting of two small villages about 1.5 km apart, is on the *old* Lisbon–Setubal main road. It is a good base for the Arrabida peninsula with a beautiful coastline, attractive beaches and the resorts of Sesimbra and Portinho. Palmela complete with castle is nearby. With the motorway and the 25 Abrile Bridge, Lisbon is an easy run (about 40 minutes). Azeitão itself is surrounded by vineyards and olive orchards. You approach the *Quinta* up a long overgrown drive between flowering shrubs. It is a beautiful rather shabby old house in its own grounds with a small ornamental lake against one wall. Our room was off a courtyard as pretty as a stage set, with a fountain in the middle and four fruit-laden orange trees at the corners. The quiet is only broken in the evenings by the competition between bullfrogs, nightingales and cicadas. The whole place is beautifully furnished with old family furniture, portraits, prints, etc. Lovely bowls of flowers everywhere. Our beds were four-posters and the big fireplace was laid ready for an immediate fire with stacks of logs beside it. A log fire blazed in the anteroom to the dining room. The food was delicious – original and well-cooked, and that very dicey Portuguese speciality, *bacalhau*, is here cooked deliciously. The *vinho de casa* is from the local vineyards. Breakfast started with huge glasses of fresh squeezed orange juice, hot rolls and big jars of honey.' *(Mrs R B Richards)*

A recent visitor, endorsing the entry, tells us that the two elderly ladies who own the hotel speak French, English and German, and the receptionist and head waiter also speak some English.

Open: All year.
Rooms: 9 double, 3 single, 2 suites – 10 with bath, all with tea-making facilities. 2 bungalows serving as annexe.
Facilities: Lounges, bar, restaurant; 30 acres grounds; 17 km to sandy beaches. English spoken.
Location: 27 km from Lisbon off the N10; in village centre; parking.
Terms (no fixed service charge): B & B 1,600–1,800 esc. Set meals: lunch/dinner 900 esc; full *alc* 900 esc. Reduced rates for children under 8; special meals provided.

Hotel do Elevador   *Telephone:* Braga (0023) 250 11
Parque do Bom Jesus do Monte

'Few tourists seem to come to the Minho, a mistake in my opinion as this tender green *vinho verde* country is glorious to drive through and has some interesting old towns and villages. There aren't many good places to stay if you want to avoid the ugly modern hotels that sprawl along the Costa Verde, apart from the old-style Portuguese hotels at Bom Jesus, a 19th-century religious shrine on top of the mountain at Braga. Braga itself, while crowded and busy, has enough historic buildings to merit one day's sightseeing, but Bom Jesus is a gem, spectacularly designed and landscaped, with stone terraces and larger-than-life statuary, gardens and little round chapels depicting the Stations of the Cross, and at the top a church and hotels, reached either by a funicular or a winding drive through dense and dripping woods. The *Hotel do Elevador*, the best hotel, is small, comfortable, with an old-fashioned elegance and a fantastic view of mountain peaks and the valley. This is more a place for the Portuguese than for tourists so it hasn't been gussied up and spoiled. The menu, alas, is the standard hotel type but the food isn't bad. Certainly the view makes up for uninspired eating and there's a good selection of the regional wines. The hotel is unique in terms of location and ambience, and definitely shouldn't be missed if you are travelling in the north.' *(Jose Wilson; also Mr and Mrs C Billings)*

Open: All year.
Rooms: 25 double – all with bath.
Facilities: Restaurant. Garden.
Location: 50 km from Oporto.
Credit card: Barclay/Visa.
Terms: Double rooms (including breakfast) 2,250–3,540 esc; full board 3,200–3,700 esc. Set meals 720–830 esc.

BATALHA, 2240 Leiria   Map 13

Estalagem do Mestre Afonso Domingues   *Telephone:* (0044) 962 60

'This *estalagem* (inn) is just off the Lisbon–Oporto road, about halfway between Lisbon and Coimbra. It faces the spectacular Abbey of Batalha, a national monument, and is also near a number of interesting places such as Nazaré and Fatima. We have stayed there a number of times before when exploring this part of Portugal. It also is conveniently situated as a stopping place when journeying from the Algarve to north Portugal. It is one of the only two inns in Portugal classified as five-star. It is very well-appointed but is too small to be classed as a hotel so the price of its rooms is much lower. It has an excellent restaurant. The service is friendly and competent. It is very popular so one usually has to make a booking some weeks ahead.' *(LMS)*

Open: All year.
Rooms: 42 double – many with bath.
Facilities: Bar, restaurant, air-conditioning.
Location: Just off the E3 between Lisbon and Coimbra.
Terms: Double rooms with breakfast 1,000–2,900 esc.

BUÇACO, 3050 Mealhada, Aveiro   Map 13

Palace Hotel do Buçaco   *Telephone:* (0031) 931 01
Mata do Buçaco

'This "de luxe" hotel is fantastic, in all senses of the word. It was a 19th-century royal hunting lodge, built with extreme examples of Manueline architecture. It stands in a large park on the Buçaco ridge, which is planted with a magnificent selection of trees, particularly "cedars of Buçaco" *(Cupressus lusitanica)* which are world famous. Originally, the park was planted by the Carmelite monks, whose monastery stands beside the hotel. Wellington spent the night in one of the monastery cells before the battle of Buçaco, when he defeated the French attempt to capture Lisbon and throw the English out of Portugal. Buçaco is only 20 km from Coimbra, a lovely university city but without a good hotel. There are also

491

a number of interesting places in the neighbourhood so it makes a good centre for exploring this part of Portugal.' *(DS)*

Open: All year.
Rooms: 60 double, 2 suites – all with bath and telephone.
Facilities: Salons, bar, restaurant, conference facilities. Garden and park, tennis court.
Location: 20 km N of Coimbra on the N234; parking.
Credit cards: Access/Euro/Mastercard, Barclay/Visa.
Terms: B & B 2,600–4,200 esc; full board 4,500–6,000 esc. Set meals: lunch/dinner 930 esc; full *alc* 1,200 esc.

CANAS DE SENHORIM, 3520 Nelas Map 13

Hotel Urgeiriça *Telephone:* (032) 67267/8

'This hotel would make a good centre for visiting the interesting town of Viseu and exploring the great mountain range of the Serra de Estrela. It is about 4 km from Nelas on the Coimbra road, though set well back so that road traffic is not disturbing. But the railway line from Coimbra does run nearby so light sleepers might be disturbed two or three times in the night. It must have been a great holiday centre at its height. Nowadays the golf course, tennis courts and swimming pool are unusable and the neglected gardens, with their beautiful trees, have a nostalgic air. However, the hotel itself has been maintained to a high standard and the lovely furniture gleams; there are flowers everywhere. There are pleasant public rooms and the bedrooms are large and well furnished (all with private bathroom). The staff were friendly and most helpful, even managing to find someone to repair our car's exhaust on a Saturday afternoon, when all garages in Portugal are officially closed. The dining room was pleasant and the menu adequate, though limited. There was a good, inexpensive, wine list. The hotel was remarkable value, with a double room and continental breakfast costing 1,500 esc (about £11.50) a night and a three-course meal 300 esc (about £2.30) [1982].' *(DSS)*

Open: All year.
Rooms: 54 double, 3 suites – all with bath, shower and telephone. (Some rooms on ground floor.)
Facilities: Lounges, card room, TV room, bar, dining room. 14 acres grounds. English spoken.
Location: 14 miles from Viseu. On National Highway No. 234, between Mealhada and the frontier at Vilar Formoso. Parking.
Credit cards: Access/Euro/Mastercard, American Express, Barclay/Visa.
Terms: B & B 1,000–1,600 esc; dinner, B & B 1,540–2,100 esc; full board, 1,960–2,600 esc. Set meals: lunch/dinner 504 esc. Reduced rates for groups of 10 or more. 50% reduction for children up to 8 years old; special meals on request.

CANIÇADA, Vieira do Minho, 4850 Braga Map 13

Pousada de São Bento *Telephone:* (0023) 571 90

'After a day exploring the huge market of Barcelos, the provincial cathedral town of Braga and the rococo gardens of the pilgrimage centre of Bom Jesus, the *Pousada de São Bento*, high above the Caniçada dam in the mountains towards the Spanish border, gives a welcome feeling of rest. It is in the south-western end of the Peneda-Geres National Park and a perfect place to pass the night – or more nights if one is in search of wildlife. It is situated 2 km or so off the Braga to Chaves road, with a stupendous view of the river valley and reservoirs below and the surrounding mountain ranges. Built as an alpine chalet, the *Pousada* is small and welcoming and a smell of pine and eucalyptus wafts throughout. Our room was modest in size but very clean and had a pretty view through the ivy-clad windows. The service was attentive, but the food unmemorable.' *(Eleo and Peter Carson)*

Another recent visitor adds a gloss or two on the above: 'The service is first class and the food in the dining room very good. The furnishings are pleasant and the bedrooms well-equipped. One should ask for a room looking outwards when booking (which is essential) as the rooms facing onto the courtyard can be rather noisy. There is a pleasant terrace overlooking the lake and a comfortable sitting room with television. There is no night life as it is in an isolated position. There are some walks, though these are rather steep, and there is a very pleasant and well maintained garden.' *(DSS)*

Open: All year.
Rooms: 22 – most with bath and telephone.
Facilities: Lounge with TV, restaurant, terrace. Garden with swimming pool and tennis court; sailing and riding nearby.
Location: 34 km from Braga.
Terms: Room (including breakfast) 1,980–4,440 esc. Set meals: lunch/dinner from 555 esc.

ESTREMOZ, 7100 Evora Map 13

Pousada de Rainha Santa Isabel *Telephone:* Estremoz 226 18
Largo D. Dinaz – Castelo de Estremoz

Estremoz, on the road from Lisbon to Badajoz, has a busy market, a barracks, a bull ring, interesting local pottery, a museum (devoted to clay figurines which are a speciality of the town) and many marble quarries. But it also has a *pousada* converted from a 13th-century castle, the chief residence of King Diniz. The *pousada* is named after his wife Isabel, who was both queen and saint. Last year, a correspondent described it as one of the two best *pousadas* in Portugal, a view to which the writer below clearly subscribes:

'The castle has been completely, expertly and expensively restored to its former glories. Every public room and bedroom is an historical experience that boggles the mind. Each room is furnished with compatible antiques – real ones. To those who don't know, it should be pointed out that many of the *pousadas* have been restored by the Government as *objets d'art* and are run at a massive loss, to the unbelievable benefit of the visitors. This *pousada* is the best, and the loss to Government must be huge. And the restaurant. A vaulted and beamed baronial hall with impeccable service and fine food at a give-away price. The place to go for the historically-minded gourmet. Oh, Estremoz isn't very interesting – but who cares!' *(John M Sidwick)*

Open: All year.
Rooms: 20 double, 3 suites – all with bath and telephone.

Facilities: Lounge, TV room, restaurant, bar; some conference facilities, air-conditioning. Garden.
Location: In town centre; parking for 40 cars.
Terms: Double rooms (including breakfast) 2,400–3,720 esc. Set meals: lunch/dinner from 721 esc.

LISBON, 1100   **Map 13**

Albergaria Senhora do Monte   *Telephone:* (19) 86.28.46,
Calçada do Monte 39   86.28.67 and 87.17.34

'An unassuming small hotel with a family feeling, run by cordial, helpful people. The reception-cum-TV room is a bit cramped, but the guest rooms are pleasant – flowered wallpaper, and a nice old-fashioned feeling. It is located in the older part of Lisbon; it feels off the tourist beat since the area is residential – roosters crowing in the morning, lettuce in the little backyard gardens. There's a bar but no restaurant – breakfast is brought to your bedrooms; there are several small, untouristy restaurants at the end of the street as well as the wonderful Lisbon streetcars to everywhere. I've saved the best till last: the hotel is almost at the top of one of the Lisbon hills with a simply magnificent view over the city and the river Tejo. The view, the interesting and convenient location and the welcoming attitude of the staff make me prize the *Albergaria Senhora do Monte* as one of the pleasantest hotels I've ever stayed in – well worth its modest cost.' *(Lucia M Atlas)*

Open: All year.
Rooms: 18 double, 5 single, 4 suites – all with bath.
Facilities: Reception/TV room, bar.
Location: Central; parking.
Credit cards: Access/Euro/Mastercard, American Express.
Terms: B & B 900–1,600 esc. (No restaurant.) Reduced rates for children.

LISBON, 1200   **Map 13**

Hotel Tivoli Jardim   *Telephone:* (19) 53.99.71
Rua Julio Cesar Machado 7   Telex: 12172

We had our first entry last year for this modern multi-storey hotel just off the main central avenue of Lisbon, the Avenida da Liberdade. (*Warning:* it should not be confused with the sister-hotel, the *Tivoli* next door.) Here is another view, equally enthusiastic:

'It is immensely useful to know of a really good and not too costly an hotel in the centre of any city. The *Tivoli Jardim*, placed with immense convenience right in the heart of Lisbon, fulfils both these qualifications and also offers a great deal more, that makes it a genuine pleasure to stay there.

'Being in the city centre, it has no spectacular views (other than the roofs of Lisbon, if like us, you were on the eleventh floor), but in all the ambience of its public rooms it is elegant and welcoming from the moment you come in off the bustling streets. The bedrooms are exceptionally comfortable and well provided, even to a slot machine affair that will set your bed to massaging you when you come in exhausted after your rounds of sightseeing. The service, both in the public rooms and for room service, we found prompt and unfailingly kind and helpful, and it did not take long for us to regard this hotel as a sort of haven to which we came back gladly from our long days of walking in Cascais and Estoril and Sintra, all of which are easily accessible by tours or bus or train if you do not have a car. The most praiseworthy aspect of the hotel, however, we thought to be the food. Being two females escorted only by a gentleman of twelve, we thought it better not to venture into the streets at night, and never for one moment regretted our decision to stay home for dinner. Cuisine, presentation and service in the restaurant fell no way short of excellent. Beautiful food. Fine Portuguese wines, and kind, attentive service. We were recommended to this hotel by a hotel manager, who told us it was the place where hotel managers themselves went to stay. There is no doubt that they know what they are about.' *(Madeleine Polland)*

Open: All year.
Rooms: 119 double – all with bath, telephone, radio, air-conditioning and TV on request.
Facilities: Main hall with bar, TV room, restaurant; 12 km to beach. 90% of staff speak English.
Location: 10 minutes from town centre; garage and car park.
Terms: Rooms (including breakfast) 3,300–8,100 esc.

LISBON 1200   **Map 13**

York House (Residencia Inglesia)   *Telephone:* (19) 66.24.35/
Rua des Janelas Verdes, 32   66.73.98

A small two-part hotel on opposite sides of the road which contains the National Art Museum and looks down over the cranes of the docks. A little off the central track, but a tram passes every few minutes and Lisbon taxis are wonderfully cheap. The main part of the hotel, containing about 44 rooms and set back from the road under trees round a courtyard, was an early 17th-century convent; later it became a hospital, and then the Protestant cathedral in Lisbon. The lower dining room was the former chapel, still complete with font and marble plaques. It has been the haunt of writers: Graham Greene stayed here, and it was the home of Antonio Nobre, the Portuguese poet; it is still much patronized by professional people, artists and writers. In the building there is much use of *azulejos*, traditional tiles, many placed round window seats and along the upper dining room. There are polished red tile floors in the rooms and huge wooden wardrobes. Along the corridors are blue and white Arraiolos rugs. The rooms that once housed the novitiates are still the cheapest. Across the street is the other part of the hotel, decorated in *belle époque* French style with lots of red plush, bric-à-brac, framed period photos and gold-plated taps in the bathrooms. 'It certainly has charm and character. It was once a convent, and it retains a feel of those origins in *very* hard beds and very plain food. But otherwise the furnishings are beautiful and antique, and shining and spotless. The lighting is particularly good. One enters through a doorway set into a high wall and winds up shallow steps to a most delightful courtyard garden, where breakfast, tea and drinks are served under the shade of huge and beautiful trees. Some bedrooms face this courtyard: if you are a light sleeper, you must certainly not take a room above the road which is noisy all night. We sampled dinner on one night only: no choice, and, as we have said, exceedingly plain. We found it much more fun to eat in little restaurants nearby which, like the taxis, are idiotically cheap. But we would certainly come here again.' *(Ray and Angela Evans)*

Open: All year.
Rooms: 47 double, 10 single, 5 suites – 45 with bath, 17 with shower, all with telephone and TV. 18 rooms in annexe.
Facilities: TV room, bridge room, 2 bars (1 in annexe), restaurant. English spoken.
Location: In city centre; no special parking facilities.
Credit cards: All major credit cards accepted.
Terms: Rooms, 1,400–2,500 esc. Set meals: lunch/dinner 480 esc.

MADEIRA, Funchal, 9000   **Map 13**

Quinta de Penha de França   *Telephone:* 29087
Rua da Penha de França 2

'This small *Albergaria* is an attractive period mini-manor house, tucked away behind a walled garden in a quiet area of Funchal; not actually right *on* the sea, but so near it it might just as well be – and with an interesting view of the harbour to one side. The house has been most skilfully adapted – without spoiling its charm, and the lovely sub-tropical garden also contains several attractive small bungalows discreetly arranged so as not to obtrude too much and spoil the whole. It is a real oasis of peace and quiet – in a fast-growing town, the absolute antithesis of the large hotels dotted around and above it. The *Quinta* provides only bed and breakfast, which happened to suit us very well, and there are three restaurants within staggering distance, and many rather better ones in the town proper – for the cost of a 60p taxi ride. Our bedroom was spacious with attractive furniture and curtains. Ample drawer and wardrobe space, and two nice little easy chairs. Intriguing antiques around too. It is just like someone's elegant home, which indeed it is. The rather beautiful Senhora Ribeiro, whose husband is a practising doctor, was born here and is a charming and attentive hostess. Breakfast can be served in your room or the tiny dining room, or better still out on the terrace, weather permitting. "Continental" is inclusive – but you can have almost anything you like – including porridge! – at extra charge. Vast sandwiches (toasted or otherwise) can be obtained at lunchtime in the garden if you wish, and the senhora's rather dishy son runs two pleasant bars within yards, one up behind with its own pretty terrace – *Joe's Bar* – and another literally poised over the sea on the edge of the road below and aptly named Bar on the Rocks. Altogether a delightful spot for a peaceful holiday and it is deservedly popular. There were at least five nationalities represented there, so obviously its fame has spread. The atmosphere is informal and friendly, and the Senhora has a well-trained staff of both sexes. Cheerful chambermaids work swiftly in pairs. Beds are turned down in the evening and nightclothes arranged with dainty waistlines – even husbands' (hilarious in our case!). There was only one snag, and I do admit we are specially susceptible to cold: the main house was unheated (though electric fires are supplied in the bungalows, I believe) and 64 degrees wasn't quite enough for us, personally, in our bedroom. However, in better weather, or perhaps a little later in the year (we were there in January) natural solar heating through the windows would be more than enough. Funchal is getting built up – like everything else, and the roads are at times quite appalling. But the flowers – even in January – are a delight, and everything else that grows. The mountainous interior is really breathtaking and still unspoilt. We didn't regret going a second time. There is much to see and one can just lie all day in great comfort in that tranquil garden.' *(Lady Elstub)*

Open: All year.
Rooms: 22 – 18 with bath, 4 with shower, all with telephone and baby-listening; 3 with cooking facilities. (8 rooms on ground floor.)
Facilities: Lounge, TV room. Large garden with sea-water swimming pool; near sea and rock beach. English spoken.
Location: 1 km from town centre; parking.
Terms: B & B £13–18. 50% reduction for children aged 2–8 sharing parents' room.

MARVÃO, 7330 Portalagre   **Map 13**

Pousada de Santa Maria   *Telephone:* (0045) 932 01

'Marvão lies about 6 km north and about 600 m above the road from Abrantes and the valley of the Tagus into Spain. The village, of tiny white houses and narrow cobbled streets, is entirely inside the walls of a castle whose keep sits above the village. It is possible to walk round the ramparts in about half an hour, looking within at the roofs, gardens, chicken runs, kitchen and television sets, or without, over the Sierra de Torrico in Spain, and the valleys below in Portugal. The *Pousada*, like everything else in Marvão, is tiny. There are eight rooms, the building is of stone with tile floors, the public rooms are well-furnished, the beds comfortable, you can see to read, and the hot water is dependable. As befits, the staff is small (when we were there meals tended to be later than the advertised times) but amiable. There is absolutely no nightlife or entertainment to be had, but the view from the bar is fine, and the local wine excellent. The price was very reasonable. If you favour quiet, remoteness, walking, reading, then Marvão will do very well; children might get bored, and there are no great sights within 50 km or so. The Portuguese know their state hotels are good and use them – so make reservations.' *(Dugal Campbell; endorsed by DS, with special praise for the restaurant – 'best crayfish dish we have ever had')*

Open: All year.
Rooms: 8 double – all with bath and telephone.
Facilities: Lounge/bar, restaurant. Garden. Riding, shooting nearby.
Location: 22 km N of Portalagre on the N521.
Credit cards: All major credit cards accepted.
Terms: Double rooms (including breakfast) 2,300 esc; full board 5,200 esc. Set meals: lunch/dinner 610–720 esc.

We ask hotels to estimate their 1983 tariffs some time before publication so the rates given here are not necessarily completely accurate. Please *always* check terms with hotels when making bookings. Portuguese prices are more approximate than most.

Estalagem Abrigo de Montanha   *Telephone:* (0082) 921 31
Corte Dereira/Estrada de Foia

'This *estalagem* is half way between the little hill town of Monchique
(about 25 km from Portimão) and the peak of Foia. It is about 1,500 feet
up with magnificent views over the hills and lush valleys with infinite
variety of green. There is a main building and a long tier of separate
apartments at the other end of a pretty garden. Wonderful mixture of
flowers. It is family-owned and run – and the employed couple who are
waiter/concierge and chambermaid respectively – are of a charm, intelligence, and sweet gentleness unparalleled. Good English spoken throughout (and French and German). We had a bedroom, a bathroom, a sitting
room with a fireplace, and a roof garden. Prices extraordinarily reasonable. Flowers were put in our room and we were told they would have lit a
fire for us had we asked. The coffee – best I have ever had outside
anyone's home – was ground when one appeared in the dining room.
When they found we liked the local honey, it was always on the table. We
ate dinner there quite frequently – wonderfully fresh fish but the menu
would become monotonous quite soon. However, they asked us once or
twice if we would be in and then served some interesting local specialities.
Hot water more reliable in the main hotel rooms, which are also cheaper
(but smaller and lacking a balcony) than the annexe suites. *Warning:* it
can be cold and wet in Monchique even when blazing on the coast.' *(Mrs R
B Richards)*
     The above entry has recently been warmly endorsed by a correspon-
dent who developed a serious fever while staying at the *estalagem*: 'The
management went out of their way to help and finally sent us off with a
bottle of good port. The regional specialities on the menu are excellent,
incidentally, and well worth the extra price.' *(Professor J M Mitchison)*

Open: All year except New Year.
Rooms: 6 double – all with bath and telephone. 4 suites in annexe.
Facilities: Salon with TV, dining room. Garden, terrace. English spoken.
Location: About 25 km inland from Portimão. Hotel is 2 km on the road to Foia
from Monchique; parking.
Terms: B & B 900–1,000 esc. Set meals: lunch/dinner 500 esc; full *alc* 600 esc.
50% reduction for children under 8.

MURTOSA, 3878 Aveiro   **Map 13**

Pousada da Ria   *Telephone:* (0034) 483 32
Ria de Aveiro   *Telex:* 26061

'A modern English-speaking *pousada*, standing on a peninsula between
the sea and the Aveiro lagoon. It has well-furnished rooms, each with a
covered balcony looking over the lagoon, so even if it is rainy, one can sit
and watch the local sailing boats going by. The hotel entrance exhibits a
number of recommendations from various gourmet clubs of different
countries; they are well-deserved. This is an ideal place for anyone
wanting a restful time, particularly if they are interested in sea birds. Its
only disadvantage is that it is 30 km from Aveiro, the nearest town of any
size, by road, though it is only about 3 km across the water.' *(D S Smith)*

Open: All year.
Rooms: 10 double, 2 suites – all with bath, telephone and balcony.
Facilities: Salon, TV room, restaurant. Garden; outdoor swimming pool. Near river with fishing; beach 2 km (but sea a bit rough). English spoken.
Location: Take N109 N from Aveiro; then turn W towards Torreira, then fork left to Murtosa; parking.
Credit cards: All major credit cards accepted.
Terms: B & B 1,165–2,200 esc; dinner, B & B 1,830–2,870 esc; full board 2,500–3,530 esc. Set meals: lunch/dinner 610–720 esc.

OLIVEIRA DO HOSPITAL, 3400 Coimbra   Map 13

Pousada de Santa Barbara   *Telephone:* (0037) 522 52
Póvoa das Quartas

'This modern government-owned inn is on the Coimbra–Salamanca road, about 80 km east of Coimbra, and 7 km east of the small town of Oliviera do Hospital. It has a magnificent view of the 6,600 feet high Serra do Estrela, the highest mountain range in Portugal, and it is a good base from which to explore this area. The rooms are standard hotel type, with baths. There are excellent public rooms. The service is essentially friendly and helpful and the cooking first-class. We always enjoy a visit here.' *(D S Smith)*

Open: All year.
Rooms: 16 double – all with bath, telephone, colour TV and tea-making facilities.
Facilities: Sitting room, TV room, restaurant. Large garden with tennis and fishing. English spoken.
Location: On the Coimbra–Salamanca road about 80 km E of Coimbra and 7 km E of Oliviera do Hospital.
Credit cards: All major credit cards accepted.
Terms: Double room with breakfast 2,200–2,300 esc; full board 3,400–4,800 esc. Set meals: 610–720 esc. Reduced rates and special meals for children.

OPORTO, 4465   Map 13

Estalagem Via Norte   *Telephone:* (02) 948 02 94
Leça do Bolio

'This five-star *estalagem* lies about 10 km north of Oporto on the main dual carriageway from the city; it is about 4 km from the airport. It provides an ideal overnight stopping place for those who wish to avoid the horrors of the central Oporto traffic system. Although the *estalagem* is on a main road, it is very well designed and there was little traffic noise in either the bedrooms or public rooms. The restaurant is comfortable and has a good menu; our food was excellent. The staff are friendly and efficient. There is a comfortable bar. Our only criticism: it seemed rather short staffed, except in the restaurant, and we had to carry our own baggage. This may have been because we were there at a weekend, when there are few guests staying the night; the *estalagem* offers a 20% discount on rooms for Friday and Saturday nights. *(DSS)*

Open: All year.
Rooms: 12 – most with bath and telephone.

Facilities: Lounge, bar, restaurant, conference facilities; swimming pool; parking.
Credit cards: All major credit cards accepted.
Terms: Rooms 2,665–3,200 esc; full board 3,605–4,770 esc. Set meals: breakfast 177 esc; lunch/dinner 1,000 esc.

OPORTO, 4000　　　　　　　　　　　　　　　　　　　　　　Map 13

Infante de Sagres　　　　　　　　　　　*Telephone:* (02) 281.01
Praça D Filipa de Lencastre 62　　　　　　*Telex:* 22378 Sagres P

'A splendid old-style Anglo-Portuguese hotel, in the centre of the city, with a magnificent table and dining room, comfortable bedrooms and attentive service. Superb ports and the best *vinho verdes* outside the Tras es Montes. A poor bar, however, and very slow breakfasts and room service. But the British connection still appreciated.' *(MW)*

Open: All year.
Rooms: 78 double, 2 single, 4 suites – all with bath, telephone and radio.
Facilities: Lifts, 2 lounges, bar, dining room; conference room. Terraces. English spoken.
Location: In town centre, near Town Hall; parking nearby.
Credit cards: All major credit cards accepted.
Terms: B & B 2,600–4,800 esc. Set meals: lunch/dinner 1,300 esc; full *alc* 2,100 esc. Special rates for groups. 50% reduction for children under 8 when sharing parents' room, and special meals on request. 30% weekend discount on B & B price.

PALMELA, 2950 Costa de Lisboa　　　　　　　　　　　　　Map 13

Pousada do Castelo de Palmela　　　　*Telephone:* (01) 253.13.95/6
　　　　　　　　　　　　　　　　　　　　Telex: 42290 PPALM P

Palmela is about an hour's drive south from Lisbon; the *Pousada* makes a useful stopover for those en route to the Algarve. Recent correspondents endorse the entry below, though with reservations about the restaurant, the 'grudging' service and the heating in a chilly April. 'When you lean out of the window on a spring day, perfumes in the air will stop you in your tracks – which is just as well as the drop from your window ledge looks to be several hundred feet. This *pousada*, opened in 1980, is a transformed monastery inside a 1,000-year-old castle. We had anticipated a sort of Tower of London with beds, but there was no hint of discomfort. The bed, the bath, the restaurant, the cloisters – set out with flowers, deck-chairs and umbrellas – were downright glamorous. The castle is perched on top of a hill and you can see for miles, even sitting on the loo. The landscape is of windmills, orange groves and the distant shore. Things in the vicinity not to miss: the sound of sheep bells as the flock is brought down the castle hill in the evening; the Paradise garden at Quinta del Bacalhoa, the white crescent of beach at Portinho where the restaurant has its feet in the water; and the luxurious tearoom at Quintande las Torres where we wondered why it took 40 minutes for our tea to come only to discover they were baking our brioches. We thought the restaurant splendid. The olives on the table were to olives what the Muscatel is to the grape.' *(Shelley Cranshaw)*

Open: All year.
Rooms: 25 double, 2 suites – all with bath, telephone and radio.
Facilities: Lift, lounge, breakfast room, bar, dining room, TV room. Large grounds with children's play area. Sandy beaches with safe bathing 15 km; river 7 km with fishing and sailing facilities.
Location: 7 km from Setúbal; parking for 40 cars.
Credit cards: All major credit cards accepted.
Terms: Rooms with breakfast 3,500–3,700 esc; full board 5,200–7,000 esc. Set meals: lunch/dinner 720–830 esc.

PRAIA DA ROCHA, 8500 Portimão　　　　　　　　　　　　　**Map 13**

Hotel Bela Vista　　　　　　　　　　*Telephone:* (0082) 24055
Av Tomas Cabreira

'A famous old hotel on the cliff top of Praia da Rocha, the Algarve's Edwardian watering-place a mile out of Portimão. The *Bela Vista* is now overshadowed by large modern hotels built recently, but it is still an oasis of calm, surrounded by palm trees. The food is very good, and the service personal and friendly. Some of the bedrooms are small, but they are all well-equipped.' *(LMS)*

Open: All year.
Rooms: 27 – 24 double, 2 single, 1 suite – 22 with bath, 5 with shower, all with telephone. (1 room on ground floor.)
Facilities: Lounge, TV room, games room, bar. Garden. English spoken.
Location: 2 km from town centre; parking.
Terms: Rooms (including breakfast) 3,300–3,900 esc. (No restaurant.) Off-season breaks available. Reduced rates for children.

SINTRA, 2710 Lisbon　　　　　　　　　　　　　　　　　　**Map 13**

Estalagem Quinta dos Lobos　　　*Telephone:* (19) 293.02.10 or 293.13.30

The small town of Sintra, only 24 km from Lisbon, is well worth a night's stop. It has a dramatically beautiful setting, built against the north face of the *serra*. There is one royal palace in the town itself, and another, a folly of Fernando II, built like an eagle's nest on one of the nearby peaks. The *Quinta dos Lobos* is an early 17th-century manor house, built by the Knights Templar from Tomar, with a 15th-century manorial annexe built by the Duke of Cadval. Both buildings have extensive grounds with stunning views – of the Atlantic coast, of the Serra of Sintra and of the plain below. 'An absolutely delightful inn, small, intimate and charmingly decorated with great taste. The owners speak English, and the inn has been converted from a private house. Breakfast only is served. There are lovely antiques and paintings, and the place has the air of a country house. It's very comfortable, with enchanting bedrooms, bathrooms that are both modern and good-looking, and all kinds of interesting touches, such as black-painted old wrought-iron benches as seats in the bar, and huge massed arrangements of blue agapanthus in big jars.' *(Jose Wilson; endorsed by D S Smith)*

Open: All year.
Rooms: 16 double, 2 suites – all with bath, telephone, TV and tea-making facilities. 8 rooms in annexe. (2 rooms on ground floor.)
Facilities: 3 lounges (1 with TV), 2 bars, breakfast room. Terraces. Large grounds with croquet, swimming pool. 10 minutes from beach; riding, tennis and golf nearby. English spoken.
Location: 28 km from Lisbon. Take the Seteais road from the old palace and turn right at Estalagem sign.
Terms: Rooms with breakfast 1,800–2,000 esc (single), 2,200–2,800 esc (double). (No restaurant.)

VALENCA DO MINHO, 4930 Viana do Castelo   Map 13

Pousada de São Teotónio   *Telephone:* (0021) 222 52

'This welcoming and efficiently-run *pousada* is built on the 17th-century ramparts of a Vaubanesque frontier fortress and commands a splendid view of the Minho river-frontier with Spain, Eiffel's road and rail bridge and the Spanish cathedral citadel of Tuy. The pleasant modern rooms in the main hotel share that view with the airy and comfortable lounge and restaurant. The *pousada* is well placed for a night or two's stop on the main road into Portugal from the north. Valenca itself is pretty if trippery. The Minho valley offers gentle classical landscapes and vinho verde. The service was quite excellent.' *(Eleo and Peter Carson)*

Open: All year.
Rooms: 22 – most with bath and telephone.
Facilities: Lounge, restaurant.
Location: On Portuguese/Spanish frontier, 37 km from Viana do Castelo, on E50.
Credit cards: All major credit cards accepted.
Terms: Rooms with breakfast 3,050–3,220 esc; full board 4,385–5,885 esc. Set meals: lunch/dinner 665–775 esc.

Hotel Alhambra Palace, Granada

Spain

ALARCÓN, Cuenca **Map 13**

Parador Nacional Marqués de Villena *Telephone:* (966) 33.13.50

There has been a castle overlooking Alarcón for many centuries; it was substantially rebuilt in the 14th century, later it fell into disrepair, but was to some extent restored during the Civil War. Now the remains of the original fortress have been turned into a comfortable *parador*, enjoying stunning views of the town, the river Júcar cutting through its deep gorge, and the rolling plains of Cuenca. 'My favourite *parador*. Not as big or as grand as Jaén or Cardona, but less messed about with – more original: a still defiant symbol of an independent and contumacious aristocracy in a kingdom stricken by faction. If you want bright lights, a disco, bars, somewhere to go at night – stay away. Once the sun goes down it is pretty dark in Alarcón; there is no disco, only one tiny bar and one small souvenir shop.' *(Jeff Driver)*

Open: 21 December–31 October.
Rooms: 10 double, 1 single – all with bath and telephone.
Facilities: Lift; salon with TV, bar, restaurant, terraces. Garden surrounded by remains of old walls. 5 km from lake with sailing and fishing. English spoken.
Location: 87 km S of Cuenca just off the N111; parking.
Credit cards: All major credit cars accepted.
Terms: B & B 2,350–3,150 pts; dinner, B & B 3,400–4,250 pts; full board 4,000–4,850 pts. Set meals: lunch/dinner 1,100 pts.

Hotel Albarracín   *Telephone:* (974) 71.00.71
Calle Azagra

'Albarracín is a little jewel of a town on the edge of the Montes Universales, which to my mind is one of the most beautiful parts of Spain – a vast empty area of forest and mountains, most of which is a state-controlled hunting reserve. Approaching the town from the Cuenca side, you go through the bottom of a gorge, sheer cliffs on either side of you, by the side of a trout stream. Then, without any warning, the road just runs right into a cliff: a great soaring wall of grey rock through which there is a tunnel about 100 metres long. On the other side is Albarracin, clinging by a brick and an odd nail or two to the cliff face. The houses are built on the side of this precipice: two storeys on the street side, and six high at the back. We asked the way to the *Hotel Albarracín*, and the man pointed vertically up into the sky. It was perched on top of an overhang, about 100 feet above the road. The streets are spattered with arms emblazoned, renaissance mini-palaces, and houses with balconies where the occupants can easily shake hands with the people living opposite. The city walls are in the process of being carefully restored. The Spanish government has declared the whole town a national monument, but it is not in the least bit tourist spoiled. As for the hotel, it is a small modern place, clean and well-furnished. There's a bit of a swimming pool but it did not seem to be much used when I was there in June. The food is quite good for Spain. It is very adequate indeed – but I go there because of its situation more than anything else.' *(Jeff Driver)*

Open: All year.
Rooms: 30 – all with bath, telephone and baby-listening.
Facilities: Salon, 2 restaurants; garden with swimming pool; direct access to river with bathing and fishing.
Location: 38 km from Teruel. Hotel is in centre of Albarracín; parking.
Credit cards: All major credit cards accepted.
Terms: Rooms 2,850–3,320 pts. Set meals: breakfast 260 pts, lunch/dinner 1,100 pts.

Parador Nacional Casa del Corregidor   *Telephone:* (956) 70.05.00
Plaza de España

This elegant house formerly belonged to a famous mayor *(corregidor)* of Arcos. It was half in ruins when it was acquired by the Spanish government, rebuilt in the style of the original and opened in 1966 as the *Parador Nacional Casa del Corregidor*. It is a fine hotel built round a typical Spanish patio. The thoughtfully furnished rooms look out on to the square or across the Quadalete river to the seemingly endless open country beyond. These latter have huge balconies and are quieter. The pleasant restaurant gives on to a large terrace. The three-course menu offers a good choice of dishes with generous helpings. The *à la carte* includes a commendable number of regional specialities. Pleasant and efficient service. Arcos itself is built on a steep hill which falls sheer away on two sides. The ascent by car to the Plaza de Espana is not for the faint-hearted

– the streets are cobbled, tortuous and narrow with few places to pass an oncoming vehicle, pedestrians have no escape but to jump into an open doorway and the many scooters seem to have priority because they make most noise. But the dangers are amply rewarded on reaching this cool, pleasant hotel with its stunning views and relaxed atmosphere.' *(Geoffrey Sharp; endorsed by the Editor)*

Open: All year.
Rooms: 18 double, 3 single – all with bath and telephone, most with balcony.
Facilities: Lift; salon, bar, dining room, patio, air-conditioning. &.
Location: Between Jerez de la Frontera and Ronda on the N342/C344. Central; no special parking facilities.
Credit cards: All major credit cards accepted.
Terms: Rooms 2,990–4,200 pts. Set meals: breakfast 290 pts, lunch/dinner 1,100 pts.

ÁVILA   Map 13

Parador Nacional Raimundo de Borgoña   *Telephone:* (918) 21.13.40
Marqués de Canales de Chozas 16   21.27.46

'One of the greatest attractions of Ávila are its old city walls, and the *parador* looks across a formal garden to these, and their towers with storks standing in their nests, to the hills beyond – a really lovely outlook. As often with *paradors*, the style is baronial – coats of armour, wide tiled floors, massive wooden and leather furniture. The feeling of space everywhere, particularly in bedrooms and bathrooms was very welcome after the cell-like arrangements of so many hotels, and the really civilized provision of towels and pillows made the place very comfortable. Unfortunately, we found the set dinner dull and mediocre and the service sullen.' *(Mrs R B Richards)*

Open: All year.
Rooms: 59 double, 3 single, 1 suite – all with bath and telephone.
Facilities: Lounges, reading room, TV room, bar, 2 dining rooms. Garden. English spoken.
Location: 500 metres from centre; garage.
Credit cards: All major credit cards accepted.
Terms: Rooms 1,810–4,025 pts. Set meals: breakfast 285 pts, lunch/dinner 1,100 pts.

AYAMONTE, Huelva   Map 13

Parador Nacional Costa de la Luz   *Telephone:* (955) 32.07.00
El Castillito

'The *parador* at Ayamonte is placed at the furthest south-west corner of Spain, with only the river Guadiana between it and Portugal, making it perfectly placed either for a jumping-off ground for a tour of that country or, as we used it, for a turning-point in a tour of some of the loveliest country we have yet seen in Spain. The main characteristic of the *Costa de la Luz* is the wonderful air of peace and tranquillity it offers at the end of a long day's driving. Situated high above the salt marshes of the Guadiana that flood dramatically with gold light at sunset, it is a modern *parador* of notably beautiful design, much enhanced by the use of growing plants like wallpaper. The bedrooms turn their backs on the views, and open instead each on to its own tiny cobbled patio of complete privacy, with one splendid rose bush in it, designed to fill the room at night with perfume. It is impossible to speak highly enough of the charm and the absolute peace and quiet of this unusual arrangement. The beautiful public rooms are almost completely glass-walled and open to the spectacular views over the river and across to Portugal. There is also a charming and strangely old-fashioned small garden. If I have carried on a bit about the building and the ambience, it is because they are really striking, but, as well as these, the *parador* offers all the essential services at very high standard. Good food, boiling bath water and invariably pleasant and attentive service. There are *paradors* more publicized; *paradors* like Jaén more incredibly dramatic; others more beautiful and spectacular. But looking at them for what they are, which is travellers' havens in the course of a long journey, we felt that Ayamonte offered more than most.' *(Madeleine Polland)*

Open: All year, except 12 January–February.
Rooms: 20 – all with bath, telephone and air-conditioning.
Facilities: Salons, bar, dining room. Garden with swimming pool.
Location: 60 km W of Huelva.
Credit cards: All major credit cards accepted.
Terms: Rooms 2,990–4,260 pts. Set meals: breakfast 290 pts; lunch/dinner 1,100 pts.

BAÑALBUFAR, Mallorca   **Map 13**

Mar I Vent   *Telephone:* (971) 61.00.25
José Antonio 49

'Of all the hotels I have seen in Mallorca (and the number runs into hundreds!) this is one of the few that I would very happily return to. It thoroughly deserves its popularity: one of the best-placed hotels on the island if beaches and bright lights are not your priority.' These words from our man in Mallorca are echoed by recent visitors: 'Exactly as described: very good value and really thoughtful attention from the owners who were particularly kind to our children.' *(Daniel Milliard)* 'We endorse all that has been written about this delightful hotel: the Vives family were most welcoming and attentive throughout our stay.' *(Mrs N Hodgson)* We repeat last year's citation:

A brother-and-sister run hotel in a small and peaceful fishing and farming village on the ruggedly picturesque west coast, the most scenic part of the island. There are wonderful views of the sea and cliffs from the hotel and from the swimming pool on the sun terrace below. For those who prefer the sea, there is good bathing from a tiny cove about 15 minutes' stroll by winding pathways through the terraced tomato fields. The hills behind the hotel offer exhilarating walking country. The *Mar I Vent* is one of the oldest hotels on the island, and has been in the same family for four generations. The building was originally 18th-century, and although it has been much renovated and modernized since, it still retains some of the older features, and there is antique furniture in both public and private rooms. Bedrooms are furnished in local style; some are on the small side but they are bright, airy and well cared for. There are only 15 rooms, and it's essential to book throughout the season. The best rooms are usually reserved for the regular clients.

Open: All year, except 1 December–1 February.
Rooms: 15 double – all with bath and telephone. 5 rooms with bath and balcony in annexe.
Facilities: 3 salons (1 with TV), bar/restaurant. Terrace with swimming pool, tennis court. Sea-bathing in nearby coves; fine walks. English spoken.
Location: 24 km NW of Palma, on the edge of the village; parking.
Terms: B & B 995–1,350 pts; dinner, B & B 1,845–2,120 pts; full board 2,200–2,575 pts. Set meals: lunch/dinner 850 pts. 10% reduction for children if sharing parents' room; special meals available.

CARMONA, Seville   Map 13

Parador Nacional Alcazar Del Rey Don Pedro   *Telephone:* (954) 14.10.10

In 1976 the King and Queen of Spain formally opened this *parador*, and it is certainly worthy of a royal opening. It has been built inside the massive walls of the ancient Moorish alcazar on the top of a hill, from which there are marvellous views over the wide green plain of the Guadalquivir valley, with mountains in the northern horizon. Although the actual hotel is new, it has been built in the Spanish renaissance manner, with Moorish influences: pierced wooden shutters and doors in the public rooms, a patio with a fountain in the middle. The walls, whitewashed or of honey-coloured brick, are sparingly punctuated with black or brown wooden and leather furniture. There is a sumptuous sitting room; the dining room is a cool, lofty hall. There is also a swimming pool – a model of good taste, with natural brick and grass surrounds; arcades to protect you from the sun; white painted garden furniture and masses of colourful flowers.

In short, a thoroughly superior example of the *parador* species. All our correspondents have enjoyed their visits, though there have been a few cavils: poor insulation in the bedrooms, for instance, inadequate heating in the public rooms in March and somewhat characterless – perhaps paradorish should be the word – menus. *(Anthony Vestrey, R H Hargreaves)*

Open: All year.
Rooms: 47 double, 7 single – 50 with bath, 5 with shower, all with telephone, some with balcony. (Some rooms on ground floor.)
Facilities: Lifts; hall, sitting room with TV, dining room, room for gatherings and banquets, air-conditioning. Patio and garden with swimming pool. English spoken.
Location: In town centre; parking.
Credit cards: All major credit cards accepted.
Terms: B & B 2,050–3,500 pts; dinner, B & B 3,150–4,600 pts; full board 3,875–5,325 pts. Set meals: lunch/dinner 1,100 pts; full *alc* 1,625 pts. Special meals for children.

CERVERA DE PISUERGA, Palencia   Map 13

Parador Nacional de Fuentes Carrionas   *Telephone:* (988) 87.00.75

'A large slightly gaunt modern *parador* in a magnificent isolated situation in the Cantabrian mountains overlooking woods and a reservoir-lake. Some 2½ hours' drive from the Santander ferry and so a perfectly placed halt on the way to the *meseta* (plateau) and León or a base for mountain air, wildlife and wildflowers – in mid-May we saw fields of wild daffodils and violas and a roadside peony. The hotel is perhaps too big for its position – there were only half a dozen guests – but maybe it fills up in summer. Large comfortable rooms with balconies – and go for those on the lake side. The usual rather gloomy reception rooms and bland *parador* food.' *(Eleo and Peter Carson)*

Open: All year.
Rooms: 80 – most with bath or shower, telephone and balcony.
Facilities: Lounges, bar, restaurant.
Location: 129 km from Santander on C 627.
Credit cards: All major credit cards accepted.
Terms: Rooms 2,900–4,260 pts. Set meals: breakfast 285 pts; lunch/dinner 1,080 pts.

CÓRDOBA   **Map 13**

Hotel Maimónides   *Telephone:* (957) 22.38.56
Torrijos 4   *Telex:* 76594 HOTM

There are a number of hotels in the Guide, of which the *Maimónides* is one, which merit an entry because of an incomparable location. It lies across the cobbled street from the Mezquita, and in the heart of the most interesting part of the old city, the Judería. The hotel has smallish rooms – often noisy if overlooking the street – but possesses the basic necessities (baths, WC, comfortable beds and good breakfasts) as well as decent service. A big plus is the garage under the hotel. *(F Joan Heyman)*

Open: All year.
Rooms: 54 double, 7 single – all with bath, shower and telephone.
Facilities: Salon with TV, bar-cafeteria; breakfast only served: no restaurant. Music in the bar at night. English spoken.
Location: In old part of city; garage.
Credit cards: All major credit cards accepted.
Terms: Rooms 2,100–2,550 pts per person; B & B 2,400–2,850 pts.

CÓRDOBA   **Map 13**

Parador Nacional de la Arruzufa   *Telephone:* (957) 27.59.00
Avda de la Arruzafa

Those who like to be in the centre of things will opt for the *Maimónides* (above). The *Parador* will suit better those who like a cool retreat after a hard day's city sight-seeing, with a swimming pool as an added bonus. It is in the hilly northern suburbs, 3½ km distance from the Mezquita – a modern building of no great architectural distinction. But most of the rooms are unusually large, with wide balconies looking down on the city and the mountains beyond. Everything works. *(HR)*

Open: All year.
Rooms: 56 double – all with bath or shower, telephone, radio and air conditioning, most with balcony.

Facilities: Lounges, bar, restaurant. Garden with terrace, swimming pool and tennis court.
Location: 3½ km N of town centre; parking.
Credit cards: All major credit cards accepted.
Terms: Rooms 3,800–4,500 pts. Set meals: breakfast 290 pts, lunch/dinner 1,100 pts.

DEYÁ, Mallorca   Map 13

Hotel Es Moli   *Telephone:* (971) 63.90.00
Carretera de Valdemossa s/b   *Telex:* 69007 Smoli E

Deyá, on the western side of Mallorca and made famous by the long residence of the poet Robert Graves, has a spectacular position in the middle of a natural amphitheatre, backed by mountains and facing the sea. *Es Moli*, a modern hotel, is one of the spectators on the banks of the amphitheatre, looking across the valley to the roofs and gardens of the village and the pattern of terrace fields which surround it. Beyond, olive and citrus groves drop away towards the distant sea. Because the hotel is built into the hillside, finding your way round can be rather confusing. The swimming pool is on the fourth floor at the rear. Floating on your back, you can stare up through the palm and fig trees at the towering honey-coloured hillside. If you don't want to take the lift to the lower floors, you can stroll down through the terraced gardens at the side of the hotel. And what gardens they are! Lemon trees shade the paths. Geraniums crowd the flower beds and brilliantly flowered creepers overflow every doorway. And they invade the hotel too, in the form of skilfully arranged flowers in many of the public rooms.

Iso Peters, manager of this idyllic hotel, adds a note to our question-naire: 'We would like to mention something that seems to be missing from your description – the atmosphere of friendliness and peace that prevails at all times, and is, I am sure, the main reason why our repeat business (we prefer to call them our friends) reaches sometimes as high as 75% of the occupancy.' That quality was not in fact missing from our description. Indeed, our final quote last year read: 'A superbly run and lovely hotel, with immaculate service, amazingly consistent standards, good eating and that indefinable quality of pleasurable ease. Only a semi-serpent could dislike this demi-Eden.' This year's postbag contains further tributes to the recuperative magic of the place. The food, the one feature which semi-serpents in the past have been prone to hiss about, is said to have improved – though still falling short perhaps of demi-Eden standards. *(Robert Heller; also Mrs J H Woakes, R and M Milner)*

Open: 15 April–24 October.
Rooms: 61 double, 11 single, 1 suite – all with bath and shower, telephone, radio and air-conditioning; most with terrace (300 pts supplement). Annexe with 9 rooms.
Facilities: Lift; several lounges (1 with TV), video room, card and reading room, dining terrace, dancing weekly. Large gardens with heated swimming pool, tennis court, ping pong, pétanque. Rock beach 6 km from the hotel (free transport by hotel minibus). English spoken.
Location: Palma 29 km; airport 37 km. Parking in front of hotel.
Terms: Dinner, B & B 3,400–4,600 pts; full board 4,000–5,200 pts. Set meals: 1,400 pts; full *alc* 2,500–3,500 pts. 25% reduction for children of 2–11 in parents' room.

Residencia Belvedere   *Telephone:* Andorra (78) 31263

A taste of England in the uplands of Andorra, this friendly informal guesthouse is run by an English couple, Terry and Jo Dixon. It is set slightly above the town of Encamp overlooking a dramatic Pyrenean valley. It caters for skiers in the winter and walkers in the summer. 'We usually prefer "local" hotels, but we had been to Andorra before and its hotels generally leave everything to be desired! Not so the *Belvedere*. The Dixons really do welcome all guests as family. It is rather spartan, but it does not pretend to be anything but a good "pension". The food is superb and the welcome unbeatable. It is unbelievably cheap: it must be great fun for young skiers.' *(David and Angela Stewart; also George Brock, R G Clark)*

Open: All year, except 1 November–15 December.
Rooms: 10 double, 1 single – 1 with bath.
Facilities: Lounge with open log fire, dining room, bar. ½ acre grounds with sun terrace, lawn and terraced garden with magnificent views; paddling pool and slides for children. Convenient for chairlift to lake, and ski slopes. English spoken.
Location: ¼ mile from Encamp in the direction of France.
Terms: B & B 1,158–1,351 pts; dinner, B & B 2,123–2,504 pts. Reduced rates and special meals for children.

Hotel Santa Marta   *Telephone:* (952) 81.13.40
Apartado 2

A delightful small hotel in the Costa del Sol set well back from the main coast road with hourly bus service. It is about 5 km from San Pedro, 12 km or so from Estepona and Marbella. The very comfortable bedrooms are mostly in separate bungalows in a pretty garden which runs down to the beach. The majority of the bungalows have two double rooms. Efficiently Spanish, and there is usually somebody at the reception desk who speaks English. There are beautiful hills just inland. The beach is mostly sandy and quite shallow. The shade on the beach is owned by the hotel which also runs a pleasant bar and fish restaurant with its own swimming pool at the end of the garden. 'Charming. A real retreat for forgetting any world outside exists. All services and performances fully up to standard, including the restaurant.' *(Madeleine Polland)*

Open: 1 April–1 October.
Rooms: 32 double, 2 single, 3 suites – all with bath, shower, telephone, colour television and baby-listening.
Facilities: TV lounge, 2 bars, 2 restaurants, bridge room. Large garden, swimming pool. Private beach club. Golf and tennis nearby. English spoken.
Location: 3 km from town centre.
Credit cards: Access/Euro/Mastercard, American Express, Barclay/Visa.
Terms: B & B 1,350–2,150 pts; dinner, B & B 2,200–3,000 pts; full board 2,850–3,400 pts. Set meals: lunch/dinner 950 pts; full *alc* 1,000 pts. Reduced rates and special meals for children.

Parador Colombino Conde de la Gomera   *Telephone:* (922) 87.11.00

The trouble with small hotels in far-away, not easily accessible places is that very few readers have a chance to try them out, and feedback is consequently sparse. According to our rules, the entry below should now come out. Friends of the *Parador Colombino Conde de la Gomera* – this is your final call!

'An island off an island – always something to be greatly desired. The Canary Islands have fair weather all year round, and the sun does indeed shine warmly on the lobster-red tourists swarming through the pizzerias and souvenir shops on the south coast of Tenerife. If you have come this far, go just a bit further, an hour and a half by ferry, to the tiny island of Gomera. This is Spain, not cardboard and concrete tourist land. Not one tourist in sight, just the locals. Whom we joined in an outdoor bar on the waterfront. A good beginning. Then up the hill to the cool luxury of the *parador*. More like a convent or an art museum than a hotel. Quiet, friendly service. A giant room with modern bath and antique furniture – and a balcony with a striking view of seaport and ocean hundreds of feet below. A cosy bar, a very complete dinner menu and surprisingly good food. Wine the best that Spain can offer which is very good indeed. Breakfast in bed in the morning, a stroll through the tropical gardens, a dip in the pool; living at its most relaxed and luxurious. A luxury well within the means of anyone familiar with London prices. We will return, happily, over and over again, whenever we are within striking distance of this warm little island.' *(Harry Harrison)*

Open: All year.
Rooms: 20 double, 1 single – all with bath and balcony or private terrace overlooking gardens and sea, telephone, tea-making facilities and baby-listening, 2 with TV. (Some rooms on ground floor.)
Facilities: 2 salons (1 with colour TV), bar, restaurant with air-conditioning. Luxuriant gardens with swimming pool; beach, fishing and sailing nearby; also underwater swimming. English spoken. &.
Location: 700 metres from town centre; parking.
Credit cards: All major credit cards accepted.
Terms: B & B 3,350–3,450 pts; dinner, B & B 4,300–4,400 pts; full board 5,025 pts.

Hotel Alhambra Palace   *Telephone:* (958) 221468
Peñapartida No 2   *Telex:* 78400.ALAM-E

The most favoured place to stay in Granada is the *Parador San Francisco* in the gardens of the *Alhambra* itself (see below). But the *Parador* is often booked weeks ahead: the *Hotel Alhambra Palace* provides an acceptable alternative in the same highish (for Spain) price bracket. It is a five-minute uphill walk to the *Alhambra* and a ten-minute steep walk down to the city. The best rooms – those at the back – have superb views over Granada, with the Sierra Nevada as a backdrop to the south. The hotel has stacks of character – it is built, unblushingly, in high Moorish camp style. The rooms are well-furnished and solidly insulated, bathrooms are splendidly

511

old-fashioned, service is smiling. Every prospect pleases – except, as so often in Spain, that the food is no more than mediocre. *(HR)*

Open: All year.
Rooms: 108 double, 12 single, 9 suites – 115 with bath, 1 with shower, all with telephone and baby-listening; TV in suites. 24-hour room service. (Some rooms on ground floor.)
Facilities: TV room, 2 bars, Arab Grill Room, restaurant, convention/banqueting halls, theatre, boutiques, terraces. Gardens. English spoken. &.
Location: 500 metres from town centre; public parking in front of hotel; garage 500 metres.
Credit cards: All major credit cards accepted.
Terms (excluding 4% tax): B & B 2,750–2,775 pts; dinner, B & B 4,100–4,125 pts; full board 6,000–6,025 pts. Set meals: lunch/dinner 1,350 pts; full *alc* 1,750 pts. Reduced rates for groups, low-season rates. Reduced rates and special meals for children.

GRANADA   Map 13

Hotel Inglaterra   *Telephone:* (958) 22.15.59
Cettie Merien, 4

A medium-sized old fashioned city hotel, one block from the Plaza de Los Reyes Católicos, and behind the Cathedral. 'We first stayed at this hotel in 1953 and were a little worried at the prospect of what time and the Spanish tourist revolution might have done to it. As soon as we came into the tiled lobby we realised with delight that nothing had changed and we were back in fact in 1923 or before! It is a most beautiful example of the very quiet, dignified southern Spanish hotel atmosphere of the 1920s–1930s, an atmosphere which had survived unchanged in Spain until the tourist explosion of the 1960s. The hotel is not air-conditioned, but then it doesn't need to be; every floor surface is white inlaid marble, including the bedroom floors, the stairs and the bathrooms. All the windows have fixed sunscreens which sensibly prevent the windows from heating up in the harsh sunlight. The fitting and furniture throughout the hotel are authentic 1920s Art Nouveau (a collector's dream!) – even the bentwood chairs and the door handles, as well as the coloured glass screens and lampshades. The somewhat elderly staff are quick and courteous, without any "click click" semi-efficient substitute for the real thing. The owner speaks a little English (and she is most anxious to be as helpful as possible), though none of the rest of the staff do. Breakfast is taken in the hotel dining room off the internal courtyard. The meal was crisp *hot* rolls, curls of butter and fresh peach jam in pots. Coffee came in large china pots as did the hot milk and the coffee pot was filled twice without our having to ask for it. The very large coffee cups were also the ancient shape which we like for *café au lait*, instead of the usual thimble size. The rooms are arranged on four floors, around a large central internal courtyard which is covered with a large skylight. This creates a beautiful soft lighting and excludes the harsh midday sun. The bedrooms have billowing white sun curtains, which can be pulled across the small balconies overlooking the courtyard. During the midday siesta these curtains provide a misty, dim, but airy tent-like atmosphere inside the cool oasis of each bedroom. The bedroom furniture would never be acceptable in a Holiday Inn, nor would

Don't rely on our printed tariffs! Check before booking.

the bathroom fittings. It is still the authentic Spain, if that is what one wants to experience at least once in a holiday. Prices are absurdly cheap. Go quickly, before it all becomes a parking lot or yet another glass box hotel chain horror.' *(Enid Robbie)*

Open: All year.
Rooms: 42 double, 5 single, 3 suites – 45 with bath, 5 with shower, all with telephone and mono TV. (3 rooms on ground floor.)
Facilities: TV room, bar, restaurant. English spoken.
Location: In town centre, behind Cathedral and 1 block from the Plaza de Los Reyes Católicos.
Terms: Rooms (including breakfast): 1,500 pts (single), 2,500 pts (double), 3,000 pts (triple). Set meal: breakfast 170 pts.

GRANADA   Map 13

Parador Nacional de San Francisco   *Telephone:* (958) 22.14.93
Alhambra

This 'fairest jewel in the *parador* crown', as one reader put it, is a former Franciscan convent on the Alhambra hill, with lovely formal gardens of its own and a romantic view from the terrace across to the Generalife. Since the Alhambra is to Spanish tourism what the Taj Mahal is to India, and the *Parador* has an incomparable setting, it is not surprising that prices are higher than elsewhere, and bookings need to be made weeks or even months ahead. The building itself, despite its monastic foundations, is to all intents and purposes modern, though the tower and the main entrance are preserved. As with other *paradors*, the architects have created and recreated the fabric with sympathy. There are impressive reception rooms, furnished with antique pieces, and the bedrooms (air-conditioned) are dependably comfortable. One correspondent this year, making a 20th-century pilgrimage from one *parador* to another, rated this the best of four very good ones. He had found no problem with the laundry (see last year's entry), had thoroughly enjoyed his meals and his only mini-complaint was that the mini-fridge was not replenished during his 3-day stay. (*R H Hargreaves)*

Open: All year.
Rooms: 26 – all with bath, telephone and air-conditioning.
Facilities: Salon, bar, dining room. Attractive gardens. Night life (flamenco dancing, etc.) in Granada; skiing in the Sierra Nevada 34 km SE by good but winding road.
Location: 3 km from town centre, on the Alhambra hill.
Credit cards: All major credit cards accepted.
Terms: Rooms 5,750 pts. Set meals: breakfast 290 pts; lunch/dinner 1,100 pts.

JAÉN   Map 13

Parador Nacional Castillo de Santa Catalina *Telephone:* (953) 23.22.87/88
Apartado de Correos 178

Opinions differ about this recently modernized *parador*, a few miles outside the provincial capital of Jaén – a colossal eagle's nest of a castle perched precariously on a mountain above the town with dizzying views.

Southern-facing rooms have balconies, but all have equally stunning vistas. One reader, while acknowledging the remarkable job of reconstruction, and despite the truly fabulous view, found the *parador* far too bleak and gloomy for any comfort as a hotel – 'like having a cheery weekend in the Tower of London'. Another reader found Jaén nonpareil: 'I stayed in six *paradors*, including Jaén. I found the same standard in all of them: friendly courtesy, surgical cleanliness, comfort, uniformly dependable cuisine. But Jaén represents the *parador* system at its best: the vision of the architect, his respect for the original structure, the harmonious, almost imperceptible blending of old and new, as well as the skill of the builders. You can easily become transported by this place, especially if, like me, you love to brood on mountain peaks. For a mountain brooder, this is the Promised Land. Oh, for a marriage of Spanish accommodation and French cuisine, and I don't think I would ever leave the place. Still, at the price I am not complaining.' *(J A Driver)*

Open: All year.
Rooms: 37 double, 6 single – all with bath and telephone, some with balconies. (11 rooms on ground floor.)
Facilities: Lift, 2 lounges, chess and card room, dining room, TV room, airconditioning. 2,000 square metres of garden with trees and seating; swimming pool. English spoken. &.
Location: 5 km from town centre.
Credit cards: All major credit cards accepted.
Terms: Rooms 3,400–4,000 pts. Set meals: breakfast 285 pts, lunch/dinner 1,100 pts; full *alc* 1,500 pts. No charge for children under 8; special meals provided.

LEÓN   **Map 13**

Hotel San Marcos   *Telephone:* (987) 23.73.00
Plaza de San Marcos 7   *Telex:* 89809 HSM LE

Unquestionably in the super-grand class, the *San Marcos* is fashioned from a 16th-century monastery and has a staggering renaissance façade, no less than 80 metres long. There are three-quarters of a mile of carpeted corridors which are lined on both sides with exquisite reproductions of Spanish furniture through the ages – a museum in itself. To gain some idea of the size of the place, one of the smallest rooms, used only for breakfast, is 69 feet by 27 feet, the smaller restaurant giving on to a summer terrace – with the river Bernesga beyond – is 78 feet long, while the main lounge, which has a polished marble floor on which are a multitude of Persian rugs, and the ceiling one enormous painting, is 84 feet square. A hotel of this stupefying magnitude is not of course to everyone's taste, but those who enjoy *paradors* are likely to find the *San Marcos parador*-plus. Others may consider it a bit formal or stuffy; some of the rooms, though luxurious in their furnishings, still retain monastic or cell-like elements. Also the cuisine is more everyday international than *haute* or grandee.

Open: All year.
Rooms: 244 double, 14 suites – all with bath, telephone, radio and mono TV, some with balconies. 24-hour room service. (Some rooms on ground floor.)
Facilities: Lifts, salons, TV room, rooms for private functions; tea room, bar, 2 restaurants; conference rooms; children's playroom. Large garden. English spoken. &.
Location: 500 metres from city centre; garages.

Credit cards: All major credit cards accepted.
Terms: B & B 4,000–5,600 pts. Set meals: lunch/dinner 1,725 pts; full *alc* 2,000 pts. Reduced rates and special meals for children.

MADRID   Map 13

Hotel Ritz   *Telephone:* (91) 221.28.57
Plaza de la Lealtad 5, Madrid 14   *Telex:* 43986 RITZ-E

Another legendary Spanish hotel – the only hotel, so far as we know, to have been built by a reigning monarch, Alfonso XIII, in 1908 – within strolling distance of the Prado. 'I have been staying at this perfect hotel for the past 13 years. Some things have gone. The old men who washed the lifts and the little boys who seized your shopping or your dog as you entered. But it has still the best service. Individual waiters for your room service. Not an anonymous voice on the telephone. The concierges never change, they all know one, and can and do work marvels over any travel problem. The last of the great hotels.' *(Mrs M D Prodgers)*

Open: All year.
Rooms: 150 rooms and 25 suites – all with bath, shower and telephone; colour TV in the suites.
Facilities: Lifts, lounge, reading/TV room, restaurant; 3 banqueting rooms. Small garden. Baby-sitting on request. English spoken.
Location: Central, near the Prado; parking.
Credit cards: All major credit cards accepted.
Terms: Rooms 5,150–12,500 pts per person, suites from 18,750 pts. Set meals: breakfast 700 pts; lunch/dinner 2,500 pts; full *alc* 3,600 pts. Reduced rates and special meals for children on request.

MADRID   Map 13

Hotel Suecia   *Telephone:* (91) 231.69.00
Marqués de Casa Riera 4, Madrid 14   *Telex:* 22313

Warm expressions of appreciation for this medium-sized Swedish-run hotel in a quiet side-street, but centrally placed for shops, opera or the Prado. It has a faithful clientele of journalists, guest stars at the opera and other discriminating parties, including (always a good sign) the Spanish. The hotel has its own restaurant, *The Bellman*, also liked by our readers. It's the sort of hotel, where, if you have to catch an early plane, the hotel will serve you a dawn breakfast. Prices are reasonable. 'I love the location – central and yet very quiet. The chambermaids are the most amiable in Spain and did our laundry beautifully at a fraction of the cost at a comparable hotel, either in Spain or Britain.' *(Lynn Hay; also F Joan Heyman)*

Open: All year. Restaurant closed August.
Rooms: 56 double, 3 single, 5 suites – all with bath, telephone, tea-making facilities, baby-listening, air-conditioning and mini-bar, TV on request.
Facilities: Bar/breakfast room, restaurant, facilities for banquets and conference. English spoken.
Location: In town centre, just off the Calle de Alcalá. Public car parks nearby.

Credit cards: All major credit cards accepted.
Terms: Rooms 4,070–5,830 pts. Set meals (excluding 4% tax): breakfast 300 pts; lunch/dinner 1,540 pts. Special meals for children.

MARBELLA, Málaga Map 13

Hotel Los Monteros *Telephone:* (52) 77.17.00
Carretera de Cadiz *Telex:* 77059

As fine an example as you could hope to find of a slap-up beach resort hotel, offering within the borders of the estate a complex of rooms and suites of varying sizes and grades surrounded by immaculately maintained gardens, swimming pools, tennis courts, a golf course and plenty of other sporting amenities. It is about 5 km out of Marbella on the Malaga road. The hotel is different in scale and character to most in the Guide, but there are not so many hotels in Spain or anywhere else in the world that can, to quote a phrase in the report below, 'float you back to the Gatsby era'.

'Everything about this hotel was pleasurable. The service was excellent, rooms spotless. Coffee can be taken on the swing loungers by the pool after dinner and one floats back to the Gatsby era as one watches the reflections in the pool and can hear the dance music playing inside. Spacious rooms include a double sink and fresh towels twice a day if needed. Breakfast can be enjoyed in the room. In the dining room you can have anything – fish, meat, ham, etc., even champagne at breakfast. Champagne cocktail parties are held every Tuesday completely free for guests to meet the management. All food was excellent. The lunch at the Beach Club is a real experience: there is a set price and you can have what you like – any grilled fish to order, a choice from 50 salads, fresh fruit, delicious cakes, other hot main course dishes, etc. Special touches like a fresh cotton mat to step out of bed on to each night make this hotel especially pleasurable. One thing to look out for are the rooms facing the road which can be noisy. Also from late June the band play outside and if you crave peace and quiet you need a room facing out to sea in the Mediterranean Suite.' *(Mr and Mrs T Gallagher)*

Open: All year.
Rooms: 168 – many with salon, all with bath and radio; colour TV and baby-listening on request.
Facilities: Salons, library, TV room, bridge room, bar, restaurant; nightly dancing to orchestra; once-a-week flamenco shows. 2 saunas, indoor and outdoor swimming pools; hotel is surrounded by sub-tropical gardens; tennis club, golf club, squash; riding nearby. Private road to sandy beach, safe bathing. English spoken.
Location: 5 km N of centre of Marbella, off the N340; parking.
Credit cards: All major credit cards accepted.
Terms: B & B 5,000–11,000 pts; half board 7,300–13,600 pts; full board 2,300–2,600 per person added. Set meals: lunch/dinner 2,800 pts; full *alc* 3,500 pts. 20% reduction for children under 5.

We should like to be able to recommend more budget-priced hotels in Madrid.

MOJÁCAR, Almería   Map 13

Parador Nacional Reyes Católicos   *Telephone:* (951) 47.82.50

Mojácar has a magnificent position dominating the plains and the Andalusian coast. It has not avoided the spoliation of development, though it still retains its maze of small Moorish alleys. 'The old town,' according to one reader, 'clings with bony hands to the summit of its barren hill while "whiter than white" bungalows flaunt themselves like tarts all over the lower slopes.' The *Parador* is a mile out of the village on the Carboneras road. Opinions vary about the food: 'paradorish' according to some, though others are more enthusiastic. 'An excellent building of modern design, below the village and just above the sea. Elegant rooms, effortless service, good food and value for money. Apart from Nerja, the only possible place to stay on the Costa del Sol.' *(Antony Vestrey)*

Open: All year.
Rooms: 89 double, 9 single – all with bath, telephone and tea-making facilities. (Some ground floor rooms.) Warning: front rooms may be noisy.
Facilities: Salon, TV room, air-conditioning. Garden, swimming pool; beach nearby. English spoken.
Location: On the N340 coast road, 2 miles from village.
Credit cards: All major credit cards accepted.
Terms: B & B 2,050–3,900 pts; dinner, B & B 3,200–5,050 pts; full board 3,960–5,810 pts. Set meals: lunch/dinner 1,150 pts; full *alc* 1,400 pts. Special meals for children.

MONACHIL, Granada   Map 13

Parador Nacional de Sierra Nevada   *Telephone:* (958) 48.02.00

'A modern Alpine-type building, 2,500 metres up in a superb position facing the south-west. Elegant and uncluttered. Good food and service. A steal for the price. Probably hard to get into during the winter skiing season when it is on the snow-line, or in high summer.' *(Antony Vestrey)*

Open: All year except 1 October–1 December.
Rooms: 20 double, 2 single, 10 4-bedded – 10 with bath, 22 with shower, all with telephone and mini-bar.
Facilities: Salon, TV room, dining room, terrace. Tennis and winter sports nearby. English spoken.
Location: 35 km from Granada; parking.
Credit cards: All major credit cards accepted.
Terms: B & B 2,050–3,900 pts; full board 3,900–5,700 pts. Set meals: lunch/dinner 1,100 pts; full *alc* 1,300 pts.

NERJA, Málaga   Map 13

Parador Nacional de Nerja   *Telephone:* (952) 52.00.50
Playa de Burriano – Tablazo

'This pleasantly run and well-maintained *parador* was opened in 1965. It is situated high up on the cliffs overlooking the beach of Burriano on the eastern edge of the town of Nerja. The hotel grounds stretch to the very edge of the cliff and the splendid view is for the most part uninterrupted. It is a long low building of an unobtrusive design. The large rooms have generous-sized balconies overlooking the sea and the mountains, and are comfortably furnished with well-equipped bathrooms and bar-fridges. It is spotlessly clean everywhere. There is a pool surrounded by a delightful garden, mainly undulating lawn but with trees for shade and flowers for colour, where there is plenty of room and facilities for sunbathing. Alternatively a lift takes you directly to the beach below. Although open throughout the year, it is very much a hotel for the sun and the sea. The restaurant also looks over the sea, and as well as an *à la carte* offers an above-average three-course menu with very generous helpings. Excellent choice of first courses, good fish and boring sweets. Slightly impersonal service. An agreeable place for a reasonably simple and quiet summer holiday. A car whilst not essential would be helpful. There are some extraordinary caves nearby (about 2½ miles) which have a mind-boggling plethora of stalactites and stalagmites in two vast caverns.' *(Anna Waley; endorsed, with reservations about the food, by F Joan Heyman)*

Open: All year.
Rooms: 38 double, 2 single – all with bath, shower, telephone, fridge-bar, balcony and air-conditioning.
Facilities: Salon/bar, reading room, games room, restaurant. Sunny terrace and gardens with swimming pool and 2 tennis courts; lift to sandy beach with safe bathing and motor boats; open-air café for meals or snacks.
Location: 2 km from Nerja, S of the CN 340 in the direction of Málaga.
Credit cards: All major credit cards accepted.
Terms: Rooms 3,800–4,500 pts. Set meals: breakfast 290 pts; lunch/dinner approx 1,100 pts.

ORIENT, Bunyola, Mallorca   **Map 13**

Hostal de Muntanya   *Telephone:* Orient 21.40.95
Bordoy 6

'In the mountains, in a remote village, it is the only hotel: 16 rooms, and a large dining room which on fiestas and Sundays is the mecca for people from the towns who rave about country-style eating. Tourists are still a rare sight for the 160 or so inhabitants and local farmers. It is ideal for an away-from-it-all holiday if what you are looking for is clean mountain air, clear skies and glorious countryside. Most nights the village goes to bed after dinner, unless some of the local characters join the hotel guests over jugs of tangy wine after they have eaten the superb dishes of *tumbet*, a tasty but meatless vegetable pot-pourri, or mutton rice *brut*, or delicious stews. Apart from the village dishes, which are the speciality of the hotel and its big attraction, there is a vast *à la carte*. There is no swimming and anyone wanting transport must hire a car in Palma before taking up residence. Paradise for those who want peace, quiet and a lazy holiday in beautiful natural surroundings.' *(Bert Horsfall)*
So ran our original entry for this remote mountain hostel. Recent visitors warmly endorse it: 'First-rate in all respects: a perfect setting and the road to Orient took us through some breathtaking scenery. The food – eaten on a terrace with a view of the countryside – was way above the usual Spanish standard, without being pretentious. Outstanding value too.' *(Brian Capstick)*

Open: All year.
Rooms: 14 double, 2 single – 1 with bath, 12 with shower.
Facilities: Salon/bar with TV, reading room, restaurant, terrace. Garden.
Location: 33 km from Palma on the southern edge of the Sierra de Alfabia; go N from Palma by the main Buñyola road, then fork NE to Orient.
Terms: Rooms 1,090–1,350 pts. Set meals: breakfast 170 pts, lunch/dinner 570 pts.

PUERTOMARÍN, Lugo   Map 13

Parador Nacional de Puertomarín   *Telephone:* (982) 54.50.25

'For 20th-century pilgrims on the route to Santiago de Compostela (100 km to the west) this smallish modern *parador* above a vast flooded valley is a welcome sight at the end of a long day. Built 16 years ago when the medieval village was flooded with the making of the reservoir, it is well situated in the modern village. We arrived without booking and were lucky to get one of its nine double rooms, though not lucky enough to have one with a picture window overlooking the beautiful countryside. The *Parador* is a few yards from the pleasant arcaded square surrounding the rebuilt 12th-century fortified church of San Juan.' *(Peter and Eleo Carson)*

Open: All year.
Rooms: 9 double, 1 single – all with bath, telephone, tea-making facilities and baby-listening.
Facilities: Salon with TV, restaurant. Garden. Public swimming pool nearby; fishing, rowing, sailing, waterskiing available in vicinity. English spoken.
Location: 26 km S of Lugo; parking.
Credit cards: All major credit cards accepted.
Terms: B & B 1,550–2,630 pts; dinner, B & B 2,500–3,580 pts; full board 3,125–4,205 pts. Set meals: lunch/dinner 950 pts; full *alc* 1,500 pts. Reduced rates and special meals for children.

SANTIAGO DE COMPOSTELA, La Coruña   Map 13

Hostal de los Reyes Católicos   *Telephone:* (981) 58.22.00 and 58.23.11
Plaza de España 1   *Telex:* 86004 HRCS E

'A cross between Hampton Court and All Souls', furnished with the best pieces from the Victoria and Albert Museum,' was how one reader has described this former hospital for pilgrims reincarnated as perhaps the grandest of all grand Spanish hotels – 500 years old, four interior courtyards, its own Chapel Royal, fountains, fourposters, and goodness knows how many miles of marbled corridors. For some, it is an ultimate experience – but, be warned, not everyone comes back equally enchanted. Last year we reported a visitor, a single woman travelling alone, who had found the staff rude and her room on the second floor small, cold and damp. This year we heard from an elderly single lady who had had a similar experience, and who had also found the fabled restaurant of the hotel less than sympathetic to her vegetarian needs. Other visitors, having been given a small dark room on the ground floor, successfully negotiated a cheaper but far nicer room on the fourth floor – bright and quiet overlooking the rooftops. They reckon that rooms on the third and fourth floors are the ones to book: the third-floor rooms, mostly suites, tend to be the most expensive. They would not have wished themselves anywhere else in Santiago, but they added that the lounges were a bit formal and gloomy, and the bar and cafeteria adequate but nondescript. It may seem like *lèse :najesté* to ask for more views about what some regard as a supremely great hotel. But there is often a considerable difference – with hotels as with statesmen – between the great and the good.

Open: All year.
Rooms: 145 double, 9 single, 3 suites – all with bath or shower, telephone, radio, and TV. (Some rooms on ground floor.)
Facilities: Salon, bar, dining room, cafeteria; conference facilities. Beauty parlour, shops. Chapel Royal with occasional concerts. English spoken.
Location: In town centre; parking.
Credit cards: All major credit cards accepted.
Terms: Rooms: 2,850–4,845 pts; dinner, B & B 5,400–7,400 pts; full board: 7,400–9,400 pts. Set meals: breakfast 456 pts, lunch/dinner 2,000 pts.

SANTILLANA DEL MAR, Santander   **Map 13**

Parador Nacional Gil Blas   *Telephone:* (942) 81.80.00
Pl. Ramón Pelayo 11

One of the showplace villages of Northern Spain, Santillana is full of fine seignorial mansions and a Collegiate Church dating from the 12th and 13th centuries.

'Santillana is still an enchanting village despite the fact that souvenir shops spread like measles across its face and a mushroom growth of bar-restaurants is appearing. There are also many little stalls that sell the regional speciality: a glass of milk with a kind of biscuit. Surprisingly, this co-exists with the traditional life of the village. The sight – and traces – of cows are ubiquitous. The *parador* is a beautiful old building; more outgoing, less introspective than those further south. It has all the comforts and amenities of *paradors* without leaving any special impression, but it is a handy place to end up at if you are catching the ferry out of Santander the following day, being only some 32 km outside the city, and is also convenient for visiting the awesome cave paintings at Altamira a mile away.' *(Jeff Driver)*

Open: All year.
Rooms: 22 rooms – most with bath, all with telephone. 21 rooms in annexe. (Many rooms on ground floor.)
Facilities: Lift, salon with TV, bar, restaurant.
Location: Central; garage and private parking.
Credit cards: All major credit cards accepted.
Terms: Rooms 3,500–4,400 pts. Set meals: breakfast 290 pts; lunch/dinner 1,100 pts.

In the case of many continental hotels, especially Spanish ones, we have adopted the local habit of quoting a price for the room whether it is occupied by one or more persons. Rates for B & B, half board, etc., are per person unless otherwise stated.

SANTO DOMINGO DE LA CALZADA, La Rioja   Map 13

Parador Nacional Santo Domingo de la Calzada   *Telephone:*
Pl. del Santo 3   (941) 34.03.00

'Santo Domingo was an 11th-century anchorite who built a bridge across
the Glera river and a causeway *(calzada)* to help pilgrims on their way to
Santiago de Compostela by the Camino Francés (French road). A town
grew up at the bridge and a hostel was built for the pilgrims. The *parador*
has been built around the former hostel, little of which now remains
except the facade and the main hall. It's nice – but noisy. When the
baroque had reached its most florid exuberance the good people of Santo
Domingo built themselves a campanile and put it on one side of their quite
tiny main square; another side being taken up with part of the front of the
cathedral and another, today, with the side of the *parador*. Added to the
usual waking noises of the Plaza Mayor we found matutinal campanology
just a little trying. Nevertheless, a good first stop in Spain for somebody
travelling south from Santander after docking in the mid afternoon, as we
did. All the usual remarks re. *paradors* apply.' *(Jeff Driver)*

Open: All year.
Rooms: 27 – most with bath, all with telephone.
Facilities: Lift, salon, bar, restaurant.
Location: Central; no private parking.
Credit cards: All major credit cards accepted.
Terms: Rooms 3,000–3,700 pts. Set meals: breakfast 290 pts; lunch/dinner 1,100
pts.

SEGOVIA   Map 13

Parador Nacional   *Telephone:* (911) 41.50.90

A modern *parador* on a hill overlooking the town, with superb views of
the golden cathedral and the romantic Alcazar. The nominator who
contributed last year's entry briefly praised the comfort and the food,
mentioned that the whole decor of the hotel was in keeping with the
modern architecture – and left it at that. A recent correspondent agreed
about the comfort, but grieved that we had said so little about the
extraordinary achievement of the *Parador*'s architect: 'It should be so
ugly since it is only concrete beams and brick walls, with no interior walls
in the public rooms. But lines in every direction give pleasure to the eye,
and the place is full of small gardens, lit by light traps from the roof to keep
them flourishing. Also, since the building is cantilevered out from the hill,
you have this lovely illusion that you are approaching the fabulous skyline
of Segovia (you must mention the aqueduct) from an approaching air-
craft. Incidentally, the restaurants of Segovia, with their ancient Guild of
Meat Roasters, are famous all over Spain. If you say you have been to
Segovia, at once you are asked did you eat at *Candido* or *Casa Duque*. We
did. Both. And it was more than memorable. If you eat only in the
Parador, that would indeed be tragic.' *(Madeleine Polland)*

Open: All year.
Rooms: 70 double, 5 single, 5 suites – all with bath, shower and telephone;
air-conditioning throughout.

Facilities: Salon, library, TV, bar, dining room; indoor swimming pool, sauna. Garden with outdoor swimming pool. English spoken.
Location: 3 km from Segovia; garage.
Credit cards: All major credit cards accepted.
Terms: Rooms 3,000–3,600 pts; suites from 6,000 pts. Set meals: breakfast 285 pts, lunch/dinner 1,100 pts. Special meals for children.

SEVILLE Map 13

Hotel Alfonso XIII *Telephone:* (954) 22.28.50
San Fernando 2 *Telex:* 72725

Seville's grandest hotel, inaugurated in 1929 and run by the same company as the *Reyes Católicos* of Santiago (q.v.). For those who like to do a city in style. 'A really wonderful hotel for a rest, in a lovely city. It is a large oblong building with an inner courtyard, just by the centre of Seville. There is traffic noise and the garden is small, but it is near the river and great parks. The public rooms are huge, the service attentive, and the atmosphere one of old-fashioned, comfortable luxury. Our room was big and well-furnished, with an elegant hand-made carpet signed "Madrid 1928", and excellent modern gouaches. The beds were very comfortable, percale sheets changed daily and good modern bathroom. The restaurant was excellent – admirable Spanish wine list, a first-class fish dish every night, and spinach souffles, Spanish gooey puddings, etc. Other guests unobtrusive and the service pleasant and courteous. Cheap all-in rates by Mundicolor (tours department of Iberian Airways).' *(Lord Vaizey; also Anthony Holden, Helge Rubinstein)*

Open: All year.
Rooms: 112 double, 18 single, 19 suites – all with bath, telephone and radio; TV and baby-listening on request.
Facilities: TV room, salons, San Fernando Bar, restaurant, convention/banqueting halls, patio. Boutiques, hairdressers, beauty parlours. Swimming pool. Gardens. English spoken. &.
Location: In town centre; parking, underground garage.
Credit cards: All major credit cards accepted.
Terms: B & B 4,525–7,200 pts; dinner, B & B 6,325–9,000 pts; full board 9,650–12,350 pts. Set meals: lunch/dinner 1,800 pts; full *alc* 2,500–3,000 pts. Special meals for children.

SEVILLE Map 13

Hotel Doña María *Telephone:* (954) 22.49.90
Don Remondo 19

A beautifully furnished bed-and-breakfast hotel in the Spanish baroque style close to the Cathedral square. Some rooms have a close-up of the awesome façade of the Giralda and Cathedral, with attendant bells, others – quieter – look out onto a sub-tropical interior courtyard. The entrance lobby leads into a large attractive lounge area, where drinks can be taken; there is also an adjoining bar; and you can also order drinks or snacks on the fifth floor rooftop swimming pool – a particularly attractive feature of the hotel. Admirable old-world service. Breakfasts are best taken in your room, as the breakfast-room is a chilly neon-lit place in the basement. You can park your car in the Cathedral square or the hotel will direct you to a nearby lockup. *(HR, F Joan Heyman, G G Bennett)*

Open: All year.
Rooms: 60 rooms – all with bath, telephone, radio; mono TV available on request at no charge.
Facilities: Lobby-cum-bar lounge; basement breakfast room; rooftop swimming pool with fine views.
Location: Central, near cathedral; no garage.
Credit cards: American Express, Barclay/Visa, Diners.
Terms: Rooms 5,200–5,750 pts. Set meals: breakfast 290 pts. (No restaurant.)

SON VIDA, Palma de Mallorca 13   Map 13

Racquet Club Hotel-Residence   *Telephone:* (971) 28.00.50
Telex: 69154 ABL

There is very much the air of a country club about this hotel – with its nine tennis courts in front of the building (one more than last year), a large swimming pool on the other side and the golf course right next door. And there is horse-riding close by too. Moreover, although you are only ten minutes by car from the hustle and bustle of Palma, the hotel is surrounded by hills, with lovely views, and has the feeling of being in the country. Inside, the hotel has an intimate elegance: there's wood panelling in the reception and bar, and plenty of leather chairs and sofas in the lounge area, as well as pretty brass lamps on small tables. The bedrooms, too, are comfortable and have balconies with side screens to prevent you from looking at your neighbours or vice versa. Most of the staff are German and notices are in German. The service is good and attentive, and the food, if not specially imaginative, is well above the island's average. In short, a thoroughly agreeable hotel in a quiet and secluded setting – ideal if you play tennis or golf, but especially tennis. It's very much a hide-away for young professional or semi-professional players.

Open: All year.
Rooms: 46 double, 5 single – all with bath and shower, radio, air-conditioning; TV and baby-sitting on request. (25 rooms on ground floor.)
Facilities: Salon, TV room, cards room, bar, terrace-bar; some conference facilities. 9 clay tennis courts, large heated swimming pool, sauna; 18-hole golf course adjoining the hotel with special rates for guests; riding school nearby; 15 km from beach. English spoken. &.
Location: Bus service to Palma 7 km.
Credit cards: American Express, Barclay/Visa.
Terms: B & B 2,260–2,900 pts. Set meals: lunch/dinner 1,000 pts. approx; full *alc* 1,600 pts approx. Reduced rates and special meals for children.

TOLEDO   Map 13

Hotel Alfonso IV   *Telephone:* (925) 22.26.00
General Moscardó 2

'This hotel is well situated by the side of the Alcazar and within easy reach of the cathedral and deserves an entry on the strength of this. It was very comfortable and the rooms were air-conditioned. Prices were similar to

paradors and I think in fact a bit cheaper. Good breakfast served in room. We couldn't get into the *parador* just outside Toledo. We called there for a drink on the way out next morning and it really must be the most beautiful site of all! However, even in October the *paradors* everywhere seem to be *very* full. The *Cardenal* (see below) was also fully booked. I therefore suggest the *Alfonso IV* as a thoroughly acceptable alternative.'
(F Joan Heyman)

Open: All year.
Rooms: 65 double, 15 single – all with bath, telephone, radio and air-conditioning.
Facilities: Lift, salon with TV, bar, restaurant; conference facilities. English spoken.
Location: In town centre beside the Alcazar; garage parking 20 metres.
Credit cards: All major credit cards accepted.
Terms: B & B 1,825–2,785 pts; dinner, B & B 2,590–3,710 pts; full board 3,515–4,635 pts. Set meals: lunch/dinner 925 pts; full *alc* 1,200 pts. Reduced rates and special meals for children.

TOLEDO **Map 13**

Hotel Residencia Cardenal   *Telephone:* (925) 22.49.00
Paseo de Recaredo 24

'Altogether delightful. Small, the old residence of a cardinal, it abuts the city walls. It is spotlessly clean, with good-sized rooms overlooking a terraced garden which extends down to one of the city gates. It is absolutely quiet and peaceful at all times – day and night. It has no restaurant of its own, but adjoins one of the same name which is independently run. The food there is very expensive, and we thought poor value for money.' *(SK)*

Open: All year.
Rooms: 24 double, 3 single – all with bath, telephone and air-conditioning.
Facilities: Reading room, TV and games room. Garden. Restaurant next door. English spoken.
Location: Central; parking. (By the old walls at the Puerto de Bisagra.)
Credit cards: American Express, Barclay/Visa, Diners.
Terms: Rooms 3,450 pts. Set meal: breakfast 250 pts; *alc* 1,400–2,700 (excluding wine).

TORDESILLAS, Valladolid **Map 13**

Parador Nacional de Tordesillas   *Telephone:* (983) 77.00.51

One of the larger *paradors*, built in 1958 and enlarged in 1975, 1 km outside Tordesillas in pine woods. It lies close to two main highways, the Madrid–La Corunna road and the road from France to Portugal which passes through Burgos. A useful stopover, therefore, but also, because of its convenience, often booked up in advance. 'We had a super room with all the usual *parador* equipment – mini-bar, good bathroom, etc. We also had a *very* good dinner there – this *parador* is more interested in food than is usual!' *(F Joan Heyman)*

Open: All year.
Rooms: 65 double, 8 single – most with bath or shower, all with telephone and air-conditioning.
Facilities: Lounges, bar, dining room. Garden with swimming pool.
Location: 1 km from Tordesillas. Near Madrid–La Corunna road and France–Portugal road; parking.
Credit cards: All major credit cards accepted.
Terms: Rooms 2,990–3,800 pts. Set meals: breakfast 290 pts, lunch/dinner 1,100 pts.

ÚBEDA, Jaén   Map 13

Parador Nacional Condestable Davalos   *Telephone:* (953) 75.03.45
Plaza Vázquez de Molina 1

'Úbeda has many interesting, old buildings; not least in this category is the *parador* itself: a large, classical, renaissance palace right on the busy main square that has two churches – each with umpteen bells. But the *parador*, though a bit noisy, is built around an interior, square courtyard and, like many Spanish buildings, seems to look inwards into itself and presents to the world beyond its wall just a few blind, unseeing eyes. It is, of course, an architectural answer to the problem of coping with the heat. Úbeda was undergoing a heatwave whilst we were there and, as this *parador* is not air-conditioned, we had to make do with such remedies as the renaissance architects could provide, which were not very effective against weather I had previously only experienced in India. I must say a word about the staff, who were outstandingly pleasant and helpful. The meal was – er, interesting. I had *gazpacho*, the regional speciality of Andalusia, and pickled quail! The rest of the dish was pickled too: French beans and some unknown vegetable that has me baffled yet. It was pleasant enough on a sweltering evening. I would not choose it again but perhaps others might like it. The usual high standard of *parador* accommodation: much antique furniture and suits of armour, that nearly all *paradors* seem to display, with something of a specialization in old chests.' *(Jeff Driver; also, with reservations about the plumbing, Antony Vestrey)*

Open: All year.
Rooms: 25 double, 1 suite – all with bath and telephone.
Facilities: Lounge with TV, bar, restaurant. English spoken.
Location: Úbeda is 9 km E of Baeza; 26 km E of Linares; 56 km NE of Jaén. Hotel is central; unsupervised parking.
Credit cards: All major credit cards accepted.
Terms: Rooms 2,450–3,200 pts for one person, 3,000–4,000 pts for 2. Set meals: breakfast 300 pts; lunch/dinner 1,100 pts; full *alc* 1,600 pts.

VIELLA, Lérida 42   Map 13

Parador Nacional del Valle de Arán   *Telephone:* (973) 64.01.00
Ctra del Túnel

'Perched above the Valle de Arán and a mile from the small village of Viella, this *parador* was built primarily for the winter skiers but its open-air pool makes it an ideal summer centre for walking and the nearby

National Park. It is only about a twenty-minute drive south of the French border and the excellent and inexpensive food makes it a popular place for Frenchmen over the border to come and have Saturday and Sunday lunch. The furnishings, the marble bathrooms, the huge fireplaces which in winter blaze with logs are those of a luxury hotel. The views on three sides are stunning. Central feature of the hotel is a circular wing which houses a lower ground floor lounge with bar and a first floor lounge both having panoramic views reminiscent of an airship. The cooking is regional and one is likely to be offered mountain trout, wild rabbit, baby lamb, excellent fish and an hors d'oeuvre which runs to 15 separate dishes. The Catalán specialities, the freshness of the food and its quality were remarkable. Viella is a ten-minute walk below the hotel and the whole of the valley is remarkably unspoilt. No doubt in winter it presents a different picture but as a summer mountain resort it takes a lot of beating. The courtesy of the staff was outstanding.' *(Derek and Janet Cooper)*

'A really good, no nonsense Spanish *parador* – when I looked at the size, decor, view from the window of my bedroom and compared it with other more expensive hotels, I realized what good value for money a good *parador* is. The staff were all helpful in their rather aloof Spanish manner, including the porter who seemed to know exactly how far an elderly lady driving herself would wish to go the next day.' *(Mrs M D Prodgers)*

Open: All year.
Rooms: 135 – most with bath, all with telephone.
Facilities: Lift, salon, restaurant, bar. Garden, swimming pool.
Location: 2 km from Viella; parking.
Credit cards: All major credit cards accepted.
Terms: Rooms 3,795–4,000 pts. Set meals: breakfast 290 pts; lunch/dinner 1,100 pts.

VILLAJOYOSA, Alicante   **Map 13**

Hotel El Montiboli   *Telephone:* (965) 89.02.50
Apartado 8

The *El Montiboli* is 3 km out of Villajoyosa on the Alicante road, and 11 km from Benidorm; but it stands on a rocky promontory over the sea: a position of privacy and calm, utterly remote from the razzmatazz of the nearby Costa Blanca resorts. It was built in 1978 in the Moorish style and has won a first prize for the best tourist building in Spain. There are a lot of sporting facilities available at the hotel – tennis, windsurfing, sailing, waterskiing, for all of which the hotel offers coaching. But if you feel like some more touristy life, a minitrain stops at the hotel hourly on the way to or from Benidorm and Alicante. 'Not a place where you expect to find a hotel with such first-class food, service and decor. The bedrooms are beautiful, with those little extra touches to make them perfect. The food is excellent.' *(John Gullidge)*

'The description in the 1982 Guide is perfect.' This endorsement for last year's entry, printed above, comes unfortunately not from a reader but from the *El Montoboli* themselves, who go on to tell us that they have improved one beach transforming it into a tropical beach with lots of palm trees – the only one of its kind on the Mediterranean coast. We are delighted to hear it, but should be glad also to hear from readers.

Open: All year.
Rooms: 32 double, 5 single, 12 suites – all with bath, telephone, radio, tea-

526

making facilities and baby-listening; TV on request; all doubles have terrace overlooking the sea. (Some rooms on ground floor.)

Facilities: Lifts, 2 salons, TV room. Large garden with children's play area, 2 swimming pools (1 heated, 1 seawater); sauna, massage; tennis, windsurfing, sailing, waterskiing and deep sea fishing. English spoken.

Location: 3 km S of Villajoyosa on the road between Alicante and Benidorm; garage, parking.

Credit cards: All major credit cards accepted.

Terms: B & B 2,900–4,600 pts; dinner, B & B 4,500–5,800 pts; full board 6,000–7,800 pts. Set meals: lunch/dinner 1,900 pts; full *alc* 2,400 pts. 20% reduction on meals for children.

Hotel Stenungsbaden, Stenungsund

Sweden

Rusthållargården   *Telephone:* (042) 462 75

'About 9 km from the E 6, the main road from Hälsingborg to Gothenberg and Oslo, Arild is a fishing village perched on the side of the peninsula jutting out into the Cattegat. The hotel is about 200 metres from the harbour and high enough to command a magnificent view of the bay, Skälderviken. The building itself is old – 17th-century – but it has been completely modernized inside and an upper floor containing bedrooms has been added. None of these bedrooms is alike; each is furnished in its own personal style and has a name of its own – Grandmother's Room, the Major's Room, Mamselle's Room, etc. We had the Poet's Room and very comfortable it was too, with good beds and chairs, plenty of cupboard and drawer space, a clock-radio and a private bathroom, alas without a window. Downstairs there are several spacious rooms: two big lounges, a TV lounge and a large restaurant. The food is excellent, particularly the fish, which is sent up fresh from the harbour every morning. The menu is not long, but diners are encouraged to talk to the chef in advance and discuss with him exactly what they would like. The wine-cellar is good. We liked the atmosphere of the hotel. Peter Malmgren, fourth generation of the family that owns it, has given it a friendly feeling. The hotel is well situated for those who like outdoor life. The whole of the peninsula from Arild to Kulla is a national park, excellent for walking and with lovely views, especially from the lighthouse on the westernmost point. There are ten golfcourses within fairly easy reach and the village has a harbour for visiting boats. The bathing there is poor, but it is only a few km to good sandy beaches. The hotel has its own tennis court, table-tennis room and sauna. We enjoyed our stay there and thought it good value for money. One pleasure we can recommend to anyone in the neighbourhood is afternoon tea or coffee in the garden of the Lundgren sisters, "Systrarna på Skäret", where you can taste some of the best pastries in Sweden. It is only a few miles from Arild.' *(Johanne Suul-Erikson)*

Open: 15 June–1 September.
Rooms: 25 – all with bath or shower.
Facilities: 2 lounges, TV room, restaurant. Table tennis, sauna; outdoor swimming pool, tennis court. Golf courses, sandy beaches nearby.
Location: About 9 km from the E6, the main road from Halsingborg to Gothenberg.
Terms: Rooms 185–230 Skr (single), 220–275 Skr (double); dinner, B & B 215–250 Skr.

GRYTHYTTAN, 710 60 Västmanland   **Map 7**

Grythyttans Gästgivaregård   *Telephone:* (0591) 143 10

'*Grythyttans* is an inn that has arisen from the dead. Originally built in 1640 in the heart of the then flourishing iron-mining district, it fell into disuse with the arrival of the railway and slowly decayed. In 1972 the local cultural association acquired it and re-opened it. Carl Jan Granqvist, the manager they installed, proved to be an inspired choice; an art-historian by profession, he has the gift of re-creating the past. He bought up the surrounding 18th-century shops and cottages, converted them into comfortable bedrooms, filled the rooms with antique furniture and art, dressed the staff in period clothes and successfully re-created the atmosphere of a hundred and fifty years ago. In the eight years that have passed since the inn was re-opened it has become well known all over Sweden.

'Gourmet is the only possible word to describe the food, the highlights being Saturday evening dinner and Sunday lunch: many of the guests are passionately interested in what they eat. Every summer a few of the regulars are allowed to work in the restaurant, and Granqvist relates the story of the distracted leader of a conducted tour who rushed in one day asking for a doctor, quick. Granqvist took him into the kitchen, pointed to four of the cooks, and asked him what sort of specialist was required. The service is efficient, excellent and friendly, with a hostess to take personal care of all arrivals. We were left with the impression that the staff took great pride in what they were doing and regarded themselves as cultural pioneers rather than as ordinary hotel employees.

'Grythyttan is off the beaten track – 46 km from the main road from Gothenburg and Dalarna and 64 km from the Gothenburg–Stockholm road, but those who take the time to visit this peaceful corner of genuine old Sweden will not regret it.' *(Michael Stevens)*

Open: All year. Restaurant closed to non-residents Sunday evening.
Rooms: 45 double, 10 single – 50 with shower, some with TV, all with telephone, radio and baby-listening.
Facilities: Salons, TV room, restaurant, sauna. Dancing Saturday night. 2 acres grounds. 150 lakes in area; bathing and fishing. English spoken. &.
Location: 39 km from Nora on Route 244. In centre of village; parking.

Credit cards: Access/Euro/Mastercard, American Express, Diners.
Terms: Rooms 150–275 Skr; dinner, B & B 280–340 Skr; full board 350–415 Skr.
Set meals: breakfast 26 Skr; lunch 65 Skr; dinner 105 Skr; full *alc* 180 Skr.

MARIEFRED, 150 30 Södermanland   Map 7

Gripsholms Värdshus   *Telephone:* (0159) 100 40 and 100 18

'Mariefred is a tiny town on the shores of Lake Mälar, 4 km from the main
highway E3, 424 km from Gothenburg and 66 km from Stockholm. The
inn, which was first opened in 1623 and is reputed to be the oldest in
Sweden, is situated by the waterside facing the historic castle of Grip-
sholm. It is not a large inn – only seven bedrooms – but the atmosphere is
cosy and friendly. Our room, though not large, was comfortably furnished
and had a superb view of the castle across the water. Plenty of good
reading lamps. We thought at first that there was no bathroom or shower,
but later discovered that there is a bathroom, but on the ground floor
while all the bedrooms (and the large dining room) are on the first floor.
Other amenities are a small TV room, a sauna, a playground for the
children and boats for hire. The price for B & B seemed good value for
money. The wine-cellar and food are excellent, though definitely not
cheap. Food plays an important part in the life of the inn, which is
well-known for its good Swedish hors d'oeuvres. Open all the year round,
the restaurant is obviously planned with the summer months in view, for
there are tables for meals and lighter refreshments on verandas as well as
under a roof in the garden.

'We thoroughly enjoyed our stay here. Not only the hotel, but the
whole town is charming; it must be one of the most unspoilt places in
Sweden. Almost all the houses (and the inn) are built of wood, beautifully
looked after, and there is not an ugly building to be seen (except perhaps
the new school, which is well tucked away). The castle, mid 16th-century,
is well worth a visit. Two further attractions that can make a visit to
Mariefred memorable are the narrow-gauge railway from the main line, 4
km away, and the steam-boat from Stockholm. The former, a genuine
antique, operates on a regular timetable in summer and the steamer, daily
except Mondays, gives you a good lunch on board.' *(Michael and Marit
Stevens)*

Open: 1 March–22 December.
Rooms: 7.
Facilities: TV room, restaurant; sauna, children's playground, boating.
Location: On the shores of Lake Malar, 4 km from the E3.
Terms: Rooms 115–185 Skr; full board 235 Skr.

STENUNGSUND, 444 00 Bohuslän   Map 7

Hotel Stenungsbaden   *Telephone:* (0303) 831 00
Stenungsön   *Telex:* 21292 Stenba S

'The west coast of Sweden enjoys a comparatively mild climate, thanks to
the Gulf Stream, and Stenungsund, 45 km north of Gothenburg, has a
particularly attractive hotel right on the waterfront, the *Stenungsbaden*.
Though large, 144 rooms, the atmosphere is caring and friendly. The
hotel is sited on a hill with beautiful views across the Hakefjord. It has a

sauna, squash court, swimming pool, a fleet of twenty Maxi sailing boats and a few motor boats for rent; there is a disco and more traditional dancing to live music in the restaurant. I enjoyed the exercise track; you follow red markers for about 3 km along the shore and through the forest. As meals are not only good but copious, it's a great idea. *Stenungsbaden*, in common with 245 other hotels, accept Swedish Hotel Cheques, purchaseable in advance in the UK for use between May and September.' *(Anne Bolt)*

Open: All year.
Rooms: 100 double, 44 single – 28 with bath, 116 with shower, all with telephone, radio and TV. (Some rooms specially equipped for the disabled.)
Facilities: Lifts, ramps for disabled, 2 restaurants, 2 bars, dancing 3 times a week; indoor swimming pool, sauna, squash court. Sea nearby. English spoken. &.
Location: 45 km N of Gothenburg, by Route 160.
Credit cards: All major credit cards accepted.
Terms: B & B 150–365 Skr. Reduced rates and special meals for children.

STOCKHOLM, 1456   Map 7

Hotel Diplomat   *Telephone:* (08) 63.58.00
Strandvägen 7 C   *Telex:* 17119 Diplhot S

'That placid bourgeois comfort, untouched by the troubles of 1914 and 1939, that pervades Stockholm is reflected in the calm of the *Hotel Diplomat*. Overlooking the harbour and standing between blocks of turn-of-the-century flats, it has an air of discretion. The hotel has recently opened its own restaurant; there is also a ground-floor tea-shop – which has for many years been a rather smart Stockholm rendezvous – where breakfast and light meals are served as well, of course, as afternoon tea. The bar upstairs is tucked away in a series of small, cosy sitting rooms, well-furnished with armchairs, newspapers and magazines. The bedrooms have a solid comfort that is particularly agreeable when snow whirls in from the Baltic. The *Diplomat* is within a few minutes' walk of the city centre.' *(Tom Pocock)*

Open: All year. Restaurant closed Saturday and Sunday.
Rooms: 70 double, 57 single, 5 suites – 98 with bath, 34 with shower, all with telephone, radio, colour TV, films on closed circuit TV, and mini-bar.
Facilities: Lounges, TV room, cocktail bar, restaurant, café, rooftop sun terrace, sauna, solarium, conference facilities. Fishing and winter sports nearby. English spoken.
Location: 5 minutes' walk from the centre. Parking.
Credit cards: All major credit cards accepted.
Terms: B & B 332.50–625 Skr. Children under 12 free of sharing parents' room.

TÄLLBERG, 79303 Dalarna   Map 7

Åkerblads   *Telephone:* (0247) 500 04 and 500 12

In the Book of Hotel Records, *Åkerblads* (pronounced 'Awkerblads') must have an honoured place. The Åkerblad family have been in continuous occupation here since the early 18th century, and the people presently running the hotel are the 14th and 15th generations. They speak good English. We liked their note which accompanied the hotel tariff: 'We are not so much for flattery to the guests but we do take care of them and want them to feel like a member of the family. They are so welcome to stay with us.' Tällberg is halfway between Leksand and Rättvik, two of the best-known towns round Lake Siljan, the heart of the holiday and tourist area in Dalarna, in the middle of Sweden. The hotel, the oldest part of which is a 17th-century farmhouse, has been tastefully converted into a comfortable and spacious building in the old style. It has a fine view of the lake. The bedrooms, both in the main building and the annexe, are pleasantly furnished, hardly any two being alike. Good beds, running h and c in all rooms and a shower, toilet, etc., in most – a few have baths. There is a sauna and a warm brine-bath (very luxurious) all the year round, a tennis court in summer and an ice-rink in winter. Other winter attractions are good skiing for everyone except really advanced slalom experts, torchlight sleigh-rides through the woods and log fires in the evening. In summer there is good bathing and fishing in the lake, boats available, and good walking country all round.

'We loved *Åkerblads*! We spent four days there in perfect weather in early June. Tällberg is a village full of meadows on the edge of Lake Siljan and the houses are all built in traditional styles in wood. Inside, *Åkerblads* had much charm – we had a lovely bedroom with verandas. It felt very Swedish painted in different shades of green and orange. The atmosphere in the hotel is easy and informal. We loved the mealtimes – all very Swedish with no compromises to an international style or cuisine. Everyone helped themselves from a central table. There were great bowls of fruit and yoghurt and lots of different rolls and breads for breakfast. Lunch seemed to be the main meal – often with several kinds of fish and potatoes with dill. It always ended with cake and excellent coffee (served from a large copper kettle) in the upper hall. When it was hot people took their food outside. Local parties coming for meals often included men and women in national costume. Christina and Arne Åkerbalds made us very welcome – it was a pleasant and somehow particularly *Swedish* experience.' *(J A Wainwright)*

Open: All year, except 24–26 December inclusive.
Rooms: 31 double, 14 single, 3 suites – 31 with shower, all with baby-listening. 26 rooms in 2 annexes. (7 rooms on ground floor.)
Facilities: Lounge, 2 TV rooms, 2 dining rooms; facilities for parties and functions. Large garden with tennis court, skating rink; bicycles; sauna, warm brine-bath, hair salon; skiing, sleigh-rides in winter; bathing, fishing, boating in summer. English spoken.
Location: 12 km from Leksand; on road between Leksand and Rättvik; parking.
Credit cards: Access/Euro/Mastercard, Barclay/Visa.
Terms: B & B 125–170 Skr. Set meals: lunch/dinner 45–70 Skr. Reduced rates for children sharing parents' room.

TANUMSHEDE 45700 Bohuslän   **Map 7**

Tanums Gestgifveri   *Telephone.* (0325) 290 10

'Tanumshede, 6 km from the sea, is a rather ordinary large village, with two supermarkets, a chemist, post office, small gift shop and tourist information office. It is however a strategic 160 km from Gothenburg and 140 km from Oslo. *Gestgifveri* means a guest house, but the standard of service and food is much higher than that suggests. The E6 runs a couple of gardens' lengths away so it is a little noisy, despite double glazing, but the 28 rooms are usually full of travelwise Swedes, Norwegians and Nederlanders, so it is wise to book ahead. The inn has been serving wayfarers since 1663, and Swedish owner manager Mr Steiner Öster personally supervises the kitchen. Waitresses and reception staff speak excellent English, Mr Öster is happier in French. Doubtless it is to his French wife that guests owe the comfort and extremely elegant decor. It is worth finding time to visit the Bronze Age rock carvings. There are several sites within 5 km and a charming little museum supplying a fact sheet in English. It is open from 10 a.m. to 7 p.m. and has a friendly cafeteria.' *(Mrs Maurice Yates)*

Open: 15 May–15 October.
Rooms: 11 double, 18 single, 2 suites – 4 with bath, 25 with shower, all with telephone and radio. (15 rooms on ground floor.)
Facilities: Lift; lobby, TV room, bar, cafeteria, pool room; small sauna with dip-pool. Fishing and sea bathing 4–6 km; golf 20 km. English spoken. &.
Location: 160 km from Gothenburg; 140 km from Oslo. In village centre; parking.
Credit cards: All major credit cards accepted.
Terms: B & B 195–235 Skr. Full *alc* 200 Skr, 50% reduction for children under 12; children under 2 free; special meals provided.

Hotel Eden au Lac, Zürich

Switzerland

AROSA, 7050 Grisons **Map 11**

Hôtel Belvédère-Tanneck *Telephone:* (081) 31.13.35

'A second-class hotel of no great pretensions, but full of robust Swiss *en pension*. Helpful staff and welcoming reception – they had two English girls from the Wirral serving as waitress and chambermaid for the season. We had a very pleasant room with a balcony giving a spectacular view in a sunny morning of snow-clad peaks bathed in a pink light. Comfortable beds, radio, good bedside lighting and very well-equipped bathroom – and the best-heated garage our car has ever rested in. We would strongly recommend guests not to eat *en pension* as the dinners looked very dull (rice pudding was the sweet of the day) but to eat in the basement *stüberl* where we had a splendid *fondue bourguignonne* and the place filled up later with locals.' *(Angela and David Stewart)*

Open: June–September, December–April.
Rooms: 70 beds – some rooms with bath or shower and kitchenette, all with radio, telephone and balcony.
Facilities: Lift, restaurant.
Location: Central; parking.
Terms: Rooms with breakfast and dinner 40–115 Sfrs (single), 80–225 Sfrs (double).

Hotel Casa Berno   *Telephone:* (093) 35.32.32
                                                            Telex: 846167

'Ascona is no longer the unspoilt fishing village of the 1920s, favourite
resort (and later refuge) of Central-European intellectuals, but its beautiful situation facing the Lago Maggiore remains, and the tastefully restored lanes of the village centre and attractive hotel terraces and cafés
facing the lake border mitigate the restless traffic of cars and the expensive
new concrete developments owned by the Central-European *nouveaux
riches* who have taken over Ascona's centre from the writers, artists and
nature apostles of bygone days. The wooded surroundings, the truly
romantic attraction of the most beautiful of Northern Italian lakes and the
limitless possibilities of excursions into the genuinely unspoilt valleys of
the Ticino, make up for the hustle and bustle of the village and the
tourist-overcrowded city of Locarno.
  '*Casa Berno* lies on the hillside between Monte Verità and Ronco,
referred to by the locals as *Monte Mercedes*, about 30 minutes' uphill walk
from Ascona's centre (15 minutes downhill, or less than ten minutes by
car, either way) and within about 15 minutes' level walking distance of
Ronco. The modern hotel has all facilities expected of a four-star establishment, yet none of the raffish décor of equivalent hotels of Ascona
itself, nor the slightly run-down character of its famous neighbour on
Monte Verità. The views from the hotel's terraces and swimming pool
over lake, islands and surrounding mountains could be called stunning,
breathtaking and soothing as well, which appears contradictory, yet
represents exactly the feeling of visitors and guests. And this view is
available to each room – all rooms face south and have a balcony or
terrace facing this ravishing aspect of Swiss–Italian beauty. The public
rooms have recently been refurbished and refurnished. The swimming
pool is admirably heated to 27–30°C, and there are ample secluded
terraced meadows for those who prefer individual quiet resting places.
The food (with choice of main courses) is of really high standard, even
recognized by those who claim to be connoisseurs of Swiss–French–
Italian cuisine. Meals, weather permitting, are willingly served on the
terrace – breakfast in the morning sun is such a beautiful experience that
one tends to linger on to forget all well-planned intentions to catch the
morning steamer or hydrofoil from Ascona to the Borromean Islands and
Stresa – ah well, a later one to the Brissago Islands will do, or a visit to the
markets of the Italian lakeside towns Luino or Cannobio, a drive to
Centovalli or Vallemaggia, or a leisurely level walk to Ronco or Arcegno
with their attractive *grottos*, for a rustic luncheon and a *boccalino* or two
of Merlot. Tours combining hotel bus drives and easy rambles are
organized by the hotel's reception. In short, *Casa Berno* presents all
characteristic attractions of the Ticino in contemporary comfort, far away
from, yet within reach of, Ascona's noise and commotion.' *(Arnold
Horwell)*

Open: March–November.
Rooms: 53 double, 7 single, 12 suites – all with bath, telephone, radio, balcony or
terrace.
Facilities: Lift; lounges (1 with TV), bar on roof-garden, grill-room, restaurant
with terrace. Sauna, solarium, fitness room. Garden with heated swimming pool.
Golf, tennis nearby. English spoken. &.
Location: Between Monte Verità and Ronco; parking.

Credit card: American Express.
Terms: B & B 98–118 Sfrs; half board 118–138 Sfrs, full board 134–155 Sfrs. Set meals: lunch 25 Sfrs, dinner 35 Sfrs. Reduced rates and special meals for children.

BASLE, 4058   **Map 11**

Hotel Krafft am Rhein   *Telephone:* (061) 26.88.77
Rheingasse 12   *Telex:* 64360

A medium-priced centrally-located modern hotel looking out on the Rhine and the Old Town. The hotel has its own restaurant, *zem Schnooggeloch*, and a broad terrace overlooking the river with the Cathedral beyond. 'The perfect Swiss family-run hotel. Extremely friendly staff. But make sure you are on the Rhine side, otherwise it can be noisy.' *(Godfrey Pilkington)*

Open: All year.
Rooms: 26 double, 26 single – 16 with bath, 32 with shower, all with telephone and radio.
Facilities: Lift, sitting room, TV room, 2 restaurants, terrace, café. English spoken.
Location: Central, on the Rhine; parking.
Credit cards: Access/Euro/Mastercard, American Express, Diners.
Terms: B & B 30–75 Sfrs; dinner, B & B 54–99 Sfrs; full board 78–123 Sfrs. Set meals: lunch/dinner 18–24 Sfrs; full *alc* 32 Sfrs. Reduced rates for children: under 6, 50%; 6–12, 30%. Special meals available.

CASTAGNOLA-LUGANO, 6976 Ticino   **Map 11**

Hotel Aniro   *Telephone:* (091) 52.50.31
Via Violetta 1

Once the retreat of a Russian Royal Duke, the *Aniro* has a magnificent position, 250 feet above the lake in a quiet cul-de-sac, 10 minutes' walk to the centre of town. Most of the rooms have balconies or a terrace overlooking the lake, and the hotel has a lift from the road. 'The meals were all set menus, but were not repeated during a fortnight's visit. The food was all first-class, as was the service and accommodation – and reasonably priced.' *(J Wilkinson)*

Open: March–November.
Rooms: 50 beds – all rooms with bath or shower, radio and telephone, most with balcony or terrace.
Facilities: Lift, reception, salon, restaurant, terrace. Garden, table-tennis, mini-golf, outdoor swimming pool.
Location: 10 minutes' walk from town centre, just off Via Cortiva; parking.
Terms: B & B 43–62 Sfrs; half board 16 Sfrs per person added to room rate; full board 26 Sfrs per person added to room rate.

We should be glad to hear of good hotels in Bern.

Hotel Eden   *Telephone:* (041) 94.32.94

'An officer of the British Ski Federation recommended this hotel to us for a Christmas and New Year holiday. We wanted somewhere small, offering good food, value for money, a friendly atmosphere and no inclusive-tour holidaymakers. We found just that. The *Hotel Eden* is central, close to the Ski School, opposite the pick-up point for the buses to the school slopes and the path for the start of mountain walks. We had a room with shower; our children did not. The beds were marvellously comfortable and everything in the bedrooms worked with typical Swiss efficiency. Yet modernization had in no way spoilt the atmosphere of this old-established hotel. A games room was a constant source of fun and things to do. Thomas and Sybil Reinhardt-Waser speak good English and were most attentive. Sybil went to great lengths in helping to get our very sick car repaired. Thomas prepared excellent and varied menus and his English staff served the food cheerfully. We ate *table d'hôte* in the restaurant but we sampled the *Stübli* once and the food (all Swiss specialities) was superb: our impression was borne out by the fact that a lot of Engelbergers patronised the *Stübli*. Interesting selection of Swiss and other wines. It cost the four of us the equivalent of £55 a day [1982] for dinner, bed and breakfast – excellent value for money indeed! The welcome was warm, and we were not hustled. One of the most enjoyable hotel experiences we have ever had.' *(Malcolm Seymour)*

Open: Mid December–mid April.
Rooms: 10 double (also let as singles) – most with shower and WC, all with telephone and radio.
Facilities: 2 salons (1 with TV), games room for children, restaurant, garden and terrace. English spoken.
Location: Central, near station and Ski School. Garage and outdoor parking.
Credit cards: All major credit cards accepted.
Terms: B & B 35–52 Sfrs; dinner, B & B 17 Sfrs per person added; full board 27 Sfrs added. Set meal: lunch about 14 Sfrs. Reduced rates for family holidays in summer and skiing holidays in winter (1 or 2 weeks).

FLIMS, 7018 Flims-Waldhaus   **Map 11**

Hotel Adula   *Telephone:* (081) 38.01.61
                                                   Telex: 74160 adula ch

Flims is a favourite medium-height (1,100 m), summer and winter resort in the Grisons, about 20 minutes' drive from Chur. The woods of the Waldhaus offer miles of easy walking for Senior Citizens (who are specially well looked after), and there is no shortage of mountain walks for the more energetic, as well as a network of chairlifts and cable cars. The *Adula*, close by the Waldhaus, is an admirable example of a medium-to-large Swiss resort hotel. It has a huge range of facilities, plus impeccable service and dependably good Swiss cooking. In the winter, the hotel provides its guests with transport to the mountain railway, and in the spring and summer it organizes conducted walks, has barbecues outside the large daylight indoor pool, and does all the things you would expect of a good resort hotel. It doesn't suit all-comers: one guest was depressed to find that, when he was staying, dinner started at 6.45, that lights were out in the dining room by 9.0 and the place deserted by 9.30. The *Adula* is adding a wing of 30 new rooms at the end of 1983, and may become too big for Guide readers. But at the moment there are plenty of adula-tors who come year after year.

Open: 18 December–18 October.
Rooms: 52 double, 31 single – 41 with bath, 30 with shower, all with telephone and radio. 22 rooms in annexe. Another wing, with 30 double bedrooms due to open at Christmas 1983.
Facilities: 2 lifts, salon, TV room, bar with pianist, 2 dining rooms, dinner-dances, games room; indoor swimming pool; sauna, steam bath. Garden with terrace and 3 tennis courts; tennis instructor at the hotel. English spoken.
Location: In the Waldhaus part of Flims; parking.
Credit cards: All major credit cards accepted.
Terms: B & B 55–110 Sfrs; dinner, B & B 75–150 Sfrs. (Annexe rooms are cheapest.) Set meals: lunch 25 Sfrs, dinner 28 Sfrs. Reduced rates for children sharing parents' room; special meals on request.

GENEVA, 1204   **Map 11**

Hôtel L'Arbalète   *Telephone:* (022) 28.41.55
3 rue de la Tour Maitresse   *Telex:* 427293

A small de-luxe hotel, well-located near the lake and the best shops, recommended for the quality of its furnishings, its excellent reasonably priced restaurant and pleasant staff. One reader last year, endorsing the entry, particularly appreciated the restaurant's courtesy in cooking a Zurichoise speciality, a favourite of her husband's which was not on their menu. The only snag about the *Arbalète*, at least on a Saturday night, is the proximity to the Piccadilly Nightclub next door. Some readers may prefer the *Hôtel Les Armures* (see below) under the same ownership. *(Jill and John Dick)*

Open: All year.
Rooms: 32 double – all with bath, telephone, radio and colour TV.
Facilities: Lift, hall, bar, restaurant, breakfast room. English spoken. 5 minutes from the lake.
Location: Central, but there are quiet rooms; parking.
Credit cards: American Express, Barclay/Visa, Diners, Eurocard.
Terms: B & B 170 Sfrs. Set meals: lunch/dinner 8–30 Sfrs. Reduced rates and special meals for children.

GENEVA, 1204   **Map 11**

Hôtel Les Armures   *Telephone:* (022) 28.91.72
Puits-St-Pierre   *Telex:* 421129

A warm endorsement for Tom Pocock's recommendation last year of this newly opened hotel in a quiet little square near the Cathedral, high up in the old town. The building itself is 17th-century, and its restaurant at the back is said to be the oldest in the city. 'Indeed all that it was cracked up to be in your former report. I was able to park just outside the front door – no fuss. The feeling of solidity and repose about the place – no oppressive rules and regulations – has a magical effect. After suffering the heat and discomfort of Germany's continental quilts (though they were at hand here for those who want them), it was a relief to find a firm but soft bed of sensible size, with sheets and blankets, a perfect bathroom, with *bath* (not merely a shower) and a built-in hair-dryer! The delicious breakfast, cheerfully served had – wait for it – *really hot coffee*, a rarity on the Continent nowadays. Everything is "Swiss clean", unoppressively new and solid. I cannot recommend it too highly.' *(James Shorrocks)*

Open: All year.
Rooms: 24 double, 4 single – all with bath, telephone, radio and colour TV.
Facilities: Lobby, salon, breakfast room, restaurant, *Stüberl* (rustic bar/restaurant). English spoken.
Location: Central, near St-Pierre cathedral; no special parking facilities.
Credit cards: All major credit cards accepted.
Terms: Rooms (including breakfast) 170–250 Sfrs. Full *alc* about 40 Sfrs. Reduced rates for children.

GENEVA, 1202   **Map 11**

Hotel Mon Repos   *Telephone:* (022) 32.80.10
131 rue de Lausanne

'Inexpensive fairly old-fashioned hotel on the right bank, within walking distance of UNO, WHO and other international agencies. Rooms at the front tend to be noisy, but the ones at the back are quiet. Very near large park (Mon Repos) and lake, and Botanical Gardens. Friendly staff. Convenient for station too (15 minutes' walk or, frequent bus, No. 5).' *(Andrew Herxheimer)*

Open: All year.
Rooms: 70 double, 20 single, 10 suites – all with bath or shower, telephone and radio; TV and baby-listening on request. (Suites with kitchenettes in annexe.)
Facilities: TV room, drawing room, bar, 2 restaurants, terrace. English spoken.
Location: On the bank of Lake Geneva facing the public parks and gardens; private garage (6 Sfrs).
Credit cards: All major credit cards accepted.
Terms: B & B 55–75 Sfrs. Set meals: lunch/dinner 20–25 Sfrs. Reduced rates for children; special meals on request.

GSTAAD, 3780   **Map 11**

Hotel Christiania   *Telephone:* (030) 45121/2/3

'With 27 beds, the *Christiania* is the smallest four-star luxury hotel in fashionable Gstaad, warmly recommended to those visitors to Switzerland who prefer a resort, with all its facilities of boutiques, sport and food shops, cafés, and lively pavements frequented by the beautiful people, to the rustic charms of a chalet village. Mrs Nopper (of *Ermitage*, Schönried fame – q.v.) has changed this old *hotel garni* as you enter on the Saanen road to a bijou hotel which satisfies the highest demands in comfort, furnishing and service. Most rooms have every conceivable facility, are spacious, and are individually furnished with taste and charm. The small yet elegant restaurant provides attractive snacks and satisfying main meals. However, the main attraction is Mrs Nopper's hospitality, extending a specially warm welcome to old friends and newcomers alike, from Britain and the USA.' *(Arnold Horwell)*

Open: All year.
Rooms: 17 double, 6 single, 3 suites – all with bath, telephone and radio, most with colour TV and balcony.
Facilities: Salon, TV room, restaurant; garden. Guests have free use of the heated swimming pool near the Palace Hotel in summer. English spoken.
Location: Central, opposite the skating rink; light sleepers might find front rooms noisy. Garage.
Terms: Rooms with breakfast 55–125 Sfrs (single), 90–210 Sfrs (double). Half board 30 Sfrs per person added. Set meals: lunch/dinner 35 Sfrs. Reduced rates for children under 12.

GUNTEN-THUNERSEE, 3654 Bern   Map 11

Hirschen am See   *Telephone:* (033) 51.22.44
                                                              Telex: 922100

'Gunten is a village on the north shore of Lake Thun, and although we had a car we had no need to use it due to the excellent boat and trolleybus services. The hotel is well-managed and comfortable with south-facing aspect. It has a lakeside garden and terrace; the lake steamers call at the adjacent landing-stage, but the rear rooms overlooking the lake are quiet. The managers, who speak good English, were most attentive, the food was excellently prepared and served, and the wine list was extensive. The lounge was light and well-furnished in an old-fashioned style. The bedrooms, although a trifle small, were comfortable and those we occupied had balconies where we enjoyed breakfast overlooking the lake and the Bernese Alps. There are numerous excursions to be made to the surrounding area and walks galore. No night-life when we were there. Warmly recommended.' *(John H Bell)*

Open: April–October.
Rooms: 47 double, 21 single – 39 with bath, 29 with shower, all with telephone and radio, many with balcony.
Facilities: Lift, lounge, 2 restaurants (one on terrace); conference facilities. Garden. Private lido; water sports, fishing and sailing; tennis nearby. English spoken. &.
Location: On the N shore of Lake Thun. Leave motorway at Thun Nord; travel towards Gunten.
Credit cards: Access/Euro/Mastercard, American Express, Diners.
Terms: B & B 53–76 Sfrs; dinner, B & B 73–96 Sfrs; full board 85–108 Sfrs. Set meals: lunch 18 Sfrs; dinner 22 Sfrs; full *alc* 38 Sfrs. Special meals provided for children on request.

KANDERSTEG, 3718 Berner Oberland   Map 11

Hotel Blümlisalp   *Telephone:* (033) 75.12.44

The holiday resort of Kandersteg, 1,200 metres up in the Bernese Oberland, at the foot of the Blümlisalp range, has plenty to offer its visitors whatever the season. And for those who want to be hoisted higher, whether skiers or walkers, there is a wide range of chairlifts and cabin lifts. The *Blümlisalp* is a middle-sized, middle-priced middle-class family hotel, in a fine scenic position and particularly well-equipped with sporting adjuncts: an indoor swimming pool with what the hotel calls underwater massage and against-current swimming, an American bowling alley (sound-proofed) as well as a games room wtih table tennis. In the summer, the hotel organizes picnic parties, walking tours and botanic trips to Stresa in Italy; in the winter there are sledge-drives and ski-tours at night with *Glühwein*. 'All round excellence.' *(J C Nicholson Belwell)*

Open: 1 December–31 October.
Rooms: 16 double, 4 single – 8 with bath, 10 with shower, 6 with radio.
Facilities: Lift, TV room, lounge, bar, 2 restaurants. Bowling alley, heated indoor swimming pool, games room, sun terrace. Walking, winter sports. English spoken.
Location: 5 minutes from centre, in main street of village; parking.
Credit cards: Access/Euro/Mastercard, Barclay/Visa, Diners.
Terms: B & B 30–55 Sfrs; dinner, B & B 44–80 Sfrs; full board 12 Sfrs added. Set meals: lunch 19 Sfrs, dinner 24 Sfrs; full *alc* 30 Sfrs. Reduced weekly rates in low season. Reduced rates for children sharing parents' room: under 6, 50%; under 12, 30%; special meals available.

KLOSTERS, 7250   **Map 11**

Hotel Bündnerhof   *Telephone:* (083) 414.50

The entry below, reproduced from last year, has been warmly endorsed by recent visitors to the *Bündnerhof*. 'All as before – if not better,' and the hotel tell us that they have now added showers to six more of the single rooms.

'Old-fashioned family hotel. Mother/daughter/son-in-law. Extremely friendly and run with typical Swiss efficiency. Bedrooms (a *few* with private loo and shower) are well-equipped and beds lovely. Sitting area restricted – stuffy little room but there is a pub bit where the locals come to eat and drink and where Frau Anderhub holds court. Son-in-law is an excellent chef – there is no choice but the food is plentiful and well-served. Daughter supervises with eagle eye – second helpings are offered and she soon gets to know individual dislikes. It's not at all grand, but they speak English and love having English visitors. A member of our party had to be left behind in hospital where he was visited by the family and given every assistance to help him get down to the valley trail on his crutches. A warm, personal welcoming place.' *(E Newall)*

Open: All year, except May.
Rooms: 13 double with bath; 6 single with shower, in annexe.
Facilities: Lift, lounge, bar, dining room, restaurant. Garden; bowling and table tennis. Close to heated summer swimming pool, mountain cable railway, ski-lift station and skating rink. English spoken. &.
Location: In town centre; private parking.
Terms: Dinner, B & B 42–80 Sfrs; full board 10 Sfrs added. Reduced rates for children sharing parents' room.

> If you have difficulty in finding hotels because directions given in the Guide are inadequate, please help us to improve them.

LUCERNE, 6000   Map 11

Hotel Royal   *Telephone:* (041) 51.12.33
Rigistrasse 22

'Those with childhood memories of huge, hushed Swiss hotels, commanding vistas of mountains reflected in still lakes, are often disappointed on return. Many of them have been converted into flats, or are seedy shadows of their former selves, kept going by casinos and night clubs. For such seekers after a reassuring echo, the *Hotel Royal* is rewarding. It stands on the outskirts of the charming old town of Lucerne, overlooking what must be the most ridiculously beautiful view of lake and mountains in Switzerland. It is high above the waterside promenade so that a short but steep uphill walk is necessary to reach it. The view makes that worthwhile. The *Royal* was the last of the grand hotels of the great days of Swiss tourism to be built hereabouts – in 1910 – and, with 80 beds, it is one of the smallest. It still has solid Edwardian calm and comfort but the cheerful ministrations of the Hofer family, who own and run it, save it from becoming museum-like. Once, Herr Hofer says, the guests were almost all English and they still make up a high proportion of his guests, although mostly in package-holiday groups and mostly over-50. The *Royal* is a quiet and unostentatious hotel for a rest, with the Hofers always ready to arrange an excursion on the lake or to the summits of Pilatus or the Rigi when activity is required.' *(Tom Pocock)*

Open: April–October.
Rooms: 80 beds – some rooms with bath or shower, all with telephone.
Facilities: Lift, bar, 2 restaurants (1 on terrace).
Location: On the outskirts of Lucerne; parking.
Terms: Rooms with breakfast 36–68 Sfrs (single), 60–115 Sfrs (double); half board 14 Sfrs per person added to room rate; full board 21 Sfrs added.

MONTANA, 3692 Valais   Map 11

Hotel du Lac   *Telephone:* (027) 41.34.14

'This hotel, which I first noticed 16 years ago, has a superb position on a shelf 1,200 metres above the north side of the Rhône valley overlooking the Valaisian Alps. It is owned and run by the Fischer family; the son now provides sophisticated comfort, informality, good food and wine at reasonable cost and a ready welcome to English guests with his total fluency in our language. There is a bar and most rooms have balconies facing south where breakfast is served on request without additional cost. Nothing seems to be too much trouble for the staff or management. Although development has made Montana less attractive it has not affected the hotel, protected by a lake on its north side and only five minutes' walk from the main ski lifts. Apart from its skiing potential the hotel offers an attractive base for a summer walking holiday with lifts rising to over 10,000 feet and tennis, windsurfing and swimming readily available.' *(G C Brown)*

Open: June–October, December–May.
Rooms: 24 double, 9 single, 14 with bath, 9 with shower – most with balcony, all with telephone, radio and TV on request.

Facilities: Bar, restaurant. Garden. Tennis, mini-golf, table tennis, windsurfing; winter sports nearby. English spoken.
Location: N of Route E2 between Sion and Sierre.
Credit cards: All major credit cards accepted.
Terms: Dinner, B & B 24–55 Sfrs; full board 7 Sfrs supplement. Special meals for children on request.

MURTEN, 3280   Map 11

Hotel Weisses Kreuz   *Telephone:* (037) 71.26.41

'Murten is a well-preserved medieval town, still with fortified towers and walls dating from the 15th century, which makes an attractive staging-post between Basel and Zürich and the French cantons. The rooms of the *Weisses Kreuz* are comfortable, with beautiful views over lake Murten and the Jura hills. It has a very good restaurant, with a splendid lakeside terrace, specialising in freshwater fish, including crayfish, *Egli, Felchen* and pike – about 20 ways of preparing them. The local white wine (Vully) is quite excellent. (Swiss wines are generally much underrated.)' *(Arnold Horwell; warmly endorsed by P G Bourne)*

Open: All year, except 15 December–31 January.
Rooms: 25 double, 1 single – 11 with bath, 7 with shower – all with telephone. 17 rooms in annexe.
Facilities: Lift, salons, terrace restaurant overlooking the lake; banqueting and conference facilities. English spoken.
Location: 50 metres from town centre; parking nearby.
Terms: B & B 46–66 Sfrs; dinner, B & B 60–86 Sfrs; full board 80–106 Sfrs. Set meals: breakfast 6 Sfrs, lunch 16 Sfrs; full *alc* 37 Sfrs.

NYON, 1260 Vaud   Map 11

Hôtel du Clos de Sadex   *Telephone:* (022) 61.28.31

A superb patrician house on lac Léman (23 km from Geneva), formerly the home of Major and Madame Louis de Tscharner, who now run it as a hotel of great character and charm. The atmosphere of the aristocratic family whose seat it was (and is) is carefully preserved in the furnishing of the public rooms and the restaurant. Beautiful lakeside garden, with breakfast and lunch willingly served on the terrace overlooking the lake and French shoreline and mountains opposite. There is a modern annexe which blends in well. The bedrooms are large and have high standards of comfort, though we did have one complaint this year about the thinness of the bedroom walls. 'A fantastic hotel in a magnificent position. The food is really first-class, and the staff and management are friendly and courteous. We fully endorse the remark quoted in your last report: "We wished we could take the hotel with us wherever we went."' *(Hugh and Elsie Pryor; also Barbara Anderson)*

Open: All year, except February.
Rooms: 15 double, 3 single – 14 with bath, 2 with shower, all with telephone. 5 rooms in annexe. (3 rooms on ground floor.)
Facilities: Hall, salon with TV, restaurant; conference room. Gardens with

terrace for meals, leading directly to the lake (the hotel has a small harbour); swimming, boating, waterskiing. English spoken.

Location: 1 km from Nyon towards Lausanne on the lake road; the hotel is on the right; parking.

Credit cards: All major credit cards accepted.

Terms: Rooms (including breakfast) 42–110 Sfrs; full board 60 Sfrs added to room rates. Set meals: lunch/dinner 35–40 Sfrs; full *alc* 55 Sfrs. Reduced rates for children sharing parents' room; special meals provided.

RINGGENBERG, Nr Interlaken, Bernese Oberland, 3852   Map 11

Hotel Seeburg   *Telephone:* (036) 22.29.61

'Ringgenberg is a very pretty flowery village, with delightful views towards the Faulhorn Schwarzhorn range, where the spurs of the Alps literally plunge into the waters of Lake Brienz. It is 3 km from Interlaken; you can take a path beside the shore of the lake and return by steamer. We have been visiting the *Seeburg* for about ten years now, and have seen it in just about every season, from the late heavy snows of Easter, baking hot June days through to the light new snow falling on the highest peaks heralding the beginning of winter. It has an idyllic situation, literally on the lakeside; the nearest road is five minutes' walk away, so there is practically no noise apart from ducks and swans squabbling for titbits thrown by the guests or the occasional arrival of the lake steamer. The hotel's lakeside gardens are most attractive, with masses of geraniums and flowery window-boxes in the summer. There are plenty of tables and chairs for drinks or lunch or even, in fine weather, alfresco dining; also beach beds for sunbathing; and the hotel has facilities for sailing, rowing and fishing.

'The Michel family have owned it for many years; Peter Michel, the present owner, took it over from his father nine years ago. He and his wife are rather quiet and shy, but run the hotel efficiently and the same guests appear year after year to enjoy a peaceful holiday. Rooms are clean and simply furnished. In the summer, there is always a race for shower and toilets, and you might do well to bring your own big towels with you as the hotel towels are uncomfortably small. Lighting in the room is appalling – a common failing, but you can remove the lampshades. The food is excellent value for money – large portions, with second helpings offered. The local fish is delicious. Vegetables vary. Service is willing though slow when the hotel is full. . . . There are faults to find with any hotel, but the gorgeous situation, friendly staff, and, above all, the value for money must offset most complaints.' *(Padi Howard)*

Open: April–October.

Rooms: 50 beds, some rooms with bath, all with hot and cold running water and central heating.

Facilities: Lift, salon, dining room, terrace, garden; on lake with facilities for watersports, sailing and fishing.

Location: 3 km SW of Interlaken, on the Brienzersee.

Credit cards: All major credit cards accepted.

Terms: Rooms with breakfast 35–40 Sfrs (single), 46–100 Sfrs (double), half board 11 Sfrs per person added to room rate; full board 19 Sfrs added.

Please don't just leave the feedback to others.

Hôtel Beausite   *Telephone:* (027) 65.15.86

'The *Hôtel Beausite* stands high up in the mountain village of St Luc overlooking the highest mountains of Val d'Anniviers which includes the Matterhorn. Rarely have we seen a view comparable to this one. The hotel is ten years old and offers modern comfortable rooms; most have their own bathrooms *en suite*, also a balcony. It is a family-run hotel with a very friendly atmosphere, and good home cooking. It is situated in an excellent walking area, which is also a well-equipped skiing centre. One *very* important point is that the hotel has a good parking area, and also a large underground heated garage with electrically operated doors, something which is rarely (if ever) found, also a lift to all floors direct from the underground car park.' *(Hugh and Elsie Pryor)*

Open: All year.
Rooms: 26 double, 2 single, 2 studios – 15 with bath, 3 with shower, all with telephone and balcony; cooking facilities in studios.
Facilities: Lift, lounge, 2 bars, 2 dining rooms, disco in season, terrace; facilities for functions; tennis, winter sports, swimming pool in summer, 4 km.
Location: Halfway between Lausanne and Milan; turn off at Sierre (22 km); underground car park.
Restriction: No children under 2.
Credit card: American Express.
Terms: B & B 30–35 Sfrs; dinner, B & B 45–50 Sfrs; full board 50–55 Sfrs. Set meals: lunch 12.50 Sfrs; dinner 15 Sfrs; full *alc* 30–35 Sfrs. Reduced rates for children sharing parents' room; special meals provided.

Hôtel Bella Tola   *Telephone:* (027) 65.14.44

'St Luc is a typical Swiss mountain village facing south towards the Matterhorn, high up on the slopes of a sunny valley, two valleys west of Zermatt. To those whose French is more fluent than their German, one of its attractions is that it is (coming west) the first of the French-speaking valleys. The views are superb, and even the Swiss themselves admit that the wild flowers in early summer are better than almost anywhere else in Switzerland. The *Bella Tola*'s cooking is supervised by the proprietor and his wife; the proprietor himself serves the wines, and helps those of his guests who do not know Swiss wines, with his advice (and he doesn't necessarily recommend the most expensive!). Unlike many continental hotels, there is an admirable lounge with (in the evenings) an open fire and also a very snug and cosy bar. At lunchtime, snacks and light dishes are served in this bar, or, in fine weather, in the garden. One of the pleasant things about the *Bella Tola* is that its guests include a representative selection from all over western Europe, so that it is never monopolized by any one nationality.' *(E M Sanders)*
   Last year's entry, reproduced above, has been endorsed by recent visitors, including one who wrote gratefully: 'Although our impression was that the hotel was used by an older clientele, our 13-month-old daughter was made most welcome, with the proprietor even going shopping for yogurt for her tea.'

Another, while enthusiastic about the welcome, the decor, the views and the overall value, did express reservations about the meals – not at all about their quality, but the helpings were, in his view, inadequate for healthy young hikers or skiers after a day in the mountains. *(Judith and David Jenkins; also P Mahrer, Roger Bennett)*

Open: 1 June–25 September, 15 December–20 April.
Rooms: 42 double – 32 with bath, 10 with shower.
Facilities: Lift, 3 salons (1 with TV), bar, restaurant, children's playroom. Garden. English spoken.
Location: 22 km from Sierre. (*Warning:* parking is available 100 metres from the hotel, but it is right by the road and there is no security; also there is an uphill walk back to the hotel.)
Credit cards: All major credit cards accepted.
Terms: B & B 25–45 Sfrs; dinner, B & B 55–65 Sfrs. Set meals: lunch/dinner 20–25 Sfrs; full *alc* 35 Sfrs. Reduced rates and special meals for children.

SCHÖNRIED, Gstaad, 3778 Bernese Oberland   **Map 11**

Hotel Ermitage-Golf   *Telephone:* (030) 4.27.27

'Schönried is a village in the Simmental, about 180 metres above Gstaad. Although now on the way to becoming a resort of repute, with marvellous winter sports facilities, it has preserved its character since the days when the Monaco Grimaldis built their chalet refuge above the village, mainly due to the far-sighted planning policy of the local authorities which permit building in chalet style only. Although unspoilt in appearance, one of the "attractions" is the neighbourhood of Gstaad – one of the most fashionable resorts of Switzerland. Only nine minutes by *Bähnli* (the Montreux–Berner Oberland Railway), or ten minutes by car, and you can enjoy (if that is the right word) the boutiques and cafés of Gstaad, or the simple attractions of the larger village of Saanen – and then you return to Schönried and are surrounded by meadows and pine woods, or unsullied snow fields, away from it all. In August there is the additional attraction of the Festival directed by Saanen's most famous citizen, Yehudi Menuhin, one of Europe's most attractive chamber music festivals.

'The *Ermitage Hotel* combines the appearance of two interconnected chalets with the facilities and comforts of a really first class hotel. *Habitués* will remember the charm of the *Ermitage* of the Sixties and early Seventies under the Nopper management. When the Noppers left, alas, the standards declined, to be brought up again to the highest level by Herr Lutz and his *Mitarbeiter*. They built the second chalet, the "new wing", with the most comfortable rooms and apartments (some of those in the old wing still require some updating). There are three restaurants – a charcoal grill restaurant, a rôtisserie and the Restaurant Français – all really beautifully furnished in best *gemütlich* Swiss style; so are the lounge and the two well-stocked bars. There are also underground garages, a sauna, a squash court, conference and "fitness" rooms. The greatest attraction, however, is the *Solbad*, a reasonably-sized swimming pool filled with briny water – Continentals firmly believe in its health-giving qualities – heated to 33°C (93°F). Amazingly, this indoor pool opens out to an outdoor pool of similar size, heated to the same temperature. It was for us a truly sensational experience in December to swim outside, the body most comfortably warmed, but the head in the nippy night air of − 10°C, the steam of the water rising to reveal the surrounding snow banks several metres high; we did, however, refrain from climbing out for a really good roll in the snow. The friendliness of the hotel's service, the variety of the meals and a sleigh ride laid on for the guests on Christmas Eve, deserve special praise.' *(Arnold Horwell)*

Open: All year, except April and November.
Rooms: 70 beds – most rooms with bath or shower.
Facilities: 2 bars, lounge, 3 restaurants, café; conference facilities; squash, sauna, solarium, fitness room, heated indoor swimming pool; garden with swimming pool and tennis court.
Location: Between Aigle and Interlaken; underground parking.
Terms: Dinner, B & B 50–150 Sfrs; full board 16 Sfrs added per person.

TEGNA, 6652 Ticino Svizzera **Map 11**

Casa Barbate *Telephone:* (093) 81.14.30

'Tegna is a small unspoiled village in the Centovalli area of the Ticino, near Locarno at the north east end of Lake Maggiore. It is an excellent centre for walking in lake, valley and mountain scenery, and with a car the scope extends to remote Alpine villages and the Italian border. The hotel, which is just off the main street of the village, is a modern one-storey building of character set in a pretty garden. It is light and spacious, and everything in it carries the stamp of the owner, Madame Jenny, who is herself Irish. The decor is restful and imaginative. The lounge has books, record-player, pictures, flowers, and the atmosphere of a private house. All the bedrooms have bathrooms and are furnished as bed-sitting rooms. Most open on to their own section of the garden, so one sunbathes in peace and seclusion. The small railway from Locarno to Domodossola passes the north side of the house, but I slept on that side and hardly heard the trains. Because there are no steps, the hotel can take guests in wheelchairs. The cooking is consistently excellent, and the service efficient and friendly. People come back year after year. Madame Jenny likes to introduce newcomers to other guests, and often joins everyone in the lounge in the evening when the talk is general. One would miss a lot by opting out of this informal, friendly atmosphere. She is interested in helping each guest to have the holiday he or she wants – lending local maps to walkers, telling one where to look for gentians, recommending a concert in Locarno, advising on local wines. She enjoys the company of artists, writers and musicians, and the hotel attracts people with similar interests. Altogether, most unusual and delightful.' *(Miss H M Dillon)*

As on previous occasions, and not just for sentimental reasons, we have quoted again from our original 1977 report, which has consistently been endorsed. Among this year's crop, one correspondent wrote appreciatively of the way in which Madame Jenny and her staff coped with a 13-month-old daughter, though her impression was that they were more used to dealing with an older clientele. Another mentioned gratefully the provision of a hot plate in the rooms for midday picnicking, and went on: 'We found *Casa Barbate* exactly as described, and Madame Jenny could not have been more welcoming and considerate. No-one need fear that the emphasis on the promotion of sociableness among her guests will discomfort those who prize privacy on their holidays or whose conversational standard in any language other than English would make them feel a misfit. Madame Jenny is too sensitive a hostess to embarrass any guest for that.' *(Judith and David Jenkins, Charles and Margaret Baker)*

Open: Mid March–30 October.
Rooms: 12 double, 3 single – 12 with bath, some with cooking facilities, all with telephone.
Facilities: Lounge, restaurant; banqueting and conference facilities. Sun terrace. Garden with pool. Bathing, boating 200 m. English spoken. &.
Location: 4 km from Locarno towards Centovalli.
Credit card: Euro.
Terms: B & B 46–75 Sfrs; dinner, B & B 68–96 Sfrs. Set meal: dinner 22–24 Sfrs. Reduced rates and special meals for children.

THUN, 3600 Bernese Oberland   Map 11

Hotel Beau-Rivage   *Telephone:* (033) 22.22.36
Aare-Quai

'The small town of Thun is the gateway to the Bernese Oberland, at the western end of Lake Thun. It is far less crowded than Interlaken, at the other end of the lake, less touristy, more genuinely Swiss, and also offers a better view of the High Alps. What lifts the *Beau-Rivage* above all others in Thun is its marvellous position. It is an imposing old building which overlooks the river Aare as it leaves the lake. There is no road for cars on either side of the Aare, so the rooms facing south (the majority – but it is worth specifying the south side when booking: rooms facing the north are noisy and without an outlook) have a spectacular view across the river and the Alps beyond. Being large and roomy, the hotel offers that solid comfort so often absent in new hotels. The bedrooms are airy. Furnishings are not luxurious, but adequate. Downstairs, there is a large lounge with easy chairs, more English than Swiss, which leads out on to a garden terrace. The hotel is run as a *garni*, i.e. no main meals provided, but there is an adjoining café serving snacks, and there are plenty of good restaurants in the town, a few minutes' walk away. And it is always a joy to come back, from the noise and bustle of town life, over the old wooden bridge with its weir to the peaceful situation of the *Beau-Rivage*, where all you hear is the water rushing across the weir. Prices are very reasonable for what is offered. The proprietors, Mr and Mrs J Wuetrich, both speak excellent English.' *(Richard Pinner)*

Last year's entry, reproduced above, has been endorsed by one correspondent, but another reader was less enthusiastic. He agreed that the hotel had a wonderful position in a glorious spot and appreciated the airy bedrooms and the modern bathrooms. But he minded the fact that the hotel lacked its own restaurant; the ones nearby were not close enough on a wet night for a couple with a 6-year-old in tow. And, in general, he felt the hotel was slightly run-down in appearance, and could do with a lick of fresh paint. More reports welcome.

Open: 1 May–31 October. (Restaurant closed Monday.)
Rooms: 20 double, 10 single, 2 suites – 22 with bath, 1 with shower, all with telephone.
Facilities: Lift, salon, TV lounge, writing room, breakfast room, dining room, bar, games and fitness rooms; heated indoor swimming pool. Garden with coffee shop and sun terrace; situated on the river, with quay. English spoken. &.
Location: On the road from Thun to Interlaken via Gunten, between the town and the casino. 300 m from town centre; garage (7Sfrs per night), free public car park for 150 cars nearby.
Credit cards: All major credit cards accepted.

Terms: B & B 30–70 Sfrs. *Plat du jour* at the *Café Maxim* in the hotel: 8 Sfrs. Reduced rates for children.

VADUZ, Liechtenstein   **Map 11**

Hotel Real   *Telephone:* (075) 2.22.22
Telex: 77809

'The *Hotel Real* is one of several on the main street of Vaduz, and we chose it because it looked clean and prosperous, with an attractive restaurant on the first floor. Inside, we found excellent use of natural materials: creamy marble and natural carved dark elm, attractive lighting, good carpets. The entrance foyer and bar are tiled in an interesting rich red glazed tile, ideal for travellers coming in straight off the snow. The room we had was well-designed, with an enormous window opening on to a narrow balcony. The linen in both bedroom and restaurant had that particular polished crispness that bespeaks a first-class laundry. There was a large and well-fitted bathroom. But the food was the most surprising of all: we had enjoyed the food at a two-rosette Michelin restaurant the evening before, but here, unheralded and unsung, we found its equal. Not quite so much panache of presentation, but perfectly cooked fish, beautiful sauces, and the most delicious mousse of passion-fruit sweet. Not surprisingly, the restaurant was the scene of local celebratory meals, and the chef emerged to carve their *boeuf-en-croûte* himself. Not really a tourist centre, but well worth a detour on the way north or south.' *(David and Angela Stewart)*

Open: All year.
Rooms: 6 double, 1 single, 1 suite – 7 with bath, 3 with shower, all with radio and telephone, some with balcony.
Facilities: Lift, bar, brasserie, restaurant. English spoken.
Location: Central; light sleepers might find traffic a bit noisy; parking.
Credit cards: All major credit cards accepted.
Terms: B & B 70–75 Sfrs. Full *alc* 85 Sfrs.

ZERMATT, 3920 Valais   **Map 11**

Hotel Garni Metropol   *Telephone:* (028) 67.32.31

The brochure says the *Metropol* offers 'consciously elegant service', but we think that misleading. What draws guests back to this hotel year after year – and we were told of one couple now on their 12th visit – is the specially warm caring attention of the English-speaking Taugwalder family who own this small unpretentious hotel on the banks of the fast-flowing Vispa, which runs close by. All the south-facing rooms offer the famous Matterhorn view. A particular attraction of the hotel is its own private garden (something of a rarity in Zermatt these days). Officially it's a breakfast-only place, but it offers a wide range of snacks. Last year, we quoted a metropolitan addict, who concluded his paean: 'I am not easily satisfied when it comes to hotels, but at the *Metropol* I cannot think of any improvement that could be made; perfection is something that does not exist where human beings are concerned, but this hotel is very close to it.' Recent visitors echo these sentiments: 'No praise too high for this small hotel and the personal and friendly attention of the young owners. Except on Mondays, when no meals are served, we took all our evening meals in the hotel, and the simple snacks were more than adequate and very reasonable. On Mondays we had a feast at the *Pollux Hotel*, owned by Herr Taugwalder's two brothers. The hotel is quiet except for the nearby stream. You soon get used to the sound of water, however.' *(R E and W C Wessely; also Richard Pinner)*

Open: 20 November–10 May, 10 June–10 October; no meals served on Monday evening.
Rooms: 20 double, 4 single – 16 with bath, 4 with shower, all with telephone, radio, colour TV and baby-listening.
Facilities: Salon, bar, dining room, TV room. Small garden on river. English spoken.
Location: In town centre, 2 minutes from the station; hotel porter will fetch you. (No cars in Zermatt.)
Credit cards: All major credit cards accepted.
Terms: B & B 35–70 Sfrs.

ZÜRICH, 8023   Map 11

Hotel Eden au Lac   *Telephone:* (01) 47.94.04
Utoquai 45   *Telex:* 52440

Not the largest, but certainly one of Zürich's grander hotels, recalling old-style opulence of the heyday of Swiss tourism: the ornate Edwardian exterior, with statues and caryatids, flower-filled urns and balconies looking across the lake, can't have changed much this century, though the lakeside promenade on which it stands has become a dual carriageway and a major thoroughfare. However, all the rooms are now double-glazed and fully air-conditioned and the hotel has been making another concession to modernity recently in the shape of direct-dial telephones. 'Possesses the discreet charm of the aristocracy' was a *mot* we quoted in a previous entry. A recent guest warmly endorses the recommendation: 'A mixture of Swiss efficiency, superb courteous service with modern conveniences. Not cheap but excellent value. To indicate the service, no taxis were available when I wanted to leave, so the hall porter, without being asked, decided to take me to the station in the hotel's limousine. Just the right size of hotel, in my view, for Zürich.' *(Brian Whittaker; also O Kromwell)*

Open: All year.
Rooms: 30 double, 21 single, 2 suites – 44 with bath, 9 with shower, all with telephone, radio, colour TV and baby-listening on request.
Facilities: Lift, reception rooms, bar, 2 restaurants; conference facilities; sauna. 7–10 minutes' walk from town centre; overlooks Zürich lake; good walking, safe bathing. English spoken.
Location: Central (just E of Bellevue Platz); parking.
Credit cards: All major credit cards accepted.
Terms: B & B 110–160 Sfrs. Set meals: 36–45 Sfrs; full *alc* 70 Sfrs.

Deadlines: nominations for the 1984 edition should reach us not later than 1 June 1983. Latest date for comments on existing entries: 31 July 1983.

Hotel Florhof   *Telephone:* (01) 47.44.70
Florhofgasse 4

A 16th-century patrician's house set in a small garden on a quiet residential street, but also a well-ordered hotel with every mod. con. It's within easy walking distance of the Kunsthaus and the old city, and a few minutes from the centre by tram or taxi. Meals in the restaurant or on the terrace are good, if not *cordon bleu*. 'A very quiet clean small hotel. Lashings of hot water and big towels. A friendly atmosphere and flowers everywhere.' *(Sheila Kitzinger; also Mr and Mrs R W Stumbo)*

Open: All year.
Rooms: 23 double, 10 single – 22 with bath, 11 with shower, all with telephone and radio; TV on request.
Facilities: Lift, small salon, restaurant. Garden with terrace for lunch and light refreshments in fine weather. English spoken.
Location: In town centre; parking.
Credit cards: All major credit cards accepted.
Terms: B & B 60–100 Sfrs. Set meals: lunch 15–20 Sfrs; dinner 20–30 Sfrs; full *alc* 40 Sfrs.

Hotel zum Storchen   *Telephone:* (01) 211.55.10
Weinplatz 2   *Telex:* 813 354

'A really civilized hotel. Most rooms, including the restaurant and the terrace, face the Limmat, and have the classic view of the cathedral and the ancient Town Hall across the river. The sides of the hotel not facing the river overlook the charming Weinplatz, with its beautiful fountain and the most elegant and charming streets of the Alstadt which have now become pedestrian precincts. All the rooms are therefore absolutely quiet. The cuisine is distinguished, of international standard with a Swiss touch. There is also a less recommendable *buvette* on the ground floor. Above all, the hotel is centrally situated, within easy walking distance of the Bahnhofstrasse and all the sights and is still a haven of comfort, peace and quietness.' *(Arnold Horwell)*

Open: All year.
Rooms: 37 double, 40 single – 55 with bath, 22 with shower, all with telephone, radio, colour TV, in-house TV films and baby-listening by arrangement.
Facilities: Lift, bar, restaurant, terrace; conference and banqueting facilities.
Location: Central; public paid parking 4 minutes walk.
Credit cards: All major credit cards accepted.
Terms: Rooms with breakfast 110–260 Sfrs. Set meals (Sundays only): lunch/dinner 35 Sfrs; full *alc* 55 Sfrs.

Grand Hotel Toplice, Bled

Yugoslavia

Hotel Moskva   *Telephone:* (011) 327 312
                                      Telex: 11505 yu moskva

'A notable building right in the centre of the city, one of the few survivors of the last war. It has been thoroughly modernized, and has the kind of gentle attentive staff that any traveller anywhere would always appreciate. If you become a favoured client, they will give you a duplex, with a sitting-room downstairs and sleeping quarters and bathroom up a little staircase.' *(Hella Pick)*

Open: All year.
Rooms: 140 – all with bath or shower, most with telephone.
Facilities: Lift, bar, café, restaurant, banqueting hall, air-conditioning.
Location: Central.
Terms (excluding tax): Rooms (including English breakfast) US$ 52.50 (single), US$ 90–107.50 (double); dinner, B & B US$ 69; full board US$ 82.50.

Grand Hotel Toplice   *Telephone:* Bled (064) 77 222
                                                  Telex: 34-588 yu toplice

'Lake Bled, as seen from the wide windows of the *Grand Hotel Toplice*
presents a perfect picture postcard view: dense trees mask many of the
hotels which edge its shores; from the wooded islet in the middle of the
water rise the tower and tall turret of an ancient castle and chapel; and on
the horizon, misty and mysterious as a well-painted scenic backdrop, rise
the peaks of the Julian Alps. This area of Slovenia, just across the border
from Austria, is a paradise for fishermen, hunters, painters, and wine
connoisseurs; the Riesling here is fabulous. The Toplice (meaning "spa")
stands right at the lake edge, and it is in the best traditions of 19th-century
Hapsburg Vienna; but though it keeps its period elegance, mod-cons have
been discreetly added. And you don't have to brave the cold lake water;
the *Toplice* has its own covered swimming pool fed by a thermal spring
and edged with columns like the Roman baths at Bath. For me, this is
simply one of the finest hotels in Europe. Superb choice of food and wine.
On this, my third visit, I received all the unobtrusive courtesy and
attention I have come to expect.' *(George S Jonas)*

Open: All year.
Rooms: 74 double, 36 single, 14 suites – all with bath and telephone, most with
balcony overlooking the lake. 45 rooms in annexe.
Facilities: Lift, salon and cocktail bar, TV room, elegant restaurant; conference
rooms, bridge room; sauna, massage, solarium, keep-fit club; indoor heated
swimming pool. Dancing 6 evenings a week. Lakeside terrace and bathing beach;
boats and fishing licences available; golf and tennis a short distance away. English
spoken.
Location: 55 km NW of Ljubljana, near the Austrian border. 200 metres from
town centre; parking. *Warning:* Rooms facing street may be noisy.
Credit cards: Access/Euro/Mastercard, American Express, Diners.
Terms: Rooms with breakfast US$ 19–32 (single), US$ 32–57 (double); full
board US$ 23–49 (min. 3 days). Reduced rates and special meals for children.

DUBROVNIK   **Map 14**

Villa Dubrovnik   *Telephone:* Dubrovnik 22 933
                                                  Telex: 27503

Of the three smart hotels on the south side of Dubrovnik, the *Excelsior*,
the *Argentina* and the *Villa Dubrovnik*, it is the last – much smaller than
the other two – which our readers seem to prefer. (There is also the
unsmart, unpackaged *Hotel Dubravka*, the only hotel in the old town,
which, alas, we have had to drop this year for lack of feedback – but if
anyone has been recently to the *Dubravka*, and thinks it should re-enter
the lists next year, would they please let us know.) To return to the *Villa
Dubrovnik*, it is a modern medium-sized hotel, perched high on a cliff,
with lovely views of the old walled town and harbour and also over to the
island of Lokrum opposite. The hotel is terraced into the cliff on at least
five different levels with lifts to all floors, except to the bathing rocks. Pine
trees, flowers and blue awnings give a Riviera flavour. The bar and dining
room both have superb views, and you can eat outdoors in fine weather.

The service is excellent and the food good by Yugoslav standards. Most bedrooms face the front with small balconies, and are well furnished. There are high standards of cleanliness. The hotel has its own 'concrete' beach with rock bathing in unpolluted water; there are plenty of chairs and beach umbrellas and a bar service. There is no nightlife on the spot, but you can wander down to the city in about twenty minutes or take the hotel's own motor-boat, and it is easy to get a taxi back. Not recommended for the elderly or infirm, as there are steps up from the hotel entrance to the road above.

'Warmly endorsed. The welcome on arrival from beautiful receptionist was really magnificent. Obviously many of the guests come back again and again, an English couple sixteen times, a Swedish couple six times. Because the hotel is fairly small, you receive personal service unlike in the larger establishments up and down the coast. Although we were on B & B terms, we enjoyed dining in the hotel's restaurant, which is beautifully sited and excellent value for set meal.' *(S D Carpenter; also Mary Ann Hamill)*

Open: 1 May–31 October.
Rooms: 56 – all with bath/shower and telephone, many with sea-facing balconies.
Facilities: Lifts, lounge, bar, restaurant; sub-tropical gardens; own bathing beach, mainly rock; sea-level bar service.
Location: On S side of Dubrovnik.
Terms: Rooms US$ 24–75; dinner, B & B (min. 3 days) US$ 20–65; full board (min. 3 days) US$ 21–70.

HVAR   Map 14

Palace Hotel   *Telephone:* (058) 74013
                                              Telex: 26235 Yu hHvar

Hotels in Yugoslavia tend to be much-of-a-muchness, but the *Palace* is an exception. We had an enthusiastic entry last year for this medium-large hotel attractively sited overlooking the island of Hvar's Venetian harbour, but one correspondent wrote to say that the place itself far surpassed our description, at least if you avoid June, July and August when the place is crowded with package tours and is disagreeably hot. 'My husband and I have travelled throughout the world. The one place we shall return to is the *Palace* at Hvar.' Another was only slightly less enthusiastic:

'Hvar is a quite delightful small harbour town on the island of the same name, an hour or so by hydrofoil from Split. The *Palace* is as centrally located as could be, overlooking the quays where everyone comes and goes. The squares, quays and steep narrow streets of the old town are paved and largely traffic-free. Prices are lower early and late in the season; the hotel could be noisy in summer, but is perfect for a spring holiday. The service is efficient and courteous, the food varied and interesting, and the décor pleasant. Some rooms at the back are rather gloomy, so it is well worth requesting (and paying extra for) a room with a sea *view*. Some sea-facing rooms are behind large trees. Altogether we thoroughly endorse your recommendation. Incidentally, there's not much left of the 16th-century Venetian palace – most of the hotel is early 20th century, architecturally not very special.' *(Dr and Mrs E A Hoyle; also Mrs B Bannister)*

Hotels are dropped if we lack positive feedback.

Open: All year.
Rooms: 63 double, 7 single, 6 suites – 45 with bath, 25 with shower, all with telephone.
Facilities: Lifts, 2 lounges, TV room, bar, restaurant. Sun terrace overlooking harbour with music and dancing every night during summer.
Location: Central; no special parking facilities.
Credit cards: All major credit cards accepted.
Terms (excluding tax): Rooms 35–89 DM (single), 50–150 DM (double); half board (minimum 3 days) 41–100 DM; full board (minimum 3 days) 45–106 DM.

LENDAVA, 69220 Slovenia
Map 14

Hotel Lipa
Telephone: (069) 75.720

Lendava is about 90 km north of Zagreb, in the north-eastern corner of Slovenia, 5 km from the Hungarian border on the road to Lake Balaton and 25 km from the Burgenland border of Austria. 'An enchanting countryside, like being whisked back 150 years: it is largely a farming community, but there are several outstanding churches and some beautiful medieval frescoes to be seen in the neighbourhood. It was an old fiefdom of the Princes Esterházy (of Haydn fame) and the rather sombre Esterházy Castle on the hilltop houses an interesting little museum. The *Lipa* is a very new (and therefore still in working order) hotel. It is run by friendly staff. The food is rather good, though of course limited. There is a mineral spring (good for rheumatism) a few km away which fills two swimming pools in pleasant open grounds, and the hotel is supposed to be building its own swimming pool soon. Don't miss the nearby town of Varazdin.' *(HC and Elsa Robbins Landon)*

Open: All year.
Rooms: 82 – mostly double – all with bath or shower and telephone.
Facilities: Lift, dining room; grounds; 2 swimming pools nearby.
Location: 90 km N of Zagreb.
Terms: Rooms: US$ 17–20 (single, US$ 27–30 (double); half board US$ 16–26; full board US$ 20–30.

OCTOČEC OB KRKI
Map 14

Grad Otočec
Telephone: (068) 21.830
Telex: 35740

'A beautiful medieval castle on an island in the middle of the romantic slow-moving River Krka, between Ljubljana and Zagreb, 8 km NE of Novo Mesto. It would be a good base for exploring this part of Slovenia which is particularly beautiful, with rolling hills and pretty old towns. You reach the hotel by a picturesque series of bridges. Restaurants and rooms, both expensive, tell of better times. The food is good, and there is a decent wine list, but service in the dining room is slow, as it frequently is in Yugoslavia, and telephoning abroad is a drama. The kitchen is run by an organization separate from the hotel, so you can't charge meals to your room, which is a bore.' *(H C and Elsa Robbins Landon)*

Open: All year.
Rooms: 17 double, 2 single, 2 suites – 8 with bath.

Facilities: Salons, dining room. Large park and river with bathing and fishing. English spoken.
Location: 8 km NE of Novo Mesto.
Credit cards: Access/Euro/Mastercard, American Express, Diners.
Terms: B & B US$16–22. Set meals: lunch/dinner US$ 6–11; full *alc* US$ 10. 30% reduction for children under 7.
Note: In addition to the castle, there is, on the northern bank of the river, a big modern hotel complex under the same management, with a motel, self-catering bungalows and camping facilities.

ZAGREB   **Map 14**

The Palace   *Telephone:* (041) 44.92.11

'Zagreb is a hotel desert. The *Palace* is the best of a poor bunch – but, in the Zagreb context, very highly commended. It is an old imperialist building, architecturally superb, with lots of character. A high-ceilinged bar with decorated ceiling and deep leather armchairs; a beautiful dining room with integral fish-pond; and lovely old-fashioned Victorian bedrooms – all with private bathrooms. It is centrally situated, within five minutes' walk of the best square in the city, with its open-air cafés and colourful market. So far so good. The trouble lies with the service and lack of facilities. Guests are tolerated with perfunctory politeness. There is nowhere to relax away from your bedroom – no comfortable lounge, no pool, no anything – but there is a pleasant public garden opposite. But, by Zagreb standards, it is the only place for Guide readers to stay. I have enjoyed it (yes, really) four times during the past year and would stay nowhere else from choice.' *(John M Sidwick)*

Open: All year.
Rooms: 91 – all with bath or shower and telephone.
Facilities: Lift; bar, restaurant; public garden opposite.
Location: Central.
Terms: Rooms US$ 31–42 (single), US$ 48–60 (double); half board US$ 49–56; full board US$ 53–67.

Our Yugoslav section is unacceptably short. Please would Yugoslav travellers tell us if they come across a good hotel.

Report of the year competition

Every year, among the many hundreds of reports that reach us, there are a few which stand out as models of their kind. Sometimes, as with Shelley Cranshaw's citation of the *Altnaharrie Inn* at Ullapool (see page 192), they are commending hotels not previously known to us; sometimes they are commenting on or endorsing an existing entry. Either type, when well done, will be both entertaining and informative and will make a place come alive. Vivid and accurate description is the essence of this sort of Guide, so we are naturally eager to persuade more readers to flex their literary muscles. As an encouragement, we are instituting this year a competition for the best report. Prize: a case of champagne. No special entry forms needed: everything we receive in the course of the year will qualify. No stipulation as to length.

The following tribute to *The Abbey*, Llanthony by G M Cameron reached us just after we had prepared the entry which appears on page 146. It seemed too good to leave out, so we include it here as a sample of the kind of report we are looking for.

'The approach to Llanthony is a haunting memory. The road follows a stream at the bottom of a lonely Welsh valley with wild skies overhead full of wheeling black birds. Tufts of sheep's wool cling to roadside branches and solitary horses strike dramatic poses in hilltop paddocks. One expects to find witches boiling cauldrons or someone in armour trying to pull a sword out of a stone. The road from Hay-on-Wye is the more spectacular though only a single track with passing-places (well-metalled). The arrival at the *Abbey* (actually priory) ruins and hotel is no let-down. One is met by a smug marmalade cat atop a stone wall and a blissful lack of people and signs. A vaulted, white-washed cellar, fitted-out as an attractive, comfortable pub serves as Reception. A few amusing touches such as the pictures of old Queen Victoria and her Prince of Wales under crossed flags give a clue to a sense of humour somewhere behind the green baize door. A group of local farmers in wellies with their dogs asleep at their feet were creating a pleasant fug while I was there. A young man with an earring showed me to my room which was at the top of the tower, up thousands of (actually 62) stone steps in a narrow spiral well. En route I passed narrow but tempting views through slit windows. My room, which deserved to be called a chamber, contained a theatrical four-poster with canopy and curtains, a washstand with ewer and basin (and a card saying "Please do not use"). And a chamber-pot, oh the thrill of it! It was so cold I could see my breath but I found a little electric heater that served well. One little

Gothic window (almost on the floor . . . one had to lie on one's stomach to enjoy the view) looked out over the beautiful ruins and the hills and valley beyond.

'I felt I knew Mrs Fancourt, the proprietor, personally, after your write-up and her endearing acknowledgement that her hotel was "rather odd". (In fact, I don't think I said more than two words to her during my stay. The Fancourts do not hover. A plus in my mind, I like to be un-entertained.) When I'd telephoned the day before to see about accommodation, Mrs F was very helpful in giving a choice of routes to Llanthony (pron. "Clan-Tony" . . . a useful bit of information to one who frequently gets lost and has to ask directions). She also suggested I stop in Abergavenny on the way because there was going to be an interesting furniture sale in the old market hall that day. A thoughtful suggestion for which I was grateful.

'I'd noted your comment about the infamous nylon sheets. And had specifically asked for them because I am perverse. They weren't the slick and slippery kind I'd expected but of a strangely spongey material that was perfectly all right except for the pillowcase in the morning that created a Velcro effect when brought into contact with an unshaven jaw.

'The loo and bathroom are on a landing at the bottom of the tower and are both in perfect working order. Older guests may wish the rooms closer to them. The hike up and down the steps is arduous and a chamber pot is amusing once.

'The only other people staying at the hotel were an attractive young couple on a romantic get-away. We were friendly but respected each other's privacy. (I think a warning here is in order about high heels: Monks didn't often wear them so the tower stairs were not constructed with them in mind. The young lady portion of the above-mentioned couple, after changing smartly for dinner, caught her high heel while descending the staircase and came flying into the dining room like a screaming ghost. Fortunately she wasn't killed.)

'I admit to being leery about the food before my meal. The menu sounded arty-smarty. Amateur cooking is so often disguised by exotic spices and strange-sounding names. It was either death or delight when I ordered Mexican *guacamole*, a Welsh soup made of seaweed and something else and lamb chops *teriyaki*. It was all very good. There appeared to be a useful wine list. And the coffee was a filtre variety that is fail-safe. The room was attractively done-up with an eclectic assortment of furniture, all in keeping with the mood and style of the place. I thought it faintly Scottish baronial for some reason; there weren't any targes or antlers around but hanging old silver dish-covers along the walls suggested an armoury. Pretty plates arranged in dressers gave the whitewashed room colour and an amazing cast-iron stove provides heat from an astonishingly elaborate grate. The single waitress, a local Welsh woman, was friendly, informal and efficient. The bar after dinner was warm, inviting and obviously attractive to the local youth, who were well-behaved and seemed to be quite happy without loud music. One suspects the *Abbey* represents the bright lights of Llanthony.

'Breakfast the following morning was vast and delicious. The fresh baked bread was an item of special interest. Separate tables were set in the pub, not the dining room, for breakfast: I liked that. I asked for my bill for the entire stay and was well pleased by its smallness. I'd recommend the

Abbey Hotel to anybody but the standard vulgarian. Who'd hate the place anyway because there isn't cello-wrap on anything and who wouldn't appreciate the slight discomforts.'

Appendix One

THE UNCOMMERCIAL TRAVELLER
by Charles Dickens

Dickens was fascinated by hotels and inns, and his fiction, most notably
Pickwick Papers, *abounds in observations, insights and anecdotes about
the whole range of hotel characters from genial landlords to impudent
boot-boys.* The Uncommercial Traveller, *written originally as a magazine
serial in 1860, is one of his lesser-known works, but it contains a particular
bravura passage about unspeakable hotels of various kinds which still rings
horribly true a century and a quarter later. If we had to sum up in a few
words our reason for compiling this Guide, we could do worse than refer
readers to the last paragraph of this extract and 'the lingering personal retail
interest within us that asks to be satisfied'.*

Mr Grazinglands, of the Midland Counties, came to London by railroad
one morning last week, accompanied by the amiable and fascinating Mrs
Grazinglands. Mr G. is a gentleman of a comfortable property, and had a
little business to transact at the Bank of England, which required the
concurrence and signature of Mrs G. Their business disposed of, Mr and
Mrs Grazinglands viewed the Royal Exchange, and the exterior of St
Paul's Cathedral. The spirits of Mrs Grazinglands then gradually beginning to flag, Mr Grazinglands (who is the tenderest of husbands) remarked with sympathy, 'Arabella, my dear, I fear you are faint.' Mrs
Grazinglands replied, 'Alexander, I am rather faint; but don't mind me, I
shall be better presently.' Touched by the feminine meekness of this
answer, Mr Grazinglands looked in at a pastry-cook's window, hesitating
as to the expediency of lunching at that establishment. . . . He might have
entered, but for the timely remembrance coming upon him that Jairing's
was but round the corner.

   Now, Jairing's being an hotel for families and gentlemen, in high repute
among the midland counties, Mr Grazinglands plucked up a great spirit
when he told Mrs Grazinglands she should have a chop there. That lady
likewise felt that she was going to see Life. Arriving on that gay and festive
scene, they found the second waiter, in a flabby undress, cleaning the
windows of the empty coffee-room; and the first waiter, denuded of his
white tie, making up his cruets behind the Post-Office Directory. The
latter (who took them in hand) was greatly put out by their patronage, and
showed his mind to be troubled by a sense of the pressing necessity of
instantly smuggling Mrs Grazinglands into the obscurest corner of the
building. This slighted lady (who is the pride of her division of the county)
was immediately conveyed, by several dark passages, and up and down
serveral steps, into a penitential apartment at the back of the house,

where five invalided old plate-warmers leaned up against one another under a discarded old melancholy sideboard, and where the wintry leaves of all the dining-tables in the house lay thick. Also, a sofa, of incomprehensible form regarded from any sofane point of view, murmured 'Bed;' while an air of mingled fluffiness and heeltaps, added, 'Second Waiter's.' Secreted in this dismal hold, objects of a mysterious distrust and suspicion, Mr Grazinglands and his charming partner waited twenty minutes for the smoke (for it never came to a fire), twenty-five minutes for the sherry, half an hour for the tablecloth, forty minutes for the knives and forks, three-quarters of an hour for the chops, and an hour for the potatoes. On settling the little bill – which was not much more than the day's pay of a Lieutenant in the navy – Mr Grazinglands took heart to remonstrate against the general quality and cost of his reception. To whom the waiter replied, substantially, that Jairing's made it a merit to have accepted him on any terms: 'for,' added the waiter (unmistakably coughing at Mrs Grazinglands, the pride of her division of the county), 'when indiwiduals is not staying in the 'Ouse, their favours is not as a rule looked upon as making it worth Mr Jairing's while; nor is it, indeed, a style of business Mr Jairing wishes.' Finally, Mr and Mrs Grazinglands passed out of Jairing's hotel for Families and Gentlemen, in a state of the greatest depression, scorned by the bar; and did not recover their self-respect for several days.

Or take another case. Take your own case. . . . And any of the numerous travelling instances in which you are, have been, or may be, equally ill served. Take the old-established Bull's Head with its old-established knife-boxes on its old-established sideboards, its old-established flue under its old-established four-post bedsteads in its old-established airless rooms, its old-established frouziness up-stairs and down-stairs, its old-established cookery, and its old-established principles of plunder. Count up your injuries, in its side-dishes of ailing sweetbreads in white poultices, of apothecaries' powders in rice for curry, of pale stewed bits of calf ineffectually relying for an adventitious interest on forcemeat balls. You have had experience of the old-established Bull's Head stringy fowls, with lower extremities like wooden legs, sticking up out of the dish; of its cannibalic boiled mutton, gushing horribly among its capers, when carved; of its little dishes of pastry – roofs of spermaceti ointment, erected over half an apple or four gooseberries. Well for you if you have yet forgotten the old-established Bull's Head fruity port: whose reputation was gained solely by the old-established price the Bull's Head put upon it, and by the old-established air with which the Bull's Head set the glasses and D'Oyleys on, and held that Liquid Gout to the three-and-sixpenny wax-candle, as if its old-established colour hadn't come from the dyer's.

Or lastly, take to finish with, two cases that we all know, every day.

We all know the new hotel near the station, where it is always gusty, going up the lane which is always muddy, where we are sure to arrive at night, and where we make the gas start awfully when we open the front door. We all know the flooring of the passages and staircase that is too new, and the walls that are too new, and the house that is haunted by the ghost of mortar. We all know the doors that have cracked, and the cracked shutters through which we get a glimpse of the disconsolate moon. We all know the new people, who have come to keep the new hotel, and who wish they had never come, and who (inevitable result) wish *we* had never come. We all know how much too scant and smooth and bright the new furniture is, and how it has never settled down, and cannot fit itself into right places, and will get into wrong places. We all know how the gas, being lighted, shows maps of Damp upon the walls. We all know how the ghost of mortar passes into our sandwich, stir our negus, goes up to bed with us, ascends the pale bedroom chimney, and prevents the smoke from following. We all know how a leg of our chair comes off at breakfast in the morning, and how the dejected waiter attributes the accident to a general greenness pervading the establishment, and informs us, in reply to a local inquiry, that he is thankful to say he is an entire stranger in that part of the country, and is going back to his own connexion on Saturday.

We all know, on the other hand, the great station hotel belonging to the company of proprietors, which has suddenly sprung up in the back outskirts of any place we like to name, and where we look out of our palatial windows, at little back yards and gardens, old summer-houses, fowl-houses, pigeon-traps, and pigsties. We all know this hotel in which we can get anything we want, after its kind, for money; but where nobody is glad to see us, or sorry to see us, or minds (our bill paid) whether we come or go, or how, or when, or why, or cares about us. We all know this hotel, where we have no individuality, but put ourselves into the general post, as it were, and are sorted and disposed of according to our division. We all know that we can get on very well indeed at such a place, but still not perfectly well; and this may be, because the place is largely wholesale, and there is a lingering personal retail interest within us that asks to be satisfied.

Appendix Two

THE UNCOMMERCIAL HOTELKEEPER
by Alison Johnson

Perfectionists in the hotel trade have a hard enough time in a metropolis, but catering difficulties are compounded when the location is remote. Alison Johnson's Scarista House on Harris must certainly rank as one of the more distant outposts of civilization. How does she contrive in the Outer Hebrides to produce every night throughout the year her highly esteemed six-course dinners? We are grateful to her for allowing us to reprint this letter, written to the author and broadcaster Derek Cooper, which testifies so eloquently to the dedication and flair of the true hotelier. The title of this Appendix, we should make clear, is entirely our own.

The Hebrides teem with good natural ingredients: heather- and seaweed-fed mutton, wild red-deer venison, a vast variety of fish from salmon to octopus, and superb shellfish (I particularly recommend those ferocious giant langoustines, recognizable by their rose-pink carapaces, who have whittled away a tedious week in a creel by devouring their smaller relatives).

Putting your hands on all this stuff is a strenuous full-time business, though. Ask the estates for salmon, and you find it's all being blast-frozen and despatched south, though aronymous phone calls offer you them by the hundredweight. Last winter I waited hopefully for my usual three prime hinds, only to find that our supplier couldn't get to his shooting for heavy snow. Scallop divers get the bends, prawn fishers lose their gear in Atlantic storms, Calum who grows our potatoes shows an unshakeable faith in beastly Kerr's Pinks.

And what of exotica? Well, everything from cream to Kiwi fruit *is* exotic in Harris, and has to be organized by letter or telephone to make its way to the post van or the twice-weekly bus. People often ask if I plan my menus during the winter, that happy season of repose and meditation in which mainlanders envisage us. Not likely! *Probably* the turbot will arrive by 5 p.m. – if not I'll still have three hours to replace it – but the stilton and grapes (to be served at 8.45) aren't scheduled to arrive till 8.15 (quick dash down the drive in the rain). I used to count on things, before the strawberry episode. They featured on the menu – the bus arrived – the cartons were there – but not the strawberries. They must have shared a back seat with one who couldn't resist temptation. Then there was the gentleman who came specially to enjoy our cheeseboard. I ordered £30 worth of the stuff from a reputable Edinburgh supplier. The cheese-loving gent came and went – no sign of the cheese. A bank holiday intervened, followed by a suppurating parcel of exploded stilton and other horrors.

One learns to make other arrangements – never order from one firm when you could order from two. It's not economic sense, but it saves embarrassment. If we wanted to make a profit, I suppose we would do what many Highland hotels obviously feel forced to – rely on frozen, portion-controlled, utterly reliable, utterly boring supplies, and forget all about the halibut too small for Billingsgate, the half-boxes of prawns, too few for market, delivered at midnight for two hours of weary preparation, the egg that Henrietta looks as if she might lay any minute so that Mrs X needn't have a battery one in her scrambled.

We couldn't stand the boredom of it, though. All the enjoyment of our work comes from doing it as well as we possibly can, and better than anyone has a right to expect in such a far-flung locality. We don't believe in 'can't', and are prepared to go on trying till we drop dead with the effort. This may not be long if we don't improve on our Mark I electrical stunner for lobsters, which consists of the mains run through a bath of salt water – to be operated with one's free hand in one's pocket.

Incidentally, lobsters thus stunned before being dropped into boiling water are full of curd and don't shed claws. It's complete rubbish that they have to be dropped in snapping and kicking to develop their best flavour. We'd like that to be publicized. The device was dreamt up by an Oxford professor, but there's no model on the market.

Our dinner menus offer no choice except for the first course, and this poses son.e problems, as we try to find out people's likes and dislikes ahead, and then work out what to do. It's nearly always someone's special occasion, so I can't risk disappointments. At the same time, I can't bear providing an unbalanced, cloying meal, so the party who asks for prawns in cream followed by Beef Stroganoff and Crème Brulée have to be gently dissuaded, unless it's the depths of winter and they're on their own, when I grit my teeth and do it.

Winter! That's the season, according to lady customers, when I must 'make all the desserts and bread and freeze them for summer'. I never know what to say. I hope I've never agreed with this horrendous misconception. I mumble that I don't have time, I think. I daren't tell these planners-ahead of twice-yearly dinner parties that the stuff would be too rancid to swallow and of a loathsome texture, and that I never freeze anything except raw quality fish and meat when this is going to be unobtainable fresh, and then for as short a time as possible. We are becoming more and more obsessive about the freshness of our food. We like salmon from the sea not the river, lobster that hasn't been ponded, fish that hasn't languished on ice, venison (but it must be a first-rate beast) that has been hung for three days, not three weeks. I won't start preparing food till the last possible minute, and many are the scenes in the kitchen when some innocent diner takes too long eating his prawns, so that his vegetables go soggy. We don't have a *bain marie* any more than a microwave, and class them together as works of the devil. The porridge does *not* brew overnight in the Aga, and we don't compose Crécy soup of yesterday's leftover veg, *pace* the Stornoway diner who confidently so asserted. As for those dishes beloved of female cookery writers which 'keep well in a refrigerator for a week or in a freezer for three months', may they and their authors go to perdition.

Exchange Rates

These rates for buying currency are correct at time of printing but in some cases may be wildly awry at the time of publication. It is essential to check with bank or newspapers for up-to-date pound and dollar equivalents.

	£1 sterling	$1 US
Austria (Schillings)	31.50	17.77
Belgium (Belgian francs)	89.80	49.08
Denmark (kroner)	15.45	8.92
Finland (Finnish marks)	9.19	5.47
France (francs)	12.47	7.15
Germany (Deutschemarks)	4.44	2.53
Greece (drachmae)	130.00	71.00
Holland (guilders)	4.84	2.76
Hungary (forints)	100.00	58.7
Ireland (punts)	1.287	0.746
Italy (lire)	2,500	1,444
Luxembourg (Luxembourg francs)	89.80	52.7
Malta (Maltese pounds)	0.74	0.4166
Norway (kroner)	12.76	7.2215
Portugal, including Madeira (escudos)	160.00	89.65
Spain, including Andorra, Balearics and Canaries (pesetas)	200.00	115.61
Sweden (kroner	13.00	7.40
Switzerland, including Liechtenstein (Swiss francs)	3.82	2.17

Tourist Offices

National Tourist Offices will supply general information and literature on request. Among the booklets and leaflets available (many of them free) are accommodation lists, regional pamphlets, catalogues of the main sights and events, and details of sporting, travel, and other facilities. Ask for the area which particularly interests you. Within each country there are information offices in all main towns and resorts, able to supply more detailed local information, maps, itineraries, etc., and sometimes to assist visitors to find accommodation.

UNITED KINGDOM	London:	The British Tourist Authority, 64 St James's Street, London SW1
	New York:	680 Fifth Avenue, New York, NY 10019
ENGLAND	London:	*Correspondence:* English Tourist Board, 4 Grosvenor Gardens, London SW1 *Personal Callers:* London Tourist Board (1) Victoria Station next to main ticket office by Platform 15 (2) Heathrow Central underground station
WALES		Wales Tourist Board, Brunel House, 2 Fitzallan Road, Cardiff CF2 1UY
SCOTLAND	Scotland·	*Correspondence:* Scottish Tourist Board, 23 Ravelston Terrace, Edinburgh *Personal Callers:* 5 Waverley Bridge, Edinburgh

	London:	19 Cockspur Street, London SW1Y 5BL
CHANNEL ISLANDS	Alderney:	Recreation and Tourism Committee, States Office, Alderney
	Guernsey:	States of Guernsey Tourist Committee, PO Box 23, St Peter Port, Guernsey
	Herm:	Tourist Office, Herm Island
	Jersey:	States of Jersey Tourism Committee, Weighbridge, St Helier, Jersey London Office: 118 Grand Buildings, Trafalgar Square, London WC2N 5EP
	Sark:	Tourist Office, Donmar, Sark.
NORTHERN IRELAND		Ulster Office, 11 Berkeley Street, London W1
REPUBLIC OF IRELAND	London:	Irish Tourist Board, 150 New Bond Street, London W1Y 0AQ
	Dublin:	Baggot Street Bridge, Dublin 2
	New York:	590 Fifth Avenue, New York, NY 10036
AUSTRIA	London:	Austrian National Tourist Office, 30 St George Street, London W1
	New York:	545 Fifth Avenue, New York, NY 10017
BELGIUM	London:	Belgian National Tourist Office, 38 Dover Street, London W1
	New York:	745 Fifth Avenue, New York, NY 10022
DENMARK	London:	Danish Tourist Board, Sceptre House, 169–173 Regent Street, London W1
	New York:	75 Rockefeller Plaza, New York, NY 10019
FINLAND	London:	Finnish Tourist Board, 66 Haymarket, London SW1
	New York:	Finland National Tourist Office, 75 Rockefeller Plaza, New York, NY 10019

FRANCE	London:	French Government Tourist Office, 178 Piccadilly, London W1V 0AL
	New York:	610 Fifth Avenue, New York, NY 10020
GERMANY	London:	German National Tourist Office, 61 Conduit Street, London W1
	New York:	747 Third Avenue, 33rd floor, New York, NY 10017
GREECE	London:	National Tourist Organization of Greece, 195–197 Regent Street, London W1R 8Dl
	New York:	Greek National Tourist Organization, 645 Fifth Avenue (Olympic Tower), New York, NY 10022
HOLLAND	London:	Netherlands National Tourist Office, 143 New Bond Street, London W1Y 0QS
	New York:	576 Fifth Avenue, New York, NY 10036
HUNGARY	London:	Danube Travel, 6 Conduit Street, London W1
ITALY	London:	Italian State Tourist Office, 1 Princes St, London W1
	New York:	Italian Government Travel Office, 630 Fifth Avenue, Suite 1565, New York, NY 10111
LUXEMBOURG	London:	Luxembourg Tourist Office, 36–37 Piccadilly, London W1
	New York:	Luxembourg Tourist Office, 801, 2nd Avenue, New York, NY 10017
MALTA	London:	Malta Government Tourist Office, Malta High Commission, 24 Haymarket, London SW1
	New York:	Malta Consulate, 249 East 35th Street, New York, NY 10016

NORWAY	London:	Norwegian National Tourist Office, 20 Pall Mall, London SW1
	New York:	75 Rockefeller Plaza, New York, NY 10019
PORTUGAL (and MADEIRA)	London:	Portuguese National Tourist Office, New Bond Street House, 1–5 New Bond Street, London W1Y 0NP
	New York:	548 Fifth Avenue, New York, NY 10036
SPAIN (and BALEARICS and CANARY ISLANDS)	London:	Spanish National Tourist Office, 57–58 St James's Street, London SW1
	New York:	665 Fifth Avenue, New York, NY 10022
SWEDEN	London:	Swedish National Tourist Office, 3 Cork Street, London W1
	New York:	75 Rockefeller Plaza, New York, NY 10019
SWITZERLAND (and LIECHSTENSTEIN)	London:	Swiss National Tourist Office, Swiss Centre, 1 New Coventry Street, London W1
	New York:	Swiss Centre, 608 Fifth Avenue, New York, NY 10020
YUGOSLAVIA	London:	Yugoslav National Tourist Office, 143 Regent Street, London W1
	New York:	630 Fifth Avenue, Rockefeller Centre, Suite 210, New York, NY 10020

Alphabetical List of Hotels

Establishment	Listed under
ENGLAND	
Abbey	Penzance
Angel	Bury St Edmunds
Arundell Arms	Lifton
Athenaeum	London
Bailiffscourt	Climping
Basil Street	London
Bay Tree	Burford
Beechfield House	Beanacre
Bell	Aston Clinton
Berribridge	Thorverton
Bibury Court	Bibury
Bishopstrow House	Warminster
Blakeney	Blakeney
Bly House	Chagford
Boscundle Manor	St Austell
Budock Vean	Budock Vean
Burleigh Court	Minchinhampton
Butchers Arms	Woolhope
Butts	Ryall
Castle	Taunton
Cavendish	Baslow
Chedington Court	Chedington
Chewton Glen	New Milton
Chilvester Lodge	Calne
Clinchs'	Chichester
Combe House	Gittisham
Connaught	London
Crantock Bay	Crantock
D'Isney Place	Lincoln
Deans Place	Alfriston
Dedham Vale	Dedham
Downrew House	Barnstaple
Duke's	London
Dundas Arms	Kintbury
Durrants	London
Eastbury	Sherborne

571

Lygon Arms	Broadway
Mains Hall	Little Singleton
Maison Talbooth	Dedham
Mallory Court	Bishops Tachbrook
Malt House	Broad Campden
Malvern View	Cleeve Hill
Marine Hotel	Salcombe
Mariners	Lyme Regis
Marlborough	Ipswich
Michael's Nook	Grasmere
Mill	Kingham
Millstream	Bosham
Millcombe House	Lundy
Miller Howe	Windermere
Millers House	Middleham
Mount Royale	York
Netherfield Place	Battle
Number Sixteen	London
Old Bridge Hotel	Huntingdon
Old Mill Floor	Trebarwith Strand
Old Vicarage	Witherslack
Old Vicarage Guest House	Rye
Parkhill	Lyndhurst
Passford House	Lymington
Peacock Vane	Bonchurch
Pengethley	Ross-on-Wye
Pheasant Inn	Bassenthwaite
Plumber Manor	Sturminster Newton
Poltimore Guest House	South Zeal
Port Gaverne	Port Isaac
Portobello	London
Priory	Bath
Priory	Wareham
Priory Country House	Rushlake Green
Priory Court	Pevensey
Prospect Hill	Kirkoswald
Quayside	Brixham
River House	Thornton-le-Fylde
Riverside	Helford
Rookery Hall	Worleston
Rose and Crown	Romaldkirk
Rothay Manor	Ambleside
Royal Crescent	Bath
Royal Glen House	Sidmouth
Russell	Harrogate
Sandringham	London
Scale Hill	Loweswater
Seatoller	Borrowdale
Sharrow Bay Country House	Ullswater
Slepe Hall	St Ives
Smuggler's	Newlyn
Somerset	Bath

573

Spindlewood	Wallcrouch
St George	Sheffield
Steppes Country Guest House	Ullingswick
Ston Easton Park	Ston Easton
Stone Green Hall	Mersham
Stratford House	Stratford-upon-Avon
Summer Lodge	Evershot
Teignworthy	Frenchbeer
Temple Sowerby House	Temple Sowerby
Thornbury Castle	Thornbury
Thornworthy	Chagford
Three Shires Inn	Little Langdale
Treglos	Constantine Bay
Trevaylor	Gulval
Wateredge	Ambleside
White House	Williton
Whitwell Hall	Whitwell on the Hill
Winterbourne	Bonchurch
Woodhayes	Whimple
Woolverton House	Woolverton
Worsley Arms	Hovingham
Yeoldon House	Bideford

WALES

Abbey	Llanthony
Bodysgallen	Llandudno
Bontddu Hall	Bontddu
Crowfield	Abergavenny
Crown	Whitebrook
Druidstone	Druidston Haven
Gallt y Glyn	Llanberis
Glansevin	Llangadog
Lake Vyrnwy	Llanwddyn
Meadowsweet	Llanrwst
Minffordd	Talyllyn
Old Black Lion	Hay-on-Wye
Porth Tocyn	Abersoch
Rhyd-Garn-Wen	Cardigan
Robeston House	Robeston Wathen
Ty'n-y-Wern	Llangollen
Warpool Court	St David's
Wolfscastle	Wolfscastle
Ynyshir Hall	Eglwysfach

SCOTLAND

Airds	Port Appin
Altnaharrie Inn	Ullapool
Ardfenaig House	Bunessan
Ardsheal House	Kentallen
Arisaig House	Arisaig
Atholl Arms	Dunkeld

Auchen Castle	Beattock
Balcary Bay	Auchencairn
Banchory Lodge	Banchory
Baron's Craig	Rockliffe
Beechwood Country House	Moffat
Ceilidh Place	Ullapool
Clifton	Nairn
County	Banff
Creggans	Strachur
Crinan	Crinan
Cringletie House	Peebles
Cromlix House	Dunblane
Crook Inn	Tweedsmuir
Culloden House	Inverness
Dunain Park	Inverness
Eddrachilles	Scourie
Eilean Iarmain	Sleat
Four Seasons	St Fillans
Foveran	St Ola
Gigha	Gigha
Glenforsa	Salen
Greywalls	Gullane
Inn on the Garry	Invergarry
Inverlochy	Fort William
Invershin	Invershin
Isle of Eriska	Eriska
Iveroran	Bridge of Orchy
King's House	Glencoe
Kinloch Lodge	Sleat
Knockinaam Lodge	Portpatrick
Ledcreich	Balquhidder
Loch Melfort	Arduaine
Lochalsh	Kyle of Lochalsh
Milton Park	Dalry
Ospreys	Kingussie
Ossian	Kincraig
Polmaily	Drumnadrochit
Pool House	Pool Ewe
Riverside	Canonbie
Roman Camp	Callander
Rufflets	St Andrews
Scarista House	Scarista
Sligachan	Sligachan
Stewart	Duror
Summer Isles	Achiltibuie
Taychreggan	Kilchrenan
Tullich Lodge	Ballater

CHANNEL ISLANDS

Aval du Creux	Sark
Dixcart Hotel	Sark
Longueville Manor	St Saviour

| Petit Champ | Sark |
| White House | Herm |

NORTHERN IRELAND
| Dunadry Inn | Dunadry |
| Nutgrove | Annadorn |

REPUBLIC OF IRELAND
Aghadoe Heights	Killarney
Arbutus Lodge	Cork
Ballymaloe	Shanagarry
Buswells	Dublin
Cashel House	Cashel
Coopershill Farm	Riverstown
Currarevagh House	Oughterard
Gregan's House	Ballyvaughan
Inislounaght Country House	Marlfield
Longueville House	Mallow
Marlfield House	Gorey
Newport House	Newport
Perryville House	Kinsale
Rosleague Manor	Letterfrack

AUSTRIA
Elefant	Salzburg
Elite	Vienna
Europa	Vienna
Freisitz Roith	Gmunden
Gams	Bezau
Gruener Baum	Hallstatt
Haus Rossmann	Mutters
Insel	Faak-am-See
Kaiserin Elisabeth	Vienna
Markus Sittikus	Salzburg
Moawirt	Wagrain
Montana	Kitzbühel
Post	Villach
Richard Löwenherz	Dürnstein
Sacher	Vienna
Schloss Drassburg	Drassburg
Schloss Dürnstein	Dürnstein
Schloss Mönchstein	Salzburg
Schwarzenberg, Im Palais	Vienna
Schwarzes-Rössl	Windischgarsten
Seewinkel	Fuschl-am-see
Senger	Heiligenblut
Sporthotel	Igls
Suzanne	Vienna
Weisses Rössl	Steinach
Zur Traube	Lans

BELGIUM

Amigo	Brussels
Balcon en Forêt	Rochehaut sur Semois
Brides, Château des	Oostkamp
Damier	Kortrijk
Duc de Bourgogne	Bruges
Groeninghe	Bruges
Hideux, Moulin	Noirefontaine
Oude Abdij	Lo
Sanglier des Ardennes	Durbuy
Shamrock, Hostellerie	Ronse
St Jorishof	Gent

DENMARK

Dagmar	Ribe
Munkebjerg	Vejle
Nyhavn	Copenhagen
Steensgaard Herregardspension	Millinge
Store Kro	Fredensborg

FINLAND

Kalastajatorpa	Helsinki
Mercur	Helsinki
Messilä Manor Hotel	Messilä
Rantasipi Summassari	Saarijärvi
Rauhalinna	Savolinna
Torni	Helsinki

FRANCE

l'Abbaye, Hostellerie de	Lessay
l'Abbaye	St-Cyprien
Abbaye de Sainte-Croix	Salon-de-Provence
l'Abbaye	Paris
l'Abbaye Saint Michel	Tonnerre
Agoult, Hôtel d'	Arpaillargues
Aigle Noir	Fontainebleau
l'Aiguebrun	Bonnieux
Alain Chapel	Mionnay
Albert et Milan	Chamonix-Mont-Blanc
Anne de Bretagne	La Plaine-sur-Mer
Arcades, Café des	Biot
Arlatan, Hôtel d'	Arles
Arnold	Itterswiller
L'Atlantic	Wimereux
d'Avangour	Dinan
Bain	Comps-sur-Artuby
Balzac	Tours
Bannière de France	Laon
Bastide de Tourtour	Tourtour
Baumanière, Oustau de	Les Baux-de-Provence
Beffroi	Vaison-la-Romaine

577

578

Commerce	Bar-sur-Aube
Corniche	Toulon
Côteau Fleuri	Grimaud
Croix Blanche	Chaumont-sur-Tharonne
Cro-Magnon	Les-Eyzies-de-Tayac
Croquembouche	Courry
Demeure des Brousses	Montpellier
Deux-Iles	Paris
Deux Lions	Vernet-les-Bains
Deux Rocs	Seillans
Dhérété	Louvie-Juzon
Diana	Vence
Diderot	Chinon
Domaine de la Tortinière	Montbazon
Écu de France	Château-Renault
l'Équipe	Molines-en-Queyras
l'Espérance	Vézelay
l'Esplanade	Domme
Esterel	Juan-les-Pins
l'Étoile-Bergerard	Chablis
Étrangers	Sospel
l'Étrier Camarguais	Les-Saintes-Maries-de-la-Mer
Europe	Avignon
Europe	Langres
Fifi Moulin	Serres
Figuière	Ramatuelle
Fompeyre	Bazas
France	Loches
France	Nantua
France	Ornans
France et Restaurant Clariond, Hôtel de	Seillans
France, Hôtel de la Bannière de	Laon
France et d'Angleterre, Hôtel de	La Rochelle
Frères Troisgros	Roanne
Gavarni	Paris
Giraglia	Port Grimaud
Gourmet Lorrain	Nice
Grac	Annot
Grand Monarque	Chartres
Grottes	Cabrerets
Halle	Givry
Herbes Blanches, Mas des	Joucas
Horizon	Cabris
l'Île Rousse	Bandol
Isola Rossa	L'Ile-Rousse
Juana	Juan-les-Pins
La Ker Mocotte	Bandol
Lameloise	Chagny
Lancaster	Paris

Pastorella	Monticello
Père Bise	Talloires
Pérouse	Nice
Pescalerie	Cabrerets
Petite Auberge	Tourtour
Pic	Valence
Pigeonnet	Aix-en-Provence
Pigeons Blancs	Cognac
Plage	Boulogne-sur-Mer
Port	Lechiagat
Poste	Avallon
Poste et Champagne	Brioude
Poste et Lion d'Or	Vézelay
Potinière	St-Raphaël
Poulard, Hotel la Mère	Mont-St-Michel
Préjoly	St-Vallier-de-Thiey
Prés d'Eugénie	Eugénie-les-Bains
Prieuré	Chenehutte-les-Tuffeaux
Prieuré	Vileneuve-les-Avignon
Provencal	Giens
P'tit Quinquin	Céaux
Pyrénées	St-Jean-Pied-de-Port
Regalido	Fontvieille
Régent	Villers-Cotterêts
Relais	Ardres
Relais de Nantilly	Nantilly
Remparts	Kaysersberg
Réserve	Albi
Réserve	Beaulieu-sur-Mer
Résidence	Narbonne
Résidence du Bois	Paris
Rétival, Manoir de	Caudebec-en-Caux
Rive	Najac
Rochecourbe Manoir-Hotel	Vézac
Roches Blanches	Cassis
Roches-Fleuries	Cordon
Roy, Tour du	Vervins
Royal	Antibes
Royal Champagne	Champillon
Rustica	Pons
Sablettes	Miomo
Safari	Bormes-les-Mimosas
St-Antoine	Albi
St Clair	St-Étienne-les-Orgues
Sainte-Foy	Conques
San Giovanni	Porto Vecchio
Saint Jeannet	St-Jeannet
Saint-Michel	Chambord
St-Pierre	Tourtour
Saône	Tournus
Sarthe	Châteauneuf-sur-Sarthe
Scandinavia	Paris

581

Scierie	Aix-en-Othe
Seignelay	Auxerre
Sole e Monti	Quenza
Solognote	Brinon-sur-Saulde
Table du Comtat	Séguret
Taillard	Goumois
Tavel	Tavel
Templiers	Les Bézards
Templiers, Le Moulin des	Avallon
Terrasse	Meyronne
Tour de L'Esquillon	Miramar
Tour du Roy	Vervins
Tourtour, La Bastide de	Tourtour
Trianon Palace	Versailles
Tribunal	Mortagne-au-Perche
Trois Barbus	Anduze
Trois Mousquetaires	Aire
Tropelen, Lou	St-Tropez
Univers, Hôtel de l'	Dieppe
Val d'Or	Mercurey
Valmarin	Saint Malo
Van Gogh	St-Rémy-de-Provence
Verte Campagne	Trelly
Vieille Ferme	Serre-Chevalier
Vieux Moulin	St-Jacut-de-la-Mer
Vieux Puits	Pont-Audemer
Vieux Relais	Airvault
Vigneraie	Levens
Vistaëro	Roquebrune-Cap-Martin
Voile d'Or	St-Jean-Cap-Ferrat
Welcome	Villefranche

GERMANY

Bären, zum	Meersburg
Bayerischer Hof	Bayreuth
Biederstein	Munich
Bristol	Bonn
Burg	Trendelsburg
Drei Könige	Bernkastel-Kues
Eisenhut	Rothenburg ob der Tauber
Engel	Todtnauberg
Franz Josef	Linz am Rhein
Garni Rokokohaus	Erlangen
Heusser	Bad Dürkheim
Kaiser Worth	Goslar
Krone	Rüdesheim-Assmannshausen
Landhaus Louisenthal	Bremen-Horn
Marienbad	Munich
Mönchs Posthotel	Bad Herrenalb
Oper, an der	Munich
Petrisberg Trier	Trier
Post	Aschheim

Prem	Hamburg
Rokokohaus	Erlangen
Schloss Hugenpoet	Kettwig
Weisses Rössle	Hinterzarten
Zoo	Berlin

GREECE

Akti Myrina	Lemnos
Apollon	Xylokastron
Castello	Dassia
Caterina	Kifissia
Doma	Chania
Helena	Nafplion
Kavalari	Fira
King Otto	Nafplion
Leto	Nafplion
Lido	Faliraki
Minoa	Tolon
Minos Beach	Ayios Nikolaos
Pantheon	Gythion
Paolo Beach	Epidaurus
St George Lykabettus	Athens

HOLLAND

Ambassade	Amsterdam
Carelshaven	Delden
Europe	Amsterdam
Hamert	Wellerlooi
Hoofdige Boer	Almen
Kasteel Wittem	Wittem
Kieviet	Wassenaar
Langoed de Rosep	Oisterwijk
Leeuwenbrug	Delft
Maastricht	Maastricht
Zalm	Gouda

HUNGARY

Astoria	Budapest
Gellert	Budapest
Silvanus	Visegrad

ITALY

Accademia	Venice
Agnello d'Oro	Bergamo
Anna, Villa	Marini di Puolo
Árethena Rocks	Gardini
Bahia	Cavoli
Balletti Park	San Martino al Cimino
Beccherie	Treviso
Bellevue	Cogne
Bel Soggiorno	San Gimignano

583

Ricavo, Tenuta di	Castellina
Roma	Bologna
Salario	Torricella Sabina
San Lorenzo	Mantua
San Michele, Villa	Fiesole
San Pietro	Positano
San Rocco	Orta San Giulio
Seguso	Venice
Serbelloni, Grand Hotel Villa	Bellagio
Sirio	Ivrea
Sitea	Rome
Soggiorno, Bel	San Gimignano
Splendido	Portofino
Stella d'Italia	San Mamete
Tirreno	Forte dei Marmi
Umbra	Assisi
Villoresi, Villa	Colonnata di Sesto Fiorento
Virgilio	Orvieto

LUXEMBOURG

Bonne Auberge	Gaichel
Moselle	Ehnen
Simmer	Ehnen
St Nicholas	Remich

MALTA

Cornucopia	Xaghra
Ta'Cenc	Sannat

NORWAY

Brekkestranda	Brekke
Bristol	Oslo
Continental	Oslo
Hankø Nye Fjordhotel	Hankø
Leikanger Fjord	Leikanger
Neptun	Bergen
Nordfjord	Nordfjordeid
Øystese Fjord	Øystese
Refsnes Gods	Jeløy
Savoy	Oslo
Solstrand Fjord	Os
Utne	Utne

PORTUGAL

Abrigo da Montanha	Monchique
Bela vista	Praia da Rocha
Buçaco	Buçaco
Castelo de Palmela	Palmela
Elevador	Bom Jesus do Monte
Estalagem via Norte	Oporto
Garbe	Armação de Péra
Infante de Sagres	Oporto
Mestre Afonso Domingues	Batalha

585

Quinta da Penha de Franca	Madeira
Quinta das Torres	Azeitão
Quinta dos Lobos	Sintra
Rainha Santa Isabel	Estremoz
Ria	Murtosa
Santa Barbara	Oliveira do Hospital
Santa Maria	Marvão
São Bento, Pousada	Caniçada
São Teotónio	Valença do Minho
Senhora do Monte	Lisbon
Tivoli Jardim	Lisbon
Urgeiriça	Canas de Senhorim
York House	Lisbon

SPAIN

Albarracin	Albarracin
Alcazar del Rey Don Pedro	Carmona
Alfonso IV	Toledo
Alfonso XIII	Seville
Alhambra Palace	Granada
Arruzafa	Córdoba
Belvedere	Encamp
Cardenal	Toledo
Casa del Corregidor	Arcos de la Frontera
Colombino Conde de la Gomera	Gomera
Condestable Davalos	Ubeda
Costa de la Luz	Ayamonte
Doña María	Seville
Fuentes Carrionas	Cervera de Pisuerga
Gil Blas	Santillana del Mar
Inglaterra	Granada
Maimonides	Córdoba
Mar I Vent	Bañyalbufar
Marques de Villena	Alarcón
Moli, es	Deyá
Monteros, Los	Marbella
Montiboli	Villajoyosa
Muntanya	Orient
Nerja	Nerja
Parador Nacional	Puertomarin
Parador Nacional	Segovia
Racquet Club	Son Vida
Raimundo de Borgona	Ávila
Reyes Catolicos	Mojácar
Reyes Catolicos	Santiago de Compostela
Ritz	Madrid
San Francisco	Granada
San Marcos	León
Santa Catalina	Jaén
Santa Maria	Estepona
Santo Domingo de la Calzada	Santo Domingo de la Calzada

Sierra Nevada	Monachil
Suecia	Madrid
Tordesillas	Tordesillas
Valle de Aran	Viella

SWEDEN

Åkerblads	Tällberg
Diplomat	Stockholm
Gripsholms Värdhus	Mariefred
Grythyttans	Grythyttan
Rusthållargården	Arild
Stenungsbaden	Stenungsund
Tanums Gestgifveri	Tanumshede

SWITZERLAND

Adula	Flims
Aniro	Castagnola-Lugano
Arbalète	Geneva
Armures	Geneva
Barbate, Casa	Tegna
Beau-Rivage	Thun
Beausite	St Luc
Bella Tola	St Luc
Belvedere-Tanneck	Arosa
Blümlisalp	Kandersteg
Bündnerhof	Klosters
Casa Barbate	Tegna
Casa Berno	Ascona
Christiania	Gstaad
Clos de Sadex	Nyon
Eden	Engelberg
Eden au Lac	Zürich
Ermitage-Golf	Schönried
Florhof	Zürich
Hirschen am See	Gunten-Thunersee
Krafft am Rhein	Basle
Lac	Montana
Metropol	Zermatt
Mon Repos	Geneva
Real	Vaduz
Royal	Lucerne
Seeburg	Ringgenberg
Weisses Kreuz	Murten
Zum Storchen	Zürich

YUGOSLAVIA

Dubrovnik, Villa	Dubrovnik
Grad	Otočec ob Krki
Lipa	Lendava
Moskva	Belgrade
Palace	Hvar
Palace	Zagreb
Toplice	Bled

Maps

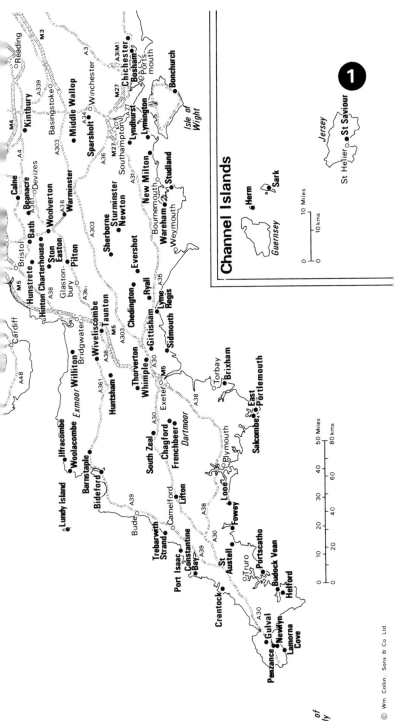

1

Channel Islands

Jersey ● **St Saviour**

St Helier ○

Guernsey

Guernsey ● **Herm** ● **Sark**

10 Miles

10 kms

Reading ○

M3

M4

Kintbury ●

Basingstoke ○

A339

Winchester ○

Sparsholt ●

Middle Wallop ●

Chichester ●

Bosham ●

Portsmouth ○

Bonchurch ●

Lyndhurst ●

Lymington ●

Southampton ○

Isle of Wight

Calne ●

Beanacre ●

Devizes ○

Woolverton ●

Warminster ●

New Milton ●

Studland ●

Bath ●

Ston Easton ●

Pilton ●

Sherborne ●

Sturminster Newton ●

Bournemouth

Wareham ●

Weymouth ○

Bristol ○

Hinton Charterhouse ●

Glastonbury ○

Evershot ●

Hunstrete ●

Cardiff ○

Chedington ●

Ryall ●

Lyme Regis ●

Wiveliscombe ●

Taunton ●

Gittisham ●

Sidmouth ●

Williton ●

Exmoor

Bridgwater ○

Thorverton ●

Whimple ●

Ilfracombe ●

Woolacombe ●

Huntsham ●

Exeter ○

Torbay ○

Brixham ●

Barnstaple ●

Bideford ●

South Zeal ●

Chagford ●

Frenchbeer ●

Dartmoor

East Portlemouth ●

Salcombe ●

Lundy Island

Bude ○

Camelford ○

Lifton ●

Plymouth

Looe ●

Trebarwith Strand ●

Port Isaac ●

Constantine Bay ●

Fowey ●

Crantock ●

St Austell ●

Truro ○

Portscatho ●

Budock Vean ●

Helford ●

Gulval ●

Newlyn ●

Lamorna Cove ●

Penzance ●

Isles of Scilly

Tresco ●
Bryher ●

50 Miles

80 kms

© Wm. Collins Sons & Co Ltd

SOUTH-WEST ENGLAND

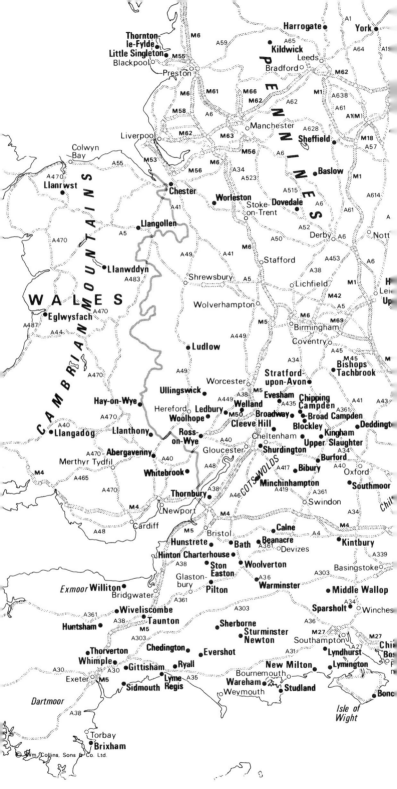

Kingston
upon Hull
A15
A18 Grimsby
A16
A158
coln
Skegness
A16
Blakeney
A17
King's Lynn
Norfolk Broads
Stamford A47 A47 Great Yarmouth
ford Peterborough
A11
A10
A12
Huntingdon A45
St Ives Bury St Edmunds
A1 A45
Bedford A14
A11
M11
Ipswich
M1 A6 A1(M)
Luton A10
A11 Dedham
Hertford A12 Colchester
A1
41
M11
M1 A127
A40 Southend-on-Sea
M4 LONDON
Margate
A23 A2
A3 A21 A2 Canterbury
M25 M26 M20 A2
Maidstone M2
Reigate Ashford
M23 A20 A20 Dover
East A20 Mersham
Grinstead Tunbridge Wells
A21
A267 Wallcrouch
rington A23 Rushlake Northiam A259
Green Battle Rye
Lewes A27
rping Hastings
nor Alfriston Pevensey
Eastbourne

0   10   20   30   40   50 Miles
0   20   40   60   80 kms

CENTRAL & SOUTHERN ENGLAND

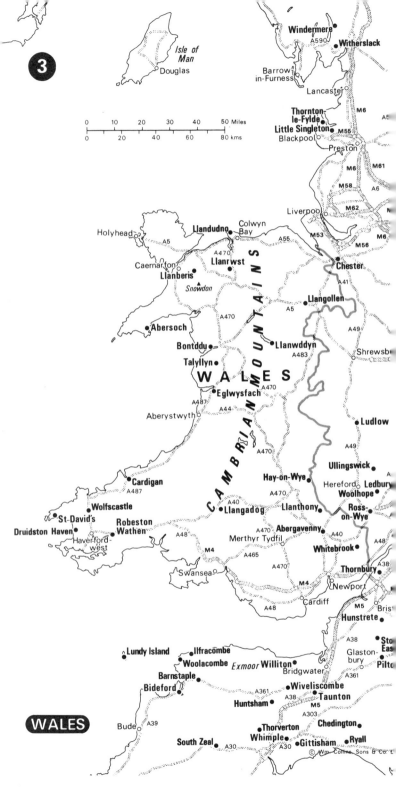

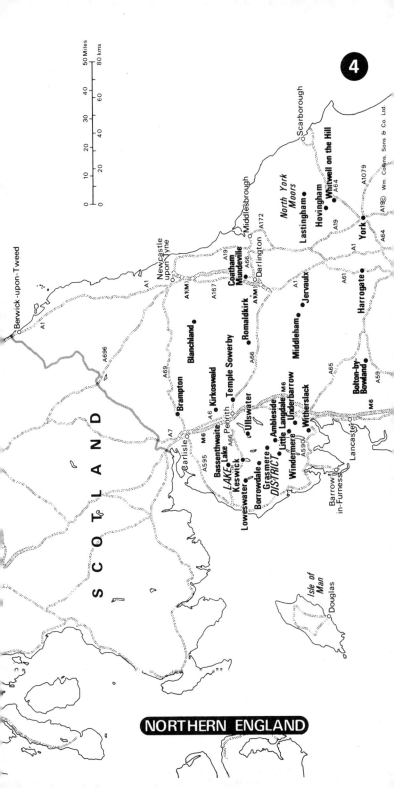

NORTHERN ENGLAND

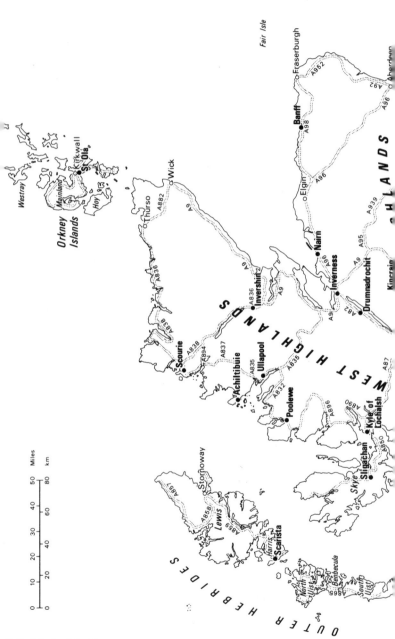

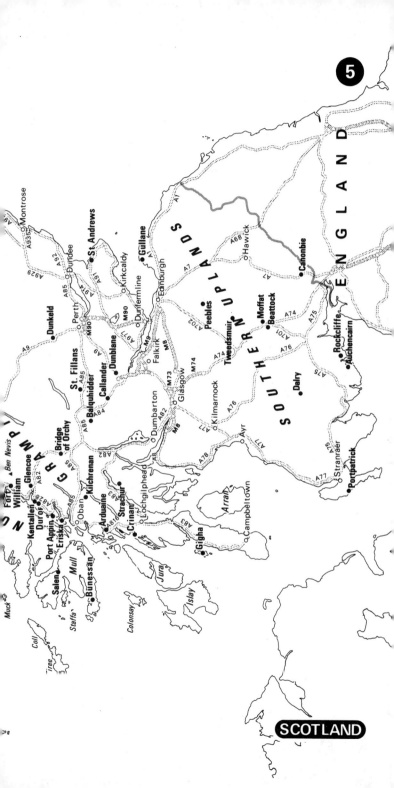

6

Coleraine
Londonderry
A2
A26
Larne
M12
N15
Dunadry ● M2
Belfas
Donegal
A5
M1
N15
A4
Ann
N16
Sligo
A4
Mourne Mts.
509
Riverstown ●
N17
N4
N2
N1
N5
N4
N3
Newport ●
Castlebar
N5
N59
Letterfrack
N4
Oughterard ●
Athlone
N6
N4
Dublin ●
N17
N59
Galway
N6
N17
Ballyvaughan ●
N7
Wicklow Mts.
N9
Gorey ●
N18
Limerick
N11
N7
Wexford
N21
N24
Cashel ●
N25
Clonmel
Tralee
N20
N8
Marlfield ●
N24
N2
Waterford
Mallow ●
N25
Killarney ●
N22
Cork ●
N71
Shanagarry ●
N71
Kinsale ●

0   20   40   60 M

0   20   40   60   80 km

IRELAND

© Wm. Collins, Sons & Co.

SOUTHERN SCANDINAVIA

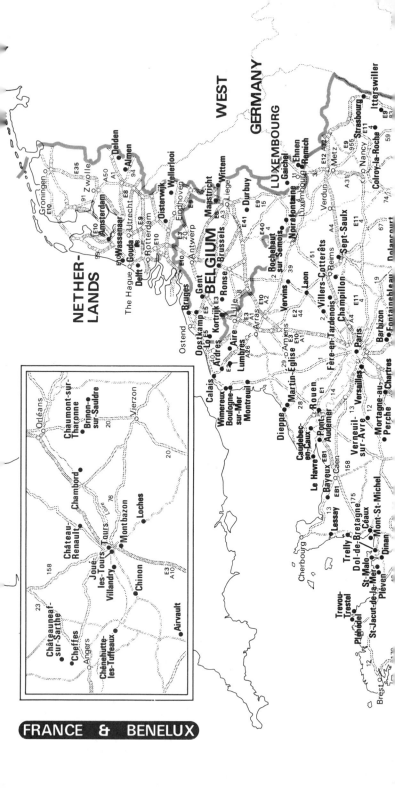

FRANCE & BENELUX

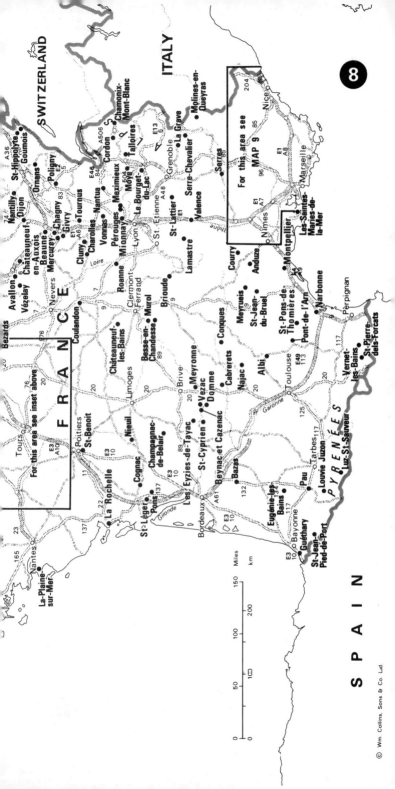

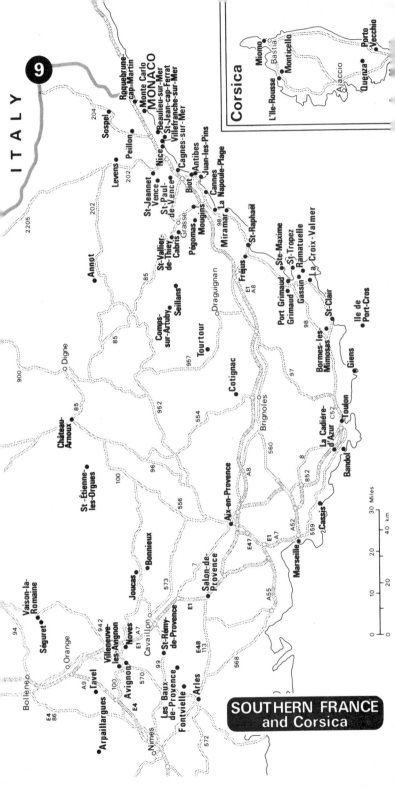

SOUTHERN FRANCE and Corsica

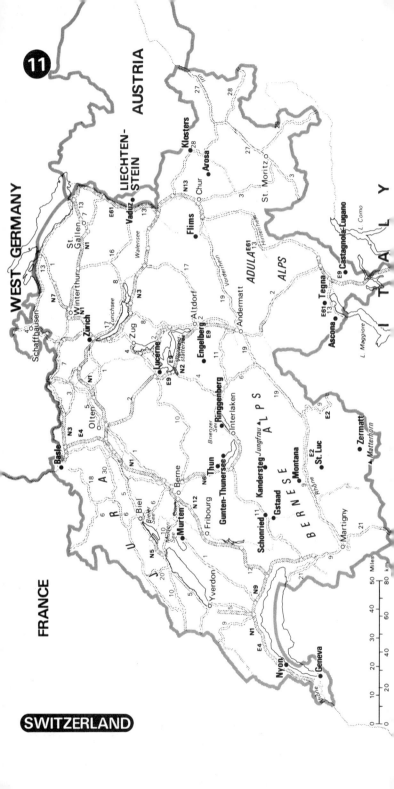

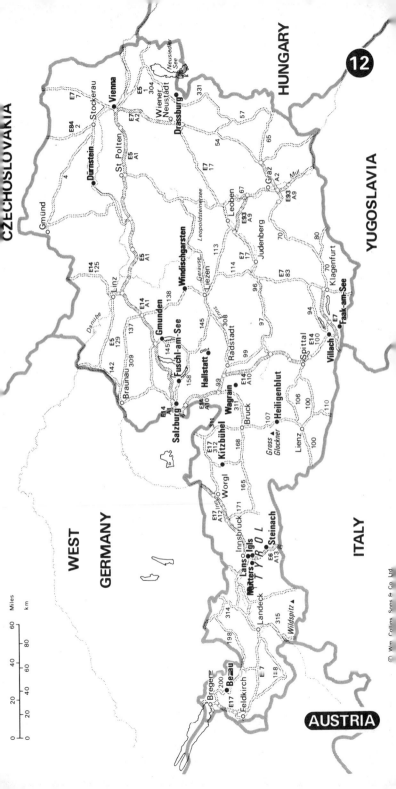

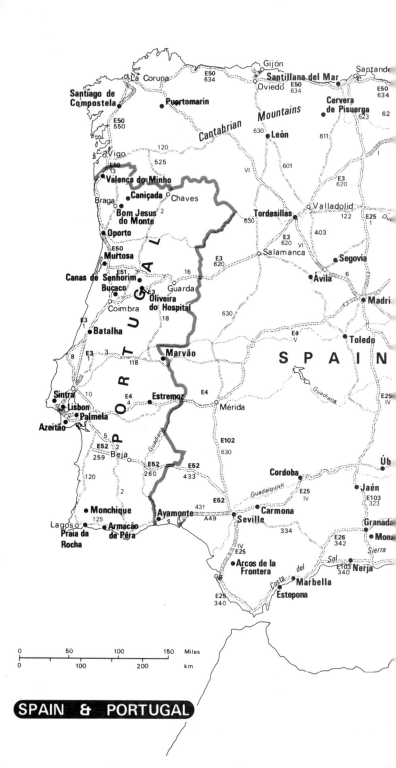

SPAIN & PORTUGAL

HUNGARY, ITALY & YUGOSLAVIA

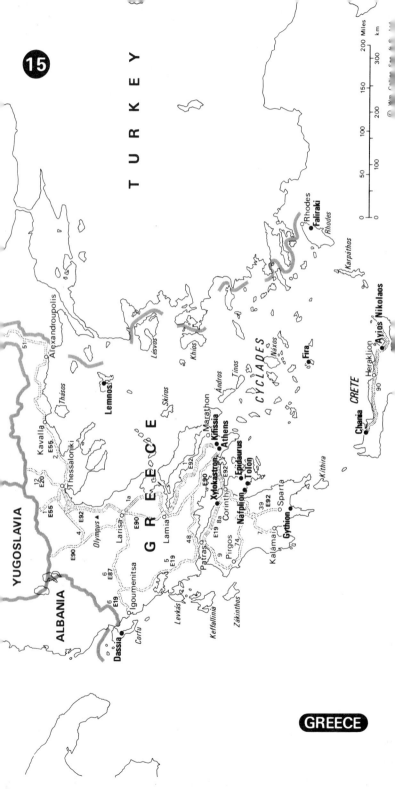

To: *The Good Hotel Guide*, Freepost, London W11 4BR
NOTE: No stamps needed in UK, but letters posted outside the UK should be
addressed to 61 Clarendon Road, London W11 4JE and stamped normally. Unless
asked not to, we shall assume that we may publish your name if you are
recommending a new hotel or supporting an existing entry, and, in appropriate
cases, that we may share your report with *The Good Food Guide*.

Name of Hotel _____

Address _____

_____

Date of most recent visit   Duration of visit
☐ New recommendation   ☐ Comment on existing entry
Report:

**(Continue overleaf if you
wish or use separate sheet)**

Signed _____

Name and address (Capitals please) _____

_____

To: *The Good Hotel Guide*, Freepost, London W11 4BR

NOTE: No stamps needed in UK, but letters posted outside the UK should be addressed to 61 Clarendon Road, London W11 4JE and stamped normally. Unless asked not to, we shall assume that we may publish your name if you are recommending a new hotel or supporting an existing entry, and, in appropriate cases, that we may share your report with *The Good Food Guide*.

Name of Hotel ———————————————————————————

Address ———————————————————————————

———————————————————————————

Date of most recent visit   Duration of visit
☐ New recommendation   ☐ Comment on existing entry
Report:

**(Continue overleaf if you
wish or use separate sheet)**

Signed ———————————————————————————

Name and address (Capitals please) ———————————————

———————————————————————————

To: *The Good Hotel Guide*, Freepost, London W11 4BR

NOTE: No stamps needed in UK, but letters posted outside the UK should be addressed to 61 Clarendon Road, London W11 4JE and stamped normally. Unless asked not to, we shall assume that we may publish your name if you are recommending a new hotel or supporting an existing entry, and, in appropriate cases, that we may share your report with *The Good Food Guide*.

Name of Hotel _____

Address _____

_____

Date of most recent visit   Duration of visit
☐ New recommendation   ☐ Comment on existing entry
Report:

**(Continue overleaf if you
wish or use separate sheet)**

Signed _____

Name and address (Capitals please) _____

_____

To: *The Good Hotel Guide*, Freepost, London W11 4BR

NOTE: No stamps needed in UK, but letters posted outside the UK should be addressed to 61 Clarendon Road, London W11 4JE and stamped normally. Unless asked not to, we shall assume that we may publish your name if you are recommending a new hotel or supporting an existing entry, and, in appropriate cases, that we may share your report with *The Good Food Guide*.

Name of Hotel _____

Address _____

_____

Date of most recent visit   Duration of visit
☐ New recommendation   ☐ Comment on existing entry
Report:

**(Continue overleaf if you
wish or use separate sheet)**

Signed _____

Name and address (Capitals please) _____

_____

To: *The Good Hotel Guide*, Freepost, London W11 4BR
NOTE: No stamps needed in UK, but letters posted outside the UK should b
addressed to 61 Clarendon Road, London W11 4JE and stamped normally. Unles
asked not to, we shall assume that we may publish your name if you ar
recommending a new hotel or supporting an existing entry, and, in appropriat
cases, that we may share your report with *The Good Food Guide*.

Name of Hotel _____

Address _____

_____

Date of most recent visit   Duration of visit
☐ New recommendation   ☐ Comment on existing entry
Report:

**(Continue overleaf if you
wish or use separate sheet**

Signed _____   _____

Name and address (Capitals please) _____

To: *The Good Hotel Guide*, Freepost, London W11 4BR

NOTE: No stamps needed in UK, but letters posted outside the UK should be addressed to 61 Clarendon Road, London W11 4JE and stamped normally. Unless asked not to, we shall assume that we may publish your name if you are recommending a new hotel or supporting an existing entry, and, in appropriate cases, that we may share your report with *The Good Food Guide*.

Name of Hotel _____

Address _____

_____

Date of most recent visit   Duration of visit
☐ New recommendation   ☐ Comment on existing entry
Report:

**(Continue overleaf if you
wish or use separate sheet)**

Signed _____

Name and address (Capitals please) _____

_____

To: *The Good Hotel Guide*, Freepost, London W11 4BR
NOTE: No stamps needed in UK, but letters posted outside the UK should be addressed to 61 Clarendon Road, London W11 4JE and stamped normally. Unless asked not to, we shall assume that we may publish your name if you are recommending a new hotel or supporting an existing entry, and, in appropriate cases, that we may share your report with *The Good Food Guide*.

Name of Hotel _____

Address _____

_____

Date of most recent visit   Duration of visit
☐ New recommendation   ☐ Comment on existing entry
Report:

(Continue overleaf if you wish or use separate sheet)

Signed _____

Name and address (Capitals please) _____

_____

To: *The Good Hotel Guide*, Freepost, London W11 4BR

NOTE: No stamps needed in UK, but letters posted outside the UK should be addressed to 61 Clarendon Road, London W11 4JE and stamped normally. Unless asked not to, we shall assume that we may publish your name if you are recommending a new hotel or supporting an existing entry, and, in appropriate cases, that we may share your report with *The Good Food Guide*.

Name of Hotel _____

Address _____

_____

Date of most recent visit   Duration of visit
☐ New recommendation   ☐ Comment on existing entry
Report:

(Continue overleaf if you wish or use separate sheet)

Signed _____

Name and address (Capitals please) _____

_____

To: *The Good Hotel Guide*, Freepost, London W11 4BR
NOTE: No stamps needed in UK, but letters posted outside the UK should be addressed to 61 Clarendon Road, London W11 4JE and stamped normally. Unless asked not to, we shall assume that we may publish your name if you are recommending a new hotel or supporting an existing entry, and, in appropriate cases, that we may share your report with *The Good Food Guide*.

Name of Hotel _____

Address _____

_____

Date of most recent visit   Duration of visit
☐ New recommendation   ☐ Comment on existing entry
Report:

(Continue overleaf if you wish or use separate sheet)

Signed _____   _____

Name and address (Capitals please) _____

_____

To: *The Good Hotel Guide*, Freepost, London W11 4BR

NOTE: No stamps needed in UK, but letters posted outside the UK should be addressed to 61 Clarendon Road, London W11 4JE and stamped normally. Unless asked not to, we shall assume that we may publish your name if you are recommending a new hotel or supporting an existing entry, and, in appropriate cases, that we may share your report with *The Good Food Guide*.

Name of Hotel _____

Address _____

_____

Date of most recent visit   Duration of visit
☐ New recommendation   ☐ Comment on existing entry
Report:

**(Continue overleaf if you
wish or use separate sheet)**

Signed _____

Name and address (Capitals please) _____

_____

To: *The Good Hotel Guide*, Freepost, London W11 4BR

NOTE: No stamps needed in UK, but letters posted outside the UK should b addressed to 61 Clarendon Road, London W11 4JE and stamped normally. Unles asked not to, we shall assume that we may publish your name if you ar recommending a new hotel or supporting an existing entry, and, in appropriat cases, that we may share your report with *The Good Food Guide*.

Name of Hotel _____

Address _____

_____

Date of most recent visit   Duration of visit
☐ New recommendation   ☐ Comment on existing entry
Report:

(Continue overleaf if yo
wish or use separate sheet

Signed _____   _____

Name and address (Capitals please) _____

_____

To: *The Good Hotel Guide*, Freepost, London W11 4BR

NOTE: No stamps needed in UK, but letters posted outside the UK should be addressed to 61 Clarendon Road, London W11 4JE and stamped normally. Unless asked not to, we shall assume that we may publish your name if you are recommending a new hotel or supporting an existing entry, and, in appropriate cases, that we may share your report with *The Good Food Guide*.

Name of Hotel _____

Address _____

_____

Date of most recent visit   Duration of visit
☐ New recommendation   ☐ Comment on existing entry
Report:

**(Continue overleaf if you
wish or use separate sheet)**

Signed _____

Name and address (Capitals please) _____

_____

To: *The Good Hotel Guide*, Freepost, London W11 4BR
NOTE: No stamps needed in UK, but letters posted outside the UK should be addressed to 61 Clarendon Road, London W11 4JE and stamped normally. Unless asked not to, we shall assume that we may publish your name if you are recommending a new hotel or supporting an existing entry, and, in appropriate cases, that we may share your report with *The Good Food Guide*.

Name of Hotel _____

Address _____

_____

Date of most recent visit   Duration of visit
☐ New recommendation   ☐ Comment on existing entry
Report:

(Continue overleaf if you wish or use separate sheet)

Signed _____   _____

Name and address (Capitals please) _____

_____

To: *The Good Hotel Guide*, Freepost, London W11 4BR

NOTE: No stamps needed in UK, but letters posted outside the UK should be addressed to 61 Clarendon Road, London W11 4JE and stamped normally. Unless asked not to, we shall assume that we may publish your name if you are recommending a new hotel or supporting an existing entry, and, in appropriate cases, that we may share your report with *The Good Food Guide*.

Name of Hotel _____

Address _____

_____

Date of most recent visit   Duration of visit
☐ New recommendation   ☐ Comment on existing entry
Report:

**(Continue overleaf if you
wish or use separate sheet)**

Signed _____

Name and address (Capitals please) _____

_____

Hotel Reports

The report forms on the following pages may be used to endorse or blackball an existing entry or to nominate a hotel that you feel deserves inclusion in next year's Guide. Either way, there is no need to restrict yourself to the space available. All nominations (each on a separate piece of paper, please) should include your name and address, the name and location of the hotel, when you stayed there and for how long. Please nominate only hotels you have visited in the past 18 months unless you are sure from friends that standards have not fallen off since your stay. And please be as specific as possible, and critical where appropriate, about the character of the building, the public rooms, the sleeping accommodation, the meals, the service, the night-life, the grounds. We should be glad if you would give some impression of the location and country as well as of the hotel itself, particularly in less familiar regions.

You should not feel embarrassed about writing at length. More than anything else, we want the Guide to convey the special flavour of its hotels; so the more time and trouble you can take in providing those small details which will help to make a description come alive, the more valuable to others will be the final published result. We are instituting this year a prize for the best report of the year (see page 558). The more entrants the better.

There is no need to bother with prices or with routine information about number of rooms and facilities. We obtain such details direct from the hotels selected. What we are anxious to get from readers is information that is not accessible elsewhere. And we should be grateful, in the case of foreign hotels, to be sent brochures if you have them available.

These report forms may also be used, if you wish, to recommend good hotels in North America to our equivalent publication in the States, *America's Wonderful Little Hotels and Inns*. They should be sent adequately stamped (no Freepost to the United States), not to *The Good Hotel Guide*, but to Congdon & Weed, 298 Fifth Avenue, New York, NY 10001, USA.